THE SCEPTER OF EGYPT · PART II

The Scepter of Egypt A Background for the Study of the Egyptian Antiquities in The Metropolitan Museum of Art

---

Part II: The Hyksos Period and the New Kingdom (1675-1080 B.C.)

BY WILLIAM C. HAYES

THE METROPOLITAN MUSEUM OF ART

FRONTISPIECE King Amun-ḥotpe wearing the Blue Crown

Library of Congress Catalogue Card No. 52-7286
First printing, 1959; second printing, 1968; third printing, 1978

Table of Contents

I. The Hyksos Domination

II. The Rise of the New Kingdom

III. The Thutmoside Pharaohs: Thut-mosĕ I to Ḥat-shepsūt

IV. The Thutmoside Pharaohs: Thut-mosĕ III and His Successors

V. Private Works of Art and Craftsmanship Produced during the Thutmoside Period

VI. The Reign of Amun-ḥotpe III

VII. The ʿAmārneh Period and its Aftermath

VIII. The Nineteenth Dynasty

IX. The Later Ramessides

X. The Art and Culture of the Ramesside Period

List of Illustrations

FRONTISPIECE

King Amun-ḥotpe III wearing the Blue Crown. Head of a quartzite statue from the great temple of Ptaḥ at Memphis. H. 13¾ in.

Chronological Table

Kings of the Hyksos Period

DYNASTY XV (Hyksos) (1675-1567 B.C.)

Maʿ-yeb-Rēʿ Sheshi	3 years
Mer-woser-Rēʿ Yʿaḳub-her	8 years
Sewoser-en-Rēʿ Khyan	
ʿA-woser-Rēʿ Apopy I	40 + years
ʿA-ḳen-en-Rēʿ Apopy II	
ʿA-seḥ-Rēʿ Khamudy	

DYNASTY XVI (Hyksos)[1] (1670?-1567 B.C.)

ʿAnat-her
Semḳen
Khaʿ-woser-Rēʿ
ʿA-ḥetep-Rēʿ
Sekhaʿ-en-Rēʿ
ʿA-mu
Neb-khopesh-Rēʿ Apopy (III?)
and others

DYNASTY XVII (Theban)

First Group (1660?-1610? B.C.)

Sekhem-Rēʿ Waḥ-khaʿu Reʿ-ḥotpe	
Sekhem-Rēʿ Wep-maʿet In-yōtef V, "the Elder"	3 years
Sekhem-Rēʿ Ḥeru-ḥir-maʿet In-yōtef VI	less than 1 year
Sekhem-Rēʿ Shed-towy Sobk-em-saf II	16 years
Sekhem-Rēʿ Semen-towy Tḥūty	1 year
Seʿankh-en-Rēʿ Montu-ḥotpe V	1 year
Sewadj-en-Rēʿ Neb-iry-er-awet I	6 years
Nefer-ku-Rēʿ (?) Neb-iry-er-awet II	less than 1 year
Semen-nefer-Rēʿ	
Sewoser-en-Rēʿ (Woser-en-Rēʿ?)	12 years
Sekhem-Rēʿ Shed-Wast	

Second Group (1610?-1567 B.C.)

Nūb-kheper-Rēʿ In-yōtef VII	3 + years
Senakht-en-Rēʿ	
Seḳen-en-Rēʿ Taʿo I, "the Elder"	
Seḳen-en-Rēʿ Taʿo II, "the Brave"	
Wadj-kheper-Rēʿ Ka-mosĕ	

1. Listed as Theban in Part I of this handbook (p. 2) in accordance with what we now believe to be faulty versions of Manetho's history.

Kings of the New Kingdom

DYNASTY XVIII (1567-1304 B.C.)

Neb-peḥty-Rēʿ Aʿḥ-mosĕ I	1570-1546 B.C.
Djeser-ku-Rēʿ Amun-ḥotpe I	1546-1526 B.C.
ʿA-kheper-ku-Rēʿ Tḥut-mosĕ I	1526-1508 B.C.
ʿA-kheper-en-Rēʿ Tḥut-mosĕ II	1508-1490 B.C.
Maʿet-ku-Rēʿ Ḥat-shepsūt	1489-1469 B.C.
Men-kheper-Rēʿ Tḥut-mosĕ III	1490-1436 B.C.
ʿA-khepru-Rēʿ Amun-ḥotpe II	1436-1411 B.C.
Men-khepru-Rēʿ Tḥut-mosĕ IV	1411-1397 B.C.
Neb-maʿet-Rēʿ Amun-ḥotpe III	1397-1360 B.C.
Nefer-khepru-Rēʿ Amun-ḥotpe IV (Akh-en-Aten)	1370-1353 B.C.
(ʿAnkh-khepru-Rēʿ) Semenkh-ku-Rēʿ	1355-1352 B.C.
Neb-khepru-Rēʿ Tūt-ʿankh-Amūn	1352-1343 B.C.
Kheper-khepru-Rēʿ Ay	1343-1339 B.C.
Djeser-khepru-Rēʿ Ḥor-em-ḥēb	1339-1304 B.C.

DYNASTY XIX (1304-1195 B.C.)

Men-peḥty-Rēʿ Ramesses I	1304-1303 B.C.
Men-maʿet-Rēʿ Sēthy I	1303-1290 B.C.
User-maʿet-Rēʿ Ramesses II	1290-1223 B.C.
Ba-en-Rēʿ Mery-en-Ptaḥ	1223-1211 B.C.
Men-mi-Rēʿ Amun-messĕ	1211-1207 B.C.
User-khepru-Rēʿ Sēthy II	1207-1202 B.C.
Sit-Rēʿ Meryet-Amūn Te-Wosret Akh-en-Rēʿ Mery-en-Ptaḥ Si-Ptaḥ	1202-1195 B.C.

DYNASTY XX (1195-1080 B.C.)

User-khaʿu-Rēʿ Sēth-nakhte	1195-1192 B.C.
User-maʿet-Rēʿ (Mery-Amūn) Ramesses III	1192-1160 B.C.
Ḥiḳ-maʿet-Rēʿ Ramesses IV	1160-1154 B.C.
User-maʿet-Rēʿ (Sekheper-en-Rēʿ) Ramesses V	1154-1150 B.C.
Neb-maʿet-Rēʿ Ramesses VI	1150-1145 B.C.
User-maʿet-Rēʿ (Akh-en-Amūn) Ramesses VII	1145-1144 B.C.
User-maʿet-Rēʿ (Mery-Amūn) Ramesses VIII	1144-1137 B.C.
Nefer-ku-Rēʿ Ramesses IX	1137-1118 B.C.
Kheper-maʿet-Rēʿ Ramesses X	1118-1110 B.C.
Men-maʿet-Rēʿ (Sotep-en-Ptaḥ) Ramesses XI	1110-1080 B.C.

THE SCEPTER OF EGYPT

I. The Hyksos Domination

1. The Hyksos

In the concluding paragraphs of the first volume of this book[1] we saw how, early in the seventeenth century before the Christian Era, the control of most of Egypt slipped from the feeble grasp of the kings of the late Middle Kingdom and rested for more than a hundred years in the hands of a succession of Asiatic chieftains known to their Egyptian contemporaries as *Ḥiḳau-khoswet*, "rulers of foreign countries," and to the Ptolemaic historian Manetho and his successors as the "Hyksos." Since both the title *Ḥiḳ-khoswet* and the other expressions—ʿAmu, Setetyu, Mentyu Setet—by which the Egyptians referred to the new ruling element had been used by them for centuries to describe the sheikhs of the Eastern Desert and the tribesmen of southwestern Asia, it would appear that the Hyksos, far from being a novelty on Egypt's horizon, were the same groups of princes and peoples who from time immemorial had raided her northeastern border and during periods of internal weakness had swarmed into the Delta in formidable numbers.

To judge from their names and their few surviving portraits the intruders appear to have been chiefly Semites; but there is no reason to suppose that they belonged to a single tribe or nation or even to a single racial stock. The view that their ascendancy over the Egyptians was the result of a concerted military invasion from without is no longer generally held. On the other hand, since it is unlikely that an Asiatic prince could have established himself as their overlord without some resistance on the part of the Egyptians, fighting must have taken place, and to carry off what appears to have been a relatively easy victory the Hyksos must have had the backing of a numerous, well-trained, and well-armed following.

In the course of the fighting it was inevitable that towns should be burned, temples damaged, and the native population subjected to hardships and cruelties. Once the Hyksos were in control they undoubtedly ruled the country with a firm hand, imposing heavy taxes upon the people of the occupied areas and collecting tribute from the vassal kingdoms to the south. Their administration, in which Egyptian officials apparently participated, seems, however, not to have been unduly harsh or oppressive and was probably accepted with complacency by the majority of their subjects. However we may evaluate them they were evidently not the ruthless barbarians conjured up by the Theban propagandists of the early New Kingdom and the Egyptian writers of later periods. The Hyksos kings of the Fifteenth Dynasty sponsored the construction of temple buildings and the production of statues, reliefs, scarabs, and other works of art and craftsmanship; and, curiously enough, some of our best surviving copies of famous Egyptian literary and technical works date from the time of these kings.

On the other hand, with the doubts recently cast by scholars upon the so-called "Hyksos forts,"

[1] Hayes, *The Scepter of Egypt*, Part I, p. 351.

the "Hyksos pottery," and other products formerly attributed to them, there seems to be little left to support the view that they possessed a distinctive culture of their own. In Egypt they borrowed extensively from the ancient civilization in the midst of which they found themselves. Their rulers wrote their names in Egyptian hieroglyphs, adopted the traditional titles of the kings of Egypt, used throne names compounded in the Egyptian manner, and sometimes even assumed Egyptian personal names. Their admiration for Egyptian art is attested by the number of statues, reliefs, and minor works which they either usurped, or had copied—probably by Egyptian craftsmen—from good Middle Kingdom originals; and their production of that peculiarly Egyptian type of seal, the scarab, was nothing short of prodigious.

The official religion of the Hyksos princes appears to have been modeled upon that of the Egyptians, and their state god, perhaps of Asiatic origin, to have been readily assimilated with Sēth of Avaris, the ancient deity of the northeast Delta town which the Hyksos made their first base of operations in Egypt. Contrary to a later tradition, other Egyptian divinities seem also to have been accepted by the Hyksos, notably the sun god Rēʿ, whom they honored in their throne names.

For the Egyptians, in return, the Hyksos did two things. They rid them once and for all of the old feeling of self-sufficiency and false security, born of a misplaced confidence in Egypt's unassailable superiority over and aloofness from the other nations of the world; and, because they themselves were Asiatics with a kingdom which appears to have embraced northern Sinai and much of Palestine, they brought Egypt into more intimate and continuous contact with the peoples and cultures of western Asia than ever before in her history. Over the Hyksos bridge there flowed into the Nile Valley in unprecedented quantity new blood strains, new religious and philosophical concepts, and new artistic styles and media, as well as epoch-making innovations of a more practical nature—the well sweep, the vertical loom, the composite bow, and, toward the very end of the Hyksos occupation, the horse and the horse-drawn chariot. Though represented as an unmitigated disaster by native historians of later times, the Hyksos domination provided the Egyptians with both the incentive and the means toward "world" expansion and so laid the foundations and to a great extent determined the character of the New Kingdom, or, as it is often called, "the Empire."

In Egypt we can recognize two principal stages in the Hyksos rise to power, the first of which had its origin in the northeastern Delta around 1720 B.C. This was the time of the Asiatic occupation of the town of Ḥat-wʿaret, or Avaris, and the founding there of a temple to the Hyksos counterpart of the god Sēth, an event commemorated on a New Kingdom stela as having taken place four hundred years before the reign of Ḥor-em-ḥēb, the last king of the Eighteenth Dynasty. For approximately forty-five years (about 1720-1675 B.C.) the first waves of Asiatic princes appear to have consolidated their position and extended their holdings in northern Egypt; but they have left us no monuments, inscribed or otherwise, which can with assurance be assigned to this initial phase of the Hyksos domination.

About 1675 B.C. a Hyksos prince whom Manetho calls Salatis ("the Sultan"?) ousted the contemporary Egyptian ruler from the capital city of Memphis, occupied most of Middle Egypt, and appears to have extended his control southward to include, for the time being at least, the whole of Upper Egypt and Nubia. With Salatis begins the succession of six Hyksos sovereigns—the so-called "Great Hyksos"—who comprised Manetho's Fifteenth Dynasty and whose names were once listed, preceded in each case by the title *Ḥiḳ-khoswet* and followed by the years of their reigns, in Column X of the Turin Canon of Kings. Their rule, according to this Canon, continued for over a hundred years, or, presumably, until the rise of the New Kingdom in 1567 B.C.

The Manethonian "Salatis" (or "Saïtes"), unattested elsewhere, was, as already indicated, probably a title or epithet applied to an early

FIGURE 1. Royal and official scarabs of the Hyksos period. L. 9/16-1 in.

Hyksos ruler of sufficient power and importance to have been recognized by posterity as the founder of the Fifteenth Dynasty. Just such a ruler was King Maʿ-yeb-Rēʿ Sheshi, whose seals and seal impressions, of early Hyksos types, are both numerous and widely distributed, examples of the latter having been found as far south as the Middle Kingdom trading post at Kermeh, near the Third Cataract of the Nile. Our own collection includes twenty-seven glazed steatite ★scarabs of this king, on which his names are preceded by the pharaonic titles the "Good God" or the "Son of Rēʿ" and followed by the phrases "given life" or "May he live forever" (see fig. 1, first row). Eleven examples bear the Egyptianizing throne name "Maʿ-yeb-Rēʿ" ("Just-is-the-heart-of-Rēʿ") and sixteen the personal name "Sheshi"—probably, though not certainly, belonging to the same ruler. The decorative motifs which fill the lateral segments of the oval fields include the interlocking-spiral border, inherited from the Middle Kingdom, appropriately chosen hieroglyphic word signs (𓊹𓄤, the "Good God"; ☥, "life," etc.), and geometric linear patterns of distinctive "Hyksos" types. Though on the whole the carving of these scarabs is of fair quality, the forms of some of the hieroglyphs in their legends are distorted and misunderstood to the point where the signs themselves can scarcely be identified. One of the Maʿ-yeb-Rēʿ scarabs is from Elephantine, and one of those with the name Sheshi is from Deir el Baḥri, where it was found in an Eighteenth Dynasty rubbish pit in front of the temple of Ḥat-shepsūt.[2] The

[2] Referred to in Part I as Ḥet-shepswet.

others, chiefly from the Davis, Murch, Carnarvon, and Timins collections, are of unknown provenience.

Four very similar ★scarabs from the Amherst, Murch, and Carnarvon collections were inscribed for another early Hyksos ruler whose personal name, Jacob-El, is written in Egyptian "Yʿaḳub-her" and is preceded in each case by the kingly title the "Son of Rēʿ" (see fig. 1, first row). Like those of Maʿ-yeb-Rēʿ Sheshi, sealings of Yʿaḳub-her have been found at Kermeh; and, in general, the two kings seem to have been closely associated in time and in the geographic areas which they controlled. Though it is difficult to equate him with the king whom Manetho calls Bnōn, or Beōn, there is some probability that Mer-woser-Rēʿ Yʿaḳub-her was Maʿ-yeb-Rēʿ's immediate successor and, as such, the second of the Great Hyksos rulers.

With King Sewoser-en-Rēʿ Khyan (or Khayana)—the "Staan" or "Iannas" of the Manethonian lists—we are, historically speaking, on firmer ground. He is known to us on monuments from Gebelein in southern Upper Egypt to Bubastis in the Delta and, outside of Egypt, on objects which somehow or other found their way as far as Baghdad in Mesopotamia and Knossos on the island of Crete. Though he was obviously one of the most powerful of the Hyksos princes, Khyan's name is not found south of Gebelein; and it is probable that in his day the Asiatics had already begun to relax their control over and withdraw their outposts from Nubia and the southernmost provinces of Egypt itself.

Five glazed steatite ★scarabs of this king in the Museum's collection carry his personal name "Khyan" preceded in four cases by the pharaonic title the "Son of Rēʿ," and in the other by the title *Ḥiḳ-khoswet*, "Ruler of Foreign Lands." The first of the two Khyan scarabs, the undersides of which are shown in figure 1 (top row, right), is set in a gold swivel mounting and once formed the bezel of a signet ring. The decorative motifs which accompany the name are the same as those seen

FIGURE 2. Signet ring and alabaster vase fragment of King Apopy I. H. of fragment 3 ⅜ in.

on the scarabs of Sheshi and Yʿaḳub-her—interlocking-spiral borders and hieroglyphic word signs (𓄹☥, "repeating life," etc.). Here too we find the same distorted and misunderstood forms of some of the hieroglyphs in the legends.

The fourth Great Hyksos ruler, with a reign, according to the Turin Canon, of forty years or more (about 1620-1580 B.C.), can only have been King ʿA-woser-Rēʿ Apopy ("Apōphis"), in whose thirty-third regnal year the Rhind mathematical papyrus was copied down by a Theban scribe and whose monuments, like those of Khyan, are known from Gebelein on the south to Bubastis in the north. The Museum is fortunate in possessing two of the more interesting objects on which this king's name is preserved: a fine human-headed scarab of glazed steatite mounted in a gold ★finger ring (fig. 2, top) and part of an inscribed alabaster ★vase found at Thebes in the tomb of King Amun-ḥotpe I of the early Eighteenth Dynasty (fig. 2, bottom). On the scarab Apopy's throne name, "ʿA-woser-Rēʿ," is preceded by a title probably intended to be the "Good God," but actually written the "Good King." On the vase fragment we find not only the titles and names of the pharaoh: "The Good God, ʿA-woser-Rēʿ, the Son of Rēʿ, Apop(y)," but also those of the "King's Daughter, Ḥerit," to whom in all probability the vase once belonged. It has been thought that this Hyksos princess may have been married to a contemporary ruler of Thebes and may even have been an ancestress of King Amun-ḥotpe I. However that may be, the presence of her vase, with its inscription intact, in a Theban royal tomb certainly bears out the evidence of the title page of the Rhind Papyrus and indicates clearly that during most of the long reign of Apopy I the Hyksos and Thebans were on good terms with one another and that the memory of the Asiatic rulers was not as hateful to the Egyptians of the early New Kingdom as some of our sources would have us believe. Apopy I is also represented in our collection by an unglazed steatite ★scarab and a white-glazed steatite ★cowroid (fig. 1, second row), each bearing his throne name incorrectly written and accompanied in one instance by a figure of the Egyptian cobra goddess Udōt and in the other by the falcon of Horus surmounting the *wedjat*-eye (see Part I, p. 313).

Toward the end of Apopy's reign the Egyptians, spearheaded, as frequently in their history, by the proud and warlike princes of Thebes, began to stand up against their Asiatic overlords. Echoes of the opening of hostilities are preserved to us in a New Kingdom legend describing a verbal quarrel, or duel of wits, which took place between "King Apopy" of Avaris and "King Seḳen-en-Rēʿ" of Thebes. Actual fighting seems to have broken out shortly thereafter; and the serious reverses suffered by the "wretched Asiatic," "ʿA-woser-Rēʿ, Son of Rēʿ, Apopy," at the hands of the embattled Thebans are described on two great stelae set up in the temple of Amūn at Karnak by King Ka-mosĕ, the last ruler of the Seventeenth Dynasty.

Sometime during the reign of Apopy I the Hyksos had withdrawn their southern boundary to Kusae, north of Asyūt; and before his death they had been routed out of most of Middle Egypt and driven back almost as far as the Fayyūm. An attempt on the part of Apopy to induce the "Prince of Kush" to come to his assistance was thwarted by the Thebans who intercepted his messenger as he was traveling southward to Nubia through the Libyan Desert. With the exception of a dagger purchased in Luxor, monuments of ʿA-woser-Rēʿ's successor, ʿA-ḳen-en-Rēʿ Apopy II, have not been found south of Bubastis in the eastern Delta; and ʿA-seḥ-Rēʿ (Khamudy?), probably the last pharaoh of the Fifteenth Dynasty, is known only from a small obelisk discovered on or near the site of Avaris itself. The fall of Avaris and the expulsion of the Asiatics from the soil of Egypt took place about 1567 B.C., and a few years later King Aʿḥ-mosĕ, the Theban founder of the Eighteenth Dynasty, wiped out the remaining vestiges of Hyksos power in southern Palestine.

Contemporary with the Great Hyksos of the Fifteenth Dynasty there appears to have been at least one other group of Hyksos rulers in Egypt, in whom we may probably recognize the "other Shepherd Kings" identified by Africanus in his epitome of Manetho's history as the Sixteenth Dynasty. Near the beginning of this group are to be placed such chieftains as ʿAnat-her, Semḳen, Wadjed, and Seket. Later in the series of minor Hyksos rulers belong "Kings" Khaʿ-woser-Rēʿ, ʿA-ḥetep-Rēʿ, Sekhaʿ-en-Rēʿ, and ʿA-mu, whose names, preceded in most cases by the title the "Good God" and followed by the words "given life," appear on ten glazed steatite ★scarabs in the Museum's collection (see fig. 1, second row). Of King Neb-khopesh-Rēʿ Apopy (III?), who is probably to be placed near the end of the Sixteenth Dynasty, we possess no inscribed monuments.

Associated stylistically and geographically with the scarabs of King Maʿ-yeb-Rēʿ Sheshi, the founder(?) of the Fifteenth Dynasty, are those of an important Hyksos official, whose Semitic name Ḥur (as in the familiar "Ben Ḥur") means "the noble," "the freeborn." On the ★scarabs, of which the Museum possesses eight examples in green-glazed steatite, the name is actually written "Ḥar" and is accompanied by the titles "Treasurer of the King of Lower Egypt," "Sole Companion (of the King)," and "Overseer of the Treasury" (see fig. 1, third row). The scarabs of this man—charged, no doubt, with the receipt of taxes and tribute for King Sheshi or for an approximately contemporary Hyksos pharaoh—have been found on many different ancient sites, all the way from the region of Gaza in Palestine to that of Kermeh in the Sūdān. Another Hyksos Treasurer, whose titles are the same as those of Ḥur and whose scarabs are almost as numerous, bore the Egyptian name Pery-em-waḥ and may have been an Egyptian in the employ of the Asiatic rulers. His six ★scarabs in our collection are somewhat crudely carved of steatite and are coated with a bluish green glaze. The title and name of a Queen Te-ty, known elsewhere from two scarabs in the British Museum and thought by some to have been a consort of one of the Hyksos rulers, appear on a large glazed steatite ★scarab of this period (fig. 1, third row), formerly in the Theodore M. Davis collection.

Many seals of the Hyksos period bear pseudo names of kingly type, sometimes enclosed within cartouches and preceded by royal titles. Such a name, to be read perhaps "Rēʿ-ʿa-em-neṭer," appears on a ★button seal of glazed steatite shown in the third row of figure 1. To the right of this seal are two scarabs with legends of the so-called *ʿnr*-type, imitation names made up of various combinations of the signs 𓂝, 𓈖, and 𓂋. In addition to the examples illustrated the Museum possesses thirty-five ★scarabs and two ★cylinder seals with inscriptions of this type.

2. The Thebans

Forced southward by the expansion of the Hyksos rule, King Dudy-mosĕ and his successors of the late Thirteenth Dynasty had managed to maintain for several decades small Upper Egyptian "kingdoms" centered around towns like Asyūt, Abydos, and Thebes. About 1660 B.C. the Theban branch of the Thirteenth Dynasty was replaced by a new and more vigorous line of Theban rulers in whom we may recognize without much doubt the "kings of Thebes or Diospolis" of Manetho's Seventeenth Dynasty. The names and years of these rulers are partially preserved in Column XI of the Turin Canon of Kings; and a number of them are listed in the Karnak table of ancestors of Tḥut-mosĕ III and on other Theban monuments of the New Kingdom. Their tombs at Thebes—small brick pyramids built along the southeastern slope of the Dirāʿ Abu'n Naga—are known to us chiefly from coffins and other items of funerary furniture which they had once contained, from references to them in the tomb-robbery papyri of the Twentieth Dynasty and other New Kingdom documents, and from the accounts of nineteenth-century explorers and travelers.

The compiler of the Turin Canon appears to have divided the Manethonian Seventeenth Dynasty into two groups, the first group embracing Sekhem-Rēʿ Waḥ-khaʿu Rēʿ-ḥotpe (Column X, 30?) and his ten successors down to and including Sekhem-Rēʿ Shed-Wast (Column XI, 9); the second group having been made up apparently of the last five kings of the dynasty, from Nūb-kheper-Rēʿ In-yōtef VII to Wadj-kheper-Rēʿ Ka-mosĕ (Column XI, 10-15?).

The territory claimed by these rulers probably coincided approximately with that ruled centuries before by the Theban princes of the Herakleopolitan period and embraced perhaps the eight southernmost nomes of Egypt from the Nubian frontier to the neighborhood of Abydos. Building operations and repairs were carried out at Abydos itself by King Reʿ-ḥotpe, the founder of the Dynasty, and by several of his successors; but the wording of a well-known decree of King In-yōtef VII at Koptos suggests that there were other ruling houses in Upper Egypt contemporary with the Theban Seventeenth Dynasty, while Middle and northern Egypt were, of course, in the hands of the Hyksos.

None of the kings of the earlier group of Thebans seems to have been of a particularly warlike nature or to have entertained any very great antagonism toward his Asiatic overlords and neighbors to the north—perhaps because none of them had as yet the means to back up sentiments of a rebellious nature. The most fully documented of the group, King Sekhem-Rēʿ Shed-towy Sobk-em-saf II, enjoyed a relatively long reign of sixteen years and, thanks probably to his building activities at Karnak and Abydos, was still remembered in the late New Kingdom as "a great ruler" whose "monuments stand to this very day."[3] One of the few monuments known from this period is a stela set up at Karnak in the reign of King Neb-iry-er-awet I, recording an inquiry into the sale to a private individual of the hereditary governorship of the province of el Kāb; it constitutes one of the most interesting juridical documents which have survived from Egyptian antiquity. Incidentally, it fixes the reign of Neb-iry-er-awet as being less than three generations removed from that of King Mer-ḥetep-Rēʿ Iny of the late Thirteenth Dynasty.

With the kings of the second group the picture changes. In a relief at Koptos King Nūb-kheper-Rēʿ In-yōtef is shown with upraised mace striking down a cluster of his enemies, and at Karnak his cartouches surmount figures of bound Nubian and Asiatic captives. The pharaoh himself was buried with his bows and arrows beside him in his coffin, and his son Nakhte bore the high military rank of a Troop Commander of the army. Though the "enemies" referred to in the king's Koptite decree are now recognized as having been not real enemies, but small magical figures which had been stolen by one Tety, son of Min-ḥotpe, the tone of the decree is both autocratic and violent. We have seen how one of the two kings named Seḳen-en-Rēʿ Taʿo battled verbally, if not actually, against King Apopy, his Hyksos adversary; and from the axe, club, and dagger wounds which appear on his mummy it is clear that King Taʿo II, "the Brave," met a violent end, quite possibly in combat against the invaders of his country.

It is not, however, until we come to the last ruler of the Seventeenth Dynasty, King Wadj-kheper-Rēʿ Ka-mosĕ, son of King Taʿo II, that a long historical text, known to us from two big stelae found at Karnak and from a slightly later student's copy of one of these, throws definite light on the progress made by the embattled Thebans in their war of liberation against the Hyksos. At the beginning of this text we are told how, despite the cautious advice of his council, Ka-mosĕ set his heart on "delivering Egypt and smiting the Asiatics" and how, with the aid of his Kushite auxiliaries, the famed Medjay troops, he captured an enemy stronghold at Neferūsy, deep in Hyksos-held territory, and chased the enemy's "horses" into the fortress at Per-shaḳ, presumably still further to the north. Here, almost at the end of the Hyksos occupation, we find our first reference in an Egyptian text to the horse, an animal which may not have been used by the Asiatics in their conquest of Egypt but which was destined in the centuries to come to play a leading role in the establishment of Egypt's Asiatic empire.

The text as preserved on the second stela goes on to tell us how Ka-mosĕ captured a fleet of Hyksos ships, laden with "all good products of Retenu" (Palestine-Syria), how he carried his conquests into the Kynopolite Nome, only fifty miles south of the entrance to the Fayyūm, and how, "to prevent the rebel from being behind me," he sent a unit of his army to occupy the strategically important oasis of Baḥaria in the Libyan Desert to the west. The taking of Avaris and the expulsion of the intruders from the soil of Egypt was not, however, accomplished by Ka-mosĕ himself, but by his younger brother and successor King Neb-peḥty-Rēʿ Aʿḥ-mosĕ, the founder of the New Kingdom.

[3] The Abbott Papyrus, 6, 3-4. See Winlock, *The Rise and Fall of the Middle Kingdom in Thebes*, p. 138.

As the liberators of Egypt and the forerunners of the New Kingdom the rulers of the late Seventeenth Dynasty were held in high honor by their successors of happier and more prosperous times, especially by their immediate descendants of the early Eighteenth Dynasty. It is a striking testimonial to the growing importance of Egypt's royal women that equal or even greater honors were extended to the wives and mothers of these rulers —the ancestresses of the Theban line—whose names and figures appear as frequently on monuments of the New Kingdom as do those of the kings themselves. Among the ladies particularly revered by subsequent generations were Queen Sobk-em-saf of Edfu, the wife of Nūb-kheper-Rēʿ In-yōtef; Queen Tety-shery ("Little Tety"), wife of King Taʿo I, mother of King Taʿo II, and grandmother of the royal brothers Ka-mosĕ and Aʿḥ-mosĕ I; and Queen Aʿḥ-ḥotpe, the wife of Seḳen-en-Rēʿ Taʿo II and the mother of his two great successors. Both Tety-shery and Aʿḥ-ḥotpe lived on into the early years of the Eighteenth Dynasty and were buried by Aʿḥ-mosĕ I in richly endowed tombs.

Like those of their Hyksos adversaries the names of the kings, queens, and princes of the Seventeenth Dynasty are found in the Museum's collection chiefly on ★scarabs (fig. 1, fourth row). With the Carnarvon collection we acquired a large and rather handsome scarab in blue-glazed steatite inscribed for the "Good God In-yōtef, the Elder," probably Sekhem-Rēʿ Wep-maʿet In-yōtef V, the second king of the dynasty; and an altogether similar scarab bearing upon its underside, likewise within an interlocking-spiral border, the title and name of a "King's Son In-yōtef." In the same collection there are also a blue faience scarab of the "King's Wife Aʿḥ-ḥotpe," apparently the queen of Seḳen-en-Rēʿ Taʿo II, and a somewhat smaller example in green-glazed steatite with the

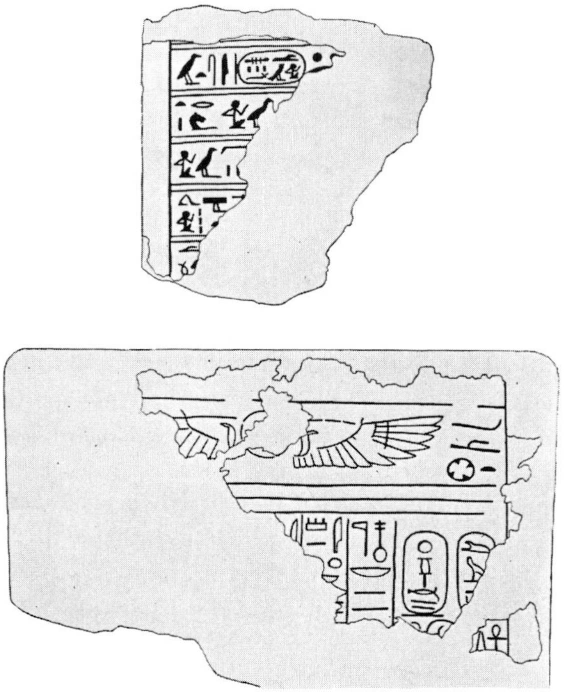

FIGURE 3. Fragmentary limestone stela and shrine with the names of King Sobk-em-saf II. L. of shrine 11 in.

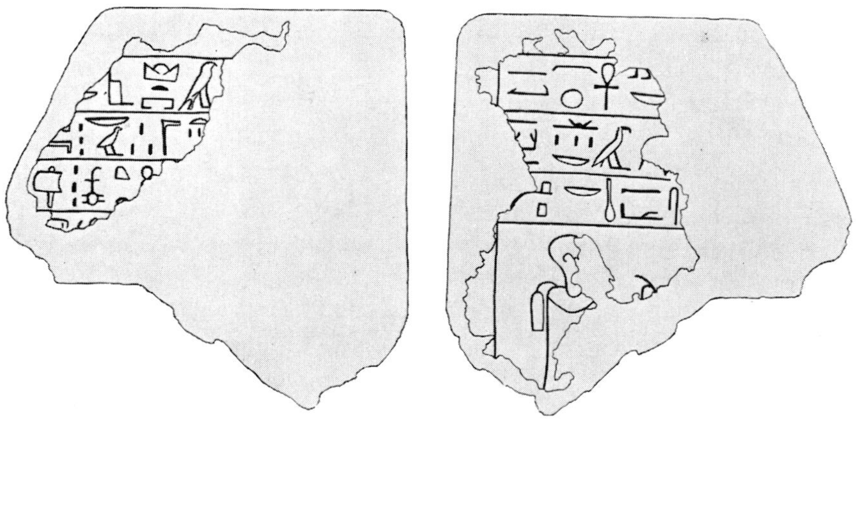

personal name of King (?) "Ka-mosĕ." From the Museum's excavations near the pyramid of Amun-em-ḥēt I at el Lisht come another scarab of Prince In-yōtef and two in faience of King "Sewadj-en-Rēʿ" (Neb-iry-er-awet I); and from the Altman collection a scarab resembling these last two, but with the throne name of Nūb-kheper-Rēʿ In-yōtef VII. A glazed steatite ★bead bearing the title and name of Queen Aʿḥ-ḥotpe enclosed within a cartouche was acquired with the Murch collection.

Through a gift of Norman de Garis Davies the long and relatively prosperous reign of Sobk-em-saf II is represented in our collection by parts of two small but interesting monuments from western Thebes, picked up many years ago on the Dirāʿ Abu'n Naga, probably not far from the site of the king's pyramid. One was a limestone tomb ★stela inscribed with the autobiography of an official of the "Son of Rēʿ, Sobk-em-saf," whose cartouche by great good fortune is preserved on our fragment (fig. 3, top). The other was a small ★shrine, also of limestone, on the back of which (fig. 3, center), below a crudely carved winged sun's disk (labeled "the Beḥdetite"), the "Good God, Lord of the Two Lands. . . Sekhem-Rēʿ Shed-towy Sobk-em-saf, given life," was once shown making offering to "Amun Rēʿ, Lord of [Kar]nak. . . ." The sides of the battered little monument (fig. 3, bottom) still carry parts of offering formulae in which Ptaḥ, Ḥor-akhty, and "all the gods of heaven" are invoked "in behalf of the spirit" of the shrine's deceased owner, whose figure probably confronted that of the god Ptaḥ on the right-hand side of the block. The accuracy of Lindsley Hall's pen permits us to see even in the line drawings of figure 3 the coarse, provincial style which characterizes nearly all the products of the Theban ateliers of this period.

The Museum possesses no monuments of Queen Tety-shery which were made during her lifetime; but her name, enclosed within a cartouche, appears on a limestone ★stela of the Eighteenth Dynasty belonging to a man named Tḥūty (see p. 170), one of whose relatives was a priest of the temple of "Aʿḥ-mosĕ, daughter of Tety-shery, the justified." If, as seems possible, the Aʿḥ-mosĕ referred to here was Queen Aʿḥ-mosĕ Nefret-iry, the wife of the founder of the Eighteenth Dynasty, then we must understand the word daughter to mean, as it sometimes does, female descendant or, in this case, granddaughter.

3. The Arts and Crafts of Northern Egypt under the Hyksos

It is probable that in the northern and central portions of the country Egyptian architects, artists, and craftsmen, trained in the Middle Kingdom tradition, continued working throughout the period of the Asiatic occupation under the appreciative patronage of the Hyksos rulers and their followers. Aside, however, from several minor objects such as a scribe's palette with the names of King Apopy I and a dagger handle with the cartouches of Neb-khopesh-Rēʿ Apopy (III?), very few original works have survived in Lower and Middle Egypt which can with assurance be dated to this period. Monumental sculpture is represented almost entirely by reinscribed royal statues and sphinxes of Middle Kingdom origin; and of the temples built by the Hyksos kings there remain only a few blocks of inscription from Bubastis, a small obelisk of King ʿA-seḥ-Rēʿ from Tanis, and a fine granite altar which Apopy II dedicated to "his father, Sēth, Lord of Avaris." Though what has come down to us is quantitatively unimpressive, the quality of the work is on the whole as good or better than that produced under the independent Egyptian kings of the Thirteenth Dynasty.

For objects of this period from northern Egypt our collection has depended chiefly on the Museum's own excavations at el Lisht, especially those conducted between the years 1906 and 1922 in the area surrounding the pyramid of King Amun-em-ḥēt I, the founder of the Twelfth Dynasty. The extensive cemetery of private pit tombs which fans out to the west and south of the pyramid enclosure appears to have continued in use until the end of the Middle Kingdom, when the site was abandoned to the mercies of the local peasantry, who used it both as a source of loot and as a quarry for ready-cut blocks of building stone. To these plunderers and their families we probably owe the founding of a settlement of small mud-brick houses and granaries clustered haphazardly around the pyramid and climbing part way up its sloping sides. This settlement, which grew at length into a considerable village, seems to have continued in uninterrupted occupancy for seven or eight hundred years, the latest datable objects found in it belonging to the time of the Twenty-Second Dynasty (950-730 B.C.). Unfortunately, the bulk of the material from the ruins of the village—chiefly utilitarian items of household equipment—cannot be dated with any exactitude. The same is true of many of the objects found in the adjoining cemetery, for these too may have been of village origin, swept into the open tomb shafts during the repeated disturbances to which the site has been subjected.

There are, however, a few groups of objects from the site of the North Pyramid at el Lisht which not only can be assigned to the time of the Hyksos occupation of northern Egypt, but which may be said to be typical of this period.

Three of the tomb pits in the North Pyramid cemetery yielded, between them, seven small pyriform ★jugs in black pottery adorned with incised and white-filled decoration in which predominate chevrons and other geometric designs made up of or filled with rows of dots. These jugs, most of which are fragmentary, belong to a well-known type of Syro-Palestinian pottery which has been found in quantity at Tell el Yahudīyeh in the southeast Delta, some fifty miles to the north of el Lisht, and is now generally known as "Tell el Yahudīyeh ware." Though it is doubtful that this pottery was a Hyksos product, most of the examples recovered are datable to the period when the Hyksos were a power in the Near East. Its presence at el Lisht, as on other north Egyptian sites, reflects the lively trade relations which existed at this time between northern Egypt and southwestern Asia.

Fragments of five of the Tell el Yahudīyeh jugs were found together in a single tomb shaft and with them was found what Helene J. Kantor has described as "perhaps the most remarkable of the foreign vessels assignable to the Second Intermediate period . . . . a ★vase unique in Egypt but belonging to a typical Palestinian and Syrian type known at the end of the Middle Bronze IIA period, but common in Middle Bronze IIB" (fig. 4). Miss Kantor goes on to say: "This vase is not merely a normal import from Palestine, however, but is outstanding for its decoration—decoration utterly unparalleled in both Egypt and Palestine. The designs are executed in a red wash, with borders and interior details incised and filled with white pigment. Though the ungainly geese seem unparalleled, the dolphins are somewhat clumsy imitations of Middle Minoan IIIB dolphins, motifs borrowed from wall paintings by the Minoan pot painters. In technique the Lisht dolphins have affinities both with their white-outlined Minoan prototypes and with the incised, white-filled decoration of Tell el Yahudiyah juglets. The synchronism between the Second Intermediate period in Egypt, Middle Minoan III in Crete, and Middle Bronze IIB in Palestine is, of course, already well established by other finds in Egypt and elsewhere, but the dolphins of the Lisht jar are the first Middle Minoan III feature to be discovered in Egypt. Thus they form a most welcome counterbalance to the evidence for Egyptian, and also Syrian, influence on the development of the representational art of Middle Minoan III. The Lisht find provides what might hardly have been expected, the epitomization on a single vase of the intimacy of connections between Egypt, Syria-Palestine, and Crete in the final phase of the Middle Bronze period."[4]

From another tomb shaft near the pyramid of Amun-em-ḥēt I come two small black pottery ★vases, one cordiform with incised palm-tree decoration, the other shaped like a bird with the outlines of the feathers and other details incised. Undecorated pottery ★jars and ★bowls of late Second Intermediate types were found in both the cemetery and the village area.

Thirty-two crude little faience ★amulets from

[4] "Chronology of Egypt," pp. 13-14.

FIGURE 4. Decorated pottery jar of foreign type from el Lisht. H. 5 ½ in.

the same site and apparently of the same period include fourteen in the form of the hippopotamus goddess Ta-weret (Thoueris), five in the shape of a recumbent lion, four flies, two birds, an ape, two scarab beetles, a human hand, a rather amorphous star, and two almost unrecognizable *wedjat*-eyes. Five ★bullae, or bottle-shaped amulets, are carved of carnelian, as are also three pear-shaped ★pendants. One of two agate ★pendants is shaped like a tooth, while the other is simply an oval pebble with a hole bored through its middle. There are, in addition, an agate ★cowroid, acacia-pod ★beads of beryl and of steatite, a glazed steatite oval ★bead with engraved scroll decoration, and long strings of faience spheroid ★beads and disk-shaped ★beads of shell. Rectangular and circular pieces of carnelian ★inlay have been somewhat vaguely dated to the period between the Twelfth and Eighteenth Dynasties.

Eight tombs in the North Pyramid cemetery produced a dozen large sections of papyrus and Ḥalfa-grass ★mats and four lengths of grass and palm-fiber ★rope, both two- and three-ply. These, also, were dated by the Museum's excavators to the interval between the Middle and New Kingdoms. A bronze ★hairpin, some five and a half inches in length, found in the ruins of the ancient village, has been given the date "XIII-XVII Dynasty."[5]

It is tempting to assign to the time of the Hyksos occupation the lower part of a large limestone ★*shawabty*-figure (see Part I, pp. 326, 350) of late Middle Kingdom type inscribed for a man named "Apopy." The name, however, is common during the Twelfth and Thirteenth Dynasties and the figure may well antedate by many years the similarly named Hyksos rulers. On the other hand, a small rectangular model ★coffin of Nile mud is so similar to examples found in tombs of the Seventeenth Dynasty at Thebes (see fig. 15) that there is every probability that it is of Second Intermediate period date. The little box and its flat lid are painted red and were once covered with a piece of linen cloth. Within there is a small and rather amorphous mud figure with eyes made of beads, wrapped in a red cloth and covered over with a piece of heavier cloth, also stained red.

The area surrounding the South Pyramid at el

[5] This, like other dates given in the same form throughout the volume, is taken from the Museum's accession card.

Lisht, that of King Se'n-Wosret I, has added nothing to the Museum's collection which can with any confidence be attributed to Hyksos times, with the possible exception of four much worn masons' *mallets found in the débris outside the western limestone enclosure wall of the pyramid. These mallets, of the usual pear-shaped type carved in one piece from a hardwood log, are apparently post-Twelfth Dynasty and may have been used during the ensuing period in quarrying operations in the abandoned royal funerary complex.

It is difficult to draw any general conclusions on the arts and crafts of northern Egypt during the Hyksos regime on the basis of the few, relatively insignificant, and in some cases uncertainly dated objects just discussed. We may note, however, the prevalence of foreign pottery probably imported from Palestine-Syria and showing in one instance motifs borrowed from the contemporary art of Minoan Crete; and, so far as the native Egyptian objects are concerned, observe the not always successful efforts to perpetuate the stylistic traditions and technical processes of the Middle Kingdom.

4. The Arts and Crafts of Upper Egypt during the Hyksos Period

In Upper Egypt the artistic and cultural picture is even less cheerful than in the North. In the Thebaid and adjoining areas the Hyksos subjugation of the northern two-thirds of the country had, for the time being, a disastrous effect on the local arts and crafts, accelerating the decline already apparent under the ephemeral pharaohs of the Thirteenth Dynasty and reducing the quality of Egyptian artistic production in these areas to—without much doubt—its lowest level in dynastic history. Not only, as in the disturbed years following the collapse of the Old Kingdom, did the native artists and artisans lose their technical ability and their sense of style, but, in the shadow of a foreign overlordship, they also lost the spirit and ingenuity which had made the art of the First Intermediate period, in spite of its crudity and provincialism, both lively and interesting. At Thebes itself the artisans attached to the poverty-stricken court of the kings of the Seventeenth Dynasty found themselves deprived of the training and patronage enjoyed by their colleagues of more fortunate periods and, at the same time, cut off by the Hyksos and the princes of Kush from nearly all the materials normally employed by the ancient Egyptians in the production of fine works of art and craftsmanship—the gold of Nubia, the ebony and ivory of the Sūdān, the copper and turquoise of Sinai, the coniferous woods of Syria, the white limestone of Tureh, and the fine alabaster of Ḥat-nūb. For their tomb monuments even the kings had to content themselves with small pyramidal superstructures built of mud brick, and for their coffins with rough anthropoid containers carved out of the knotty, coarse-grained logs of the local sycamore-fig tree. No monumental sculpture in the round appears to have been attempted, and building operations seem to have been confined largely to the upkeep and repair of existing structures. Occasionally, however, fine small objects were turned out by the Upper Egyptian ateliers; and when, under the last kings of the Seventeenth Dynasty, the Theban rulers began to regain control of their country, we note a very marked upswing in the quality of the works produced, an upswing which carried over with uninterrupted momentum into the early years of the New Kingdom. It is, in fact, often impossible to say whether certain coffins, weapons, musical instruments, pieces of jewelry, and the like produced at the end of the Hyksos period belong to the late Seventeenth or to the early Eighteenth Dynasty.

In contrast to northern Egypt, Thebes and other Upper Egyptian sites have furnished the Museum's collection with a substantial corpus of objects datable to and characteristic of the period when the Hyksos ruled in the North and the Seventeenth Dynasty in the South. Our Theban material, which includes several complete burials, comes chiefly from excavations conducted by the Earl of Carnarvon and by our own Egyptian Expedition in cemeteries of the Second Intermediate

FIGURE 5. Painted limestone triad from Thebes. H. 6 7/16 in.

period and early New Kingdom at the eastern end of the ʿAsāsīf valley and along the lower slopes of the Dirāʿ Abu'n Naga (see Part I, p. 202).

It will make for clarity if we study this material more or less according to the subject grouping adopted for our Middle Kingdom objects in Chapters XII to XV of the first volume of this book, taking up in order the people as they appear to us in their sculpture and painting, and then their personal possessions and pastimes, the furnishings of their houses, their weapons and implements, and finally their burials and funerary equipment including their coffins, canopic chests, and *shawabty*-figures.

A painted limestone ★triad (fig. 5), less than six and a half inches in height, introduces us to three members of a Theban family of the late Seventeenth Dynasty. Offering formulae written in black ink on the back and sides of the back pilaster and invoking in each case the god Osiris tell us that the woman at the center of the group bore the very common name Aʿḥ-mosĕ, but leave us in some doubt as to the names of her companions—perhaps "Sen(i)" and "Wadjet"—and in complete doubt as to their relationship to her. A mother with her son and daughter seems the most plausible guess, but the possibilities, of course, are manifold. The man is conventionally attired in a small, caplike wig and a short, goffered kilt with pendent tab in front. The long, full headdresses of the women are represented as bound over the top and around the sides with broad, ribbonlike bands. Interesting is the painstaking, if not completely successful, treatment of the clasped hands. The flesh of the man is painted the customary dark red, that of the women an ocher yellow (see Part I, p. 107). With the photograph before us it is unnecessary to harp upon the overly squat proportions and the other technical shortcomings of the little group; but its close adherence (or attempted adherence) to the typological and stylistic traditions of the Middle Kingdom is worth noting, especially since it is probably to be dated just before, or possibly just after, the rise of the Eighteenth Dynasty. It was found in 1916 by the Museum's Expedition in a tomb court three-quarters of a mile east of the temples at Deir el Baḥri.

A pit in this courtyard gave access to several subterranean tomb chambers, and in the débris on the floor of one of these chambers was found a rather badly damaged wooden *statuette of a standing man wearing a short wig and kilt almost exactly like those of the man of the limestone triad. The figure in this case, however, is tall, slenderly proportioned, and in general more characteristic of the work of the New than of the Middle Kingdom. The man's right hand, provided with a very long, down-projecting thumb, hangs straight down at his side and at one time evidently held a scepter in horizontal position, while the bent left arm probably reached toward a staff. The statuette, seven and five-eighths inches in height, had been attached by tenons on the undersides of the feet to a wooden base, but this had been almost entirely devoured by white ants. As frequently, the forward half of each foot was carved as a separate piece and tenoned in position.

From a tomb of the "XIIIth-XVIIth Dynasties"[6] at Abydos cleared in 1901 by the Egypt Exploration Fund comes a pair of unusual little female *statuettes in limestone, one preserved to the height of the breasts (three and five-eighths inches), the other to a point a trifle above the knees. Each figure, clad in a long, tight-fitting dress which reveals the form beneath it, stands upright against a square pilaster in the center of a broad, flat base. Since on the more complete figure there is no sign of the arms it is clear that these were raised above breast level, perhaps in a gesture of protection or adoration. Without the arms, the heads, or an inscription to guide us, it is difficult to know whether we have here representations of women (the tomb owner or her servants) or of goddesses. The facts, however, that the statuettes are a pair and that their arms were raised make it not improbable that they represent the sister goddesses Isis and Nephthys, who figure so prominently in the funerary rituals and tomb art of the ancient Egyptians (see Part I, pp. 318, 347; figs. 207, 228).

By Hyksos times the so-called "doll" or "dancing-girl" statuettes of the Middle Kingdom (see Part I, p. 219) had been reduced to a single type —the elongated female figure grotesquely modeled in clay, usually exaggeratedly nude, but nearly always provided with an elaborate coiffure and jewelry. Variously described in the past as "concubines," as "fertility goddesses," and as "characterizing . . . the universal concern with generation," it is probable that the principal purpose of such figures was to stimulate and perpetuate the procreative powers of the deceased Egyptians with whom they were buried.[7] An elaborate example in the Museum's collection comes from a typical Seventeenth Dynasty burial in western Thebes, that of a man named Pu-Ḥor-Senbu. It comprises

[6] Randall-MacIver and Mace, *El Amrah and Abydos*, pp. 100 f.

[7] For full discussions see the works of Bruyère and Desroches-Noblecourt, Bibliography, § 22.

the terra-cotta ★figures of a woman and her child found swathed together in linen bandages (see fig. 6) and placed beside the head of the deceased. The child, held in front of the mother and exhibiting the same hideous crudity in the rendering of the face and body, is also a female. Like the "paddle dolls" of the Eleventh Dynasty (Part I, pp. 219-21) the woman wears a coiffure of Nubian type, in this case a great disk-shaped mass of clay "curls" with pellets of clay suspended on strings from the top of the head, and, looped twice around her neck, a heavy necklace of primitive appearance. Her figure, which tapers downward to a point, with the merest suggestion of the feet at the lower end of the legs, measures seven and three-quarters inches in height; that of the child, slightly over four inches. Three similar ★"dolls" (see fig. 6), of which one is certainly and the other two probably from Thebes, are somewhat smaller and are not accompanied by figures of children. One has its hair dressed in two widely flaring lateral sections which are bound together, above the narrow, wedge-shaped face, by a fillet. The second is without its head, but exhibits on the stomach and abdomen pricked dot patterns which probably represent tattooing. The third figure has a pointed, birdlike face, a wide headdress, flat on top and

FIGURE 6. Crude female figures from Thebes and Koptos. Terra cotta. H. of largest figure 7¾ in.

with loops descending on either side of the head, and across the abdomen a row of dots which may in this case indicate the presence of a bead girdle. All wear heavy necklaces. To our more or less complete figures are to be added two terra-cotta ★heads acquired by Albert M. Lythgoe, the Egyptian Department's first curator, at Ḳuft (the ancient Koptos), some twenty-five miles to the north of Thebes. One head wears the divided, flaring coiffure surmounted by a fillet and a small cone; the other shows a disk-shaped headdress and has the lobes of the ears pierced for earrings. It is worth noting that the barbaric crudity exhibited by these figures is a characteristic of the class of object to which they belong, not primarily of the period in which they were made, since altogether similar figures, indistinguishable from our Seventeenth Dynasty specimens, were produced during both the Twelfth and the Eighteenth Dynasties. Nor were these grotesque doll-like statuettes of nude women with elaborate headdresses local to Egypt only: they are found in quantity in other parts of the Near East, notably in Persia, in Syria, and on the island of Cyprus.

The rough form, childish draughtsmanship, and limited colors of the painted limestone ★stela of figure 7, on the other hand, do fairly exemplify the work of the provincial artisans of Upper Egypt during the period of the Hyksos domination in the North. Stylistically, perhaps, the greatest interest of the rather lifeless little painting lies in the very slender proportions of the figures, one of the several characteristics which, as we shall see, differentiate the art of the New Kingdom from that of the preceding great eras of Egyptian history. Coming in all probability from a plundered burial of the Seventeenth Dynasty, the stela was found during the winter of 1918-1919 in the surface rubbish to the east of the tomb of the Chief Steward Pe-Bēs, a Theban official of the Saïte period. On it we see a man named Tetu, son of Oḳeret, seated at the right with "his beloved wife, Nefer-tjentet, born of Bet," and confronted by his two sons, Amūny and Si-Amūn, and his seven daughters, Sit-Amūn, Dedyet-Amūn, Iket-Amūn, Oḳeret (I), Bet, Oḳeret (II), and Yaʿḥ. The cursive hieroglyphic labels, including that over Tetu's pile of food and drink offerings ("a thousand of bread and beer, a thousand of beef and fowl"), are written in black; and the figures, offerings, and accessories, including the mirror and casket under the couple's elaborately grained chair, are painted in red, yellow, black, and white.

Almost equally crude is a small, round-topped ★stela of limestone on which the spindly, angular figures of a man named Mery-en-Ptaḥ and a woman named Ina are silhouetted in low, flat-surfaced relief, with the details of their forms and clothing scratched in or added in paint. The man, clad in a long, diaphanous over-kilt, sits behind a table of offerings, smelling a lotus flower, while the woman stands facing him, holding in her extended right hand the branch of a shrub or small tree. Above, in the lunette of the stela, is a pair of large *wedjat*-eyes flanking a *shenu*-symbol; and below, a brief and unevenly written *ḥtp-di-nsw* formula calling upon Osiris, Lord of Busiris, to provide Mery-en-Ptaḥ with the customary funerary offerings. The front of the stela is framed by a low, flat band raised slightly in relief above the enclosed surface. Though the name Mery-en-Ptaḥ is not common until well along in the New Kingdom, the style and iconography of the little monument point clearly to a date in the Second Intermediate period. A gift of Darius Ogden Mills, the stela came to the Museum in 1904 without indication of its original provenience.

A fragmentary limestone ★stela of the very late Seventeenth or early Eighteenth Dynasty, on which are preserved portions of two registers of figures executed in shallow *relief en creux*, or sunk relief, shows a return on the part of the Upper Egyptian draughtsman and sculptor to the uniformity of proportions, technical sophistication, and sense of established style which we associate with the "classic" periods of Egyptian art. The figures, sharp-faced and slenderly proportioned, include, in the upper register, the lower portions of two men and a woman seated on chairs side by side and, standing facing them, a man wearing a

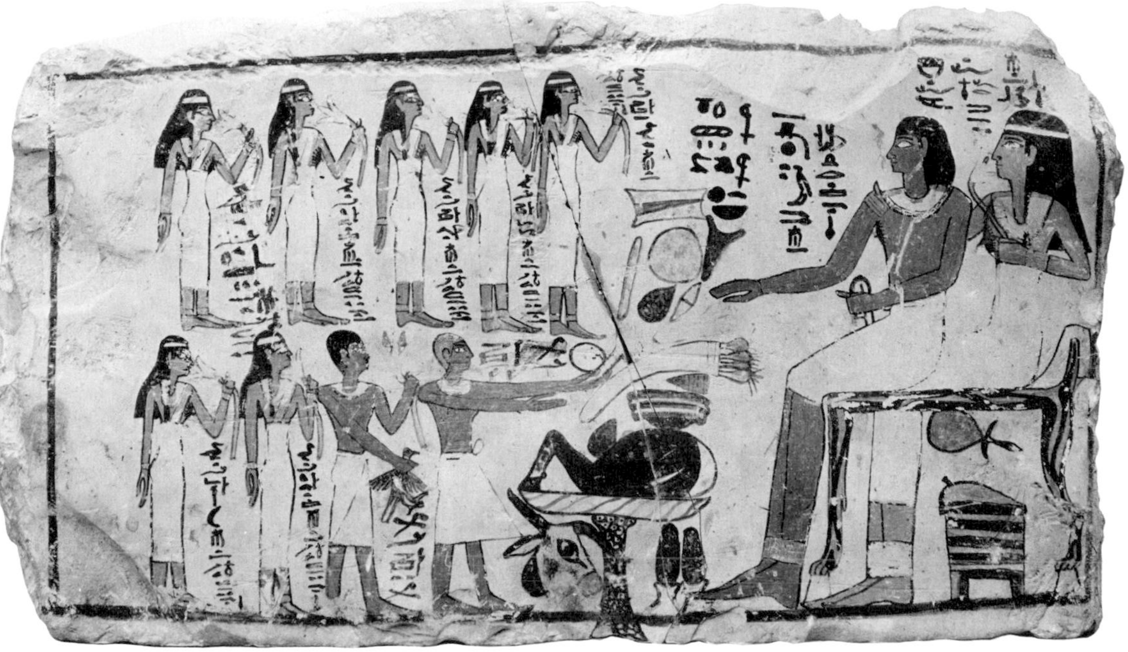

FIGURE 7. Painted limestone stela of Tetu and his family. L. 16 ⅛ in.

short under-kilt and a long, transparent overskirt. In the lower register we see, according to the accompanying hieroglyphic labels, the "King's Son Aʿḥ-mosĕ" and another man, named Tḥūty, each presenting a duck as an offering, and behind them three women, Aʿḥ-ḥotpe, Aʿḥ-mosĕ, and "Sit- . . . ," offering, respectively, a conical loaf of "white bread," a *ḥes*-vase (𓏁) of "beer," and a small jar of "wine." It should be noted that at this period the title King's Son did not necessarily indicate royal birth, but was borne by many quite ordinary citizens of Egypt, such as the offering bearer Aʿḥ-mosĕ of our present fragment. The piece, presented to the Museum in 1890 by James Douglas, is probably, though not certainly, from Thebes. It measures nine and a half by nine inches.

Of articles of clothing which had belonged to people of the Hyksos period we possess nothing except two large fragments of an openwork leather ★loincloth cut in one piece from a gazelle skin. The openwork pattern consists of horizontal rows of small, closely spaced, rectangular slots, and the effect is that of a fine lattice rather than of an open net as is the case with the cutwork leather loincloths of the New Kingdom. An exactly similar garment was found at Balabish (near Abydos) in the burial of one of a group of Sudanese soldiers, the so-called "pan-grave people" (see pp. 39 ff.), and it is not unlikely that this type of loincloth was a military or semimilitary garment of Sudanese or Nubian origin. Our two sections of loincloth belonged to a man whose only other worldly possession was a boomerang and who was buried, in a typical Seventeenth Dynasty *rishi* coffin (see pp. 29 f.), in the lower ʿAsāsīf valley in western Thebes.

Altogether similar burials in the same locality produced many interesting, though rarely fine, pieces of personal jewelry—★scarabs, ★cowroids, ★plaques, ★amulets, bead ★necklaces and ★girdles, and metal ★earrings. On the body of a man named Pu-Ḥor-Senbu (the owner of the mother-and-child "doll" figures discussed above) were found a glazed steatite scarab with a decorative design on its underside, tied by a cord to a finger of the left hand, and a matching cowroid of the same material and with a similar design, attached with a loop of cord to the left wrist. On the right hand was a roughly shaped scarab of haematite, and around the neck two long cords, one supporting three alabaster amulets (a falcon and two "hearts") with a big cylindrical bead at the back serving as a counterpoise, the other having eight kidney-shaped ★seeds tied to it at intervals. Around the waist of the same mummy there was a girdle of small shell and carnelian disk beads and, scattered in the wrappings, a long cylindrical bead of blue faience and a quantity of loose disk beads. An adjacent burial yielded a small rush basket containing, among other items, three scarabs with "heraldic" devices (a falcon, a clump of papyrus, etc.), a *wedjat*-eye plaque with the name of the god Amūn inscribed on the back, and a little plaque in the form of a cartouche bearing apparently the legend "Sobk-Rēʿ, Lord of Shedet"—all of blue faience, except for one scarab of glazed steatite, and all strung together on a loop of thread. Outside the basket but in the same coffin was found a green-glazed steatite scarab inscribed for the "Accountant(?) of the God's Offering Amun-ḥotpe." The only object from a third burial of the same group was a faience scarab with a decorative pattern on the base.

A series of burials in the reused Middle Kingdom tomb court referred to above has furnished eleven scarabs and three cowroids in glazed steatite, faience, glass, and various fine stones, adorned for the most part with scrolls, plant forms, and other purely decorative elements or with hieroglyphic signs (𓋹, 𓄤, 𓎿, 𓆣, 𓋳, 𓎟, 𓇓, 𓆤) used in simple mottoes or in heraldic arrangments. Most interesting is a scarab beautifully carved in a fine brownish green stone and having engraved upon its underside the crouching figure of a winged griffin, a Helladic motif found also during this general period on the Cairo Museum's famous axe from the near-by tomb of Queen Aʿḥ-ḥotpe.

From the same series of burials come a blue faience amulet in the form of a couched lion and the majority of our Seventeenth and early Eighteenth Dynasty bead necklaces and girdles. Among the more striking necklaces is one composed of 444 pale gold disk beads with, at the ends, specially designed hemispherical gold caps to which the last four disks are soldered. A long string made up in equal parts of small gold ball beads and blue paste disk beads has at either end a blue paste leopard's head, and a similar string of minute faience disk beads is punctuated at intervals by long silver barrel beads. Twenty-six silver and greenish blue faience beads in the form of small semicircular pods (?) are strung together to form a necklace eleven inches in length. A short string of eight ball beads, graduated in size, includes two in amethyst, two in faience, three in glass, and one in glazed crystal. A necklace composed of grayish paste ball beads has as its central ornament an amulet in the form of a falcon. There are not only single faience beads in the forms of melons and periwinkle shells, but also a necklace found by Lord Carnarvon in which periwinkle beads and small ball beads have been strung together with a melon bead and a long drop-shaped bead in an elaborate and rather effective combination. There are, besides, a very large spherical bead of bluish green faience decorated with black bands, several large cylindrical beads with two or more rings marked at the ends, and 130 blue paste ball beads forming a string over thirty inches in length. Far and away the favorite type at this period was the plain, small disk bead, and of these we possess, in addition to the ones already mentioned, four necklaces and a girdle in faience, paste, shell, and mica. Having been found in organized excavations, all of the beads and amulets discussed above either are on their original strings or have been restrung in their original order. They comprise, then, actual ancient necklaces and girdles, not simply modern assemblages of miscellaneous, often unrelated beads which not infrequently pass for "necklaces" on the antiquities market.

The earring, an ornament probably of Asiatic origin newly adopted by the Egyptians of Hyksos times, is represented in our collection by twenty examples (ten pairs) found on burials of the Seventeenth and early Eighteenth Dynasties. Ten of these (five pairs) are small doughnutlike rings made of solid gold or of sheet gold over bronze cores. Each is composed of a short, cylindrical bar of metal bent into a tight circle, but usually with a minute gap left between the ends. They average about three-quarters of an inch in outside diameter and something over a quarter of an inch in thickness. The other type of earring of which we possess five pairs consists of a length of gold or silver wire coiled into a tight, springlike spiral of two or three turns. Both types could probably be worn either clipped onto the ears or threaded through holes pierced in the ear lobes, the latter apparently being the more usual.

The final item in our Theban jewelry of this period is a thin, slightly curved silver ★wire, nine and a quarter inches in length, found partially encircling the waist of its deceased owner.

From the excavations of the Egypt Exploration Fund at Diospolis Parva (Hu), seventy-five miles north of Thebes, come a bottle-shaped ★amulet, or bulla, in carnelian and a string of brown and blue faience ★beads varying in shape between disks and globes. At Abydos the same tomb which yielded the pair of small female statuettes discussed above produced two ★girdles and a ★necklace of tubular beads, disk beads, and multiple-disk beads of light and dark blue faience and blue paste.

Like many of the foregoing, the remaining objects which we shall study in this section are, with very few exceptions, from intact burials of the Seventeenth or very early Eighteenth Dynasty in western Thebes. These burials, to which we have already referred several times, were cleared by our Egyptian Expedition under the direction of Ambrose Lansing during the seasons of 1915-1916, 1918-1919, and 1934-1935, and between 1907 and 1914 by the Earl of Carnarvon and Howard Carter.

Among the possessions of these Thebans of Hyksos times ★combs were something of a rarity; but two examples were found, both of the small, short-toothed type carved from hardwood and adorned with simple incised decoration. The complete example, just over three inches in length, has a straight back with four small trapezoidal spurs projecting upward from it. The back of the fragmentary comb, decorated with a row of concentric circles, was triangular and had at either end a crudely carved duck's head. A long, straight bone ★hairpin has a head in the shape of a crowned cobra, or uraeus, with the tail of the serpent winding down around the shaft of the pin.

Two handsome bronze ★mirrors, one small, one large, have handles of the traditional form, that of a papyrus column with a gracefully spreading umbel. In one case the handle is of copper, cast in one piece and slenderly proportioned; in the other it is of wood, the engraved shaft and umbel made in separate pieces and tenoned together. In both examples the tang of the slightly elliptical mirror disk is let into a deep slot in the top of the handle and fastened in place with a single rivet. What chiefly distinguishes the handles of these mirrors from the Twelfth Dynasty examples illustrated in the first volume of this book (figs. 154, 155) is the spread and slenderness of the papyrus umbels. A third ★mirror disk, just under four inches in diameter, may never have had a handle, its tang not being drilled for a fastening of any sort.

Among the articles which our Seventeenth Dynasty Egyptians used in applying cosmetics and otherwise making themselves presentable, major interest attaches to a slender wooden ★spoon elaborately carved over the whole eight inches of its length. This ornate and somewhat rococo object has a bowl in the form of a human hand holding a shell and a long slender handle carved with a continuous spiral design and ending in a duck's head turned back upon its own neck. Bronze ★tweezers, averaging around two inches in length, are fairly common, and we possess half a dozen examples of this period from western Thebes. A puzzling little bronze ★instrument, usually called either a "tweezer razor" or a "hair curler," consists of a small razor of the chisel type, to the side of which, one-third of the way along its length, a hollow, pointed prong has been attached by a single rivet, allowing the two parts of the implement to be manipulated like a pair of scissors or, perhaps more accurately, tongs. It is obviously a composite instrument designed for several different purposes, among which may have been the curling and trimming of small locks of hair on a wig or natural coiffure. A lump of ★pumice stone found in a box containing cosmetics was perhaps used as a cleansing agent. In the same box were a crystal of rock ★salt, some chips of aromatic ★wood, a fossil ★shell, a dried ★fig, a large quantity of ★raisins, and some of the small ★fruits of the nabk, or sidder, tree. Five little ★hones of sandstone were evidently for sharpening razors and other small instruments of that general category. A slate blade with rounded ends and slightly convex sides, from a tomb of this period at Abydos, also was probably a ★hone rather than a spatula, as was once thought.

Of twenty-eight cosmetic ★vessels found in our Theban burials (see fig. 8), twenty-two are *koḥl*-jars, or *koḥl*-pots, that is, small, squat vases of distinctive shape designed to hold a black eye cosmetic equivalent to, but not identical with, the modern Arabic *koḥl* (see Part I, p. 242). Three similar ★jars from a burial at Abydos include a fine example in alabaster in which the vessel is represented as resting on a small ring stand. As usual, the great majority of our *koḥl*-jars are carved in "Egyptian alabaster" (calcite), but there are three examples of serpentine, two of pink limestone, one of "blue marble" (anhydrite), one of pottery, and one of wood. Many of the jars retain their flat, disk-shaped lids, some are stoppered with cloth, some still contain "*koḥl*" (galena) or, in one case, green eye paint (malachite), and some are accompanied by the slender stick with one bulbous end used in applying the cosmetic to the eyes. The ★*koḥl*-sticks, including eight examples from Abydos, are more often than not of ebony, but several are made of other hardwoods, a few of haematite, one of ivory, and one of bronze. The bronze stick,

FIGURE 8. Cosmetic vessels of alabaster and other fine stones. H. 1 3/16-3 1/4 in.

which has a tiny circular bowl at the top end of its handle, could also be used as a cosmetic spoon. Besides the *koḥl*-containers in the form of jars there are two ★*koḥl*-tubes, one a double-barreled affair carved in wood and provided with a swivel lid, the other simply a length of thick reed plugged at one end and covered at the other with a scrap of cloth tied in place with string. Each tube is equipped with a short wooden ★*koḥl*-stick. The other cosmetic vessels include two small blue faience ★bowls, one carinated and flat-bottomed, the other having a curved profile and four small lug handles projecting horizontally from its rim. The first bowl once had black line decoration, but both it and its companion are now badly faded and discolored. In alabaster there are a large carinated ★bowl with a flat bottom, a disk-shaped ★jar lid slightly hollowed on the underside, and a pair of broad drop-shaped little ★jars, resembling in their form the huge, bulbous pottery storage jars of the Twelfth Dynasty (see Part I, p. 262). An oval slate ★dish, when viewed from above, is seen to have the form of the royal cartouche (⊂⊃). Finally, there is a container which consists simply of a blown ostrich ★egg with a circular hole neatly cut in one end. By way of decoration this hole has been surrounded by a ring of little circular cavities in each of which a tiny ring of bone has been inserted.

Many of the smaller personal possessions described above had been kept by their owners in little circular ★baskets made of continuous coils of grass sewn with strips of rush. The three examples brought back by the Museum's Expedition in 1916 and 1919 average slightly over five inches in diameter. Each is provided with a low conical lid which fits inside the mouth of the basket, resting on a ledgelike inner rim.

Considering their rarity in tombs of other periods a rather surprising number of stringed musical instruments, especially harps, were found in our late Seventeenth and early Eighteenth Dynasty Theban burials. The five ★harps from these burials in the Museum's collection are light, mostly four-stringed instruments ranging in length from twenty-seven to forty-seven inches (see fig. 9). Their gently curving necks and long, boat-shaped soundboxes (once covered with skin membranes, or drumheads?) have caused them to be classed by musicologists as "arched," "naviform" harps; and since they were frequently held, when being played, against the harpers' shoulders, they have also on occasion been called "shoulder-harps." In four of our five examples the entire harp, with the exception of the suspension rod and the string-pegs, is carved from a single piece of dark, rather coarse-grained wood. The longitudinal suspension rod, to which the lower ends of the gut strings were once fastened, was movable, its point fitting loosely into a socket on the inside of the squared end of the soundbox, its butt attached by an adjustable loop of cord to the knob projecting from the curved end of the box. The upper ends of the strings were wound around the neck of the instrument and made fast to the small hardwood pegs, or pins, driven into its back. The tension of the strings and hence the tuning of the harp were controlled not by these pegs, which were immovable, but by tightening or slackening the cord holding down the butt end of the suspension rod—in other words, by raising or lowering this end of the rod. The hide drumheads, which must have passed under the suspension rods, seem in some cases to have been lashed in place with cords which have scored the rounded undersides of the soundboxes. The smallest of the five harps, though of the same type, is of unusual construction. Its neck and soundbox are separate pieces united by means of an ingenious, lashed lap joint; and, since the end of the soundbox away from the neck was open, the butt of its suspension rod was tethered to a slender, transverse bar fitted into the box near the end. In spite of its modest size this is the only instrument of the lot to have had five strings. An almost exactly similar harp in the Cairo Museum was published some years ago by Dr. Hans Hickmann.

In the same tomb with two of the harps was found a boat-shaped soundbox rounded at both ends and evidently once provided with a long, straight neck (see fig. 9). This, then, was not a

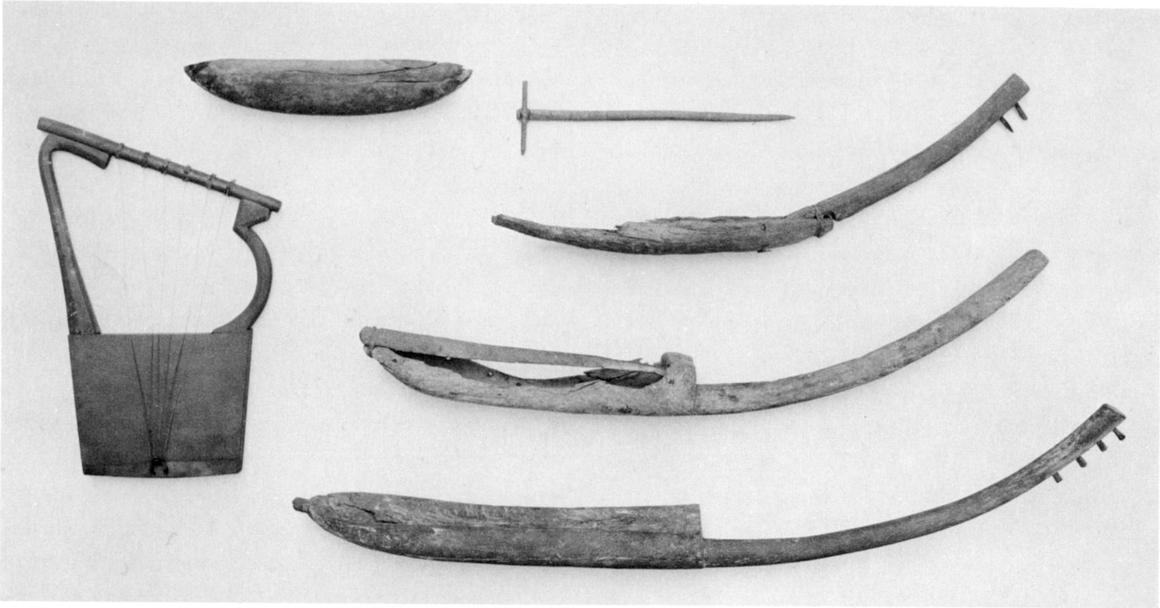

FIGURE 9. Musical instruments, including three harps, a lyre, and the soundbox of a lute. L. 13 ½-47 ¼ in.

harp, but a ★lute, a three-stringed instrument of somewhat more advanced type, known to us chiefly from examples and representations of the mid-Eighteenth Dynasty and later times. The present soundbox is thirteen and a half inches in length. It is nicely made of a fine, ornately grained wood, reddish brown in color, and has a smooth finish inside and out. All around the outside of the rim there is a clean band where the edge of the raw-hide(?) drumhead overlapped the sides and ends of the box, and along the lower edge of this band are streaks of pitch, probably used to fill the seam between the hide and the wood. The lute, a musical instrument unknown in Egypt before the New Kingdom, was, like the horse, the composite bow, and other innovations, probably imported from western Asia during the latter years of the Hyksos domination. If, as seems likely, our present fragmentary example is to be dated to the end of the Seventeenth or the very beginning of the Eighteenth Dynasty, it is the earliest Egyptian lute of which we now have any record.

The lyre, another stringed instrument of unquestioned Asiatic origin, was adopted by the Egyptians at about the same time; and it is not surprising to find it represented, with the lute and the naviform harp, among the musical instruments in vogue at Thebes immediately before and during the rise of the New Kingdom. Of the two examples found by our expedition in 1915-1916 the more complete was retained in the division of finds by the Cairo Museum. The other ★lyre (fig. 9, left), now in New York, has had much of its soundbox, parts of its yoke, and all of its strings and cord loops restored. Typologically it is an "oblique," or "asymmetrical," lyre with arms of unequal heights and different forms and with the crossbar of its yoke slanting sharply downward from one side to the other, so that the over-all height of the instrument on the left side is seventeen and a quarter inches and on the right side only thirteen inches. The shallow, trapezoidal soundbox consists of a stout wooden frame covered with a thin veneer of dark brown wood. It is open at the bottom and has projecting from near the lower edge of its front a bronze staple to which the lower ends of the six gut strings were made fast. At the top the strings were fastened to loops of cord hitched tightly around the crossbar in such a manner that by rotating these loops in one direction or the other the tension of the strings could be altered and the instrument tuned as desired. A special advantage of the oblique lyre was that the tension of its strings could be changed by simply moving the loops up or down the slanting crossbar. When played, this lyre was usually held in a horizontal position, one hand sweeping down across all the strings with a plectrum, the other hand muting the strings which were not to be sounded. For many years after its introduction into Egypt it continued to be regarded as a "foreign" instrument, and is often represented in tomb paintings of the Eighteenth Dynasty being played by a Syrian.

Of the three instruments, then, the arched harp was the only one indigenous to Egypt, where from the Old Kingdom onward it had been used mainly to provide accompaniment for songs, often sung by the harper himself. Though we have the texts, or lyrics, of several of these songs—including one described as being "in the House of King In-yōtef (of the Seventeenth Dynasty), before the singer with the harp"—we have little or no idea what the melodies were like. Musical notation of any sort seems to have been unknown in dynastic Egypt, the melodies being handed down from one generation to another, as they are today. From the harps themselves and the other, similarly limited instruments in use before the New Kingdom it has been surmised that the Egyptians of the earlier periods had only the simple five-tone scale, without half tones, and that their music in general was austere, mild, and lacking in volume, characterized by quiet, tinkly rhythms and soft, flutelike sounds. During the Hyksos period and the early New Kingdom, constantly intensified contacts with the music and musical instruments of western Asia brought about a great change. It is probable that at this time Egyptian music not only became livelier and shriller, but also that the introduction of instruments like the multistringed harp, the multifretted lute, and the oboe with its numerous, closely spaced finger holes brought with it a much more elaborate system of tuning and a far greater flexibility and scope in the handling of tone.

The continuing popularity of board games among the Egyptians of late Hyksos times is indicated by the presence in one of our Seventeenth Dynasty Theban burials of a handsome little ★game box overlaid with ivory. Dampness and termites in the tomb had severely damaged the wood of the box, and this has been restored in the Museum with, we believe, a very fair degree of accuracy. On one side of the box the little rectangles and strips of ivory are arranged to form three rows of ten squares each, the layout, or "board," for the ancient game which the Egyptians called *senet* and which modern writers sometimes refer to as "the game of thirty squares." The other and better preserved side of the box (fig. 10) carries the layout for a companion game, newly

FIGURE 10. Underside of a game box overlaid with ivory, from Thebes. L. 9 ½ in.

introduced from Asia and called in antiquity *tjau* ("robbers"?). An unusual and interesting feature of this board is the incised decoration of the long panels flanking the central "ladder." On one panel we see a crouched lion and two gazelles and on the other a lion confronted by a lop-eared hound in the much discussed pose known as the "flying gallop," possibly, though not certainly, borrowed from Helladic art. Both *senet* and *tjau* seem to have been games of position, like our parchesi or backgammon. Both were played with two sets of five or more pieces each, the moves being determined by throwing knucklebones or sets of wands, the equivalent of dice. The present game box is provided at one end with a small drawer locked by means of an ivory bolt (—•—) sliding in three bronze staples. In this drawer were found twelve ivory ★playing pieces for the games, six conical, six spool-shaped, as well as six ivory ★game wands, pointed at both ends, and a pair of ★knucklebones. An adjacent burial yielded a set of larger and more elaborate ★game wands nicely carved in hardwood. The four wands comprising the set average slightly over eight inches in length. Two have rounded ends like fingertips and two have pointed ends carved in the form of fox or jackal heads. All are flat on one side and slightly convex on the other, and each is adorned with three bands of closely spaced incised lines. It was apparently the way in which such wands fell when tossed that indicated the moves of the men in an associated board game. A leather-covered ★ball for an outdoor game is made of four segments of hide laced together with leather thongs and tightly stuffed with barley husks. Like the Eleventh Dynasty balls discussed in the first volume of this book (p. 251) it is smaller, lighter, and softer than a modern baseball, to which, however, it bears a marked resemblance.

The crude, but rather appealing, little figure of a heavily laden pack ★donkey (fig. 11), found by the Earl of Carnarvon on the hill slope northeast of Deir el Baḥri, is believed with considerable plausibility to have been a child's toy rather than a funerary model. Both the animal and the nine oval sacks which make up its load are modeled in Nile clay, the sacks being supported on four vine-leaf stalks thrust into the back of the beast. Fortunately, the figure had been packed in a small, wide-mouthed pottery ★jar of a type well known in the Second Intermediate period, and may be assigned with some assurance to the interval between the Twelfth and Eighteenth Dynasties. A second ★donkey, in this case of red pottery, painted white, was found not far away, on the lower slopes of the Dirāʿ Abu'n Naga. Three and a half

FIGURE 11. Toy pack donkey of clay. L. 2 9/16 in.

inches in length, it carries no load, but is provided on its back with two looplike projections, perhaps part of a packsaddle. Both figures had undoubtedly once been associated with burials. Comparable to our two examples is a pottery donkey with packs discovered by Petrie in a tomb of the Twelfth Dynasty at Diospolis Parva (Hu).

Though in many cases the types of housefurnishings recovered from our Theban burials continued in use well down into the Eighteenth Dynasty, the great majority of the pieces which we are about to inspect were found in association with coffins of the straight *rishi* type and are dated by their discoverers to the "IInd Intermediate Period," "Dyn. XVII," or, at the latest, "Dyn. XVII-XVIII."[8]

Ten wooden ★headrests are of the conventional columnar type (𓊫) popular throughout the greater part of Egypt's dynastic history (Part I, pp. 120, 258). Most of them are made in three parts—the curved wooden "pillow," the rectangular or octagonal column, and the wide, flat base—joined together by a long square tenon running vertically up through the center of the headrest and occasionally capped, at the middle of the pillow, with a small square of ivory. A pair of bronze ★studs, their hemispherical heads overlaid with sheet gold, were probably used to fasten the pillow and shaft of a headrest to the central tenon.

The form of the little ★table shown in figure 12 was evidently inspired by one of the pair of great rectangular towers which flank the gateways of Egyptian temples and which, with the gateway proper, are generally referred to as the pylon. We see, in any case, in this gracefully proportioned small piece of furniture the salient characteristics of the pylon tower—the oblong rectangular shape, the sloping sides and ends, and the crowning cavetto-and-torus cornice. Made up of numerous pieces of fine hardwood, skillfully joined together with pegged tenons, the table shows on its top and along the edges of its legs the effective use of strips of light-colored veneer. Well designed, well made, and handsomely finished, it is a worthy forerunner of the many admirable works of craftsmanship produced during the great centuries of the New Kingdom.

Three small square ★stools of a common type (see fig. 12) have plaited rush seats and short, sturdy legs suggesting in their form the hieroglyph 𓎿, "protection." Though just over a foot square and less than six inches in height such stools were apparently employed as seats, not as footstools, an article of furniture which did not come into use in Egypt until well along in the Eighteenth Dynasty. As can be seen in the photograph, the ends of the rails forming the frames of the stools are let into mortises running through the heavy upper sections of the legs. The rushes of which the seats are made are interlaced so as to produce a diagonal pattern, each rush passing under the first two to four cross strands, then over the next ten to twelve strands, and so on. At the edges the strands are looped entirely around the seat rails and secured with a row of knots. A stubby rectangular ★leg from a fourth stool of the same type measures only five and a quarter inches in height. Four slender cylindrical legs, their lower parts waisted and decorated with bands of incised rings, are from two higher ★stools of a variety well known during the first half of the Eighteenth Dynasty. Light horizontal stretchers found with the legs indicate that each of the two stools measured approximately the same in all three of its principal dimensions—in one case fifteen inches, in the other twelve inches. Both legs and stretchers are of some dark, heavy hardwood—perhaps tamarisk. The

FIGURE 12. A small table and a stool with a rush seat. L. of table 25 in.

[8] See the works of Carnarvon and Carter and of Lansing, Bibliography, §§ 20 and 22.

missing seat rails were probably of pine or a similar soft wood and the seats themselves of rushwork, string mesh, or leather.

What was once a handsome ★chair is now represented only by numerous fragments of its dark wood veneer and ebony and ivory overlay. The decoration of the back of the chair evidently consisted of alternating vertical bands of ebony and ivory topped by a horizontal panel of ivory, some sixteen inches in length, on which was engraved the winged sun's disk flanked on either side by the sun god's epithet "the Beḥdetite," written in monumental hieroglyphs. Other bits of the chair which had resisted the effects of dampness and proved unpalatable to the ancient termites include the ivory overlays for the angle braces joining the back to the seat, thin strips of hardwood veneer which had served as edging for the back and seat, and a great quantity of small notched pieces of ebony inlay of undetermined use. In view of their length and straightness no special knowledge is needed to conclude that the panels of ivory used in the adornment of the chair were sawn from the tusks of an elephant, not from those of a hippopotamus. This, no less than the lavish use of ebony in its construction and decoration, indicates that at the time this chair was made trade relations existed—perhaps had recently been re-established—between Upper Egypt and the lands to the south. Of a similar chair from an adjacent burial there remains only one front ★leg, skillfully carved in a hard, dark wood in the shape of the foreleg of a lion resting on a ribbed and tapered block. A short section of cylindrical wooden ★rail ending in a knob is perhaps also from a chair; and a very much larger ★knob, some three and a half inches in its maximum diameter, is known to have come from the end of a funerary bier. One final item of furniture is a very small wooden ★drawer, lap-jointed at the corners, which must have belonged to a game box, a cosmetic casket, or a jewel case.

The same adverse conditions which destroyed so much of the furniture must also have been responsible for the disappearance of most of the household baskets of this period. All that remain are a shallow, open ★basket plaited of palm-leaf strip and indistinguishable from its modern descendant, a conical ★lid from a grass-coil basket sewn with strips of rush, and a circular basketry ★tray made of a thick grass coil lashed at intervals with two-ply grass cord. Four fragments of a coarse linen ★sheet, which had been used as a pall, preserve one selvage edge, one fringed edge, and one end with the usual long warp fringe, in this case braided.

Twenty-five pottery ★vessels give us a fair cross section of the types and wares in use in Upper Egypt during the Hyksos period. Among the larger vessels, elongated ovoid jars of greenish white desert clay ("*ḳulleh*-ware"; see Part I, p. 147) predominate and some of these show incised linear or "combed" decoration on the lips and shoulders. Drop-shaped jars and degenerated *ḥes*(𓎿)-forms in fine red ware with polished red slip are particularly characteristic of the period; and the squat, carinated jar with red and black line decoration, so well known in the Eighteenth Dynasty, is beginning to make its appearance. Two slender-necked, cordiform vases in fine light-red ware are from the tomb in which was found Carnarvon Tablet I, a hieratic copy of a famous historical text dealing with the wars of King Kamosĕ against the Hyksos (see p. 9). A pottery ring stand shows little advance over the Middle Kingdom model, but two little one-handled pitchers are similar to those seen in Eighteenth Dynasty banquet scenes. Other types include small flasks with long, corrugated necks, squat cordiform and drop-shaped jars with wide mouths, flat-bottomed bowls in coarse red or fine brown ware, and rough little saucers in soft reddish brown pottery. A beaker of polished black ware and three deep-red bowls with polished black tops, though found in ordinary Seventeenth Dynasty Theban burials, may be products of the so-called "pan-grave people," soon to be discussed. A fragment of a large *ḳulleh*-ware jar bears part of an incised hieroglyphic inscription referring to the "King's ḥarīm."

Some of the jars and bowls contained supplies

of ★food, including small cuts of meat, grains of wheat, flat peas (*gilban*), figs, dates, and raisins. The fruits, or ★nuts, of the dōm palm, which Winlock has described[9] as "a favorite food of the ancient Egyptians, frequently found in burials, especially in the period just before the Empire," do, in fact, occur in some quantity in our Seventeenth Dynasty Theban burials, both in and out of pottery vessels.

Turning from housefurnishings to the equipment of some of the professions and trades, we encounter first a small group of weapons dated by their discoverers to the years immediately preceding the rise of the New Kingdom. Among these, major interest attaches to a composite ★bow, a powerful, long-range weapon of Asiatic design which in Egypt had only recently begun to replace the old, one-piece self bow of the Middle Kingdom and earlier periods (see Part I, pp. 279 ff.). The present, somewhat fragmentary specimen is a reflex bow, just under six feet in length, showing in its relaxed, or unstrung, state two arched limbs meeting at an angle at its center and curving away from the direction in which the bow was to be strung. It is made up of thin layers of horn glued to the front and back of a grooved wooden core and is bound the whole of its length with birch bark. The tree from which the bark was obtained, the European white birch, is not found in the Near East south of Cappadocia, and it is practically certain that the bark or possibly the bow itself was imported from some country well to the north of Egypt. Two large hardwood ★boomerangs, twenty - four and twenty - seven inches in length, were hunting weapons probably used chiefly for knocking over birds and small animals. Their thin, carefully shaped blades, though showing a marked twist, or skew, from one end to the other, are only slightly curved, and it would seem that these particular weapons are of the nonreturn type which has great range, but which has to be retrieved after every throw. A heavy bronze ★axe head from Hu shows the slender, waisted shape characteristic of the late Seventeenth Dynasty and seen in the well-known axe of King Ka-mosĕ. The longer of two forked ★staves is an interesting example of ancient nature-faking, the "knots" at its lower end having been carved by the maker and the lateral leg of the "fork" being a separate piece of wood doweled in place.

The simple equipment of the Theban painter of this time is represented by a rough ★mortar and pestle of Nile mud stained with red pigment, an equally rough wooden ★paddle for mixing paint, and a lump of red ★ocher. A scribe's writing ★palette, or pen case, nine and a half inches long, is carved in one piece from a narrow slab of hardwood capped at either end with a little plaque of ivory. Red pigment is caked in one of the two small, circular ink depressions near the top of the palette, and the thin wooden slip is still in position over the lower section of the pen slot. A second ★palette of exactly the same type is represented by a fragment only. Other items of the scribe's equipment include a small ★water jar of buff pottery with brown linear decoration, and two large bivalve ★shells which had been used as inkwells.

The most noteworthy development in Egyptian burial customs during the period of the Hyksos domination was the widespread adoption by kings and commoners alike of the anthropoid, or man-shaped, coffin, the popularity of which now began rapidly to surpass that of the earlier, rectangular type. At Thebes the provincial craftsmen, unable to obtain good structural lumber, adopted the expedient of carving the boxes and lids of the coffins out of the rough, coarse-grained logs of the sycamore-fig tree in much the same manner as dugout canoes are produced in other parts of the world. Projections, such as the foot pieces of the anthropoid lids, were often shaped separately and doweled to the carved logs in the appropriate places, and rough patches, their joints smeared over with coarse plaster, are numerous. The highly distinctive form and decoration of these Seventeenth Dynasty coffins is well described by Ambrose Lansing, the discoverer of four of our eight ex-

[9] On a label written before 1920 to accompany a group of food supplies exhibited in one of our galleries.

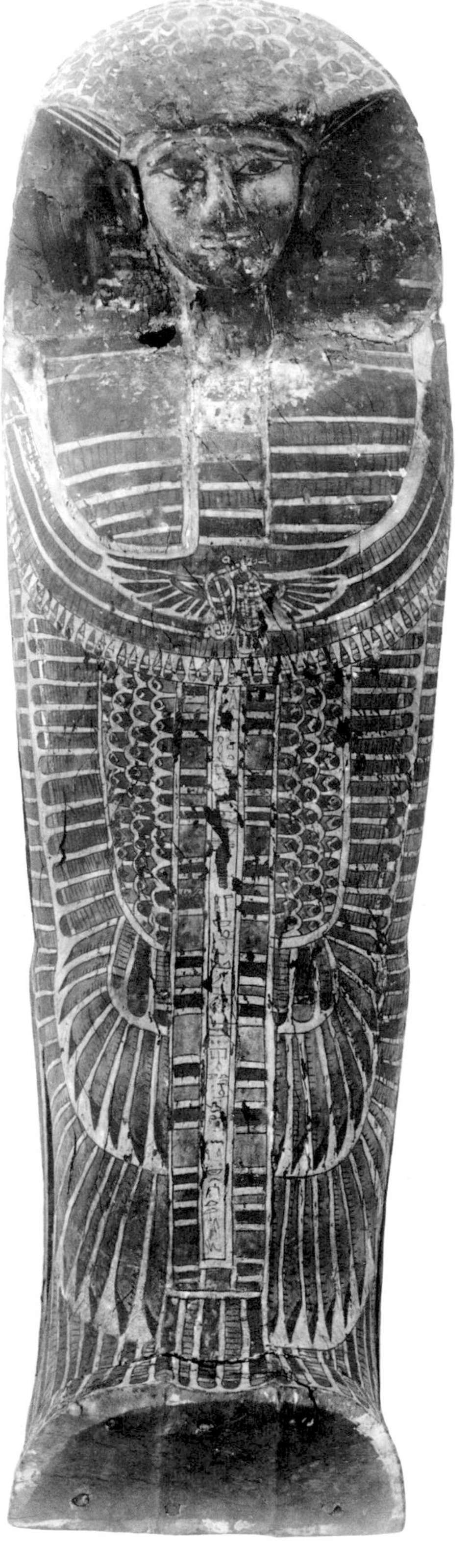

FIGURE 13. *Rishi* coffin inscribed for the House Mistress Reri. L. 75 in.

amples, in his excavation report: ". . . the coffins were of the type known as 'Rishi,' a name taken over from the Arabic of the native workmen of earlier excavators into the vocabulary of Egyptology, and meaning 'feathered.' It aptly describes their appearance. They are anthropoid in shape, with a decoration representing the wings of a vulture spread protectively over the body, and the same motive repeated on the wig. The feathers are colored red, blue, and green, recurring in the same order, with black, or white and red tips, the whole on a yellow ground. This decoration is confined to the lid, the bottom of the coffin being commonly plain, or simply painted with broad bands of different colors. The faces, usually poorly modeled, may best be described as 'wedge-shaped' in appearance, a characteristic peculiar to the coffins of this period. On the chest a broad semicircular band is painted to represent the ordinary bead collar with pendants, sometimes replaced by a band imitating a braid of hair and hawk's-head shoulder pieces. A small vulture with outspread wings forms the center of the necklace, and a similar representation often occurs on top of the headdress. Down the middle of the lid, between the wings of the vulture, a band with a border on either side is left for the inscription. This is the ordinary 'nisut-dy-hotep' offering formula—but it is usually omitted in the poorer coffins. The arms are not suggested, nor do the hands appear except in coffins of a time so late that the influence of the Eighteenth Dynasty is apparent in other respects also, notably the shape of the face and the treatment of the wig. The first reigns of the Eighteenth Dynasty mark the disappearance of the true Rishi coffin. . . ."[10]

The Museum's eight *rishi* ★coffins range in length from just under six feet to just over seven feet, the great majority being within four inches one way or the other of six feet. For illustration we

[10] *M. M. A. Bulletin*, XII (1917), May, *Supplement*, p. 16.

have chosen a typical example of the *rishi* class (fig. 13) and one of exceptional interest because of the painted scenes on its sides (fig. 14). Though most of the coffins are inscribed down the center of the lid with a crudely written offering formula invoking Osiris or, more rarely, Ptaḥ, in only three instances have the names of their owners been filled in. The coffin shown in figure 13 belonged to the House Mistress Reri; another, not illustrated, to the King's Servant Res; and a third example—rather above average in quality—to a man named Pu-Ḥor-Senbu, whose other belongings have been discussed in the foregoing pages. On the rest the space either for the name or for the whole inscription has been left blank, or where the name should be the group *mn*, "so-and-so," has been written in. Besides the elements noted by Lansing four of the coffins have, on the flat foot ends, large amuletic symbols (𓊽, etc.) or, more often, kneeling or standing figures of the goddesses Isis and Nephthys, accompanied in one case by a speech of assurance addressed by the goddesses to the deceased.

The painted scenes on the sides of the coffin of figure 14 show us in somewhat crude, but most interesting, fashion the funeral procession and the presentation of meat offerings at the tomb. On the left side the boat-shaped bier, containing the anthropoid coffin lashed in place under a canopy and attended by figures of the goddesses Isis and Nephthys, is seen being dragged to the tomb by a team of oxen. It is accompanied on its way by male and female mourners and preceded, at the extreme right, by two offering bearers—a woman

FIGURE 14. Funeral scenes on the sides of a *rishi* coffin. L. 86 in.

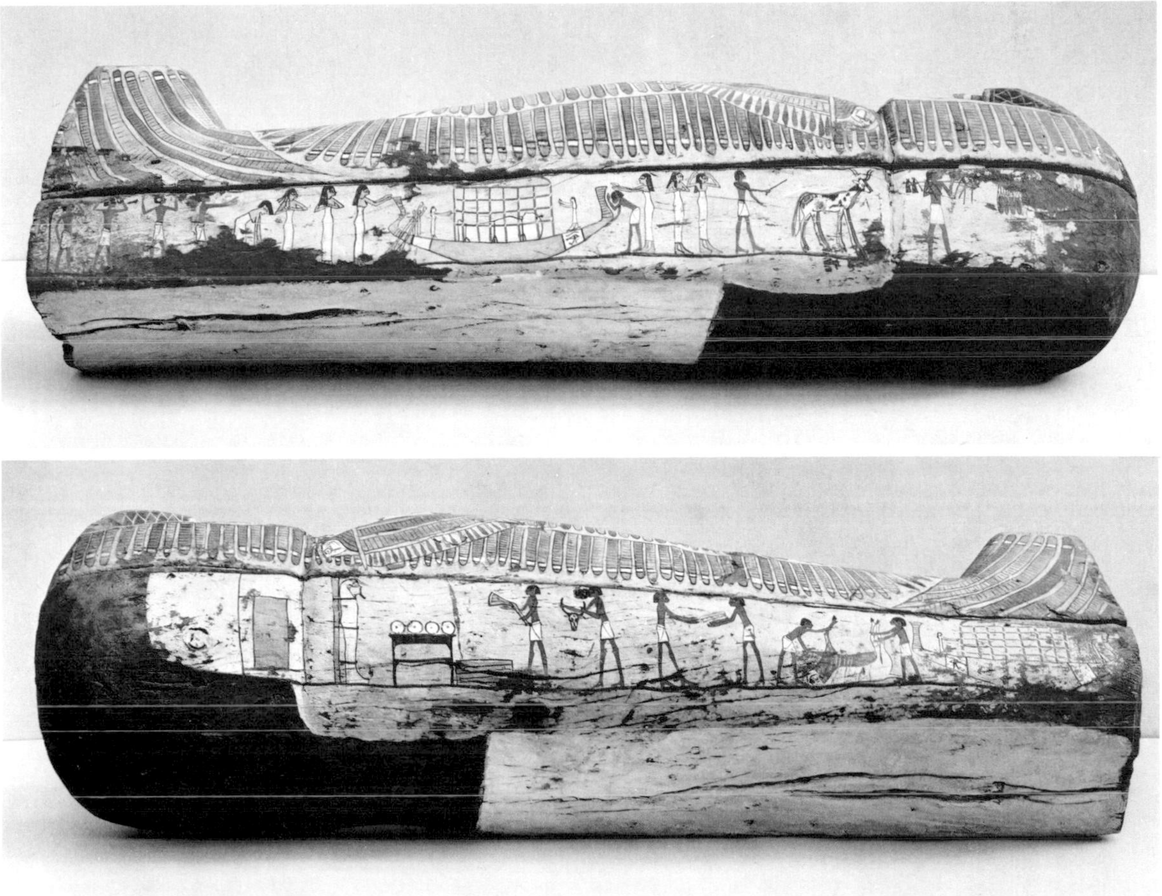

with pottery jars slung from a yoke across her shoulders and a man carrying hoes and adzes in similar fashion. At the left end of the other scene we see the tomb doorway and, before it, the mummy of the deceased wrapped in white linen and lashed upright to a pole or stake. A light table bearing circular loaves of bread has beside it what appears to be a pile of meat offerings. To this pile three men are bringing the foreleg (*khopesh*), head, and ribs of the slaughtered ox which the butchers on the right are in the act of dressing. At the extreme right the bier stands emptied of its burden but with the figures of the two goddesses—evidently statues—still in position. The products of a provincial folk art, these little scenes show, nevertheless, in the slenderly proportioned and at times graceful figures as well as in the clear, uncrowded compositions some of the qualities that we associate with the tomb paintings of the earlier New Kingdom.

Part of another funeral scene is preserved on a ★fragment of an approximately contemporary coffin. The major interest here centers in the fact that the coffin over which, in the painted scene, the female mourners are shown lamenting is itself a *rishi* coffin, with plain, dark box and elaborately "feathered" lid. Interesting also are the women's skirts, with ornamental bands at waist and hem, and the way in which they have discarded their upper garments and allowed their long hair to hang down in eloquent disarray. Other parts of anthropoid coffins of this period include a painted plaster ★face, formerly in the Murch collection, and two alabaster ★eye inlays from our Theban excavations, in one of which the black iris disk is of basalt, in the other of ebony.

A rectangular ★coffin from a tomb chamber of the late Seventeenth Dynasty on the Dirāʿ Abu'n Naga, though resembling superficially its Middle Kingdom forerunners, is flimsily constructed of light, coarse-grained planking and is gaudily decorated in a crude, "village" style. The narrow, rectangular box, six feet in length, is dovetailed at the corners and its low, vaulted lid was provided with heavy, transverse end boards, only one of which has survived. The decoration consists largely of an over-all checkerboard pattern in red, white, and black on a brown background; but down the center of the lid there is a long offering formula in behalf of the coffin's owner, the House Mistress Tety, on the ends of the lid there are pairs of *wedjat*-eyes, on the ends of the box an Anubis animal and figures of the goddesses Isis and Nephthys, and on the sides of the box rectangular panels containing crudely painted little scenes. In the panel on the right side of the coffin we see the spindly figures of four women with arms upraised in mourning, a row of eight tall pottery jars on stands, and a row of four smaller jars above an altar from which flames appear to be rising. One of the two panels on the left side of the box shows us a funerary ship of ancient type with the mummy of the deceased standing upright under a canopy amidships. A man carrying pottery jars suspended from a long yoke across his shoulders occupies the upper register of the other panel, and below, a very badly drawn little male figure guides a plow drawn by a team of spotted oxen. In spite—or perhaps because—of the childish naïveté of its decoration this is without much question one of the most interesting examples of this class of coffin which has come down to us.

No canopic equipment was found with our Second Intermediate period Theban burials; but in 1886 the Museum obtained from Sir Gaston Maspero's work at Gebelein the canopic, or visceral, ★chest of a woman named Sit-Rēʿ, who, in spite of her typical Eighteenth Dynasty name, almost certainly lived and died during or even slightly before the Seventeenth Dynasty. The chest, made of thin sycamore planks, is dovetailed at the corners and provided with two floor battens. One of the end boards of its high, vaulted lid is integral with the lid itself, the other board being attached permanently to the box and grooved to take the end of the lid vault. The whole is painted a dull ocher yellow with black trim and carries, down the center of the lid vault, an offering formula written in black hieroglyphs and invoking the god Osiris, Lord of Busiris, in behalf of "the spirit of Sit-Rēʿ, the justified." There were no canopic jars, but four compartments on the interior of the chest contained its deceased owner's viscera wrapped in linen cloth.

The Seventeenth Dynasty, a period in many ways transitional between the Middle and New Kingdoms, marks an interesting stage in the development of the *shawabty*-figures, the small, mummiform statuettes which since the Eleventh Dynasty had been buried with the dead and since the Thirteenth Dynasty had come to be thought of as substitutes for their owners in the work gangs of the hereafter. A large pottery **shawabty* of Seventeenth or early Eighteenth Dynasty date (fig. 15) was purchased in 1912 from a native of the village of Ḳurneh and is probably from a tomb in western Thebes. Ten inches high, it is clumsily modeled in fine pinkish brown ware and is coated with a polished red haematite slip, on which the wig stripes, eyes, beard, bracelets, and inscription have been drawn in black. The face and the heavy wig are reminiscent of the Middle Kingdom; but the proportions and general style indicate a later date, as does also the fact that the text is a developed, if somewhat carelessly written, version of Spell VI

FIGURE 15. *Shawabty*-figures and coffins from western Thebes. H. of largest figure 10 in.

of the Book of the Dead (see Part I, p. 350), the so-called Chapter of the *Shawabty*. As is sometimes the case, the owner of the figure, the Scribe Neb-seny, is referred to in the third person in the body of the spell, which is here said to be recited by a man named Heny, perhaps a close relative. A slender alabaster ★*shawabty* has the name of its owner, "ʿAbūt," written on its front in black ink, but is otherwise uninscribed. The long, full wig, the beardless face, and the feminine form of the name suggest that the person represented was a woman. As with the *shawabty* of Neb-seny just discussed, the hands are shown, in this case crossed over the breast, the right hand holding a folded handkerchief.

A type of *shawabty* popular at Thebes during the latter part of the Hyksos period and the early years of the New Kingdom is the small, mummiform figure crudely whittled of sycamore wood and usually enclosed within an equally crude miniature coffin of wood or Nile mud (see fig. 15). A few attempt to reproduce the angular mummy shape seen in the *rishi* coffins; but in most cases the figure is little more than a tapered stick with a pointed, featureless face at the broad end and a rectangular ledge, to suggest the feet, at the narrow end. The half-dozen Seventeenth Dynasty ★*shawabtys* of this type in our collection range in length from about four to about eight inches. An unusual example, represented as lying upon a small rectangular coffin, the whole carved from a single block of wood, has a length of just under six inches. Two of the figures carry hieratic inscriptions in black ink: in one case an offering formula invoking Osiris, Lord of Abydos, in behalf of a Theban named Nefer-ḥotep-it; in the other, the *shawabty*-spell recited by a man named Djab. The little ★coffins show considerable variation in their forms. Some are rectangular with flat or vaulted lids, in both cases provided with upward-projecting end boards. Some are of the anthropoid *rishi* type. Others are merely split and hollowed replicas of the stick-like little figures which they contain. Several of the wooden coffins are whitewashed inside and out; one of the mud coffins has the outlines of a bearded face, a headdress, and bands of decoration scratched upon its lid. Ink inscriptions on the lids of two of the rectangular mud coffins tell us that their owners were named Sebet and Khonsu-ḥotpe, "the Little."

FIGURE 16. Genre figure of a woman in red faience. H. 1 ¾ in.

As early as the Eleventh Dynasty it had become the practice in the Theban necropolis to adorn the fronts of tombs with two or more rows of elongated pottery cones, set point first in the masonry near the tops of the tomb façades in such a manner that only the flat, circular bases were visible. The effect was that of the ends of closely spaced roof poles, and this was perhaps the intent of the arrangement from the outset. The individual cones, of soft, coarse, brown or reddish brown pottery, average around a foot in length and three and a half to four inches in maximum diameter. During the Middle Kingdom the bases of the cones were left plain, but toward the end of the Seventeenth Dynasty the Theban tomb owners began to stamp their names and titles on the ends of the cones before the latter were fired, using for the purpose circular or, more rarely, oval or square stamps probably of hardwood. This practice, confined to Thebes, continued far down into Late Dynastic times and has provided us with a vast corpus of Theban names and titles, many of which would otherwise be unknown. In our collection there are, all told, 370 funerary cones of which 183 were presented to the Museum in 1930 by Norman de Garis Davies, 33 were purchased at the sale of the Rustafjael collection in 1915, and the balance are for the most part from our Theban excavations. Twelve ★cones from excavations in the ʿAsāsīf valley have been assigned by their discovererers to the Seventeenth or very early Eighteenth Dynasty. Four of these bear an oval impression with the title and name of the Steward Abety. The impressions on the other cones are all circular. They contain the titles and names of, respectively, the Herald Ibety (four examples), the Steward Kuy-em-Rēʿ, called Isy (two examples), and the Prophet Yaʿef-yeby (two examples).

5. Objects of Unknown Provenience Datable to the Hyksos Period

No period is represented in the Egyptian collection entirely by excavated objects of known source and pedigree. Many of our finest and most interesting pieces came to the Museum as gifts or purchases. Among the objects so acquired a not inconsiderable number can be attributed stylistically or on other grounds to the interval between the end of the Thirteenth and the beginning of the Eighteenth Dynasty. The fact that in most cases we have no background information, geographical or otherwise, on such objects is frequently offset by the intrinsic beauty or interest of the pieces themselves, that is, by the qualities which first attracted the attention of their experienced purchasers, whether private collectors or museum curators. Most of the pieces which we shall take up in this section came to us, in point of fact, as parts of three great private collections: the Murch collection acquired in 1910 as a gift of Miss Helen Miller Gould, the Carnarvon collection purchased in 1926 with funds provided by Edward S. Harkness, and the Theodore M. Davis bequest which became the property of the Museum in 1930.

From the Carnarvon collection comes an attractive little genre ★figure in red faience of a woman carrying her babies(?) in a basket on her back and leaning forward to grasp with her right hand the neck of a small dog (fig. 16). If the contents of the basket are, indeed, one or a pair of infant children, then it is probable, as has been pointed out elsewhere, that the statuette is intended to represent a Sudanese or Syrian woman, for Egyptian women did not normally carry their offspring in this fashion. Unencumbered by the conventions and formalities which governed more serious works, this unimportant little figure gives us a refreshing insight into the tastes and capabilities of the Egyptian artist when left to his own devices.

Of some five hundred and fifty scarabs, cowroids, button seals, cylinder seals, and plaques assignable to the Second Intermediate period we have already had occasion to discuss those bearing the names of Hyksos and Theban kings, their families, and their officials, as well as a number found in position in a series of intact burials of the Seventeenth Dynasty at Thebes. The balance, numbering about four hundred and twenty examples and consisting almost exclusively of scarabs of glazed steatite, come chiefly from the three collections just referred to and from the Farman and Ward collections of scarabs acquired for the Museum in 1904 and 1905 through the generosity of Darius Ogden Mills and J. Pierpont Morgan. Some others are from open excavations at Thebes and el Lisht, but are best considered with their numerous undocumented fellows of the same types, especially since with an object as small and readily portable as a scarab provenience is not a matter of much significance. For convenience in treatment these nonhistorical ★seals may be divided into several classes according to the subjects and designs engraved on their undersides.

Far and away the most interesting and, at the same time, the most characteristic of the period of Asiatic domination are those carved with figures of human beings or animals, sometimes grouped together into simple compositions (see fig. 17). Though Egyptian deities and Egyptian motifs occur on these "picture scarabs" we feel that both in style and subject matter they are much more

FIGURE 17. Scarabs and other seals of the Hyksos period. L. 9/16-1 in.

closely affiliated with the art of western Asia than with that of the Nile Valley. This is particularly clear in the draughtsmanship, poses, and proportions of the figures and in the often extensive use of crosshatching on their bodies and limbs. Among the deities represented we recognize the crocodile-headed Sobk, the falcon-headed Horus, and the horned Ḥat-Ḥor—unless, as has been suggested, the last two are, in fact, Asiatic divinities (Ḥaurūn and ʿAstarte?) like some of the other male and female figures shown. Among the animals the lion is the one most commonly represented, more often than not in victorious combat with one or more crocodiles or with several human adversaries. In two of our scarabs the animal seems to be a standing androsphinx rather than a lion. Antelopes occur with some frequency, and in one instance we find three of the graceful beasts in a circular composition with a pursuing lion. Bulls, hippopotami, and apes are less commonly shown, but an example of each may be seen in figure 17 and there are others in our collection. Beetles, birds, goats, and uraei are also represented on scarabs of this class with varying degrees of frequency. Sometimes the backs of the seals are carved with figures and decorative motifs, an especially elaborate example, with a sphinx couched amid papyrus plants, appearing at the lower right-hand corner of our illustration. Professor Hanns Stock of Munich believes that many of the compositions on these scarabs may have been adapted from wall paintings or reliefs and that some of them may embody in partial or abbreviated form mythological and even political themes.

The symbols or names of leading Egyptian deities make up the legends on another fairly large class of scarabs of this period. The sistrum with the head of the goddess Ḥat-Ḥor, the Khepri beetle trundling before it the solar disk, and the squatting ape of the god Tḥōt all occur with some frequency, while the name of Rēʿ is repeated over and over again on a series of scarabs from el Lisht and the name of Wen-nefer appears once on a seal from the Murch collection. These and similar scarabs of Hyksos times are the earliest to be engraved with divine figures, symbols, and names, which, though exceedingly common from the Eighteenth Dynasty on, are unknown on seals of the Middle Kingdom.

One of several classes of inscribed scarabs bear kingly titles and epithets—the "Good God," "Lord of the Two Lands," "Son of Rēʿ," "Son of Amūn," "given life"—used decoratively to fill the oval fields. A far larger class, numbering in our collection ninety-two examples, is made up of scarabs and other seals on which hieroglyphic signs with amuletic significance—"life," "goodness," "well-being," "stability," "protection"—are grouped so as to form decorative or heraldic designs. Within the designs the hieroglyphs, from two to fourteen in number, are usually arranged symmetrically, the paramount consideration obviously having been the ornamental effect, rather than the meaning, of the combinations. Understandably popular was the handsome and elaborate device symbolizing the union of the Two Lands and consisting of the papyrus of Lower Egypt and the heraldic plant of Upper Egypt knotted together around a 𓄤-sign. The same two plants, especially the papyrus, are also employed in various combinations in a long series of purely decorative patterns. Other patterns are made up of intricately interlaced and knotted ribbons or cords, sometimes combined with plant forms or with hieroglyphs. The spiral, or scroll, ornament, first seen in Egypt on seals of the First Intermediate period, had by Hyksos times reached a high state of development and achieved great popularity. It occurs in many forms and numerous combinations, some undoubtedly inspired by contemporary Aegean art, as the principal motif on over fifty scarabs in our collection and in borders and the like on many others. The forms include the S-spiral, the C-spiral, and the oval scroll, used as separate elements or linked together in continuous border or over-all patterns. Frequently the scroll patterns are interspersed with plant forms and other types of ornament. To this already extensive repertory of decorative motifs found on our Hyksos period scarabs are to be added the looped cord, the cord edge, the square knot, the loaf pattern, concentric circles, crisscross patterns, and geometric linear designs of several different kinds. In themselves these scarabs offer a rich field of investigation for the student of ancient ornament, the designs on their undersides including not only traditional Egyptian elements, but also many motifs borrowed from other eastern Mediterranean peoples.

It was apparently during the Second Intermediate period that it first became customary to place on the breast of the deceased Egyptian a large scarab of dark stone inscribed on the underside with Chapter XXXB of the Book of the Dead, a "spell for preventing the heart" of the deceased "from creating opposition against him" in the judgment hall of the Underworld. Our collection includes a fragmentary ★heart scarab, as this type of amulet is now commonly called, datable to the Hyksos period and, like many scarabs of this period, having on its back a human face carved in place of the head of the insect. It is of polished basalt and is inscribed on the underside with parts of six horizontal lines of incised hieroglyphic text. In the inscription the legs of all bird hieroglyphs have been omitted for superstitious reasons—a practice particularly characteristic of the late Middle Kingdom and the Second Intermediate period. The text, though incomplete, was clearly a version of Spell XXXB of the Book of the Dead similar to the one selected by Sir Alan Gardiner for translation in his *Egyptian Grammar* (p. 269): "O my heart of my mother! O my heart of my mother! O my heart of my different ages (lit. my forms)! Stand not up against me as a witness. Create not opposition against me as a witness. Create not opposition against me among the assessors. Do not weigh heavy (lit. make inclination) against me in the presence of the keeper of the scales. Thou art my soul which is in my body, the Chnum who makes to prosper my limbs." The scales referred to are presumably those in which, in a well-known Underworld scene, the heart of the deceased is weighed in his presence against a figure or emblem symbolizing "right." A rubric appended to this spell in Books of the Dead stipulates that the heart scarab shall be made of nephrite(?) and shall be mounted in gold and provided with a silver suspension ring. Many heart scarabs of the New Kingdom and later times, as we shall see, still retain their gold mountings and the gold chains or wires by means of which they were once suspended from the necks of their deceased owners. Very few, however, are made of nephrite.

The Murch collection, especially, is rich in small ★amulets of the period extending from the end of the Twelfth to the beginning of the Eighteenth Dynasty. These are carved for the most part of such fine, hard stones as carnelian, agate, beryl, feldspar, lapis lazuli, quartz, rock crystal, haematite, and diorite; but two examples, a *wedjat*-eye and a fly amulet, are of chased sheet gold. Nearly all are pierced for stringing. Besides the ever-popular *wedjat*-eyes (𓂀) and numerous double-sided, beetle-shaped amulets (𓆣), the forms include a desert hare (𓃹), a crouching lion (𓃬), two falcons (𓅃) and a falcon's head, two frogs (𓆏), two tortoises (𓆉), a fly (𓆦), a claw or talon, and a number of drop-shaped, tooth-shaped, and bottle-shaped pendants.

From the same collection come nine strings of necklace ★beads, of which seven are composed of spheroid, disk, or barrel beads of conventional types and materials, the latter including carnelian, faience, and paste. There are, besides these, a string of hexagonal barrel beads made of wood covered with gold foil and eleven large and abnormally thick wooden disk beads also overlaid with gold. Two large barrel ★beads, one of sheet gold, the other of gilded wood, and a big cylindrical ★bead of glazed quartz are not attached to strings. Fifty-one amethyst barrel ★beads strung together with an amethyst ★scarab and a gold ★eye amulet came as a gift to the Museum in 1949 without external evidence of date, but may tentatively be assigned to the interval between the Middle and New Kingdoms. The same is true of a circular ★bracelet carved in one piece of pink limestone and a small green faience collar ★terminal of the plain semicircular type provided along its straight lower edge with eight string-holes. Two fragmentary bone ★hairpins are topped by minute carved figures of the hippopotamus goddess Taweret. One of these was purchased at Luxor in 1907; the other is from the Theodore M. Davis collection. Both have been dated "Dyn. XII-XVIII."

Sixteen ★*koḥl*-jars of alabaster, anhydrite, serpentine, and basalt came to us, without indications of their original proveniences, from the Douglas, Drexel, and Murch collections. Among these there are, needless to say, a number of fine and interesting examples, including a small alabaster jar mounted on four short, domical feet. Two wide-mouthed little ★jars of somewhat similar type, one of alabaster, the other of steatite, were probably designed to hold some other cosmetic besides *koḥl*. A thickset, flat-bottomed ★flask of alabaster is almost a duplicate of one found by Dr. George A. Reisner at Kermeh in the Sūdān and dated by him to the Hyksos period. Our flask, having been purchased at Luxor, is probably from Thebes or its vicinity. Two polished haematite ★*koḥl*-sticks and a bronze ★hair curler, all from the Murch collection, are similar to those found in our Theban excavations and discussed in the preceding sections of this chapter.

Games are not well represented in the material of this period acquired by purchase or gift. All that has reached our collection from a game of "hounds and jackals" (see Part I, p. 250) is one of the jackal-headed ★playing pins, nicely carved in hardwood and resembling in its form the hieroglyph 𓄊.

A drop-shaped pottery ★jar of coarse buff ware is accompanied by a rough pottery saucer which serves as its lid.

Three ★axe heads, two of bronze, one of copper, came to the Museum in 1932 as an anonymous gift. One of the bronze heads, of the heavy, deep-bladed type developed during the Twelfth Dynasty, was almost certainly a weapon. The other two heads, probably tools, are thin blades of the old-fashioned discoidal form known at least as early as the Old Kingdom. The example in bronze is solid; but the copper blade has two rectangular sections cut out of its middle, producing a simple openwork design—the forerunner of the similar, but more elaborate, cutout designs which we shall see on the ceremonial axe heads of the New Kingdom.

One final Hyksos period object of well-known type, but of unrecorded provenience, is a scribe's ★ink-grinder, or pestle, of serpentine, acquired in 1941 as part of the bequest of W. Gedney Beatty.

FIGURE 18. Pan-grave and Nubian C-Group pottery. H. of jar in bottom row 6 ¼ in.

6. The Pan-Grave People and Their Possessions

Contemporary with the Hyksos occupation of northern Egypt we find in the South, between Asyūt and Aswān, copious evidence of the immigration into this area of a Nubian people of mixed Hamitic and Negro blood, whose homeland was probably the region around the Second Cataract of the Nile. Fifteen Upper Egyptian sites, from Deir Rifeh on the north to Daraw on the south, have yielded the characteristic circular or oval graves of these immigrants, and at Mustagiddeh and Ḳau are the scanty remains of small settlements occupied by them. At Hu, near Abydos, where the presence of this people first became known to modern excavators, their graves are shallow, panlike cavities in the desert surface and,

although this is not the case in the majority of their cemeteries, the name "pan grave" has been retained as a convenient term, applied both to the graves themselves and to the culture which they represent.

In common with other Nubian cultures of this period that of the pan-grave people still preserves characteristics originated, millenniums earlier, in the predynastic civilizations of southern Upper Egypt. It is closely related to, but not identical with, the latest phase of the so-called C-Group culture found in Lower Nubia between the Old and Middle Kingdoms and also shows less well defined affiliations with the civilization of the Kermeh people of the northern Sūdān.

The homogeneity of the pan-grave culture is accented rather than weakened by the occurrences at different sites of minor variations in the forms of the graves and their contents. The graves, ten to fifteen inches deep at Hu, range in depth at other sites to as much as six feet. The bodies, clad in leather garments (see p. 19) and adorned with primitive jewelry, usually lie on their right sides in contracted position with the heads to the north and the faces to the west. Among the more distinctive items of jewelry are bracelets made of strips of shell or mother-of-pearl threaded together side by side. Pan-grave pottery is confined almost entirely to small, deep bowls of red, black, and black-topped ware with or without incised decoration. Near the graves, in shallow deposit pits, were stacked more pottery bowls and skulls of various horned animals crudely adorned with painted decoration.

The Museum's small, but representative, collection of pan-grave material includes two complete ★bracelets and six loose ★bracelet plaques acquired as gifts in 1916 and 1910. Our pan-grave ★pottery consists largely of bowls and cups of polished black-topped red ware, of both the deep, thin-walled type with flaring rim and the heavier, roughly hemispherical shape, sometimes with incised decoration around the rim (see fig. 18). Three of the deep bowls, purchased in 1920, are from Professor John Garstang's work at Abydos, while three bowls of the shallower type and the polished black beaker come from a *rishi* burial in western Thebes and have already been referred to in the fourth section of this chapter. A pink pottery dish with burnished black inside and incised decoration on the exterior was purchased at Luxor in 1912, but the small black-topped jar with pointed bottom is of unknown provenience and may actually be predynastic rather than pan-grave. For comparison and because they were omitted in the first volume of this book there are included, in the bottom row of our figure, a few pieces of Nubian C-Group ★pottery found by the Oxford expedition to Faras in 1912 and probably to be dated to the Middle Kingdom. Bowls and jars of much the same types with very similar incised decoration occur also in pan-grave burials in Upper Egypt.

Of twenty-four pairs of animal ★horns from pan-grave deposits a selection is shown in figure 19. Among these we recognize without difficulty the horns and frontal bones of the longhorn steer (*Bos Africanus*), the longhorn sheep (*Ovis longipus palaeoaegyptiacus*), the fat-tailed sheep (*Ovis platyra aegyptiacus*), the Mambrine goat (*Hircus mambricus*), the gazelle (*Gazella dorcas*), and (not shown in the figure) a young specimen of the Nubian ibex (*Capra Nubiana*). Both horns and frontal bones are usually decorated with crudely painted designs, the former with broad rings of solid color or with bands of dots applied with a fingertip, the latter with red crosses surrounded by spots. Soot and red ocher appear to have been the only pigments used. It is believed that these barbarous and typically "African" ornaments or amuletic devices were intended originally to be hung on the walls or over the doors of their owners' houses.

Numerous weapons recovered from the relatively small number of unplundered graves indicate clearly that the pan-grave people were a warrior race and suggest the conclusion that they were imported into Upper Egypt as professional soldiers. This conclusion is supported by the types of weapons, which are all of Egyptian design and manufacture, and by the presence in the same graves of gold jewelry and other objects of intrinsic value. Most significant is the fact that the cemeteries and settlements of the pan-grave people, though widely distributed throughout southern Upper Egypt, do not extend northward into Hyksos territory, but are confined to the country south of Kusae—in other words, to the realm governed by the Theban rulers of the Seventeenth Dynasty. They must, then, have been Nubian troops who served as auxiliaries in the armies of Thebes and are in all probability to be identified with the famous Medjay, used as scouts and light infantry by the Egyptians from the late Old Kingdom onward and twice mentioned by King Kamosě in the account of his campaign against the Hyksos. If the identification, suggested by Professor Torgny Säve-Söderbergh, is correct, we must abandon the old conception of the pan-grave people as casual, seminomadic settlers on the fringes of the Nile Valley and recognize them as active participants in Egypt's struggle for independence and in that phase of Egyptian history which led to the founding of the New Kingdom.

By the end of the Second Intermediate period the Nubian immigrants had apparently become completely Egyptianized and in the New Kingdom their presence in Egypt is no longer demonstrable on purely archaeological grounds. Men of Nubian race, however, have continued to serve in the Egyptian army and police force until the present day, and we may be sure that throughout the dynastic period many Nubian and Sudanese tribesmen, particularly the warlike Medjay, resided with their families within the boundaries of Egypt itself.

FIGURE 19. Animal horns and frontal bones from a pan-grave cemetery. W. of largest pair of horns 29½ in.

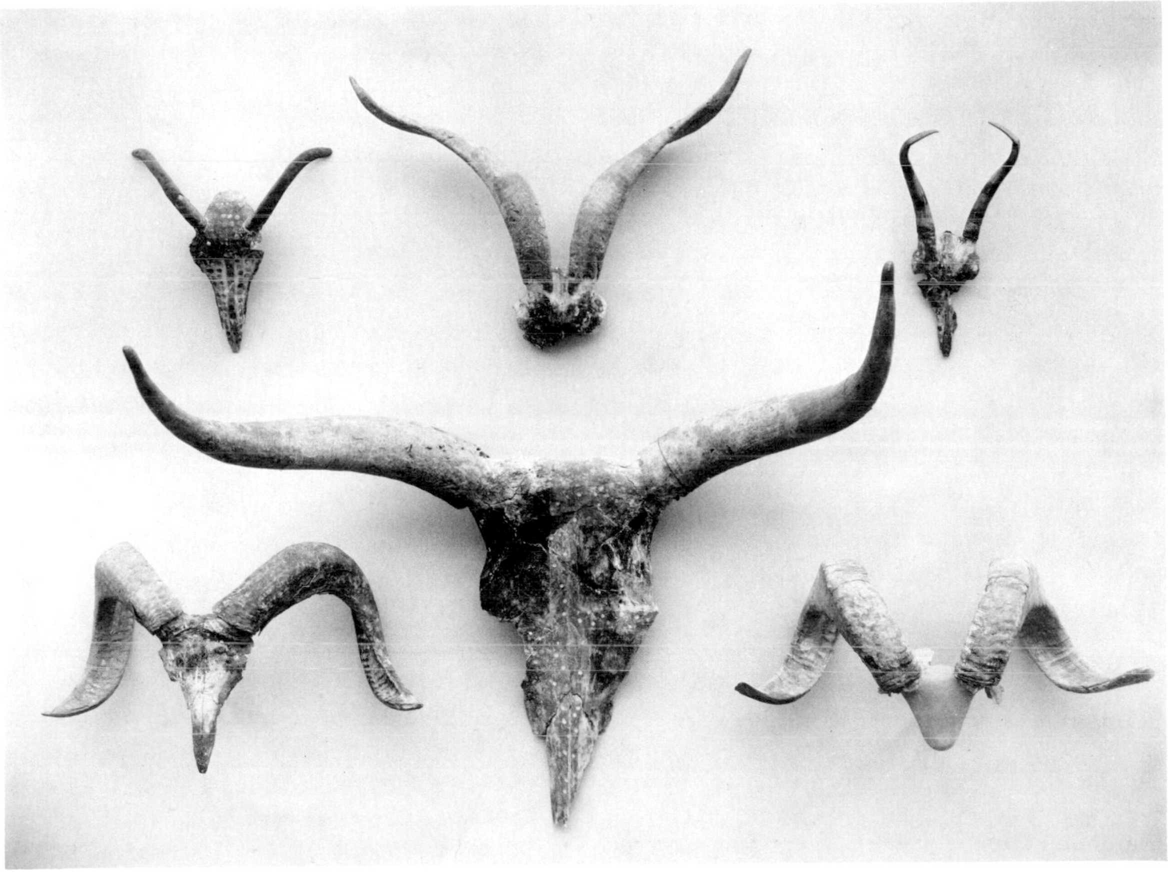

II. The Rise of the New Kingdom

1. Aʿḥ-mosĕ I and Queen Aʿḥ-mosĕ Nefret-iry

The capture of Avaris about 1567 b.c. marked the end of the Hyksos rule in Egypt and the inauguration of the great era in Egyptian history which we call the New Kingdom. At Thebes the throne had passed from the redoubtable Ka-mosĕ to his younger brother, King Neb-peḥty-Rēʿ Aʿḥ-mosĕ I; and it was he who in the third or fourth year of his reign besieged and sacked the enemy capital, breaking the power of the Asiatic rulers and depriving them of their last foothold within the boundaries of Egypt. Our only eyewitness account of the taking of Avaris is a somewhat subjective version preserved at el Kāb in the tomb of one of the king's marines, Aʿḥ-mosĕ, son of Ebana, who, in itemizing his own deeds of valor, lets it be known that the city fell after a series of assaults by land and by water and provided, when finally taken, a very gratifying amount of plunder.

King Aʿḥ-mosĕ I, hailed by posterity as the father of the New Kingdom and the founder of the Eighteenth Dynasty, was evidently a man of exceptional vigor and ability. Characteristic is the manner in which he followed up his victory at Avaris by his three-year siege and capture of the Hyksos base at Sharuhen in southern Palestine and by his pursuit of the enemy northward into Syria, moves successfully designed to forestall once and for all any recurrence of the disaster from which Egypt had just extricated herself. Characteristic, too, is the way in which, with the Asiatic menace removed, he instantly set about recovering control of Nubia, which during the Second Intermediate period had broken free from Egypt and in the time of King Ka-mosĕ was, as we have seen, governed by a local ruler called the Prince of Kush. Without encountering serious resistance Aʿḥ-mosĕ in his first campaign upriver regained control of Wawat, or Lower Nubia, probably as far south as the Second Cataract, and may even have reached the island of Sai, between the Second and Third Cataracts; but was forced to return twice to crush rebellions fomented apparently by relatives of the deposed native princes. As governor, or viceroy, of the newly recovered province the pharaoh appointed his son, Aʿḥ-mosĕ Si-Ta-yīt, with the title King's Son and Overseer of Southern Countries. Once established, the viceroyalty of Nubia continued to exist throughout the New Kingdom as one of the most important offices in the pharaonic administration and its incumbents continued to bear the title King's Son or, later, King's Son of Kush. The successors of Aʿḥ-mosĕ Si-Ta-yīt and his son Tjuroy appear, however, not to have been members of the royal line, but high-ranking civilian officials selected for their administrative ability and their unquestioned loyalty to the crown.

The rebuilding and refurnishing of the temples of Egypt's gods, neglected and probably damaged and looted during the Hyksos regime, ranked high on the list of Aꜥḥ-mosĕ I's activities. A great stela from Karnak records his splendid gifts to the temple of the state god Amun Rēꜥ, and an inscription in the Muḳattam Hills near el Maꜥṣareh tells how in the twenty-second year of his reign the famous limestone quarries "were opened anew" and blocks were extracted for the temple of Ptaḥ at Memphis(?) and the temple of Amūn at Luxor.

At Abydos, the Upper Egyptian cult center of the great funerary god Osiris, the monuments of Aꜥḥ-mosĕ include a pyramidal cenotaph adjoined on its eastern side by a small mortuary temple. The temple was chiefly of brick, but contained rectangular piers of limestone on the sides of which the king was represented in painted relief confronted and embraced by various deities. A fragment of one of these ★piers, which came to us in 1906 as a gift of the Egypt Exploration Fund, preserves the head of the pharaoh wearing the crown of Lower Egypt (fig. 20). At the back of the king's neck, projecting upward from behind the right side of his broad collar, is the hand of a destroyed figure of the god Rēꜥ Ḥor-akhty who stood facing him on the pier and whose name is preserved along the left side of the fragment. At the extreme top edge of the piece are parts of hieroglyphic signs in the familiar formula "given life, stability, and well-being," which in this case, as always, must have been preceded by the cartouches and titles of the king. In this interesting representation of the Red Crown the complex form of the upright element at the back is carefully delineated and the neck-flap at the base of the crown is carried forward under the ear as in the Old and Middle Kingdoms. In general the relief shows little advance over its Middle Kingdom models and on the basis of style alone might well be dated to the Twelfth or even to the late Eleventh Dynasty. Though hardly a portrait in the modern sense, the face of the king—particularly the long, straight nose—is consistent with the very few other representations of Aꜥḥ-mosĕ I which have come down to us. The king's face is painted dark red and traces of red paint are still visible on the crown. The corners of the original pier were beveled and a section of beveled corner may be seen along the right edge of our piece.

A fragment of very fine limestone ★relief found by Edouard Naville in the ruins of the Eleventh Dynasty temple at Deir el Baḥri preserves what may also be a figure of Aꜥḥ-mosĕ I. Here again the king wears the Red Crown, treated as in the Abydos relief, and, in addition, a short ceremonial garment of archaic type with a strap over one shoulder, a broad collar and a pair of bead bracelets, and on his chin the long, curved beard of a god. He stands facing right, holding in his left hand what was evidently a tall staff or scepter and in his right hand a mace with a pear-shaped head. A symbol of "life" (☥) dangles before the royal nose from the neck of a uraeus serpent which descends from some object now lost, probably a solar disk. Feminine hands appearing at the king's shoulder and waist belong undoubtedly to a queen or goddess who stood behind him. The relief is bold, assured, and rich in detail, but rather small in scale, the height of our fragment, on which

FIGURE 20. King Aꜥḥ-mosĕ I, painted limestone relief from Abydos. H. 17¾ in.

two-thirds of the king's figure is preserved, being less than eleven inches.

Not far from his own cenotaph at Abydos Aʿḥ-mosĕ I caused to be erected a chapel for his grandmother, Queen Tety-shery. A magnificent stela found in this chapel speaks of his affectionate remembrance of Tety-shery and of the pyramid and funerary foundation which he provided for her in the "Holy Land," or cemetery of Abydos.

Even greater was the respect and devotion evinced by the founder of the New Kingdom for his mother, Queen Aʿḥ-ḥotpe, and for his sister and wife, Queen Aʿḥ-mosĕ Nefret-iry. The treasure of jewelry and jeweled weapons which he caused to be buried with his mother has for almost a century been one of the marvels of the Egyptian Museum in Cairo. Among the many honors which he heaped upon his wife was the office of Second Prophet of Amūn which he permitted her to assume temporarily and for the relinquishment of which she was handsomely reimbursed. The relinquishment and the lists and values of the property involved are recorded on a block of limestone recovered not many years ago from the fill of the third pylon of the temple of Amūn at Karnak. Frequently represented in the company of her husband and, later, of her son King Amun-ḥotpe I, Queen Aʿḥ-mosĕ Nefret-iry was evidently one of the most able, respected, and beloved women of her time. Deified shortly after her death, she became identified as a patron of the Theban necropolis, her cult and that of her son, Amun-ḥotpe I, remaining popular throughout the whole of the New Kingdom and down into the Late Dynastic period.

After reigning, according to Manetho, over twenty-five years, Aʿḥ-mosĕ I died before reaching the age of fifty and was succeeded on the throne by Amun-ḥotpe I, the eldest of his surviving sons. Aʿḥ-mosĕ's tomb has not been discovered; but his mummy, rewrapped in the Twenty-First Dynasty, was found in 1881 in the Cache of Royal Mummies at Deir el Baḥri.

Few museums boast many monuments of Aʿḥ-mosĕ I. Of objects bearing his name which were made during his reign our own collection contains only fragments of three inscribed alabaster *jars found in the tomb of Amun-ḥotpe I, six *scarabs, a *cowroid, a cartouche-shaped *plaque, an oblong *plaque, and three funerary *cones from the tomb of a contemporary Theban official. The incised hieroglyphic inscriptions on the jar fragments give the titles and names of the king—the "King of Upper and Lower Egypt, Neb-peḥty-Rēʿ, Son of Rēʿ, Aʿḥ-mosĕ, given life forever"—accompanied in one case by the name of a queen, of which only the letter *ḥ* now remains, and in another instance by a fragmentary text in which occurs the name of the eastern country, Ḳedem, followed immediately by the words "seeking recreation." The cowroid, the plaques, and five of the scarabs are inscribed with the king's praenomen, "Neb-peḥty-Rēʿ," the sixth scarab bearing his personal name, "Aʿḥ-mosĕ." Most of these seals are from private collections and are of unknown provenience; and, with the exception of two scarabs of blue and yellow faience, all are made of blue- or green-glazed steatite. The oblong plaque, from Lord Carnarvon's excavations in western Thebes, has carved upon its back in high relief the upright figure of a winged sphinx, a motif strongly reminiscent of the winged griffin on Aʿḥ-mosĕ's famous axe head in the Cairo Museum. The funerary cones are inscribed for the "First Prophet (i.e., High Priest) of Amūn and Overseer of Treasurers Tḥūty," but make prominent mention of the reigning pharaoh, either as the "Good God, Neb-peḥty-Rēʿ" or as the "Son of Rēʿ, *Ḥiḳ-towy*," in both cases said to be "given life forever." *Ḥiḳ-towy*, "Ruler of the Two Lands," is here substituted for the king's personal name and was evidently a recognized way of referring to Aʿḥ-mosĕ I. The funerary cult of the founder of the Eighteenth Dynasty clearly continued for a considerable time after his death; and on the stamped *bricks of Seni-men, a prominent official of the reign of Ḥat-shepsūt, we find among their owner's titles that of "Page of (King) Neb-peḥty-Rēʿ."

Queen Aʿḥ-mosĕ Nefret-iry survived the death

of her husband and lived on well into the reign of her son, so that some at least of her many monuments are to be dated to the time of Amun-ḥotpe I rather than to that of Aʿḥ-mosĕ I.

The drop-shaped alabaster ★jar, shown in figure 21 restored from fragments in the Museum's collection, was found in the tomb of Amun-ḥotpe I. In the panel on its shoulder we read in well-cut, incised hieroglyphs: "The King's Daughter, the Sister of the Sovereign, the God's Wife, the King's Great Wife, the King's Mother, Aʿḥ-mosĕ Nefret-iry, may she live forever!" This elaborate titulary reminds us that the queen was a daughter of King Seḳen-en-Rēʿ Taʿo II, the sister and principal wife of King Aʿḥ-mosĕ I, the mother of King Amun-ḥotpe I, and, in theory, the consort of the god Amūn. The form of the jar is an early version of an exceedingly common Eighteenth Dynasty type—one which we shall encounter again and again in the pages to follow. Fragments of four other alabaster ★jars from the same tomb also bear the names and titles of Aʿḥ-mosĕ Nefret-iry. Among the latter, besides those already listed, "King's Sister" occurs twice and "She Who is United to the White Crown" once. On one fragment the name of the royal lady is followed by the words "beloved of [Amun] Rēʿ, Lord of Karnak." The rubbish in the tomb also yielded fragments of a serpentine statuette of a lady, believed at one time to be the great queen herself, but which, to judge from its style and its elaborate costume, probably belonged to an "intrusive" burial or votive group of the late Eighteenth or early Nineteenth Dynasty (see p. 311).

From a chapel erected by Amun-ḥotpe I at Deir el Baḥri and subsequently engulfed by Ḥatshepsūt's terraced temple come mud ★bricks, almost a foot in length, each bearing on its broad upper surface an oval stamp impression with the name of Aʿḥ-mosĕ Nefret-iry, who evidently shared the proprietorship of the building with her royal son.

A faience ★counterpoise inscribed for Queen Aʿḥ-mosĕ Nefret-iry belongs to a type of ceremonial necklace which was associated, at least as early as the Middle Kingdom, with the cult of the goddess Ḥat-Ḥor and is frequently found in the possession of her female devotees or, as a votive object, in the ruins of her temples. Called a *menyet*, or "*menat*," such a necklace was composed of multiple strands of small beads attached at the ends to single strands of larger beads, from each of which depended a long counterpoise of stone, faience, or metal. In votive *menyets* of the New Kingdom the two counterpoises are usually combined into one with, however, a groove running around the outside edge to suggest two elements placed together; and the counterpoise itself is nearly always given the distinctive form which we see in the *menyet* hieroglyph, , and in the late Eighteenth Dynasty example of figure 153. Once believed to have been a musical instrument, like the Hathorian sistrum with which it is often associated, the *menyet* is now generally recognized as a magical, amuletic object thought to have been imbued with the same beneficial and protective powers as the divine being whose symbol it was.

FIGURE 21. Inscribed alabaster jar of Queen Aʿḥ-mosĕ Nefret-iry. H. 9¾ in.

More recently the shape of its counterpoise has been compared with that of the "paddle dolls" of the Middle Kingdom and emphasis has been placed upon the role of the *menyet* as a symbol of fecundity and upon its association with the birth of the god Horus and hence, with the idea of birth and rebirth in general. Our present counterpoise, made of fragile blue faience, was probably an ex-voto or funerary model and, as such, complete in itself, though its squared end is pierced with two holes so that it could actually have been attached to a necklace. Over seven inches in length, it is inscribed on both sides with the title and name of the queen, the "God's Wife Aʿḥ-mosĕ Nefret-iry—may she live!" who is said to be "beloved of Ḥat-Ḥor," in one case "Mistress of Dendereh" in Upper Egypt, in the other "Mistress of Tepēḥu," an important cult center of the goddess near the Fayyūm. The disk-shaped end of the counterpoise is adorned on each side with a rosettelike design drawn in black outline. A fragment from the mid-section of another blue faience ★counterpoise of the same type preserves on one side the cartouche of Aʿḥ-mosĕ Nefret-iry preceded by the title "[King's] Mother," and on the other side what appears to be part of Amun-ḥotpe I's throne name, "Djeser-ku-[Rēʿ]." This piece, like many other fragments of faience ex-votos, comes from the shrine of Ḥat-Ḥor at Deir el Baḥri, having been found by our expedition in a rubbish pit immediately in front of the shrine. Part of a glazed steatite ★rod, seven-eighths of an inch in diameter, is also inscribed for the "King's Mother, Aʿḥ-mosĕ Nefret-iry" and, like the other monuments on which she bears this title, must obviously have been made during or after the reign of her son.

On her numerous ★seals the great queen is usually referred to as the "God's Wife Nefret-iry," this being the case with a duck-shaped seal, six scarabs, and three cowroids of green-glazed steatite and with a fine scarab of red jasper once part of the Timins collection. On three other scarabs of glazed steatite she is called, respectively, the "King's Wife Nefret-iry," "Aʿḥ-mosĕ Nefret-iry" without title, and simply "Nefret-iry," the last name, however, being enclosed within a cartouche. One of two steatite cylinder seals is inscribed for the "King's Daughter, God's Wife, and King's Sister Nefret-iry"; and the other for the "Hereditary Princess, great of favor, Aʿḥ-mosĕ Nefret-iry." "The God's Wife Nefret-iry" is inscribed around the circumference of a large, gold-mounted carnelian ball ★bead, and four similar ★beads of glazed steatite bear the same name preceded by one or another of the titles "King's Wife," "God's Wife," and "She Who Is United to the White Crown."

The funerary ★cones of a Theban named ʿAb-em-weskhet tell us that he was a Doorkeeper of the Granary of the God's Offering (i.e., temple property) of Amūn and Overseer of the Magazine of the God's Wife Aʿḥ-mosĕ Nefret-iry; and the Steward of Amūn, Ro-au, whose tomb ★doorjambs (see p. 129) were provided for him by King Tḥut-mosĕ III, was also a steward of the estates of our early Eighteenth Dynasty queen.

Among our facsimile color ★copies of Theban tomb paintings of the Eighteenth and Nineteenth Dynasties are four in which Aʿḥ-mosĕ Nefret-iry and Amun-ḥotpe I appear together as deities receiving the offerings and prayers of the tomb owners, and one in which a statue of the deified queen is shown being brought out of a temple on the occasion of an important annual festival.

2. Amun-ḥotpe I and His Family

The reign of King Djeser-ku-Rēʿ Amun-ḥotpe I is fairly well fixed, both as to date and duration. The Papyrus Ebers, an early Eighteenth Dynasty copy of one of the great medical compilations of Egyptian antiquity, bears on the verso a calendrical table dated to the ninth year of the king's reign and embodying a record of the heliacal rising of the star Sothis (Sirius) on the ninth day of the eleventh month of the Egyptian civil calendar (see Part I, pp. 39 f.). This enables us to identify the year in question with considerable probability as 1537 B.C., to place the king's accession nine years earlier, in 1546 B.C., and, on the basis of an inscription of one of his officials, to set his death in the twenty-first year of his reign, or 1526 B.C.

A worthy successor of his father, whose program of recovery and whose internal and foreign policies he vigorously carried forward, Amun-ḥotpe I appears to have merited well the reputation for greatness which culminated, as we have seen, in his being made a tutelary divinity of the Theban necropolis. Though probably more concerned with the organization of the kingdom than with foreign wars of conquest, the new ruler found time to consolidate and expand the conquest of Nubia so that in the seventh and eighth years of his reign his Viceroy, Tjuroy, was able to carve inscriptions near the Middle Kingdom border forts at Semneh and Uronarti at the southern end of the Second Cataract. Inscriptions of Amun-ḥotpe I have been found also at Sai, below the Third Cataract. The king is credited with having crushed an uprising of the Libyan tribes of the Western Desert and with having made important progress toward the conquest of Palestine, though the last-named accomplishment is at the moment more a matter of supposition than of record.

Architecture and the allied arts began to flourish again on a grand scale during his reign, and the buildings which he erected, particularly in the temple enclosure of the state god Amun-Rēʿ at Karnak, were monuments of great dignity and beauty. Especially striking is a small shrine built entirely of alabaster from the famous quarry at Ḥat-nūb and designed as a way station for the barque of Amūn during its processions around the temple area. This little structure, recovered piecemeal from the fill of the third pylon of the Amūn temple, is adorned with fine reliefs and inscriptions, not only of Amun-ḥotpe I himself, but also of his successor King Tḥut-mosĕ I, who may for a short while have shared the throne with him.

A limestone building of more monumental proportions was also erected by Amun-ḥotpe I at Karnak, and it was perhaps from this structure that there came a fragment of fine limestone ★relief with an over life-size portrait head of the king (fig. 22). In the relief, formerly part of the Alphonse Kann collection, the pharaoh wears a close-cropped, caplike wig and a diadem, probably of metal, but reproducing in its form the *seshed*, or "boatman's circlet," a fillet of ribbon tied in a bowknot at the back of the head with the ends pendent. The hooded head of the royal cobra, or uraeus, rises from the front of the circlet and appears again on the streamers at the back. The loops of the bow, as almost always in circlets of this type, have been given the form of two papyrus umbels springing from a circular boss. The subtly modeled face exhibits all the characteristics which we find in other good portraits of the king: the prominent, arched nose, the small, tight mouth, the hard, narrow eyes, and the high, massive cheekbones. Further identification is provided by the bit of cartouche at the upper left-hand corner of the fragment which preserves the final *p* (□) in the pharaoh's personal name as it is normally written, without a following epithet. The small human foot above the head is undoubtedly part of the *b*-hieroglyph (𓃀) in the expression *snb*(*w*), "May he be healthy!" The quality of this relief tells us most eloquently how far Egyptian art had progressed on the road to recovery by the time of

FIGURE 22. King Amun-ḥotpe I, a block of limestone temple relief. H. 17 ⅜ in.

Amun-ḥotpe I; and the style, though retaining much that reminds us of Twelfth Dynasty work, is already beginning to show the softer and more generalized modeling of royal temple sculpture of the New Kingdom.

Allowing for the slight difference in appearance occasioned by the fact that in the relief the sculptor has depicted the king's eye in full front view and has shown more of the mouth than would normally appear in profile, we have no difficulty in seeing that the same face is represented in three fragmentary sandstone ★heads found by the Museum's Egyptian Expedition in western Thebes, one of which is shown in figure 23. These heads are from over life-size statues of Amun-ḥotpe I, in the guise of the mummiform god Osiris, which once stood along the avenue leading up to the small brick chapel erected by the king and his mother, Aʿḥ-mosĕ Nefret-iry, at Deir el Baḥri on the site of the forecourt of the later temple of Queen Ḥat-shepsūt. A complete statue of this series in the British Museum stands nine feet two inches in height and wears on its head the Double Crown (𓋖) of Upper and Lower Egypt. In all three of our head fragments the faces are painted red, the eyes black with white corneas, and the beard straps blue. The blocks for these statues were probably quarried at Gebel Silsileh, ninety-five miles upriver from Thebes, where the king himself is represented in a relief of later date and whence his successors drew the bulk of the stone for their gigantic temples. Two mud ★bricks from the Deir el Baḥri chapel are stamped with Amun-ḥotpe I's throne name, "Djeser-ku-Rēʿ"; and this is found also on a fragmentary faience *menyet* ★counterpoise from the adjoining shrine of the goddess Ḥat-Ḥor.

Faced with the plundering of the royal pyramids of the Old and Middle Kingdoms, which during the Hyksos period must have reached wholesale proportions, the founders of the Eighteenth Dynasty adopted the policy of separating their mortuary temples from the underground burial complexes of their tombs and concealing the latter in the desert hills behind the Theban necropolis, where, unmarked by superstructures of any kind, it was hoped that they might escape detection. The tomb of Amun-ḥotpe I, its entrance pit half hidden under an overhanging boulder, was excavated high up on the rocky slope overlooking the Dirāʿ Abu'n Naga, more than eight hundred and fifty yards north-northwest of the king's mortuary chapel in the plain below. In its general form and arrangement the tomb is the prototype of subsequent royal tombs of the Eighteenth Dynasty. From the foot of the entrance shaft a corridor over thirty feet in length leads to a square chamber having its floor cut away to form a deep well, a protective device found also in the tomb of Queen Aʿḥ-mosĕ Meryet-Amūn and in those of Kings Tḥut-mosĕ III to Amun-ḥotpe III inclusive. Thence a second long passage, at a slight angle with the first, gives access to the oblong burial chamber, a big rectangular room with two square, rock-cut piers left standing in its middle. A small chamber opening from one side of the first corridor is perhaps to be equated with the antechamber found in all later royal tombs.

Repeatedly plundered in spite of the precautions taken to conceal it, the tomb nevertheless yielded, when cleared by Lord Carnarvon and Howard Carter in 1914, a quantity of broken antiquities belonging to the period of its original occupancy. Among these, besides the vase fragments of Aʿḥ-mosĕ I and Queen Aʿḥ-mosĕ Nefret-iry already discussed, are five fragmentary ★jars of alabaster inscribed with the names and titles of Amun-ḥotpe I himself. The jars show a certain amount of variation in their forms, but their panels of inscription are the same throughout, reading in every case: "The Good God, Djeser-ku-Rēʿ, the Son of Rēʿ, Amun-ḥotpe, given life forever." Fragments of at least forty uninscribed ★jars and several provision ★boxes shaped like trussed ducks are of alabaster and include a piece adorned with engraved lotus flowers the calices of which are inlaid in faience.

Much of this interesting and historically important material came to the Museum as a gift of Lord Carnarvon in 1921. The rest was acquired with the Carnarvon collection in 1926.

FIGURE 23. Head of a sandstone Osiride statue of King Amun-ḥotpe I from Deir el Baḥri. H. 8 in.

Among the objects obtained with the Carnarvon collection is a small royal head in gray basalt (fig. 64) which was once identified as a portrait of Amun-ḥotpe I and represented as having come from his tomb. Aside from the fact that sculptures in stone do not normally form part of royal tomb equipment of this period, there seems to be no compelling reason to associate this head with Amun-ḥotpe I, its type and style pointing, rather, to a date late in the reign of Tḥut-mosĕ III (see p. 123).

The Murch collection includes, on the other hand, the ★head of a large alabaster statuette of a king datable by its style and the form of its headdress and uraeus to the early Eighteenth Dynasty, with the strong probability that the pharaoh represented is Amun-ḥotpe I. The headdress, only the front of which is preserved, was either a plain *nemes* (see Part I, p. 71) or, more probably, the *khat* (see p. 97), with a curious double line marking the top of the forehead band. On his chin the king wore the usual artificial beard, supported by straps running up the sides of

FIGURE 24. Limestone stela of the cult servant Ḳen-Amūn, from Thebes. H. 17 ¼ in.

his face. From the crown of the headdress to the point, just below the top of the beard, where it was broken away from the statuette, the head measures two and a quarter inches. Its provenience, unfortunately, is not recorded.

Part of what was probably a ★cartouche-shaped dish in glazed steatite has a brief titulary of Amun-ḥotpe I engraved down the center of its interior. Preserved are the words "The Good God, Lord of the Two Lands, Djeser-ku-Rēʿ, the Son of Rēʿ, Amun-ḥotpe." To judge from the existing fragment the dish, when complete, was seven to eight inches long and three to four inches wide. Its provenience is unknown, but its style suggests that it was carved during the reign of Amun-ḥotpe I himself.

Twelve ★scarabs, three steatite ★plaques, and a cylinder ★seal carry the king's praenomen, "Djeser-ku-Rēʿ," either alone or, more often, in company with figures and motifs of varied types. On one scarab of blue faience the pharaoh himself appears as a small standing figure wearing the *kheperesh*-helmet, or Blue Crown (see figs. 80, 186, 216), and holding in his extended hand what looks like a miniature obelisk. On two others he is represented as a crouching sphinx and his name is preceded by the title "Lord of the Two Lands" and followed by the phrase "given life." The cartouche containing the royal name is sometimes surmounted by the sun's disk and double plume, the winged disk, or the vulture with outspread wings, and is occasionally flanked by figures of divinities. A green paste scarab shows Amun-ḥotpe I's name and titles surrounded by an interlocking-spiral border of Middle Kingdom type; and on a fine big scarab of green jasper the hieroglyphic legend has been expanded to read: "The Good God, Djeser-ku-Rēʿ, the Son of Rēʿ, Amun-ḥotpe." A glazed steatite ★scarab on which a cartouche with the personal name "Amun-ḥotpe" is embraced by the arms of the *ku*-sign (; see Part I, p. 79) and surmounts the two little pavilions associated with the *ḥeb-sed*, or jubilee festival (see Part I, pp. 126 f.), may possibly refer to one of the later Amun-ḥotpes, though its style suggests a date early in the Eighteenth Dynasty. The same is true of a large cylindrical ★bead of glazed steatite and a faience necklace ★pendant on which the royal cartouche is painted in black.

After a reign of approximately twenty-one years Amun-ḥotpe I died, apparently before he had reached the age of fifty. His badly damaged mummy, twice rewrapped in the Twenty-First Dynasty, was found with that of his father in the Royal Cache at Deir el Baḥri. Encased in what may be one of the king's original set of anthropoid coffins, the mummy has not been unwrapped, but in 1932 was examined and photographed by X-ray.

The Priest of Amūn, Amun-em-ḥēb, on whose funerary ★cones the throne name "Djeser-ku-Rēʿ" appears, curiously preceded by the title "Son of Rēʿ," was apparently a contemporary of Amun-ḥotpe I; but the rest of the private monuments in our collection which refer to the deified pharaoh by name were made after his death. The earliest of these monuments, a limestone ★stela datable to the first half of the Eighteenth Dynasty (fig. 24), shows the cult servant Ḳen-Amūn presenting offerings to two deceased and deified pharaohs, Amun-ḥotpe I and, enthroned beside him, King Se'n-Wosret I of the Twelfth Dynasty. Both kings hold the crook scepter and the symbol of "life" and wear on their heads the royal *nemes* which, in the case of Amun-ḥotpe I, is surmounted by an elaborate version of the Osirian *atef*-crown (). Above, in the lunette, a sun's disk with a single, down-sweeping wing hovers protectively over the two "gods," while, on the right, the lone mortal is protected from above by the amuletic *wedjat*-eye. The principal text on the stela is an offering formula recited by Ḳen-Amūn and invoking Amun Rēʿ, King of the Gods, in behalf of the "*ku* of the Good God, Djeser-ku-Rēʿ, justified [with Osiris]." To the latter part of the Eighteenth Dynasty belongs the ★stela (fig. 94) of a certain Amun-ḥotpe who, among many other priestly functions, performed that of *ku*-servant, or mortuary priest, of the "Good God, Djeser-ku-Rēʿ." During the late Nineteenth or Twentieth Dynasty a Theban named Pe'n-Amūn had himself represented on a small limestone ★stela (see p. 384) kneeling in adoration before Osiris and before the "Lord of the Two Lands, Djeser-ku-Rēʿ," who is represented standing behind his mummiform fellow deity and clad in the elaborate costume of a pharaoh of the late New Kingdom. The stela, donated to the Museum by Theodore M. Davis, was found by him in the Valley of the Tombs of the Kings, where the cult of Amun-ḥotpe I was particularly strong. On a Theban ★stela (see p. 384) of the Twentieth Dynasty belonging to a treasury official named Pa-nakht-(em-)Opet, King "Djeser-ku-Rēʿ Amun-ḥotpe, the Heart's Heart (i.e., Image ?) of Amūn," is invoked in the principal offering formula together with the great gods Rēʿ, Ptaḥ Sokar, and Osiris.

One of the latest and in many respects the most interesting object in our collection on which the figure and names of Amun-ḥotpe I appear is a painted wooden ★pectoral apparently made in the late Twentieth Dynasty and used in the reburial of an infant boy named Amun-em-ḥēt who seems to have been a son of our early Eighteenth Dynasty pharaoh. The ★mummy of the year-old baby, wrapped in Twentieth Dynasty ★linen and enclosed in a reinscribed child's ★coffin of the same period, was found by our Egyptian Expedition during the winter of 1918-1919 high up in a bay of the towering cliffs south of Deir el Baḥri. The pectoral, found tied with a cord to the breast of the small mummy, is carved with an openwork design in which we see the "Lord of the Two Lands, Djeser-ku-Rēʿ, the Lord of Crowns, Amun-ḥotpe" standing and grasping by their topknots two enemy chieftains, a bearded Asiatic and a swarthy, kinky-haired African (fig. 268; see also p. 420). Curiously enough the inscription on the coffin lid, as hastily rewritten by a Twentieth Dynasty scribe, calls the royal occupant of the coffin the "King, the Lord of the Two Lands, Amun-em-ḥēt"; and, though this can be attributed to a scribal error, there is a possibility that this child may actually have been designated by his father as Egypt's future king and may even have served for a few fleeting months as his father's nominal coregent.

Near the spot where his small coffin was discovered there is a rock-cut shaft and chamber, in and around which was found a great quantity of ★meat and ★fowl offerings, coming in all probability from the original burial of the royal infant and belonging, therefore, to the reign of Amun-ḥotpe I. Among the seventy-six items retained by the Museum there are joints, steaks, and briskets of beef, as well as beef hearts and livers and whole dressed fowls, the latter including geese, ducks, and quail. Each is carefully mummified and wrapped in linen bandages and many are still in their white-stuccoed wooden cases. These are carved in two halves in the forms of the trussed fowls or cuts of meat which they were designed to contain, the lids and boxes of the cases having been held together by pegs, by crisscrossed linen bandages, and by a black, resinous substance with which their interiors and rims were coated.

The existence of a child king who died prematurely would explain the otherwise puzzling title of King's Mother borne by Amun-ḥotpe I's sister and principal queen, Aʿḥ-ḥotpe, the daughter of Aʿḥ-mosĕ I and Aʿḥ-mosĕ Nefret-iry. Usually called Aʿḥ-ḥotpe II to distinguish her from her similarly named grandmother, this lady was not the mother of Tḥut-mosĕ I, her husband's successor, nor, so far as I can discover, of any hitherto identified person who could reasonably be called a king.

The queen herself is known to us from any quantity of monuments, including her enormous anthropoid coffin in the Cairo Museum, which is similar in size and style to that of her mother, Queen Aʿḥ-mosĕ Nefret-iry, and to that of her sister(?), Queen Aʿḥ-mosĕ Meryet-Amūn. In our collection her name, accompanied by the title "King's Wife," occurs on a fragmentary faience *menyet* counterpoise from Deir el Baḥri, on a big spheroid ★cap from a *menyet* necklace (followed here by the epithet "beloved of Ḥat-Ḥor"), on a large ball ★bead of glazed steatite, and on a steatite ★plaque, the back of which is carved in the form of a fly. Preceded by the title "King's Mother," Aʿḥ-ḥotpe II's cartouche appears also in the lunette of a painted limestone tomb ★stela from western Thebes belonging to the "Herald of the King's Mother, ʿAmotju," who calls himself a "Real and Beloved Familiar of the King." The stela, probably made during Aʿḥ-ḥotpe's lifetime, shows her herald seated on a lion-legged chair, attended by "his beloved son, Renef-sonbe," "his wife, the House Mistress Aʿḥ-mosĕ," and "his beloved daughter, Ren(?)-nefer." The four-line offering formula below calls upon the composite deity Ptaḥ Sokar Osiris to provide ʿAmotju's spirit with "bread, beer, beef, fowl, and all things good and pure on which a god lives, that which heaven gives and that which the earth creates, at the month feast, the half-month feast, the *wag*-feast, and at all feasts of eternity." Wholly typical of run of the mill private tomb sculpture of its period, the stela shows clearly the superposition on good Middle Kingdom models of habits and mannerisms developed in the provincial ateliers of Thebes during the interval of foreign domination.

Queen Aʿḥ-mosĕ Meryet-Amūn, who, like Aʿḥ-ḥotpe, bore the title King's Great (or Chief) Wife, appears also to have been a sister and wife of Amun-ḥotpe I. On two ★scarabs and a green jasper ball ★bead in our collection she is referred to, as frequently elsewhere, simply as "Meryet-Amūn," the name in one case preceded by the titles "King's Daughter" and "King's Wife." Though not so reported at the time, it is almost certainly her tomb which the Museum's Egyptian Expedition discovered during the winter of 1929-1930 beside and partially under Ḥat-shepsūt's temple at Deir el Baḥri. The tomb, which bears a very striking resemblance to that of Amun-ḥotpe I, had been plundered during the New Kingdom, but in the Twenty-First Dynasty the mummy of the queen had been rewrapped and restored to her coffins, and much of the equipment which formed part of the original burial was found more

FIGURE 25. Baskets and duck case of Queen Aʿḥ-mosĕ Meryet-Amūn, from her tomb at Thebes. H. of largest basket 18 in.

or less intact. Of this equipment the Museum received in the division of finds with the Egyptian Government a fine linen ★sheet from the original mummy wrappings, ingeniously woven in the shape of a human being, a linen ★label from an oil jar, a small, decorated ★basket containing ★braids of human hair, three large, undecorated ★baskets, a circular basketry ★tray, a wooden ★case in the form of a dressed duck, and twenty-six cuts of ★meat wrapped in linen bandages. The linen jar label is inscribed in hieratic with the words "Resinous oil, 5 *hin*-measures." (The *hin* was approximately equal to one pint.) The small basket and its lid are made of spiral coils of grass wrapped with grass and are decorated with black and red triangles (see fig. 25). The basketry tray is also of grass, but the larger baskets are entirely of palm-leaf strip. The lids of all the baskets were held in place by loops of two-ply linen cord rising from the rims of the baskets proper and tied together over the centers of the lids, the ties being further secured by stamped mud sealings. The duck case is of sycamore wood, covered with white stucco inside and out, and then with black pitch inside. The meat offerings comprise a shoulder of beef, three beef hearts, twenty-one cutlets or steaks, and the leg of a large duck. Evidence for the existence during the New Kingdom of a cult of this queen includes the funerary ★cones of a man named Meḥ who was "Second Prophet of (the goddess) Amūnet" and "First Prophet of (Queen) Meryet-Amūn."

A third, and evidently much younger, sister of Amun-ḥotpe I was known to her contemporaries simply as the "King's Sister, Aʿḥ-mosĕ," without an accompanying epithet. There is no definite record of her parentage, but she seems to have been a daughter of Queen Aʿḥ-mosĕ Nefret-iry and probably of King Aʿḥ-mosĕ I. Upon her brother's death—her elder sisters and younger brother, Amun-em-ḥēt, being presumably already dead—she was the only surviving legitimate heir to the throne. Some time previously, however, she had been married to another of Amun-ḥotpe I's younger contemporaries, a middle-aged soldier named Tḥut-mosĕ, whose mother, Seni-sonbe, was neither a king's wife nor a king's daughter; and it was he who in 1526 B.C. acceded to the throne as King ʿA-kheper-ku-Rēʿ Tḥut-mosĕ I. Tḥut-mosĕ himself may have belonged to a collateral branch of the royal line or may have been descended from an earlier family of Theban kings. He may also have received his appointment to the kingship from Amun-ḥotpe I in person. These possibilities, however, do not alter the fact that the legitimacy of his claim to the throne depended almost entirely upon his marriage to the Princess Aʿḥ-mosĕ, a circumstance which, as we shall see, produced a certain amount of friction among his first three successors of the so-called Thutmoside line.

One of the royal ladies of the early Eighteenth Dynasty—probably one of those whom we have just been discussing—is represented in our collection by the upper part of a large seated ★statuette admirably carved in indurated limestone, or, as it is sometimes called, Egyptian marble (fig. 26). The face, unfortunately somewhat battered, is characteristically Theban, the slanting eyes, high cheekbones, and full, slightly protruding lips calling to mind the royal portrait heads of the Twelfth Dynasty (see Part I, pp. 175 f., 198 ff.). More powerfully and more carefully modeled than the rest of the statuette, it catches the eye immediately, standing out with great clarity above the slender, cursorily handled figure and from the heavy frame of the elaborate headdress. The latter consists of a massive wig, over the top and front of which is worn a coif in the form of the skin and wings of the vulture of the goddess Nekhābet of el Kāb, one of the most ancient emblems of Egyptian royalty. Worn by queens of Egypt since as early as the Fourth Dynasty, this headdress frequently replaces the head of the vulture with that of the equally ancient royal emblem, the cobra, or uraeus. This was apparently the case here, though, as can be seen, the ornament over the brow of our queen or

FIGURE 26. A queen or princess of the early Eighteenth Dynasty. Upper part of a statuette of indurated limestone. H. 11 in.

princess has been almost completely broken away. Exceptionally graceful in its general form, the present headdress shows the most meticulous detail in the treatment of the feathers of the bird's wings and body. The same detail may also be seen in the handling of the individual wavy locks of the wig and in the beads of the broad collar which appears at the lady's throat between the straps of her simple, close-fitting dress. The way in which the back of the figure is entirely broken away suggests that it was once attached to a wide back pilaster, perhaps as one of a group of two or more figures.

3. Officials and Other Prominent Citizens of the Time

The suppression of the power of the hereditary nobility in the late Twelfth Dynasty and the virtual disappearance at that time of the feudal conditions which had characterized the Old and Middle Kingdoms led, with the return of Egyptian autonomy in the early New Kingdom, to the growth of a new state and a new society, both completely dominated by the king and, under him, by a vast hierarchy of crown officials whose primary function was to see that the pharaonic will was carried out to the last detail. Among these officials must be included not only the members of the administrative branches of the government—the civil service, strictly speaking—but also the military officials and officers in command of Egypt's now highly organized army and navy, the priesthoods of her great temples, especially those of the state god, Amūn, the overseers in charge of her thousands of craftsmen and laborers, and the stewards responsible for the management of the huge personal estates of the king and his family.

Much of our knowledge of these civil servants, soldiers, churchmen, and master artisans and of the world in which they lived comes from the painted or carved decoration of their tomb chapels, especially from those hewn in the slopes of the desert hills to the west of the capital city of Thebes. Here the typical private tomb of the Eighteenth Dynasty consists of a rectangular courtyard and T-shaped chapel, rock-cut in the side of a hill and containing, at the rear of the chapel or in a corner of the court, a hidden shaft descending to one or more subterranean burial chambers. The pyramidal superstructure, abandoned by the kings, had been taken over by private individuals, and a small pyramid of whitewashed brick with a capping of limestone appears to have been a regular feature of the New Kingdom tomb chapel. Pottery cones, stamped on the base with the name and titles of the tomb owner and embedded point first in the masonry, were frequently used to form friezes across the top of the chapel façade and around the upper part of the pyramid (see p. 34). The painted or sculptured decoration of the chapels was distributed on their walls according to a more or less set plan, the transverse forehall being given over to scenes taken from the daily life of the tomb owner, the longitudinal passage and the sanctuary to subject matter of an almost exclusively funerary nature. Painted scenes from the Theban tomb chapels may be studied in three hundred facsimile color ★copies prepared for the Museum by Nina and Norman de Garis Davies, Charles K. Wilkinson, H. R. Hopgood, and others; and many scenes may be consulted in line drawings by the same artists and in the admirable photographs of Harry Burton.

In the New Kingdom, to perhaps an even greater extent than in the preceding periods, the co-ordinator and mainspring of the pharaoh's government was his vizier, an exceedingly busy official who seems to have exerted at least supervisory control over every branch of the national administration. Under King Tḥut-mosĕ III the duties of the vizier were divided on a geographical basis between two great functionaries, a Vizier of the South and a Vizier of the North; but during the first five reigns of the Eighteenth Dynasty a single Vizier managed the affairs of both Upper and Lower Egypt.

One of the earliest of the Eighteenth Dynasty viziers, the "Overseer of the City, the Vizier Yuy," is known to us almost entirely from monuments in the Metropolitan Museum. These include a glazed steatite ★scarab formerly in the Murch collection and a number of objects from Yuy's tomb in western Thebes, which was discovered and cleared by our Egyptian Expedition during the winter of 1922-1923. Among the latter are the bent left ★arm, the ★feet, and one of the ★eye inlays of what must have been a magnificent life-size statue carved of hardwood. It is evident from what remains that this was a standing figure holding in its clenched left hand a long walking stick. The big wooden ★statuette of figure 27, though lacking its face and feet, is also an admirable piece of early New Kingdom sculpture. In it we see the shaven head, corpulent body, and distinctive robe of office of the elderly Vizier rendered with the restrained realism which characterizes the private portrait statues of this period. Less restraint in the treatment of the creased and sagging torso appears in a similar, but much smaller, ★statuette of limestone. Headless, this statuette still retains on its back pilaster traces of a cursive hieroglyphic inscription written in black ink. Near the entrance to Yuy's tomb were found two attractive little pottery ★vases (fig. 28), one in the form of a goose, the other made up of two pitcherlike small jars jointed together and fitted with a single loop handle. Both are of red pottery covered with a glossy black slip and both are adorned with incised and white-filled decoration, that of the double vase comprising conventionalized palm trees and a band of continuous, interlocking spirals. Also found in the tomb were a small painted wooden ★figure of a pig(?) and fragments of three coffins, including a gilded anthropoid case of late *rishi* type, inscribed with Yuy's name and titles. Elsewhere the Vizier Yuy is named as the maternal uncle of a certain Khonsu, the owner of a sandstone stela of Eighteenth Dynasty style in Vienna.

A prominent Theban of the time of the pharaoh Aʿḥ-mosĕ I was the King's Son, the Mayor of the Southern City (Thebes), Tety-ky, whose interesting decorated tomb on the southern slope of the Dirāʿ Abu'n Naga was discovered in 1908 by the Earl of Carnarvon. Among other antiquities a considerable number of model coffins containing

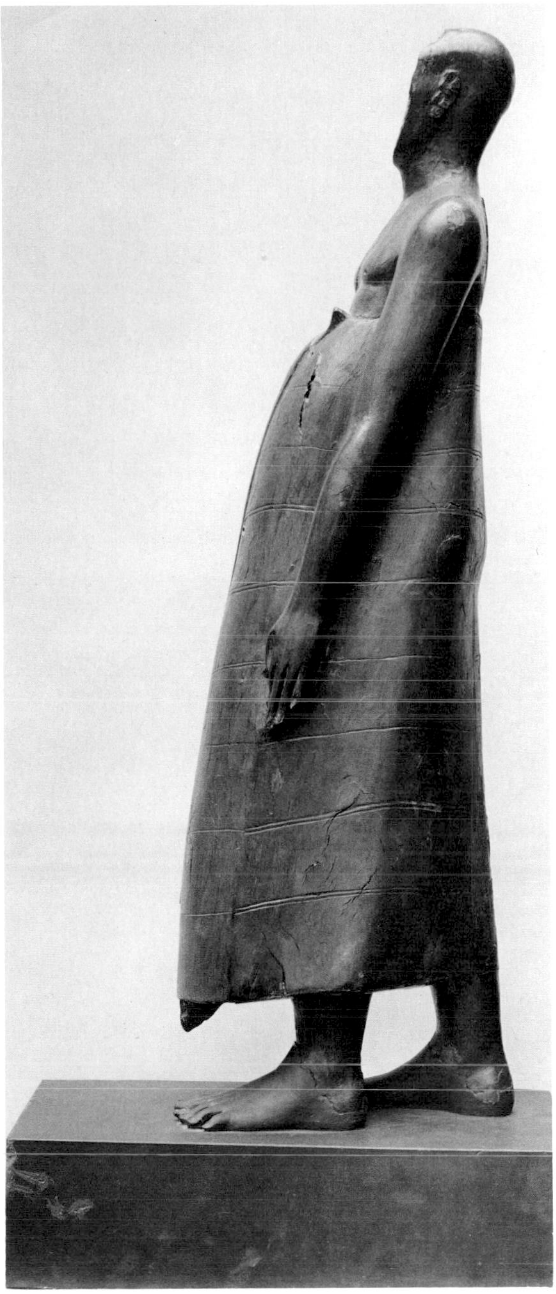

FIGURE 27. The Vizier Yuy, a large wooden statuette from his tomb at Thebes. H. (feet restored) 35 in.

crude wooden *shawabty*-figures were found, deposited in five small niches in the west wall of the courtyard of the tomb. This class of *shawabty*, which apparently originated during the Seventeenth Dynasty (see p. 34), continued in use well down into the early decades of the New Kingdom. Nine of the eleven ★figures and six of the nine ★coffins from the tomb of Tety-ky in our collection are inscribed in hieratic with the names of their owners—Tety (four examples), Tety-ʿan, Tety-nefer, Pa-nefer, Aʿḥ-mosĕ, Teyu, and Nena, daughter of Pa-rekhty—in five cases incorporated in offering formulae invoking the gods Osiris or Sokar. The two remaining figures, one of which is enclosed within a miniature coffin of Nile mud, are uninscribed. An altogether similar ★*shawabty*, lying in a small rectangular coffin of sycamore wood, is of unknown provenience. The figure bears the *shawabty*-spell written in eight horizontal lines and the underside of the lid of the little coffin is inscribed in cursive hieroglyphs for the Sculptor Nefer-ḥēbef.

The large and handsome ★*shawabty*-figure shown in figure 29 was found in a bay of the Theban cliffs, near the burial of the child king Amun-em-ḥēt who, as we have seen, is believed to have been a son of Amun-ḥotpe I. It is of early Eighteenth Dynasty type and is inscribed for the Chief Steward and Scribe Sen-yu, a man who may well have been charged with the management of the estates of the royal infant. The figure is carved of steatite and is coated with a fine greenish blue glaze, the wig being painted black over the glaze. The text, engraved in seven horizontal lines around the lower part of the figure, is the usual *shawabty*-spell (Chapter VI of the Book of the Dead) and differs in no essential respect from the late Middle Kingdom versions of the same spell mentioned in the first volume of this book (p. 350). It is recited by Sen-yu himself, who addresses his small mummiform double, saying: "O you *shawabty*, if the Scribe Sen-yu is registered for work which is to be done in the necropolis, as a man under obligation, to cultivate the fields, to irrigate the banks, to transport sand of the east and of the west—'Here am I!' you shall say."

Ineni, an official whose long and eventful

FIGURE 28. Small pottery vases from the tomb of the Vizier Yuy. H. 3 ½ and 3 in.

career began under Amun-ḥotpe I and lasted well into the reign of Tḥut-mosĕ III, is best remembered as an architect and builder. His principal function, however, seems to have been the administration of the vast grain supplies assigned to the god Amūn, and on the stamped pottery ★cones from his Sheikh ʿAbd el Ḳurneh tomb he calls himself the "Mayor, the Overseer of the Two Granaries of Amūn, the Scribe Ineni." "The Inspector of Scribes Ineni," known to us from eight similar ★cones, was possibly, though not certainly, the same man.

Among a number of other early Eighteenth Dynasty dignitaries represented in our collection by funerary cones from their tombs at Thebes, we have already had occasion to refer to the First Prophet of Amūn and Overseer of Treasurers Tḥūty, who held his high office under King Aʿḥ-mosĕ I, and the *Wēʿb*-priest (see Part I, pp. 76, 102) of Amūn, Amun-em-ḥēb, an evidently well-to-do churchman of the reign of Amun-ḥotpe I. Nine other ★cones of the period, seven of which are from known Theban tomb chapels, introduce us to the King's Scribe and Treasury Overseer Tḥut-nofre; the Steward of the King's Mother, Aʿḥ-ḥotpe, called Pe'n-yaty; the (Royal) Page Pa-ḥiḳ-men, called Benia; the Overseer of the Two Granaries in the Southern City, Ḥery-iry; and the Overseer of Waterfowl Runs (?) Tjay. Their owners' names suggest that the ★cones of the (Royal) Page Ka-mosĕ, and the *Weʿb*-priest of Amūn, Si-pe-ir, are also to be assigned to the early part of the dynasty.

4. Products of the Early Eighteenth Dynasty Ateliers

Unlike those discussed in the preceding sections of this chapter, the works of art and craftsmanship to which we now direct our attention were not associated with members of Egypt's royal family or with her great officials, but with ordinary and for the most part untitled citizens of Thebes and other communities. The beauty and technical excellence of many of these works show that the country's rapidly growing prosperity and the accompanying rise in her standards of taste were

FIGURE 29. Glazed steatite *shawabty* of the Chief Steward Sen-yu. H. 10¾ in.

no longer confined to certain privileged classes, but were shared to a great extent by her people as a whole. They are, moreover, eloquent testimonials to the availability even at this early stage in the development of the New Kingdom of large numbers of highly trained artists and artisans, already vying with one another in skill and imagination to meet the demands of an ever more numerous and more sophisticated clientele.

It must, for example, have been a sculptor of considerable ability who produced the charming and sensitive ★statuette of a nude youth shown in figure 30. The figure, that of a young Theban named Amun-em-ḥēb, was found, together with a statuette of the boy's elder brother Ḥu-webenef, in the coffin of their mother, Aʿḥ-ḥotpe, who was called Ta-nedjem(et), "the Sweet," and who evidently lived and died during the early part of the Eighteenth Dynasty. Both statuettes, we learn from the inscriptions on their somewhat crude wooden bases, were dedicated by the boys' father, Tḥūty. The offering formulae which precede the dedications and which in both cases invoke the god Osiris are of the usual funerary type, a fact which suggests that the figures were designed or at least inscribed as tomb statuettes. It seems clear that we have stumbled upon an ancient family tragedy involving the premature deaths of two youths much beloved of their parents.

The figure of Amun-em-ḥēb, just over five inches in height, was solid cast in a metal which appears to be an alloy of silver and copper, only the lotus bud held in the boy's left hand being of pure silver. Following the casting the figure was carefully worked over with a tool, evidently after the metal had thoroughly chilled. Except for the highly individualistic face and head, which are executed in considerable detail, the statuette exhibits an adept and obviously studied simplification of the slender, boyish form which would do credit to our best modern practitioners of this same type of graceful plastic understatement. It is certainly one of the masterworks of its period, if not of Egyptian art as a whole.

FIGURE 30. The brothers Amun-em-ḥēb and Ḥu-webenef. Silver-copper alloy and wood. H. 5 1/8 and 12 1/4 in.

The much larger ★statuette of Amun-em-ḥēb's brother, Ḥu-webenef (fig. 30, right), though "wooden" in more senses than one, is not without a certain rigid charm. The close-cropped head and youthful face are carved with subtle delicacy and the enormously elongated figure, in spite of its stiff and wholly conventional pose, has both dignity and grace. Since he wears the formal *shendyet*-kilt, in this case interestingly adorned with vertical bands of pleats, Ḥu-webenef had, technically at least, achieved man's estate and was therefore distinctly older than his brother to whom in other respects he bears a close resemblance. Though carved in a handsome, fine-grained wood, Ḥu-webenef's figure was once painted—the flesh red, the hair, eyes, and eyebrows black, and the corneas of the eyes white.

In the attractive limestone ★statuette of figure 31 we meet an early Eighteenth Dynasty lady named Ta-weret, who stands before us clad in a full, braided wig and long simple dress, holding in her left hand the stem of what was probably a large flower. Again we find the sculptor treating the figure proper in somewhat cursory fashion and concentrating his attention on the elaborate head-dress and on the pleasant, typically Theban face with its large, wide-set eyes, straight nose, and fine, slightly smiling mouth. At the back of the figure a rectangular pilaster is inscribed with an offering formula in which Osiris is called upon to "give everything good and pure to the spirit of Ta-wer[et]"; and on the right side of the base there is a second inscription which tells us that "it is her daughter, Ḥenwetiroy, who causes her name to live." The rims and irises of Ta-weret's eyes are painted black and patches of black paint still remain on her wig. The statuette is from the ʿAsāsīf valley in western Thebes, having been found there in 1912 by the Earl of Carnarvon.

From a plundered tomb of the very early Eighteenth Dynasty in the same neighborhood, cleared by the Museum's Expedition in 1916, comes an uninscribed and much battered wooden ★statuette almost nine and a half inches in height, representing a man kneeling on both knees. The head is broken away and the arms, which were made separately and tenoned in place, are also missing. Its wasp waist and full hips give the figure a curious hourglass shape which appears to be a carry-over from the mannered provincial art of the Second Intermediate period. The short kilt is of unusual form, divided down the front and with the left half painted red.

FIGURE 31. The Lady Ta-weret, a limestone statuette from western Thebes. H. 7 in.

A shrine in the same cemetery yielded a number of votive offerings including a miniature ★stela of blue-glazed steatite inscribed for a woman named Aʿḥ-mosĕ and her husband, whose name, confusingly enough, was also Aʿḥ-mosĕ. Like its larger counterparts the crude little monument carries in its lunette a pair of *wedjat*-eyes flanking a Ω-sign. Below these symbols we see the two Aʿḥ-mosĕs, female and male, seated on chairs and holding lotus flowers to their noses; and, at the bottom, a four-line inscription which reads: "An offering which the King gives (to) Osiris, Lord of Busiris, that he may give invocation (consisting of) bread and beer, beef and fowl to the spirit of Aʿḥ-mosĕ. It is Ky-ky who causes (her?) name to live." A similar stela from the same shrine is now in the Cairo Museum.

Jewelry datable to the first two reigns of the Eighteenth Dynasty was found in some profusion on the persons or in the burials of the Theban men and women buried at the foot of the ʿAsāsīf. ★Necklaces, ★girdles, and ★bracelets predominate. These are made up for the most part of long strings of small disk and ball beads often supporting groups of little amulets—*wedjat*-eyes, flies, bullae, scarabs, cowroids, heart amulets, tooth amulets, palmettes, and drop-shaped pendants. In a series of well-to-do burials cleared by the Earl of Carnarvon the beads and amulets are of gold, carnelian, lapis lazuli, and shell, while those recovered by our own expedition from the burials of persons of more modest means are chiefly of paste, faience, and glazed steatite. Among the latter is a necklace of large blue faience lenticular beads, a type rarely found before the rise of the New Kingdom, but exceedingly common thereafter, especially during the Eighteenth Dynasty. Isolated elements include three colored glass ★cowroids, handsomely set in gold swivel mounts with beaded edges, and two very large blue faience ball ★beads decorated with black segments. A pair of bronze ★rings, perhaps earrings, consist simply of lengths of heavy bronze wire bent to form loops three-quarters of an inch in diameter, with the tapered ends of the wires overlapping.

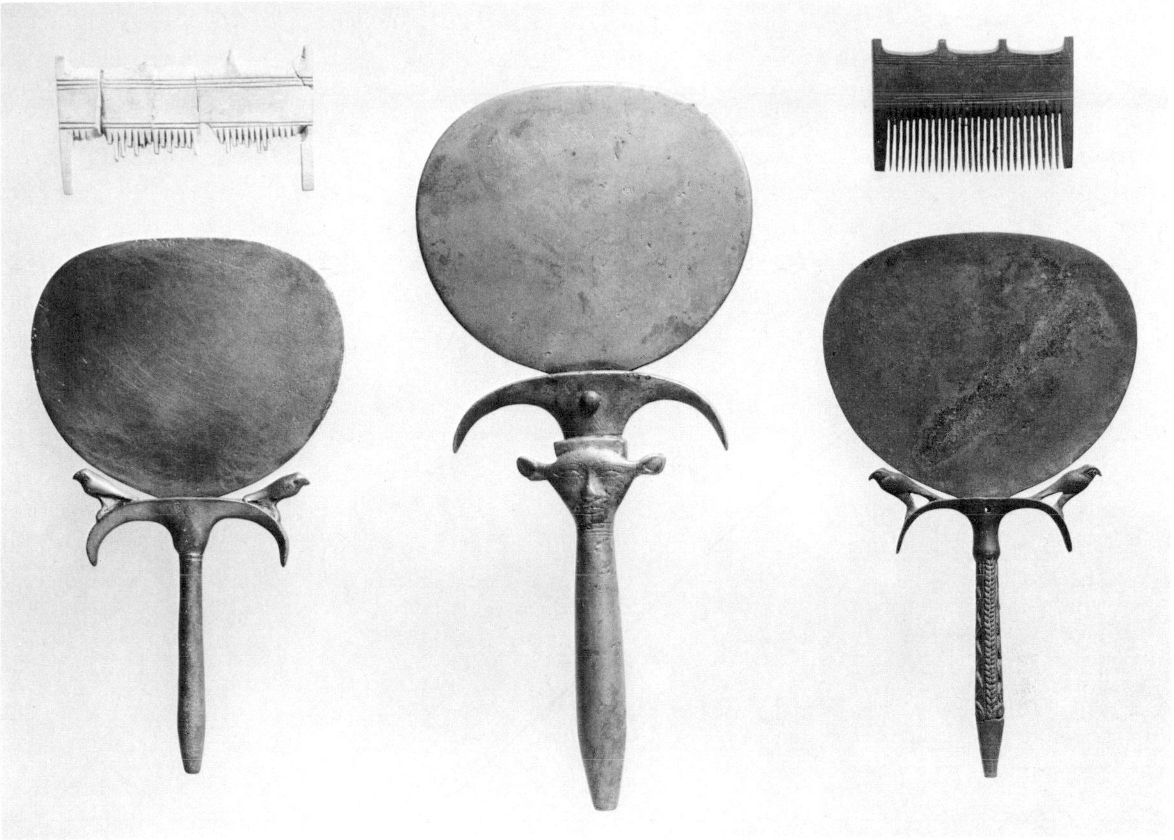

FIGURE 32. Mirrors of bronze and copper and combs of hardwood and ivory. Early Eighteenth Dynasty. H. of large mirror 10¾ in.

Four ★combs, one of hardwood, perfectly preserved (see fig. 32), and three fragmentary examples in ivory are of the same rectangular, short-toothed type found on slightly earlier burials of the Seventeenth Dynasty (see p. 21). Their handles are decorated on both sides with groups of incised parallel lines, and four spurs rising from their otherwise straight backs provide a better grip for their users' fingers. Two long, straight ★hairpins of ebony are from early Eighteenth Dynasty tombs near the pyramid of King Tety of the Sixth Dynasty, at Saḳḳâreh. Both are adorned with incised line decoration and the top of one is skillfully carved in the form of the hooded head and neck of a uraeus serpent.

Also from the "Tety Pyramid Cemeteries" is a small bronze ★mirror, its slender papyriform handle—in this case of copper—surmounted by two little figures of falcons (see fig. 32). In a similar, but more elaborate, ★mirror from Lord Carnarvon's work in western Thebes the shaft of the handle is ornamented with zigzag and cord patterns in relief. Egyptian mirror disks, as we have seen, are never true circles, and the two present examples show, in addition to a very pronounced flattening of the top of the disk, a tendency to taper the lower part in toward the handle, rather like the lower half of a palm-leaf fan. The large ★mirror of figure 32 is made up of two very heavy bronze castings. Its handle is of composite form, the papyrus column being interrupted just below the spreading umbel by a Ḥat-Ḥor head with projecting bovine ears. In every case the tang of the mirror disk is fastened in place by a single bronze rivet passing through the top of the handle.

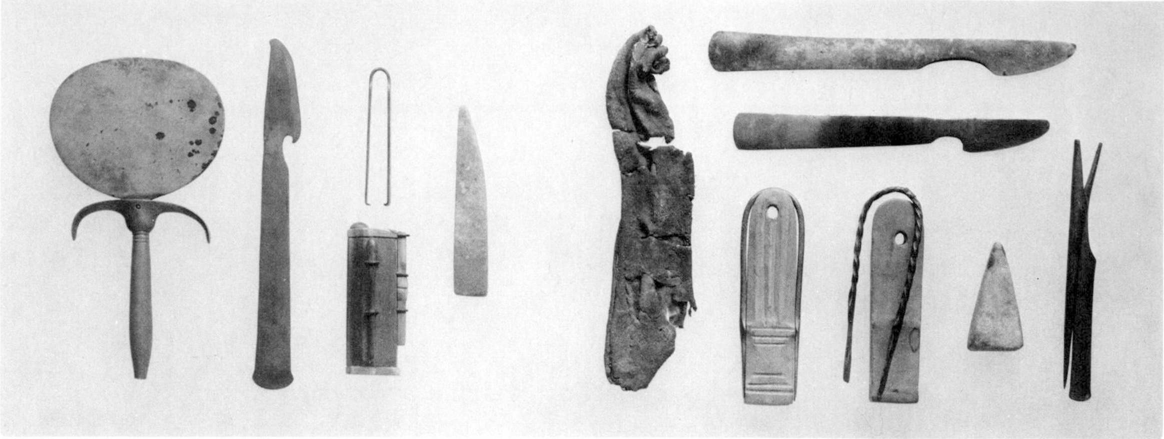

FIGURE 33. Two "shaving sets" from Theban burials of the early Eighteenth Dynasty. L. of leather case 9 7/8 in.

The smallest and simplest of our four early Eighteenth Dynasty ★mirrors belongs to a set of "dressing-table" accessories (fig. 33, left) which includes also a bronze knife-shaped ★razor, a pair of bronze ★tweezers, a small quartzite ★whetstone, or slipstone, and a wood and ivory ★*koḥl*-tube. The set, from a Theban burial of the reign of Amun-ḥotpe I, came to the Museum in 1926 as part of the Carnarvon collection. The razor, which resembles a modern surgical instrument, has, besides its principal, straight cutting edge, a convex, chisel-like edge at the lower end of the handle. Of this razor Howard Carter has said, "The preservation is so good that the knife edges are still keen, and the prints of the ancient finger-marks are still visible upon its polished surfaces."[1] The bronze tweezers, to judge from the curved ends, were designed expressly for extracting superfluous hair. Nicely carved in a fine, dark brown wood resembling cedar, the octagonal *koḥl*-tube is provided with an ivory base plate and an ivory lid swiveling open and shut on a single hardwood peg. The lid is locked by means of a vertical ⊸ bolt sliding in copper staples on one side of the tube. On another side a pair of similar staples holds the ebony *koḥl*-stick with which the black cosmetic contained in the tube was applied to its owner's eyes.

Another set of the same general date and provenience comprises two bronze ★razors, two pairs of bronze ★tweezers provided with wooden formers on which they were kept when not in use, a bronze ★hair curler (or tweezer razor?), and a small triangular ★hone, or whetstone, of quartzite (fig. 33, right). One of the razors and one pair of tweezers, the latter in position on its wooden former, were found lashed together with a strip of leather, and the whole set was contained in an oblong leather ★case. A pair of ★tweezers with incurved ends, a ★hair curler, and a tubular ★object of undetermined use, all of bronze, come from a Theban tomb chamber where they were found, together with a small bronze ointment ★spoon, in the metal cup shown in figure 34. The tweezers had been clipped around a former of hardwood, but of this only a fragment was preserved. A bronze ★razor, altogether similar to our Theban examples, is from a tomb discovered by the Egypt Exploration Fund at Abydos. Also from Abydos are three small, pointed ★hones of the kind usually found with shaving sets.

Like its Seventeenth Dynasty predecessor discussed above on page 21, a large wooden cosmetic ★spoon has a bowl in the form of a bivalve shell held by a human hand, and a long, slender shaft ending in a duck's head curved down to form a

[1] Carnarvon and Carter, *Five Years' Explorations at Thebes*, p. 72.

hook. The spoon, acquired by purchase in 1926, is from a tomb of the early Eighteenth Dynasty at Saḳḳāreh. A circular ivory cosmetic ★dish is provided with a swivel lid decorated with a geometric flower-petal design surrounded by an incised zigzag border. Two knobs, one on the lid (now missing) and one on the side of the container, could be lashed together with cord and the dish thereby fastened securely shut. Though of well-known type the dish is noteworthy both for the high quality of its workmanship and for its almost perfect state of preservation. It comes from a tomb of the early Eighteenth Dynasty near the foot of the ʿAsāsīf valley in western Thebes.

Two oval rush, or Ḥalfa-grass, ★baskets, fourteen and eighteen inches in length, are of the usual sewn coil type. Both are provided with convex lids and on the larger one colored strands have been inserted into the stitching at intervals to form triangular markings. In this basket were found a much smaller, circular ★basket and lid together with one of the combs and shaving sets already discussed and the green jasper scarab with the names of King Amun-ḥotpe I (see p. 51). All are from a great Theban tomb ("Tomb 37") discovered by Carnarvon and Carter in 1911.

A remarkable series of metal vessels recovered by the Museum's Egyptian Expedition from a near-by tomb includes a shallow, one-handled bronze ★cup, a wide bronze ★basin with two flat loop handles, and a bronze and copper ★situla, or bucket, found with the basin (fig. 34). The cup and the basin were beaten to shape from single, thin sheets of bronze and the surfaces of the latter were given a mat finish, apparently by being dipped in a solution containing both acid and salts. On the inside the basin has a convex circular boss at its center, and at one point a reef has been taken in its rim, the overlapping folds of metal being fastened with a rivet. The handles of both vessels are riveted in place. The hammered copper lower half of the situla was joined by a row of rivets to its overlapping bronze upper part, which was then given a thorough burnishing, the process

FIGURE 34. Bronze and copper vessels from a Theban tomb of the early Eighteenth Dynasty. Diam. of basin 17⅝ in.

rendering the flattened ends of the rivets all but invisible. The rim of the vessel was rolled to shape over a heavy bronze ring and the two suspension rings for the missing bucket handle were fastened in place by two rivets each. These types of metal vessels, especially the cup and the situla, remained popular into Late Dynastic times, though variations on the basic shapes are numerous and often marked. The situla and basin, evidently a set, were found empty; but the cup had been pressed into service as the container of a quantity of small items of tomb equipment including some of the bronze instruments mentioned above and a little cylindrical cosmetic ★vase carved in hardwood and just over three inches in height.

Fourteen other cosmetic and ointment ★jars from the same group of early Eighteenth Dynasty tomb chambers are for the most part of alabaster (calcite), but there are two of serpentine, one of yellow limestone, and three of pottery decorated with simple linear designs. The types, a selection of which is given in figure 35, are wholly characteristic of their period and recur again and again throughout the greater part of the Eighteenth Dynasty. Most common are the heavy drop-shaped jar with flaring neck and lip, the squat cordiform or carinated vase with a small foot and a high, cylindrical neck, and the flat-bottomed beaker with flaring rim and foot, which is the New Kingdom version of the cylindrical oil jar of hoary antiquity. A broad, carinated jar of yellow limestone with a cord molding around the base of the neck and a squat little jar of alabaster with a very wide, flat base and rim provide us with interesting variations of known shapes. Two alabaster *koḥl*-pots and a third example in serpentine are of the traditional type (cf. fig. 8), as are also two wooden *koḥl*-sticks found in association with the little jars.

Four inscribed pottery ★jars including a drop-shaped vase, a small situla, and two squat little vases, are also well-known early Eighteenth Dynasty types and the hieratic texts inscribed on them may be dated by their handwritings, orthography, and phraseology to the same general period. The three small jars come from the chamber and courtyard of a tomb in western Thebes. The provenience of the larger jar is not recorded, but it too may well be of Theban origin. The texts in all four cases are brief letters, those on the small jars being scarcely more than repetitions of standard formulae of greeting addressed to a man named Amun-mosĕ (the deceased tomb owner?) by his friends Neb-em-seni and Si-Amūn. The best preserved of these rather dull little texts—the one written around the shoulder of the neckless cordiform jar—is typical: "Neb-em-seni says 'Hail to you! Hail to you! I greet Amun-mosĕ. Further: Hail to you! Hail to you!' " The letter on the tall, drop-shaped jar, which probably referred to its contents, is of a more practical nature and of somewhat greater interest: "Senu speaks to Amun-ḥotpe, saying 'I have caused to be brought to you good lapis lazuli, 20 *deben*, lapis lazuli of Libya(?), 40 *deben*, malachite, 10 *deben;* total, 70 *deben;* (also) galena, 4 *deben*, good black pigment, 10 (*deben*?).' " Since the *deben* was a unit of weight equal to only about 91 grams it is quite possible that all the minerals (or mineral pigments?) listed could have been contained in the jar itself, their total weight amounting to only slightly over sixteen and a half pounds. Parallels to the formulae and other expressions used in these texts occur in the well-known letters of Aʿḥ-mosĕ of Pe'n-Yaty, an Upper Egyptian official whose career began under Amun-ḥotpe I and ended under Tḥut-mosĕ III.

Three ★knucklebones, used like dice to determine the moves in a board game, are from the floor of a Theban tomb chamber where they lay amid the rotted remains of the board on which the game was played.

The fragments of two tufted linen ★pads were found near Deir el Baḥri in the rubbish thrown out of the early Eighteenth Dynasty cliff tomb which in later times served as the principal cache for the royal mummies of the New Kingdom. Such pads are not infrequently included among the household equipment buried in tombs of the Eighteenth Dynasty and it is probable that their uses in and about the house were manifold. They could, for example, be employed as rugs, as chair

FIGURE 35. Cosmetic vessels from Theban tombs of the early Eighteenth Dynasty. Alabaster and yellow limestone. H. 1 ¾-6 ⅝ in.

and bed covers, as mattresses, as packcloths, and as donkey saddles. Our two present examples were evidently large rectangles of very coarse linen cloth composed in one instance of double and in the other of triple warp and weft strands combined in a simple over-and-under weave. Bunches of six to eight threads, eight inches long, were looped through the fabric at intervals, leaving patterns of small, knotlike bosses on one side and long, closely spaced double tufts, resembling the coat of a long-haired animal, on the other side. On one pad the tufts are arranged in parallel rows ten weft strands apart. On the other they are grouped so as to form an elaborate, over-all diamond pattern. Unlike those of our modern pile carpets the patterns are discernible on one side only, disappearing entirely on the tufted, or wrong, sides of the pads.

The weapons shown in figure 36 are without exception from burials of the early Eighteenth Dynasty found in close proximity to one another in a reused Middle Kingdom tomb court at the foot of the ʿAsāsīf in western Thebes. Of the two full-size battle ★axes one is of unusual interest because of the preservation of its wooden handle and because enough remained of its intricately plaited rawhide

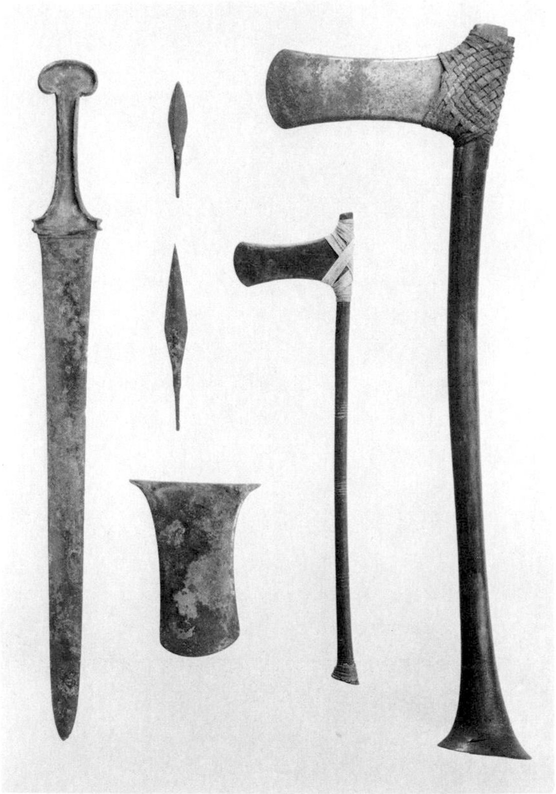

FIGURE 36. Weapons of the early Eighteenth Dynasty. L. of larger axe 21 ½ in.

lashing to allow it to be accurately restored. The lashing, probably applied in a moist, or green, state, was tightened, first by driving a long, narrow wedge between it and the back of the handle, and second, by the natural shrinkage of the hide as it dried, the two successive steps producing a union of great strength and rigidity between the heavy bronze head and the slender, whippy haft of the weapon. At the head end the underside of the handle is rabbeted to take the straight back of the axe blade which, as can be seen on the unhafted blade, is provided with two laterally projecting spurs for the lashing to bear against. The miniature ★axe shown with its full-scale counterparts may have been a toy since it was found in the coffin of a child. Here again, both the bronze head and the wooden handle, tipped at the butt end with a ferrule of gold foil, are well preserved, while the lashing has been restored. This type of axe is one of the most common and most characteristic of all New Kingdom weapons, appearing in the hands of Egyptian foot soldiers and marines in tomb paintings and temple reliefs throughout the Eighteenth and Nineteenth Dynasties. It was used, presumably, in hand-to-hand fighting and for dispatching wounded enemies laid low by missiles, and may, like the Indian tomahawk, have been employed as a throwing weapon, a use to which its short, springy handle and heavy head make it admirably suited.

In late Hyksos times the old lenticular pommel of the Egyptian dagger was replaced by a straight grip cast in one piece with the blade. This basic change in the design and structure of the weapon permitted the blade to be lengthened until there was achieved the type of arm shown at the left of figure 36, which can properly be called a short ★sword. An even cubit (20.5 inches) in length, the sword is made of a single piece of bronze, the grip having been once inlaid with carved(?) wooden plates, only rotted traces of which now remain. Both the construction and the design of the weapon appear to have been borrowed by the Egyptians from their Asiatic enemies, the method of casting and the hilt type closely paralleling slightly earlier short swords and daggers of undoubted Asiatic design, including the well-known Hyksos dagger from Saḳḳāreh with the names of King Neb-khopesh-Rēʿ Apopy and another, from Thebes(?), with the name of King ʿA-ḳen-en-Rēʿ Apopy. Its plain grip and blade and slightly rounded point mark our sword as belonging to an early stage in the development of arms of this class, later examples having their grips provided with finger notches and their blades reinforced by longitudinal midribs. Since relatively few swords have survived from the time of the New Kingdom —especially the early New Kingdom—our weapon is something of a rarity. Of its condition Ambrose Lansing, its discoverer, has said, "Wood inlays in the handle have decayed, but the polish is for the most part undimmed and the blade still retains its keen edge and ancient flexibility."[2]

[2] *M. M. A. Bulletin*, XII (1917), May, *Supplement*, p. 24.

Six bronze ★points ranging in length from two and nine-sixteenths to five and three-sixteenths inches are probably from light javelins rather than from arrows as has been thought (see fig. 36). Arrows with pointed bronze tips were certainly used by the kings of the mid-Eighteenth Dynasty and later times; but the typical New Kingdom arrow, like its predecessors of the Old and Middle Kingdoms, was a very light missile of reed tipped with minute flakes of flint or quartz or with slender points of ivory, bone, or hardwood. Bronze points exactly like the ones we are now considering have actually been found on the shafts of javelins, but none, so far as I know, has been discovered on a short, feathered shaft or in direct association with a bow. The points, as can be seen, have elongated diamond-shaped blades strengthened along the center lines by flat, tapered midribs. They are provided with slender tangs, square in section, which fitted into, rather than around, the ends of the wooden shafts.

Not many craftsmen's tools datable to the first two reigns of the Eighteenth Dynasty have reached our collection. The tomb chamber of the Overseer Khay, a Theban contemporary of King Amun-ḥotpe I, yielded a stout bronze adze ★blade, six and a half inches long, having the tapered form, the knobbed top, and, at the bottom, the slightly curved cutting edge characteristic of this type of tool. A bronze netting ★needle, or shuttle, from an adjoining chamber in the same tomb, is a somewhat elongated version of the hieroglyph ⟜. In this particular implement, which measures eight inches in length, the longitudinal planes of the open loops at the ends of the rod are at right angles to one another, a characteristic which is not apparent in the hieroglyphic sign.

The transition from the Seventeenth to the Eighteenth Dynasty brought with it a number of changes in Egyptian funerary beliefs and customs which are reflected in the Theban tombs of the period, especially in the design and decoration of the coffins and other items of funerary equipment found in these tombs.

Though the *rishi*, or "feathered," coffin adorned with the protective wings of the heaven(?) goddess survived in modified form into the early years of the New Kingdom, the characteristic type is now the white anthropoid coffin decorated with inscribed longitudinal and transverse bands repro-

FIGURE 37. Coffin of Aʿḥ-mosĕ, son of the Lady Nakhte, from western Thebes. Early Eighteenth Dynasty. L. 90 in.

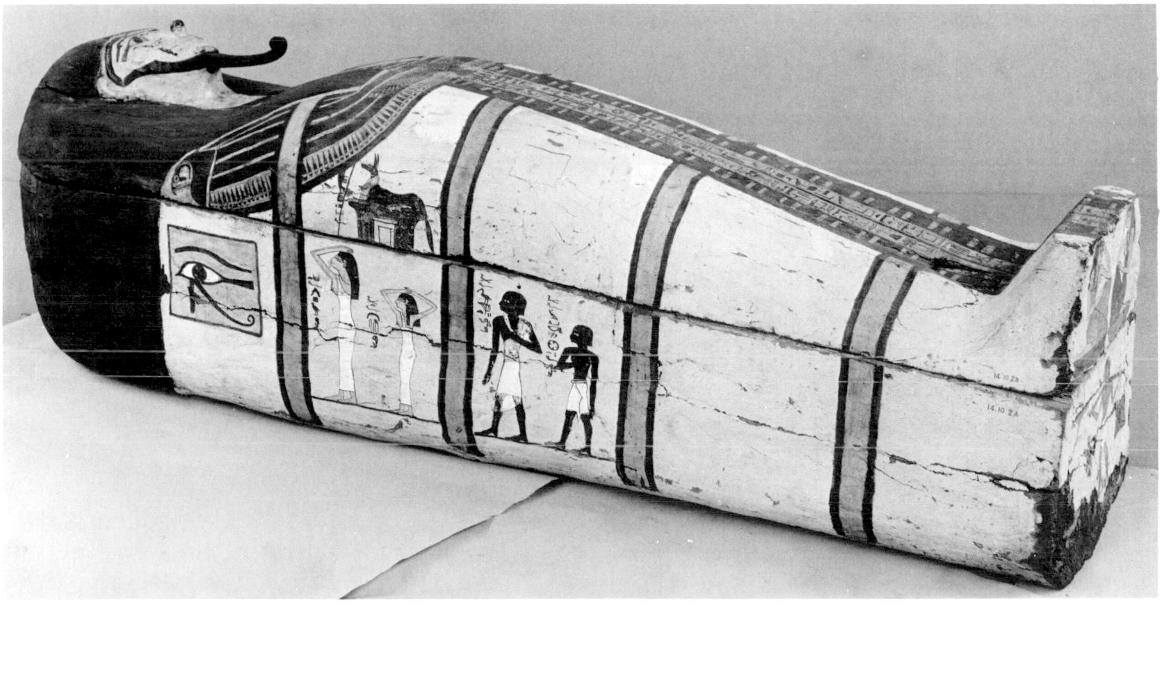

ducing the broad binding tapes of the bandaged mummy within and recalling, at the same time, the inscribed bands which on the rectangular house coffins of the Old and Middle Kingdoms appear to represent the principal upright members and the beams of the "eternal dwelling." No longer roughly hewn out of sycamore logs, the coffins are constructed of planks skillfully joined together with tenons and dowels, and each is covered on the outside with a coating of white stucco that serves both as the ground color of the coffin and as the base for its painted decoration. The earlier examples still retain to some extent the wedge-shaped faces and angular forms of their *rishi* predecessors and, like these, continue to show on their sides little groups of mourners and other funeral scenes.

Such a ★coffin is that of the Theban Aʿḥ-mosĕ (fig. 37), son of the House Mistress Nakhte, whose burial in a tomb on the southern slope of the Dirāʿ Abu'n Naga was found almost fifty years ago by the Earl of Carnarvon. The deceased is represented in this hollow, mummiform effigy as wearing on his chin the long, curved beard of the god Osiris, his prototype in immortality, and on his breast, above a vulture with wings outspread, a huge broad collar with falcon-head terminals. Though perhaps regarded as amuletic in nature, the single large *wedjat*-eye in a panel on either side of the coffin box would appear to be a now functionless carry-over from the rectangular coffins of the Middle Kingdom (see Part I, pp. 312 f.). A cursive hieroglyphic label tells us that the lean, black, canine animal crouching upon a shrine in the first panel on the right side of the lid is the god "Anubis who is on his mountain." The two women below, with their hands to their heads in gestures of mourning, are the dead man's wife Ḥapu, and "his daughter Aʿḥ-mosĕ." Behind, with their hands on their hearts, come "his son Tḥūty," and "his son Meky-niwetef," the name of the latter meaning "Protector-of-his-town." The wife appears again, on the left side of the coffin, accompanied by a daughter, Tet(?), and by two sons, Neb-seny and Si-Amūn. Figures of the goddesses Isis and Nephthys (the wife and sister of Osiris), kneeling in mourning upon ⏝-signs, adorn the foot end of the lid; and below, on the foot end of the coffin, we see a male offering bearer carrying by means of a long yoke across his shoulders a rectangular basketry hamper and a red pottery jar in a rope sling. The two vertical texts which occupy the long, double band down the center of the lid are both offering formulae. The one on the right which calls upon Osiris, the "Great God who is in the midst of Abydos," is of commonplace type; but the one on the left which invokes the powerful god of Thebes is sufficiently interesting to bear quoting: "An offering which the King gives (to) Amun Rēʿ, King of the Gods, the Lord of Life who grants what is desired, the lord of burial after old age, that he may give glory in heaven, power on earth, and a coming and going in the necropolis to the spirit of Aʿḥ-mosĕ, born of the House Mistress Nakhte, the justified." The distribution of the colors, which include a dark greenish blue, an ocher yellow, a pinkish red, chalky white, and black, can be determined with a fair degree of accuracy from the photograph.

The ★coffin of another Aʿḥ-mosĕ, in this case a woman, is also from a Theban tomb chamber of the early Eighteenth Dynasty and is similar in most respects to the one we have just described. Now, however, a figure of and prayer to the sky goddess Nūt have been added to the decoration of the lid, the transverse bands are inscribed with texts referring to or spoken by tutelary divinities of the dead, and figures of the so-called Four Genii of the Dead have replaced those of the mourners in the lateral panels between the bands of inscription (see Part I, pp. 314 ff.). The positions, or stations, of the Four Genii are indicated by references in the transverse bands to the deceased as "one in honor with" such and such a genius, Imsety and Ḥapy as usual flanking the shoulders of the mummy, Dewau-mautef and Ḳebeḥ-snēwef the legs. On the left side of the coffin, for example, the transverse band nearest the head contains the words "one in honor with Ḥapy" and in the adjoining panel stands one of four identical human-headed male figures, clad in a short kilt and long wig of archaic type and representing in this

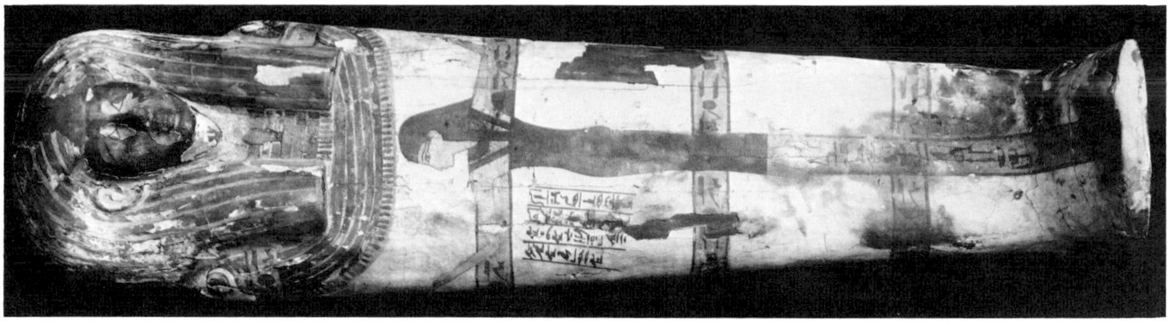

instance the genius Ḥapy. The inscribed band behind the figure contains the speech traditionally addressed to the deceased by this particular genius: "I am Ḥapy. I have come that I might be your protection, that I might bind to you the chief of your members, that I might place your enemies beneath you, and that I might give you your head forever." Dewau-mautef comes next, preceded by his name and followed by his speech, and on the right side of the coffin we find Imsety and Ḳebeḥ-snēwef presented in similar fashion. A large standing figure of the goddess Nephthys with arms outspread in protective gesture occupies the foot end of both coffin and lid, the figure accompanied by a brief speech of assurance similar to those of the Four Genii. The goddess Isis is not represented, but on the left side of the coffin near the foot end we find the words "Recitation: 'Ho my mother Isis, come that you may remove the bindings which are on me . . .' " The texts which on this coffin are preserved to us in somewhat corrupt form we shall find repeated again and again on royal and private

FIGURE 38. Coffin of Aʿḥ-ḥotpe Ta-nedjem(et) from western Thebes (above and below). Early Eighteenth Dynasty. L. 74 in.

coffins and sarcophagi throughout most of the Eighteenth Dynasty and not infrequently thereafter. Some of them derive ultimately from the Pyramid Texts of hoary antiquity (see Part I, p. 82) and most of them occur together in a version of Spell CLI of the Book of the Dead, the so-called Chapter of the Sepulchral Chamber. Being that of a woman, the coffin is beardless. Its length is just over seventy-seven inches, its maximum width (at the shoulders) almost twenty inches.

With the *coffin of Aʿḥ-ḥotpe Ta-nedjem(et) (fig. 38), whose burial equipment included the two handsome statuettes of her sons (fig. 30), we are approaching the fully developed Eighteenth Dynasty type. The salient characteristics of this box and lid—the long, slender proportions, the large, well-modeled face, the rounded contours of the striped headdress, the graceful profile of the

high foot end—have no longer anything in common with the crude and angular *rishi* type. The decoration, too, in spite of a lingering awkwardness in its style, has nearly achieved the well-articulated, rational arrangement which is to remain standard for centuries to come. On the lid the sky goddess Nūt stretches her arms in a gesture of embrace over the body within the coffin. On the head end the goddess Nephthys and on the foot end the goddess Isis repeat the same protective gesture. Four transverse bands of inscription, springing from either side of the central lid band, indicate the positions of eight tutelary divinities who take their stations on the sides of the coffin and its contents—the Four Genii on either side of the shoulders and legs of the deceased and the great deities Horus, Gēb, Shu, and Tefēnet flanking the mid-section. In the six panels formed by the transverse bands are the identical, human-headed figures of Horus, Gēb, and the Four Genii, all wearing long, curved beards, long, old-fashioned headdresses, and garments of archaic type appropriate to their status as gods. The figure of every deity represented on the coffin is accompanied by a speech, written in cursive hieroglyphs, which he or she addresses to the deceased person, assuring the latter of various forms of protection.

The canopic, or visceral, jar, rarely present in burials of the Second Intermediate period, reappears at the beginning of the Eighteenth Dynasty and is represented in our collection by a set of uninscribed pottery ★jars and ★stoppers (fig. 39) belonging to a Theban of this time named Katy-nakhte. The jars, one of which was missing, were found in the remains of a canopic chest of early Eighteenth Dynasty style in a chamber of the tomb from which came also Carnarvon Tablet I, the well-known writing board with the account of the struggles of King Ka-mosĕ against the Hyksos. Their date is significant since they appear to be the earliest known examples in which the stoppers vary in form according to the particular

FIGURE 39. Canopic jars of Katy-nakhte from a tomb of the early Eighteenth Dynasty at Thebes. Pottery. H. 11 3/8-12 in.

Genius of the Dead with whom each jar is associated (see Part I, p. 321). As can be seen, the Imsety jar, like the genius Imsety himself, has a bearded human head, the Dewau-mautef jar a dog or jackal head, and the Ḳebeḥ-snēwef jar a falcon head, while the missing jar—that of the genius Ḥapy—had in all probability a stopper in the form of the head of a cynocephalous ape. Stoppers of this type do not seem to have come into general use before the late New Kingdom, all the other Eighteenth Dynasty canopic jars in our collection and most of those datable to the Nineteenth Dynasty adhering to the Middle Kingdom practice of having human-headed stoppers throughout. In the present set the jars, which are of the squat Middle Kingdom shape, are covered with a semilustrous buff slip while their stoppers are painted to imitate limestone or, perhaps, alabaster. Remains of the bundles containing Katynakhte's viscera are still preserved inside the jars.

Aside from those already discussed, very few of our New Kingdom *shawabty*-figures are datable to the first two reigns of the Eighteenth Dynasty. Among the exceptions is a fragmentary ★figure in rich blue faience found near Deir el Baḥri, in the valley below the Cache of Royal Mummies. It is inscribed in horizontal lines with the *shawabty*-spell, the name of the owner having been apparently Ta-ʿa(t). Interesting characteristics of this figure are its extreme slenderness and the fact that, though it is mummiform, the division between the legs and feet is clearly indicated. Of much the same date but of quite a different type is a painted pottery ★*shawabty* contained in a small rectangular ★coffin, also of painted pottery. The figure, six inches in length, is colored yellow and black and has a shape not unlike that of a *rishi* coffin. Another painted pottery ★*shawabty*-coffin, having a vaulted lid with upward-projecting end pieces, was found empty and broken in a reused late Middle Kingdom tomb at the foot of the ʿAsāsīf valley. A wooden ★*shawabty*-coffin of anthropoid type, seventeen inches in length, crudely carved from a sycamore log, came to us many years ago with the Farman collection.

Through the generosity of Edward S. Harkness the Museum acquired in 1935 an uninscribed alabaster ★*shawabty* of Middle Kingdom type, but probably of early Eighteenth Dynasty date. The admirably carved mummiform figure, six and three-quarters inches in height, wears on its head a full, striated wig with long tabs pendent over the breast and has the enormous, high-set ears so characteristic of the sculptured heads of the Twelfth Dynasty. The proportions and style of the figure, coupled with the fact that the arms are shown crossed over the breast with the hands open, tend, however, to suggest a date subsequent to the Middle Kingdom, and the sophistication and high standard of technical excellence exhibited by the piece seem unlikely to have been achieved during the Hyksos period.

The heart ★scarab of the Overseer Khay, a Theban official of the reign of Amun-ḥotpe I, is, for its class, relatively small, measuring only an inch and three-sixteenths in length. It is of green jasper, nicely carved and highly polished; but the inscription on its underside is incomplete, giving only the title and name of its owner and the opening words of Chapter XXXB of the Book of the Dead.

In the present chapter we have confined our study to works of art and craftsmanship which can with some confidence be assigned to the first two reigns of the Eighteenth Dynasty. There is probably much additional material, especially small objects such as scarabs, amulets, and beads, which may also belong to this period, but which, lacking any positive indication of date, is more safely and advantageously considered with the mass of similar objects produced under the great rulers of the Thutmoside line.

III. The Thutmoside Pharaohs:

THUTMOSĔ I TO HAT-SHEPSŪT

1. Thut-mosĕ I and II

With King Thut-mosĕ I (1526-1508 b.c.) Egypt entered upon what from many points of view must be regarded as the most glorious period in her long history—the period of her greatest military strength, greatest territorial expansion, and greatest material prosperity. Under the military pharaohs of the Thutmoside line the protective countermeasures initiated by the first two rulers of the dynasty were expanded into wars of conquest, inspired by a new realization of the economic advantages of an Asiatic and African empire and made possible by the possession of the most efficient and mobile fighting force in the then known world. Spearheaded by the newly developed chariot divisions and led by kings trained from early youth in the arts of war, the Egyptian armies thrust their way southward to the Fourth Cataract of the Nile and northeastward to the farther bank of the Euphrates. From the conquered areas a steady stream of slaves, gold, and raw materials poured into Egypt's labor compounds, treasuries, and storehouses, adding constantly to the vast wealth of natural commodities and manufactured goods which the country itself, under its highly efficient internal administration, was now producing. A third and most important source of essential materials as well as luxuries was trade, conducted both overland and by sea, often with regions lying outside the scope of Egypt's military and administrative control—Central Africa, Arabia, Mesopotamia, Asia Minor. In the conduct of this trade it was Egypt herself who played the dominant role, her caravans penetrating far into the continents of Africa and Asia, her fleets of seagoing ships ranging up the Red Sea to Somaliland and northward, not only along the Syrian coast, but also to Cilicia and Ionia and across open water to Crete, Cyprus, the Aegean islands, and perhaps even to the mainland of Greece. Nor were material riches all that the once isolated land of the Nile gained from her now active participation in world affairs: foreign customs, foreign philosophies and religious cults, and a not inconsiderable quantity of foreign blood insinuated themselves into a society which a new-found security and leisure rendered particularly receptive to exotic influences.

Head and shoulders above this new society tower the often heroic, always arresting figures of the Thutmoside pharaohs, ambitious, intelligent, and energetic as rulers, vain, self-indulgent, headstrong, and occasionally ruthless as individuals, but consistent in their pious devotion to the god Amūn and his fellow deities and in their enthusiastic patronage of their country's arts and crafts. We may achieve some understanding of these rulers by sketching briefly their careers and by studying at first hand those of their monuments which have found their way into our collection.

The beginning of the reign of Thut-mosĕ I was announced in a circular letter dated Regnal Year 1, Month 3 of Prōyet, Day 21, the day of his accession to the throne, and issued apparently to all the key officials of the realm. In this letter, known to us from the copy sent upriver to Tjuroy, the Viceroy of Nubia, the new ruler proclaimed his kingship, prescribed the oath to be taken in his name, and published his royal titulary, including his praenomen and cult name ʿA-kheper-ku-Rēʿ. The son of a woman of nonroyal origin named Senisonbe, Thut-mosĕ I appears to have achieved the kingship chiefly through his marriage to the hereditary princess Aʿh-mosĕ, the sister and daughter, respectively, of his two predecessors. He is, however, associated as king with Amun-ḥotpe I on an alabaster chapel at Karnak and may have been designated by the latter as his successor following the death of the infant crown prince referred to on page 52.

In two important campaigns undertaken early in his reign, one in Upper Nubia, the other in western Asia, the founder of the Thutmoside line showed himself to be a military leader of exceptional ability and a builder of empire second only to his distinguished grandson Thut-mosĕ III. In the Nubian campaign, to which he devoted the entire second year of his reign, he extended Egyptian control southward, beyond the Middle Kingdom outpost at Kermeh, to the island of Argo far above the Third Cataract of the Nile, overcoming the greatest military and navigational difficulties and opening the way for the final thrust to the region of the Fourth Cataract. Returning northward with the body of a Nubian chieftain whom he had killed in personal combat hanging head downward from the bow of his flagship, the pharaoh left behind him in Upper Nubia and the Sūdān a string of newly constructed fortresses and a new governmental system based on the division of the southern provinces into five administrative districts. The Asiatic campaign carried Thut-mosĕ I and his army (including the two Aʿh-mosĕs of el Kāb) to the Euphrates where a crushing defeat was inflicted on the powerful Mitanni of Naharīn, a land which lay for the most part to the east of the great river. Having set up his boundary stela beside the Euphrates the king returned slowly homeward, pausing in northern Syria long enough to hunt wild elephants in the lake district of Niy, where herds of the great beasts were then to be found.

The building activities of Thut-mosĕ I and his successors and the new architectural trends developed under them may be studied to greatest advantage in the additions which they made to the temple and temple precinct of the state god Amūn at Karnak. The first major enlargement of the temple proper was carried out in behalf of Thut-mosĕ I under the inspired direction of the king's architect, Ineni. The square, brick and limestone shrine of the Middle Kingdom and an extensive area to the west of it was enclosed within a girdle wall of sandstone, adorned on its four inner surfaces with columned porticos and with statues of the king in the guise of the mummiform god Osiris. Across the front, or western end, of the great oblong court so formed was built the present fifth pylon of the temple—a monumental gateway, flanked by broad rectangular towers of masonry crowned with brilliantly painted cavetto cornices and provided with two tall wooden flag masts mounted in slots in their sloping forward walls. The tips of the masts were sheathed "in fine gold" and the portal between the massive towers was fitted with "a great door of Asiatic copper whereon was the 'shadow' of the god wrought in gold."[1] Later in the reign of Thut-mosĕ I the now firmly established east-west axis of the temple and the processional way leading along it were extended by the construction, fourteen yards to the west of Pylon V, of a second and much larger pylon, IV. The space between the pylons was converted into

[1] Inscription in the tomb of the architect Ineni (No. 81).

a hall by the addition of side walls of stone and a wooden roof supported on five slender papyriform columns, also of wood. Before the outer pylon, in commemoration of the king's *sed*, or jubilee, festival, were erected two sixty-four-foot obelisks of red Aswān granite, their sides inscribed with the names and titles of Tḥut-mosĕ I, their pinnacles encased in burnished sheet gold to catch the rays of the sun. Here, then, at the very outset of the Thutmoside period we have the essence of the great processional temple of the New Kingdom and later times and all of its component parts: the ancient sanctuary enclosed within screening walls, the deep, colonnaded courtyard, the hypostyle reception hall of the god, and the monumental entrance feature, the pylon, repeated with each new re-establishment of the temple façade. Here, too, we find the already extensive use in temple construction of brown Nubian sandstone, usually overlaid with white stucco and adorned with brightly colored relief sculpture.

The site selected by Tḥut-mosĕ I for his burial lies more than a mile and a quarter west of the tomb of Amun-ḥotpe I, on the far side of the lofty cliffs behind Deir el Baḥri, at the inner end of a long and tortuous valley famous today as the Wādy el Bibān el Molūk, the Valley of the Tombs (literally "Doors") of the Kings. Here, "in solitude, without being seen or heard,"[2] the architect Ineni supervised the excavation of the tomb of his royal master and here in the course of the next four centuries were hewn the tombs of almost all the pharaohs of the Eighteenth, Nineteenth, and Twentieth Dynasties. The tomb of Tḥut-mosĕ I, the smallest and simplest of the series, comprises an entrance stair well cut down into the bedrock at the base of a cliff, a sloping tunnel leading downward to a rectangular antechamber, a second stairway and corridor descending to the pillared sepulchral hall, a big, cartouche-shaped room which contained at its inner end the king's sarcophagus; and finally a small storeroom, or "treasury," opening off the sepulchral hall.

[2] *Ibid.*

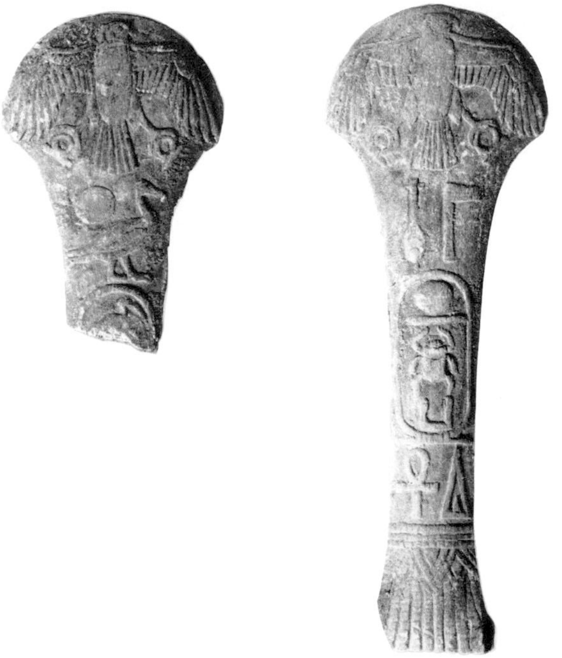

FIGURE 40. Sides of a dagger handle with the names of King Tḥut-mosĕ I. Wood. L. 4¾ in.

Tḥut-mosĕ I's mortuary temple, called the "Mansion-of-ʿA-kheper-ku-Rēʿ-which-is-united-with-life" or, in abbreviated form, simply "United-with-life," was built far from his tomb, on the edge of the Theban plain probably in the neighborhood of Medīnet Habu. The building itself has not yet been found and the only part of it which has so far come to light is the upper part of an inscribed wooden ★door (see pp. 82 f.; fig. 44) dating from the period of the joint reign of Ḥat-shepsūt and Tḥut-mosĕ III. To the same period belongs a series of stamped mud ★bricks bearing the throne name of Tḥut-mosĕ I side by side with that of Ḥat-shepsūt, the former followed by the epithet "justified" (i.e., deceased), the latter by the expression "given life." The heavy, cylindrical mud ★sealing of a large jar, on the other hand, may well date from the reign of Tḥut-mosĕ I himself. It is stamped in three places with a long oval containing the throne name "ʿA-kheper-ku-Rēʿ" followed by the hieroglyph [hieroglyph], referring perhaps to Lower Egypt, whence the contents of the jar (wine?) probably came.

A pair of handsome wooden ★cheek plates from the handle of a dagger (fig. 40) are elaborately carved with the names and titles of Ṭhut-mosĕ I surmounted in each case by a falcon with wings and legs outspread, holding in each claw a *shenu*-sign. In shape the handle conformed to one of the several popular post-Hyksos types and was not unlike the handle of the early Eighteenth Dynasty sword of figure 36. On the complete handle plate we read the "Good God, ʿA-kheper-ku-Rēʿ, given life" and on the fragmentary plate the "Son of Rēʿ, Ṭhut-mosĕ. . . ." The pieces were found southwest of Deir el Baḥri, in one of a series of pit tombs of the reign of Ṭhut-mosĕ I excavated in the unfinished and abandoned platform of the temple of Seʿankh-ku-Rēʿ Montu-ḥotpe of the Eleventh Dynasty. The owner of the tomb in question, a soldier named Aʿḥ-mosĕ Pe'n-ḥat, son of Aʿḥ-ḥotpe, had been given the dagger by his king, perhaps as a reward for valor upon the field of battle.

"ʿA-kheper-ku-Rēʿ," the praenomen of Ṭhut-mosĕ I, is engraved on a small wooden ★plaque in the form of a cartouche, perhaps a piece of inlay. It occurs also on fourteen ★scarabs and two ★cowroids of green-glazed steatite, on four ★scarabs and a ★cowroid of blue faience, and on a little ★seal of glazed steatite in the form of a cat seated on a cartouche. Frequently the name is preceded by the title the "Good God," less often by other titles such as the "Lord of the Two Lands" and "King of Upper and Lower Egypt," and in several cases it is followed by the expression "May he live!" or "given life forever." On some of the larger scarabs (see fig. 41) the royal name appears with protective or heraldic motifs of a more or less elaborate nature: the crowned falcon with wings stretched forward to protect the king's cartouche, the spread falcon crushing with either claw a bound foreign enemy, the winged sun's disk above a pair of uraeus serpents, and the king himself in the form of a sphinx couched beneath a winged disk. The legend on a glazed steatite ★scarab which came to the Museum as a gift in 1946 is apparently to be read: "The King of Upper and Lower Egypt, ʿA-kheper-ku-Rēʿ, to whom is given life, power, and stability." The distinctive nomen "Ṭhut-mosĕ Khaʿ-mi-Rēʿ" is found on four ★scarabs, two of which are of glazed steatite, one of blue faience and one of green paste. It is twice preceded by the title the "Good God," and is once accompanied by the epithet "Strong bull"—perhaps an elided version of the king's Horus name—and by a rather elaborate figure of the uraeus serpent wearing the crown of Lower Egypt. Ṭhut-mosĕ I's Horus name, "Strong-bull-loving-right," appears alone on a ★scarab of glazed steatite (fig. 41, lower right); and two similar ★scarabs preserve his Golden Horus name, "Goodly-of-years," the latter being found also, together with the throne name, on one of the first group of scarabs.

The king's name occurs also on pottery funerary ★cones from the tombs of eight Theban dignitaries, at least two of whom were his contemporaries. These two were, to quote from the inscriptions on their cones, the "Chief Steward of ʿA-kheper-ku-Rēʿ, Bak," and the "Steward and Overseer of

FIGURE 41. Scarabs of King Ṭhut-mosĕ I in glazed steatite and faience. L. 7/16-3/4 in.

Cattle of ʿA-kheper-ku-Rēʿ, the Scribe Pe'n-Rēʿ." The six other men were all priests of the pharaoh's mortuary cult which survived at least into the Nineteenth Dynasty. They include the First Prophets of ʿA-kheper-ku-Rēʿ, Amun-mosĕ and ʿA-kheper-ku-Rēʿ-sonbe; the Scribe of the God's Offering of the House of Amūn and First Prophet of ʿA-kheper-ku-Rēʿ in the temple "United-with-life," Ny-to; the Scribe and Chief Lector Priest of ʿA-kheper-ku-Rēʿ, Nedjem; the One Pure of Hands in the Presence of ʿA-kheper-ku-Rēʿ, Amun-ḥotpe; and the Prophet of Smiter-of-the-Nine-Bows (Tḥut-mosĕ I), Ḳen-Amūn, the owner of a glazed steatite ★scarab formerly in the Davis collection.

Further evidence of the honor in which Tḥut-mosĕ I was held long after his death are scenes in two Theban tombs of the early Nineteenth Dynasty of which we possess facsimile color ★copies by Norman de Garis Davies and Charles K. Wilkinson. In a scene from the tomb of Woser-ḥēt, who was First Prophet of the Royal Spirit of Tḥut-mosĕ I, we see an elaborate re-enactment of the king's funeral procession, with a colossal statue of the long-dead pharaoh taking the place of his mummy and coffin. The other scene is from the tomb of a First Prophet of Amun-ḥotpe I named Amun-mosĕ and shows offerings being made to the statues of two famous queens and twelve well-known kings, the fourth of whom is identified by the cartouche before his face as Tḥut-mosĕ I.

Six handsome ★scarabs in our collection have engraved upon their undersides the title and name of Tḥut-mosĕ I's queen, the "King's Great (or Chief) Wife, Aʿḥ-mosĕ," the royal heiress on whom, as we have remarked, the legitimacy of his claim to the throne very largely depended. Five of the scarabs are of green- or blue-glazed steatite and of these three, set in gold swivel mountings, once served as the bezels of signet rings. One was found at Thebes on the body of a woman who had served the queen's daughter Ḥat-shepsūt. The sixth scarab is carved in a hard, yellowish green stone which has not yet been identified.

Another of Tḥut-mosĕ I's royal contemporaries was the Princess Aʿḥ-mosĕ Tu-meri-sy, a daughter of Amun-ḥotpe I and Queen Aʿḥ-ḥotpe II. Her tomb was one of a dozen or so which during the reign of Tḥut-mosĕ I were cut in the unfinished temple platform of King Montu-ḥotpe II of the Eleventh Dynasty. It had been extensively and savagely plundered, but some of its contents were recovered by our expedition, including the two arms of the mummy of the princess still bearing the imprints of her stolen bracelets. A length of linen★bandage from the wrappings of the mummy has on it a short, cursive hieroglyphic inscription written in black ink: "One in honor with Osiris, the King's Daughter Aʿḥ-mosĕ Tu-meri-sy, the justified." Three attractive little objects in blue faience were also found in the tomb and these are shown in figure 42. They include a model ★head-rest, a small four-legged ★stand for a dish, and a ★ring stand for a jar, its rims accented with narrow bands of black.

Though they do not bear royal names, mention may be made of a ★scarab of Tḥut-mosĕ's Vizier I-em-ḥotep, and of two funerary ★cones of the "King's Son and Overseer of Southern Countries, Seny," who in the third year of the reign succeeded Tjuroy as Viceroy of Nubia.

Prince Wadj-mosĕ and Prince Amun-mosĕ, the two eldest sons of Tḥut-mosĕ I, having died during their father's reign, the crown passed at the king's death to his third son, Tḥut-mosĕ, the child of a royal princess named Mūt-nefret, who was perhaps a younger sister of the queen. To strengthen his right to the throne the boy, now known as Tḥut-mosĕ II, had been married to his half sister, Ḥat-shepsūt, the elder of two daughters born to Tḥut-mosĕ I and Queen Aʿḥ-mosĕ. Together the young couple buried their royal father in his tomb in the Valley of the Tombs of the Kings and together, as king and queen, ruled Egypt for at least eighteen years, their reign ending about 1490 B.C. when Tḥut-mosĕ II, still in his early thirties, died—presumably of an illness.

Though hampered by a frail constitution which restricted his activities and shortened his life, the king during his reign acquitted himself creditably,

FIGURE 42. A model headrest and two small stands in blue faience from the tomb of the Princess A‘ḥ-mosĕ Tu-meri-sy. H. of headrest 4⅝ in.

crushing a revolt in Nubia in his first regnal year and later quelling an uprising among the Bedawīn of southern Palestine. Like his father before him he built his mortuary temple on the edge of the cultivated land north of Medīnet Habu and in the Valley of the Tombs of the Kings prepared for himself a rock-cut tomb which, however, was never inscribed and in which he appears not to have been buried. A ★foundation deposit at the entrance of this tomb contained objects bearing the names of Queen Meryet-Rē‘ Ḥat-shepsūt and her husband King Tḥut-mosĕ III, and in the tomb were canopic jars and other stone ★vases of Senet-nay and her husband, Sen-nefer, Mayor of Thebes under King Amun-ḥotpe II (see p. 146).

"‘A-kheper-en-Rē‘," the throne name of Tḥut-mosĕ II, appears with that of his father on the wooden door from the latter's mortuary temple referred to above (p. 76); but, as on many other monuments once assigned to him, the feminine title and verb ending which accompany the name show that it was surcharged over that of Ḥat-shepsūt, probably by Tḥut-mosĕ III long after Tḥut-mosĕ II's death.

Aside from this door panel the few monuments in our collection on which the name of the second Tḥut-mosĕ occur are small and relatively unimportant. A fragment of a blue faience *menyet* ★counterpoise from the shrine of Ḥat-Ḥor at Deir el Baḥri preserves on one side part of the cartouche with the king's praenomen followed by the phrase "given life," and, on the other side, the feminine name Meryet-Nūb which, since it is also enclosed within a cartouche, must be that of a hitherto unrecorded member of the royal family. A small blue faience ★saucer inscribed for the "Good God, ‘A-kheper-en-Rē‘, given life," was found near by, in the tomb of the parents of Ḥat-shepsūt's great official Sen-ne-mūt. From the same tomb come two rough little ★cowroids in bright blue faience bearing only the name "‘A-kheper-en-Rē‘." This, too, is the sole name that occurs on our nine ★scarabs of Tḥut-mosĕ II. Here, however, it is sometimes accompanied by a title—the "Good God," "King of Upper and Lower Egypt," "Lord of the Two Lands"—occasionally by figures of falcons with wings spread in protective gestures, and once by a couched figure of the canine animal of the god Anubis. On three scarabs the name is enclosed within a cartouche which surmounts a "gold"-sign and is in turn surmounted by the ram's horns and double plume or rests in the curve of a broad collar with falcon-head terminals or is surrounded by a wide border made up of an intricate loop pattern. One scarab is carved of haematite. The rest are of steatite coated with a smooth, clear bluish green glaze which we have come to recognize as characteristic of scarabs—especially royal scarabs—of early and middle Thutmoside times.

Though the mortuary cult of Tḥut-mosĕ II was evidently not maintained on the same scale as those of his more famous predecessors and successors, his statue appears between that of his father and that of his son in our color *copy of the Nineteenth Dynasty tomb painting referred to above, and we know of at least one lector priest who during the New Kingdom was attached to his funerary foundation.

FIGURE 43. Alabaster ointment jars and a multiple *koḥl*-tube inscribed with the name of Queen Ḥat-shepsūt. H. of tall jar 9 in.

Throughout the lifetime of her husband and during most of the first two years of the reign of her stepson Tḥut-mosĕ III, Ḥat-shepsūt used on her monuments only the titles appropriate to her rank as a royal princess and queen consort. It was presumably during this period in her career that two alabaster *jars (see fig. 43) found in a royal tomb (see pp. 130f.) of the reign of Tḥut-mosĕ III were made and inscribed. The panel of inscription engraved on the side of the graceful drop-shaped jar names the "God's Wife, the King's Great Wife whom he loves, the Mistress of the Two Lands, Ḥat-shepsūt, may she live!"—while on the wide, globular jar she is called the "King's Daughter, King's Sister, God's Wife, King's Great Wife Ḥat-shepsūt, may she live and endure like Rēʿ forever!" Earlier still may be an

alabaster ★jar fragment from the Murch collection on which Ḥat-shepsūt does not as yet bear the titles of queen, but only those of crown princess, namely, "King's Chief Daughter" and "God's Wife of Amūn in Karnak(?)." It was apparently during the period of her queenship that she added the epithet Khnemet-Amūn, "united to Amūn," to the cartouche containing her personal name, since it appears, following her early title "God's Wife," on a multiple ★*koḥl*-tube of alabaster (see fig. 43) purchased in Luxor by the Earl of Carnarvon. Nicely carved from a single piece of the ornately grained stone, this interesting little object comprises a circle of six cylindrical tubes surrounding a seventh, drilled in the center of the block. It has been suggested that the form of the container reproduces a cluster of seven lengths of hollow reed of the kind often used to hold *koḥl* and other eye cosmetics. A fragmentary *koḥl*-stick, carried in a tube of its own at the back of the container, is of bronze as were also the fittings of the missing lid. The simple personal name "Ḥat-shepsūt," preceded by the titles "God's Wife" or "Mistress of the Two Lands," occurs on a ★scarab of carnelian and three ★scarabs of glazed steatite, two mounted in silver rings and all from private tombs at Thebes. It is found also, alone or accompanied by the titles "God's Wife" or "King's Daughter," on thirty-five similar ★scarabs which, though they come from foundation deposits of Ḥat-shepsūt's temple at Deir el Baḥri, belong by type and inscription to the earlier stage of her career. On the underside of a ★scarab of unknown provenience, formerly in the Murch collection, the name Ḥat-shepsūt is curiously written and is followed by the phrase "beloved of Amūn."

Ḥat-shepsūt's association with her great official Sen-ne-mūt and his family apparently began during the lifetime of Thut-mosĕ II or shortly thereafter. A stamped cornice ★brick from Sen-ne-mūt's tomb on the ʿIlwet esh Sheikh ʿAbd el Ḳurneh gives his titles as "Overseer of the Two Granaries of Amūn," "Overseer of the Fields of Amūn," "Steward of the God's Wife Ḥat-shepsūt," and "Overseer of the Audience Chamber." On stamped mud ★bricks from his own near-by tomb, his brother Seni-men calls himself "Page of Neb-peḥty-Rēʿ (Aʿḥ-mosĕ I)," "Administrator of the God's Wife, Nefru-Rēʿ," "Tutor of the Daughter of the God's Wife, Ḥat-shepsūt," and "Steward of the King's Daughter." Since Nefru-Rēʿ was the daughter of Ḥat-shepsūt and Thut-mosĕ II, the last three titles would seem to refer to her. Another interesting survival of Ḥat-shepsūt's name and title as queen is on the sealing of a large pottery ★amphora from the tomb of Sen-ne-mūt's parents, Raʿ-mosĕ and Ḥat-nūfer. The jar, according to a hieratic label written on its shoulder, was sealed in "Regnal Year 7" (of Thut-mosĕ III). Four big oval seal impressions on the cylindrical mud stopper give the title and name of the "God's Wife Ḥat-shepsūt," indicating that the jar and its contents were drawn from one of the queen's own estates. Side by side with this oil jar, in the same tomb chamber, was found another and closely similar ★amphora, the stopper of which was stamped with the name Maʿet-ku-Rēʿ, Ḥat-shepsūt's praenomen as king of Egypt. Since two inscriptions at Karnak prove conclusively that Ḥat-shepsūt had assumed this name and the other prerogatives of kingship five years earlier, in Thut-mosĕ III's second regnal year, the sealings with her name and title as queen must refer, not to Ḥat-shepsūt personally, but to "(the Estate of) the God's Wife, Ḥat-shepsūt," which continued functioning under its original name long after the queen herself had abandoned her earlier titulary.

Knowing the temper of his ambitious consort, Thut-mosĕ II contrived before his death to have his only son, Thut-mosĕ III, who was born to him of an obscure ḥarīm girl named Isis, appointed as his successor; and when he "went up to heaven in triumph" this son, a mere child at the time, "stood in his place as King of the Two Lands" and "ruler upon the throne of him who begat him." In a text composed many years later Thut-mosĕ III describes how as a young priest in the temple of Amūn he was singled out by the god as Egypt's future ruler and proclaimed coregent with his father. Aside from this account, which may be partly or wholly fictional, there is little reason to suppose that such a coregency actually existed. The legitimacy of the young king's claim to the throne may have been reinforced by marriage to his little half sister Nefru-Rēʿ, apparently the only child of Ḥat-shepsūt and Tḥut-mosĕ II. Lunar dates preserved from his reign permit us to place Tḥut-mosĕ III's accession to the throne in 1490 B.C.

FIGURE 44. Wooden door panel from the mortuary temple of King Tḥut-mosĕ I. H. 46 in.

2. Ḥat-shepsūt

Since at the time of his accession Tḥut-mosĕ III and his consort Nefru-Rēʿ were children, it was only natural that the dowager queen, Ḥat-shepsūt, should have acted as regent and, in the words of the royal architect Ineni, should have "settled the affairs of the Two Lands by reason of her plans." For a brief while nothing untoward occurred. At the beginning of the reign Ḥat-shepsūt allowed herself to be represented on public monuments standing behind her stepson and bearing only the titles of queen which she had acquired as the wife of Tḥut-mosĕ II. It was not long, however, before this vain, ambitious, and unscrupulous woman showed herself in her true colors. Stressing the purity of her royal ancestry and relying on a group of powerful officials whose support she had gained by innumerable favors, she contrived, late in the second regnal year of Tḥut-mosĕ III (1489 B.C.), to have herself crowned king with full pharaonic powers, regalia, and titulary, calling herself the Female Horus Wosret-kū, She of the Two Goddesses Wadjet-renpowet, the King of Upper and Lower Egypt Maʿet-ku-Rēʿ, the Daughter of Rēʿ, Khnemet-Amūn Ḥat-shepsūt. A few years later work was started on her temple at Deir el Baḥri, in the reliefs and inscriptions of which attempts were made to justify her seizure of the throne by scenes purporting to represent her divine birth and by equally fictitious accounts of her appointment and coronation as king under Tḥut-mosĕ I. As the key figure in his daughter's propaganda the long-dead Tḥut-mosĕ I was subjected to a series of highly publicized attentions, including reburial in Ḥat-shepsūt's own tomb in the Valley of the Tombs of the Kings and a share in the mortuary services conducted in her Deir el Baḥri temple.

Since it bears the names of Tḥut-mosĕ I and II we have already had occasion to mention the upper part of a wooden ★door panel (fig. 44) contributed by Ḥat-shepsūt to her father's funerary temple. The panel, just under four feet high

FIGURE 45. Model of the temple of Ḥat-shepsūt at Deir el Baḥri (restored at a scale of 1:100). L. of model 156 in.

and two feet wide, is made up of stout vertical planks, two inches thick, once held together at the back by heavy, closely spaced battens, the positions of which are indicated by five horizontal rows of peg holes. Painted dark red, the door shows at its top and sides bands of black which, to judge from the lines of small bronze nails along their inner edges, were once overlaid with sheet metal applied apparently over a layer of linen cloth. The hieroglyphs in the incised panel of inscription, now painted white, were at one time gilded. In the text we are told that the panel was dedicated to the "Good God, Lord of Rites, ʿA-kheper-ku-Rēʿ" and "Amun Rēʿ, Lord of Thrones-of-the-Two-Lands (Karnak), in the Mansion-of-ʿA-kheper-ku-Rēʿ-which-is-united-with-life," by the "King of Upper and Lower Egypt, the Mistress of the Two Lands ʿA-kheper-en-Rēʿ, (may she be) given life." From the feminine title Mistress of the Two Lands and the feminine ending of the verb form "given," as well as from the evident reworking which the right-hand cartouche has received, it is clear that this cartouche originally contained Ḥat-shepsūt's kingly praenomen Maʿet-ku-Rēʿ, not that of Tḥut-mosě II as it now does. The change was almost certainly made, as already suggested, by Tḥut-mosě III after Ḥat-shepsūt's fall from power.

Ḥat-shepsūt's own mortuary temple at Deir el Baḥri (fig. 45), constructed almost entirely of limestone, is remarkable in many respects. Built under the supervision of the queen's steward Sen-ne-mūt, in accordance with a design evidently inspired by the adjoining Eleventh Dynasty shrine of Neb-ḥepet-Rēʿ Montu-ḥotpe, this temple is composed, as can be seen in the model, of two broad, retreating terraces fronted by well-proportioned double colonnades and preceded, on the east, by a deep, walled forecourt. The central sanctuary, rock-cut in the towering cliff against which the temple is built, was dedicated to the god Amūn and there are, in addition, shrines to Anubis and Ḥat-Ḥor, the divinities of the necropolis, an open altar court for the worship of the sun god Rēʿ Ḥor-akhty, and vaulted funerary chapels for Ḥat-shepsūt and her father, Ṭhut-mosĕ I. Eastward a long, walled avenue, lined with painted sandstone sphinxes, led down to a small Valley Temple on the edge of the cultivated land; and halfway down this avenue was built a small peripteral way station for the barque of Amūn on its annual journey from Karnak.

At the laying-out of the temple plan, probably early in the eighth regnal year of Ṭhut-mosĕ III, a rock-cut or brick-lined pit, a yard in diameter and four to five feet deep, was dug at every important point in the perimeter of the proposed structure, and in each pit were placed food offerings contained in pottery jars and bowls, alabaster unguent jars, samples of the materials and models of the tools to be used in the construction of the temple, magical and amuletic objects of several kinds, and, in four of the pits, over three hundred beautifully carved scarabs and cowroids. Of these so-called ★foundation deposits (see fig. 46) nine were discovered within the confines of the main temple and its forecourt and five others in the Valley Temple, near the foot of the ʿAsāsīf valley. Nine of the fourteen deposits were found by our own Egyptian Expedition between the years 1915 and 1927; two are from the excavations conducted in 1911 by the Earl of Carnarvon; one is from the work of the Egypt Exploration Fund in 1896; and at least two have been uncovered and looted since

FIGURE 46. Reconstruction of a foundation deposit from the temple of Queen Ḥat-shepsūt at Deir el Baḥri. Diam. 35 in.

1927 by natives of the modern village of Ḳurneh. The contents of all except the last two deposits are for the most part in the Metropolitan Museum and constitute in themselves a considerable corpus of objects, selected examples of which are shown in figures 47 and 48.

From five of the deposits come seventeen alabaster ointment *jars of the traditional beaker form ([hieroglyph]) containing the remains of resinous unguents and bearing on their sides and on the tops of their flat, disk-shaped lids incised hieroglyphic inscriptions, once filled with blue pigment. All the inscriptions give the names and titles of Ḥat-shepsūt as king—the "Good Goddess, Mistress of the Two Lands, Maʿet-ku-Rēʿ," the "Daughter of Rēʿ, Khnemet-Amūn Ḥat-shepsūt" —followed either by the expression "beloved of Amūn in Djeser-djeseru" or by the statement "she made it as her monument to her father, Amūn, on the occasion of stretching the cord over Amūn-Djeser-djeseru, may she live, like Rēʿ, forever!" Djeser-djeseru, "Holy-of-Holies," and Amūn-Djeser-djeseru were common shortened versions of the name of the Deir el Baḥri temple, the full form of which was the "Mansion-of-Maʿet-ku-Rēʿ-(called-) Amūn is-the-Holy-of-Holies." The expression "stretching the cord" refers, of course, to the temple foundation rites when the king ceremonially outlined the plan of the projected building by driving stakes at its principal angles, stretching a cord around them, tracing with a pick the line of the foundation trenches, and laying the foundation deposits. In these jar inscriptions the god is frequently referred to as "Amūn who resides in Djeser-djeseru," and occasionally as "Amūn, Lord of the Throne(*sic*)-of-the-Two-Lands (Karnak)," "Amūn, Chief of the Two Lands," and "Amun Rēʿ, Lord of Heaven." The longer of the two types of inscription, with the reference to the stretching of the cord, occurs also on an alabaster *saucer and on two alabaster

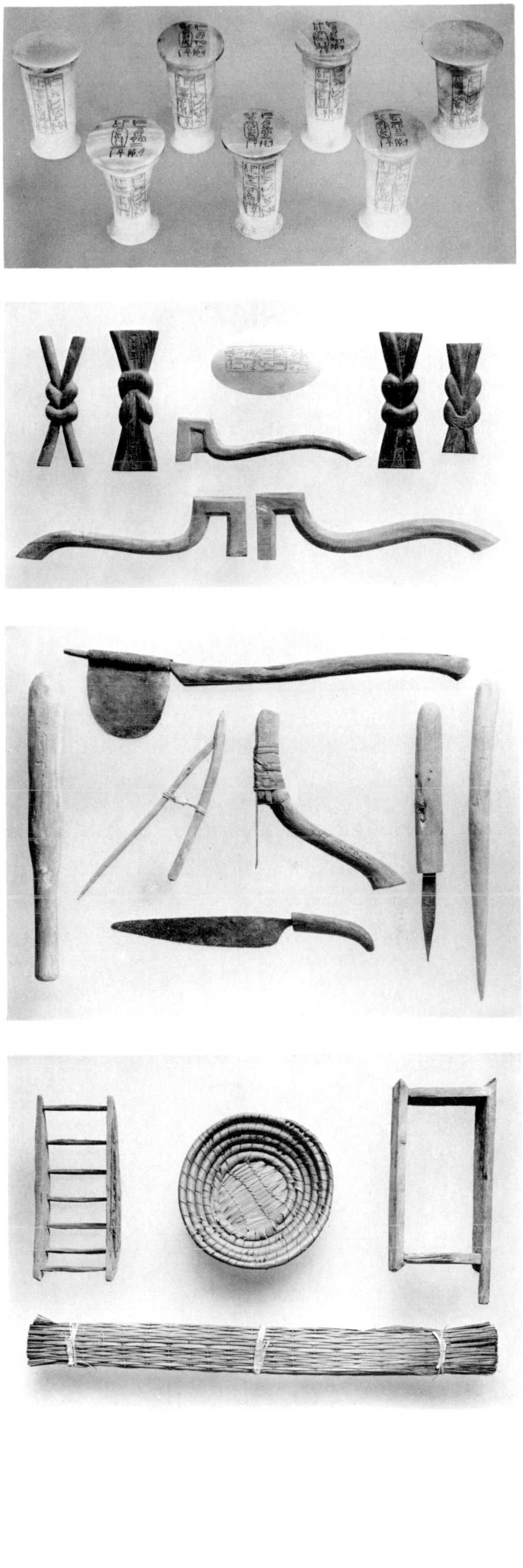

FIGURE 47. Alabaster ointment jars, magical emblems, and model tools from foundation deposits of Ḥat-shepsūt. L. of rolled mat 24 in.

★"clamshells," the latter perhaps intended to reproduce the actual bivalve shells used by scribes and draughtsmen to hold their writing and drawing pigments (see Part I, p. 296). Two rectangular ★plaques of blue faience, a little over three inches in width, might well have come from foundation deposits of Middle Kingdom date. They are, however, from a deposit in the forecourt of Ḥat-shepsūt's temple and are inscribed in black with her praenomen, followed by the words "beloved of Amūn who resides in Djeser-djeseru." Two flat, rectangular ★slabs of copper, six and a half by three and a quarter inches, are uninscribed and are perhaps to be classed with the metalworkers' materials and tools.

The ★food offerings which had been placed in the deposit pits included the heads and forelegs of slaughtered bullocks, trussed quail, circular and conical loaves of bread, grapes, figs, dates, jujubes, and currants. The fruits and a substance identified as butter were contained in small and often rough ★pottery jars, bowls, and saucers—many of them undoubtedly models of larger vessels—and in shallow circular and oval ★baskets and basketry ★trays made of spirals of rush sewn with strips of papyrus bark or palm leaf. Two pottery bowls contained lumps of ★resin and two others small supplies of ★natron, a form of soda used by the Egyptians as a detergent and as a preservative.

Many different kinds of tools, chiefly models, and many examples of each type of tool were piled up in the deposits. For the symbolic laying-out of the temple plan there are miniature surveyors' ★stakes and hardwood ★mallets for driving them, and for digging the foundation trenches and sifting the sand used in their fill there are wooden ★picks ( ) and circular basketry ★sieves. Present, too, are the quartzite ★mauls and long, solid bronze ★chisels of the stonemasons, as well as little models of the heavy wooden ★rockers and long wooden ★levers with which they maneuvered the blocks of stone into position, and the wooden ★brick molds used in the production of sun-dried mud bricks. The bronze blades of the carpenters' ★adzes are lashed to their curved wooden handles with leather thongs, tinted red, and the bronze carpenters' ★axes, ★saws ( ), ★chisels ( ), and ★reamers ( ) are hafted into hardwood handles of appropriate shapes. A burnishing ★pebble of chert is probably also part of the carpenters' equipment. The metalworkers' craft is represented by tubular ★crucibles of baked clay accompanied by lumps of copper ore (★malachite), lead ore (★galena), and ★charcoal used as fuel in the smelting process. A plain block of ★wood, a piece of bull's ★hide, two rolled-up ★mats made of the rind and pith of the papyrus plant, and eight little folded rectangles of linen ★cloth probably exemplify the materials and fittings used in the finishing and furnishing of the temple. Many of the implements, as can be seen in figure 47, are inscribed either on the blades or on the handles, the inscription nearly always reading: "The Good Goddess, Maʿet-ku-Rēʿ, beloved of Amūn who resides in Djeser-djeseru."

From a deposit cleared by the Museum's Expedition in 1924 come four examples of a ceremonial wooden instrument shaped like the handle of an adze ( ) and called in ancient Egyptian a *mesekhtyu* (fig. 47, center). Such instruments were used in an ancient funerary rite called the "opening of the mouth," usually performed on a statue and intended apparently to induce the soul of the person represented to enter into the stone or wooden image. Each of our four ★*mesekhtyu*-instruments has engraved on its back one of Ḥat-shepsūt's names as king of Egypt—the "Female Horus Wosret-kū," "(She of) the Two Goddesses Wadjet-renpowet," "Maʿet-ku-Rēʿ," and "Khnemet-Amūn Ḥat-shepsūt." A fifth ★instrument of the same type, but from another deposit, was found by the Egypt Exploration Fund in 1896. The large wooden ★*tjeset*, or knot amulet ( ), occurred in several of the temple deposits, the four examples in our collection being nicely carved of either

FIGURE 48. Scarabs and cowroids from the foundation deposits of Ḥat-shepsūt's temple at Deir el Baḥri. L. ½-⅞ in.

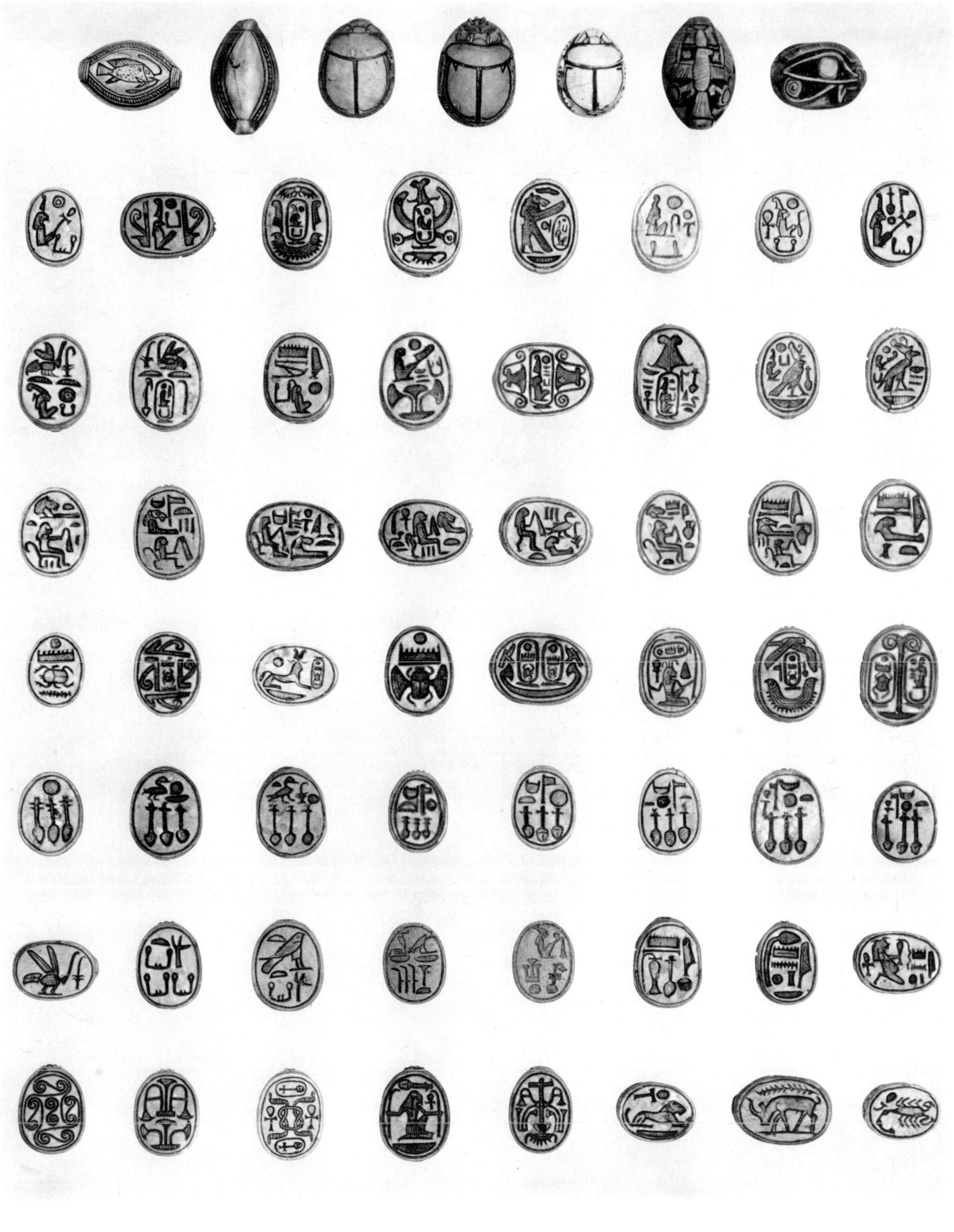

cedar or ebony. In three cases the names of Ḥat-shepsūt, including her Golden Horus name "Net-jeret-khaʿu," are engraved in the wood of the amulet, but in the example with the freestanding ends the name is written in ink on one of the "cords." Four small Ḥat-Ḥor-head ★amulets in blue faience and one in the form of the dwarf god Bēs were found in Deposits 7 to 9, and with them were found forty-four blue faience ★rosettes and great quantities of ★beads, the last including bottle-shaped, barrel-shaped, and cylindrical beads of blue and black faience and tubular beads of gold and silver.

The same three deposits and a fourth, outside the southeast corner of the temple forecourt, yielded, between them, 306 exquisitely carved ★scarabs and ★cowroids in green-glazed steatite and faience—one of the most remarkable finds of royal seals ever made. The beauty, technical perfection, and faultless condition of these seals can be seen in the examples selected for illustration in figure 48, but their fine, clear, bluish green color is lost in the black and white reproduction. More than half of the scarabs bear the names and titles of Ḥat-shepsūt, including not only her five "great names" as king of Egypt, but also, in thirty-five cases, her earlier titles and simple personal name as queen consort of Ṭhut-mosĕ II and as dowager queen after his death (see pp. 80f.). The name of Ḥat-shepsūt's coregent King Men-kheper-Rēʿ (Ṭhut-mosĕ III) appears on only thirty-one scarabs, while eighteen carry the titles and name of her daughter, the "King's Daughter, King's Sister, and God's Wife Nefru-Rēʿ," and two the praenomen of her deceased father, King ʿA-kheper-ku-Rēʿ (Ṭhut-mosĕ I). The god Amun Rēʿ is named on eighteen of the remaining seals and the undersides of the rest are given over to mottoes and to heraldic and decorative designs of many different types, some obviously carried over from the Middle Kingdom and the Hyksos period. A number of these scarabs, including the two with the name of Ṭhut-mosĕ I, were retained in the division of finds by the Egyptian Government, but the great majority of them are in the Metropolitan Museum.

In common with other Theban structures sponsored by Ḥat-shepsūt, her mortuary complex at Deir el Baḥri, particularly the Valley Temple, seems to have had incorporated in its rough-built foundation and retaining walls scores of small, inscribed votive stones which for lack of a better term we have called ★"name stones." Out of forty-six stones of this type found in the Museum's excavations or acquired by purchase we have retained in our permanent collection two dozen examples. The stones are rough slabs of limestone, quartzite, or (in one case) diorite having one artificially flattened surface on which is incised with varying degrees of skill and care Ḥat-shepsūt's throne name, Maʿet-ku-Rēʿ, enclosed within a cartouche. Remains of ink lines on some of the slabs show that the cartouche was laid out inside a rectangle and then carefully drawn in black ink outline before being carved. In a few cases the royal name is accompanied by a title (the "Good God," the "Son of Rēʿ," the "Mistress of Foreign Lands") or by the words the "Fortress of Thebes," presumably an epithet of Ḥat-shepsūt and perhaps part of the name of an actual building or enclosure. Nearly all of our name stones have, in addition, a hieratic docket written in black ink beside or, more rarely, in the cartouche. These dockets, most of which are dated, indicate that the stones were sent by citizens of Thebes (perhaps the sculptors who made them) to the officials who, we may assume, were in charge of the construction of Ḥat-shepsūt's mortuary buildings at Deir el Baḥri. The officials to whom the stones were addressed or in behalf of whom they were contributed include the Vizier (Ḥapu-sonbe?), the Steward of Amūn, Sen-ne-mūt, the treasurers Ṭḥūty and Ṭhut-nofre, the First Herald Dewa-enḥeḥ, the Second Prophet of Amūn, Puy-em-Rēʿ, and the Scribe Tety-em-Rēʿ, all of whom, in addition to their other duties, functioned as the queen's architects. The senders, or makers, bore such ordinary names as Amun-ḥotpe, Amun-em-weskhet, Amun-em-Opet, Min-ḥotpe, Min-mosĕ, Sobk-ḥotpe, Sen-em-Rēʿ, and Nefer-menu, in no case preceded by a title. The stones, then, appear to have been in a sense ex-votos, contributed by private individuals to the building of the temple. The dates, unfortunately, are given only in terms of the day, month, and season of the Egyptian civil year, including in one instance one of the five epagomenal days, the "Birth(day) of Isis" (see Part I, p. 39).

Consistent with her program of representing herself as the chosen coregent and successor of her father, Tḥut-mosĕ I, Ḥat-shepsūt, as we have seen, frequently linked his name with her own on her monuments. Good examples of this are the stamped mud ★bricks from her Valley Temple at Deir el Baḥri, on which the cartouches containing her praenomen, "Maʿet-ku-Rēʿ, given life," and that of her father, "ʿA-kheper-ku-Rēʿ, justified," appear side by side within a single outer cartouche. From the five fragmentary examples in our collection it is evident that complete bricks of this type measured something over a foot in length, six and a half inches in width, and three to three and a half inches in thickness.

A fragment of painted limestone ★relief, found by our expedition in the area once occupied by Ḥat-shepsūt's Valley Temple, comes undoubtedly from a wall of this structure. On it we see the upper part of a symbolic coronation scene in which Ḥat-shepsūt (at the right) receives the Double Crown from the Heliopolitan sun god Atūm, himself wearing the Double Crown and the long, curved beard indicative of his divinity. Stylistically the relief harks back in its clean outlines and delicacy of detail to the royal temple sculpture of the Twelfth Dynasty; but it shows a new graciousness of concept, a greater simplification and generalization in the modeling of the forms, and, on the whole, a greater tendency toward idealization in the presentation of the subject matter. At the same time, despite the fact that it is treated in an idealistic and conventional manner, the face of the god is recognizable as a royal Thutmoside type, the prominent, slightly arched nose and curious, half-smiling mouth being, as we shall see, especially characteristic of Ḥat-shepsūt herself and of the other immediate descendants of Tḥut-mosĕ I. Since Atūm was a solar divinity of Heliopolitan origin his figure has been left unscathed by the Atenist iconoclasts of the late Eighteenth Dynasty (see p. 280); but, as elsewhere, the figure of Ḥat-shepsūt has been intentionally destroyed—in this case, hacked out with a narrow chisel or punch—by agents of her coregent Tḥut-mosĕ III.

The erasure which we see on this fragment of relief is a sample of what befell the whole of Ḥat-shepsūt's magnificent funerary complex at Deir el Baḥri, particularly her great terraced temple at the head of the valley. Since, like other royal mortuary temples of this time, it was dedicated to the service of the god Amūn and his fellow deities, the building itself was spared; but the name and figure of its owner were savagely and methodically obliterated wherever they occurred. This involved the destruction not only of much of the temple's superb relief sculpture, but also of the more than two hundred statues and sphinxes with which its colonnades, courts, and avenue of approach were adorned. Though systematically defaced and then smashed to pieces by Tḥut-mosĕ III's workmen and subsequently picked over by generations in search of hammerstones, millstones, and the like, fragments of most of these statues and sphinxes have been recovered from quarries and other hollows on either side of the temple avenue and from adjoining areas of the Theban necropolis. In 1845 a seated statue and three colossal heads were acquired by Richard Lepsius for the Berlin Museum and in 1869 a granite torso was taken to Holland by Prince Henry of the Netherlands. The bulk of the pieces from which the Ḥat-shepsūt statues and sphinxes have been restored, however, come from excavations conducted during the seasons of 1922-1923 and 1926-1928 by our own Egyptian Expedition under the brilliant direction of Herbert E. Winlock.

At each end of the temple's lowest and uppermost colonnades, on every one of the latter's twenty-four front pillars, in each of ten niches at the rear of the uppermost court, and in each of the four corners of the sanctuary stood a painted limestone statue of Ḥat-shepsūt in the guise of the mummiform god Osiris (see fig. 45). Since these figures were actually part of the temple structure,

FIGURE 49. Ḥat-shepsūt represented as Osiris: parts of two painted limestone statues from the uppermost porch of her temple at Deir el Baḥri. H. 40 in.

built up in courses with the pillars or walls against which they stood, their carving probably antedated by a number of years that of the freestanding statues and sphinxes—a circumstance which students of New Kingdom sculpture have used to explain the slight differences in style discernible between the two groups of statuary. In height Ḥat-shepsūt's Osiride statues ranged from eleven feet, or about twice life size, for those in the sanctuary and in the upper court niches, to twenty-six feet for the two gigantic figures at the ends of the lower colonnade. All were slenderly proportioned and each was in the shape of a bandaged mummy with only the crowned and bearded head and the crossed hands, holding the usual Osirian emblems, projecting from the tall white form.

Flooding of the low-lying hollows into which the temple statuary had been dumped by Thutmosĕ III had severely rotted most of the limestone blocks from the bodies of these statues; but for our own collection we were able to salvage three ★heads and a pair of ★shoulders from the eighteen-foot figures of the upper colonnade pillars, three ★heads from the eleven-foot figures of the upper court niches, and three of the ★heads from the four similar figures in the sanctuary. Each head wears either the tall White Crown of Upper Egypt or the Double Crown, depending on whether it comes from a statue to the south or to the north of the temple axis, and each has hanging from its chin the long, curved Osirian beard, painted blue and obviously artificial since it appears to have been supported by straps passing up the cheeks to tabs on the sides of the crown. In figure 49 we see one of the great, fragmentary heads from an upper colonnade statue placed on the shoulders of a colossus of the same series, the whole measuring over a yard in height and almost four feet in width. Around their necks and crossing over their breasts these larger figures wear colored braces, rather like ecclesiastical stoles, and in their hands hold the *was*-scepter, symbol of "well-being," and the sign of "life" combined with the crook and *ladanisterion* (see Part I, pp. 286 f.) of Osiris. Their throats and faces are red with white and black eyes and blue eyebrows, and the various attributes which they wear or hold are red, blue, and yellow. The smaller heads shown, rather extensively restored, in figure 50 come, as has been said, from statues eleven feet in height which stood in the niches looking out into the uppermost court of the temple. The face of the head wearing the White Crown is orange yellow, while that of the head with the Double Crown is painted red. Because it was a symbol of Ḥat-shepsūt's royalty the uraeus emblem on the front of the crown or other headdress was invariably one of the first parts of the statues smashed or knocked off by Tḥut-mosĕ III's agents, the partial preservation of the one on our White Crown head being unusual. The three much battered heads from the main sanctuary of the temple are in most respects exactly like those from the niches, but instead of being red or yellow, their faces and other exposed flesh parts are painted a pale pink. Though the faces of some of these statues are delicately modeled and nearly all are endowed with Ḥat-shepsūt's slightly receding chin and prominent, arched nose, they are, on the whole, too generalized and too idealized to be classed as portraits. Indeed, it would be surprising if anything so fussy as detailed portraiture had been attempted in figures which were designed first and foremost to provide massive and rhythmically repeated accents in a vast architectural scheme. Here, even more than in the freestanding statues, the existence of many examples of each type and size of head and figure has enabled the individual pieces in our collection to be restored with accuracy and with assurance, the restored portions being fully recorded in drawings and photographs and easily discernible upon close inspection.

The freestanding statues and sphinxes were for the most part stationed along the processional way on which the god Amūn on his annual visit to the temple would be carried in his portable barque in passing from the entrance gateway to the sanctuary, and the majority of them were designed and carved with this in view. Their original positions in the temple have been determined on the basis of evidence of various sorts—the numbers, sizes, and types of the figures themselves, carvings or sketches of them on adjacent architectural elements, and occasionally the discovery of a uraeus or other small fragment of a statue *in situ*.

In Ḥat-shepsūt's day, when the barque of Amūn reached the top of the first ramp it was flanked on either side by a small, human-faced *lion in painted limestone, crouched upon the newel block at the head of the ramp balustrade. Three and a half feet in length, these guardians of the entrance to the temple's middle court probably represent the twin lion divinities who, among other functions, watched over a gateway of the Underworld. In each case the face, provided with the ponderous pharaonic beard and surmounted by the royal uraeus, is a generalized portrait of Ḥat-shepsūt; but the rest of the head with its massive, fringed mane and high-set animal ears is completely leonine, as is also the lithe, muscular body of the crouching beast. The type was already ancient in Ḥat-shepsūt's time, being found in the rather brutish royal "sphinxes" of the late Twelfth Dynasty from Tanis and Edfu. An incised hieroglyphic inscription which starts on the breast of the animal and runs forward onto the top of the high, rectangular base tells us that this is "(King) Maʿet-ku-Rēʿ, beloved of Amūn and given life

forever." The body of the lion is painted a tawny yellow, with the mane, the kingly beard, and the signs in the inscription picked out in blue. The better preserved of the pair of figures was retained in the division of finds by the Cairo Museum, our lion consisting of large fragments of the second figure set into a plaster cast of its mate in Cairo.

The way across the second court of the temple to the foot of the second ramp was lined on either hand by three colossal sphinxes of Ḥat-shepsūt in red Aswān granite, or, as it is some times called, syenite. Of the six great figures, reassembled from the fragments left us by Tḥut-mosĕ III's workmen, one more or less complete ★sphinx (fig. 51) and the ★head and shoulders of another are now in the Metropolitan Museum.

Like the Great Sphinx at Gīzeh and its numerous Old and Middle Kingdom descendants, these are true sphinxes, representing Egypt's ruler with the body of a lion and a completely human head, wearing in this case the royal *nemes*, or striped wig cover, and the long, square-cut, pharaonic beard. The conception of the king as a lion, one of the most majestic and powerful animals with which the Egyptians came into contact, goes back into prehistory, and the superposition of the ruler's head on the animal's body probably dates at least as early as the beginning of the Fourth Dynasty. The association of the human-headed lion with various solar divinities and the identification of the Great Sphinx with a form of the sun god called Ḥor-em-akhet (Harmakhis) were probably secondary developments, the latter dating apparently from the Eighteenth Dynasty itself. The closest existing prototypes of our Ḥat-shepsūt sphinxes are those of the kings of the late Middle Kingdom. On them, as here, we find, among other details, the highly conventionalized treatment of the mane of the lion, which appears from under the royal

FIGURE 50. Ḥat-shepsūt as Osiris: two heads from painted limestone statues which once stood in niches in the uppermost court of the queen's temple at Deir el Baḥri. H. of each as mounted 49 in.

headdress like a striated cloak extending in points over the shoulders and down over each side of the chest of the animal.

Over eleven feet in length and weighing in the neighborhood of seven and a half tons, our reassembled sphinx is a massive piece of architectural sculpture. Though highly stylized as becomes such a work, it exhibits upon close inspection a deft and knowing treatment of the structure and musculature of the lion's powerful body, and surprisingly subtle modeling in the attractively idealized royal face. The rear half of the figure is still a solid piece of stone, but the head, shoulders, and forelegs, which were the principal targets of the demolishers' sledge hammers, are a mosaic of small fragments, and the uraeus, battered away from the front of the headdress, was never recovered. On this, as on other works of Egyptian sculpture executed in a hard, ornately grained stone, paint was used sparingly and was confined to the blue and yellow striping of the headdress, the black and white details of the eyes, the blue eyebrows and corner strokes, and the blue hieroglyphs in the inscription. Little of the paint now remains, and through exposure at one time to fire, the yellow has turned red. The inscription was very largely hacked out, but enough is left on the chest of the sphinx and on the top of the base to show that it once read: "The King of Upper and Lower Egypt, Maʿet-[ku-]Rēʿ, [belov]ed of [Amūn who is in the midst of] Djeser-djeseru [and given life] forever."

Of our second granite sphinx all that could be salvaged was the head, the beard, small portions of the chest, shoulders, and back of the lion, and a fragment of the base. Though badly battered and lacking the uraeus, the nose, and much of the mouth and one cheek, the head is still a single large piece of stone, and the paint, especially the blue of the beard and the blue and yellow of the *nemes*, is better preserved than on our other example. This head is slightly smaller than that of the reassembled sphinx, but seems to have been similar to it in all other respects and may well have been carved by the same sculptor. Only parts

of the inscription are preserved: "The Good Goddess . . . beloved of . . . may she live forever!"

The courts and chapels of the temple's uppermost terrace were adorned with twenty-seven freestanding statues of Ḥat-shepsūt, for the most part of red granite. In all but three of these she is represented, like her predecessors and successors on the throne of the pharaohs, as a male figure clad in the costume and equipped with the attributes traditionally associated with Egyptian kingship. This was merely a concession to the conventions governing the form in which a king of Egypt was habitually represented in temple sculpture, and in no way implies that Ḥat-shepsūt ever pretended, officially or otherwise, to be a man or ever actually wore male attire or assumed male attributes.

The first of the freestanding statues encountered by the god Amūn or any other visitor to the temple was a magnificent pair of colossal red granite figures standing, with hands lowered in an attitude of adoration, before the gateway leading into the uppermost, peristyle court. Though smashed to pieces, the figures were recovered almost in their entirety from a great quarry, or borrow pit, north of the temple avenue; and since they are to all intents and purposes duplicates, only one was retained by the Cairo Museum. The other *statue, brought to New York in 1928, is shown mounted upon a new cement base, but otherwise very little restored, in figure 52. Eight feet in height without the base, it retains something of the massive ruggedness of its Middle Kingdom prototypes, but shows the blander, more idealized facial type and the more rounded and less detailed modeling of the limbs and torso characteristic of New Kingdom temple sculpture as a whole and of over lifesize figures in particular. Perhaps because it was difficult to reach, the uraeus atop the handsomely proportioned royal *nemes* has lost only its head. The elaborate and ultraformal dress kilt seen on this statue is of a type worn by the kings of Egypt at least as early as the Fifth Dynasty. It consists apparently of the usual goffered *shendyet*-kilt ( ) with a pleated triangular apron added to the front, and over this, suspended from the belt, a "spor-

FIGURE 51. Colossal red granite sphinx of Ḥat-shepsūt from her temple at Deir el Baḥri. H. 64½ in.

ran" of tubular beads adorned on the edges with representations of the royal cobra, probably of metal. A loop supporting the underfold of the kilt projects prominently from the right side of the top of the belt, and on the belt clasp is inscribed Ḥat-shepsūt's throne name preceded by the titles the "Good Goddess, Mistress of the Two Lands," and followed by the words "given life forever." The back pilaster is also inscribed and here we find a longer version of the royal titulary: "The King of Upper and Lower Egypt, Lord of Rites, Maʿet-ku-Rēʿ, [the Son of Rēʿ], Khnemet-[Amū]n Ḥat-shepsūt, beloved of Amun Rēʿ, who is in the midst of Djeser-djeseru, and given life forever."

Of eight colossal ★kneeling figures which lined the way leading across the uppermost court to the door of the sanctuary, the Museum acquired from its own work at Deir el Baḥri and through an exchange with the Berlin Museum three more or less complete examples (fig. 53), two wearing the *nemes* and one the tall crown of Upper Egypt. It was the head of the last-named statue which was taken by Lepsius to Berlin in 1845 and which came to our collection in 1930 as part of the exchange referred to. Ranging in height from eight and a half to nine feet and averaging around four and a half tons in weight, these massive pieces of architectural sculpture show the same stylization and the same simplified modeling which we have observed in the standing colossus and in the big granite sphinx. The pose, in which the pharaoh is represented as kneeling before his god and holding in each hand a small, globular offering jar (○), is known from earlier periods but did not achieve real popularity until the Eighteenth Dynasty, when it began to be used with great frequency for both royal and private statues. In working out the pose the Egyptian sculptor has elongated the legs and other portions of the figure to an absurd degree—a fact which is not apparent until we imagine such figures as unfolding and standing upright. The precise actions being performed by these kneeling colossi are described in short inscriptions on the tops of two of the bases. They tell us in one case that this is "[The Good

FIGURE 52. Colossal statue of Ḥat-shepsūt in red granite from her temple at Deir el Baḥri. H. without base 8 ft.

Goddess], Maʿet-ku-[Rēʿ], offering fruit before Amūn," and in the other, that this is "Maʿet-ku-Rēʿ presenting Right *(Maʿet)* to Amūn." Of the longer inscriptions on the back pilasters of the three figures, the most complete occurs on the one wearing the White Crown: "The Horus Wosret-kū, [the King of Upper and Lower Egypt, Maʿet-ku-Rēʿ, the Daughter of Rēʿ,] Khnemet-Amūn Ḥat-shepsūt, [beloved of] Amun Rēʿ, who is in the midst of Djeser-djeseru, and given life." The goffered *shendyet*-kilt worn by all three of our kneeling figures is provided with a wide belt decorated with wavy lines and inscribed at the middle of the front with a title and name of Ḥat-shepsūt. In two cases the figure wears a knot amulet of ancient type suspended over its breast on a cord. It will have been noted that, to bring them up to the over-all height of their mates with the tall crowns, the statues wearing the *nemes* (of which there were four) have been given exceptionally high bases. In the initial defacement of these statues by the agents of Tḥut-mosĕ III only the heads of the lofty uraei were knocked off, and in one instance the eyes were methodically pecked out with a small chisel or punch. Subsequently they were all smashed to pieces and the fragments of some of them scattered far and wide over the ʿAsāsīf.

Five small kneeling ★statues, also of red granite but averaging less than three feet in height, had been broken up and are without their bases, but in two cases are otherwise complete and undamaged, with the uraei on their headdresses still intact and the white and black coloring of their eyes still fresh. On their heads the little figures wear a type of soft kerchief or wig cover called a *khat*, and each holds before it a *nemset*, or lustrations, vase fronted by a symbol of "stability" (𓊽). Little attempt at portraiture is discernible in the faces, and the bodies are summarily modeled, a circumstance attributable in some degree to the very coarse-grained crystalline stone in which they are carved. The short inscriptions on the pilasters running up the backs of the figures are of two types, one reading: "The Good God, Lord of the Two Lands (or Lord of Rites), Maʿet-ku-Rēʿ, beloved of Amūn and given life"; the other: "The Son of Rēʿ, of his body, Khnemet-Amūn Ḥat-shepsūt." There were at least a dozen of these small statues, and they seem to have stood around the upper court of the temple, perhaps in the spaces between the columns of its peristyle.

Except for the face, which was almost completely obliterated by Ḥat-shepsūt's enemies, a big red granite seated ★statue, seven feet in height and coming perhaps from one of the shrines of the upper terrace, is well preserved, even to the blue and yellow striping of the *nemes* and the blue, red, and yellow coloring of the elaborate broad collar. Though representing a king, wearing the *shendyet*-kilt and having the symbols of the "Nine Bow" peoples (see Part I, p. 181) carved on the base beneath his feet, there is in the slenderness and softly rounded forms of this figure something of a feminine quality which we shall find even more pronounced in the smaller seated statues of Ḥat-shepsūt soon to be discussed. The folded "handkerchief" held in the figure's clenched right hand, the block borders around the edges of the throne, and the panels on its sides with the heraldic knotting-together of the plants of Upper and Lower Egypt are traditional elements handed down from the Old and Middle Kingdoms but not previously treated in so light and graceful a manner. The inscriptions, in which, as usual, Ḥat-shepsūt is accorded full kingly titles and is referred to as "beloved of Amūn, who resides in Djeser-djeseru," are confined to the front of the throne, the uninscribed and undecorated back of the statue suggesting that it was designed to be placed immediately against a wall surface of some sort or in any case was not intended to be seen from the rear.

The same is true of the seated ★statue shown in figure 54, which, because it is unique in scale and material and because it is without question the finest of all the temple sculptures, is thought to

FIGURE 53. Red granite colossi of Ḥat-shepsūt from the uppermost court of her Deir el Baḥri temple. H. of center statue 9 ft.

FIGURE 54. Ḥat-shepsūt. An indurated limestone statue, probably from her funerary chapel in the Deir el Baḥri temple. H. 77 in.

have come from Ḥat-shepsūt's own funerary chapel on the south side of the uppermost terrace. Slightly over life size and carved in a hard, marble-like limestone, the figure and throne together measure six feet five inches in height. Here again the Female Horus is presented to us as a pharaoh, wearing the *shendyet*-kilt and the kingly *nemes*, but beardless and with a form so slender, so graceful and so essentially feminine in feeling that little doubt could exist as to the true sex of the ruler portrayed. Cyril Aldred speaks of this statue as giving "an idealisation of feminine grace which is yet in the Theban tradition"; and goes on to remark that "this and other similar statues of the queen may have been a contributory factor in giving to the sculpture of the dynasty a pronounced twist towards a tradition of femininity which develops throughout the period."[3] Though certainly idealized, the face of our statue, with its broad forehead, softly rounded cheeks, pointed and slightly receding chin, small, pleasant mouth, and delicately arched nose, gives us without doubt one of the best portraits of Ḥat-shepsūt now in existence. The head, broken and with the uraeus missing, the forearms, and parts of the throne were unearthed by the Museum's Expedition during the winters of 1926 to 1928. The rest of the statue, found almost intact three-quarters of a century earlier, was in the Berlin Museum from 1845 to 1929, when it was acquired for our collection in the exchange to which we have already referred. As with the granite statues, the headdress, the eyes and eyebrows, the broad collar, and the inscriptions were carefully painted in appropriate colors, patches of which still remain. The inscriptions give Ḥat-shepsūt's kingly names and titles followed by the expression "beloved of Amun Rēʿ," but make no reference to the Deir el Baḥri temple (Djeser-djeseru), Amūn in one case being described as the "King of the Gods" and in the other as the "Lord of Thrones-of-the-Two-Lands (Karnak)." May we conclude from this that the statue was not made originally for the queen's mortuary temple, but for a chapel or other structure which she had planned to contribute to the great temple of Amūn at Karnak?

The lower half of a much smaller but otherwise similar seated ★figure in black porphyritic diorite was found, not far away, in the great shale quarry north of the temple avenue. About half life size, the statue is preserved in one piece from the waist down, but of the upper portions only small fragments of the torso and arms were recovered. Though it is not inscribed there can be no doubt that this slender, somewhat effeminate male figure represented Ḥat-shepsūt herself in her role as king.

Less certainty attaches to the upper part of what was once a magnificent royal ★statue in milky white, indurated limestone found at Deir el Baḥri by Edouard Naville and presented to the Museum in 1907 by the Egypt Exploration Fund. Seventeen inches in height from the pit of the stomach to the crown of the head, the statue was rather under life size. It represents an Eighteenth Dynasty king wearing a blue and white striped *nemes* and wavy pharaonic beard supported by straps, outlined in red, running up the sides of the cheeks. It is not inscribed, and unhappily the entire face, from the crown of the head to below the chin, was sheared away and is missing—a loss which, in view of the extraordinarily high quality of the remaining portions of the figure, is much to be deplored. The breaking away of the face and forehead has revealed a small hole bored vertically into the top of the head and partially plugged with wood. If, as seems likely, this hole was for the attachment of a metal uraeus, possibly of gold or silver, the splitting-off of the front of the head could have been the work of thieves intent on acquiring the valuable emblem, and not an act intended to dishonor and consign to oblivion the royal owner of the statue. Though the style is not unlike that of the larger Ḥat-shepsūt statues, the figure is heavier and more masculine than those which we have just been studying and could easily have belonged to some other early New Kingdom

[3] *New Kingdom Art in Ancient Egypt*, p. 47.

ruler, such as Amun-ḥotpe I or Tḥut-mosĕ III, each of whom built a chapel at Deir el Baḥri.

In only two of her temple statues, both life-size seated figures probably from the shrine of the goddess Ḥat-Ḥor, is Ḥat-shepsūt represented as a woman, and even in these she wears kingly insignia and is referred to in the inscriptions as a pharaoh. Thus the headdress of the red granite ★statue of figure 55 is the pharaonic *nemes*, with the uraeus, as frequently, battered away, and in the inscriptions on the front of the throne the owner of the statue is called the "Good Goddess, Maʿet-ku-Rēʿ" and the "Daughter of Rēʿ, Khnemet-Amūn Ḥat-shepsūt, beloved of Amūn, who resides in Djeser-djeseru." Unlike the seated statues already discussed, this one is decorated on the back, the rear surface of the throne being adorned with two standing figures of the hippopotamus goddess Ta-weret (Thoueris) executed in *relief en creux* and, above these, with a vertical column of inscription descending from the top of the back pilaster and giving again the titles and names of the female pharaoh. In the face of this statue we have a less flattering, but perhaps more accurate, portrait of Ḥat-shepsūt than the obviously idealized version of the statue shown in figure 54. Here the face is narrower, the eyes smaller and closer together, the recession of the chin more pronounced, and the mouth and general expression less pleasant—still a handsome face, but one not distinguished by the qualities of honesty and generosity. The head, forearms, and lower half of this figure were found by our Egyptian Expedition in 1928, but the torso had long before been taken to Holland by Prince Henry of the Netherlands and is now in the Rijksmuseum van Oudheden in Leiden.

The second of the two statues in which Ḥat-shepsūt appears in her true sex is a fragmentary seated ★figure in black diorite, estimated to have been about five feet in height. The plain block throne and most of the slender female figure, clad in a simple, tight-fitting dress, is preserved; but of the head only enough of one side remains to show that the headdress was the softly rounded *khat* surmounted by the serpentine form of the royal

uraeus. Over her throat the queen is shown wearing an elaborate broad collar of polychrome beads, and suspended from her neck a knot amulet on a beaded cord. Like Ḥat-shepsūt's other seated statues, the figure, though that of a woman, has incised on the base block beneath its feet the "Nine Bow" emblems of Egypt's traditional enemies; and the names and titles in its inscriptions, in spite of their feminine endings, are those of a king of Egypt. The long vertical inscription descending from the back pilaster onto the back of the throne is interesting in that it gives all five of Ḥat-shepsūt's official names: "The Horus Wosret-kū, She of the Two Goddesses Wadjet-renpowet, Horus of Gold Netjeret-khaʿu, King of Upper and Lower Egypt Maʿet-ku-Rēʿ, Daughter of Rēʿ, Khnemet-Amūn Ḥat-shepsūt."

An interesting profile portrait of Ḥat-shepsūt, executed in sunk relief (fig. 56), is preserved on the side of a fragmentary limestone ★statue base thrown out of the Deir el Baḥri temple by Tḥut-mosĕ III and recovered by our expedition in 1923. The base, some twenty-six inches square and al-

FIGURE 55. Ḥat-shepsūt. Head and shoulders of a seated statue of red granite. H. of face 6 in.

most eighteen inches high, had carved on each of its two sides a representation of the female pharaoh in the form of a crouching sphinx, surmounted by a ⊟ -sign and having before it a large cartouche with one of Ḥat-shepsūt's principal names. As with the rest of the temple sculpture, the style and workmanship of this relatively insignificant detail are of the highest caliber, and as a portrait the small face seems to reflect to an extraordinary degree both the appearance and character of the shrewd and strong-willed woman ruler.

From the foot of the ʿAsāsīf, not far from the site of Ḥat-shepsūt's Valley Temple, comes the *nemes*-clad ★head of a king broken from a red granite temple statue about one and a half times life size. Once dated to the later New Kingdom, the head has been recognized by Aldred as a conventionalized portrait of Ḥat-shepsūt herself—a conclusion amply borne out by the facial type, the style, and the form of the *nemes* and uraeus. It measures thirteen and three-quarters inches in height from the base of the neck to the top of the headdress and, in spite of its badly battered nose, mouth, and chin beard, is an imposing piece of sculpture. Traces of blue and yellow paint still remain on the stripes of the *nemes*. The right half of a much smaller ★head in dark gray diorite seems also to have the features of Ḥat-shepsūt and has been tentatively assigned to her. Of unknown provenience, it was presented to the Museum in 1941 by Elisha Dyer in memory of his son George R. Dyer.

Two small fragments of painted limestone ★relief, a gift of Mrs. Morton C. Nichols, are without much question from the main temple at Deir el Baḥri. On the larger fragment appear the close-shaven head of one of the queen's henchmen and, above, part of a line of monumental hieroglyphs describing Ḥat-shepsūt's (?) embellishment of the capital city and including the words ". . . [Th]ebes with silver . . ." The smaller piece preserves the hieroglyph ☥, carved in great detail and over three and a half inches in height—clearly from an inscription of royal temple proportions.

Besides those purporting to record her affiliation with the god Amūn, the reliefs in the Deir el Baḥri temple commemorate what, in the absence of any important military activity, were probably the major achievements of Ḥat-shepsūt's reign: namely, her trading expedition to the "incense land" of Pwĕnet, or Pūnt, on the east coast of Africa near the southern end of the Red Sea, and the quarrying and transport of a pair of her Karnak obelisks. The Pwĕnet expedition, composed of five fast sea-going ships, set sail in Ḥat-shepsūt's sixth or seventh year on the throne (Year 8 or 9 of Tḥutmosĕ III), and after an interesting sojourn in tropical surroundings returned laden with rich cargoes, including aromatic gum for use as incense in the temple rites of Amūn and living "myrrh" trees for replanting in the temple groves of the god. Seven years after the return of the fleet from Pwĕnet Ḥat-shepsūt dispatched a much larger expedition to the quarries of red granite at Aswān to obtain the second of two pairs of obelisks which she

FIGURE 56. Cartouche and profile head of Ḥat-shepsūt represented as a sphinx on a fragmentary limestone statue base. H. of fragment 8 ¼ in.

erected in the temple of Amun Rēʿ at Karnak. One obelisk of this pair, ninety-seven and a half feet high, still stands where it was set up, in the hall of Tḥut-mosĕ I between the fourth and fifth pylons of the temple; on its shaft is the statement that the queen "made (it) as her monument for her father, Amūn. . . (when) she celebrated [for] him the first occurrence of the *sed*-festival." An admirably worded inscription on the base block of the huge monolith tells how it and its fallen mate were freed from the quarry in seven months, being ready for loading and transport downriver to Thebes in Regnal Year 16 of Tḥut-mosĕ III. In the Deir el Baḥri temple reliefs we see the two great shafts lying butt to butt on an enormous barge, fully 270 feet in length, which is being towed downstream by 27 ships deployed in three columns and propelled by an estimated 864 oarsmen. Aside from her obelisks Ḥat-shepsūt's most important additions to the great temple complex at Karnak were the massive eighth pylon on the southern processional way and a magnificent quartzite sanctuary for the barque of the god, the latter built originally on a raised platform immediately in front of the Middle Kingdom temple and flanked by groups of small sandstone cult chambers. Other temples bearing her name, usually in conjunction with that of her youthful co-regent Tḥut-mosĕ III, exist at Medīnet Habu in western Thebes and at Buhen and Semneh near the Second Cataract of the Nile.

From the Medīnet Habu temple come in all likelihood a red jasper ★nose and ★thumb broken from a life-size statue of superb quality. It is probable that only the face, hands, and other exposed flesh parts of this statue were of jasper, the clothing, headdress, and accessories of the figure being made of other materials. The exact shape of the delicately formed, slightly arched nose is such that it is difficult to think of it as having belonged to anyone except Ḥat-shepsūt; and the fact that a red jasper hand, apparently from the same statue, was found at Medīnet Habu not far from the Eighteenth Dynasty temple tends to support the identification. The red flesh color need cause us no concern, for in her temple statues, as we have seen, the Female Horus usually had herself represented as a male ruler.

In a desert valley near Beni Ḥasan Ḥat-shepsūt dedicated two rock-cut shrines to the lioness goddess Pakhet, and on the façade of the larger shrine, generally known as the Speos Artemidos, caused to be carved a long inscription in which she records her restoration of a number of temples of Middle Egypt, damaged or destroyed during the Hyksos occupation of the region. "I have raised up what was ruined," says the great queen, "in that earlier time when the Asiatics were in Avaris of the Northland with wandering outlanders among them overthrowing what had been made."

The activity of Ḥat-shepsūt's mining expeditions in the copper and turquoise mines of Sinai is attested by a rock tablet in the Wādy Maghāreh and ten inscriptions in the temple at Serābīt el Khādim. Dates in Regnal Years 11 and 16 (counted from the accession of Tḥut-mosĕ III) occur among these inscriptions; and a stela of Year 20 erected at Serābīt in behalf of Ḥat-shepsūt and Tḥut-mosĕ III is the latest dated monument of the queen which we now possess, antedating by only a short time her disappearance early in Year 22.

Having abandoned a small cliff tomb made for her as queen consort of Tḥut-mosĕ II, Ḥat-shepsūt early in her reign had her "vizier," Ḥapu-sonbe, prepare for her in the Valley of the Tombs of the Kings a much larger and more elaborate sepulcher appropriate to her newly acquired dignity as pharaoh. The new tomb, almost 700 feet in length, comprises a series of sloping rock-cut passages and stairways leading, 320 feet below ground level, to a rectangular sepulchral hall, its roof supported by three square, rock-cut pillars. Here were found the quartzite sarcophagus and canopic chest which Ḥat-shepsūt had planned to use for her own burial, and a slightly earlier sarcophagus,[4] also made for her, which she had had reinscribed for her father, Tḥut-mosĕ I. The extraordinary length of the tomb and the position of its entrance, in the corner of the royal valley nearest to Deir el Baḥri, suggest that Ḥapu-sonbe had once planned to extend it beneath the intervening mountain wall and bring its sepulchral hall squarely under the queen's mortuary temple. For practical reasons this scheme was soon abandoned, and the tomb actually turns almost back on itself in a long curve.

Excavation of the tomb, initiated by Theodore M. Davis in February 1903, uncovered directly in front of the entrance stair well a single foundation deposit containing over one hundred and eighty objects, many of them bearing the cartouches of Ḥat-shepsūt. With the acquisition of the Davis collection in 1930 a selection of these ★objects became the property of the Museum. Similar, though inferior in quality, to the contents of the Deir el Baḥri temple deposits, the pieces in our collection include a model adze, axe, chisel, reamer, and saw of bronze with wooden handles, a mason's float and a brick mold of wood, a wooden *mesekhtyu*-instrument ( ), a wooden *tjeset*-knot ( ) and a tiny wooden *ladanisterion* ( ) both overlaid with gold foil, three miniature linen sheets, five papyrus mats rolled up and tied together in a bundle, a model basket of grass and palm leaf, an alabaster unguent jar with a flat lid, and a rough little pottery beaker. The jar is inscribed for the "Good Goddess, Maʿet-ku-Rēʿ, the Daughter of Rēʿ, Khnemet-Amūn (*sic*), given life forever," and the same inscription appears on the back of the *mesekhtyu*-instrument, except that here the nomen is written out in full, "Khnemet-Amūn Ḥat-shepsūt." The throne name "Maʿet-ku-Rēʿ," is scratched on the wooden *tjeset*-knot and on the bronze blades of most of the tools.

Ḥat-shepsūt's name occurs also on an alabaster ★clamshell from one of five foundation deposits associated with the Deir el Baḥri tomb of her favorite official, the Steward Sen-ne-mūt. The shell, smaller and more roughly made than those from the queen's own deposits (see fig. 47), appears to have been acquired by Sen-ne-mūt from the material destined to be used in the founding of a temple to the god Montu, for in the inscription Ḥat-shepsūt is called the "Good God, Maʿet-ku-Rēʿ, beloved of Montu, Lord of Thebes, the bull who is in the midst of Hermonthis." A rough little alabaster ★saucer from another of the deposits is inscribed for the tomb owner himself, the "Overseer of the Fields of Amūn, Sen-ne-mūt, justified with Osiris." The rest of the ★material from Sen-ne-mūt's deposits, numbering, exclusive of the pottery, some sixty items, consists for the most part of smaller and coarser versions of the objects found in the royal deposits. Besides the clamshell with the name of Ḥat-shepsūt there are two uninscribed examples. Of four crudely carved *tjeset*-knots two are of ebony and two are of cedar. The carpenters' tools include two miniature bronze axe heads, two adzes, three saws, and three chisels, all of bronze with crude wooden handles, a wooden block, an alabaster whetstone, and nine quartzite rubbing stones. The masons' and builders' equipment is represented by a model hoe ( ) made of a natural tree fork, a wooden brick mold, and two levers; and that of the metalworkers by a clay crucible accompanied by lumps of copper ore (malachite) and charcoal. Eight alabaster oil jars are uninscribed except for one which has the numeral "16" written on its side in black ink. Of eleven basketry trays, made up of coils of grass wrapped with strips of palm leaf, eight are circular and three are roughly oval in shape. By way of food

[4] Now to be seen in the Museum of Fine Arts in Boston.

supplies there were provided a whole pigeon with the wings and legs tied together, a conical loaf of bread and two others shaped like a leg and a side of beef, and five pottery saucers containing, respectively, barley grains, jujubes, dates, grapes, and figs.

Also from the tomb of Sen-ne-mūt is a low, domical jar ★stopper of Nile mud stamped in some twenty places with the praenomen of Ḥat-shepsūt, accompanied by the words "beloved of Amūn." The small, oval seal impressions, each flanked by a pair of little, rounded dents, were evidently made by a scarab mounted in a heavy metal finger ring. The impressions on a second ★stopper, made by a signet ring with a square, metal(?) bezel, are, unfortunately, illegible.

Near by, in the rubbish thrown out of the Deir el Baḥri temple, were found two ★sketches drawn in black and red ink on small fragments of pottery jars. In one sketch the winged scarab beetle of the sun god Khepri holds between its forelegs a small cartouche containing Ḥat-shepsūt's praenomen, "Maʿet-ku-Rēʿ," while with its hind legs it grasps the disk of the sun, from which, in turn, is suspended the symbol of "life." The whole device is mounted on a *neb*-sign (⌓) and is surmounted by a winged sun's disk. The drawing is clearly the work of a trained draughtsman and was probably the preliminary sketch of an element actually used in the decoration of the temple. The second drawing, by an unskilled hand, comprises the small figure of a seated man holding a lotus flower and two very crudely drawn cartouches evidently intended to read "Maʿet-ku-Rēʿ" and "Khnemet-Amūn Ḥat-shepsūt."

Sometime during the coregency of Ḥat-shepsūt and Ṭhut-mosě III, three members of the latter's ḥarīm were buried together in a tomb in one of the desolate valleys west of Deir el Baḥri (see pp. 130 f.); and among the gold funerary jewelry found in this tomb was a pair of ★bracelets inscribed with Ḥat-shepsūt's name and title as king of Egypt. The bracelets are made of concave bands of light and extremely soft sheet gold seven-eighths of an inch wide, bent into circular loops and provided with hinged sleeve clasps locked together by means of removable gold pins. In a short hieroglyphic inscription incised in the metal on the outside of each bracelet we read: "The Good God, Maʿet-ku-Rēʿ, beloved of Amūn who resides in his Ḥarīm"—the last expression apparently referring to the temple of Amūn at Luxor. From the same tomb comes a ★scarab of lapis lazuli mounted in a heavy gold finger ring and having inscribed upon its base the throne name cartouches of Ḥat-shepsūt and Ṭhut-mosě III, set side by side and preceded in each case by the title the "Good God."

A ★draughtsman, or playing piece, of red jasper exquisitely carved in the form of the head of a lion shows, for so small an object, an extraordinary amount of delicate modeling and fine detail. Carefully incised on the top of the animal's head is the cartouche containing Ḥat-shepsūt's throne name, Maʿet-ku-Rēʿ, and on the back of the head and neck are the words "(Long) live the Daughter of Rēʿ, [Khnemet-Amūn] Ḥat-shepsūt, may she live forever!" The piece, of unknown provenience, passed in 1911 from the Hilton Price collection to the Carnarvon collection and with the latter in 1926 to the Metropolitan Museum.

A rectangular ★seal of glazed steatite and six small, cartouche-shaped ★plaques of faience, glazed steatite, and hard glazed paste carry Ḥat-shepsūt's throne name or personal name combined in two instances with the praenomen of Ṭhut-mosě III ("Men-kheper-Rēʿ"), and in another with the name of a building called the "House-of-Amūn-in-the-Colonnade." The personal name is once written simply "Khnemet-Amūn," with the "Ḥat-shepsūt," as occasionally elsewhere, omitted. Two of the plaques, which range in length from three-quarters of an inch to just over an inch, have been thought to be from foundation deposits, and this may have been the case with most of them, though in no instance is the provenience actually known. A rectangular ★plaque of green jasper, set in a gold finger ring, is inscribed on one side for the First Prophet of Horus of Nekhen, Tjeny, and bears on the other side the praenomen cartouches of Ḥat-shepsūt and Ṭhut-mosě III. The name Maʿet-ku-Rēʿ enclosed within a cartouche appears also on the backs of three handsome little *wedjat*-eye (𓂀) ★amulets made, respectively, of polished carnelian, blue-glazed steatite, and green faience; and around the side of a small carnelian ★amulet in the form of a plumb bob we read in minute, incised hieroglyphs: "The Good God, Maʿet-ku-Rēʿ, beloved of Amūn. . . ." Two large ball ★beads of white amethyst are inscribed, respectively, for the "King of Upper and Lower Egypt, Maʿet-ku-Rēʿ," and for the "Good God, Maʿet-ku-Rēʿ, beloved of Ḥat-Ḥor who is in (the midst of) Thebes and who resides in Djeser-djeseru"; on the second bead, below the titles and name of the queen, have been added those of the "Hereditary Prince and Count, the Steward Sen-ne-mūt." Ḥat-shepsūt's praenomen cartouche appears alone on an even larger ★bead of the same type in light blue faience, in this case measuring over an inch and a half in diameter. On all of these beads the inscriptions are incised, but on a long ★pendant bead of blue faience the hieroglyphs in Ḥat-shepsūt's name are drawn in somewhat cursive fashion in a black overglaze.

Besides the hundreds of examples discussed in the preceding pages and illustrated in part in figure 48, there are in our collection nineteen ★scarabs and three ★cowroids bearing Ḥat-shepsūt's kingly names and titles which came to us chiefly from private collections and are, without exception, of unrecorded provenience. Like those from the Deir el Baḥri foundation deposits, fifteen of the scarabs and all three of the cowroids are of green-glazed steatite, one of the remaining scarabs being of green paste and the other three of faience. Among the last there is a scarab, formerly in the Timins and Carnarvon collections, on which the throne names of Ḥat-shepsūt and Tḥut-mosĕ III appear in company with a cartouche containing the name of Meni, or Menes, the traditional founder of Egypt's first historic dynasty. Interestingly enough, this seems to be the earliest undisputed occurrence of the name of Menes now known, though it is common enough in kings' lists and other monuments of the later New Kingdom. The cartouche of Menes is supported by a winged scarab beetle—a motif which we have just seen in an ink drawing from Deir el Baḥri—and below this is a kneeling god(?) holding in either outstretched hand a papyrus plant on which the cartouches of Ḥat-shepsūt and Tḥut-mosĕ III appear to rest. Ḥat-shepsūt's personal name, written either "Khnemet-Amūn Ḥat-shepsūt" or simply "Khnemet-Amūn," occurs on three of the remaining scarabs and on one of the cowroids and is once preceded by the title "Daughter of Rēʿ." Otherwise Ḥat-shepsūt is referred to in this series of seals only by her throne name, Maʿet-ku-Rēʿ, combined more often than not with a title, an epithet, or one or more heraldic motifs, the last comprising the crowned and winged uraeus, the winged sun's disk, and the kneeling god of "Millions-of-years." The titles are commonplace—the "Good God," "Lord of the Two Lands," "Mistress of the Two Lands"—but some of the epithets are not without interest, including, for example, "Fresh-of-years" (Ḥat-shepsūt's Two Goddesses name), "fair of years," "protector of the gods," "beloved of Amun Rēʿ," and "born of Mūt and Amūn." Two of the smaller scarabs are mounted in finger rings, in one case of gold, in the other of bronze.

Aside from the already mentioned funerary cones and bricks of her guardians Sen-ne-mūt and Seni-men (see p. 81), and the scarabs from her mother's foundation deposits (see p. 88), the name of Ḥat-shepsūt's daughter, the young princess Nefru-Rēʿ, occurs in our collection on four ★scarabs of green-glazed steatite and on two marked linen ★sheets from the wrappings of the mummy of Sen-ne-mūt's father, Raʿ-mosĕ. On the sheets the cartouche with the name "Nefru-Rēʿ" is written by itself in black ink. On the scarabs it is twice accompanied by the title the "God's Wife," and once by a kneeling figure with hands raised in an attitude of adoration. Three of the scarabs are from the Deir el Baḥri temple or its vicinity, but the fourth was found tied to the hand of an old woman buried in the chip heaps in front of the tomb of Sen-ne-mūt on the ʿIlwet esh Sheikh ʿAbd el Ḳurneh. Nefru-Rēʿ, who seems to have died while still a young girl, between Tḥut-mosĕ III's eleventh and sixteenth regnal years, is known to us from inscriptions at el Kāb and Serābīt el Khādim, from group statues in which she appears as a child with her tutors Sen-ne-mūt and Seni-men, and from a relief in the sanctuary of the Deir el Baḥri temple, where her slender, youthful figure, loaded with royal attributes, is seen standing behind the much larger figures of her mother and her half brother. In this scene carved near the end of her short life, she bears the titles "King's Daughter [of his body, whom he loves], Lady of the Two Lands, Mistress of Upper and Lower Egypt, [Wife of the God,] and Holy [Image] of Amūn"; but neither here nor elsewhere is she called a King's Wife—a fact which leaves us in some doubt as to whether she was ever actually married to Tḥut-mosĕ III. It is sometimes stated that young Meryet-Rēʿ Ḥat-shepsūt, who became Tḥut-mosĕ III's principal queen, was also a daughter of the elder Ḥat-shepsūt, but there is no evidence to support this belief, which on the face of it seems extremely unlikely.

3. Sen-ne-mūt, His Family, and His Associates

The person chiefly responsible for Ḥat-shepsūt's success was apparently her Chief Steward Sen-ne-mūt, a canny politician and brilliant administrator who, having entered the royal household during the reign of Tḥut-mosĕ II as the tutor and steward of the Princess Nefru-Rēʿ, rose to be the queen's most favored official, adding one important office to another until he had become, in his own words, "the greatest of the great in the entire land." The holder of more than eighty titles, chiefly in the administration of the vast properties of the royal family and of the state god Amūn, Sen-ne-mūt in his capacity as High Steward probably controlled in the names of these two great powers a large part of the total resources of the Egyptian empire. As chief royal architect he was in charge of all building construction undertaken by Ḥat-shepsūt and her youthful coregent, not only at Deir el Baḥri and at Karnak but also at other important temple sites up and down the Nile, and it was he who supervised the quarrying and transport of at least one pair of the queen's gigantic obelisks. As confidant of the female pharaoh and guardian of her daughter he was evidently on the most intimate terms with Egypt's ruling family and was permitted to conduct himself almost as if he were a member of that family, enjoying privileges and prerogatives never before extended to a mere official, particularly to one whose origin, like that of Sen-ne-mūt, was of the

FIGURE 57. The Steward Sen-ne-mūt offering a votive sistrum to the goddess Mūt. Statuette in black porphyritic diorite. H. 8⅝ in.

humblest. He was, for example, allowed by his royal mistress to represent himself at least seventy times in out-of-the-way places in her mortuary temple, to quarry and execute for himself a quartzite sarcophagus of the contemporary royal type, and, under the forecourt of the Deir el Baḥri temple, to excavate for himself a long, sloping corridor tomb, totally unlike those of his fellow officials but strikingly similar to Ḥat-shepsūt's own tomb in the Wādy el Bibān el Molūk. His power, however, did not long survive the death of his royal ward Nefru-Rēʿ, and by the nineteenth year of the reign (1472 B.C.) his downfall was complete, his great new tomb at Deir el Baḥri abandoned unfinished, and many of his monuments defaced or smashed to pieces.

Though it has suffered less than some of his other monuments, a diorite ★statuette representing Sen-ne-mūt kneeling and presenting a votive sistrum to the goddess Mūt (fig. 57) appears to have been roughly used, portions of its delicately carved and highly polished surfaces being worn and battered. Acquired in 1948 through the generosity of Mr. and Mrs. George D. Pratt, the figure is a miniature version (for a tomb or private shrine) of a big red quartzite statue which during the coregency of Ḥat-shepsūt and Tḥut-mosĕ III was set up in the temple of Mūt at Karnak and which is now in the Cairo Museum (No. 579). In both figures Sen-ne-mūt wears a heavy, shoulder-length wig and a short, wavy chin beard, obviously artificial since on the statue it is seen to be supported by straps running up his cheeks; and in both his middle-aged torso is festooned with rolls of fat indicative of a life of prosperous ease. The giant sistrum held before him is of elaborate design, comprising a large *tyet*-symbol, its loop replaced by a head of the goddess Ḥat-Ḥor carved in great detail and surmounted by a small temple façade with a doorway opening in which, in a real sistrum, the bars and plates of the rattle would be suspended. In our votive sistrum this space is occupied by a uraeus coiled between the arms of a ⊔-sign and wearing on its head a solar disk—a well-known cryptographic writing of Ḥat-shepsūt's praenomen, "Maʿet-ku-Rēʿ." The inscriptions carved on the top, sides, base, and broad back pilaster of our statuette are abridged versions of those found on the Karnak statue and are interesting enough to bear being quoted, at least in part. On the upper surface of the sistrum a five-line text tells us that, like its larger counterpart, this statuette was "given as a favor of the King's bounty to the Hereditary Prince and Count, the confidant of the Female Horus Wosret-kū (Ḥat-shepsūt), the trusted one of the Horus Khaʿ-em-Wast (Tḥut-mosĕ III), who executed their eternal monuments and remained in favor with them every day." Short inscriptions on the sides of the sistrum tell of the adoration which Sen-ne-mūt bestows on the goddesses Mūt and Ḥat-Ḥor "in behalf of the life, prosperity, and health of" Ḥat-shepsūt and Tḥut-mosĕ III and in behalf of a "good burial" for himself; and below, his name appears twice, preceded by the titles Overseer of Works (i.e., chief architect) and Overseer of the Fields of Amūn. The principal text, preserved in somewhat damaged condition on the back pilaster, is an offering formula addressed to the goddess Mūt, Lady of Ishru, "[that she may give] glory in heaven and power on earth to the spirit of the [Chief Steward of] the King, Sen-ne-mūt, the justified; that she may give the offerings which are in the Southland to the spirit of the Magnate of the Tens of Upper and Lower Egypt, Sen-ne-mūt; that she may give the food which is in the Northland to the spirit of the greatest of the great, the noblest of the nobles, the Chief in the Mansion of the Red Crown, Sen-ne-mūt; that she may give everything which comes forth from upon her offering table in Most-select-of-places (Karnak) and in [the temples of the gods of Upper and Lower Egypt to the spirit of the Privy Councilor] in the Temples, Sen-ne-mūt; that she may give evocation of bread and beer, beef and fowl, and a drinking of water at the flood to the spirit of the Chief Steward of Amūn, Sen-ne-mūt, who filled the storehouses and enriched the granaries, the Overseer of the Double Granary of Amūn, Sen-ne-mūt, the justified, engendered of the worthy Raʿ-mosĕ, the justified, and born of Ḥat-nūfer...."

Of the once magnificent quartzite ★sarcophagus which Sen-ne-mūt prepared for his first tomb (No. 71) on the hill of the Sheikh ʿAbd el Ḳurneh, over twelve hundred fragments, representing approximately half of the original monument, were recovered by our Egyptian Expedition in this tomb and in its vicinity. As reassembled and restored from these fragments the sarcophagus is seen to have consisted of an oblong chest seven feet eight inches in length, rounded at both ends and provided with a low, flat lid slightly vaulted on the underside. Both box and lid were carved from single blocks of the intensely hard, brown crystalline stone, the exterior of the sarcophagus being painted dark red, probably to give the impression that the stone used was the much admired, but rather rare, deep red quartzite. The paneled decoration, comprising funerary texts inscribed in graceful, incised hieroglyphs and slender figures of tutelary divinities executed in *relief en creux*, is essentially the same as that which we have already studied on the private coffins of the early New Kingdom and derives ultimately from that seen on the exteriors of the rectangular wooden coffins of the Middle Kingdom (see Part I, pp. 312 ff.). In the second panel on the left side of the box we find the pair of great eyes which on the earlier coffins marked the position of the face of the deceased and was therefore the point around which the rest of the decoration was composed. The deities represented included, on the floor of the box and probably also on the lid, the heaven goddess Nūt, with arms outstretched in a protective gesture; on the ends of the sarcophagus, the sister goddesses Isis and Nephthys, each kneeling upon a large  -sign; and on its long sides, standing figures of the canine-headed god Anubis, and of the Four Genii of the Dead, all with bearded human heads. Besides the longitudinal and vertical bands of inscription with dedications of the deceased to these deities and the usual brief speeches addressed by the gods and goddesses to the occupant of the sarcophagus, the texts on the exterior of the box include Chapters VIII, XXXIV, XLV, LXII, and LXXXVI of the Book of the Dead—one of many indications of the growing popularity during the early New Kingdom of this particular series of funerary spells. Like those of many Middle Kingdom coffins, the interior surfaces of the walls of Sen-ne-mūt's sarcophagus were completely covered with narrow, vertical columns of inscription, in this case incised and comprising the whole of Chapter CXXV of the Book of the Dead, a long and important spell designed to enable the deceased to enter and to exonerate himself in the courtroom of the Underworld, the so-called Hall of the Two Maʿets. Except for this feature, the fact that it is oval, not cartouche-shaped, in plan, and some minor differences in details and dimensions, this sarcophagus is so like the second of the two prepared for Ḥat-shepsūt as king of Egypt (Cairo Museum, No. 620) that there can be little doubt that the two monuments were quarried and executed at the same time, probably about the eleventh year of the reign of Ṭhut-mosĕ III (1480 B.C.). From the score of titles preserved on the fragments of his sarcophagus we learn that Sen-ne-mūt was not only a Steward of Amūn (his most common title) and a Chief Steward of the King, but also an Overseer of the Treasury, Granary, Fields, and Cattle of Amūn, a Controller of Works, a Prophet of the Barque Woser-ḥēt-Amūn, and an Overseer of the Prophets of Montu. Four titles not found on any of his other monuments are Overseer of the Administrative Office of the Mansion, Overseer of Administrative Offices, *Imy-weret* Priest, and Conductor of Festivals.

Of some ninety ★name stones recovered from Sen-ne-mūt's Sheikh ʿAbd el Ḳurneh tomb a few representative examples have been retained in our permanent collection. Related in concept to those of Ḥat-shepsūt discussed above, these stones are rough flakes or lumps of limestone of various sizes and shapes, clearly waste material from the original cutting of the tomb. After being inscribed on one surface with the name and often also with a title of Sen-ne-mūt, the stones were incorporated into the roughly constructed revetments of the tomb's courtyard and the retaining walls of its terrace, where they were immediately lost to view

FIGURE 58. Portraits of Sen-ne-mūt. Two trial sketches in black ink on a flake of limestone. L. 6 ¾ in.

among their thousands of uninscribed mates. Though invisible when once in place, the purpose of such stones was apparently to establish a magical bond between the walls and their owner, the identification being made all the more forceful by the fact that the identifying elements were component parts of the structures they identified. Our name stones range in size from a modest slab, eight by seven by three inches, to a massive lump nineteen inches long, eleven inches wide, and eleven inches thick. On four examples the inscriptions are carved (incised) on the stones in formal hieroglyphs. On the others they are merely drawn in cursive hieroglyphs on the rough surfaces with black or red paint, the draughtsmanship varying considerably in quality. On two of our stones the name "Sen-ne-mūt" appears alone, and on one of these it is followed by the Osirian epithet, "the justified." The titles which on the remaining stones precede the owner's name include Steward, Overseer of the Double Gold House, Overseer of the Garden of Amūn, and Overseer of the Fields of Amūn. The four titles borne by Sen-ne-mūt on the stamped pottery funerary ★cones from this same tomb are Steward of Amūn, Priest of (the Barque) Woser-ḥēt-Amūn, Steward of the King's Daughter Nefru-Rēʿ, and Overseer of the Cattle of Amūn.

The appearance of the great official is preserved to us in particularly lively fashion in two profile heads sketched in black ink on a ★flake of limestone (fig. 58) which was acquired in 1931 as an anonymous gift but which is known to have come from the vicinity of Sen-ne-mūt's second tomb, at Deir el Baḥri. With the exception of the small and probably artificial chin beard the head at the right is practically a duplicate of a well-known profile portrait of Sen-ne-mūt in the first corridor of the Deir el Baḥri tomb. Both drawings show the sensitive, aquiline nose, the nervously pursed lips, and the deep wrinkles about the mouth and chin which seem to have been Sen-ne-mūt's most arresting facial characteristic. The headdress in both cases is a close, caplike wig made up of rows of short, wavy locks, and in both we see the unadorned neckline of a plain linen shirt. On our ostrakon the draughtsman evidently sketched the left-hand profile first—possibly from life, but more probably from a model of some sort—and, being dissatisfied with it, drew the second head partially over it, details like the corner of the eye and the side of the wig of the preliminary sketch showing through the more finished drawing. On the reverse of the flake there is an admirable drawing in black ink of a lean, hairy rat with prodigiously long whiskers.

Three ★flakes of limestone from Sen-ne-mūt's earlier tomb (No. 71) carry profile heads drawn in black ink outline which, though differing considerably from one another and from the heads of the Deir el Baḥri ostrakon, were evidently studies for portraits of the tomb owner. All show his rather prominent, arched nose, protruding lips, and slight double chin, and in the two more complete examples the wig is of the small, caplike type which seems to have been favored by the great man. The drawing which is probably the least accurate likeness of the three is interesting because in its unfinished state it shows the stages involved in its production. The basis of the drawing is a square, three and three-quarters inches on a side, divided by ruled red lines into sixteen smaller and approximately equal squares. On this the head was drawn first in heavy red outline and subsequently in heavy black outline, the second outline deviating from the first in several places. Thin, horizontal black guide lines for the rows of locks were ruled on the headdress, but only the upper three rows of locks were filled in. The proportions of this head and the method employed in obtaining them correspond closely with those used in other New Kingdom tombs in the Theban necropolis; and the same system of squares was used in laying out the portrait of Sen-ne-mūt in his Deir el Baḥri tomb. A man's head drawn in very heavy black outline on another ★ostrakon from Tomb 71 is difficult to class as a portrait of Sen-ne-mūt, though it may in fact have been intended as such.

A fifth ★ostrakon, a flake of limestone four by three and an eighth inches, is interesting in that it carries the sketch layout for the painted decoration of the inner surface of the lintel and jambs of the main doorway of the tomb. On the lintel, as shown on the ostrakon, are two panels each containing the common scene of a priest dedicating a funerary meal to a seated couple. With the help of the finished painting, which happens to be still preserved in the tomb, we can identify the seated figures as Sen-ne-mūt, his father, Raʿ-mosĕ, and his mother, Ḥat-nūfer, and one of the standing figures as a brother, the *Wēʿb*-priest Min-ḥotpe. The drawings on a dozen other ★ostraka from Tomb 71 and from Sen-ne-mūt's later tomb, now in our collection, are, in the main, preliminary studies of figures, scenes, or decorative elements which were, or were to have been, painted on the walls of the tomb. Some are extremely sketchy and summary, but this only means that we have caught the study of the subject at an early stage. Human faces and figures, either alone or as parts of scenes, naturally predominate. Animal and bird forms are also well represented, and in these we can distinguish both naturalistic treatments of the subjects, to be used in scenes, and conventionalized renderings to be employed either as decorative elements or as hieroglyphs. Sketches of inanimate objects, except those held, worn, or otherwise used by human figures, are rare. On the other hand, a great deal of ostrakon space was devoted to preliminary drawings of the famous ceiling patterns of Tomb 71.

Five fragments of the actual painted plaster ★ceilings were found by Norman de Garis Davies lying on the floor of the longitudinal passage and tranverse forehall of the tomb. They range in size from thirteen by seven inches to twenty-eight by twenty-seven inches and show three widely different ornamental designs: lines of yellow diamonds and triple zigzags of blue, red, and green, bordered by yellow bands inscribed with blue hieroglyphs; alternating concentric squares and square rosettes of blue, red, yellow, and white, with borders formed of continuous blue and white S-spirals on a red ground; and quadruple spirals of red and yellow, and red, white, and blue rosettes on a white ground with white-on-red zigzag borders. While there can be no doubt that spiral patterns like these, known in Egypt as early as the Twelfth Dynasty, were derived ultimately from Minoan Crete, it is difficult to say whether their widespread use during the New Kingdom was, as Helene Kantor has put it, "an indigenous development based solely on the traditions inherited from the Middle Kingdom, or whether these designs may have been conditioned, in part at least, by renewed stimulation from the Aegean."[5]

Besides the sarcophagus, the name stones, the ostraka, the ceiling fragments, and the stamped bricks and funerary cones of Sen-ne-mūt and his brother Seni-men discussed in the foregoing pages, our excavations in and around Tomb 71 yielded fragments of the blocks of painted limestone relief with which the elevated statue niche at the inner end of the great chapel had once been lined. The walls of this niche, made to contain a well-known statue of Sen-ne-mūt, at one time in the Berlin Museum, were adorned with offering and banquet scenes in which members of the great man's family seem to have participated. On the largest fragment of ★relief recovered—from the south wall of the niche—we see "his [belov]ed [sist]er, [Aʿḥ]-ḥotpe, the justified," seated on a mat behind an offering table and holding to her nose the flower of a blue lotus. A mummiform wooden ★statuette probably of this same Aʿḥ-ḥotpe was picked up on the hill slope in front of the tomb; and it may have been she whose mummy, uninscribed anthropoid ★coffin, and other belongings were found near by in a rough little chamber built of chunks of limestone from the cutting of her brother's great tomb above.

On the same hill slope, in an area subsequently covered by the artificial terrace thrown out in front of Tomb 71, were buried other members of Sen-ne-mūt's family and household, including, in a small rock-cut chamber on the axis of the larger tomb, his father and mother, Raʿ-mosĕ and Ḥat-nūfer, and further down the slope to the south, also in a tiny rock chamber, a boy named Amun-ḥotpe, who would seem to have been a much younger brother. Near the burial which we have tentatively identified as that of his sister Aʿḥ-ḥotpe was found a white anthropoid ★coffin containing the mummy of Sen-ne-mūt's minstrel, Ḥar-mosĕ, and, lying beside the coffin, the lute which the latter had used to accompany himself in his songs. Not far away was the uninscribed coffin of a male member of the great steward's household, the wrappings of the otherwise unidentified mummy including two ★sheets inscribed with the names Amun-mosĕ and Weʿbet-Amūn; and, a little further to the north, a youth buried in a reed mat, and an old woman encased in a cheap rectangular coffin, but wearing tied to one of her fingers a handsome ★scarab inscribed for the "God's Wife, Nefru-Rēʿ" (see p. 105). Nor were Sen-ne-mūt's human companions the only ones to be interred beneath the terrace of his great tomb. Here also were discovered one of his horses—a little mare scarcely twelve and a half hands high—and a cynocephalous ape, each swathed in linen bandages, enclosed within a rectangular coffin, and provided with food contained in pottery bowls. Aside from these subsidiary tombs and "surface burials," all of which were found undisturbed, the hill slope yielded four intact deposits of weapons and other objects, obviously associated with the burial of Sen-ne-mūt or some member of his family. A wooden ★statuette of his mother, Ḥat-nūfer, similar to that of Aʿḥ-ḥotpe referred to above, was acquired by purchase in Cairo, but comes almost certainly from this same area and probably from our own excavations. Though once the property of an important official and his household, little of the material from the burials and deposits below Tomb 71 is in itself of historical significance; and most of the individual pieces can and will be represented to greater advantage in Chapter V, on the arts and crafts of the period.

Except for its foundation deposits, which we have already discussed, Sen-ne-mūt's unfinished second tomb, under the forecourt of the Deir el

[5] *The Aegean and the Orient*, p. 30.

FIGURE 59. Whip handle of Sen-ne-mūt's Skipper, Neb-iry. Hardwood. L. 17¾ in.

Baḥri temple, produced no portable objects which can be associated directly with its owner. The glory of this tomb is its inscribed antechamber which boasts, among other interesting features, the earliest and one of the finest astronomical ceilings now known—a great chart of the heavens complete with a decan table and a list of monthly festivals, laid out and "drawn by the most skilful penmen of the mid-Eighteenth Dynasty."[6] In the only partially hewn lowermost chamber of the tomb was found a canopic jar ★stopper of pottery in the form of a bearded human head, probably of Eighteenth Dynasty date but not necessarily of the time of Sen-ne-mūt. The corridors of the tomb, which totaled over a hundred yards in length, produced two traprock ★mauls, three quartzite ★whetstones, and three small pottery ★lamps, evidently left behind by the workmen who had been engaged in cutting the tomb. Two of the lamps are little open bowls of special design with wide, horizontal rims to support the wicks. The third is merely the bottom of a broken pottery jar which had been pressed into service as a lamp. A hieratic ostrakon bearing parts of two columns of accounts, found not far from his tomb, provides striking evidence of Sen-ne-mūt's stature as a national figure. Four great powers are involved in these accounts: the "Pharaoh" (Ṭhut-mosĕ III), the "Estate of the Queen" (Ḥat-shepsūt), the "Overseer of the (National) Treasury," and, last but by no means least, "Sen-ne-mūt," the only one of the four whose name alone was regarded as sufficient identification. Of the unspecified items accounted for, the Treasurer is credited with thirty-five, Sen-ne-mūt with thirty-four, Ḥat-shepsūt's Estate with twenty-nine, and Ṭhut-mosĕ III with only seventeen.

The heavy wooden ★whip handle shown in figure 59 completes the objects in our collection on

[6] Winlock, *M. M. A. Bulletin* XXIII (1928), February, Section II, p. 37.

which the name of Ḥat-shepsūt's great official appears. The carved and blue-filled inscription on the thick upper part of the handle tells us that its owner was "Sen-ne-mūt's Skipper Neb-iry"; the size of the slot at the top and the marks around it make it evident that the whip's two leather lashes were broad and thick; and the well-worn grip at the lower end of the handle shows that it had enjoyed long and strenuous use. The handle was found among the huts of a workmen's settlement in a hollow south of the Ḥat-shepsūt temple avenue.

Besides Sen-ne-mūt, Ḥat-shepsūt counted among her devoted supporters many other influential and high-ranking officials: the Vizier (?) and High Priest of Amūn, Ḥapu-sonbe, the Chancellor Neḥesy, the Viceroy of Nubia Inebny, the Treasurer Tḥūty, the Chief Steward Wadjet-renpowet, the Chief Steward Tḥut-ḥotpe, the Second Prophet of Amūn, Puy-em-Rēʿ, and, as we have seen, Sen-ne-mūt's brother the Steward Seni-men. Of Ḥapu-sonbe, whose rank surpassed and whose power must have rivaled that of Sen-ne-mūt, the Museum possesses five pottery funerary ★cones from his tomb (No. 67) in western Thebes. His titles as preserved on these cones are Hereditary Prince and Count, Treasurer of the King of Lower Egypt, First Prophet of Amūn, Overseer of the Priests of Upper and Lower Egypt, and Overseer of All Works of the King. In connection with the last title we may recall that it was Ḥapu-sonbe who supervised the excavation of Ḥat-shepsūt's huge tomb in the Valley of the Tombs of the Kings. Five ★name stones of Wadjet-renpowet were found in the chip heaps below Sen-ne-mūt's Sheikh ʿAbd el Ḳurneh tomb, and of these two—one with a carved and one with a painted inscription—were brought to New York in 1936. In the carved inscription Wadjet-renpowet bears only his principal title, "Chief Steward of the King." On the other stone a second title, "Overseer of Works of the House of Amūn," has been added, but the Chief Steward's name has been left unwritten. Another High Steward of Ḥat-shepsūt, less well known than his two distinguished colleagues, is represented in our collection by the curved bronze ★blade of a small knife of the type used by scribes to trim their brushes, cut sheets of papyrus, and the like. An inscription engraved on the blade and inlaid with strips of thin sheet gold identifies the owner of the knife as the "Chief Steward of the Good Goddess, Tḥut-ḥotpe." Puy-em-Rēʿ, one of Ḥat-shepsūt's officials who appears to have survived her reign and continued in office under Tḥut-mosĕ III, appears, as we have seen on page 88, to have been one of the architects of the queen's Valley Temple. We are, therefore, not surprised to find his title and name, the "Second Prophet of Amūn, Puy-em-Rēʿ," written in hieratic on a limestone ★block from this temple—one of several such blocks found in 1910 by the Earl of Carnarvon. Another functionary who seems to have served under both Ḥat-shepsūt and Tḥut-mosĕ III, though in a minor capacity, was the "Scribe and Accountant of the Bread of Upper and Lower Egypt, Sen-em-yaʿḥ," who is named with his titles on a funerary ★cone from his tomb (No. 127) at Thebes. A glazed steatite ★scarab inscribed for another minor official, the "Scribe and Overseer of Crafts, Ḳen-Amūn," turned up among the hundreds of royal scarabs in one of the Deir el Baḥri foundation deposits (see p. 88). Finally, we have in our collection a limestone ★doorjamb discovered at Abydos in 1900 by the Egypt Exploration Fund. It comes from the tomb of a nomarch of Thinis named Si-tep-iḥu, who, since he is referred to in the inscription as "one praised of the Lord Wadjet-renpowet," is presumed to have held office under Ḥat-shepsūt. The well-cut hieroglyphic text on the jamb, a rather interesting offering formula, runs as follows: "An offering which the King gives (to) Ptaḥ Sokar, Lord of Shetyet, and (to) Anubis, Lord of Rosetau, that he (*sic*) may give the sweet breath of the north wind to the spirit of the Hereditary Prince and Count, the Overseer of Priests in Thinis of the Abydene Nome, one praised of the Lord Wadjet-renpowet, Si-tep-iḥu, the justified."

IV. The Thutmoside Pharaohs:
THUTMOSĔ III AND HIS SUCCESSORS

1. Thut-mosĕ III, Forger of Empire

IT WAS APPARENTLY well along in the twenty-second year of his reign (1469 B.C.) that King Men-kheper-Rēʿ Thut-mosĕ III, now rid of his detested stepmother, found himself at last the sole master of Egypt. Our evidence does not tell us what became of Ḥat-shepsūt. It is quite possible that she died a natural death. We know, however, of several incidents which could have led to her downfall, the last and most damaging of which was the revolt of the Asiatic provinces in the twenty-first or twenty-second year and the pusillanimous withdrawal of all of Egypt's Asiatic garrisons to Sharuhen in southern Palestine, a step which the Female Horus evidently preferred to entrusting her energetic and resentful coregent with the leadership of Egypt's armed forces. Fortunately, the army seems to have been maintained during her reign in reasonable readiness for combat, and with Ḥat-shepsūt out of the way Thut-mosĕ III was able to embark forthwith upon the first of a long series of campaigns which were to bring the principalities of Palestine and Syria firmly under the Egyptian yoke and to instill into the other great nations of the Near East a profound respect for Egypt's newfound military might.

The immediate problem was the checking of the widespread revolt already referred to, a revolt fomented by a confederation of local rulers under the leadership of the prince of the powerful north Syrian city of Ḳadesh on the river Orontes. The action taken by Thut-mosĕ III was characteristically swift and effective. Proceeding posthaste to Gaza, the Egyptian administrative center in southern Palestine, in time to celebrate there the commencement of his twenty-third year on the throne, the pharaoh pressed on toward the strategically important and heavily fortified city of Megiddo (in the district of Ḥar Megiddon, the Biblical Armageddon), where the prince of Ḳadesh and his allies had assembled their forces. Profiting from the stupidity of his enemies he bulled his way through the narrow and dangerous pass of ʿAruna, arrived unmolested in the plain before Megiddo, and in a brief encounter routed the Syrian dynasts and chased them back into the city, which was promptly invested and subsequently forced to surrender. Though the prince of Ḳadesh escaped and the other chieftains were released under obligation to pay tribute, the revolt was crushed and Egyptian prestige in western Asia, already built up under Thut-mosĕ I, was re-established on a firm basis. Furthermore, the material plunder from Megiddo and the adjoining camp was not only huge, but included furnishings and luxuries of types with which the Egyptians of the early New Kingdom were as yet unacquainted. The sack of

Megiddo was followed by a swing northward into the region of the Lebanon, where the king topped off his first campaign by capturing three towns and over twenty-six hundred prisoners before returning to Thebes to celebrate a victory feast and to dedicate a generous portion of the rich spoils to Amūn.

None of the ensuing Asiatic campaigns are so fully described, either in the king's Annals at Karnak or in our other sources, and some were certainly little more than tours of inspection or expeditions sent out primarily to collect tribute. Others, however, included actions of considerable military interest and historical significance. Among the latter, special prominence should be accorded the sixth campaign, in Regnal Year 30, when Thut-mosĕ extended his conquests to the realm of his archenemy the prince of Kadesh, and the eighth campaign, in Year 33, when he led his army across the Euphrates and ravaged Naharīn, the western province of the empire of the Mitanni, at that time Egypt's most powerful rival in the Near East. Like his grandfather Thut-mosĕ I, he set up a boundary stela on the east bank of the Euphrates, and on his way home gratified his enthusiasm for big-game hunting by laying low 120 elephants in the north Syrian lake district of Niy, risking his life on at least one occasion in the midst of a herd of the great beasts. In Year 35 and again in Year 42 he defeated armies sent into northern Syria by the king of Mitanni, but ended by reaching an agreement with the latter which seems to have led to a suspension of hostilities between the two great states.

The administration of the conquered regions, including responsibility for delivery of the annual tribute, was left largely in the hands of selected native princes, watched over, however, by resident Egyptian commissioners and under the over-all supervision of a high commissioner for the whole area. Further to ensure the loyalty of the native rulers and to provide, upon their deaths, thoroughly Egyptianized successors, the children of many of them were taken to Egypt and brought up with the pharaoh's own children in the courts at Thebes and Memphis. Royal marriages were also arranged with the daughters of the Asiatic kinglets, and among Thut-mosĕ III's minor wives were a number of Syrian princesses, including three whose jewelry and other personal possessions now form part of our collection.

Impressed and probably not a little disturbed by Thut-mosĕ III's conquests, most of the other nations of western Asia and the eastern Mediterranean area hastened to make friendly overtures to the pharaoh. Delegations came from Babylonia, Assyria, and Mitanni on the east of Egypt's Syrian provinces, from the land of the Hittites to the north and northwest, and from the more remote, island kingdoms of Cyprus and Crete. With them they brought gifts which the Egyptians naturally chose to regard as tribute, but which seem actually to have been presented in the well-founded hope of receiving from the pharaoh in exchange even richer consignments of Egyptian commodities—above all, gold, of which Egypt controlled the greater part of the world's supply.

Most of the gold which made Egypt the envy of the ancient world was mined, as we have seen, in the desert valleys of Nubia and the Sūdān, and it was thither, following his subjugation of Syria, that Thut-mosĕ III turned his attention. A massive granite stela which he erected far up the Nile, at Gebel Barkal, shows that before the forty-seventh year of his reign the Egyptians had occupied the district of Karoy, immediately below the Fourth Cataract, and had founded there the important fortified town of Napata. Beyond this point Egyptian political control was never extended, and all subsequent royal campaigns in Nubia and the Sūdān, including that of Thut-mosĕ III's own fiftieth year, were clearly no more than disciplinary expeditions, directed not against the peaceful and largely Egyptianized inhabitants of the river valley, but against the wild and predatory tribesmen of the adjoining deserts. The administration of the pharaoh's southern provinces was, as before, in the hands of his Viceroy of Nubia, who made his official residence at Miʿam (modern ʿAnība), one hundred and forty miles south of the

First Cataract, and who was assisted by two deputy governors, one in charge of the old Nubian province of Wawat, the other administering the affairs of the more recently subjugated territory of Kush. The system of fortresses and fortified settlements developed during the Middle Kingdom was enlarged and extended southward, and through these fortresses there passed during each year of the reign of Thut-mosĕ III between six and eight hundred pounds of raw gold. In addition to gold the principal imports which reached Egypt from or by way of Nubia were elephant ivory, Sudanese ebony and other fine African woods, fragrant gum resins for use in perfumes and incense, ostrich plumes and ostrich eggs, and panther and leopard skins. Animals, including three breeds of cattle, hunting dogs, leopards, giraffes, and apes, were imported in some quantity; and each military expedition brought in fresh batches of male and female captives destined to serve as slaves in Egypt or in Nubia itself.

Although numerically these captives were surpassed many times over by the hordes of Asiatic prisoners taken in the great campaigns in Palestine and Syria, both they and other classes of immigrants from the southern provinces played an important role in the economic and military organization of the New Kingdom. In the Eighteenth Dynasty we find Nubians and Sudanese in Egypt not only as workers, house servants, and personal attendants, but above all as soldiers and police. Many appear to have enjoyed the status of free citizens, and a few, like Thut-mosĕ III's Fanbearer, Mai-her-peri, attained positions of wealth and influence.

An important result of the expansion of the Egyptian empire southward to Napata was that for the first time in world history direct contact was established with the Negro peoples of central Africa, whose natural habitat then, as now, was confined to the regions south of the Fourth Cataract of the Nile. Groups of true Negroes as well as Hamitic half-breeds were met with by Hat-shepsūt's trading expedition to the Somali coast; but it is from the independent reign of Thut-mosĕ III onward that we begin to find numerous representations of authentic Negro types in Egyptian art (see fig. 164) and hear of men of the black race employed in the mines and quarries and attached to the fortresses and temples of Nubia.

At home the king ruled his country with the same absolute power, the same taut efficiency, and the same meticulous attention to detail which had characterized his command of the army in the field, his amazing versatility and vigorous personality making themselves felt in every branch of the government and every phase of the national life. One of the important reforms which he appears to have introduced into the national administration was the division of the office of vizier between two great functionaries: a Vizier of the South, who had his headquarters in the capital city and administered the ancient realm of the Theban kings northward to Asyūt; and a Vizier of the North resident at Heliopolis (or Memphis?), whose jurisdiction extended over Middle and Lower Egypt—that is, over the whole of the territory recently recovered from the Hyksos.

Incontestably the greatest pharaoh ever to occupy the throne of Egypt, Thut-mosĕ III appears to have excelled not only as a warrior, a statesman, and an administrator, but also as one of the most accomplished horsemen, archers, and all-round athletes of his time. He is even credited with having designed a set of vases for a temple and, though the evidence for this is a trifle tenuous, there can be no doubt that he was an ardent and discriminating patron of the arts, under whose sponsorship the most notable advances were achieved in Egyptian architecture, sculpture, and painting. A serious, methodical, and industrious ruler, his reign—with the exception of one childish outburst of rage directed against the memory of Hat-shepsūt—was singularly free of acts of brutality, bad taste, and vainglorious bombast, and his records, for their period, are for the most part moderately phrased and sincere in tone. Physically he cannot have been very prepossessing. His mummy shows him to have been a stocky little man, under five feet four inches in height, and his portraits are almost unanimous in endowing him with the largest and most beaked of all the Thutmoside noses (see figs. 60, 62).

The tomb of Thut-mosĕ III (No. 34), its entrance hidden in the southernmost cleft of the Valley of the Tombs of the Kings, is modeled on those of Thut-mosĕ I and II and is only slightly larger and more elaborate than the latter. The walls of its cartouche-shaped sepulchral hall are adorned with scenes and texts from the so-called "Book of Him Who Is in the Underworld" (*Imy-Dēt*) drawn and written in cursive fashion on a yellowish brown background in obvious imitation of an unrolled papyrus version of the book; and on one of the hall's two square piers the king is shown accompanied by his mother, Isis, his queen, Mery-et-Rēʿ (Hat-shepsūt II), two other wives, Sit-Yaʿh and Nebet-u, the latter labeled "deceased," and a deceased daughter, Nefret-iru. Toward the rear of the hall the pharaoh's cartouche-shaped quartzite sarcophagus still rests on its broken alabaster base block, and scattered through the tomb's lower chambers were found bits of other items of his original funerary equipment.

The long line of temples, fortresses, and towns founded, rebuilt, or enlarged by Thut-mosĕ III stretches from Kōm el Hisn in the northwest Delta to Gebel Barkal, deep in the Sūdān, and embraces almost every important cult center, strategic point, and center of population along the Nile. In the temple of Amun Rēʿ at Karnak the king, having first defaced and later removed Hatshepsūt's quartzite sanctuary and surrounding chambers, converted the space so gained into a Hall of Annals, in the midst of which, during or after his forty-sixth regnal year, he constructed a red granite sanctuary of his own. Earlier in his reign his architects had replaced the colonnades along the sides and back of Thut-mosĕ I's court with rows of little chapels, and near the western end of the enclosure had inserted a shallow, colonnaded courtyard and a small pylon (VI). Between Pylons V and VI he installed two rooms containing lists of feasts and offerings, and behind Pylon VI the so-called First Hall of Records, its roof supported by two handsome granite piers with the heraldic plants of Upper and Lower Egypt carved in high relief on their sides. Across the eastern end of the temple, behind the enclosure of Thut-mosĕ I, was built Thut-mosĕ III's great Festival Hall with its complex of adjoining chambers; and this, together with the rest of the temple as far west as the fourth pylon, was surrounded by a heavy girdle wall of sandstone. In the Festival Hall the massive sandstone columns of the central aisle have the bell-shaped tops and inverted taper of the tent poles used in the light pavilions in which the *sed*-festival was traditionally celebrated. Thanks to the height of these columns the roof of the three central aisles is raised above those of the side aisles, thus providing an ample clerestory through which the hall is lighted.

On the occasions of his first, second, and fourth *sed*-festivals (Years 30, 33, and 40) Thut-mosĕ III embellished Karnak with a pair of granite obelisks, the first pair (now in fragments) having been set up before the fourth pylon in front of those of Thut-mosĕ I, the third pair (now missing) near the Festival Hall at the eastern end of the temple. The obelisks of the second pair seem to have been erected before the great pylon (VII) which the king added to the temple's southern processional way. Of this pair one is represented by fragments found near the pylon and the other is perhaps the huge shaft now in Istanbūl, which was originally about a hundred and fifteen feet in height. The Lateran obelisk in Rome (height 105.6 feet) appears to have been prepared for Thut-mosĕ III's fifth *sed*-festival (Year 42) and to have stood by itself between Pylons V and VI until it was removed by Thut-mosĕ IV, thirty-five years after the death of its owner, and re-erected at the extreme eastern end of the temple axis.

Sometime prior to the reign of Akh-en-Aten (Amun-hotpe IV) the ancient shrine of Rēʿ Atūm at Heliopolis appears to have been converted into a full-fledged processional temple with three big courts, each preceded by a pylon; and before one of these pylons Thut-mosĕ III in the thirty-sixth year of his reign (third *sed*-festival) is known to have erected the obelisk which now stands on the Thames embankment in London, and its mate, the Central Park obelisk in New York. The latter, taken to Alexandria by the Romans in 13-12 B.C., was brought to New York in 1879 by Lieutenant Commander Henry H. Gorringe and on January 22, 1881, was set up in its present position behind the Museum. The tapered red granite shaft measures 69½ feet in height and 7¾ feet across the base. Its estimated weight is 448,000 pounds, or 224 tons. The sides of the pyramidion at the top are adorned with square panels in which Tḥutmosĕ III appears as a sphinx presenting offerings to Rēʿ Ḥor-akhty and to Atūm, Lord of Heliopolis; while the great vertical inscriptions down the centers of the sides of the shaft give the names, titles, and epithets of the king, followed on the front by the statement: "He made (it) as his monument to his father, Atūm, Lord of Heliopolis, when he erected for him two great obelisks, the pyramidions (overlaid) with fine gold. . . ." The inscriptions on either side of the central columns were added by King Ramesses II of the Nineteenth Dynasty almost two hundred years after the obelisk was first erected. The bronze crabs under the broken corners of the shaft are replicas of those provided by the Roman prefect Barbarus at the time the obelisk was moved to Alexandria. Two of the original crabs are in the Metropolitan Museum and will be discussed in our final volume.

Two mud ★bricks in our collection, stamped with Tḥut-mosĕ III's praenomen, Men-kheper-Rēʿ ("Established-is-the-form-of-Rēʿ"), and the words "beloved of Amun Rēʿ (in) Ḥenket-ʿankh" are probably from the king's mortuary temple in western Thebes, the full name of which was Ḥe-Men-kheper-Rēʿ-ḥenket-ʿankh, the "Mansion-of-Men-kheper-Rēʿ-endowed-with-life." The name is found again on a fragment, from the side of the throne, of a seated ★statue of the king, in a black basaltic stone, which came to the Museum in 1950 as a gift of Mrs. Morton C. Nichols. Here we read in well-carved, monumental hieroglyphs: "[The Lord] of the Two Lands, Men-kheper-Rēʿ, [the Son of Rēʿ, of] his [body], Tḥut-mosĕ, given life

FIGURE 60. King Tḥut-mosĕ III. Fragment of limestone relief from western Thebes. H. 12⅝ in.

forever, beloved of Amūn who resides in the Mansion-endowed-with-life." The funerary ★cones in our collection include examples from the tomb (No. 121) of the Second Prophet of Amun Rēʿ, Aʿḥ-mosĕ, who was also the First Prophet of Amūn in Ḥenket-ʿankh; from that of Ḥiḳ-nefer, a *wēʿb*-priest of Amūn and Attendant of the Royal *Ku* of Men-kheper-Rēʿ in Ḥenket-ʿankh; and from that of the Overseer of the Granary of Upper and Lower Egypt and Scribe of the God's Offering of Amūn in Ḥenket-ʿankh, Men-kheper-Rēʿ-sonbe (Tomb No. 79). Of Aʿḥ-mosĕ, the owner of Tomb 121, we also have the head and shoulders of a large ★*shawabty*-figure, excellently modeled in fine white limestone and with the details of the eyes emphasized with black paint. Other ★cones from Theban tombs are inscribed for the Second Prophet of Men-kheper-Rēʿ, Amun-em-ka, and for the Fourth Prophet of Amūn, Ka-em-Amūn, and his son the Second Prophet of Men-kheper-Rēʿ, Se-ḳed. An inscribed wooden ★staff (see p. 215) belonged to a "*Wēʿb*-priest of (the) Amūn of Men-kheper-Rēʿ in [Ḥenket-ʿankh ?], Montu." A "*Ku*-servant of the Good God Men-kheper-Rēʿ" named Amun-ḥotpe, whose interesting sandstone

★stela (see pp. 172 f.) shows him to have been also a *ku*-servant of Amun-ḥotpe I and of Ṭhut-mosĕ I, was certainly attached to the funerary cult of Ṭhut-mosĕ III and probably to his mortuary temple.

The temple itself, on the edge of the cultivated land south of Deir el Baḥri, seems to have been inspired in its design by the Ḥat-shepsūt temple. Even in its present ruined state we can see that it comprised three courts which rose one behind the other in terraces, that the Amūn sanctuary on the upper terrace was approached through a colonnaded court and hypostyle hall, and that there were subsidiary chapels including one on the south side of the main temple dedicated to Ḥat-Ḥor, and on the north an open altar court for the worship of the sun god Rēʿ Ḥor-akhty. The whole of the temple enclosure, 162 yards from front to back and 93 yards across, was surrounded by a heavy brick wall and fronted by a massive brick pylon.

In the northwest corner of the Montu-ḥotpe temple platform at Deir el Baḥri Ṭhut-mosĕ III built (or rebuilt) a shrine to Ḥat-Ḥor which, like the larger temples on either side of it, was provided with a long, walled avenue leading eastward, down to a little Valley Temple on the edge of the cultivated land. From the latter in all probability comes a fragment of fine limestone ★relief (fig. 60) with a profile head of the king wearing the long, pharaonic beard and a soft wig cover adorned with a coiled uraeus. The piece, which still bears traces of red and blue paint, was found by the Earl of Carnarvon in the foundations of the unfinished mortuary temple of Ramesses IV, a structure built in part upon the site once occupied by the lower end of Ṭhut-mosĕ III's avenue. A somewhat idealized portrait of the great king, the head is remarkable for the delicacy of its outline and for the amount of subtle modeling achieved in the very low relief. Though there is an undoubted family resemblance between this head and our portraits of Ḥat-shepsūt, there are, at the same time, some very marked points of difference, both in the details of the faces and in their general feeling and appearance.

Also from Deir el Baḥri and probably from the same group of buildings are a rough piece of sandstone—perhaps a ★name stone—painted yellow and inscribed in black ink with the praenomen cartouche of Ṭhut-mosĕ III, a fragmentary model ★stone-rocker from a foundation deposit, inscribed for the "Good God, Men-kheper-Rēʿ, beloved of Amūn," and a small foundation deposit ★plaque of blue faience in the form of the cartouche containing the king's praenomen. A foundation deposit in front of Tomb 42 in the Valley of the Tombs of the Kings—apparently that of Ṭhut-mosĕ III's father, Ṭhut-mosĕ II—yielded, besides some model vases bearing the name of Queen Meryet-Rēʿ Ḥat-shepsūt, a small alabaster ★clamshell roughly inscribed for the "Good God, Men-kheper-Rēʿ, beloved of Osiris."

The site of a temple built by Ṭhut-mosĕ III in the ancient temenos of Osiris at Abydos was excavated in 1902 by Sir Flinders Petrie, and among the finds from this temple allotted to the Metropolitan Museum were a group of model tools and other objects from a foundation deposit, part of an inscribed limestone doorjamb, and an inscribed block of limestone, probably from the foundations of the building. The model ★tools, comprising a saw blade and two adze blades, are inscribed for the "Good God, Men-kheper-Rēʿ, beloved of

FIGURE 61. Limestone block from a temple of Ṭhut-mosĕ III at Abydos. L. 18½ in.

FIGURE 62. King Tḥut-mosĕ III, a colossal red granite statue from Medamūd. H. 128 in.

Osiris(?)." With them are two small and heavily oxidized bronze ★tablets and the ★handle of a model basket, also of bronze. The section of ★door-jamb bears, in two columns of monumental hieroglyphs, portions of one of the so-called jubilee titularies of Tḥut-mosĕ III, found normally on monuments associated with his *sed*-festivals: "The Horus Strong-bull-beloved-of-Rēʿ, the Good God. . . He of the Two Ladies Great-of-dignity-in all-lands, the Son of Rēʿ. . . ." The foundation ★block (fig. 61), believed to have been incorporated into the temple's substructure as a hidden means of identification and an insurance against appropriation of the building by later rulers, is inscribed in carefully incised hieroglyphs with the king's personal name, "Tḥut-mosĕ, Ruler of Thebes," preceded by the title "Son of Rēʿ, of his body, whom he loves," and followed by the words "given life forever." As can be seen, both the block and the inscription are complete in themselves. Similar blocks have been found in position in the subfoundations of the great Abydene temple of King Sēthy I of the Nineteenth Dynasty; and the roughly shaped name stones of Ḥat-shepsūt and Sen-ne-mūt, discussed in the preceding chapter, seem to have been intended for much the same purpose. A further parallel which suggests itself is the practice adopted by Ramesses II of having his cartouches carved on the butt ends of his obelisks, where they could neither be seen nor tampered with by would-be usurpers of the great shafts.

The long oval stamp impressions on three fragmentary mud ★bricks, unfortunately from an unidentified building, contain Tḥut-mosĕ III's throne name, Men-kheper-Rēʿ, followed in two cases by the epithet "Lord of Strength," and in one by the title "Ruler of Thebes." A small glazed pottery ★tile, probably from a foundation deposit, also bears the Men-kheper-Rēʿ cartouche, incised upon one of its broad surfaces and preceded by the simple title "King."

Three and a half miles northeast of Karnak lies the ancient Theban suburb of Medu, the modern Medamūd, with its temple to the great war god Montu. Founded under King Se'n-Wosret III of the Twelfth Dynasty on the site of a much earlier shrine, this temple was added to by Thut-mosĕ III and his successors, the Eighteenth Dynasty additions extending along an east-west axis line and including a monumental granite doorway which, having been re-erected under the Ptolemies, is still standing. It was in the pavement to the west of this doorway that Daninos Pasha in 1914 uncovered a colossal red granite *statue (fig. 62) of Thut-mosĕ III wearing the tall crown of Upper Egypt; it probably once stood, with a companion figure wearing the crown of the North, before the doorway, one statue on either side of the temple's processional way. Acquired for the Museum through the generosity of Edward S. Harkness, the statue has been restored and set up in our sculpture court as a pendant to the standing statue of Ḥat-shepsūt (fig. 52), to which, with the obvious exception of the headdress, it is similar in almost every respect, though perhaps slightly more elegant in its proportions and displaying an even higher degree of conventionalization. Aldred in his description of this statue points out that "in a side view a slight thrusting forward of the head

FIGURE 63.
King Thut-mosĕ III as a sphinx.
Quartzite. L. 13 in.

FIGURE 64. Small head of a Thutmoside pharaoh, in gray basalt. H. 2 in.

(seen also in several statues of the period. . .) may be observed."[1] Our restorations, carried out in cement and tinted plaster, include the nose and mouth of the figure, the beard, the left arm, the left leg below the knee, and all except the rear portion of the base. The uraeus, broken away from the front of the crown, and the characteristic knoblike tip of the crown itself have been left unrestored. Fortunately, the back pilaster is practically undamaged, and here we read in a long, vertical column of monumental hieroglyphs: "The Horus Strong-bull-appearing-in-Thebes, the King of Upper and Lower Egypt, the Lord of the Two Lands, Men-kheper-Rēʿ, the Son of Rēʿ, of his body, Tḥut-mosĕ Goodly-of-forms, beloved of Montu, Lord of Medu, and given life forever."

A large kneeling ★statuette of Tḥut-mosĕ III skillfully executed in polished black diorite has lost not only its *nemes*-clad head, but also its hands, together with the globular offering jars which they must have held. In pose and costume the figure is exactly similar to the kneeling colossi of Ḥat-shepsūt shown in figure 53, but when complete measured only about twenty inches in height. Two lines of incised hieroglyphic inscription on the top of the base ask eternal life for the "Good God, Men-kheper-Rēʿ, the Son of Rēʿ, Tḥut-mosĕ, Prince of Right, beloved of Amun Rēʿ, Lord of Thrones-of-the-Two-Lands (Karnak) and King of the Gods." The statuette was probably dedicated in a temple of Amūn, perhaps in the great shrine at Karnak. Despite its modest size it would seem to have occupied a public position in the temple, since in its inscription the name of the god has been erased—presumably by agents of Amūn's archenemy the pharaoh Akh-en-Aten—and subsequently restored.

The last two remarks apply equally well to a small quartzite ★sphinx (fig. 63) inscribed on its breast for the "Good God, Men-kheper-Rēʿ, beloved of [Amūn]," except that here no effort has been made to restore the almost completely obliterated divine name. Like most of the larger sphinxes, this one is of the conventional Egyptian type, comprising the body of a crouching lion surmounted by the head of the pharaoh wearing the graceful, kingly *nemes*, but lacking the usual royal beard. When compared with the colossal sphinx of Ḥat-shepsūt (fig. 51) the head is seen to be somewhat smaller in relation to the body and to be perched a little higher above the shoulders of the animal, while the paws and certain other details seem disproportionately large. The loss of the forelegs of the lion has given the crouching form an unhappily truncated appearance and the destruction of the nose has done away with whatever portrait quality the small face may have had. The workmanship, on the other hand, is of the highest

[1] *New Kingdom Art in Ancient Egypt*, p. 48.

quality and the surface finish obtained in the hard, gritty, brown stone is remarkably fine. Remarkable, too, is the feeling of dignity and monumentality achieved in a piece of sculpture which was not more than sixteen inches in length and is just over nine inches in height. Above all, there is about this figure and the kneeling statuette of Ṭhut-mosě III a new quality of grace and elegance which is to become more and more the keynote of New Kingdom art.

The same qualities and much the same facial type appear in the sensitive little basalt ★head of figure 64, which would seem to have been intended as a conventionalized portrait either of Ṭhut-mosě III himself or of one of his immediate successors. Here again the headdress is the royal *nemes* surmounted, as usual, by the uraeus, the upreared head of which has been broken away, probably in the same accident which damaged the tip of the king's nose. Exquisitely carved in the fine-grained, dark gray stone, this small masterpiece was acquired by the Earl of Carnarvon in Cairo during the winter of 1912-1913. The once prevalent belief that it came from the tomb of Amun-ḥotpe I at Thebes and is a representation of that king appears to be without foundation.

Besides the few and relatively unimportant architectural elements and works of sculpture just discussed, and the treasure of royal jewelry and precious vessels for which a separate section of this chapter is being reserved, the name of Egypt's greatest pharaoh appears in our collection on miscellaneous small objects of varying degrees of interest. One of the most attractive of these is a cosmetic ★dish of green-glazed steatite (fig. 65) in the form of a Nile fish with one side hollowed out to provide a shallow oval receptacle. The fish represented is easily recognizable as the common *bolti*, or *Tilapia nilotica* (𓆛), though in real life the tail of this species is rounded, not forked as—probably in the interest of better design—it has been made to appear here. The scales, fins, gills, and other details of piscine anatomy are executed with the most meticulous care, and thanks to the almost perfect state of preservation of the dish are clearly visible in our photograph. The color of the glaze is for the most part a deep olive green. A small cartouche, engraved on the left side of the fish below the pectoral fin, contains the by now familiar throne name of Ṭhut-mosě III, written, as nearly always, with the three hieroglyphs 𓇳 𓏠 𓆣.

This name occurs on two little faience finger ★rings found near the pyramid of King Amun-em-ḥēt I of the Twelfth Dynasty at el Lisht, and on the backs of seven small *wedjat*-eye ★amulets, chiefly of glazed steatite, but including an example in carnelian and one in red jasper. In the openwork design of a large cylindrical ★bead, exquisitely carved of steatite and adorned at either end with a gold cap (fig. 66, top row), we see the god Amūn placing the Blue Crown (𓋙) on the head of a kneeling figure of Ṭhut-mosě III. To the right of this group a second kneeling figure of the king, wearing the Blue Crown, offers a pair of 𓏌-jars to the god. Almost microscopic inscriptions carved above and beside the figures identify the

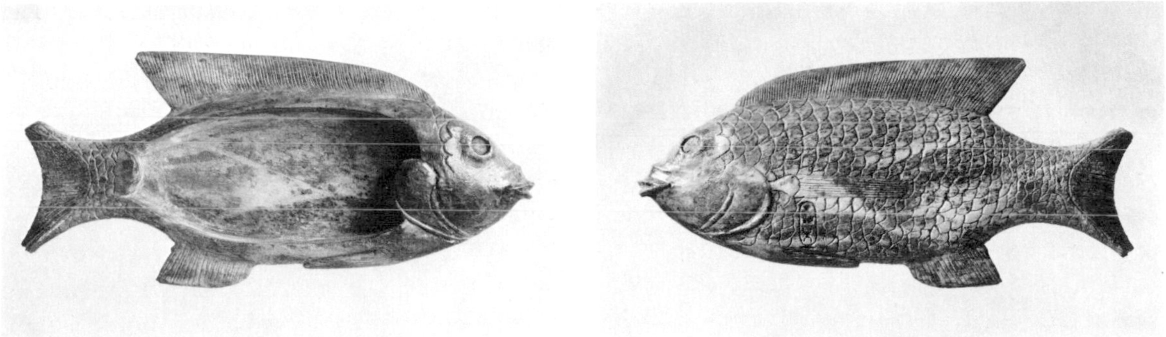

FIGURE 65. Glazed steatite cosmetic dish with the name of Ṭhut-mosě III. L. 7 in.

god as "Amūn" and the king as the "beloved of Amūn" and as the "Good God, Lord of the Two Lands, Men-kheper-Rēʿ, beloved of Amūn forever."

Among objects usually classed as seals, but which were probably in most cases worn by their owners as amulets or simply as ornaments, are three small ★cylinders inscribed with Tḥut-mosĕ III's praenomen, one of bronze, one of faience, and one of green-glazed steatite. The design on the steatite cylinder (fig. 66, top row), by far the most interesting of the three, is made up of four panels containing, respectively, engraved figures of the god Ptaḥ, a large scorpion, a decorative design composed of two crowned uraei and a scroll, and the name Men-kheper-Rēʿ. On the faience cylinder a crouching dog with a feather on its back (the nome standard of Kynopolis) has replaced the scorpion, and the panel with the uraei and scroll has been omitted. The bronze cylinder bears simply the name and title of the king. Three hemicylindrical ★seals of glazed steatite are engraved on their long, flat undersides, two with Tḥutmosĕ III's throne name, flanked by feathers of "right" (𓆄) or accompanied by a little standing figure of the king and followed by the epithet "image of Amūn." Here, as on most of the seals in our collection, the pharaoh is represented wearing the Blue Crown and holding the crook scepter (𓋾). The third seal, found at el Lisht, is adorned with figures of two divinities local to the region of Memphis, the lioness-headed goddess Sakhmet and her son Nefer-tēm. The name Men-kheper-Rēʿ is inscribed on the four sides of two small rectangular ★prisms of steatite, in one instance written with a scarab beetle (*-kheper-*) flanked by uraei, in the other preceded by the titles the "Good God, Lord of the Two Lands," and followed by the words "beloved of Amūn." It is found also on eight flat, cartouche-shaped ★plaques, chiefly of blue faience, accompanied in one case by the rare epithet "establisher of houses," and by the expression "beloved of Sobk-Rēʿ, Lord of Sumenu." Several of these plaques have on their reverse sides the king's personal name, Tḥut-mosĕ Nefer-khepru. A circular ★seal of glazed steatite is decorated on the back with a rosette carved in high relief and on its underside with four tiny praenomen cartouches of Tḥut-mosĕ III symmetrically disposed between four uraei which radiate from the central point of the design.

Forty-five ★plaques of simple forms—ovals, oblongs with rounded corners, and rectangles—share in common the characteristics that they are flat or nearly so on both sides, that the designs on one or both sides are almost always incised, and that somewhere in these designs we find the throne name of Tḥut-mosĕ III. The range in size of the plaques can be gauged from the examples selected for illustration in figure 66. The materials used are interestingly varied, including not only the common green-glazed steatite and blue and green faience, but also green and red paste, dark blue glass, and such fine, hard stones as serpentine, carnelian, and olive green jasper. In most cases it is not difficult to differentiate between the back and the underside of a plaque, the latter being normally the side on which the king's name is engraved. Designs used on the backs include the name or figure of the god Amun Rēʿ, figures of the Memphite deities Sakhmet and Nefer-tēm clasping hands, figures personifying Upper and Lower Egypt, their heads surmounted by their distinctive plants, the head of the goddess Ḥat-Ḥor, the plumed falcon head of the god Montu, a lion or royal sphinx trampling on a fallen Asiatic, a frog, a pair of crocodiles, and groups of four to eight uraei arranged to form symmetrical patterns. The horse, an animal relatively new to the Egyptians, appears with some frequency on these little monuments, either alone or driven in pairs to the king's chariot. On a large, square steatite plaque shown in figure 66 (fourth row) we see a plumed horse, urged on by an armed rider who sits well back on the animal's rump, trampling to earth a bearded foreigner; and on a smaller carnelian plaque (in the same row) the king appears in his chariot with bow drawn, driving his span of horses over a lion which he has shot. More often than not the name Men-kheper-Rēʿ dominates

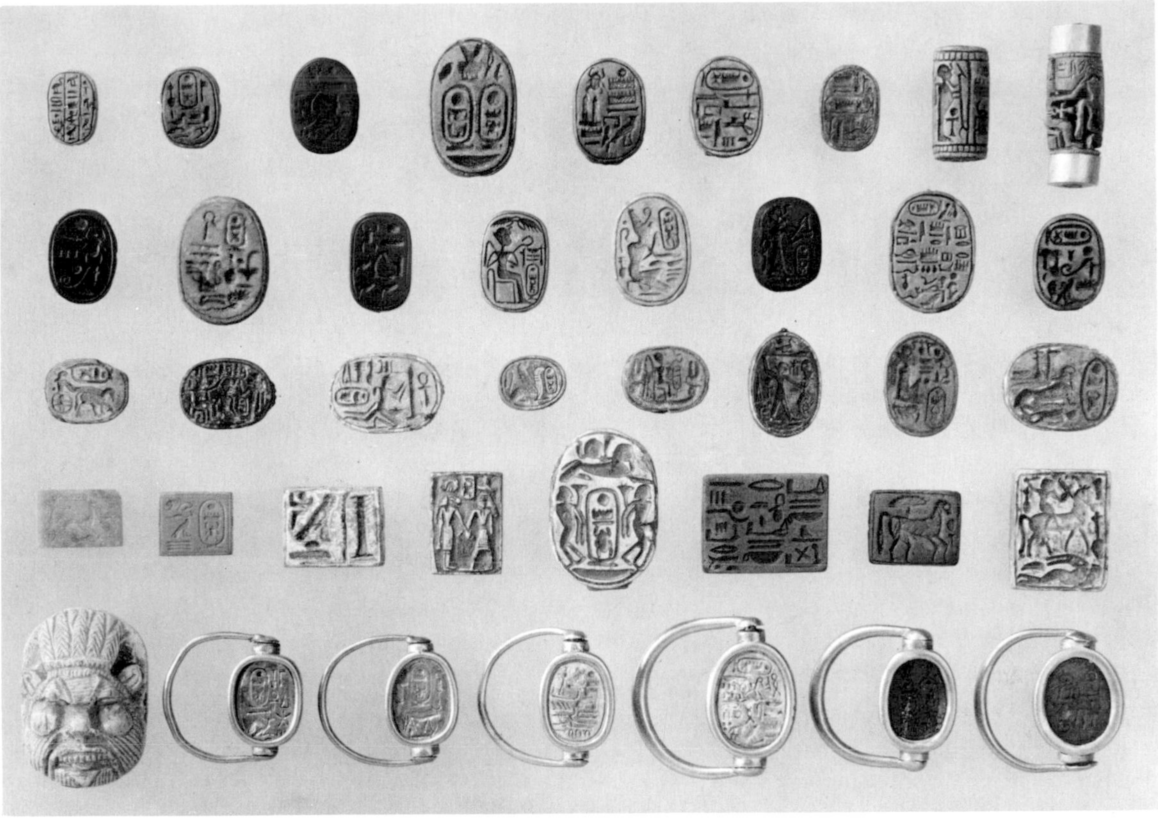

the design on the underside of a plaque. Occasionally we find the writings "Men-kheper-ku-Rēʿ" or "Men-kheper-en-Rēʿ," variants derived from the throne names of Thut-mosĕ I and II and used by Thut-mosĕ III from time to time during the early years of his reign. Sometimes the element *kheper* is written with a flying scarab, with wings outspread, instead of with the ordinary form of the beetle hieroglyph. Seated or standing figures of the king, complete with crown and scepter, often appear beside the cartouche and in one case the pharaoh holds before him a small obelisk, as if in the act of presenting it to a god. Falcons, uraei, sistrums (𓏣), and the hieroglyphic symbols for "life," "stability," "well-being," "unity," "goodness," and "right" are used to fill the oval or oblong fields. The titles which frequently accompany the royal names are of a few, familiar types; but some of the epithets are interesting enough to bear citing. Among these we find "image of Amūn,"

FIGURE 66. Scarabs and other seals of King Thut-mosĕ III. H. ½-2 1/16 in.

"image of Rēʿ," "truly enduring of years in the horizon of the god," "gilder of Thebes," "mighty in his strength," "fear of whom is in the lands," and "fighter of hundreds of thousands" (see fig. 66). In a three-column inscription on the underside of an exceptionally large plaque of glazed steatite a falcon god, represented on the back of the plaque, speaks to the king, saying, "I give to you strength against the South; I give to you might against the North." The text on another steatite plaque also runs to three columns, but the hieroglyphs are so small and so summarily rendered that, except for a reference at the end to an "offering for Men-kheper-Rēʿ," it is not certainly legible. A small faience plaque, which bears, in addition to the name of Thut-mosĕ III, that of the late Eighteenth Dynasty queen ʿAnkhes-en-Amūn, was clearly made long after the death of the ruler whom it honors, and this is true of a number of the other plaques, the style and content of which point to dates ranging from the Nineteenth to the Twenty-Sixth Dynasty. A few examples are probably to be assigned to the High Priest of Amūn, Men-kheper-Rē‛, who in the time of the Twenty-First Dynasty assumed kingly titles; but the vast majority were inscribed in honor of Tḥut-mosĕ III, either in his own day or later. It goes without saying that exactly the same remarks apply to the numerous seals of other types on which the name Men-kheper-Rē‛ appears.

Eighteen of these ★seals are distinguished from the plaques just discussed by the fact that the figures and devices which adorn their backs are not engraved in flat surfaces but are carved either in the round or in very high relief. Here we find tiny, sculptured figures of the dwarf god Bēs, and a head of the same divinity (see fig. 66), as well as a head of the goddess Ḥat-Ḥor and figures of various animals and birds—the baboon, the hedgehog, the cat, the frog, the falcon, the duck, and the pigeon. The convex backs of three faience seals are decorated in relief with a palm-branch pattern and on three others the back is given the form of the amuletic *wedjat*-eye. The legends on the undersides of the seals are similar to those on the plaques and are, on the whole, less interesting. On a big rectangular seal with a *wedjat*-eye back the praenomen cartouche of Tḥut-mosĕ III is engraved on either side of the grotesque figure of Bēs, and on a similar seal it shares the rectangular field with what appears to be a cryptic writing of the praenomen of Ḥat-shepsūt, "Ma‛et-ku-Rē‛" (see p. 107).

In the Museum's collection, as in all others the world over, the scarabs of Tḥut-mosĕ III outnumber by far those of any other pharaoh. The distinctive throne name of this deified conqueror was evidently regarded as a potent talisman centuries after his death, and scarabs bearing this name continued to be produced until almost the end of Egypt's dynastic history. During the last century or so the production of Men-kheper-Rē‛ scarabs has, unfortunately, been revived on a grand scale and modern forgeries are almost as numerous as the by no means rare ancient examples.

Nearly all of the three hundred ★scarabs of Tḥut-mosĕ III which have been retained for our permanent collection are of glazed steatite or, less frequently, of blue or green faience, with only a few isolated examples in other materials—blue glass, lapis lazuli, ivory, and gold. A dozen, including seven handsome specimens from the tomb of three wives of the king, are mounted in gold, silver, or bronze finger rings and several others still retain the loops of string whereby they were tied to their owners' hands. The scarabs on which the names of Ḥat-shepsūt and Tḥut-mosĕ III appear together have been discussed in Chapter III, as have also the scarabs of Tḥut-mosĕ III found in Ḥat-shepsūt's temple deposits (see fig. 48, fifth row). Of the others, more than two hundred came to the Museum from well-known private collections (Murch, Davis, Ward, Timins, Farman, Carnarvon, and Morgan) and many of these have been published by Ward, Newberry, Mace, and others. The rest are largely from our excavations at el Lisht and Deir el Baḥri, from those of the Egypt Exploration Fund at Sedment, Abydos, and Deir el Baḥri, and from the work of the Oxford University expedition to Napata in the Sūdān.

In general, the designs and inscriptions on the undersides of our Tḥut-mosĕ III scarabs add nothing to what we have already encountered on the plaques and other seals, consisting for the most part of the throne name of the king, alone or accompanied by the conventional titles, epithets, and heraldic or decorative motifs. There are, however, some thirty scarabs which because of the intricacy and unusual nature of their subject matter or because of the length and interest of their texts merit our special attention. The undersides of twenty-four of these are shown in figure 66. In the little scenes here presented to us at minute scale, but in amazing detail, we see the king kneeling and worshiping Amūn in the form of an obelisk; dispatching with his mace a kneeling foreigner; driving forth in his chariot; riding in the falconprowed ship of the god Montu; kneeling, squatting, or seated in full regalia before his own name and titles; and receiving his crown from the god Amun Rēʿ and the goddess (Mūt) Sakhmet in a tiny but elaborate coronation scene complete with labels identifying the participants. More often than not the pharaoh is represented wearing the *kheperesh*, or Blue Crown, but he is twice shown with the elaborate *atef*-crown ( ) of Osiris, and once with the Double Crown of Upper and Lower Egypt. On one scarab Tḥut-mosĕ III's cartouche is surmounted by a royal androsphinx and flanked by bearded foreign captives, and on another the cartouche is attended by a winged griffin of Helladic type. Some of the scenes on these scarabs would appear to commemorate actual events in the king's reign, such as his coronation, a victory over a specific foreign enemy, the erection of one or a pair of obelisks, or some outstanding achievement on the hunting field.

A similar function was evidently performed by a series of scarabs bearing inscriptions of a historical or semihistorical nature which have been recognized as the forerunners of the large commemorative scarabs of Amun-ḥotpe III and other late Eighteenth Dynasty kings. Among the scarabs of this type in our collection one refers to "Men-kheper-Rēʿ, whose two obelisks are established in the House of Amūn," another to "Men-kheper-Rēʿ, Lord of Strength, who smote the Nine Bows and twice destroyed the Bedawīn," and a third to "Men-kheper-Rēʿ, harpooner of the hippopotamus, powerful of arm when he takes the spear." The four-line inscription on a glazed steatite scarab (fig. 66, second row), formerly in the Murch collection, reads: "How happy is Men-kheper-Rēʿ when he carries Amūn to the Valley (Deir el Baḥri?) to receive the monuments which he (the King) has made! Rēʿ sees his happiness." On nine other scarabs the king is variously described as the "strong bull, the divine power," the "Son of Amūn, whom he loves," the "Good God . . . whom the people worship," the "possessor of life (in) the House of Amūn," "great of wonders in the House of Amūn," the "goodly image of Rēʿ, appearing in Thebes," the "Good God . . . appearing (as) King," the "Ruler of Heliopolis," and the "crusher of rebellions in all lands."

Besides those on which he is associated with Ḥat-shepsūt (and once with King Menes of the First Dynasty) there are a number of scarabs in our collection on which the name of Tḥut-mosĕ III appears together with that of Amun-em-ḥēt II of the Twelfth Dynasty ("Nub-kū-Rēʿ") and with that of Sētḥy I of the Nineteenth Dynasty ("Men-maʿet-Rēʿ Chosen-of-Rēʿ"). A steatite scarab and a gold signet ★ring, on both of which the praenomen of Tḥut-mosĕ III is written above a kneeling male figure holding aloft a divine barque, have been dated to the Twenty-Sixth Dynasty. The basis for this is chiefly the form of the ring, which consists of a flat, engraved plate fused to a plain loop of gold wire. Five small lumps of Nile mud used to seal rolled-up documents ( ) bear the impressions of scarabs and plaques with the throne name of Tḥut-mosĕ, accompanied in one case by the figure of a lion and in the others by titles and epithets of familiar types. Four of these ★sealings are from the ruins of the palace of Amun-ḥotpe III in western Thebes. The fifth was acquired in 1917 at Deir el Ballās.

Among our color ★copies of painted scenes in the tomb chapels of Theban officials is one made by H. R. Hopgood in the tomb of the Second Prophet of Amūn, Puy-em-Rēʿ, showing part of the red granite shaft of one of Tḥut-mosĕ III's Karnak obelisks. The names and titles of the great pharaoh appear on the shaft itself—much as they did on the original monument—and to the left is an accompanying label referring to the "[fine] gold" with which the pinnacles of the "two great obelisks" were overlaid. Long after his death statues of Tḥut-mosĕ III were represented with those of other Theban kings in the tombs of Amun-mosĕ (No. 19) and I-mi-sība (No. 65), the former datable to the early Nineteenth Dynasty, the latter to the end of the Twentieth Dynasty. The scenes in question may be studied in facsimile copies by Charles K. Wilkinson and Nina de Garis Davies.

The title and name of Tḥut-mosĕ III's queen,

the "King's Great Wife, Ḥat-shepsūt Meryet-Rēʿ, the justified," are written in black ink on a model ★bowl and two model ★jars of alabaster, coming from a foundation deposit at the entrance of Tomb 42 in the Wādy el Bibān el Molūk. This tomb, which lies just below and to the north of that of Tḥut-mosĕ III, was probably prepared originally for Tḥut-mosĕ II, but was not used by him and may, some time after his death, have been taken over by his daughter-in-law. In the same deposit, as we have already had occasion to note, was found an alabaster clamshell with the title and name of Tḥut-mosĕ III. The names "Ḥat-shepsūt Meryet-Rēʿ" occur in that order and without an accompanying title on a blue-glazed steatite ★scarab, formerly in the Theodore M. Davis collection. Though she was Tḥut-mosĕ III's principal wife and the mother of his successor, Amun-ḥotpe II, there is no evidence that Meryet-Rēʿ was a daughter either of the elder Ḥat-shepsūt or of Tḥut-mosĕ II. Her titles include God's Wife, King's Great Wife, Mistress of the Two Lands, and King's Mother, but she is never referred to as a King's Daughter or a King's Sister.

The Museum's collection boasts no monuments of Tḥut-mosĕ III's Southern Vizier Rekh-mi-Rēʿ, or of his Viceroy of Nubia Neḥy, but most of the other great men of his reign are represented—by funerary ★cones from their tombs at Thebes if by nothing else. A run-through of the names and titles preserved on the cones not only introduces us to the top-ranking Thebans of this period, but also throws a good deal of light on the complex and highly organized system of government built up under the Thutmoside pharaohs. Through their cones we meet such important administrative officials as Rekh-mi-Rēʿ's predecessor, the Overseer of the City and Vizier Woser (Tombs 61 and 131), the King's Scribe and Overseer of the Double Granary Min-nakhte (Tomb 87), the Steward and Overseer of the Treasury Sen-nefer (Tomb 99), the King's Scribe and Overseer of the

FIGURE 67. Doorjamb from the tomb of the Chief Steward of Amūn, Ro-au. Limestone. H. 57 ½ in.

Magazine Amun-mosĕ (Tomb 251?), and the Hereditary Prince and Count, the Overseer of the Treasury, Mīn. From Tomb 109 come the cones of a prominent provincial administrator, also named Mīn, who was Mayor of Thinis, Governor of the (Great) Oasis, and Overseer of the Priests of Onuris, a retired soldier, perhaps best known to us as the archery instructor of the future king, Amun-ḥotpe II. The steadily growing class of army officers and military officials is represented in our series of cones by such men as the Lieutenant Commander of the Army Amun-em-ḥēb (Tomb 85); the Chief Royal Heralds Yamu-nedjeḥ (Tomb 84), In-yōtef (Tomb 155), and Rēʿ (Tomb 201); the King's Scribe and Scribe of the Recruits Tjanuny (Tomb 74); and the Standard-bearer Amun-mosĕ (Tomb 42?). An important police officer, the Chief of the Medjay, Royal Envoy, and Overseer of the Deserts on the West of Thebes, Dedu, was apparently the owner of Tomb 200. Four cones from an as yet unlocated tomb are inscribed for the "King's Craftsman, clean of hands, Nefer-peret." Most numerous are the cones of members of the clergy and "vestry" of the state god Amūn: the *Wēʿb*-priest of Amūn and Overseer of the Granaries of Upper and Lower Egypt Men-kheper-Rēʿ-sonbe, also called Men-kheper (Tomb 79); the Scribe and Accountant of the Grain of Amūn, the Steward of the Vizier, Amun-em-ḥēt (Tomb 82); the Scribe and Accountant of the Grain of Amūn, Neb-Amūn (Tomb 146); the Overseer of the Fields of Amūn, Overseer of Accounts and Weigher of Amūn, Woser (Tomb 260); the Overseer of the Goldworkers of Amūn, Neb-seny; the Temple Attendant of Amūn, Amun-em-ḥēt (Tomb 53); and last but by no means least, the First Prophet, or High Priest, of Amūn, Men-kheper-Rēʿ-sonbe (Tombs 86 and 112). Of the last-named dignitary we possess, besides his funerary cones, a graceful limestone ★vase inscribed with his titles and name and said to have come from Saḳḳāreh, and a handsome steatite ★scarab on which he is referred to by one of his secondary titles, "Overseer of the Crafts of Amūn."

The monument shown in figure 67 is the right-hand one of a pair of limestone ★doorjambs from the tomb of a man named Ro-au who held the important office of Chief Steward of Amūn and who was also a steward of the estate of the deceased Queen Aʿḥ-mosĕ Nefret-iry (see p. 44). The jambs were purchased in 1926 from a native of Luxor and come allegedly from a tomb "near Dirāʿ Abu'n Naga" in western Thebes.[2] From their inscriptions we learn that the tomb in question was "given as a favor of the King's bounty" by Tḥut-mosĕ III "on the occasion of the founding of Djeser-akhet," the chapel built by the pharaoh for the goddess Ḥat-Ḥor at Deir el Baḥri. This probably meant that in preparing his tomb Ro-au was permitted to avail himself of the services of the masons and sculptors attached to the royal ateliers—a fact which would account for the high quality of workmanship seen in these doorjambs. On the bottom of each jamb, carved in delicate *relief en creux*, is the fashionably dressed figure of the tomb owner seated behind a table of offerings and holding in his hand an *ʿaba*-scepter (see Part I, p. 287). The inner column of inscription is in each case an offering formula which, on the right jamb, invokes the gods Amun Rēʿ, Lord of Karnak, and Osiris, Ruler of Eternity; and, on the left jamb, calls upon Amun Rēʿ Ḥor-akhty and Anubis to cause Ro-au's spirit to "go forth as a living soul." The outer columns tell us of the king's donation of the tomb, that on the jamb illustrated reading: "Given as a favor of the King's bounty in the form (literally, "likeness") of a proper tomb by the Good God, the King of Upper and Lower Egypt, Men-kheper-Rēʿ, to the Chief Steward of Amūn, true of heart, Ro-au." As can be seen in the photograph, the name of the god Amūn, wherever it appeared on the tomb doorway, was hacked out by agents of the pharaoh Akh-en-Aten (Amun-ḥotpe IV) and subsequently somewhat roughly restored, probably in early Ramesside times.

The guardian of Tḥut-mosĕ III's daughter, the

[2] So recorded on the accession card in the Museum's catalogue.

FIGURE 68. Double *shawabty* of the royal architect Beny-meryet, and his mother. Serpentine. H. 8¾ in.

Princess (later Queen) Meryet-Amūn, was a royal architect named Beny-meryet, known to us from a statue in the Cairo Museum in which he is represented with his young charge. In our collection he appears with his mother, the House Mistress Ikhem, in a handsome double ★*shawabty* of polished serpentine (fig. 68). Except for the fact that Beny-meryet's *shawabty* wears a long, Osirian chin beard, the two figures are practically duplicates, though the woman's beardless face does seem a trifle fuller, softer, and more feminine than that of her companion. The spell inscribed in horizontal lines on each of the figures is, as usual, a version of Chapter VI of the Book of the Dead; but, since it varies slightly from those which we have already encountered, is not without interest. On the left-hand figure it goes: "O you *shawabty* of the Overseer of Works and Craftsman of the King, Beny-meryet, if Beny-meryet be called and registered by name to do work which is done in the necropolis, restraints being imposed upon him there, as a man under obligation to cultivate the fields, to irrigate the banks, to transport sand of the east and of the west, 'I will do (it)! Here am I!' you shall say." The text on the other figure is the same, except that feminine forms are used in referring to both the owner of the *shawabty* and the *shawabty* itself. In the first line of this text and in the column of inscription on the back pilaster the name of Ikhem has been written over an erasure, apparently replacing her other name, Tekhy-em-Akhet, which, since it means "Intoxicated-in-the-inundation-season," may have been regarded as insufficiently dignified for use on a funerary monument.

The monuments of some of Tḥut-mosĕ III's less important contemporaries include a steatite ★plaque of the Servant of the Overseer of the Treasure, Min-nakhte, and a ★linen sheet inscribed with the name of Nefer-khēwet's son-in-law, Baki.

2. The Treasure of Three Wives of Tḥut-mosĕ III[3]

We have already had occasion to mention three members of Tḥut-mosĕ III's extensive ḥarīm who, because of their non-Egyptian names, Menhet, Menwi, and Merti, are thought to have been the daughters of Syrian chieftains. These three women, each of whom bore the title King's Wife, were buried together in a small rock-cut tomb hidden away at the head of the Wādy Gabbānet el Ḳurūd, a desert valley two miles west of Deir el

[3] Published by H. E. Winlock in *The Treasure of Three Egyptian Princesses,* source of the quotations (excepting translated inscriptions) throughout this section.

Baḥri. The tomb, periodically flooded by rain torrents and thoroughly plundered in modern times by villagers of Ḳurneh, has yielded little or no information on its occupants. They probably died sometime during the coregency of Ḥat-shep-sūt and Tḥut-mosĕ III, but we do not know the exact date or the manner of their deaths. Although much of their jewelry, funerary equipment, and other possessions has been acquired bit by bit for the Metropolitan Museum, a considerable number of elements from all three categories are in other collections or are simply "missing." The intermittent dampness to which the contents of the tomb had been exposed had destroyed almost everything that was not made of either stone or precious metal, including practically all faience and glass inlay used in the jewelry; and careless handling by the modern plunderers has resulted in the loss or destruction of much in addition. There seem at one time to have been three more or less complete and similar sets of objects—one for each lady—and many, though by no means all, of the remaining pieces, especially those designed for funerary use, are preserved in triplicate.

Of the jewelry which these royal women wore during their lifetimes the most striking and best preserved items are two ★headdresses of gold inlaid with colored glass and semiprecious stones. The more elaborate headdress (fig. 69) is made up of between eight and nine hundred inlaid gold rosettes combined with an inlaid gold skull plate to form a flexible metallic cowl descending at the back and sides to the level of its wearer's shoulders and covering nearly the whole of the long wig or coiffure worn beneath it. The rosettes, supported between strings of small gold tubular beads by means of interlocking tubes soldered to their sides, are arranged in vertical rows graduated in size from top to bottom. At the top each row ends in a diamond-shaped element made in one piece with the first rosette, and at the bottom in a triple lunette similarly combined with the last rosette. The skull plate is adorned on its upper surface with an engraved palm-tree design, once inlaid with bars of colored glass, and at the center of its front edge there is a small ring from which one or more pendent ornaments may have been suspended over the wearer's forehead.

The second headdress, a circlet, shown in figure 70 as it would have appeared when worn over a coiffure of New Kingdom type, consists of a T-shaped band of heavy sheet gold finished at its tapered ends with small gold leopard heads holding in their mouths the rings for the cords by means of which the circlet was tied in place. Like its companion headdress and its Middle Kingdom predecessors, the circlet is adorned with gold rosettes once inlaid with a variety of different colored materials, of which only the red carnelian now remains. Winlock in his *Treasure of Three Egyptian Princesses* has pointed out that the pair of little gold gazelle heads rising from the front of this headdress were emblems traditionally associated with the graceful, gazelle-like inmates of the king's ḥarīm who, unlike the reigning queen, were not entitled to wear the royal vulture or uraeus head. Below the gazelle heads a row of seven little rings suggest that small pendants once dangled from the forehead band of the circlet. The pair of corrugated gold ★rings shown in figure 70 being worn as hair rings were actually earrings. They are slightly open at the back, and behind the projecting floral ornament each narrows suddenly to a slender prong apparently designed to pass through a pierced ear lobe. Two pairs of similar but narrower ★rings have in place of the flower-shaped lugs, gold rosettes inlaid with carnelian and colored glass. The triple ★necklaces appearing in both of our illustrations are made up of lenticular beads of blue faience, of which enough were recovered from the burials of the three ladies to form strings totaling over five feet in length.

Hundreds of beads and inlaid gold elements from an indeterminate number of broad ★collars () include a pair of shoulder pieces of the traditional falcon-head type, a second pair adorned with flowers of the blue lotus () flanking the title and praenomen of Tḥut-mosĕ III (fig. 71), and an element shaped like an inverted lotus flower which was probably the top of a bead

FIGURE 69. Inlaid gold headdress of one of Tḥut-mosĕ III's wives. It is mounted on a cast of a late Eighteenth Dynasty head and a modern wig. H. of headdress 14 3/16 in.

counterpoise (*mʿankhet*) designed to be worn with one of the collars. The falcon heads are inlaid with turquoise, have eyes of obsidian and markings of carnelian, and are engraved on their backs with the details of the birds' heads and with the words "Long live the Good God, Men-kheper-Rēʿ, given life forever!" Though the holes along their lower edges indicate a collar made up of seven rows of short cylindrical (?) beads, they have been strung together with five rows of long, drop-shaped gold pendants, now devoid of their inlays, to form a collar which, if nothing else, is certainly striking in appearance. The second pair of shoulder pieces, also provided with string-holes for seven rows of beads, have been combined with five rows of little gold elements shaped like the hieroglyph 𓄤 ("good") and a row of thirty-six small gold palmette pendants (fig. 71). Half of the 𓄤- signs were inlaid on one side with colored glass, now largely rotted away, but "to give a uniform appearance" all were strung with their gold backs forward. A third collar as assembled in the Museum uses the lotiform counterpoise top and a modern replica of it as shoulder pieces and, with these, miscellaneous drop-shaped, petal-shaped, and semicircular elements of gold and silver inlaid with carnelian, green feldspar, turquoise, and lapis lazuli. Also included in the composition of this collar are 161 cylindrical beads of carnelian and turquoise—recovered from the thousands which must at one time have existed—and several hundred little tubular and ring beads of gold.

Gold ★necklace beads, which the tomb produced in great quantity, are of several different types. The most numerous and most remarkable are little ring beads each of which is composed of five tiny pellets of gold "soldered together in a circle about the thread hole in such a fashion that, when the beads are strung together, the pellets interlock, and the beads seem to make a flexible rod of gold rather than a string of independent units." Of these enough have been acquired to have provided each of the three King's Wives with a necklace thirty-one and a half inches in length. Hollow gold beads in the forms of flies (𓆦),

FIGURE 70. Gold circlet with gazelle heads, and other items of jewelry belonging to a minor wife of Tḥut-mosĕ III. H. of circlet 3 in.

crowned Horus falcons, and little standing figures of the hippopotamus goddess Ta-weret have been strung together to form four interesting and attractive necklaces. Still another necklace includes as its principal feature sixteen flat, shrine-shaped gold plaques, each somewhat crudely engraved with a squatting figure of the goddess Maʿet (𓁦). Of eighty-four roughly shaped ball ★beads, which were probably worn as or in a necklace, thirteen are of green quartz and the rest are of some sort of paste covered with hemispherical plates of thin sheet silver.

Four tubular amulet ★cases of gold and silver, lined with copper and studded on the outside with rows of little drops of metal, were probably worn suspended from the neck on cords. So also were a variety of large metal ★amulets—six hollow gold *wedjat*-eyes, a hollow gold flower with seven petals, a gold bivalve shell and another of silver, and five flat gold plaques, three of which are engraved with crude representations of the cow of the goddess Ḥat-Ḥor, one with a seated figure of the

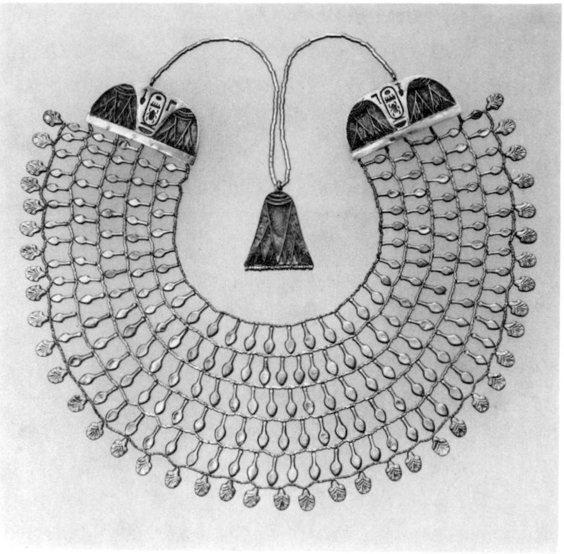

FIGURE 71. Broad collar made up of gold and inlaid elements, from the tomb of three wives of Tḥut-mosĕ III. W. 10 in.

lioness-headed goddess Mūt Sakhmet, and one with a squatting figure of the goddess Maʿet. An inlaid gold ★*shenu*-amulet (Ω) has a center of carnelian, and a cylindrical ★amulet of solid gold has running around it from end to end a spiral channel, once filled with blue or green paste. Three large, uninscribed ★scarabs, two of gold and one of lapis lazuli, are unusual in that the holes for suspension run through them not vertically but laterally, from side to side. It has been suggested that they were worn together, suspended on a single cord, the lapis scarab in the center flanked by its gold mates.

Each of our three ladies seems to have had a pair of bead ★armlets fitted with gold clasps and adorned in every case with five little figures of cats crouched in a row on a wide gold bar at the center of the armlet (see fig. 72). Transverse rows of thirteen to sixteen slender gold barrel beads, soldered together side by side to form spreaders, or stiffeners, alternated in the broad, flexible bands which made up the armlets proper with rows of similar beads of carnelian, feldspar, and lapis lazuli. The existing cats, crouching with forepaws crossed and heads turned to one side, are of carnelian (two examples) and gold (eight examples), the missing figures having probably been of blue or green faience. Similar groups of cats adorn the gold armlet spreaders of Queen Sobkem-saf of the Seventeenth Dynasty (see p. 10), and the use of cats, lions, and sphinxes as amulets or ornaments on armlets and bracelets reaches back at least as far as the Middle Kingdom. Just as the pairs of gold lions on bracelets of the Twelfth Dynasty have been thought to represent the twin lion divinities Shu and Tefēnet, so also may the cats on our present armlets have been associated in the minds of their wearers with goddesses like Bastet or with the solar cat who slays the sun god's arch-enemy ʿApep.

Three pairs of inlaid gold ★bracelets resemble in appearance the wide bead bracelets of the Old and Middle Kingdoms (see Part I, pp. 230 ff., 306 ff.), which are made up of rows of cylindrical beads separated by metal spreaders and fitted with metal clasps. In the present instances, however, each bracelet is composed of two curved plates of heavy sheet gold inlaid on the outside with rows of small rectangular plaques of carnelian, feldspar or turquoise, and, at one time, blue glass or faience. The two halves of the bracelet are hinged together and fastened with a long gold pin on the side opposite the hinge. On the inside each bears the names and titles of Tḥut-mosĕ III carefully engraved on the polished gold surfaces. One of two pairs of plain gold ★bracelets is similarly inscribed, while the other pair, as we have seen (p. 104), bears the throne name and kingly titles of Ḥatshepsūt. Of three flexible bead ★bracelets two were made up of seven strands and one of three strands of small globular beads of carnelian, lapis lazuli, and glass. Though the light gold separators from all three of these bracelets have survived, only enough beads were recovered to allow the three-strand bracelet to be reassembled. Short tubes soldered to the ends and sides of a dozen little hollow gold figures of the god Bēs and the goddess Ta-weret suggest that they had been combined with horizontal and vertical strings of similar tubes to form yet another small flexible ★bracelet, in this case entirely of gold and only an inch and three-quarters in width. Four plain blue faience rings, square in section and matching in color the strings of lenticular beads referred to above, were almost certainly worn as ★bracelets—perhaps on a single occasion. They belong, in any case, to the class of cheap and fragile "costume" jewelry which during the Eighteenth Dynasty was presented as favors to guests at banquets.

The burials of the three royal ladies yielded eight very handsome ★scarabs—three of gold, three of glazed steatite, and two of lapis lazuli—all but one mounted, with the usual swivel settings, in gold finger rings. The unmounted scarab is of gold, bears a 𓄤-sign and scroll pattern on its underside, and once had its back and wings inlaid with colored glass or faience. One of the steatite scarabs carries the legend "May Amūn give life, well-being, and the breath of life to his (the king's) nostrils." The inscriptions on the other six examples have been discussed above and appear in the bottom row of figure 66.

Of the ornaments which Menhet, Menwi, and Merti wore about their undoubtedly slender waists or hips the most striking were two broad, openwork ★belts made up entirely of fairly large beads shaped like acacia seeds. Nine sets of seven gold acacia beads, soldered together to form rigid bars, served as the spreaders for the belts, and between these were strung seven rows of carnelian, turquoise, and probably blue glass beads of the same type, producing the red-green-blue-gold color sequence so dear to the ancient Egyptians. The gold clasp bars at the ends of the belts are similar to those seen on the cat armlets of figure 72, except that their locking pins are silver, not gold. A third gold ★clasp, slightly longer and made in such a manner that "its two halves have to slide their entire length past one another when the clasp is fastened," is probably from a somewhat larger belt of the same kind, the beads and spreaders of which are missing.

A narrow ★girdle composed of two strands of large beads had an inlaid gold buckle in the form of the two hieroglyphs 𓊵𓎟, "all contentment," the 𓊵-sign once inlaid with glass, the 𓎟-sign consisting of a piece of agate framed in gold. The beads shown in figure 73 strung with this buckle are of gold, lapis lazuli, and green feldspar and include plain ball and drop-shaped beads and beads imitating in their forms nasturtium seeds and small, spiral shells. Each of two other ★girdles also shown in figure 73 is made up of three strands of very small beads of gold and red glass combined in one case with twenty-two hollow gold *bolti*-fish (𓆛) and in the other with large beads of gold and lapis lazuli which seem to represent disks of leather folded over and stitched around the edges —a type of bead used apparently only in girdles. Neither of these girdles has a buckle or clasp, but each, as Winlock has remarked, is "long enough for a girl to slip over her shoulders and let fall around her hips."

It is reasonably certain that most of the jewelry which we have been discussing was worn by our three ladies during their lifetimes. Nearly all of the pieces are sturdily constructed and fitted with strong, practical fastenings and many of them are nicked, rubbed smooth, or otherwise marked by wear. Though belonging to traditional categories and employing traditional elements in their composition, the headdresses, necklaces, bangles, and

FIGURE 72. Bead armlet of gold and semiprecious stones mounting cat figures of gold and carnelian. H. 2 in.

FIGURE 73. Girdles of gold and semiprecious stones once worn by three wives of King Ṭhut-mosĕ III. L. of gold and agate buckle 1 9/16 in.

girdles are of designs originated in and typical of the New Kingdom and are without exact parallels in the earlier periods of Egyptian history. Striking and effective as some of the individual ornaments are, they are inferior in taste and incomparably inferior in technique to those produced during the Twelfth Dynasty and exemplified in the treasures of the royal ladies of Dahshūr and el Lāhūn. The rather surprising lack of care or technical ability exhibited by Ṭhut-mosĕ III's royal jewelers was to some extent corrected before the end of the dynasty, and some of the ornaments and other small objects produced under Amun-ḥotpe III and his immediate successors are, as we shall see, marvels of fine craftsmanship. The un-Egyptian floridity and overelaboration seen in some of the pieces which we have been studying have an undeniably "oriental" flavor and may be attributed —in part, at least—to Egypt's now intimate and continuous association with the exotic and luxury-loving peoples of western Asia.

The funerary jewelry, designed to adorn the mummies and provide for the well-being of the spirits of the three women, is represented by three almost complete sets of amuletic ornaments. Each set (see fig. 74) comprised a *seweret*-bead (see Part I, p. 308) and a row of spherical beads strung on two gold wire necklaces, a gold-mounted heart scarab suspended from a loop of heavy gold wire, a falcon collar, a vulture pectoral, and a "cloth" amulet of sheet gold, a pair of sheet gold sandals, and twenty finger and toe stalls of gold. The ★*sewerets*, as usual, are large barrel beads of carnelian, while the spherical ★beads, in one instance corrugated, are of faience. The three heart ★scarabs, nicely carved of dark green schist, are inscribed on their undersides with a longer and more elaborate version of Chapter XXXB of the Book of the Dead than that quoted on page 37, the spell here being recited in one case by the King's Wife Menhet, in another by the King's Wife Menwi, and on the third scarab by the King's Wife Merti. A detail not readily apparent in the photograph is the finishing of the curved ends of the gold supporting wire in the form of small ducks' heads. The dummy broad ★collars with falcon-head terminals, and the matching ★pectorals in the form of vultures with wings spread protectively to the sides, are of heavy sheet gold with the details carefully incised or pressed into the metal. It is clear that they had been bandaged in place over the throats and breasts of the three mummies with the forked ★cloth symbols probably placed, in each case, among the wrappings over the embalmer's incision on the left side of the abdomen. On their bandaged fingers and toes the deceased women wore ★stalls, or cappings, of sheet gold with the nails and joint-creases of the digits carefully delineated, and on their feet gold ★sandals imitating closely the stamped leather sandals which they had worn during their lives. Besides the groups of incised lines around the edges of their soles, the sandals are decorated with stamped rosettes and, on the broad straps which pass over the wearers' insteps, with "incised bands of straight- or cross-hatching, ending in little two- or three-lobed tabs which project beyond the top" edges of the straps. Similar amuletic adornments and items of funerary apparel were found in position on the mummy of King Tūt-ʿankh-Amūn, a ruler who was laid to rest some one hundred and thirty years after the time of our three ḥarīm ladies.

As part of her burial equipment each of the latter was provided with a set of four ★canopic jars, rather crudely carved of limestone and surmounted by limestone stoppers in the form of beardless human heads. The inscription engraved in three or four columns on the side of each jar is the usual canopic formula whereby the human organ presumed to be contained in the jar is identified with one of the Four Genii of the Dead and placed under the protection of one of four great tutelary goddesses (see Part I, pp. 321, 325). Typical is the "recitation" inscribed on the second jar of the set: "Isis, you do cover with your arms him who is in you, you protect Ḳebeḥ-snēwef and the one in honor with Ḳebeḥ-snēwef, (namely) the Osiris, the King's Wife Merti, the justified." Blue paint is still preserved in the incised hieroglyphs and touches of black remain in the eyes of the faces on the stoppers. Traces of gold foil and gesso-coated cloth found inside the jars suggest that the bandaged viscera which they once contained were encased in little cartonnage coffins or surmounted by small gilded stucco masks. The same inferior stone and hasty workmanship are found in the canopic jars of a similar group of ḥarīm ladies who during the reign of Amun-ḥotpe III were buried in a tomb not far from the one which we are discussing.

Aside from their jewelry the personal possessions of Tḥut-mosĕ III's three wives included two heavy silver ★mirrors with gold-plated wooden handles of the usual papyrus-column type, but with the curious, composite head of the cow goddess Ḥat-Ḥor inserted below the spreading papyrus umbel (see fig. 75). Above the Ḥat-Ḥor head on the smaller mirror we find engraved the praenomen cartouche of the king, and above this appears the gilded head of the copper pin by means of which the mirror tang was fastened in place in the handle. The wooden cores of both handles were badly decayed and have had to be restored, but the bronze rims and faience inlays of the eyes of the larger Ḥat-Ḥor head are well preserved.

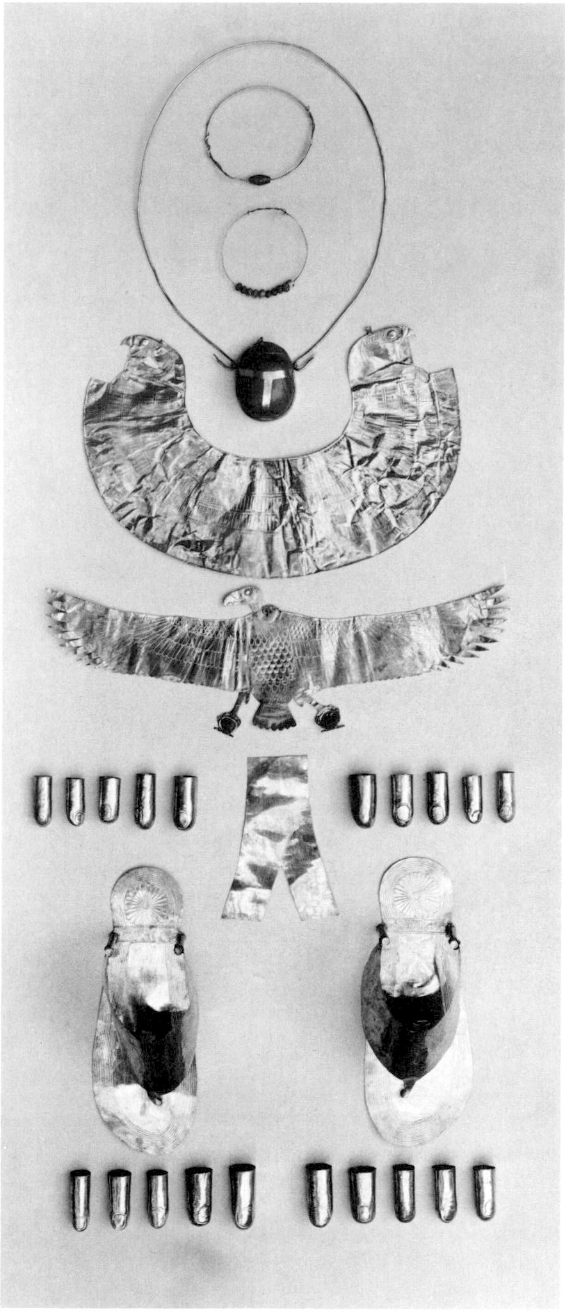

FIGURE 74. Gold funerary trappings and gold-mounted heart scarab from the mummy of a wife of King Tḥut-mosĕ III. W. of vulture pectoral 16 ½ in.

Ten small, gold-mounted cosmetic ★jars, nicely carved of alabaster, serpentine, feldspar, haematite, breccia, and fine glazed paste, show considerable variety in their forms. Three heavy, squat little vases with flat bottoms and wide, flat rims are unmistakably *koḥl*-jars, their tubelike interiors still containing traces of the fine black powder used by women and men alike to protect and to enhance their eyes. Two beakers, one of serpentine and one of alabaster, have the flaring foot and deeply incurved sides acquired by this type of vase in the New Kingdom (cf. figs. 35, 47). Of four little globular jars with tall necks, three are footed, two have wide mouths and two slender necks and broad, discoid rims. The series is completed by a small, drop-shaped jar of mottled black and white breccia. Mose of the jars have flat, disk lids, and there are, in addition, two similar ★lids of alabaster from vases now lost. All have bands of polished sheet gold fitted around the edges of their lids, rims and feet, and all are inscribed for Tḥut-mosĕ III, the inscription in nearly every case reading: "The Good God, Men-kheper-Reʿ, given life." A horizontal line of hieroglyphs enclosed within an elongated cartouche, which encircles the glazed paste vessel, gives a fuller version of the king's titulary: "The Horus Strong-bull-appearing-in-Thebes, the Good God, Lord of the Two Lands, King of Upper and Lower Egypt, Men-kheper-Rēʿ, the Son of Rēʿ, Tḥut-mosĕ Goodly-of-forms, given life, stability, and well-being like Rēʿ forever." In height these handsome little vases range from two and three-quarters to five and five-sixteenths inches. Some doubt exists concerning the provenience of eight uninscribed cosmetic ★jars of the same general class, size, and date. Of these two are of alabaster and one of serpentine. The remaining five are rough little flasks partially hammered to shape from lumps of poor-grade, light-colored amethyst.

Twenty-four larger ★jars of alabaster and serpentine contained an unguentlike mixture composed of "animal or vegetable oils and lime (or possibly chalk)," which was probably used as a cleansing cream. Two of these jars, inscribed with Ḥat-shepsūt's name and titles as queen, have already been discussed and are illustrated in figure 43. Of the others sixteen, including the five examples in serpentine, are drop-shaped with flaring rims, and one of these (fig. 76) is provided with a handle. There are two broad, squat vases, one cordiform, the other nearly globular, a tall jar with straight sides and a high, broad shoulder, and two large, uninscribed beakers of alabaster. In nineteen cases the titles and names of Tḥut-mosĕ III are engraved on the sides of the jars, usually framed within a rectangle, and below this in six instances the capacity of the vessel is given in *hin*, an ancient Egyptian liquid measure roughly equivalent to our pint. From these notations we learn that the smallest of the jars so labeled contained three and a half *hin* (1.664 quarts) and the largest six and a half *hin* (3.091 quarts). Besides the jars of this class in our collection there are at least seven others from the same tomb, one of which is now in the Minneapolis Institute of Arts.

The handsome and costly table services of the three ḥarīm favorites consist chiefly of ★drinking vessels of gold and silver. Each lady had two cups, a drinking bowl, a beaker, and a footed goblet of gold, hammered to shape from sheets of the precious metal and engraved on the outside with the title and throne name of Tḥut-mosĕ III. With the exception of the goblet, an example of each of these little vessels appears in the right and left foreground of figure 77, and in the right background we see one of two surviving silver goblets shaped and proportioned almost exactly like their gold mates. The large silver canister in the center of the illustration, as the inscription engraved on its side tells us, was "given as a favor of the King's bounty to the King's Wife Merti, the justified." Two others are similarly inscribed for the "King's Wife Menhet" and the "King's Wife Menwi" respectively. Though as readily smelted as gold, silver was still not used nearly as commonly as it is today and, as Winlock has remarked, these good-sized silver vessels of the mid-Eighteenth Dynasty are objects of considerable interest. The same is true of two gold-mounted glass ★goblets (fig. 77, left background) which are certainly as early as any vessels of that material which have survived. The lotiform goblet, with the praenomen of Tḥut-mosĕ III inscribed on its side, is of turquoise blue glass with a band of sheet gold around its lip and had in all probability another around its now restored

FIGURE 75. Silver mirror with gold-plated handle. H. 13 in.

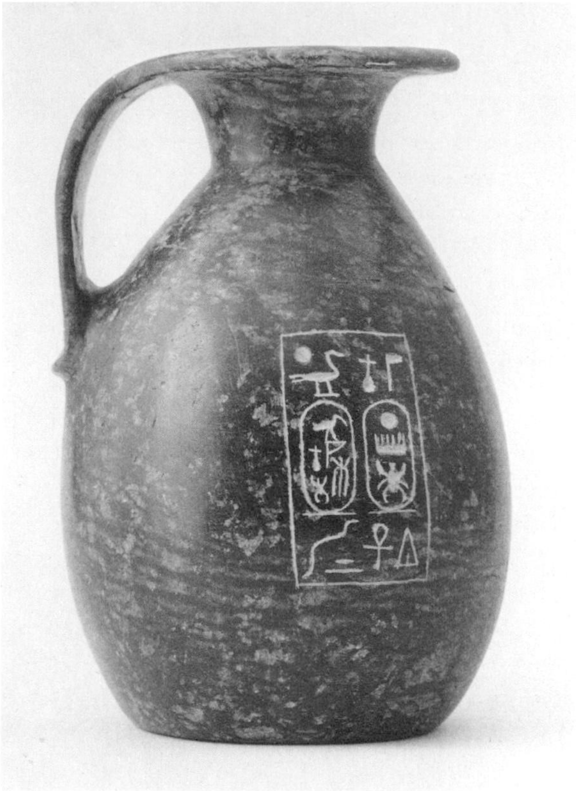

FIGURE 76. Serpentine unguent jar with the names of Tḥut-mosĕ III. H. 9 in.

foot. The second glass goblet, its rim and foot also sheathed in gold, was made up of bits of red, green, white, and yellow glass fused together around an earthen core which was subsequently ground away from the inside. Glass at this period seems to have been regarded as a kind of artificial stone, and it is not surprising to find a third gold-mounted ★goblet of the same series made of real stone, in this case a milky white alabaster (fig. 77, right center). Two shallow, thin-walled ★cups of green feldspar might easily be mistaken for glass. Though both are fragmentary and neither is inscribed there is considerable probability that they are from our royal tomb.

The table services of the three royal ladies were completed by seven or more uninscribed wine ★jars of alabaster, of which five were acquired for our collection. The latter range in height from seven to nine and three-quarters inches and are of three types: a small amphora carved in one piece with its supporting ring stand, a broad, long-necked jar with horizontal handles (three examples), and a long-necked jug with its handle represented as lashed to its neck with a double turn of rope. All five of these vessels are rough and unsightly on the inside, and all but one contain the thin, grayish sediment left behind by wine which evaporated over thirty-four centuries ago.

Though many of the possessions of Tḥut-mosĕ III's three Syrian wives are characterized, as we have seen, by inferior workmanship, the raw materials embodied in these possessions must have amounted in ancient times to a not inconsiderable fortune. Winlock has estimated the modern value of the gold and silver alone at $6,800, and the purchasing power of this sum in Eighteenth Dynasty Thebes must have been many times what it is today. Such an outlay is an eloquent testimonial, not only to the extraordinary wealth available to even relatively unimportant members of the pharaoh's entourage, but also to "the expense which the ancient Egyptian was willing to lavish on his dead."

3. Amun-ḥotpe II and Tḥut-mosĕ IV

The death of Tḥut-mosĕ III was announced on the last day of the third month of Prōyet in the fifty-fourth year of his reign (March 13, 1436), and on the following day, "when the morning brightened," his son Amun-ḥotpe II, a youth of eighteen at the time, ascended the throne and plunged energetically into the difficult task of replacing his great father as the ruler of the Egyptian empire. Born to Tḥut-mosĕ III by the King's Great Wife Meryet-Rēʿ Ḥat-shepsūt, the new pharaoh was possessed of great physical strength and had inherited, presumably through his mother, a stature exceeding that of the other Thutmoside pharaohs. A famous sportsman and athlete, he prided himself particularly on his skill as a trainer and driver of horses, as a ship handler, and above all as an archer, and in the official inscriptions of his reign we find frequent references to his allegedly unparalleled achievements in these fields.

In his youth he had been appointed by his father as commandant of the principal base and dockyard of the Egyptian navy at Peru-nefer, near Memphis, where he seems to have maintained large estates and in the vicinity of which he and his successors appear to have resided for extended periods of time. As a soldier the young pharaoh distinguished himself in three or four eminently successful, if somewhat ruthless, campaigns in Syria, and in the Sūdān he formally established his frontier at Napata, near the Fourth Cataract of the Nile. The rise to prominence of the solar deity Aten has been traced back to his time, as has also the establishment in Egypt of the cult of the Syrian storm god Resheph. As a builder and patron of the arts Amun-ḥotpe II has left us many handsome monuments at Karnak and elsewhere throughout Egypt and Nubia, and it is under him that marked changes in Egyptian sculpture and painting begin to be apparent. His reign was long and prosperous, exceeding twenty-five years and including at least one celebration of the *sed*-festival. His well-preserved tomb (No. 35) in the Valley of the Tombs of the Kings differs from those of his predecessors chiefly in the form of its columned sepulchral hall, which is no longer cartouche-shaped but rectangular in plan, with a sunken crypt at its western end for the king's brightly painted quartzite sarcophagus.

The remains of Amun-ḥotpe II's mortuary temple, called Shesep-ʿankh, "Receiver-of-life," lie southwest of that of his father on the edge of the cultivated land in western Thebes. From a foundation deposit of this temple comes a slender little ★beaker of alabaster, standing less than five and a half inches in height and provided with a small, disk-shaped lid on which is inscribed the king's praenomen, "ʿA-khepru-Rēʿ." A two-column inscription, somewhat roughly engraved on the side of the jar and once filled with green pigment, reads: "The Good God, ʿA-khepru-Rēʿ, beloved of Amun Rēʿ, on the occasion of stretching the cord in his Mansion of the West, (the temple called) Receiver-of-life (of?) ʿA-khepru-Rēʿ." A similar beaker, similarly inscribed, is in the Louvre (E 5331). Ours came to us in 1890 as a gift of James

FIGURE 77. Tableware of three wives of King Tḥut-mosĕ III. Gold and silver and gold-mounted glass and alabaster. H. of silver canister 7 in.

Douglas. A small limestone ★stela, purchased in 1920 from a native of Ḳurneh, was made for a man named ʿA-kheper-ku-Rēʿ-sonbe, who was a *weʿb*-priest of Amūn in the "Mansion of ʿA-khepru-Rēʿ in Thebes," again, in all probability, the king's mortuary temple. On the stela its owner is shown pouring a libation to the god Ptaḥ, who stands upright in a small, open pavilion at the left of the scene. In Berlin there is (or was) a similar stela, belonging to another priest of the same temple, which is also dedicated to Ptaḥ; and among the stelae found in the ruins of the mortuary temple of Tḥut-mosĕ II the majority likewise honor Ptaḥ. We meet with ʿA-kheper-ku-Rēʿ-sonbe again, on a funerary ★cone from his tomb at Thebes, whereon he is entitled "*Weʿb*-priest of Amūn," "Leader of the First (Temple) Phyle," and "Privy Councilor." Two other ★cones are inscribed for another of Amun-ḥotpe II's mortuary priests, the "Prophet of ʿA-khepru-Rēʿ, Nefer-ḥēbef." The funerary cults of the king and his consort, Queen Tiʿa, seem to have survived at least as late as the Twentieth Dynasty, both their mortuary temples being mentioned as active institutions in documents of that period.

The bronze ★blade of a model adze, inscribed for the "Good God, ʿA-khepru-Rēʿ, beloved of Osiris," is probably from a foundation deposit of the king's tomb in the Wādy el Bibān el Molūk. This is suggested, not only by the reference to the funerary god Osiris, but also by the fact that the blade once formed part of the collection of Theodore M. Davis, well known for his excavations in the royal valley. From the tomb itself comes a beautiful little three-handled ★vase of deep blue glass brilliantly adorned with wavy bands of light blue, yellow, and white glass; and from near by a fragment of a purple glass ★bowl engraved with the king's praenomen. A fragmentary mud ★brick, seven and a half inches in width and about half that in thickness, is stamped on its broad upper surface with two long ovals containing the throne name "ʿA-khepru-Rēʿ" and the kingly nomen "Amun-ḥotpe, the God, Ruler of Thebes." It was found by the Earl of Carnarvon on the Dirāʿ Abu'n Naga and comes, presumably, from a structure erected by Amun-ḥotpe II in that general vicinity.

FIGURE 78. Sandstone sphinx of King Amun-ḥotpe II. H. 4 in.

Three attractive small sculptured figures of Amun-ḥotpe II make up to a great extent for the Museum's lack of larger statues of the king. A little ★sphinx (fig. 78), skillfully carved in pale gray sandstone, is remarkable not only for the amount of modeling and fine detail which it possesses, but also for the restrained yet definite portrait quality in the tiny face. Here, framed by the graceful royal *nemes*, we see the wide, slightly tilted eyes, the long, straight nose, the small chin and pleasant mouth, and above all the aura of youthful freshness which characterize most of the known portraits of this pharaoh. On the breast of the crouching lion figure, between the striated bands which represent the mane of the beast, is the beginning of a short vertical inscription to the "Good God, ʿA-khepru-Rēʿ. . ."—the balance of which has been lost, together with the forward end of the base and the forelegs of the lion. When complete our sphinx was about eight and a half inches in length—four inches shorter than a similar sphinx of Amun-ḥotpe II from Karnak, described in the catalogue of the Cairo Museum (No. 42.079) as being made of white sandstone. Having once formed part of the Davis collection, assembled chiefly in Thebes, there is some probability that the New York sphinx, like its mate in Cairo, came originally from Karnak.

The kneeling limestone ★statuette of figure 79 also has a close parallel, in this case a small, indurated limestone figure of Amun-ḥotpe II, the head and body of which are at the moment on opposite sides of the Atlantic Ocean, the former in Boston, the latter in the Louvre. Our figure, less carefully finished than the Paris-Boston statuette, is uninscribed except for the praenomen of Amun-ḥotpe II lightly engraved on the front of the belt. Other features which do not appear in our profile view are the incised diaper pattern with which the belt is decorated and the way in which the back pilaster tapers to a pyramidal point near the top of the Double Crown. The statuette, acquired by purchase, is from Deir el Medīneh in western Thebes, where it was found in 1912 together with a similar figure of Tḥut-mosĕ III, now in Cairo.

The upper part of a much larger royal ★statuette in polished black diorite (fig. 80) has been convincingly dated by Cyril Aldred to a period extending from the latter years of the reign of Tḥut-mosĕ III to the end of the reign of Tḥut-mosĕ IV, with the strong probability that the pharaoh represented is Amun-ḥotpe II. The dating is based on the facial type, the distinctive form and proportions of the Blue Crown, the treatment of the coiled uraeus, the pyramidal top of the back pilaster, and the precise degree of idealized naturalism which characterizes this superb piece of New Kingdom sculpture. Despite the damaged nose, the rather soft, youthful face seems to exhibit all the features which we have associated above with Amun-ḥotpe II, but more accurately and in far greater detail than do those of the two little figures already discussed. The same treatment of the upper torso, and the identical pose with the crook scepter held in the left hand and slanting upward to the left shoulder, are found on a seated diorite statuette of Amun-ḥotpe II from the Karnak Cache (Cairo 42.076). This statuette, which is headless, is twenty-four inches high, was evidently of the same scale as our fragmentary figure, and, like it, probably wore the Blue Crown.

On other monuments in our collection Amun-ḥotpe II appears wearing the Blue Crown, once, for example, on a limestone stela, dedicated in behalf of an unidentified private individual, and again in Charles Wilkinson's color ★copy of a well-known scene in the Theban tomb chapel of the Chief Steward Ḳen-Amūn. The ★stela, a round-topped slab nineteen and a quarter inches in

FIGURE 79. Statuette of Amun-ḥotpe II wearing the Double Crown. H. 11 7/8 in.

height, carries a scene in which the king stands on the right of a well-provided offering table and presents two small, globular jars to a seated statue of the god Amun Rēʿ which faces him across the heaped-up food offerings. Besides the *khepereshcrown* the pharaoh wears the elaborate dress kilt with pendent tail behind and paneled "sporran" in front, while the figure of the god wears on its head Amūn's tall, two-plumed headdress and holds in its extended hands the *was*-scepter (𓌀) and the symbol of "life." Their figures, slender to the point of being spindly, are carved in *relief en creux*, which was once painted. Columns of incised hieroglyphs above their heads identify them, respectively, as the "Good God, Lord of the Two Lands, ʿA-khepru-Rēʿ, the Son of Rēʿ, whom he loves, Amun-ḥotpe, the God, Ruler of Heliopolis, given life, stability, well-being, and joy, like Rēʿ forever," and as "Amun Rēʿ, Lord of Thrones-of-the-Two-Lands," adding "may he (Amūn) give all life and well-being and all health." A solar disk with long, down-curving wings occupies the shallow lunette at the top of the slab. At the bottom, below the scene, are traces of a three-line offering formula composed in behalf of the owner of the stela, whose name, together with most of the rest of his inscription, has been methodically and thoroughly chiseled away—probably by someone who wished to appropriate the monument for his own use.

In the color ★copy of the Theban tomb painting, Amun-ḥotpe II, though represented as an adult king in full pharaonic regalia, appears as he had in his infancy, seated on the lap of his nurse, Ḳen-Amūn's mother, Amun-em-Opet. His feet rest on what would seem to have been an elaborate mechanical toy, composed of bound and kneeling figures of nine foreign enemies—five Africans and four Asiatics—whose heads could be made to move by means of strings held in the hand of the royal child. Ḳen-Amūn's principal office was that of High Steward of the pharaoh's estates at Peru-nefer, but, thanks to the function once performed by his mother, he sometimes refers to himself in his inscriptions as the "Foster Brother of the King." H. R. Hopgood's facsimile ★copy of another scene in the same tomb shows us the pharaoh, now grown to man's estate, seated with the goddess Maʿet on an elaborate throne dais receiving as New Year's "gifts" the finest products of the royal ateliers. In Ramesside times a temple statue of Amun-ḥotpe II was represented with those of his predecessors and successors in an oft-cited scene in Tomb 19, a scene which can be studied in the Museum in Wilkinson's full-scale color ★copy.

Twenty-six ★scarabs, two ★scaraboids, ten ★plaques, and four *wedjat*-eye ★amulets in our collection bear the throne name of Amun-ḥotpe II, in most cases either alone or accompanied by the same titles, epithets, figures, and designs which we have already encountered on the seals of his predecessors (see especially figs. 41, 48, 66). As usual, most of the little monuments are of green-glazed steatite, with only eight examples in faience and two in green stone (slate and jasper). Special interest attaches to two plaques, one bearing the names of both Amun-ḥotpe II and Tḥut-mosĕ III, the other inscribed on its underside with a short hymn to Amūn and having its back delicately carved in an openwork design in which Amun-ḥotpe II appears as a crouched sphinx protected from above by a winged uraeus. On the green slate scarab we see the king, wearing the Double Crown and the *shendyet*-kilt, in the act of clubbing to death a kneeling foreigner, while a second enemy begs for mercy and two others lie slain between the royal feet. From the minute inscriptions which fill the remainder of the oval field we learn that this is the "Good God, ʿA-khepru-Rēʿ, Smiter-of-the-Nine-Bows, Lord of Strength, and Divine Ruler." A large faience scarab covered with a violet glaze and set in a gold mounting is inscribed for "ʿA-khepru-Rēʿ" (written with three scarab beetles), "a valiant lion, a white bull when he crushes the Iuntiu." On yet another scarab the pharaoh is described as "a lion against him who

FIGURE 80. King Amun-ḥotpe II (?) wearing the *kheperesh*, or Blue Crown. Porphyritic diorite. H. 11 ½ in.

attacks him," and on a fourth we see him enthroned with all his regalia on the barque of the god Montu, readily identified by the plumed falcon heads which adorn its bow and stern posts. A mud ★sealing, bearing the impression of a scarab of the "Good God, ʿA-khepru-Rēʿ, beloved of Mīn of Koptos," is from a box of offerings contributed by the king to one of the shrines at Deir el Baḥri, probably that of the goddess Ḥat-Ḥor.

Queen Tiʿa, the half sister and wife of Amun-ḥotpe II and the mother of his successor, King Tḥut-mosĕ IV, is represented in our collection by a fragmentary ★*shawabty*-figure of green-glazed faience and part of a ★*shawabty*-coffin in blue and yellow faience, both from the Valley of the Tombs of the Kings. The *shawabty*, when complete, was less than five inches in height, and, like some of those found in the tomb of Tḥut-mosĕ IV, is curiously crude, its coarsely worked face framed by the heavy, twisted locks of a long wig. Horizontal lines of incised hieroglyphic inscription, covering the whole length of the figure from breast to ankles, contain a developed, New Kingdom version of the *shawabty*-spell, recited in behalf of the "King's Great Wife Tiʿa," whose name, as elsewhere, is written in a cartouche. The little coffin was evidently anthropoid in form and, like its larger counterparts, was adorned with vertical bands of yellow-inlaid inscriptions, between which stood figures of Anubis and the Four Genii of the Dead. In the three columns of inscription preserved to us Tiʿa is referred to as "the Osiris" and is given the titles "God's Wife" and "King's Mother." The last title indicates that she outlived her husband and was buried during the reign of her son, Tḥut-mosĕ IV.

Of Amun-ḥotpe II's prime minister, the "Overseer of the (Residence) City, the Vizier Amun-em-Opet," we are fortunate in possessing, besides a funerary ★cone from his Theban tomb (No. 29), a handsome gold signet ★ring, mounting a green jasper scarab, and a water-color ★palette of polished boxwood inscribed with the great man's name and titles. A narrow compartment in the back of the palette, once provided with a sliding cover, held the Vizier's paintbrushes, and on the top are eight oval cavities containing the much used blocks of dry pigment: red, black, white, red (traces only), blue, green, yellow, and red. The painting of pictures presumably was a hobby with the Vizier Amun-em-Opet as it has been with many distinguished statesmen before and since his day—including a recent prime minister of Great Britain and a president of the United States.

Amun-em-Opet's brother, Sen-nefer, was the contemporary Mayor of Thebes and is well known to students of Egyptian art as the owner of one of the most attractively painted tombs (No. 96) in the Theban necropolis. He and his wife, the King's Nurse Senet-nay, appear, however, not to have been buried there, but in the Valley of the Tombs of the Kings, in an abandoned royal tomb (No. 42) prepared originally for Tḥut-mosĕ II, but never used by him (see p. 79). Here were found, besides the canopic jars of Senet-nay and parts of two other sets, a number of small limestone ★vases inscribed with the titles and names of both Sen-nefer and his wife, five of which are now in the Museum's collection. Ranging in height from just under five to just over eleven inches, the vessels include a slender, flat-bottomed ewer, a tall vase of the [hieroglyph]-type, and three drop-shaped jars. Their inscriptions, somewhat roughly engraved and filled with blue pigment, are arranged on the sides of the jars in two or three vertical columns. The three-column inscriptions (on the *ḥes*-vase and the ewer) read in both cases: "The one in honor with Osiris, the Mayor of the Southern City Sen-nefer, (and) his wife, the King's Nurse Senet-nay, the justified"; while of the two-column inscriptions two refer to Senet-nay alone and one to Sen-nefer alone. From the same tomb comes a necklace ★pendant in the form of a gold rosette inlaid with green faience, red jasper, and blue glass. A funerary ★cone of Sen-nefer from Tomb 96 gives his titles as Steward and Overseer of the Cattle of Amūn.

Two mummiform wooden ★figures of Ḳen-Amūn, the steward of Amun-ḥotpe II's northern estates, were found with scores of others of the same type buried in the desert sand some five miles south of the pyramids of Gīzeh—a fact which suggests that Ḳen-Amūn, besides his tomb at Thebes (No. 93), may have prepared for himself a second burial place in the vicinity of Memphis. Both of our figures are carefully carved of a fine coniferous wood and both have painted faces (yellow), wigs (blue and yellow), and broad collars. Inscriptions engraved in two columns down the fronts of the figures begin in both instances with the words "Made as a favor of the King's bounty for the Prince and Count, one praised of the Good God." On the larger of the two figures (height thirteen and three-quarters inches) the inscription continues, "the Foster Brother of the Lord of the Two Lands, the Overseer of the Cattle of Amūn, Ḳen-Amūn, the justified"; and on the smaller figure, "the Overseer of the Cattle of Amūn, the Chief Steward Ḳen-Amūn." We have already noted that Ḳen-Amūn probably derived his title Foster Brother of the Lord of the Two Lands from the fact that his mother was one of Amun-ḥotpe II's nurses. On two ★cones from his Theban tomb Ḳen-Amūn is referred to as the "Steward of Perunefer and Overseer of the Cattle of Amūn."

Other dignitaries of the reign of Amun-ḥotpe II whose funerary ★cones are to be found in our collection are: the First Prophet (or High Priest) of Amūn, Amun-em-ḥēt (Tomb 97); the First Prophet of Amūn, Mery (Tombs 95 and 84); the latter's Scribe of the Offering Table Tḥūty (Tomb 45); the King's Scribe Tḥut-nofre (Tomb 80 or 104?); the King's Butler, clean of hands, Su-em-niwet (Tomb 92); the King's Butler, clean of hands, Amun-ḥotpe (Tomb 101?); the Commander of Henchmen and Troop Commander Pa-sēr (Tomb 367), and the Servant of Amūn, Woser-ḥēt (Tomb 176).

King Men-khepru-Rēʿ Tḥut-mosĕ IV, a son of Amun-ḥotpe II and the King's Great Wife Tiʿa, came to the throne about 1411 B.C. and died while still a fairly young man after a reign which probably lasted as much as fifteen years. A granite stela which he caused to be erected between the paws of the Great Sphinx at Gīzeh tells how as a young prince he used to rest from hunting and target practice in the shadow of the great figure and how on one occasion the god Harmakhis, with whom the sphinx was then identified, had spoken to him in a dream, promising him the kingship as a reward for freeing the god's image from the encumbering sands of the desert. This fanciful tale, which must have prefaced a record of restorations actually effected at Gīzeh by the king, suggests that Tḥut-mosĕ IV was not his father's heir apparent, but had obtained the throne through an unforeseen turn of fate, such as the premature death of an older brother.

The military career of the youthful pharaoh, though not comparable to those of his father and grandfather, included an armed tour of the Asiatic provinces which carried him over the boundaries of Naharīn, and a Nubian expedition which he sent upriver in the eighth year of his reign to check an incursion of desert tribesmen in the region of the province of Wawat. As a builder he was active at Karnak, where, among other projects, he was responsible for the removal and re-erection of an obelisk of his grandfather, Tḥut-mosĕ III (see p. 117). A pillared hall in the temple at Amada in Lower Nubia appears to have been built to commemorate the second of his two *sed*-festivals.

In the field of foreign relations Tḥut-mosĕ IV's most notable achievement was, perhaps, the marriage which, with some difficulty, he arranged between himself and a daughter of Artatāma, ruler of the influential Asiatic state of Mitanni and, potentially at least, Egypt's most valuable ally against the rising power of the Hittites. Unhappily, we do not know the name of the Mitanni princess, and her identification with Queen Mūt-em-weya, one of Tḥut-mosĕ IV's chief wives and the mother of his successor, King Amun-ḥotpe III, rests on no very substantial basis.

The ruins of the king's mortuary temple in western Thebes are more extensive than those of his predecessors, and his tomb (No. 43) in the Wādy el Bibān el Molūk is larger and more elaborate than any previously hewn in the royal valley

—a great subterranean complex of passages, stairways, and chambers, culminating in a pillared sepulchral hall and sunken crypt where stands the pharaoh's massive quartzite sarcophagus. Two shallow pits cut in the bedrock before the entrance stair well contained the usual foundation deposits. The tomb was cleared during the winter of 1903 at the expense of Theodore M. Davis, and in recognition of his contribution Mr. Davis was allowed to take with him to America many of the objects from both the foundation deposits and the tomb itself. Of these objects twenty-five were bequeathed by him to the Metropolitan Museum and form one of the most important and attractive groups in our collection.

From the foundation deposits come two model ★beakers of alabaster, three and an eighth inches in height, and two model ★bowls of the same material, measuring only two and a quarter inches in diameter. The beakers, though somewhat cursorily finished, are fairly well shaped, but the little bowls are rough and to a great extent amorphous. All bear hastily carved hieroglyphic inscriptions which identify their owner as the "Good God, Men-khepru-Rēʿ, beloved of Osiris."

Three of the many blue faience ★*shawabty*-figures found in the tomb show considerable variation in their types and sizes, and two of them, in view of the fact that they were made for a king of one of Egypt's most prosperous and sophisticated periods, are of surprising crudeness. One of these, a dumpy little figure under five and a half inches in height, wears a long, striped wig cover with rounded tabs and has drawn on its breast in heavy black outline a pair of crossed hands holding the hoes (𓌸) and baskets with which it was expected to labor in the corvées of the hereafter. Below the baskets, also in heavy black outline, is the title the "Good God," and the praenomen cartouche of Thut-mosě IV. A second figure, more slenderly proportioned, but otherwise of much the same type, is uninscribed. It is, however, provided with a small, anthropoid ★*shawabty*-coffin of blue faience, on the lid of which the king's titulary appears in the confused form of the "Good God. Lord of the Two Lands, Khaʿ-Thut-mosě-khaʿu, the Son of Rēʿ, Men-khepru-Rēʿ." The third *shawabty*, shown in figure 81, is well made, well proportioned, and generally more typical of the royal funerary figures of the second half of the Eighteenth Dynasty. On its head the figure wears the kingly *nemes* with uraeus, and its eyes, beard, and inscription are picked out in black glaze. In

FIGURE 81. *Shawabty*-figure of King Thut-mosě IV. Blue faience. H. 7¼ in.

the inscription the "Good God, Lord of the Two Lands, Men-khepru-Rēʿ" is said to be "justified" and "beloved of Osiris." Though one hesitates to speak of a portrait in so small and so standardized an object, it is probable that, even without the inscription, we should be able to recognize in this figure a conventionalized representation of the youthful Tḥut-mosĕ IV.

Most of the royal burials of the Eighteenth Dynasty were provided with amuletic devices, model weapons, and vessels of faience, which, being valueless to the average tomb robber, have survived in considerable numbers. Of the scores of such objects recovered by Davis from the débris in Tḥut-mosĕ IV's extensively plundered tomb, our own collection boasts two large ★*ʿankh*-signs (see fig. 82), a fragmentary model ★throw-stick, a ★lotus bud, a ★*koḥl*-tube, and five small ★vases of bright blue faience adorned with linear details and ornamentation in black glaze (fig. 83). The ☥-sign, thought to represent a knotted tie of some sort, perhaps a sandal strap, had the same phonetic value in Egyptian as the word for "life" (*ʿankh*). It almost certainly appears here, as it does elsewhere, in its role as a symbol of the eternal life with which the deceased pharaoh was, or hoped to be, endowed. Besides the interesting details of the sign itself, the smaller of our two *ʿankh*-symbols (not shown in the illustration) has the praenomen cartouche of Tḥut-mosĕ IV drawn in black outline upon its front. The model throw-stick fragment, oval in section, is from a recurved missile weapon of the nonreturn type, used from the earliest times for knocking down birds and small animals. Besides pairs of transverse black lines, simulating lashings(?), the faience model bears the king's throne name Men-khepru-Rēʿ, and one of a pair of large *wedjat*-eyes. The largest of the faience ★"papyrus rolls," inscribed on the side with the cartouche of Tḥut-mosĕ IV, is not quite five inches long, the smaller rolls measuring only two inches in length. On the latter the overlapping end edge of the papyrus is represented as a longitudinal ridge on the side of the roll, while black concentric circles on the ends of the cylinder suggest the layers of a rolled-up document (cf. p. 342). The lotus bud, slightly over four inches long, has its petals and other details outlined in black. The slightly domed top of a squat cylindrical libation vase is decorated with a band of lotus flowers and buds alternating with palmettes of Syrian type. On the sides of the vase the cartouches of Tḥut-mosĕ IV appear between symbols of "stability," the latter provided with outstretched human arms from which hang signs of "life." Three slender *ḥes*-vases (𓏀), complete with their conical faience stoppers, range in height from six and three-quarters to nine and seven-eighths inches. Two are

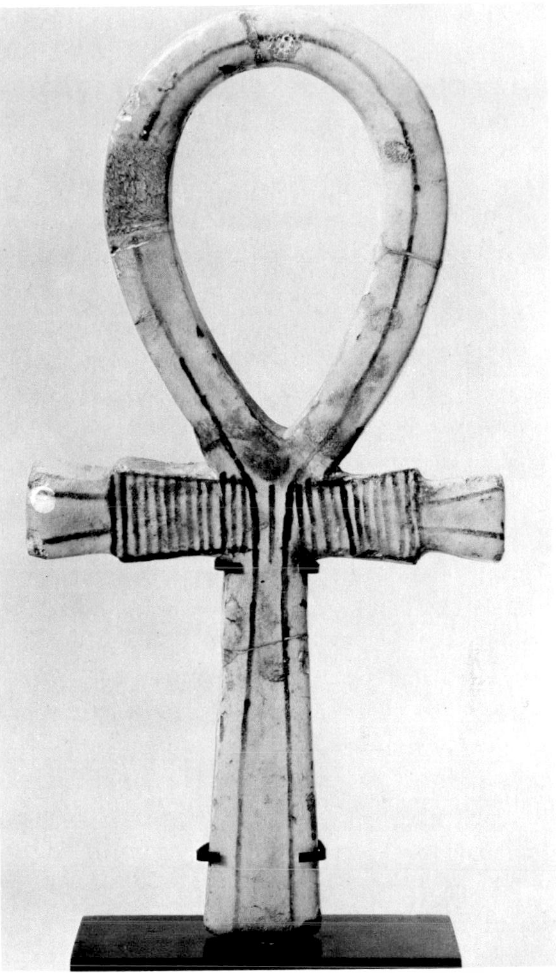

FIGURE 82. Symbol of "life" in blue faience from the tomb of King Tḥut-mosĕ IV. H. 11 in.

elaborately decorated in black line with lotus flowers, feather or scale patterns, and long drop-shaped ornaments, and one is inscribed for the "Good God, Lord of the Two Lands, Men-khepru-Rēʿ." Except for a black band around its rim and foot the third vase is undecorated, but carries on its side the cartouche of Tḥut-mosĕ IV enclosed within a small rectangle. Like those found on the *ḥes*-vases, two extra stoppers are shaped and decorated to resemble inverted flowers of the blue lotus. A small, straight-sided cup of blue faience is unadorned except for pairs of black lines just below its rim and just above its flat bottom. The little faience *koḥl*-tube, as frequently with this class of container, is shaped like a miniature palm column with tapered shaft and flaring, foliate top. On the side of the tube, somewhat carelessly written in black glaze, we read: "The Good God, Khaʿ-Tḥut-mosĕ-khaʿu, beloved of Osiris."

A small footed *vase (fig. 83, right background) of very fine, light turquoise blue glass, though fragmentary and lacking its handles, is the most complete of all the glass vessels found in the tomb. As was customary, it was made around a sandy clay core and was decorated with slender rods of yellow, violet, and white glass applied while still soft to the semimolten surface of the vase proper and then dragged up and down to produce the characteristic polychrome zigzag patterns. Subsequently the surface was smoothed and made uniform by being rolled on a stone(?) slab, the rim, foot, and handles were added, and the clay core was carefully scraped out.

Next to the body of a chariot, retained by the Cairo Museum, the most important and interesting objects recovered from the tomb of Tḥut-mosĕ IV are the carved wooden arms, or side panels, of a chair of state. One of these nearly identical panels is now in the Museum of Fine Arts in Boston, while the other is in our own collection (fig. 84). To judge from the glue stains on its surfaces the panel was once overlaid with sheet gold. Nevertheless, the carving of the fine low relief was carried out with great delicacy and with the utmost attention to detail. On the outside of his chair arm the "Son of Rēʿ, Khaʿ-Tḥut-mosĕ-khaʿu," appears as a striding sphinx striking down with its paws representatives of various African peoples, including several Nubian chieftains. The hieroglyphic groups over the back of the royal beast tell us that this is the "Horus with powerful arm, effective (in) crushing all foreign countries"; and the falcon which hovers protectively overhead is described as "the Beḥdetite, the Great God, variegated of plumage, who gives life and well-being." Behind the sphinx a symbol of "life" endowed with small human arms holds an ornate fan, or sunshade, an emblem of divine and royal pomp. On the inner side of the panel the "Good God, Men-khepru-Rēʿ," is seen seated upon his throne, with Weret-ḥekau, a lioness-headed goddess associated with the royal crowns, standing before him and stretching out her hand to the crown of Lower Egypt which he wears upon his head. To the left stands the ibis-headed god "Tḥōt, Lord of Hermopolis," holding the symbol of "life" and the tall, curved emblems of "years" and saying to the king, "I bring to you millions of years, life, well-being, and the attainment of eternity." Just behind the seated pharaoh is a tall sunshade in the form of a lotus pad and below his throne we see the familiar motif in which the knotted plants of the South and the North symbolize the union of Upper and Lower Egypt. Though difficult to parallel exactly, our scene quite evidently represents an important stage in the king's coronation or in the re-enactment of the coronation performed as part of the *sed*-festival.

Stylistically we see in these reliefs a trend toward softer, more graceful, and more naturalistic forms, a growing interest in elegant details of clothing and accessories, and a general air of sophistication and refinement attributable in part to the astounding technical skill of Tḥut-mosĕ IV's court artists. Even more remarkable are the superb battle scenes preserved to us on the king's chariot body in Cairo. Here for the first time we see the pharaoh charging in his chariot into a confused mass of stricken foreign enemies, whose bodies, horses, and chariots are distributed helter-skelter

over the field with no regard for ground lines or division into registers. This naturalistic and highly dramatic type of composition, thought to have been inspired by contemporary Helladic art, we shall find extensively employed in Egyptian relief sculpture and painting from the end of the Eighteenth Dynasty onward.

Also from the Davis collection, but not apparently from the king's tomb, is a fragmentary cylindrical ★cap of alabaster, perhaps the top of a staff, bearing on its side the nomen cartouche of Tḥut-mosĕ IV. A stamped mud ★brick on which

FIGURE 83. Vases and other objects in blue faience and glass, from the tomb of Tḥut-mosĕ IV. H. of tallest vase 10 in.

the praenomen Men-khepru-Rēʿ is spelled with three *kheper*-beetles, came as a gift to our collection in 1890 and is of unrecorded provenience.

A dozen ★scarabs, three ★plaques, and two *wedjat*-eye ★amulets bearing the throne name of Tḥut-mosĕ IV make use in their legends of the same figures, designs, titles, and epithets seen on the scarabs of Tḥut-mosĕ III and Amun-ḥotpe II.

FIGURE 84. Carved wooden panel from the side of a chair of King Tḥut-mosĕ IV. H. 10 in.

A rectangular plaque, on which the king is described as the "Smiter of Retenu" (Palestine-Syria), is of blue glass, but all the rest of his seals and amulets are of blue-, green-, or gray-glazed steatite. Representations of the pharaoh as a sphinx trampling on his enemies and references to his prowess as a warrior still occur, but are now far less common than the legends in which he is associated with the god Amūn, either as the "beloved of Amūn" or as the "image" or "Son of Amun Rēʿ."

A sandstone ★stela or lintel on which the *Weʿb*-priest of Amūn, Woser-ḥēt, and "his beloved sister," Ta-rowy, are shown "giving praise to" a statue of the canine-headed Anubis, "Lord of the Holy Land," carries, behind the figure of the god, a large cartouche of Tḥut-mosĕ IV. The cartouche, which contains the king's praenomen Men-khepru-Rēʿ, rests upon a "gold"-sign and is surmounted not only by the ostrich plumes and ram's horns of the god Osiris, but also by the sun's disk and cow's horns of the goddess Ḥat-Ḥor. The erasure in the inscription of the name of the god Amūn indicates that the slab was carved sometime previous to the "Aten heresy," and the style of the relief suggests the reign of Tḥut-mosĕ IV himself, rather than that of Amun-ḥotpe III.

In a badly damaged scene in the chapel of the Theban tomb (No. 75) of the Second Prophet of Amūn, Amun-ḥotpe-si-se, Tḥut-mosě IV appears, enthroned on an elaborate, canopied dais, surveying the "royal gifts" which, under the supervision of the tomb owner, have been prepared for the temple of Amūn. In the second of two fine color ★copies of the scene, made by H. R. Hopgood, we can see that among the gifts displayed are two standing and two kneeling statues of the king himself. Two funerary ★cones from the same tomb are inscribed for the "Second Prophet of Amūn, Amun-ḥotpe."

Among the very few examples of original Theban tomb painting in the Museum's collection is a rectangular section of painted mud-plaster wall (fig. 85) from the tomb (No. 63) of the Chancellor Sobk-ḥotpe, an official of Tḥut-mosě IV, better known, perhaps, as the Mayor of the Southern Channel and the Channel of Sobk. The ★painting, executed in tempera on a surface coating of white plaster, shows us two male offering bearers, wearing the characteristic wigs and clothing of the period, bringing up live ducks, leeks, lotus flowers, and papyrus plants adorned with twining vines. The black headdresses, dark red flesh, and white garments of the men stand out more sharply against the blue-gray background than do the paler shades of light red and blue, yellow and gray used for the birds and plants. In the block borders

FIGURE 85. Part of a wall painting from the tomb of the Chancellor Sobk-ḥotpe at Thebes. Tempera on mud plaster. L. 29 in.

the color sequence is red, blue, yellow, green, red, and so on. From the vertical column of detailed hieroglyphs at the right edge of the panel we learn that the tomb owner was the "Mayor, the Treasurer of the King of Lower Egypt, the Sole Companion, the Overseer of Treasurer(s) [Sobk-]ḥotpe, son of the Overseer of Treasurer(s) Mīn." It is of interest to note that the name of the god Sobk in the first of the two personal names has been intentionally chopped out, evidently by the Atenists, whose proscription must have extended to other of Egypt's older gods besides Amūn. Thanks to information provided by Miss Rosalind Moss we know that our painting is from a vertical band of narrow panels adjoining the left side of Sobk-ḥotpe's great painted stela. It was removed from the tomb over a century ago and until 1930 was in a private collection in England.

Another of Tḥut-mosĕ IV's contemporaries, the First Prophet of Onuris, Neb-seny, is represented in our collection by a pottery ★cone and two dummy ★vases coming from his tomb (No. 108) in the Theban necropolis. The vases, acquired by purchase in 1941, are of wood covered with gesso and painted to imitate stone—in one case alabaster, in the other a mottled black and white breccia. Both are of the familiar globular shape with a low foot and tall, cylindrical neck, and each bears on its side a panel of inscription in which the words "one in honor with Osiris," are followed by Neb-seny's title and name. The Scribe Djeser-ku-

Rēʿ, named on a green-glazed steatite ★scarab, is perhaps to be identified with the Scribe and Accountant of the Grain of Amūn, Djeser-ku, the owner of Tomb 38 at Thebes and of a funerary ★cone from this tomb. A larger ★scarab of gray steatite is inscribed for the Fanbearer on the Right of the King, Tjua, who appears also to have served under Tḥut-mosĕ IV.

Funerary ★cones from the tombs of six other prominent Thebans of the time of Tḥut-mosĕ IV include those of the Page of the Inner Palace and Commander of Cavalry Ḥiḳ-er-enḥeḥ (Tomb 64); the Standard-bearer of (the Ship) "Beloved-of-Amūn" and Overseer of the Deserts on the West of Thebes Neb-Amūn (Tomb 90); the Overseer of the Audience Chamber Amun-em-Opet (Tomb 276); the Astronomer(?) of Amūn, Nakhte (Tomb 52); the Scribe Paroy (Tomb 295), and the Steward of Amūn, Nakht-Sobk.

Finally, we find mention on a hieratic ★ostrakon, formerly in the Amherst collection, of an Overseer of the City and Vizier named Tḥut-mosĕ who held his high office under either Amun-ḥotpe II or Tḥut-mosĕ IV.

V. Private Works of Art and Craftsmanship Produced during the Thutmoside Period

In private, as in royal, sculpture and painting the era of imperial expansion under Tḥut-mosĕ I and his successors witnessed the transition from the somewhat austere artistic traditions of the Middle Kingdom to the elegant and vivacious style characteristic of the late Eighteenth Dynasty. To enable us to follow this development throughout the series of monuments at our command the descriptions of these monuments will include whatever external evidence we possess on their dates and places of origin. In the many instances where no such evidence exists we must fall back on what the style and content of the pieces themselves have to tell us.

1. Statues and Statuettes

A type of private tomb sculpture particularly popular during the reigns of Tḥut-mosĕ III and his immediate successors was the pair statue or statuette, comprising the figures of a man and his wife (or other female relative) seated side by side on a broad, high-backed throne, each with an arm around the other's shoulders. This gesture of mutual affection and respect and the fact that the figures are always equal in size are among the many indications which we possess of the new importance enjoyed by women in the New Kingdom, and contrast strongly with the treatment seen in the group statues of the Old and Middle Kingdoms, wherein the wife, clinging unnoticed to the waist or leg of her husband, is frequently represented at a much reduced scale (see Part I, frontispiece).

The heads and upper portions of two life-size ★statues in painted sandstone (fig. 86) evidently belonged to a group of this class, each figure being still attached to a portion of the common throne back and showing on the outside shoulder the clasping hand of the companion figure. The remnants of a long offering formula, engraved on the back of the throne below two pairs of *wedjat*-eyes, invoke the god Amūn of Thebes and mention the Overseer of the Cattle of Amūn, Nūfer, in such a way as to suggest that he was the owner of the group and of the tomb on the Dirāʿ Abu'n Naga from which it is reputed to have come. To judge from the pleasantly bland but otherwise rather expressionless faces, Nūfer and his wife lived during the first half of the Eighteenth Dynasty, their prominent, slightly arched noses having perhaps been borrowed from one of the earlier Thutmoside rulers. Such a dating is borne out by the man's short chin beard and simple, shoulder-length wig

FIGURE 86. The Overseer of the Cattle of Amūn, Nūfer, and his wife. Painted sandstone. H. 17 in.

and by the woman's perfectly plain white dress and long, wavy wig with the single, thick, braided locks framing the face in front. The colors, applied over a white filler, are conventional. Nūfer's flesh is dark red, that of his wife ocher yellow, while the wigs of both figures and the rims and irises of their eyes are black. Black is used also for the man's beard and deep blue for the brows and corner streaks of his eyes and those of his wife. The old-fashioned broad collars worn by the couple are polychrome—blue, green, red, yellow, black, and white. On both figures there are remains of a shiny, brown-red varnish, evidently once transparent but now opaque in places, especially on the woman's face where it hides some of the original color. As can be seen in the photograph, Nūfer's right eye and part of the forehead and wig above it have been restored.

A ★pair statuette in black diorite, complete except for the front of the base and the toes of the figures, measures only ten and five-eighths inches in height, but appears in other respects—the facial types, the forms of the wigs, the man's beard, etc. —to have been almost exactly similar to our fragmentary sandstone group. In it, as probably also in the larger pair, the man wears, besides his wig and collar, only a short, simple kilt, while the woman's plain, tight-fitting dress is seen to extend downward to just above her ankles. The embracing, inside arms of the couple cross one another over the back of the throne and in each case the outside hand rests on the outside knee, the woman's hand open, palm down, the man's clenched and holding a folded handkerchief. Said to have been purchased in Luxor, the little pair came to the Museum in 1925 as a gift of Mrs. S. W. Straus. The diorite ★head of a woman from a slightly larger group of the same type and presumably of the same general period wears the characteristic long wig with the prominent braided locks in front and has a face which is strikingly like that of Nūfer's wife. It was acquired in 1897 from the Egypt Exploration Fund and is known to have come from the neighborhood of Deir el Baḥri.

The painted sandstone ★group of figure 87 was probably carved at Thebes during the reign of one of the later Thutmoside kings—Amun-ḥotpe II or Tḥut-mosĕ IV. The man's shoulder-length wig, with the spiral under-curls appearing in a shingled, or stepped, arrangement in the front, seems to have first come into fashion under Amun-ḥotpe II, and the group as a whole is remarkably like one in the Vatican which bears the cartouche of Tḥut-mosĕ IV. The woman's massive headdress, with the heavy locks "whipped" to form points at their ends, is also of a late type, only a step away from the huge and elaborate wigs affected by the ladies of the court of King Amun-ḥotpe III (cf. fig. 161). On the other hand, the garments worn by the pair are still quite plain, though the man's kilt has been extended downward almost to his ankles. The color scheme is exactly the same as that seen on our first, fragmentary sandstone pair. The long and rather interesting hieroglyphic texts carved on the sides of the throne inform us that the group was dedicated by the Scribe of the Treasury of Amūn, Woser-ḥēt, in behalf of his parents, the Scribe of the Treasury of Amūn, Neb-waʿw, and the House Mistress Tenet-ḥat; but the inscriptions on the skirts of the figures proper have been carefully erased, suggesting that the group was made originally for another couple. On the right side of the throne the offering formula invokes "Amūn, Lord of Karnak, and Mūt, Mistress of Ishru, that they may grant a receiving of the food offerings which go forth in his presence, an assumption of whatever forms he desires on earth, glory, power, and justification, a fourfold eating of bread and drinking of beer in the presence(?) of the soul after old age and death, to the spirit of the Scribe of the Treasury in the House of Amūn, Neb-waʿw"; and on the left side, the "Council which is in the Mansion of Sokar, Ptaḥ, the great, dwelling in Tjenenet, and Anubis, Lord of Ro-setau, Lord of Life, Judge of the Underworld, that they may make an abode for the soul of the Scribe of the Treasury of Amūn, Neb-waʿw, the justified, in the House of Sokar, in the following of him who transfigures the soul in the fourth month of Akhet; that they may advance his position, making true his voice, so that he may be known and his mouth may be opened in the lands(?) which are in them, that he may be flooded with . . . and that he may have power over everything which he desires." The unattractive, almost crude quality which we note in this group is attributable, in part at least, to the unsympathetic, gritty brown stone in which it is carved. Acquired by the Museum in 1919, it was formerly in the collection of Lord Amherst of Hackney and before that, as far back as 1833, in the collection of Mr. John Lee of Hartwell House, Aylesbury.

In a similar but smaller ★group, in this case of painted limestone, a daughter of the couple represented is shown seated between them on a low block which projects slightly forward from the center of the front of their throne, the head of her little figure rising only slightly above the knees of her parents. The child, whose name was Mūt-nefret, wears her hair close cropped on top, but hanging in groups of braids down the back and right side of her head and descending in a short, curly bang over her forehead. Like her mother, the House Mistress Nebet-Yunet ("Lady-of-Dendereh"), she wears a long, simple dress reaching downward to her ankles, but lacks the older woman's bead collar and long, elaborate wig. Her father, the Storekeeper of Amūn, Amun-ḳed, also wears an ankle-length skirt, but is nude from the waist up. His wig is similar to that of Neb-waʿw of figure 87, and in his clenched right hand he holds a rolled and folded handkerchief. Inscriptions down the fronts of the skirts of the two figures speak of "everything which goes forth from upon the offering table of Amūn" for the man and "of Ḥat-Ḥor" for the woman, while offering formulae on the sides of the throne invoke Osiris, "King of the Living," and Ḥat-Ḥor, "Mistress of Thebes," in their behalf. A longer text, engraved in four columns on the back of the throne, calls upon Amūn

FIGURE 87. The Scribe Neb-waʿw and his wife Tenet-ḥat. Painted sandstone. H. 28 in.

and Osiris, "Ruler of Eternity," to provide "bread and water, the breath of incense on the flame, libations of wine and milk, geese, *khopesh*-joints, and choice cuts of meat" to the spirits of Amun-ḳed and his wife, who is here called "the house mistress whom he loves." Everywhere in the inscriptions the name of Amūn has been chiseled out by the agents of the Aten. In the last column of text on the back of the throne we are told that the statuette was dedicated in behalf of the deceased couple, not by their "elder" daughter, Mūt-nefret, who is represented with them, but by another daughter named Dewat-nefret, or "Fine-morning." A Theban provenience is strongly indicated by the names and epithets of the deities mentioned in the inscriptions.

A fragmentary alabaster ★group statuette, a gift of Mrs. J. E. Childs, comes in all probability from a tomb in the neighborhood of Aswān at the First Cataract of the Nile. Shown standing side by side against a wide back pilaster are the Overseer of the Great Prison Amun-em-ḥēt, and his wife, the King's Ornament Aʿḥ-mosĕ Baket-Amūn, their figures tall, slender, and elegantly carved in the best stylistic tradition of the mid-Eighteenth Dynasty. The style and proportions of the figures are, in fact, highly reminiscent of a well-known granite pair in the Cairo Museum representing Thutmosĕ III's Vizier Amun-wosre and his wife. In our group the man holds a folded handkerchief in his right hand and the woman's long, pleated dress is finished with a patterned hem band above her broad, beaded anklets. The couple evidently had their adjoining arms, which do not appear in our fragment, around one another's shoulders. The deities invoked in the offering formulae which separate and flank the figures are the cataract god Chnūm, and the goddesses Satis, Mistress of Elephantine ([hieroglyphs]), and Anukis, "dwelling in Nubia," the local triad of the cataract region and the Nome of Elephantine. Each of the goddesses is asked to give to the deceased Amun-em-ḥēt and his wife "every offering from upon her offering table"; while Chnūm is to provide Amun-em-ḥēt with the "cool water which comes forth from Elephantine and the contentment which comes forth from the Lord of the Primaeval Waters." The great, or main, prison, an institution which rose to prominence during the Second Intermediate period, was at Thebes, and it was here, in the capital city, that Amun-em-ḥēt, though a native of the Nome of Elephantine, probably spent most of his official life. There must have been during the centuries of its existence many an Overseer of the Great Prison, but curiously enough the title as we have it here appears to be otherwise unknown.

A small monolithic ★shrine of painted sandstone, containing the standing figures of a man and his wife, is from the Eleventh Dynasty temple at Deir el Baḥri, where it had been deposited during the early decades of the Thutmoside era as an ex-voto

FIGURE 88. The Queen's Steward Roy, singing a hymn to the sun god. Painted limestone. H. 12 ½ in.

to the goddess Ḥat-Ḥor and to the deified owner of the temple, King Neb-ḥepet-Rēʿ Montu-ḥotpe. Looking into the open front of the little monument we see the statuettes of the owner and his wife carved in high relief and measuring just under eleven inches in height. They stand together, hand in hand, the man clad in a flaring, shoulder-length wig and a long kilt with a starched triangular front, the woman wearing a long, plain wig and a perfectly simple white dress. On the exterior, the sides and back of the shrine are taken up with standing figures of the couple's four sons and six daughters, executed in low relief and painted in conventional colors—blue, red, yellow, black, and white —against a grayish blue background. Each figure holds before its face a flower of the blue lotus and above each is the designation "his son" or "his daughter" and a personal name. The names of the sons include Aʿḥ-mosĕ, Amun-em-ḥēb, and Neb-waʿ; those of the daughters, Wēʿbet, called Wedja, Nebet-Ishru-em-ḥēt, Khēwetef-. . ., Aʿḥ-ḥotpe, and Amun-ḥotpe. Two horizontal lines of inscription running around the top of the shrine contain fragmentary offering formulae in which Ḥat-Ḥor, "who is in the midst of Thebes," Isis, "mother of . . .," and the "Son of Rēʿ, Montu-ḥotpe" are invoked in behalf of the owner and his wife. The names of the couple are almost completely obliterated, but that of the man may have been Rēʿy and that of the woman appears to have ended with the element *yōtes*, "her father." Though badly battered and with many of its inscriptions chiseled out, the shrine shows in its figures and reliefs the firm draughtsmanship, clean profiles, bright colors, and simple, static compositions typical of early Thutmoside sculpture and painting.

A by-product of the resurgence under the Thutmoside rulers of the solar religion of Heliopolis was the representation of the tomb owner as a kneeling figure in the act of singing a hymn to the sun god, his hands raised before him in an attitude of adoration, or perhaps to shield his face from the brightness of the deity. Occasionally the words of the hymn are inscribed on the kilt of the figure itself, but more often they are carved on a stelalike slab which stands upright before the kneeling adorant, touched, but not supported, by his upraised hands. The type is admirably exemplified by our painted limestone ★statuette (fig. 88) of the Queen's Under Steward Roy, datable by its style, its facial type, and the form of its wig to the period embraced by the reigns of Amun-ḥotpe II and Tḥut-mosĕ IV. Here the hymn, introduced by the words "Adoration of Rēʿ when he rises until it comes to pass that he sets in life," consists of a number of phrases lifted from a longer psalm of the type found in Eighteenth Dynasty Books of the Dead: "I have provided a free passage for the great barque, I have repelled the attack of the serpent Grim-face, so that the sailing of the *mesektet*-barque (see Part I, p. 272) might take place each day. It is the Scribe and Under Steward of the King's Great Wife, Roy, who says, 'Homage to you, Ḥor-akhty Amūn, leader of the gods! May you cross the sky in peace in the course of every day!'" In the lunette, above, the Ω-sign between the *wedjat*-eyes is the symbol of the endless and all-embracing circuit of the sun, and in motifs of this type is probably to be taken as an expression for the sun god himself. Davies is inclined to regard the ripples of water and the bowl below the emblem as symbols of the "homage paid to the adumbrated deity, either by the cup of incense and water of libation or by offerings of food and drink."[1] The attractive little statue, with its bright, conventional colors well preserved, was acquired at Luxor in 1909 by J. Pierpont Morgan and was presented to the Museum in 1917.

A second and somewhat earlier ★statuette of the same type and material, a gift of Mrs. Lucy W. Drexel, has formed part of our collection since 1889. Nine and a half inches in height, it wears the plain bagwig which we associate with the first half of the Eighteenth Dynasty. The name of the owner

[1] *Tomb of Nakht*, p. 47, note 4.

has been lost with the lower part of the slab bearing his hymn; but the beginning of the hymn itself is preserved: "Giving praise to Amūn and kissing the ground before Ḥor-akhty and Osiris, Ruler of the Two Banks, that they may give the sweet breath of . . . which is in them, until Rēʿ rises over my breast. . . ." Despite the difference in their formats, indicative of the lapse of time between them, the hymns on both our statuettes present the Theban god Amūn in his new guise as a sun god, that is, as a cosmic deity endowed with the universal power and the universal appeal appropriate to the god of a vast and cosmopolitan empire.

Though less than an inch and a half in height, a haematite ★statuette, representing a fashionably dressed man kneeling and holding before him a votive sistrum, is carved with as much style and in almost as great detail as the larger versions of this popular type. Here the man's extended hands are held, palms down, at the top of the sistrum. Otherwise there is a marked similarity between this figure and the statuette of Sen-ne-mūt shown in figure 57, and it is not improbable that the two are closely contemporary in date. A hole passing through the little figure just inside and above the right elbow suggests that it was worn suspended on a cord either as an ornament or possibly as an amulet.

The upper part of a large ★statuette in polished black gabbro, though evidently inspired by a Middle Kingdom prototype, is probably to be dated to the middle years of the Thutmoside era. The shawl wig, the large ears set high on the head, the strong, slightly grim face, and the lack of clothing above the waist all hark back to the Twelfth Dynasty; but the small goatee, the minute, shingled locks of the wig, the tendency toward idealization in the face, the generalized and restrained modeling of the torso, and the rather slick finish betray the hand of the New Kingdom sculptor. To the same period belongs a beardless male ★head in gray diorite wearing a flaring, shoulder-length wig of simple form and having a broad, heavy-featured face devoid of any expression whatsoever. From the forehead band of the wig vertically downward to the chin the face measures just under three and a half inches, which means that the statuette from which the head was broken was about one-half life size.

The ★head and shoulders (fig. 89) of a youthful official wearing a short chin beard, a bobbed wig, and a fringed mantle, comes from a diorite statuette of about the same scale as the foregoing, but of slightly later date, the style and facial type pointing to the latter half of the reign of Amun-ḥotpe II or the early years of Tḥut-mosĕ IV. Though modeled with the utmost delicacy, the strong young face lacks altogether the slightly effeminate quality which we find in heads of the late Eighteenth Dynasty. Five inches in height from crown of head to collarbone, this admirable piece of sculpture was purchased in Cairo and is of unknown provenience. The upper part of a seated ★statuette in mottled gray and white gabbro, which also represents a young official wearing a shoulder-length wig, is similar in type and style, but very much smaller, measuring less than four inches from the waist to the top of the head. In both cases the facial expression is serious almost to the point of sadness.

An interesting male ★head of limestone seems to have belonged to a statue of the Nile, or inundation, god Ḥaʿpy (cf. fig. 145). The headdress is of the long, striated variety worn during the New Kingdom almost exclusively by deities, and attached to the chin of the bland and youthful face is the top of what appears to have been a long, braided beard of divine type. Purchased in 1907 from a well-known Luxor dealer in antiquities, the head, in spite of its battered nose, is an engaging piece of Thutmoside sculpture.

From the excavations of the Egypt Exploration Fund in the Middle Kingdom temple at Deir el Baḥri comes the left side of a life-size ★head in painted limestone representing a man wearing his hair close cropped to his skull. The strong, handsome face is admirably carved and smoothly finished and the eyes and eyebrows are enlivened with black paint. Edouard Naville, its discoverer, is probably correct in assigning the piece to the

FIGURE 89. An official of the late Thutmoside period. Diorite. H. 5 in.

Eighteenth Dynasty, though neither an earlier nor a later date is out of the question.

A pair of little standing female ★figures, carved in ivory and coming in all probability from an ornate article of furniture, have their heads surmounted by large floral emblems, in one case a palmettelike plant with curling leaves, in the other a flower of the blue lotus. It has been suggested that they represent the goddesses or personifications of Upper and Lower Egypt, and while this is possible it is far from certain. Each figure stands stiffly at attention with the arms at the sides and each is clad in a plain, skintight dress and a long, simple wig. The emblems on their heads were made of separate pieces of ivory and tenoned in place, and the figures themselves were once attached to bases, rails, or other elements by means of tenons projecting downward from under the soles of their feet. Only four and a quarter inches in height over all, they are difficult to date exactly, but seem to belong stylistically to the early years of the Thutmoside period or perhaps even earlier.

A number of small doll-like ★figures in blue faience had, sometime before the middle of the reign of Tḥut-mosĕ III, been offered as votives in the shrine of the goddess Ḥat-Ḥor at Deir el Baḥri. Crudely formed in one-piece molds, open at the back, they represent for the most part slender young women, nude except for their long, black, tripartite coiffures and the narrow bead girdles about their hips. The ★head of a similar figure was found by the Museum's Expedition near the pyramid of Amun-em-ḥēt I at el Lisht, and not far away, in the same stratum, was found a very primitive, violin-shaped ★figure of clay devoid of legs and with only two stumplike projections to serve as arms. Attenuated figures of nude women or goddesses wearing on their heads short, caplike wigs are carved in high relief on the fronts of two small, shrine-shaped ★plaques of limestone—unhappily of unknown provenience and of somewhat uncertain date.

The votive figure of a ★cow, from the Ḥat-Ḥor shrine at Deir el Baḥri, was found with inscribed objects which tend to place it in the first half of the Eighteenth Dynasty. The animal, represented as standing, is summarily modeled in blue faience and is adorned with prominent black spots, crosses, and other markings. Minus its head, it measures just over an inch and three-quarters in length.

2. Tomb Reliefs, Paintings, Stelae, and Votive Plaques

Far and away the richest source of material for a study of both the art and life of the New Kingdom is the painted or sculptured decoration of the private tomb chapels of the Theban necropolis (see p. 56). Of the ninety chapels datable to the period with which we are dealing, more than half were executed during the lifetimes of Ḥat-shepsūt and Tḥut-mosĕ III, the other forty-odd examples belonging to the reigns of Amun-ḥotpe II, Tḥut-mosĕ IV, and Amun-ḥotpe III. In style, composition, and coloring the decoration of the chapels of the earlier group shows a general similarity to the royal temple reliefs, especially to those in the temple of Ḥat-shepsūt at Deir el Baḥri. The figures, drawn with firm, clean outlines, are widely spaced in quiet, rather stiff compositions which are not closely interrelated but arranged serially like the parts of a long, continuous narrative. The backgrounds are a pale bluish gray and the colors, including blue, canary yellow, pink, and brick red, are fresh, clear, and light in tone. The diversity of content which is characteristic of these earlier tomb paintings is particularly well exemplified in the great chapel of Tḥut-mosĕ III's Vizier Rekh-mi-Rēʿ, long recognized as the masterpiece of its type and period. The tomb of Ḳen-Amūn, executed a few years later, in the reign of Amun-ḥotpe II, is distinguished by a new richness in design and coloring; and in the succeeding tomb chapels we find a growing tendency toward livelier, more rhythmic, and more integrated compositions and toward figures in which grace and suppleness are combined with a new feeling of depth and plasticity. Individual incidents intimately connected with the life and career of the tomb owner tend to replace the broader and more diversified representations of the world at large seen in the earlier tombs. The backgrounds are now a chalky white and the colors bright and harmonious, changing, however, to duller tones as the end of the dynasty is approached. Relief sculpture, fairly common in private tombs during the reigns of Ḥat-shepsūt and Tḥut-mosĕ III, disappears entirely under Amun-ḥotpe II and Tḥut-mosĕ IV; but is revived on a grand scale in the great rock-cut chapels of the reign of Amun-ḥotpe III, where it is characterized by the utmost delicacy in both the draughtsmanship and the modeling. Numerous stelae of the period, both royal and private, carry small-scale reliefs often of great beauty; and no study of Egyptian painting is complete which does not take into consideration the fine, colored vignettes of the funerary papyri and the hundreds of lively sketches which are preserved to us on potsherds and flakes of limestone.

The largest and most interesting piece of Thutmoside ★relief in our collection comprises parts of two registers of farming scenes (fig. 90) from the

FIGURE 90.
Activities on a Theban farm. Painted relief from a private tomb chapel of the mid-Eighteenth Dynasty.
L. 40 in.

forehall of a Theban tomb chapel of the time of Ḥat-shepsūt. The style of the work—especially the type and proportions of the tall, slender figures—closely resembles that seen in the much damaged chapel of the tomb (No. 125) of Ḥat-shepsūt's First Herald Dewa-enḥeḥ; but the fragment has passed through many hands since the time, long ago, when it was sawn out of the rock-cut tomb wall, and its exact source has long been forgotten. The stone is the unmistakable flinty, gray limestone native to large areas of the Theban necropolis and especially characteristic of the Hill of the Sheikh ʿAbd el Ḳurneh, and the surface of the painted relief has been blackened by smoke from the cooking fires of modern, or relatively modern, squatters in the ancient tomb. The agricultural activities represented—the newly sown seed being turned under by gangs of ox-drawn plows and (above) the sheaves of wheat or barley being transported to the threshing floor—are familiar subjects, known to us from scores of other Egyptian tombs; but certain details in our present scenes are remarkable and, so far as can be discovered, unique. Instead of the usual pair of long-horned African cows, the plow here is drawn by a team of humped bulls, animals related to the zebu, or Brahmany bull, of India, which had only recently been imported into Egypt from the hinterlands of Asia. Moreover, the yoke of the interesting, two-handled plow is not lashed to the horns of the beasts, as was the Egyptian custom, but rests upon their necks forward of their upward-projecting humps.

Even more extraordinary is the two-wheeled oxcart appearing in the register above. Though by this time the wheel was well known in Egypt, its use was confined almost exclusively to the light, fast-moving chariot, the demand for wheeled work vehicles being practically nonexistent in a land dominated by a great river and made up of narrow, muddy fields flanked by rocky or sandy deserts. Normally, in scenes of this type the barley or wheat is taken to the threshing floor either in bulging donkey bags or in huge network hampers slung from carrying poles between pairs of muscular peasants. Our cart, a vehicle large and ponderous enough to require two oxen to pull it, is provided with four-spoked wheels similar to those seen on chariots, but of much heavier construction. The position of the wheels, well back under the center of the open, latticework body, suggests that there were only two. The pole also is like those of contemporary chariots, being curved so as to pass under and form a longitudinal support for the body. The upper half of the contents of the cart is painted yellow, and below this a high band of red, passing behind the oxen and through the cart, suggests a field of standing grain. In the lower register both the bulls and the flesh of the men are red, while the tree (𓆭), inserted between the two central figures to provide a bit of landscape, is bluish green with slender red branches. The small size of this tree and the fact that it is placed high up in the field indicate clearly that it was thought of as being in the background of the scene and provide us with a good example of the rudimentary perspective not infrequently attempted by the Egyptian artist.

Three smaller fragments of painted limestone *relief, preserving in each case the upper part of a female figure, are attractive examples of the private tomb sculpture of the earlier decades of the Thutmoside era. All retain characteristics handed down from the Middle Kingdom and, were it not for the wig and facial type and the slender proportions of the figure, the largest of the three pieces (seventeen by ten inches) might well be assigned to the Twelfth or even to the Eleventh Dynasty. Here we see the familiar figure of the tomb owner's lady seated on a carved chair and holding before her nose a large flower of the blue lotus. In this case the long, full wig, falling far down over its wearer's shoulders, is composed of twisted locks of hair whipped at the lower ends with multiple turns of hair or fine cord. Behind the figure there is a raised band of incised hieroglyphic inscription containing part of an offering formula. The upper portion of a similar figure, similarly posed with a lotus flower, appears on the second fragment, but here the long, plain wig divides over the lady's shoulder, part hanging down her back, part over her breast. Her name, of which there now remains only a final *w*, was written in incised hieroglyphs beside her head. The small scale of the figure—the entire fragment measures only seven by six and three-quarters inches—may indicate that our piece is from a stela or from a subsidiary register showing, for example, female guests at a banquet. The figure on our third fragment is without much doubt that of a goddess, wearing a long, massive headdress and a fillet with ends pendent behind, and having her arms extended forward and downward as if to embrace or receive the body of the dead tomb owner. Though the destruction of the top of the headdress has removed whatever emblem the deity may have been wearing on her head, we think either of the goddess of the West or of one of the mourning sister goddesses Isis and Nephthys. The face, like that of the woman on the preceding fragment, is typically Theban, with narrow, slanting eyes, a slightly retroussé nose, a small, firm chin, and a strong, slightly protruding mouth. In all three cases the breast of the figure, goddess or mortal, is exposed above the top of the plain, tight-fitting dress.

The section of painted sandstone ★doorjamb shown in figure 91 is from the tomb of a Theban official who served under one of the earlier Thutmoside pharaohs, probably Tḥut-mosĕ III. In each of the two partially preserved panels we see a fashionably dressed couple seated side by side, the woman on a chair much lower than that of her husband, so that in the lower panel the top of her head reaches barely to his shoulder. In this panel, as the columns of detailed painted hieroglyphs tell us, the couple are the "Scribe and Accountant of the Cattle and Fowl of Amūn, the confidant of [his] lord, Tḥut-nofre, called Senu," and "his beloved wife, (the object) of his affection, Ben-bu, the justified," shown in the act of "diverting the heart, gladdening the eye, and receiving the food [offerings which go forth in the presence . . .]." In the upper scene a son or other male relative, clad in a long, transparent over-kilt, stands facing the

FIGURE 91. Part of a painted sandstone doorjamb from a tomb chapel in the Theban necropolis. W. 15¾ in.

seated man and woman, whose chairs and feet rest upon a narrow reed mat conventionally represented as if seen from above. Aside from the fine, clean draughtsmanship our painting is distinguished by the freshness of its well-preserved colors —blue, green, yellow, red, black, and white against the pale, bluish gray background usual in the tomb chapels of this period. Tḥut-nofre, from whose tomb the painting probably came, is known from a number of other monuments, including a funerary ★cone in our collection on which he is called the Scribe and Accountant of the Cattle and Fowl on the Estate of Amūn. Whether, as has been suggested, he was identical with the Overseer of Peasants Tḥut-nofre, the owner of a tomb on the northeast slope of the Dirāʿ Abu'n Naga, is uncertain.

The style and technique of mid-Eighteenth Dynasty wall painting may be studied also on a small rectangle of ★painted mud plaster from an unidentified Theban(?) tomb chapel, on which appears the figure of a manservant carrying two bunches of geese suspended from the ends of a slender yoke. At the right edge of the piece is part of a light shelter in which sits another servant probably engaged in plucking and cleaning the waterfowl brought to him from a near-by bird net. Here again the tempera colors, laid on a thin over-coating of fine white plaster, are wonderfully well preserved.

The attractively painted fragment of figure 92 is part of a votive(?) ★wall hanging of yellow leather, from the shrine of Ḥat-Ḥor at Deir el Baḥri, on which were depicted erotic dances and other activities related to the cult of the goddess. Particularly charming is the slender figure of the girl musician who sits on her heels beneath an arching grape arbor, providing music for the dances on a great bow harp. Among a number of interesting details we may note the stand on which the harp rests, the girl's frivolously betasseled coiffure, and the curious, black, streamerlike objects which descend from the arm of the nude dancer. The corner of the hanging is reinforced with a small square of red leather and provided with a leather tie by means of which it was, presumably, suspended on the temple wall. A fringed and painted rectangle of linen ★cloth, ten by five and a half inches, had also been offered as an ex-voto in the Deir el Baḥri shrine. On it the goddess, labeled "Ḥat-Ḥor, who is in Thebes," appears as a cow standing on a barque in the midst of a tall thicket of papyrus reeds. Facing her stands the donor of the cloth, the "House Mistress Tuy," burning incense on a tall brazier and accompanied by two other women whose coiffures, like her own, are long and black and whose dresses are long and white. The little scene, deftly drawn in red and black outline and colored red, blue, black, and white, is framed, just inside the fringed edges of the cloth, by a white border striped in black and red.

The drawing of a young man driving his chariot and pair through a garden, which decorates the cover of this book, is executed in crisp black line on a ★plaque of deep greenish blue faience. Both the driver and his galloping steeds are drawn in a style which suggests the period of Tḥut-mosĕ IV or perhaps a little earlier, and this dating is borne out by the fact that the chariot wheel has only four spokes, not six as in later times (see fig. 175). Dr. Alfred O. Hermann of Bonn, who drew this to my attention, has suggested that the plaque may have been inlaid in the lid of a chest used to contain papyrus rolls with love songs or texts of a similar nature. The grapevine and wonderfully graceful little tree which provide the landscape setting for the scene are paralleled in the mural and vase paintings of the period. One of the latter, a drawing in heavy black outline on a ★fragment of a blue faience funerary jar, shows us a young woman kneeling with hands upraised beside a pool with lotus plants. In a column of cursive hieroglyphs before the figure are preserved the words "born of the House Mistress. . . ."

From an Eighteenth Dynasty tomb court on the north slope of the hill called el Khōkheh, in western Thebes, come the ★capstone and part of one ★jamb of a whitewashed sandstone gateway inscribed for the Overseer of the Workshop of Amūn, Wesy. The capstone, topped by a cavetto-and-torus cornice, is L-shaped in plan, with the socket for the upper pivot of the gate cut on its underside inside one arm of the L. Since in Wesy's title the name of the god Amūn has been erased, the gateway was evidently erected before the time of Akh-en-Aten (Amun-ḥotpe IV), and its style points to a date fairly well back in the Thutmoside period.

Fourteen private funerary ★stelae of Thutmoside date conform more or less to a type—a type developed, to be sure, during the late Middle

FIGURE 92. Fragment of a painted leather wall hanging. W. 7 in.

Kingdom, but treated now with a style and taste which are unmistakably of the early "Empire." They are, almost without exception, upright slabs of limestone, three to four inches thick, with straight, vertical sides and rounded tops. In one case the stela proper is represented as enclosed within a rectangular door frame, inscribed across the top and down the sides and crowned with a cavetto-and-torus cornice. Of the complete examples one is almost twenty-eight inches high, but the majority are of modest size, averaging around a foot and a half in height. More often than not, the owner of the stela is shown seated with his wife and other members of his family, smelling a lotus flower and regarding the food and floral offerings piled up on a table before him. Occasionally, however, he appears standing or kneeling, with hands upraised before him in the act of reciting a hymn to the sun god or to Osiris, and on a stela (fig. 24) which we have already had occasion to discuss, the Servitor Ḳen-Amūn burns incense and pours a libation before statues of the deified kings Amun-ḥotpe I and Se'n-Wosret I. When only mortals are represented, the motif in the lunette above their heads is the pair of *wedjat*-eyes flanking the *shenu*-symbol and offering bowl; but in three instances where men and gods appear face to face, the former are protected by a single eye, while a sun's disk with one wing hovers over the latter.

The brightly painted ★stela of figure 93, probably dedicated during the reign of Tḥut-mosĕ III, is typical. In the uppermost of the three registers His Majesty's Chariot-fighter Nen-waf and his wife the House Mistress Irenena sit facing one another across a table of offerings. Below, their son and daughter, Meru and Demi-wedja, appear in a similar grouping, the daughter, evidently a little girl, perched on the seat of her low chair with both feet drawn up as if she were sitting on the ground. It is amusing to note that while the ladies grip their lotus buds in realistic fashion, the flexible stems held by the men are made to curl up in a conventional (and highly improbable) manner so that the flowers come just in front of their holders' faces. The third register is taken up, as almost always, by a *ḥtp-di-nsw* formula calling upon Osiris to supply the family with the usual funerary offerings. Said to have come from Ḳau el Kebīr in Upper Egypt, Nen-waf's stela has retained its original colors—light and dark red, yellow, blue, brown, black, and white—in a remarkable state of preservation.

In the upper of two registers of a very similar ★stela we see a standing figure of the owner's son, the Scribe Amun-ḥotpe, presenting a table of offerings to his parents, the Scribe and Accountant of the Cattle of Amūn, Ḥu-my, and the House Mistress Senet-nefret, who sit side by side on lion-legged chairs, the man smelling a huge lotus flower, the woman's hands resting in an affectionate gesture on her husband's left shoulder and right arm. In the register below, a second seated couple, labeled the "Scribe Pa-ḥered" and the "Chantress of Amūn, Amun-ḥotpe," are confronted by a standing man ("His Majesty's Chariot-fighter Amun-ḥotpe") and a youth clad in a short kilt ("his son, the Scribe Amun-em-ḥēt"). The small figure of a girl named Amun-em-Opet kneels beneath the lady Amun-ḥotpe's chair and reaches up to touch the older woman's leg. The clothing and coiffures of the men appearing in these small scenes, though not elaborate, are interestingly varied. All the adult males wear, over a short kilt, a long over-kilt, the transparency of which has been most successfully rendered by the ancient sculptor and painter. Ḥu-my wears, in addition, a thin shirt with tight sleeves reaching to just above the elbows, and his wig, like that of Pa-ḥered in the register below, is long, full, and quite plain. The wigs seen on the two standing men, on the other hand, are of the short, caplike type with rows of short, square-cut locks, or tufts, while the youthful scribe Amun-em-ḥēt wears no wig, but only his own close-cropped hair. Except for the short labels with the names and titles of the people represented, the stela is not inscribed.

A third ★stela of the same type, but with its rather spindly figures executed in *relief en creux*, acquaints us with an Upper Egyptian family composed of a *Wēʿb*-priest of Kheper-ku-Rēʿ (the deified King Se'n-Wosret I) named Pa-ḥu-ro, his similarly titled son Amun-em-Opet, two other

FIGURE 93.
Painted limestone stela of the Chariot-fighter Nen-waf and his family. H. 22 ¼ in.

sons, Men-kheper and Mery, and "his beloved sister" (i.e., wife) Mery. Like guests at New Kingdom banquets Pa-ḥu-ro and his wife have their long wigs surmounted by cones of perfumed ointment. In the lower of the stela's two registers Amun-em-Opet, who functions as mortuary priest for his parents and his elder brother, wears a leopard skin with long pendent tail. His name has twice been damaged by agents of Akh-en-Aten in their efforts to obliterate all mention of the god Amūn.

A ★stela abandoned unfinished by one of the sculptors of Ḥat-shepsūt's temple at Deir el Baḥri shows in its single scene a man seated with two women and confronted by another man who stands extending his hand toward the trio across a small table of offerings. Above, in the lunette, are the *wedjat*-eyes and *shenu*-symbol and, below, a two-line offering formula, only partially carved and with the space for the name of the owner of the stela left blank. A similar ★stela, on which, however, a single couple sit facing one another across a table of offerings and above a five-line offering formula, is interesting because the owner and his wife, though represented in conventional Egyptian attire, are shown by their names to have been Semites—probably Syrians. The man's name, Yetʿa(?)-Baʿal, has been thought to mean "Baʿal's-friend." That of the woman, Mesutu, has not been translated. The offering formula in this case invokes the gods Sokar and Osiris, "Ruler of Eternity."

Of the same general period but more elaborately inscribed is a ★stela dedicated by Aʿḥ-mosĕ, a sanctuary priest of Montu in Hermonthis, in honor of his father, the Lector Priest Tḥūty, his uncle(?) also named Tḥūty, his mother, Rui-nofret, and a dozen other members of his extensive family. In the uppermost of three crowded registers Aʿḥ-mosĕ stands before the two Tḥūtys and Rui-nofret, who sit together at the left of the scene, the men, as usual, smelling lotus flowers. In the middle register the donor appears again, this time in the presence of his maternal aunt and his sister, both named Ru. The central portion of this register is taken up by six vertical columns of inscription containing Aʿḥ-mosĕ's dedication and an offering formula invoking the triad of Hermonthis—Montu, Tjenenyet, and Yuny(et)—in behalf of "Tḥūty, whose mother is Neḥi and whose father is Mosĕ." Twelve additional beneficiaries are named in the four lines of text at the bottom of the stela. Besides the Lector Priest Tḥūty and his wife, and the mortuary priest of Queen Tety-shery's royal daughter Aʿḥ-mosĕ, referred to in our first chapter, nine men are listed here, six of whom were butcher priests, one a simple *wēʿb*-priest, and one a *Wēʿb*-priest of Montu. The home of this priestly family, so many of whom served the god Montu of Hermonthis, was presumably Hermonthis itself, the present-day Erment, on the west bank of the Nile some eight miles south of Thebes.

The ★stela which we have mentioned as being enclosed within a rectangular door frame and which, in point of fact, is represented only by a large fragment, was carved for the Temple Attendant of Amūn, Ipu-nefer, and his wife the House Mistress Ashayet—evidently contemporaries of one of the earlier Thutmoside rulers. On the stela proper an offering formula, written in vertical columns above the seated couple, invokes the god Osiris in their behalf, while on the outer frame Amūn, Lord of Karnak, is called upon to give to their spirits "a coming and going in the necropolis, the food offerings which go forth in the presence of the Lord of the Gods, and everything which goes forth from upon his offering table." As on all our other early Thutmoside stelae the inscriptions are incised and the figures are carved in low relief.

This is true also of a fragmentary stela of excellent quality donated to our collection by James Douglas. Here, however, we see the owner and his wife standing in adoration before a mummiform figure of the god Osiris, who sits enthroned at the left of the scene, wearing the *atef*-crown and holding in his hands the *was*-scepter and the crook and *ladanisterion*. He is described in the text above as "Osiris, Ruler of Eternity, the Great God, King of the Living," and is addressed by the stela's owner, the Overseer of the Magazine of Amūn, Neb-Amūn, in the following words: "Homage to you,

Bull-of-the-West, kindly ruler, Lord of Eternity. I have come to you to exalt you and worship your goodness. Let me rest in the Place-of-eternity, in the necropolis, and in the favor of Amūn, for my heart is without falsehood." Over the head of the deity hovers a sun's disk with one down-sweeping wing, and above Neb-Amūn and his wife the "House Mistress Ḥuy" is a single large *wedjat*-eye. Though the style of the relief is like that of the stelae which we have been discussing, the facial types, wig types, and clothing of the two mortals point to a date fairly well down in the Thutmoside era. This is particularly true of the figure of the lady, who wears a very long, tight dress with the hem line slanting downward to her heels, and a huge and elaborate wig crowned by a fillet from which a lotus bud hangs down over her forehead.

Much the same scene occupies the upper register of a small limestone ★stela inscribed for the "Servant of [Amūn] . . . and his wife the House Mistress Ḥenwet-nefret"; but here the figures are carved in sunk relief, the adoring couple are separated from the seated god by a table of offerings, and the inscriptions in the rounded lunette of the little monument give only the name and epithets of Osiris and the titles and names of his worshipers. In what remains of the lower register a young man with shaven head and three scantily clad young women, wearing long, full wigs bound with fillets and crowned with cones of perfume, are seen moving toward the left carrying long-stemmed papyrus plants and other offerings. Again, the style of the work and the types of garments shown suggest a relatively late date. Since, however, the name Amūn is erased in the title and probably also in the name of the owner of the stela, its carving must have antedated the reign of Akh-en-Aten, though perhaps by only a few decades. It is said to have come from near the pyramid of Meidūm.

On another ★stela, acquired in 1890 as a gift of Mr. Douglas, the object of the owner's devotions is a standing Osiride figure of a deified king wearing on his head the White Crown with uraeus and on his chin the straight, square-cut beard of pharaonic type. Over him the solar disk hovers on a single wing and in his hands he holds the attributes of Osiris, the crook and *ladanisterion* together with a long *was*-scepter which slants diagonally downward across the slender mummiform figure. The decoration of the stela is completed by a small offering table attended by the figure of a man with close-cropped hair who wears a long, simple kilt and holds in his hands a slender libation vase and a brazier with burning incense. Short hieroglyphic labels which once identified the king and his worshiper have been chopped away and the gouges left by their removal have been filled with plaster.

The upper half of a large sandstone ★stela, formerly in the Amherst collection, shows us the Keeper of the Treasury of Amūn, Ḥuy, in the act of pouring a libation and burning incense before seated figures of the gods Osiris and Anubis. Behind the two great Underworld deities stands the goddess Ḥat-Ḥor wearing on her head the symbol of the "West" (𓋀) and described in the text above her as "Ḥat-Ḥor, Mistress of the Necropolis of the West, Opposite-its-lord." The last phrase is a well-known expression for western Thebes (opposite, or across from, its lord, Amūn of Karnak) and discloses the provenience of the stela, which is otherwise unrecorded. Ḥuy, his hair close cropped, and clad only in a long kilt with a plain triangular apron, pours his libation over a table of offerings which separates him from the divine trio. The slender figures and their accessories are executed in *relief en creux* in a crisp and wholly conventional style. Thirteen columns of incised hieroglyphic text in the rounded lunette above their heads comprise offering formulae invoking each of the deities represented. The longest and most interesting of these calls upon Osiris to grant to the spirit of our treasury official "a following of Sokar . . . on the day of going round the walls (of Memphis)" and other boons of a similarly mystical nature. Of the lower register of the stela all that remains are the tops of the hieroglyphic labels which accompanied the figures of Ḥuy's sons and other members of his evidently extensive family.

Except for the *wedjat*-eyes of its lunette, a ★stela believed to be from Ḳau el Kebīr is entirely taken up with the standing figures of the owner and his wife, executed in *relief en creux*, and by a long hymn which the man, his hands raised before him, is in the act of addressing to the deities of the sun and the moon. Though the hymn, which is engraved before the figures in five long vertical columns of hieroglyphs, is entitled "Praising Rēʿ Ḥor-akhty and Tḥōt, fair one of the eight," it begins "Homage to you, Atūm Khepri, the self-produced." Continuing, we read: "You have risen from the High Place and have shone forth from the *benben*-stone (see p. 281) and the eastern horizon of heaven. (Now) you go to rest in the western horizon of heaven and those who are in the Barque-of-the-morning and the Barque-of-the-evening, the spirits of the Westerners and the spirits of the Easterners, and the shrines of Upper and Lower Egypt (rejoice?). Rēʿ Ḥor-akhty sets in life, his rays on the breasts of the *Wēʿb*-priest Imen, and his wife Inet-Ḥaʿpy. . . . Rēʿ Ḥor-akhty goes to rest as one justified after he has overthrown his enemies each day." An interesting sidelight on the persistence of Egyptian religious ideas is the fact that the opening lines of this hymn go back to the Pyramid Texts of the Old Kingdom (see Part I, pp. 82 f.). Inet-Ḥaʿpy does not join her husband in his worship, but stands behind him languidly smelling a lotus flower. Her coiffure and dress are dully conventional, but his close-cropped head, the flaring apron of his short kilt, and the elaborately stylish sandals which he wears on his feet give his figure an air of almost foppish elegance.

On the big sandstone ★stela of figure 94 the owner is twice represented kneeling in adoration before the sun god. On the right he faces the east and is seen, as the short, horizontal caption near the top of the stela tells us, "adoring Rēʿ when he rises on the eastern horizon of heaven"; on the left he faces west and pays his respects to the deity as the latter "sets in life on the horizon which is on the western mountain." The vertical columns of inscription start with the preposition "by" and simply repeat the owner's name, Amun-ḥotpe, preceded in each case by a different title or group of titles and followed, in the outside columns, by

FIGURE 94. Stela of a many-titled official named Amun-ḥotpe. Mid-Eighteenth Dynasty. Sandstone. H. 27¾ in.

the names of his parents and grandparents. Besides being an Overseer of Priests of Mīn and Isis, Amun-ḥotpe held many offices in the administration of Amūn's temples and estates, serving the god as overseer of the latter's "foreign lands," gardens, and granaries, as keeper of his storeroom and chief of his weavers, and as a temple attendant "in the second phyle." He was also a *ku*-servant, or mortuary priest, of three Eighteenth Dynasty kings, Amun-ḥotpe I, Tḥut-mosĕ I, and Tḥut-mosĕ III—mention of the last-named pharaoh supplying, incidentally, a *terminus a quo* for the dating of the stela. A *terminus ante quem*—that is, before the death of Amun-ḥotpe III—is provided by the erasure throughout the inscription of the name of Amūn; but this is scarcely necessary, since the style and iconography of the monument has already told us that it belongs well back in Thutmoside times, perhaps even in the reign of Tḥut-mosĕ III himself. In serving the god Amūn, Amun-ḥotpe seems to have been following a family tradition, for his father, Bak, was a Temple Attendant of Amūn, his mother, Roy, was a Chantress of Amūn, and both his grandfathers, Kames and Ruru, bear the priestly title First King's Son of Amūn. Besides the eyes and the usual axial symbols the lunette of our stela contains, at the corners, the hieroglyphic signs  and , standing presumably for "anointing oil" and "incense." This tends to bear out the belief that the bowl and ripples of water between the eyes also represent offerings.

Of a somewhat different nature from those which we have been studying is a small limestone votive ★stela dedicated by the Overseer of the Magazine Neb-iry to the sky goddess Nūt, whose figure, carved in relief, appears alone on the little slab seated beside a table of offerings. Represented as a woman, but wearing a wig and dress of archaic type, the goddess holds in her hands the *was*-scepter and the symbol of "life," while over her head hovers the solar disk with pendent uraei and great, down-sweeping falcon wings. The name "Nūt," having as its determinative the coiled uraeus (), is engraved beside her head, and below her feet a single line of hastily incised hieroglyphs gives the title and name of her devotee—probably added after the stela was purchased from a stock of similar votives.

Comparable in purpose, though much more modestly conceived and rarely of any artistic pretensions, are some sixty small ★plaques of stone, faience, sheet copper, and wood which had been deposited as ex-votos in the shrine of the cow goddess Ḥat-Ḥor at Deir el Baḥri. The cult of the Theban Ḥat-Ḥor, one of the principal divinities of the capital's vast necropolis, reached the peak of its popularity during the reigns of Ḥat-shepsūt, Tḥut-mosĕ III, and Amun-ḥotpe II, and it is probably to this period that the majority of our votive plaques are to be assigned. Most numerous are the plaques with representations of the goddess in the form of a long-horned cow, carrying between her horns the disk of the sun and having suspended from a collar about her neck either the symbol of life or a large lotus flower. On an interesting limestone plaque, seven inches in length, three such cows, carefully carved in low relief, stand side by side on a pedestal, while over their heads arches a large papyrus reed symbolizing the thickets of Chemmis, where the infant Horus was born. A single cow figure, molded in relief on a plaque of bright blue faience, has its horns, hoofs, and body markings picked out in black glaze. On nineteen rough little plaques of sheet copper the figure of the animal is engraved in outline with varying degrees of skill and is sometimes accompanied by a small table of offerings or by a large pair of human eyes. Two elongated oval plaques, also of copper, carry in each case a pair of Ḥat-Ḥor cows face to face. All are provided near their top edges with holes for suspension. There are, in addition, four little figures of cows and one duck cut out of copper sheeting and equipped with tubes or holes by means of which they could have been suspended from cords. The characteristic full-face human head of the goddess, with its massive headdress and projecting cow's ears, occurs twice on an oblong strip of copper and once on a tiny silver plaque, while a pentagonal piece of copper sheet bears the same head surmounting a crudely drawn female figure. On a small rectangular bronze plaque the goddess or one of her devotees appears as a standing female figure engraved in outline in the surface of the metal. Our votive representations of Ḥat-Ḥor are completed by a barbarously modeled head in gray faience.

To assure their being seen and heard by the great tutelary goddess many supplicants at her Deir el Baḥri shrine presented plaques engraved with or carved in the forms of human eyes and ears. Of the eye plaques twenty examples of copper bear one or two pairs of eyes incised in outline on their surfaces, while single examples of gritstone and faience, shaped like small, round-topped stelae, have eyes carved upon them in low relief. More often than not the ear plaques consist simply of the

FIGURE 95. A hippopotamus painted in three colors on a flake of limestone. L. 4 ¾ in.

ears themselves, molded of faience or cut out and beaten to shape from sections of copper sheet. In one case, however, a pair of ears is carved in relief on the front of a little round-topped stela of wood, which for purposes of suspension has a hole drilled through it from side to side.

3. Ostraka with Paintings, Drawings, and Inscriptions

In fourteen little ★paintings and ★sketches, done chiefly on flakes of limestone, we catch the draughtsmen of the Theban necropolis in a far more relaxed mood than they exhibit in their finished work as preserved to us on tomb and temple walls and in costly illustrated papyri. Whether the drawings are preliminary studies of elements for tomb or temple scenes or merely works produced for their own sakes—to display the draughtsman's skill, to edify a pupil, or merely to provide amusement—they share in common an engaging lack of restraint, a freshness of feeling, and a lightness and boldness of execution which reveal the Egyptian artist at his charming and talented best.

Having been produced for the most part by draughtsmen employed in and about Ḥat-shepsūt's temple at Deir el Baḥri and in Sen-ne-mūt's tomb chapel on the Hill of the Sheikh ʿAbd el Ḳurneh, the ostraka of the present series belong to the middle decades of the Thutmoside era and probably to the half century between 1500 and 1450 B.C. As already implied, the flakes of limestone and shale used for these drawings are small, the largest measuring only seven by four inches.

A little painting of a hippopotamus (fig. 95), probably to be used as a model for a detailed hieroglyph ( ), was neatly drawn in crisp black outline and skillfully painted in attractive solid colors, the body of the beast a purplish brown, his belly, eyes, and ears a bright pinkish red. The head of a bull, drawn on a grid of proportion squares and painted in five colors, may also have been intended as a hieroglyph ( ). Drawn first in thin red outline and then in thin black outline, the head was subsequently painted: the horns blue green, the neck brown, the muzzle red, the face brown, black, and red. Finally a pale blue wash was applied to the surface of the stone in a rectangle around the head. On the sides of the flakes are red and greenish blue practice strokes and "palette blobs." In a delicate, colored drawing of a sparrow ( )—a hieroglyph used chiefly as a determinative for words meaning "small," "poor," "bad," and the like—the little bird is given a pink body with red details and black legs, eye, and beak. Another much used bird hieroglyph, the duckling ( ), is sketched rapidly but deftly in heavy black outline on a flake of limestone four inches in height. In figure 96 we see the preliminary drawing for a group of signs which occurs frequently at Deir el Baḥri and in other Egyptian temples following the name of the king and which wishes him (or, in this case, her?) "all life, stability, and well-being." To ensure the proper proportions and spacing for the large, formal hieroglyphs the draughtsman has laid them out in thin red outline on a grid of proportion squares, also drawn in red, and has subsequently corrected and consolidated their outlines with black ink. Proportion squares, ruled, as usual, in thin red line, were used in the production of a fairly large, formal, and extremely detailed drawing of the falcon hieroglyph 𓅃, and even for a sensitive little sketch of the head of a donkey, though the latter is less than an inch and three-quarters in height.

A small flake of limestone from the earlier of Sen-ne-mūt's two tombs (No. 71) carries a well-drawn sketch in black line of a bound and slaughtered bull, exactly like several which occur in the reliefs of Ḥat-shepsūt's temple. It is a second attempt, traces of an earlier version of the same subject, erased by the draughtsman himself, appearing on the back of the limestone flake. The figure of a walking ibex, outlined in charcoal on a potsherd, was evidently being held in leash by one of a procession of offering bearers. Close parallels to this also are to be found in the southern hall of offerings of the Deir el Baḥri temple.

Of four informal sketches destined for no more serious purpose than to amuse their authors and their authors' companions, one of the most interesting is a valiant, if unsuccessful, effort to represent a seated dog with head turned sharply backward, scratching its chin with a hind foot. Two crude little drawings found in or near Sen-ne-mūt's Deir el Baḥri tomb show a workman seated on the ground, holding before him a large rectangular object, and a hideously ugly dignitary seated on a chair, holding to his snub nose what is probably to be identified as a long-stemmed lotus flower. In a deftly drawn caricature the "Scribe of the Garrison Troops Pa-shenu-ro," whose title and name are written above his head in an excellent hieratic hand, is portrayed as a ridiculous, fat little figure brandishing a shield in one hand and an axe in the other. Even the name assigned to the pseudo warrior, which means the "Ailing-of-speech" or something of the sort, seems to be part of the gibe.

The architect's ★plan of figure 97 is not a sketch, but part of a finished drawing executed with considerable care upon a stucco-covered wooden panel which was once joined by pegged battens to another panel of about the same size. On the basis of its style the drawing has been dated by Norman de Garis Davies to the early part of the Eighteenth Dynasty. It was, thus, contemporary with the ostraka which we have just been considering. From the extremely detailed measurements written in here and there, it would seem to have been a drawing, made roughly to the scale of 1:225, of an already existing complex of buildings. The principal building, seen in plan at the upper left-hand corner of our panel, is a rectangular structure designated as being "29 cubits" (about fifty feet) in length and "23 cubits, 3 palms, 2 digits" (about forty feet) in width, mounted apparently on a raised podium, approached from either end by a short flight of steps. Both the form and the size of the building suggest one of the small, raised chapels provided as stations, or resting places, for the portable barque of the god Amūn and placed at intervals along the processional way to be followed by the sacred vessel, not only on its tours of the temple precinct at Karnak, but also on its annual trip across the Nile to visit the temples of western Thebes. The chapel here is surrounded by a row of trees and, at a distance of "10 cubits" (about seventeen feet) by a light wall of mud brick (?) which is joined on the right by a much heavier wall bounding a tree-lined alley "32 cubits" or

FIGURE 96. A group of hieroglyphs. Limestone ostrakon. H. 6 ¼ in.

roughly fifty-five feet in breadth. The broad band of wavy lines at the bottom of the board indicates that our chapel was situated on the bank of a large body of water, probably the Nile itself, and suggests that the small structure between the chapel and the water's edge was a landing stage which, like the one before the great temple of Amūn at Karnak, was surmounted at the front by a small, rectangular altar. The board, presented to the Museum by Mr. Davies, was acquired by him in western Thebes. All things considered, it seems not improbable that we have here the plan of a small propylaeum complex built by Ḥat-shepsūt or Tḥut-mosĕ III at the foot of the ʿAsāsīf valley, on the edge of the Nile flood plain, to serve as a point of arrival for the barque of Amūn at the end of its voyage across the river from Karnak on the opposite bank.

FIGURE 97. Part of an architect's plan drawn in red and black ink upon a stucco-covered board. H. 13 ⅞ in.

Some twoscore ★ostraka of Thutmoside date in the Museum's collection are inscribed in hieratic with work reports, lists of people and supplies, memoranda exchanged between the scribes and foremen of the Theban necropolis, and, in rare instances, bits of literary and religious texts. They come chiefly from rubbish mounds east of Ḥat-shepsūt's temple at Deir el Baḥri, from a workmen's village at Deir el Medīneh, three-quarters of a mile to the southwest, and from the Valley of the Tombs of the Kings. Typical of the daily reports on the progress of the work at Deir el Baḥri is the ostrakon of figure 98, which is written in the small, neat, business hand characteristic of the reigns of Ḥat-shepsūt and Tḥut-mosĕ III. The first part of this document (lines 1-5) is dated to "Month 2 of Prōyet, Day 10," and is entitled "Work of this day: . . ." It records the preparation by stonemasons of fifteen blocks of stone of two varieties and the speedy transportation by "porters" of twenty-one blocks "to the sanctuary," and includes a progress report on an excavation(?) being carried out by the masons. The second half of the report (lines 6-10) is dated to "Month 2 of Prōyet, Day 11," and reads: "Work of this day: the porters, 5 men, transported 30 blocks of stone to the sanctuary. The stonemasons, 2 men. Work on the bricks, [1] man: the mason Amun-ḥotpe, 40 (bricks)." Another flake of limestone, inscribed on both sides and dated simply to "Day 12," lists by title and name forty-two middle-class Thebans who contributed (to the temple?) a total of "176 stones"—perhaps votive name stones of the type described on page 88. Included in this most interesting and varied roster are *wēʿb*-priests, boat skippers, chiefs and employees of the royal magazines, gardeners, doorkeepers, hairdressers, a herald, a king's scribe, a confectioner, a bouquet(?) maker, a housewife, and a number of untitled citizens with more or less common Theban names. In a brief work memorandum written by a harried foreman to his superior we read: "To the effect that Aʿḥ-mosĕ does not allow us to haul paving blocks (but) sets the people to hauling pillars; we have hauled (only) one paving block, which was put into the ramp(?)." On the back of the flake, in the same handwriting, a "list of the serfs who came to haul stone" includes "40 men" who were under the jurisdiction of the "Second Prophet," an official probably to be identified with the well-known architect and Second Prophet of Amūn, Puy-em-Rēʿ (see pp. 88, 113). Even briefer is a communication written on a small lump of limestone and entitled "Further to ʿAby (a man's name): . . ." It reads: "Give those who are not provided 10 staves likewise, that they may be equipped. See to it! See to it!" A much longer note, appended to a list of people, begins: "Behold, Mesdjer ('the Ear') arrived with a man of Medu (Medamūd) and said, 'Have him make for you 3 staves'; and he placed the loincloth in the hand of Inebna. I measured a staff for him, (but) I heeded the proverb (about) the child who was in the burning town and went to have a look . . ." and rambles on and on, ending with the injunction: "If he speaks to you of his work, pay attention! Pay attention! Listen to him!"

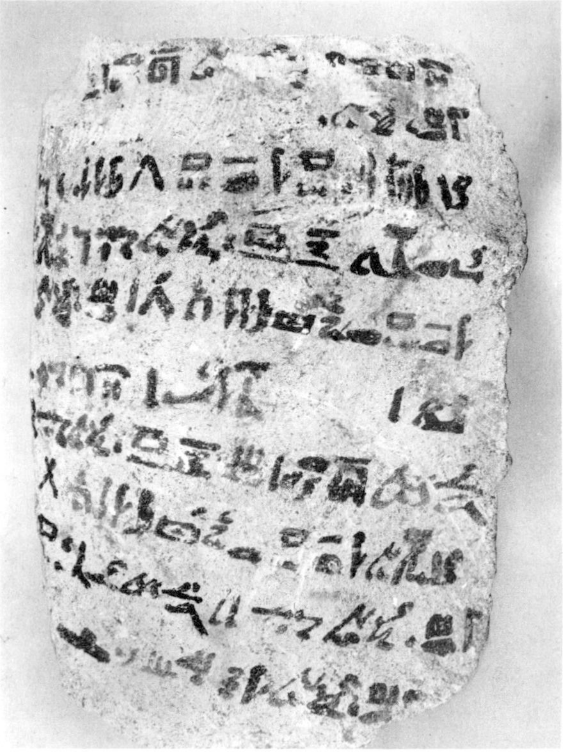

FIGURE 98. Hieratic ostrakon from western Thebes. Limestone. H. 4½ in.

An ostrakon of unknown provenience, acquired in 1890, was once thought to be a medical prescription, but has long been recognized for what it is: an inventory of painters' pigments and vehicles. Listed are "blue pigment," "green pigment," "lampblack," "white pigment of Kush," "gum," and so on, the last entry being the summation "all colors." From the Valley of the Tombs of the Kings comes an ostrakon recording the issuance of supplies over a period of six months or more in the twenty-fifth regnal year of an unnamed king—probably Thut-mosĕ III.

On an ostrakon supposed to have come from Deir el Medīneh a similar list is preceded by four lines copied from a popular literary text of the type known as a "teaching" or "instruction," addressed in this case by an unnamed man to his son. Other copies of the same text are preserved in a leather manuscript in the British Museum, a papyrus in the Louvre, and numerous ostraka of the Eighteenth Dynasty and later times. The passage selected by the copyist of our ostrakon runs: "You have achieved greatness. Behold, you have passed your life in accordance with the will of the God concerning you. (Now) worship the King of Upper Egypt and glorify the King of Lower Egypt. . . ." On a pottery ostrakon from the ʿAsāsīf valley we recognize without difficulty parts of three lines from the beginning of a well-known hymn to Ḥaʿpy, the god of the inundation of the Nile, a hymn most completely preserved in two British Museum papyri of the later New Kingdom.

The remaining thirty or so ostraka of Thutmoside date in the Museum's collection conform more or less closely to the types discussed above. So also do the hundreds of examples found by our expedition in western Thebes, which, after being photographed, copied and transcribed by our staff, were turned over to the Egyptian Museum in Cairo.

Four potsherds bearing hieratic dockets in black ink were evidently inscribed while they were still parts of the shoulders of large store jars and are therefore to be classed not as ostraka but as ★jar labels. Two are dated to "Regnal Year 2" and "Regnal Year 28" respectively, of a king or kings whose names are not given. All specify the contents of their jars, in two instances a liquid called *shedet*, associated in one case with a man named Seni-mosĕ and said to be "from the House (i.e., the estate) of the King." One label consists of the single word "Incense," and the fourth lists "wine of the estate . . . from the storehouse of the chief vintner. . . ."

In 1927 the Museum's Expedition recovered from the rubbish in the court of Ḥat-shepsūt's temple a brief but complete ★letter, written in hieratic on a strip of papyrus (fig. 99), as well as two fragments of a second ★letter of the same period though of somewhat different type. Both documents belong without much doubt to the joint reign of Ḥat-shepsūt and Tḥut-mosĕ III. The complete letter, found neatly folded and addressed on the outside from a man named Tet "to his master, Tḥūty," refers to some jurisdictional friction between the addressee and a fellow official in the Memphite-Heliopolitan area over a group of workmen(?) brought to Thebes from that area. "Tet," runs the text of the letter, "greets his master, Tḥūty—may he live, prosper, and be well!—in the favor of Amun Rēʿ. It is a dispatch to acquaint my master with the word concerning Ptaḥ-Sokar, forasmuch as it is you who has transgressed against him in the matter of the people of Heliopolis. Discuss (the matter) with the Herald Goreg-Men-nefer, so that you may send a letter concerning him to the Greatest of Seers." The writer of the note is difficult to identify, but the addressee was probably Ḥat-shepsūt's well-known chancellor and architect Tḥūty. To judge from their names, both Ptaḥ-Sokar and the Herald Goreg-Men-nefer were Memphites. The latter has long been known to us as the owner of two alabaster canopic jars in the Museum of Art in Cleveland. Though a Greatest of Seers existed at this time at Karnak and elsewhere in Upper Egypt, the one referred to here was in all probability the high priest of Rēʿ at Heliopolis.

The second letter, written by a woman to her brother Khaʿ, has the name of the addressee inscribed on the outside of the larger of the two fragments of papyrus. On the inside the following phrases from the beginning of the letter have survived: ". . . -khrod greets her brother, [Khaʿ, in life,] prosperity, and health, and in the favor [of Sokar, Lord of Shet]yet, and says, 'Hail to you!' . . . their . . . to the effect that I have caused to be brought. . . ." If the god invoked in the formula of greeting was indeed Sokar, Lord of Shetyet, there is considerable probability that the letter was written from the region of Memphis, a hypothesis supported by the handwriting, which differs markedly from the Theban hand of our other letter.

FIGURE 99. Administrative letter from Deir el Baḥri, written in hieratic script on a strip of papyrus. L. 7 in.

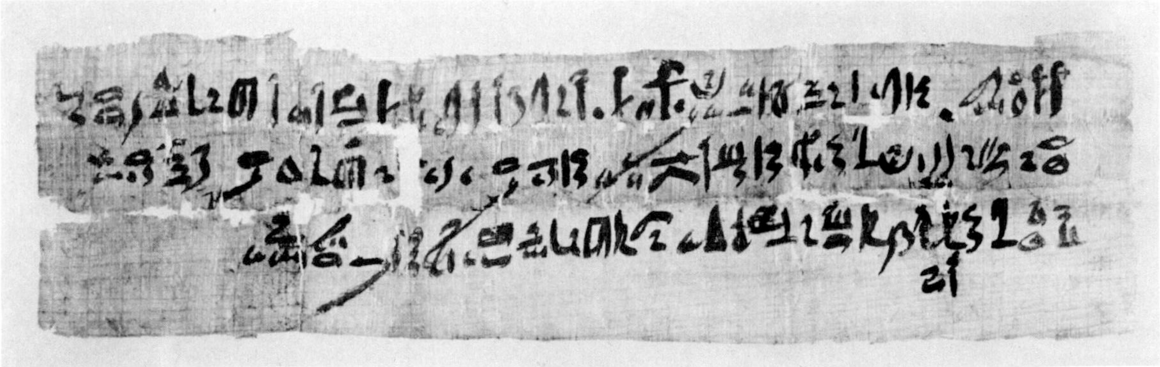

4. Jewelry

In contrast to that found in the royal burials of the Middle and New Kingdoms, the bulk of the jewelry worn in life and death by the subjects of the Thutmoside pharaohs and their successors consisted of small beads and amulets strung together on linen threads to form light, flexible, and relatively unpretentious items of adornment. Though worn primarily as ornaments, the ancient necklaces, bracelets, and girdles so composed were probably always thought of as possessing protective powers, whether made up of the simple spherical, cylindrical, or discoid forms which we normally classify as beads or of the more elaborate elements which we recognize as amulets. In many cases the amuletic power of the individual elements depended as much upon the materials of which they were made—gold, silver, semiprecious stones, or faience—as upon their shapes. In considering this jewelry, therefore, we shall be well advised not to attempt too strict a differentiation between beads and amulets, especially since, as in the scaraboid and drop-shaped forms, such a differentiation is frequently not possible.

Before taking up the different classes of assembled ornaments represented in our collection it will, however, be useful to run rapidly through the types of individual elements used in the composition of these ornaments, many of which are preserved to us in single examples or in unstrung groups. Among the simpler forms the spherical, cylindrical, disk-shaped, ring-shaped, barrel-shaped, and drop-shaped ★beads (and/or amulets) remain as popular as they were during the Middle Kingdom and the Hyksos period, but tend to be smaller and more slenderly proportioned than in the earlier periods. Exceptions to this are the large, hollow balls of blue- and black-glazed faience (see fig. 100), strings of which seem to have been offered as votives in the shrine of the goddess Ḥat-Ḥor at Deir el Baḥri. Other hollow ball beads, also of blue faience, are perforated with rectangular and triangular holes, producing an attractive openwork effect, while an isolated spherical bead, half an inch in diameter, has a band of *wedjat*-eyes molded in relief around its middle. Besides the true spheres there are roughly shaped beads of the same general class, best described as spheroids, and corrugated globes to which the name "nasturtium seeds" has been applied. Rhomboid, cowroid, and lozenge-shaped beads are found in limited numbers, as are also flat beads having the form of small square or oval plaques. Large lenticular beads strung on stout cords to form one or a series of short necklaces, or chokers, on the other hand, are exceedingly common and continue popular down into Ramesside times (see figs. 70, 100). Particularly characteristic of the earlier Thutmoside age are necklace beads of scarablike or scaraboid shape, usually made of bright blue faience and not infrequently inscribed with a good wish, the name of a divinity, or the like (see fig. 100). Single and double cylindrical beads are occasionally adorned with incised crisscross patterns or are grooved to present a ringed or corrugated appearance; and from western Thebes come several groups of light tubular beads made of sheet gold and silver. Besides the common drop, lozenge, pear, and ball shapes, pendant beads begin to branch out into the natural forms—leaves, flower petals, cornflowers, palmettes, grape clusters, dates, pomegranates, and flies—which are so characteristic of the jewelry of the late Eighteenth Dynasty and the Ramesside period. Flat, semicircular beads, believed to represent disks of leather folded once and stitched around the edges, occur with some frequency, not only in girdles (see fig. 73), but also occasionally in bracelets (see fig. 101). A few isolated fancy shapes include a four-petaled flower of blue faience, and beads in the form of double frogs, which, however, are only with some doubt assigned to Thutmoside times. Natural ★shells used as beads are far less common than in the earlier periods, and a string of small, spiral shells from an Eighteenth Dynasty tomb at Abydos is something of a rarity. On the other hand, shell is among the more common materials employed in the manufacture of the ubiquitous small disk and ring beads. Of the other materials represented in our Thutmoside bead series the outstanding favorite is faience, which occurs not only in various shades of blue and green, but also in red, purple, yellow, black, and white. Beads carved of such hard, semiprecious stones as carnelian, lapis lazuli, agate, garnet, emerald matrix, and red and green jasper, however, are far from rare, and we also find scattered examples in glazed steatite, blue paste, glass, bone, gold, and even gold-plated wood. A pair of small conical objects fashioned of the last-named material seem to be the ★tips from the ends of a necklace. Also probably from a necklace is a set of twelve ★spacers, each composed of four small tubes of sheet gold soldered together side by side. The remnants of two or more broad collars similar to those of the three Syrian wives of King Tḥut-mosĕ III (see pp. 131, 133) comprise not only lozenge-shaped beads of carnelian and cylindrical and drop-shaped beads of gold, but also flat gold ★elements, both scale-shaped and drop-shaped, inlaid with light and dark blue glass.

The more elaborate ★amulets, made of the same materials as the foregoing and apparently worn at this period by both the living and the dead, occur either singly or combined with strings of the simpler elements described above to form what we nowadays call charm necklaces and bracelets (see fig. 101). They divide themselves by form and purpose into several fairly well defined groups. Figures of divinities in human or semihuman form are far less common at this period than in later times, but our Thutmoside amulets include minute statuettes of the gods Osiris, Thōt, and Horus the Child (Harpokrates), of the goddesses Bastet, Sakhmet, Mūt, Ḥat-Ḥor (head only), Maʿet, and Thoueris, and of the grotesque little demigod Bēs. Far more numerous are those which represent animals, birds, fish, and insects. Here we encounter not only animals associated with readily identifiable divinities, but others not so associated whose strength, courage, or other characteristics it was hoped to achieve; and still others, of a dangerous and inherently hostile nature, which must be propitiated or warded off. Included in this general category are small figures, rendered with varying degrees of realism and detail, of apes, beetles, bulls, calves, cats, cows, ducks, falcons, flies, foxes (heads only), frogs, ibexes, ibises, ichneumons, jackals, leopards (heads only), lions, locusts, pigeons, rams, scorpions, snakes, tadpoles, and vultures. Though not nearly as numerous as in the Middle Kingdom and preceding periods, amulets in the form of parts of the human body—the eye, the ear, the face, the hand, the heart, and others—continued to be produced and to be worn either as strengtheners or as possible substitutes for the members represented. Several, including the hand, undoubtedly served also to ensure the general health and safety of their wearers. The ever-popular *wedjat*-eye of the god Horus occurs with great frequency, carved in the round or silhouetted in openwork plaques. Familiar symbols, such as the sign of "life," the *djed*-pillar (for "stability"), the *was*-scepter (for "well-being"), the *nefer*-sign (for "goodness"), the *shenu*-loop (for "universal power"), the *sa*-sign (for "protection"), the *tjeset*-knot (for "cohesion"), and the hieroglyph for "eternity" retain a popularity as amulets which in most cases dates back to the Old Kingdom. Miscellaneous amulets, difficult to classify or to assign specific powers, are the crescent, the star, the bulla, and the cylinder. Other classes of amulets, such as royal emblems and models of various ornaments and implements, do not apparently become current until Late Dynastic times, and the same is true for the elaborate composite forms, such as multiple *wedjat*-eyes, eyes combined with figures of deities, and the like.

Not only do all the materials used in the manufacture of the beads occur also among the amulets, but we find, besides, examples of the latter in alabaster, serpentine, haematite, obsidian, syenite, porphyry, breccia, and two unidentified blue stones, in violet faience and blue, red, yellow, brown, and white glass, and even in bronze. With the Murch collection the Museum acquired two tubular amulet ★cases of gold and silver evidently intended to hold charms written on small rolls of

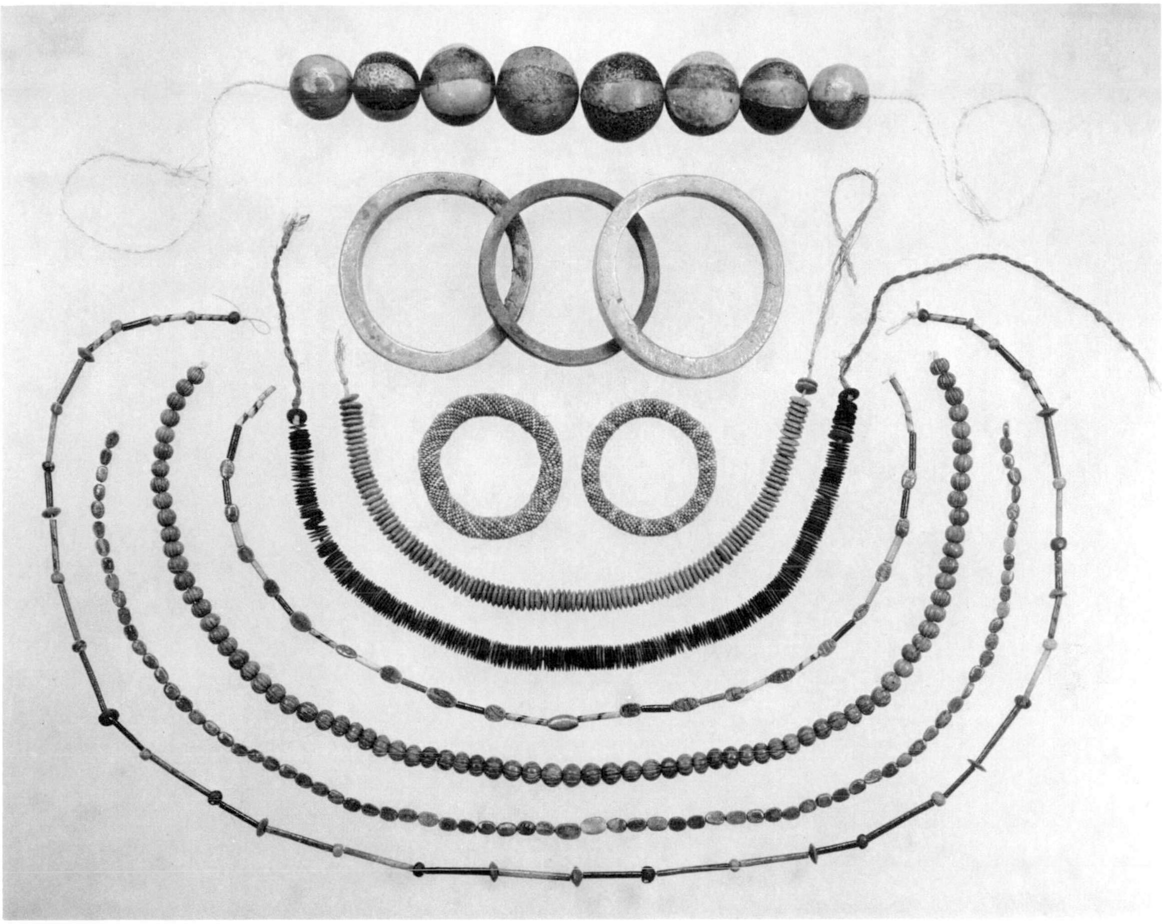

FIGURE 100. Necklaces, bracelets, and bangles of blue faience, chiefly from western Thebes. Diam. of bangles 4 3/8 in.

papyrus. Each is provided with a suspension ring so that it could be hung from the neck on a cord or necklace.

Under the Thutmoside pharaohs the scarab retained its tremendous popularity both as a seal and as an amuletic ornament, and was worn, not only by itself on a loop of cord or as the bezel of a signet ring, but combined with beads and other amulets, and frequently with other scarabs, to form bracelets and necklaces. The form of the scarab itself had become more refined and more decorative, with the various parts of the insect—the head, the back, the wing case, and the legs—often rendered in exquisite detail. Green-glazed steatite continues to be the favorite material for scarabs and other seals, with blue faience a poor second, and other substances such as carnelian, jasper, glass, ivory, bronze, gold, and silver represented only by an occasional example. Though, as we have seen, scarabs with royal names are more numerous than ever before, those inscribed with the names and titles of private individuals, so copious during the Middle Kingdom, are now relatively rare. Aside from the few mentioned in the preceding chapters only fifteen of our hundreds of *scarabs, *plaques, and other small *seal amulets of Thutmoside date bear the names of their owners. The persons referred to, none of whom appears to be otherwise identifiable, include the Overseer of the Granary Aʿḥ-mosĕ; the Overseer

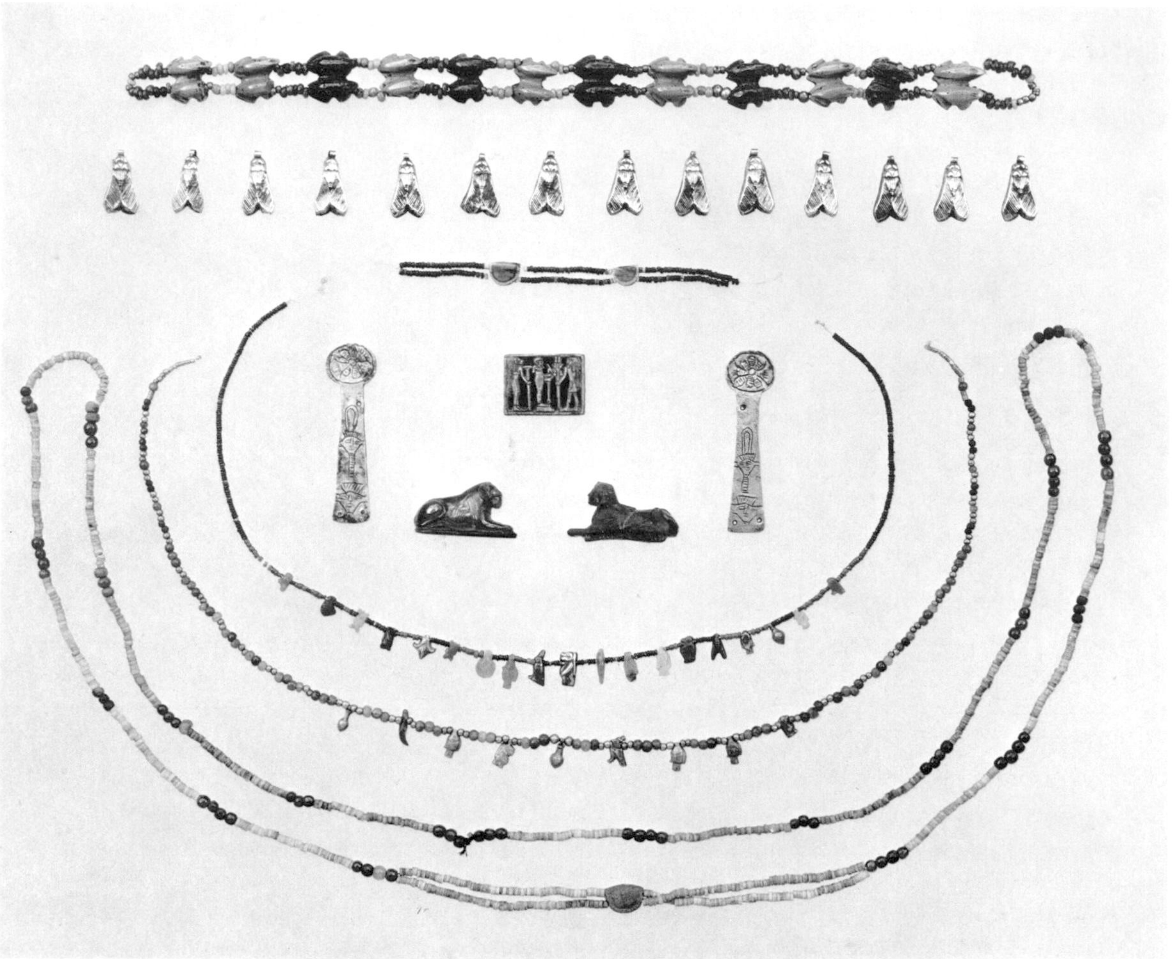

FIGURE 101. Necklaces, bracelets, and elements from both. Gold, faience, and semiprecious stones. L. of necklace at top 11 5/8 in.

of the Cattle of Amūn, Yebi-em-netjeri; the Steward of the King's Wife, Pe'n-Tjebu; the Servant Tjeḥetjy; the Overseer of the Double Granary of Amūn, Tḥūty; the Scribes Ḥumetju, Tety, and Tḥut-mosĕ; and five untitled persons named Amun-mosĕ, In-yōtef, Baket-Amūn, Nūb-ḥotpe, and Seʿankh-Tḥut-mosĕ. Twenty scarabs of "Amun-ḥotpe" and five of "Tḥut-mosĕ" are probably to be assigned to Eighteenth Dynasty kings rather than to their similarly named subjects.

The names or figures of divinities, on the other hand, appear with great frequency on the scarabs and seals of this and succeeding periods, either engraved on their undersides or, occasionally, carved on their backs. Far and away the most popular are the ancient sun god Rēʿ, and the powerful state god Amūn (or Amun Rēʿ), the former being referred to on well over a hundred scarabs, the latter on nearly as many. Beside the name "Rēʿ," written in hieroglyphs, the sun god appears as a falcon-headed figure or simply as the solar disk, sometimes riding in a barque with high-rising bow and stern, sometimes trundled between the forefeet of a scarab beetle. Amūn is rarely represented, but his name is found over and over again, often accompanied by appropriate symbols or followed by well-known epithets. Some twoscore of our scarabs and seals are inscribed with short spells in which one or the other of these great gods is invoked. Many of these little texts are of a cryptic nature, difficult to interpret; but the type is well illustrated in a few of the simpler examples, such as "The city which Rēʿ loves endures," "When Rēʿ is at hand there is no fear," "Amūn causes the heaven of Thebes to shine," "Amūn hearkens to the suppliant who has (gained) his favor." Forty scarabs show us Horus as a falcon or falcon-headed deity and sixteen Thoueris as a female hippopotamus reared up on its hind feet. Ṭhōt, ibis-headed or ape-headed, and the associated goddess Maʿet come next with ten scarabs each, and then Ptaḥ with eight. Sixteen other divinities whose figures are found on from one to five scarabs each, include Anubis, Bastet, Bēs, Ḥaʿpy, Ḥeḳet, Isis, Khonsu, Mīn, Montu, Nesret, Sakhmet, Serḳet, Sēth, Shu, Sobk, and Wen-nefer. Besides these we meet with a number of unspecified cobra goddesses and other female divinities, a being referred to simply as "the god," four unidentified male deities, and two divine barques of uncertain ownership.

Scarabs inscribed with mottoes and good wishes are not as numerous as in later times, only forty-two of this class being datable to the Thutmoside period. In many cases faulty or jumbled writings make the inscriptions difficult to understand, but the boons promised include "favor" (with a god or king), "goodness," "life" or the "breath of life," "health," and "millions of years." The legends of thirty-four of our scarabs and seals consist solely of royal titles and epithets, unaccompanied by names—the "Good God, Lord of Strength," the "Son of Rēʿ endures," the "King's Great Wife, whom he loves," the "King's Daughter," and so on; occasionally we find a similarly isolated priestly or official title, such as the "First God's Father of Amūn," the "Henchman (held) in affection." Other scarabs, clearly carved during the Eighteenth Dynasty, carry the names of pharaohs of the Old and Middle Kingdoms (see Part I, pp. 65, 176, 195, 201, 344), and, in some instances, imitation names of kingly type (see p. 8). Still others are inscribed with place names—"Heliopolis," "Memphis," the "Theban City"—and with these may be classed a number of examples of the official seal of the Theban necropolis, the canine animal of Anubis couchant above nine bound enemies. Single hieroglyphs of familiar types and almost without exception of amuletic significance adorn the undersides of fifty-five of our Eighteenth Dynasty scarabs, and on ninety others we find two or more of the same signs arranged in meaningful and, at the same time, highly decorative groupings. Often the hieroglyphs are effectively combined with conventionalized plant forms, among which the graceful lotus and the stately papyrus naturally predominate. Just as often these and other plants are used by themselves in intricate decorative designs. Though somewhat less popular than in the Middle Kingdom, scroll and cord patterns are well represented on our Thutmoside seal amulets, where they show a surprising range of forms and combinations, involving linked and unlinked scrolls of three distinct types, scroll and lotus groupings, looped cords, twisted cords, and knotted cords. Cross patterns continue popular, as do also interlaced uraei, concentric circles, and any number of linear designs—crosshatching, parallel lines, asterisks, and tree-branch motifs.

The rich and varied repertory of devices found on the undersides of our Eighteenth Dynasty scarabs is completed by an important series composed exclusively or almost exclusively of figures of human beings and animals. The human figures are limited for the most part to representations of the king, who more often than not at this period wears the Blue Crown and who is shown in a variety of poses and activities (see, e.g., fig. 66): standing, kneeling, seated on his throne or on a carrying chair, drawing his bow, riding in his chariot, and striking to earth an enemy chieftain. Frequently the unnamed pharaoh appears in the form of a lion or of a human-headed sphinx wearing on its head the royal *nemes* or one of the crowns and having in one instance a pair of wings springing from its back. The only other human figures seen on the scarabs of this period and on the backs of contemporary seals are Nubian and Asiatic captives who appear either alone, kneeling and with their arms tied behind them, or prone beneath the feet of the royal lion or the hooves of the pharaoh's horses. The animals, birds, fish, and insects represented on the undersides of the scarabs or carved on the backs of the seals include nearly all of those found among the amulets and several more in addition. The goat and antelope family, for example, is represented not only by the ibex but also by the oryx and the addax, the latter appearing as the prey of a lion on an interesting cylinder ★seal of blue glass. Thirteen scarabs bear figures of a crouched winged griffin of Syro-Aegean type, three the figures of horses, and one the figure of a giraffe. The scorpion (see fig. 102, lower left) occurs on the undersides of nine scarabs and cowroids, including a number found on Theban burials of the time of Ḥat-shepsūt and Tḥut-mosĕ III. Fish are very popular, no less than thirty-four scarabs and two seals being engraved with representations of the *bolti* (see fig. 102, lower row, second from left) and other species, often combined with twining water plants. The backs of twenty-one scaraboid seals are carved in the shape of hedgehogs, while the backs of three others are adorned with locusts or grasshoppers. Other creatures frequently represented at this period are the lion, the falcon, the vulture, the cobra, the crocodile, the scarab beetle, and the desert hare; while those which appear much more rarely include the bee, the ox, the cow, the dog, the duck, the fly, the hippopotamus, the lizard, the mouse, and the pigeon. Forty-five of our Thutmoside scarabs are completely plain on their undersides and another twenty-eight are so fragmentary or so badly worn as to render their legends unrecognizable. ★Heart scarabs, of which the Museum possesses over thirty examples datable to the New Kingdom, are items of funerary rather than of personal jewelry, and will be considered below in the section devoted to funerary equipment. To still another category belong the large ★commemorative scarabs, issued for the most part during the reign of King Amun-ḥotpe III (see Chapter VI).

Out of such elements as those listed in the foregoing paragraphs—beads, amulets, scarabs—the jewelers of Thutmoside times assembled the modest but attractive items of parure which the ordinary citizens of Egypt wore during their lifetimes and which in most cases they took with them to their tombs. Unfortunately, owing to the fragility of the linen cords and threads on which they were strung, relatively few of the necklaces, bracelets, and girdles of this period have come down to us intact.

Thus, though our collection contains more than sixty ★strings of necklace beads datable to the reigns of Tḥut-mosĕ I to IV, only twenty-one of these are, properly speaking, necklaces, that is, assemblages of elements either still on their original strings or known to be still in their original order. The examples selected for illustration in figures 100 and 101 include two necklaces of lenticular beads from the burials of Sen-ne-mūt's parents and younger brother (see p. 111), a long string of faience scaraboids from a family tomb of the time of Tḥut-mosĕ III, and a series of simple bead and amulet combinations found chiefly by the Earl of Carnarvon in Theban burials of the earlier Thutmoside period. With them is shown a string of the huge faience ★ball beads offered by pious Thebans at the shrine of Ḥat-Ḥor at Deir el Baḥri. Rubbish thrown out of the same shrine yielded, amid the remnants of other offerings, three ★counterpoises from votive *menyet*-necklaces (see pp. 45 f.), two of copper engraved with Hathorian symbols, one of wood painted brown to imitate copper.

Though many of our loose beads and amulets of Thutmoside date probably once formed parts of girdles, bracelets, and armlets, very few entire ornaments of these classes, other than those associated with Tḥut-mosĕ III's three Syrian wives, have reached the Museum's collection. Indeed, our only complete ★girdle of this period is made up, not of stone or faience beads, but of small, diamond-shaped elements, composed of folded strips of glossy palm leaf, strung together on knotted cords to form an attractive, flexible belt two inches wide and twenty and a half inches long. Were it not for the fact that it comes from a rubbish pit at Deir el Baḥri known to have been

abandoned during the reign of Tḥut-mosĕ III, this unusual ornament would be difficult to date.

One of two ★bracelets is composed of a double strand of small black and white ring beads interrupted in two places by a large semicircular girdle bead of green-glazed steatite (see fig. 101). It comes from the coffin of a woman buried at Thebes in the tomb of Sen-ne-mūt's parents. The second bracelet, consisting of four steatite scarabs strung together on a short loop of cord, was found at Asyūt on the wrist of another woman who died during the reign of Tḥut-mosĕ III. Five thousand two hundred and seventy tiny faience ring ★beads from a Theban burial of the same period represent the remains of a pair of the beadwork bracelets popular at this time, shown restored in figure 100. Elements readily identified as coming specifically from bracelets include a small carnelian ★lion, a very handsome lapis lazuli inlay in the form of a couched ★sphinx, and a rectangular openwork

FIGURE 102. Earrings and finger rings of gold, silver, bone, and various semiprecious stones. Diam. of largest earring 1 in.

★plaque of glazed steatite with the figures and names of the Memphite triad, Ptaḥ, Sakhmet, and Nefertēm (see fig. 101). The burials of Ḥat-shepsūt's Theban archivist, Nefer-khēwet, and of Sen-ne-mūt's brother Amun-ḥotpe, yielded five rigid bracelets, or ★bangles, consisting of rings of blue faience, square in section and four inches in diameter; and three fragmentary ★bangles of the same type, but carved of wood and ivory, were found in a tomb of the reign of Tḥut-mosĕ III at Abydos.

Like their predecessors of the late Middle Kingdom and Hyksos times, the dated ★finger rings of the Thutmoside period consist for the most part of scarabs, cowroids, plaques, and other seal amulets fitted with short loops of linen cord or swiveled on rings of gold, silver, or bronze (see fig. 102). In other words, they are, almost without exception, signet rings with movable bezels. In the simpler rings an unmounted scarab or other bezel is strung on a loop of tapered wire, the ends of which, having been passed through the scarab in opposite directions, are wound around the ring proper. In the more elaborate examples the bezel is mounted in a metal frame, or funda, often fitted at the ends with cylindrical bearings, which swivels between the discoid or globular terminals of a tapered, U-shaped ring of specialized design. Sometimes the funda and the ring are of different metals, the former of gold, the latter of silver. Conversely, there are in our collection four rings with movable plaque bezels in each of which the whole ornament, including both bezel and finger loop, is made of a single material, in three cases gold, in one instance silver.[2] From this type it is only a step to the familiar signet ring with fixed bezel, soldered to or made in one piece with the ring proper. Two general forms of such rings achieved popularity during the New Kingdom. In one type the bezel is a rectangular or oval metal plate and the ring a thin band of the same metal, more often than not silver. The other, and somewhat more common, type consists of a massive ring of metal or hard stone with a thickened upper segment flattened on the outside to form an elongated oval surface on which the signet proper is engraved. Though both forms of ring appear to have been in use under the earlier Thutmosides, few of the many examples in our collection can with assurance be dated before the reign of Amun-ḥotpe III and most of them belong to the so-called ʿAmārneh period (see below, fig. 180). The same is true of numerous rings of faience or other materials which were not intended to function as signet rings, but were designed to be worn as amulets or in many instances as ornaments pure and simple. The bezels of these rings, molded in high relief or carved in intricate openwork designs, include such devices as the *wedjat*-eye, the rosette, the palmette, and similar floral motifs.

★Earrings, though rather more common than heretofore, had changed but little since late Hyksos times (see pp. 20 f.). Some twoscore examples (including at least four pairs) of Thutmoside date are all of the penannular, or cleft ring, type (see fig. 102), designed to be clipped onto the ear or passed through a perforation in the lobe. The majority are plain, slightly open rings, circular or trapezoidal in section, carved of shell, bone, carnelian, or red jasper or molded in green or red faience. Included among these are twenty-six examples purchased by Albert M. Lythgoe at Deir el Ballās. An alabaster ring, also from Deir el Ballās, is broad and flat in cross section, like a thick strap, and a large carnelian ring of unknown provenience is adorned around the outside with a serrated ridge. There are, in addition, three plain hollow rings, two of gold and one of gilded bronze; a gold ring inlaid with lapis lazuli and fitted with a locking pin; and six fine examples of the wide, ribbed-band type of gold earring, in four cases inlaid with strings of tiny lapis lazuli beads. The latter come, respectively, from the excavations of the Egyptian Research Account at Tell el Yahudīyeh in the southeastern Delta and from those of Lord Carnarvon in western Thebes.

Small disk-shaped ★ornaments of metal and faience, which occur in some quantity as early as the reign of Ḥat-shepsūt, were evidently used in the decoration of garments, temple draperies, funerary palls, and the like. A type of short jacket worn by the pharaoh is not infrequently represented as studded with circular ornaments colored yellow or blue, and the tomb of King Tūt-ʿankh-Amūn yielded a pall, a linen headdress, and several other garments with rows of disk-shaped sequins of gold and silver still sewn to them. The seventy-eight ornaments of this type in our collection come largely from the foundation deposits and rubbish pits associated with the temple of Ḥat-shepsūt at

---

[2] Amun-mosĕ, whose name appears on the silver ring, was probably the owner of Tomb 89 at Thebes. He appears to have served as an army officer under Tḥut-mosĕ III and to have died in the reign of Amun-ḥotpe III. On the back of the bezel of our ring he is described as "one who followed his lord in every foreign country."

Deir el Baḥri and with the adjoining shrine of the goddess Ḥat-Ḥor. Two examples were found by Sir Flinders Petrie in the ruins of the Eighteenth Dynasty temple at Ahnāsyeh, the site of ancient Herakleopolis, and twenty-eight are from private collections. All are pierced with holes or provided with rings or lugs for attachment to the fabrics from which they came; and nearly all have the form of a rosette with engraved petals radiating from a central boss or, in the case of a few ring-shaped examples, from a central hole. The great majority are of blue faience with details sometimes picked out in black, green, and yellow overglazes; but the two disks from Ahnāsyeh are of gilded copper and one of the examples from Deir el Baḥri appears to be of silver. The diameters range from three-eighths to one and three-eighths inches. To the same class of ornament probably also belongs a small, lozenge-shaped ★plaque of blue faience with the figure of a hovering vulture silhouetted at the center of its openwork design.

5. Clothing, Coiffure, and Cosmetics

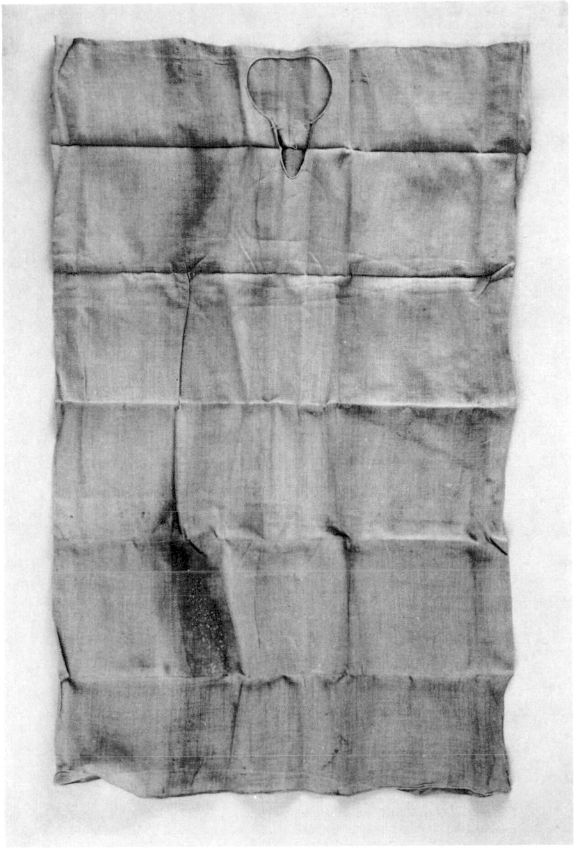

FIGURE 103. Linen shirt from a private burial of the time of Ḥat-shepsūt. L. 42 ½ in.

Though the reigns of Tḥut-mosĕ I and his successors witnessed a most interesting transition from the relatively severe fashions in dress current at the outset of the Eighteenth Dynasty to the voluminous and frivolously elaborate costumes affected by well-to-do Egyptians of the later New Kingdom, few actual garments of Thutmoside date have come down to us. Those that have reached our collection, chiefly from the Theban tombs of middle-class contemporaries of Tḥut-mosĕ I and Ḥat-shepsūt, are of simple designs and unpretentious materials.

Sleeveless shirts (see fig. 103) from the burials of Sen-ne-mūt's mother and other members of his family are simply inverted bags of linen sheeting with slits left at the tops of the sides to serve as armholes and a keyhole-shaped neck opening finished with a rolled hem and provided at the top of the vertical throat slot with a pair of light tie cords. Of the same type, but somewhat larger than the examples found in Theban tombs of the Middle Kingdom (see Part I, p. 240), our Eighteenth Dynasty shirts range in length from three and a half to over four feet and in width from thirty to thirty-five inches. The broad section of medium-weight linen sheet of which each is made has usually one selvage edge, one hemmed edge, and two hemmed ends; but occasionally one end preserves the long warp fringe of the original sheet, or bolt. Owing to variations in shade in alternate groups of warp threads, one of our shirts has pronounced, if somewhat irregularly spaced, vertical stripes of pale and dark brown color. A flimsy linen ★shawl, which also once belonged to a member of Sen-ne-mūt's household, consists of a strip of light, loosely woven cloth seventy-four inches long and not quite twenty-two inches wide. Like the strips used for the

FIGURE 104. Sandals for an adult and three children. Basketry and leather. L. of large pair 11 3/4 in.

shirts, it has one selvage edge and three hemmed edges. Because they are, properly speaking, household rather than personal equipment, the great sheets, or bolts, of cloth from which such garments were made will be taken up a bit later on in this chapter.

The burial of Sen-ne-mūt's young brother Amun-ḥotpe and the surface fill near by yielded two pairs of children's ★sandals (see fig. 104) with soles of tooled oxhide and straps of calfskin and sheepskin. In both cases the upper surfaces of the soles are adorned with simple linear decoration, lightly incised in the surface of the leather; and in both cases the ankle straps are complete loops, passing not only over the insteps but around and behind the heels of the wearer. Amun-ḥotpe's sandals, the larger of the two pairs, are of red leather and measure seven and three-quarters inches in length. The smaller pair, of white leather, are only five and a quarter inches long and were evidently made for a very young child. With them were found a pair of basketry ★sandals of the same minute size neatly woven of palm-leaf strip and Ḥalfa grass over a core of papyrus pith and provided with simple Y-type harnesses of papyrus pith. Two pairs of similar basketwork ★sandals, made, however, for a full-grown man and measuring almost twelve inches in length, come from a small cemetery of pit tombs excavated during the reign of Tḥut-mosĕ I in the Seʿankh-ku-Rēʿ temple platform, a few hundred yards southwest of Deir el Baḥri.

Complete wigs of this period rarely find their way into museum collections, and the few examples which we possess are much later in date. The burial of one of Sen-ne-mūt's female relatives, however, yielded a small, colored grass basket containing, among other items, six bundles of human ★hair, dark brown in color and including both loose, wavy locks and long, slender braids (see fig. 111), "clubbed at the ends and liberally greased to make them hold their shape."[3] Like the similar locks and braids found in the tomb of Queen Meryet-Amūn (see p. 54), these had probably been used on occasion to fill out their owner's elaborate coiffure or perhaps to effect repairs on her wig. To give it a pleasant odor the hair had been packed in the basket with chips of ★aromatic wood.

Five small ★combs, tentatively dated to the earlier New Kingdom, are carved of ivory, Sudanese ebony, and some other dark, close-grained wood, probably acacia. Ranging in width from one to three and three-eighths inches, they include three examples of the double comb, with a row of coarse, widely spaced teeth on one side and a row of fine teeth on the other side, and three single combs with, respectively, straight, wavy, and rounded backs. All three of the latter are from the area surrounding the pyramid of King Amun-em-ḥēt I at el Lisht. From here also come four long, slender ★hairpins of bone and hardwood, one plain, two decorated with incised rings, and the fourth flaring gradually at the top to form a knob on which is the stub of a carved figure now missing. A steatite ★hairpin of unknown provenience has

[3] Winlock, *Tomb of Queen Meryet-Amun at Thebes*, p. 9.

on its disk-shaped top the almost microscopic figures of two lions, and the top of a bone ★hairpin from the Davis collection is conical with engraved parallel rings. Combs and hairpins alike show relatively little development over those of earlier times and without context are often very difficult to date. The same is true of the little bronze instruments which have been identified with some justification as ★hair-curlers (see pp. 21 f.). Fortunately, many of the examples in our collection, including one or two pairs of Thutmoside date, were found in undisturbed burials of known period. A pair of small bronze ★tweezers, suitable for plucking the eyebrows and operations of that sort, is from an Eighteenth Dynasty tomb at Abydos.

★Razors of the period are of two types: a slender, scalpel-like implement, entirely of bronze, with a curved cutting edge on the butt end as well as on the side of the blade proper; and a broad, oblong blade of thin sheet metal usually provided with a curved wooden handle attached by means of rivets to one side of the blade. In the second type of razor the rounded lower end of the blade is the cutting edge. The handles are usually of hard, fine-grained woods, in one case boxwood. All except one of the razors belonged to men and women who were buried at Thebes during the first few decades of the reign of Tḥut-mosĕ III. Most of them were accompanied by small ★hones, or slipstones, of quartzite or sandstone, some pointed, some rounded at the ends, and one shaped like a small round-topped stela.

Three of four ★mirrors from the tombs of these people and their near contemporaries are of types which we have already seen in figures 32 and 75. They have disks of polished bronze, shaped like a modern palm-leaf fan, and handles in the form of a papyrus column made of wood or, more frequently now, of bronze like the mirror itself. In two cases a double-faced Ḥat-Ḥor head is interposed between the top of the shaft and its gracefully spreading capital, and in one instance the triangular spaces between the ends of the umbel and the lower edges of the mirror disk are taken up by pairs of small bronze falcons. In the fourth mirror (fig. 105) the shaft of the bronze handle has been given the form of a nude girl wearing about her slender hips a girdle of cowrie shells and having her hair dressed in the elaborate tripartite coiffure (see fig. 6) associated from the late Middle Kingdom onward with women in childbirth and with fertility goddesses. The arms of the figure, which were attached to the shoulders by means of tiny bronze pins and which are now missing, probably reached upward in a graceful gesture to touch the tips of the down-curving papyrus umbel above. A mirror ★disk without a handle, but fitted with a long, tapering tang, was found at el Lisht in a

FIGURE 105. Bronze mirror of the first half of the Eighteenth Dynasty. L. 9 in.

coppersmith's hoard of scrap metal which during the reign of Tūt-ʿankh-Amūn had been sealed up in a piece of linen cloth, placed in a cord mesh basket, and cached against the north side of the pyramid of King Se'n-Wosret I. The hoard itself, made up of some seventy implements, fittings, and vessels of copper and bronze, had been garnered chiefly from tombs of the Thutmoside period, only one or two pieces going back in date to the Twelfth Dynasty. Besides the mirror disk it included one of the razor blades referred to in the preceding paragraph, and many of the other metal objects which we shall have occasion to discuss in the course of this chapter. An ivory *figure of the dwarf god Bēs, somewhat indifferently carved from a hollow tusk and measuring four and three-eighths inches in height, was evidently once part of the handle of a mirror, as was also a *head of the same divinity skillfully molded in violet and green faience and having in the top of the head a slot for the tang of the mirror disk. Part of an ivory papyrus umbel pierced vertically with three large and numerous small holes seems to be from the top of the handle of a feather *fan or sunshade.

A score of little cosmetic *spoons and *dishes (see fig. 106), mostly of later Thutmoside times, exhibit a variety of amusing forms and materials. The earliest and simplest type of spoon has a plain oval bowl and a straight, slightly tapered handle rarely over three inches in length. It occurs in bone, wood, and bronze in tombs of the time of Tḥut-mosĕ III at Thebes and at el Lisht. Because of their minute size some spoons of this class have been thought to be earpicks. A larger and somewhat more elaborate example in wood, from el Lisht, has a bowl nicely carved in the form of a cupped human hand; and two, of ivory and bronze, derive their shape from the hind leg of an ox. A New Kingdom tomb near the pyramid of King Tety at Saḳḳāreh produced two scooplike ointment spoons of wood, one with a pointed bowl, the other with a rectangular bowl and a handle carved to resemble a papyrus column. Spoons in the form of a swimming girl, unclad and supporting on her extended arms a small rectangular basin, occur in both faience and serpentine; and a fancifully conceived scoop, or dish, in the latter material represents a nude young woman kneeling on a mat between a pair of papyrus plants and supporting on her head a large ovoid jar, the front of which is hollowed out to form a shallow basin. Three delicate little ivory spoons have elongated ovoid bowls supported on the heads of tiny nude figures of women standing or kneeling on slender papyrus columns, only one of which is preserved in its entirety. With them the Museum acquired a minute ivory dipper, its long, thin handle topped by the figure of an upreared uraeus serpent. An attractive type of cosmetic dish, represented in our collection by seven examples in faience, glazed steatite, and ivory, has the form of a *bolti*-fish or of a crouching or trussed animal with a shallow basin scooped out in one of its sides. In three such dishes the animal represented is a bound oryx, in one a mouse, and in another a lop-eared hound crouching with one forepaw crossed over the other. Two graceful dishes of alabaster, four and three-quarters and six and a half inches in length, are shaped like trussed ducks with the turned-back head and projecting tail of the bird serving in each case as the handles of the dish. A similar example in schist, six and a quarter inches long, has, when seen from above, the outline of a pair of ducks, back to back. Even more attractive is a small dish carved of black steatite (fig. 106, right) in the shape of a lotus flower and two buds, their stems tied together and curled round to form a flat, loop handle. The handle of a fragmentary alabaster dish, or spoon, is in the form of a stalking lioness seen in profile. From Meidūm comes a shallow slate cosmetic saucer unadorned except for four square lugs projecting horizontally from its rim, and from tombs of early Thutmoside times at Thebes and Saḳḳāreh two covered wooden dishes similar in all respects to the example in ivory described on page 65. One of two little dishes of blue faience, made during the reign of Tḥut-mosĕ II, is decorated in black outline with a radiating petal design. The other dish is undecorated, but segments of its lip are folded in to form four small spouts around the rim.

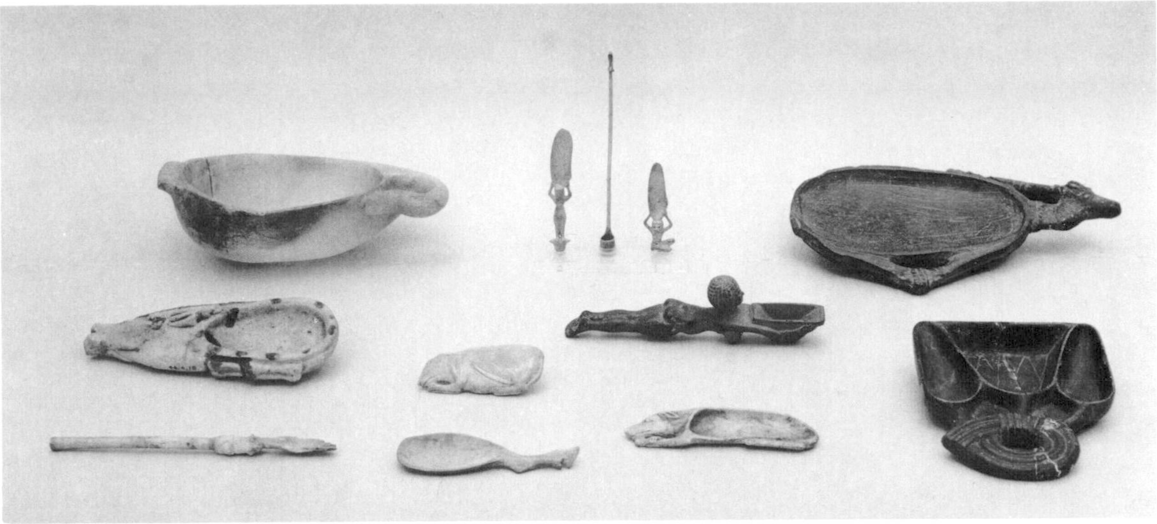

FIGURE 106. Cosmetic spoons and dishes of stone, ivory, wood, and faience. L. of alabaster duck dish 6 ½ in.

As containers of their indispensable eyesalves and cosmetics, the Egyptians of the Thutmoside era continued to use not only the squat little *koḥl*-jars of traditional type, but also tubes made up of lengths of hollow reed stoppered at both ends and sometimes bound together in pairs or larger groups. Two six-inch ★sections of castor-oil reed in our collection are stated, in the neatly drawn, black ink inscriptions on their sides, to have contained "Very good eyesalve for effusion of water in the eyes" and "Very good eyesalve as a remedy for inflammation of the eyes." Remains of the actual contents of the reeds enabled Arthur C. Kopp, the Museum's chemist, to identify the first salve as galena or white lead ground up and mixed with an oily, organic solvent, and the second as iron oxide similarly treated. A tomb at Saḳḳāreh yielded a plugged ★section of reed containing powdered galena and having a ★*koḥl*-stick of light blue glass thrust into its open end; and in 1941 the Museum acquired by purchase a bundle of four similar ★reeds lashed together with cord, rushes, and strips of cloth sewn securely in place.

From such containers it was only a step to ★reproductions of the natural reeds in faience and other materials, to single, double, and multiple ★*koḥl*-containers of tubular type made of wood, ivory, stone, faience, and glass, and to small ★blocklike containers of wood and glazed steatite drilled with two or more tubular cavities. One of the more interesting of the single *koḥl*-tubes in our collection is a small cylinder of turquoise blue faience mounted in gold and equipped with a *koḥl*-stick of polished haematite. It is inscribed on the side for the High Priest of Tḥōt, Tḥut-mosĕ, and may have come originally from Hermopolis. Four double and five quadruple tubes are carved from blocks of light wood with inlays and lids of ebony or from blocks of ebony inlaid, covered, and trimmed with ivory. In eight cases the lid swivels horizontally on a single peg and is fastened shut by means of the ebony *koḥl*-stick which, when not in use, passes through a hole or slot in the cover down into a tubular hole or slot in the side or center of the block. In the eighth example, a rectangular block container attractively inlaid with bands of dark and light wood, the lid slides horizontally in grooves, but is locked in the same manner as the swiveled lids. One type of double or triple container, usually molded of blue faience, consists simply of two or three plain tubes of equal height bound together with simulated tapes of the same material. In a similar but more elaborate type, molded in faience or carved from a single block of

FIGURE 107. Container for eye cosmetic. Green-glazed steatite. H. 2 3/8 in.

wood or ivory, the tubes, spaced slightly apart, are represented as if enclosed within a wide, flat binding which extends two-thirds of the way up their lengths and which is decorated on the front and back with figures and ornamental motifs engraved or carved in low relief. A wooden container of this type has engraved on its front a nude figure of the goddess Anukis (?), accompanied by a gazelle and holding in her hands a papyrus scepter and a small, one-handled jug. On the back, in a panel similarly framed by block borders and friezes of petals, two small animals (cats or monkeys?) appear on either side of a composite tree or large bouquet. Relief figures of the dwarf god Bēs, executed with great skill and delicacy, adorn the sides of a double-barreled *koḥl*-container of glossy, green-glazed steatite (fig. 107), which, like many other small objects of the same outstanding quality, came to the Museum with the Carnarvon collection. Little faience and serpentine figures of squatting monkeys, holding in one instance a narrow tubular receptacle and in the other a tiny, straight-sided bowl, were almost certainly intended to contain eye cosmetic. So also, presumably, was the hollowed-out figure of a kneeling Asiatic captive with pointed beard and arms bound behind him, adeptly carved in a fine, dark hardwood and measuring only three and three-quarters inches in height.

A type of *koḥl*-tube which appears to have been first produced in quantity during the latter half of the Thutmoside period, but which continued to be popular for centuries thereafter, has the form of a miniature palm column with the tapering shaft and flaring, foliate capital characteristic of this kind of column (see fig. 109, right). The majority of the known examples of this peculiarly graceful class of cosmetic container are of opaque, polychrome glass adorned with brilliantly striped wave and zigzag patterns. Seven such tubes in the Museum's collection, datable to the period bounded by the reigns of Tḥut-mosĕ III and Amun-ḥotpe III, are of dark or medium blue glass with white, yellow, green, and pale blue decoration; an eighth example, formerly in the MacGregor collection, is of violet faience with details of the palm capital picked out in yellowish white glaze. Better proportioned and more elaborately decorated than these hollow glass columns is one carved of ebony or a similar hard, dark wood (fig. 108, left). Here, in a broad frieze of figures which encircles the midsection of the shaft, are two girls dancing to the music of a seven-piece orchestra also made up of girls and including three flute players, two harpists, a lute player, and a lyre player. Above and below are bands of lotus flowers and petals and at the base of the column a paneled dado. The decoration, executed in a graceful, easy style which heralds the approach of the ʿAmārneh period, is lightly incised and was once filled with colored pastes, only traces of which now remain. Even more elaborate is an openwork holder or ornamental outer case for a *koḥl*-tube (fig. 108, right), exquisitely modeled in a rich, dark blue faience, in the form of a squat but most intricately decorated palm column. In the principal register of the fragile shaft, which miraculously has come down to us unbroken, figures of the cat of Bastet and the hippopotamus of Thoueris flank a uraeus-trimmed head of the goddess Ḥat-Ḥor, while below, long-stemmed lotus flowers and buds form a high, lacy dado. Said to have come from the district of Tūneh, near Tell el ʿAmārneh, this extraordinary piece may have been made during the so-called ʿAmārneh period, though technically, stylistically, and iconographically it could belong as well to the reign of Tḥut-mosĕ IV or even earlier.

Superseded by such light and attractive containers as those just described, the traditional stone *koḥl*-jar of the type shown in figure 8 lost its popularity and before the death of Tḥut-mosĕ III had apparently passed out of existence. Our collection, however, includes ten characteristic examples of alabaster, serpentine, and steatite from the burials of Theban contemporaries of Ḥatshepsūt and Tḥut-mosĕ III and one in limestone from a tomb of the same period at Abydos. The Abydos jar, acquired in 1901 from the Egypt Exploration Fund, is stained black (in imitation of ebony?) and is decorated with a fringe of mythological figures and plant forms, the engraved outlines of which have been colored yellow, possibly to suggest gold inlay. One of six little alabaster *koḥl*-vessels from a tomb of early Thutmoside times on the Dirāʿ Abu'n Naga has the rectangular block shape of a wooden *koḥl*-container, while two others of the same series show considerable deviation in form from the standard type. A tiny beaker of blue faience, formerly in the Davis collection, appears also to have been used as a *koḥl*-jar. Many of the little jars still retain their flat, discoid lids; and we have, in addition, an unattached ★lid of steatite engraved on the top with a symmetrical cross-and-petal design.

To the ★*koḥl*-sticks found with the tubes and jars must be added a dozen isolated examples of the same period in ebony, haematite, bone, and black and dark blue glass, some of which come from well-dated burials at Abydos and Thebes, while others are from the surface rubbish near the North Pyramid at el Lisht. Two double-ended bronze sticks and one of the ebony sticks are very long and slender, averaging over six inches in length; and a haematite stick from Abydos is unusual in having a prominent rectangular handle or grip.

As containers of their other cosmetics—pomades, unguents, lotions, and paints—the Egyptians of the Thutmoside age used jars of four principal types and four principal materials. The types, most of which were originated in earlier periods, include the graceful beaker with incurved sides, the wide-mouthed, footed vase with bulbous body and cylindrical neck, the heavy drop-shaped jar with flaring rim, and the globular or cordiform jar with short neck and wide, flat lip (see figs. 35, 43, 76). Stone continued to be one of the favorite materials for such vessels, and alabaster (calcite) the favorite stone. Out of twenty stone ★cosmetic jars from tombs of this period seventeen are of alabaster and only three of other stones—serpentine, anhydrite, and gabbro.

A dozen small ★examples of the footed vase in colored glass (fig. 109), their heights ranging from two and an eighth to three and three-quarters

FIGURE 108. Wooden *koḥl*-tube and faience holder for a *koḥl*-tube. H. 4 7/8 and 4 in.

FIGURE 109. Polychrome glass vases and *koḥl*-tubes. H. of largest vase 6 3/8 in.

inches, were probably used to contain perfumes or other valuable cosmetic substances, their minute size making it unlikely that they could have served as tableware unless possibly as condiment jars. Many of them are provided with small glass handles, and the majority are adorned with rainbow-like bands of waves and zigzags, usually light blue, bright yellow, and white against the darker blue, violet, or gray ground color of the vessel. A few, however, are monochrome—greenish white, blue, or ocher yellow—with narrow black and white or blue and white striped rims and foot moldings; these, to our modern eyes, are likely to be more attractive than their somewhat gaudy mates. Though glass vases of this type were known in Egypt as early as the reign of Tḥut-mosĕ III and were common under his two successors, they were not confined to this era, but continued to be produced throughout the greater part of the New Kingdom. It is therefore not improbable that several of our examples, while characteristic of the period with which we are now dealing, are actually later in date, belonging perhaps to the late Eighteenth or even to the Nineteenth Dynasty.

A fragmentary ★flask of blue glass with a tall, thin neck of "Syrian" type (see fig. 123) is paralleled by an example found in the tomb of Amunḥotpe II. So also are two slender, amphoralike ★vases with pronounced shoulders and long, tapered bodies, made respectively of blue and plum-colored glass with vivid green, yellow and white bands of decoration. To the same period are probably to be assigned a slender one-handled ★jug of turquoise blue glass decorated with wavy bands of dark blue, yellow, and white, and a two-ribbed carinated ★cup of violet glass with blue and white striped edgings. The ★beaker, a shape rarely found in materials other than stone, is represented by a very small example in turquoise blue glass, formerly in the Hood collection and said to have been found at Ḳurneh sometime before 1860. Twenty-seven ★fragments of polychrome glass vessels, coming with only two exceptions from the Valley of the Tombs of the Kings, exhibit a great variety of patterns and colors, the latter including light and dark blue, violet, purple, green, yellow, brown, red, and white. Perhaps the greatest value of such fragments is the light which they throw on the techniques employed by the Egyptian workers in glass (see pp. 410 f.).

Neither faience nor metal seems to have been used extensively at this period for cosmetic vases, nearly all of the vessels in these two materials being flower bowls, drinking cups, and other household containers (see pp. 205 ff.). Exceptions are a small

FIGURE 110. Anthropomorphic vials in red pottery. H. of woman with child $5\frac{15}{16}$ in.

★footed vase of blue faience from the burial of Ḥat-shepsūt's archivist, Nefer-khēwet, a faience ★*ḥes*-vase ( ) from the burial of the latter's son Amun-em-ḥēt, and two small cylindrical ★unguent jars of the same material but of unknown provenience. Another ★footed vase, from a Theban tomb of the time of Tḥut-mosĕ I, is of green paste. Mention may also be made here of a curious little hollow ★globe of yellow faience, an inch and three-eighths in diameter, its tiny, circular mouth surrounded by a ring of blue petals—perhaps an imitation of a small, yellow fruit or berry. A second ★globular container of exactly the same size but of blue paste may be meant to represent a hedgehog. It is covered with a network of deeply incised lines and is topped by the forelegs and head of an animal. A disk-shaped ★lid of blue faience, less than two inches in diameter and probably from a small cosmetic vase, is decorated on its upper side with a geometric design in heavy black line.

Though pottery, too, was a material used at this time almost entirely for household vessels, the burials of Sen-ne-mūt's family and contemporaries produced a dozen small ★jars of fine buff, pink, or brownish red pottery which had actually contained cosmetic oils and salves. The types include a squat, carinated jar with a short neck and wide mouth, sometimes coated with a burnished dark red slip; a bulbous, footed vase with a high, cylindrical neck and one or more handles, usually made of a light-colored clay and decorated with linear designs in black, purple, and red; and a little globular, one-handled jug in smooth, grayish pottery resembling modern *ḳulleh*-ware. The mouths of many of the jars were covered with inverted brown-ware saucers and/or with pieces of linen cloth knotted on one side of the neck of the vessel and occasionally secured with a mud sealing bearing the impression of a scarab. Their contents, remnants of which still survive, consisted either of resinous gums or dark, oily liquids, and in one instance are identified by a hieratic label on the shoulder of the vessel as ben, or Moringa, oil, used, according to Lucas, "for making cosmetics, for extracting perfumes from flowers and for cooking."[4]

A type of small pottery ★vial in the form of a seated woman holding on her lap an infant child has been identified as a container for "the milk of a woman who has given birth to a male child,"[5] used in medical prescriptions and mentioned in magical incantations against ailments of women and children. The single example in our collection (fig. 110) is of polished dark red pottery and measures not quite six inches in height. Similar in material, size, and style is a small red pottery ★jug with a top in the form of a human head wearing a short, caplike coiffure, painted black, and having about the throat a bead collar crudely drawn in black outline. Fitted, like its companion vase, with a single loop handle, the little vessel was found in the rubbish of an Eighteenth Dynasty cemetery at Saḳḳāreh.

Like their predecessors of the Middle Kingdom the men and women of Thutmoside times kept their jewelry, their make-up kits, and other of

[4] *Ancient Egyptian Materials and Industries*, p. 384.

[5] Papyrus Ebers, 69, 3-7. See Desroches-Noblecourt, *Revue d'Égyptologie*, IX (1952), p. 59.

FIGURE 111. Colored rush basket containing the personal belongings of Sen-ne-mūt's sister(?). Diam. 11 in.

their smaller and more intimate possessions in attractively decorated little wooden ★caskets or in small, gaily colored ★baskets (see fig. 111). A sister of Sen-ne-mūt, for example, possessed a compartmented box of cypress wood with two little sliding lids and four boxwood legs; while Nefer-khēwet's wife, Ren-nefer, had a casket with a hinged lid, made of cypress and boxwood and inlaid with rectangular and triangular panels of turquoise blue faience. The contents of these two boxes are more or less typical. In the first was found a drop-shaped ★ornament of faience, a small lump of bright blue ★pigment, a chunk of rock salt, and five purple berries; and in the second, seven glazed steatite scarabs (including one of Ṭhut-mosĕ I), wrapped in a piece of linen cloth, and two *koḥl*-sticks, one of cypress and one of ebony. From tombs of the Eighteenth Dynasty at Gebelein, seventeen miles upriver from Thebes, come a very small box with a hinged lid, made entirely of polished ebony, and a cartouche-shaped box with a swivel lid, carved from some other fine, dark wood. The sliding lid of a dark wood casket from Saḳḳāreh is trimmed with panels of ivory engraved with rows of circles and dots. Standing on four short legs, the casket measures just over three inches in height and less than four and a half inches in length. With it, in the same tomb, was found a scarab of Ṭhut-mosĕ III. A fragment of engraved ebony ★overlay from a small box preserves part of a cavetto-crowned panel in which a figure of the hippopotamus goddess Thoueris, brandishing a knife, stands beside a large symbol of "protection" ([hieroglyph]). The piece, datable stylistically to the Eighteenth Dynasty, comes from the vicinity of the pyramid of Amun-em-ḥēt I at el Lisht. A strip of flat ivory ★inlay inscribed in hieroglyphs with the words "May every enemy fail!" is probably also from the top or side of a small casket.

Besides the larger hampers and baskets in which clothing and household effects were stored (see pp. 204 f.), almost every Egyptian of this period possessed a small basket of Ḥalfa grass (rush) or palm-leaf strip which, like the caskets just discussed, was used for the safekeeping of bead necklaces, scarabs, rings, cosmetic sets, and multifarious other small personal treasures. Seven such baskets in our collection are characterized by their modest size—the largest is scarcely a foot in diameter, the smallest four and a quarter inches—and by the fact that nearly all of them are decorated with simple, geometric designs—rectangles, triangles, chevrons, checker patterns—in red, black, and dark brown. In most cases both the basket and its lid are made of continuous coils of rush whipped and stitched together with strips of the same material or with strips cut from palm leaves. More often than not the basket is circular, with a low, conical lid which rests on a flange inside its rim and is held in place by an ingenious system of cord loops (see fig. 120). An oval basket from Erment and another of unknown provenience have long, convex lids not unlike a low mansard roof in appearance. An inventory of the contents of one of the larger baskets of this class, an exceptionally well preserved example which had belonged to Sen-ne-mūt's sister(?), is both instructive and amusing. Neatly packed in its circular interior were found the small double casket referred to in the preceding paragraph, a switch, three bundles, and two braids of false hair, an alabaster *koḥl*-jar and ebony *koḥl*-stick, twenty small edible tubers of *Cyperus esculentus*, a mass of aromatic wood chips, pieces of castor-oil reed, two lumps of resin, a few lumps of refined Nile mud such as was used for sealings, and a quantity of fine black dust (fig. 111). One of three ★model baskets from Gebelein is composed of an openwork mesh of fine rushes laced together with narrow strips of split rush. The two others are of palm-leaf strip reinforced with grass cord and bound around the rim with strips of rush. Each is provided with two cord handles and one contained three little ★model *koḥl*-jars carved from single blocks of wood and having their rims and bases painted red.

6. Musical Instruments and Games

In keeping with the marked advances in Egyptian music which accompanied the rise of the New Kingdom and which stemmed for the most part from western Asia (see p. 25), we should expect to find during Thutmoside times musical instruments of more developed and elaborate types than those which we have hitherto encountered. In this we are not disappointed, though our knowledge of such instruments is based more on representations of them in Eighteenth Dynasty tomb paintings than on the relatively few actual examples which have come down to us.

Precisely the kind of elaboration referred to is found in an arched, naviform ★harp (fig. 112) of undoubted Thutmoside date in our collection. The long, boat-shaped soundbox and adjustable suspension rod of the instrument differ in no essential respect from those of the earlier harps illustrated in figure 9; but the number of strings has been increased from four (or at the most five) to sixteen,

FIGURE 112. Wooden harp of the mid-Eighteenth Dynasty. Twelve of the strings, nine of their pegs, and parts of soundbox restored. W. 32 ¼ in.

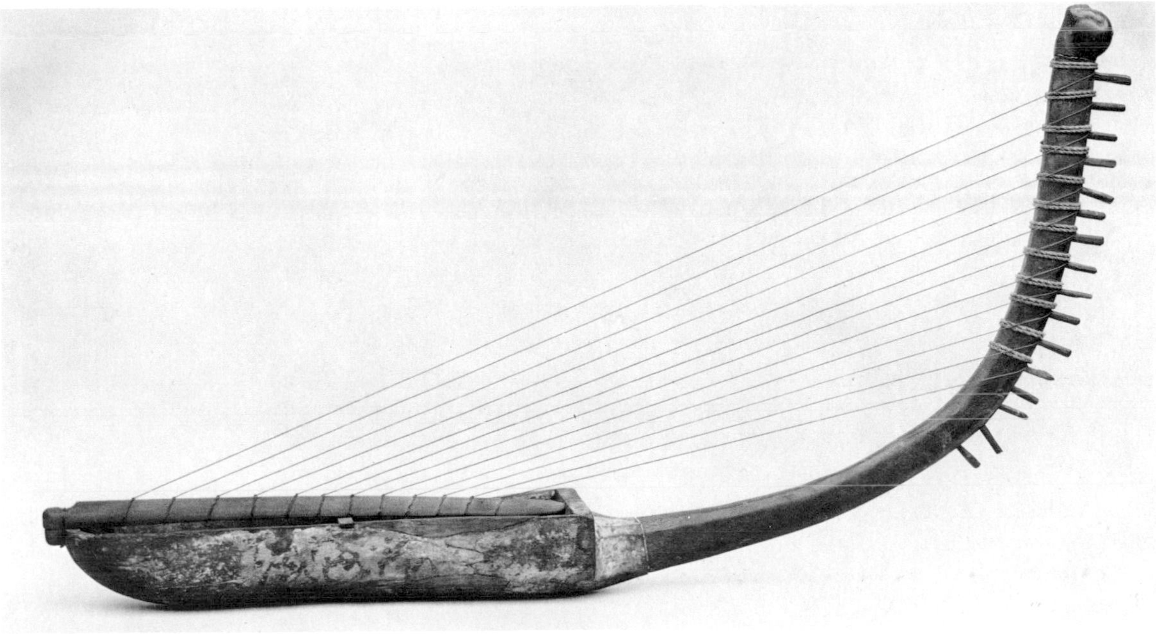

and to accommodate these the neck, made of a separate piece of wood, has been given the pronounced curve seen at an earlier period on vertical arched harps of Mesopotamian origin. As frequently on harps of the New Kingdom, the end of the neck is adorned with a small human head skillfully carved from a block of dark hardwood and attached by means of a tenon. Such heads more often than not represent divinities, and in the present instance the subject may well be the goddess Maʿet wearing a short coiffure with a hole in the top for the feather which is the distinguishing mark of this particular deity. Incidentally, the way in which the small face looks straight out from the end of the neck of the instrument suggests that the harp was held in a more or less vertical position when being played.

Aside from this harp and three bone ★pegs from another harp or perhaps from a lute, the only objects of Thutmoside date in our collection which may be classed among musical instruments are fragments of three votive ★sistrums of faience decorated with heads of the goddess Ḥat-Ḥor, near whose shrine at Deir el Baḥri they were found. A large angular ★harp and a small barrel-shaped ★drum, once assigned to the New Kingdom, are now recognized as belonging to a much later period.

The games of the New Kingdom Egyptians, especially the always popular board games, are, happily, somewhat better represented. The handsome ★draughtboard, or game box, shown restored in figure 113 was found at Abydos in the tomb of the Scribe Mery-Maʿet, a contemporary or near contemporary of King Tḥut-mosĕ III. Inlaid with squares and panels of bright blue faience, it carries on its top the layout, or board, for the ancient game of *senet* and on its bottom that for the "game of twenty squares," recently imported from western Asia and called by the Egyptians *tjau* (see fig. 10). The hieroglyphs drawn in black outline on the first five squares of the *senet*-board show, as in other examples of the game, that special significance was attached to these squares. The single sun disk (☉), the pair of men (𓀀𓀀), and the trio of *ba*-birds (𓅽) on the first three squares may only indicate their numerical values or order, 1, 2, and 3; but the symbol for "water" (𓈗) on the fourth square certainly suggests a pitfall, or penalty square, and the group meaning "goodness" (𓄤𓄤𓄤) on the fifth square points to its being either an advantageous square or perhaps the goal, or winning square, of the game. Though during the New Kingdom *senet* seems usually to have been played with ten pieces, five to a side, the present set includes eight conical ★draughtsmen and seven spool-shaped ★draughtsmen of blue and black striped faience. These were kept, when not in use, in a small drawer housed in one end of the long box and locked by means of a hardwood —○— bolt sliding in bronze staples. The players appear to have sat one on either of the long sides of the board, which in this case are designated as "south" and "north" by little drawings of the heraldic plants of Upper and Lower Egypt at the centers of their faience inlay panels.

A second ★draughtboard, carved from a single block of dark brown wood, is not inlaid, but the playing squares of the *senet* and *tjau* games are recessed in its top and bottom surfaces. Eighteen and a half inches in length, it is similar in almost every respect to a board found in the well-known tomb of the architect Khaʿ, a Theban official who served under King Amun-ḥotpe II and his two successors. Our board, too, was the property of a royal architect, or Overseer of Works, named Teya, and is inscribed on its top and sides with offering formulae invoking the divinities of Thebes in behalf of this man and his family. On the sides Amūn, "sweet of love," and two or more other deities whose names have been destroyed are asked to assure to Teya himself a favorable memory and a well-deserved reputation for virtue; while on the top Amūn, the "King, high of plumes," and "[Ḥat-Ḥor], Mistress of the Necropolis," are called upon to care for the needs of his parents, Teya (the Elder) and Yuwy. In a little scene engraved on the solid end of the block we see the owner and his wife the House Mistress Tekhy seated side by side and confronted, on the opposite side of a table of

FIGURE 113. Draughtboard and playing pieces of the mid-Eighteenth Dynasty. Wood (restored) inlaid with panels of faience. L. 15¾ in.

offerings, by "her mother, Aʿḥ-mosĕ," who sits alone, holding before her nose a large lotus flower. The other end of the block is hollowed out to provide a housing for the usual small bolted drawer, which in this case is empty. However, an important clue as to how one of the games was played or scored may be supplied by two lines of numerals, from 1 to 10, written in hieratic on the inner end of the drawer and arranged in the following order:

6	9	2	5	8
1	4	7	10	3

A set of faience ★draughtsmen from the tomb of Nefer-khēwet at Thebes comprises five conical and five spool-shaped pieces, the former averaging an inch in height, the latter under three-quarters of an inch. In a second set from the same tomb only the five conical ★draughtsmen are of faience. The spool-shaped men, carved of a fine, dark wood like the boards which they accompanied, had been almost completely destroyed by damp rot and termites. Nine conical and three spool-shaped ★playing pieces, acquired with the Murch collection, are from three or four different sets and show a number of interesting variations in their forms. All are of blue or green faience, sometimes decorated with black stripes or spots. A single conical ★draughtsman of alabaster is a trifle larger than the average, measuring an inch and three-sixteenths in height. Two rough little spool-shaped ★pieces of faience come in one case from near the North Pyramid at el Lisht and in the other from Medīnet Habu in western Thebes. A small ★cone-shaped object of bone with a rounded top is also from el Lisht and may also be a playing piece, though the game involved is difficult to identify.

Two ★game pegs found by the Museum's Expedition at el Lisht are topped by the heads of canine animals, one clearly a hound with large, pendent ears, the other perhaps a jackal or another breed of dog with upstanding, pointed ears. They are carved, respectively, of ivory and of wood and measure two and an eighth and three inches in height. Though dated by their finders to "the Empire," they come from a game known as "hounds and jackals" which is more characteristic of the Middle Kingdom than of later periods. With

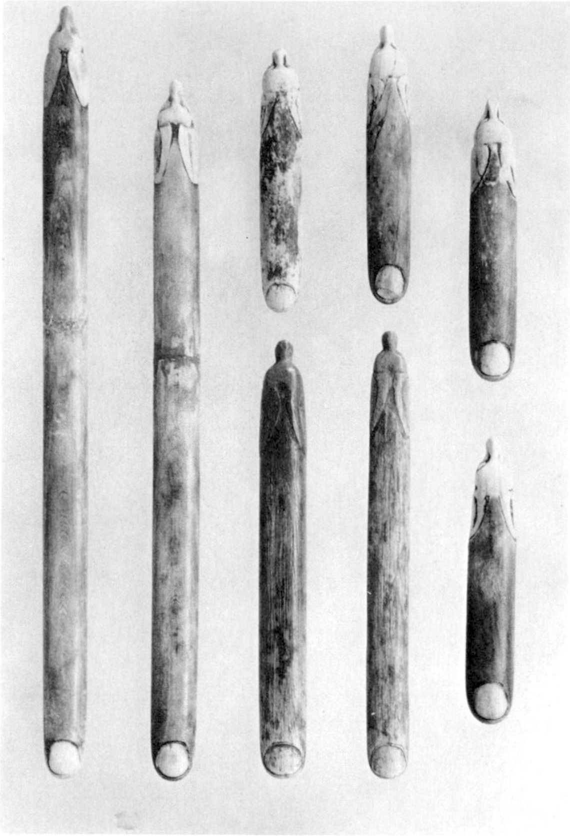

FIGURE 114. Game wands, or casting sticks, of tinted ivory. From Thebes. L. 3¼-9 in.

them was found a smaller ivory ★peg with a plain, disk-shaped head, which has also been thought to be from a game of some sort.

Knucklebones and, later, dice were used in conjunction with Egyptian board games, but during the earlier New Kingdom the moves in *senet*, *tjau*, and related games were usually determined, as they are in the modern game of *tāb es sīgeh*, by throwing sets of four or more slender, wandlike rods, generally known nowadays as casting sticks. Nine such ★sticks (see fig. 114), purchased at Luxor in 1919, are carved of ivory, their flat undersides left white, their slightly convex backs tinted red. It is clear that, as with modern sets, the value of the cast depended to a great extent on the number of white sides which fell uppermost. In our present set (or sets), however, not only the sides but also the ends of the wands are differentiated from one another, one end in each case having the form of a human fingertip, while the other is adorned with the carefully carved head of a long-eared canine animal, probably a fox. Some significance must also have been attached to the lengths of the sticks, five of which are short (three and a quarter inches), two long (nine inches), and two of medium length (five inches).

Eleven small balls, or ★marbles, made of alabaster, pink limestone, breccia, and diorite have been tentatively assigned to "the Empire," but may be of much earlier date, resembling those belonging to games of Early Dynastic times found by Petrie at Ballās and Gīzeh. Each of two ★game balls acquired from a native of Ḳurneh is made of two segments of rawhide sewn together and tightly stuffed with barley chaff. Two and three-quarters inches in diameter, they differ in no important respect from the balls found and depicted in tombs of the Middle Kingdom (see Part I, p. 251, and above, p. 26). New Kingdom surface rubbish near the pyramid of Amun-em-ḥēt I at el Lisht yielded two solid wooden ★spheres, an inch and a quarter and an inch and five-eighths in diameter, which must also have belonged to a game. The surfaces of both are covered with incised designs, in one case an over-all pattern of circles and dots, in the other simply haphazard stippling. Care has been taken in each instance to produce a sphere of sufficient regularity and balance to be used in a game of skill, such as a marble game or some miniature form of bowling.

7. Housefurnishings

Though our knowledge of the Egyptian dwelling house in the time of the Thutmoside pharaohs is limited to artisans' dwellings in the ancient village at Deir el Medīneh and to representations of larger and more elaborate houses in the tombs of contemporary Theban officials, the furnishings of such houses have come down to us in greater quantity and variety than from any of the preceding periods of Egyptian history.

Of furniture, properly speaking, our own collection is fortunate in possessing a handsome ★chair of boxwood and ebony which had belonged to Sen-ne-mūt's mother, Ḥat-nūfer, and was found broken up and cached outside the doorway of her tomb. The chair, shown reassembled in figure 115, has a well-preserved seat of string mesh composed of triple strands of linen cord interwoven in a herringbone pattern. Its legs are carved with care to represent those of a lion, and its paneled back displays at the top an openwork design comprising a figure of the god Bēs carved in boxwood and flanked on either side by ebony *tyet*-symbols (of Isis) and boxwood *djed*-symbols (of Osiris?). Less ornate, but equally well made, is a ★chair of the same type and size said to have come from an early Eighteenth Dynasty tomb on the slopes of the Dirāʿ Abu'n Naga. In this case the back of the chair is not carved nor adorned with marquetry work, but is made up of a plain rectangular frame enclosing five perfectly plain vertical slats, one of which, together with most of the string mesh seat, was missing when the chair was acquired by the Museum. Constructed throughout of a light-colored, fine-grained hardwood, the chair is in other respects strikingly similar to Ḥat-nūfer's and must have been closely contemporary with it. From a plundered burial shaft under the south wall of Sen-ne-mūt's tomb courtyard come half a

FIGURE 115. Ḥat-nūfer's boxwood and ebony chair, with its original cord mesh seat. H. 21 in.

FIGURE 116. Folding stool of hardwood inlaid with ebony and ivory. W. 16 in.

dozen fragments of a third ★chair, also of the same type and size as that of Ḥat-nūfer, but made of a dark red wood (cypress?) inlaid with boxwood, ebony, and ivory. As reconstructed on paper the chair appears to have had an over-all height of nineteen and a quarter inches and a width of between seventeen and eighteen inches. Its legs are carved in the forms of the fore and hind legs of a lion and its light and dark paneled back is framed by a laminated border of light yellow and dark red strips. The L-braces supporting the back are tipped with boxwood, edged with ebony, and inlaid with squares of ebony flanked by ivory triangles. The seat, like those of the other chairs, was apparently of string mesh, though nothing of this now remains.

With seats barely eight inches above the ground, all three of these chairs are of the low, broad type favored by a people who were probably more comfortable squatting on or near the floors of their houses than sitting upright in a chair of what we regard as normal proportions. Both types of chair appear in use on the stela of figure 93 where, in the second register, the owner's daughter is seen sitting with feet drawn up on a chair no higher than those we have been discussing. Fragments of a larger ★chair with a curved back and a seat height of fourteen and a half inches were recovered by our expedition from the tomb of the Fanbearer Aʿḥ-mosĕ Pe'n-ḥat (see also p. 77), a Theban contemporary of King Tḥut-mosĕ I. Sturdily made of a dark, reddish brown hardwood, this chair was once veneered with panels and strips of ebony and ivory. The single leg which remains has the form of the foreleg of a lion resting on the usual corrugated block. With the pieces of the chair were found bits of a marquetry ★table, similar in form to the table of figure 12, but larger and more intricately inlaid with bands and rectangles of white and brown wood. Estimates based on the remaining fragments have placed the minimum length of this table at thirty-three inches and its minimum width at nineteen inches.

The folding ★stool of figure 116, to judge from the perforations in its rails, was once provided with a woven seat, not with the leather seat more often found with this class of furniture. Both the ends of the legs and the ends of the lower rails are skillfully carved in the forms of ducks' heads with their characteristic markings inlaid in ebony and ivory. At the crossings the legs are held together by bronze rivets which are provided with washers to save wear and tear on the wood. As popular as it is graceful, this type of stool seems to have been particularly characteristic of the Eighteenth Dynasty, and most of the datable examples belong to this period.

Though our collection is lacking in full-size examples, the forms of bed used by the Egyptians of the earlier New Kingdom are revealed to us in four interesting ★funerary models of beds, one with the figure of a slender young woman reclining upon it (fig. 117). This model, carved of limestone, shows us a low, heavily constructed couch with upward-projecting footboard and short, turned legs. At the head end, under the head of the sleeping girl, can be made out a heavy columnar headrest. Traces of pigment here and there indicate that the bed was painted red in imitation of wood and that the eyes and short, bobbed coiffure of its occupant were once black. A pottery bed model, from a tomb in the ʿAsāsīf valley, has four thick cylindrical legs, a rectangular footboard, and at the head end, two small pillows, or bolsters, modeled in clay on its upper surface. Five and a

FIGURE 117. A bed with headrest and reclining female figure. Painted limestone. L. 16¾ in.

half inches long, it is somewhat cursorily modeled in a fine, soft brown ware and is painted white, with red crisscross lines on its top to represent a string mesh. Most interesting is a twelve-inch model of a folding bed (fig. 118) carefully constructed of painted wood and coming in all probability from a tomb of the Eighteenth Dynasty at Gebelein. Hinges in the longitudinal rails of the bed over the middle pair of legs allow the head section to be folded up and over onto the foot section, thereby appreciably shortening the length of the bed and facilitating its storage and transportation. A perforated flange around the inside of the frame indicates that the "springs" consisted, as usual, of a network or mesh of cords such as is used in the Sudanese *angarīb* of the present day. Hinges, angle pieces, and edgings, which on full-size beds of this type are of bronze, are here painted black, the rest of the model being white. Parts of a second model of the same type and provenience are painted red. Several bronze ★hinges from full-size beds of this sort form part of the coppersmith's hoard from el Lisht referred to on page 190.

Two of our four Eighteenth Dynasty ★headrests are of the usual columnar type (⌶), carved in one case from a single block of wood and made up, in the other case, of two parts joined together by a vertical tenon. They come, respectively, from a tomb on the Dirāʿ Abu'n Naga cleared by the Earl of Carnarvon and from the burial of Sen-ne-mūt's singer, Ḥar-mosĕ (see p. 111). Though purchased in Luxor, the delicate ivory headrest shown in figure 119 is of unknown provenience and of somewhat uncertain date. Its slender shaft has the form of a small, fluted column, above which a pair of outspread human hands form graceful supports for the curved ivory pillow. As might have been expected, the base, shaft, and pillow of this headrest are carved from separate pieces of ivory and are joined together by a long, slender dowel. Our fourth headrest, coming from a tomb of the Eighteenth Dynasty at Abydos, is made of limestone and, though full size, is perhaps to be regarded as a funerary model rather than as an actual article of furniture. Basically, it consists of a trapezoidal slab of stone on which the form of a columnar headrest has been carved in high relief.

One of two wooden ★linen chests from the tomb of Sen-ne-mūt's parents is a plain rectangular box with a flat lid, made of heavy and somewhat rough sycamore boards. Just under thirty inches in length, it is sturdily built, with dovetailed corners and stout battens on the undersides of its floor and lid. The second chest is not only more elaborate in form but is of better material (pine) and is more carefully constructed and finished. Provided with a double-pitched, gable lid and standing on four short legs, it measures twenty-seven and a half inches in length, fourteen and a quarter inches in width, and seventeen and a quarter inches in height. Both chests are painted white inside and out and each is equipped with two stout knobs, one on the end of the lid and one on the corresponding end of the box. By means of these the lid

FIGURE 118. A folding bed. An ancient funerary model or toy in painted wood. L. 12⅛ in.

in each case had been lashed in place with cord, the knotting of the cord between the knobs being secured by a stamped mud ★sealing.

The chests contained, between them, fifty-five long, fringed ★sheets, or bolts, of linen cloth, each sheet folded to form a neat rectangular bundle. The cloth differs in spin and weave, so that the sheets vary in texture from a very coarse material like burlap to a remarkably fine, filmy, weblike cambric, and in color from medium brown to almost pure white. Each sheet is woven in one piece, in lengths ranging from fourteen to fifty-four feet. In addition to weavers' marks, worked in the fabric, twenty-six of the sheets bear identification marks in black ink. Nearly all the latter are marks of the government and temple linen stores, whence, we may assume, Raʿ-mosĕ and Ḥat-nūfer drew or purchased the cloth. The only private name which occurs among these marks is that of an individual named Amun-mosĕ. There is not much doubt that the sheets—clean and neatly pressed—represent not embalmers' equipment but Ḥat-nūfer's supply of household linen. Their amazing state of preservation allows them to be unfolded and refolded at will.

Though empty at the time of its discovery, a third ★chest, found by the Earl of Carnarvon in the ruins of Ḥat-shepsūt's Valley Temple, probably contained, among other items, a quantity of clothing. Four different varieties of garments, in any case, are listed in a hieratic inscription written in black ink on the underside of its lid. This inscription is in the form of a memorandum addressed by the "Scribe Tety" to a man named Meryu. It is dated to "Month 3 of Prōyet, Day 4" and is entitled "Account for the Feast of the Valley." In addition to the clothing, which belonged apparently to the "Chief of Craftsmen Amun-ḥotpe," it mentions "Upper Egyptian barley" and other commodities "which are in the possession of the Overseer of the Forehall of the Temple in the [Southern?] Sanctuary (Luxor)."

Besides the inscribed sheets contained in the linen chests our collection includes eight★marked pieces of what was originally household linen used

FIGURE 119. An ivory headrest. H. 6 7/8 in.

in the wrappings of the mummies of various members of Sen-ne-mūt's family. On the mummy of his father were found two sheets (p. 105) bearing the cartouches of Ḥat-shepsūt's daughter, the Princess Nefru-Rēʿ, and two marked simply with a 𓊽-symbol. Sheets from the bodies of two female members of the great man's household are labeled as having belonged to the "Treasury"; while two others, from the burial of a male relative(?), are inscribed with the personal names Amun-mosĕ and Weʿbet-Amūn. Several sheets bear, in addition, the designation "real (linen?)" and several a mark shaped like a plus sign, perhaps another indication of quality. The kingly epithet "Ruler of Right," written on a ★sheet from one of the Sen-ne-mūt embalmers' caches (see p. 226) and on many of those from Ḥat-nūfer's linen chests, was probably a mark of the royal linen store.

For the storage and safekeeping of household supplies and miscellaneous items of household equipment the New Kingdom Egyptian, like his ancient predecessors and modern descendants, had recourse to large baskets and hampers made chiefly of grass or palm leaf. An oval ★basket of this class (fig. 120) which had belonged to Sen-ne-mūt's mother combines both materials, the coils of the lid and upper part of the basket being wrapped with Ḥalfa grass, while the bottom, inner rims, and other parts of both basket and lid which were required to stand special wear or strain are whipped with palm-leaf strip. The decoration, composed of black and red chevrons, bars, and rectangles, is not painted on, but was achieved by weaving into the fabric strands of grass which had previously been dyed either black or red. Four double loops of linen cord, rising from the rim of the basket and tied together over the center of the lid, served to hold the latter firmly in place. When opened the basket was found to be packed with ★loaves of bread, ★dates and ★raisins disposed in three small ★pottery dishes, and lumps of black matter, also containing raisins, which looked as wedding cake might if kept for three thousand years. The bread is of two kinds, one light brown with a hard, glossy crust like that of modern Vienna rolls, the other dark, grayish brown, with a rough surface. The four types of loaf include rings, disks, cones, and a long, flat form of fancy shape, possibly intended to suggest a human figure. Another large oval ★basket, also once the property of Ḥat-nūfer, is sewn entirely with palm-leaf strip and is reinforced with extra strands of the same material. Though undoubtedly designed for household use it contained when found nothing but a jumbled mass of dirty, oil-soaked bandages, probably used in the process of embalming Ḥat-nūfer's mummy. Two small, oval ★basketry trays, suitable for holding small fruits or berries, are made of palm fiber and palm-leaf strip and one is decorated with geometrical designs woven in colored grass. They come from the neighborhood of the ʿAsāsīf in western Thebes, as does also the ★lid of a small rectangular hamper constructed of reeds and palm ribs covered with sewn palm-leaf matting. A fragment of plaited ★matting of the same material is either from a similar hamper or from a floor or wall covering. Two flat rectangular ★panniers, or donkey baskets, measure twenty-two by sixteen and fourteen and a half by ten inches. The larger, woven of two-ply grass rope, was found beside the South Pyramid at el Lisht and contained the coppersmith's hoard of scrap metal previously mentioned. The smaller, from the fill near Sen-ne-mūt's second tomb, at Deir el Baḥri, is made of strips of palm fiber laced at intervals with grass cord, and is fitted at the top with two small loop handles.

Some ninety household vessels of Thutmoside date in our collection include flower bowls of bronze, faience, and painted pottery; drinking cups and ewers of bronze, faience, and stone; dishes, jugs, wine jars, and storage jars of pottery; jar stands of bronze and faience; mortars and pestles of stone; and several small containers carved of wood and ivory. The interesting bronze ★flower bowl of figure 121, found with two others in the forecourt of the tomb of the Vizier Rekh-mi-Rēʿ, was apparently designed as a votive

FIGURE 120. Grass and palm-leaf basket containing loaves of bread and other food supplies. L. 25 in.

FIGURE 121. Bronze flower bowl of the mid-Eighteenth Dynasty. Diam. 8 ⅝ in.

offering to the goddess Ḥat-Ḥor and has as its centerpiece a little bronze figure of the Ḥat-Ḥor cow crowned with the solar disk and double plume and raised above the bottom of the bowl on a small metal bridge. When the bowl is partly filled with water and with flowers the animal appears to be standing in the midst of a marshy thicket, reminiscent of the thickets of Chemmis, where Ḥat-Ḥor is reputed to have nursed the infant Horus (see p. 403). Eight ★bowls of turquoise blue faience and ★fragments of three others are decorated on their interiors with open and closed lotus flowers, fish, and birds conventionally drawn in heavy black line and symmetrically grouped in the circular fields. The blue backgrounds, suggesting water, are well suited to the aquatic character of the decoration, which in turn is appropriate to vessels intended to contain liquids. It is not unlikely that flowers similar to those depicted in the bowls were once arranged in them. In most cases the exteriors of the bowls are decorated with simple lotus-petal patterns, but in one instance the arrangement is reversed and the principal decoration—groups of flying waterfowl—appears on the exterior of the vessel. Bowls of this class, ranging in diameter from five to eleven inches, were especially common during the reigns of Ḥat-shepsūt and Tḥut-mosĕ III, but continued to be produced throughout the greater part of the Eighteenth Dynasty.

The drinking bowls of this period (see fig. 122) are for the most part small, shallow vessels rarely more than seven inches in diameter and usually round-bottomed, especially when made of metal. Three of our bronze ★drinking bowls have simple, rounded profiles, while three others are of the necked type, with sharply defined shoulder and vertical or recurved lip—a form with a history reaching back to the days of the Old Kingdom. A blue faience ★bowl from a Theban burial of the time of Ḥat-shepsūt is adorned around the rim with a row of black triangles, perhaps intended as lotus petals. Somewhat deeper ★bowls with flat bases occur in both faience and alabaster; little round-bottomed ★cups are made in one instance of alabaster and in another of gabbro; and, about the middle of our period, a broad, carinated ★cup with gracefully incurved sides is found in alabaster. Small globular and cordiform ★vases of bronze with wide, cylindrical necks are probably to be classed as drinking vessels, as are also two slender, highly polished alabaster ★situlae. Several fine examples of the footed lotiform ★goblet in blue and green faience, formerly dated to the Eighteenth Dynasty, are now recognized as belonging to a later period.

The minute size of six little one-handled ★pitchers and ★jugs of metal and stone suggests that they were designed to contain small amounts of spiced liquids such as were used, for example, in the flavoring of wine. In banquet scenes of the early New Kingdom we not infrequently see serving girls spicing the guests' drinks from pairs of tiny ovoid pitchers of the type shown in the foreground of figure 122. The little bronze vessel illustrated, coming from the tomb of Ḥat-shepsūt's archivist, Nefer-khēwet, measures less than four inches in height. Though even smaller, the miniature copper jug shown with it has its handle adorned with the skillfully modeled head of an ibex. Two of our stone jugs, one of alabaster, the other of serpentine, are small, footed vessels with high, cylindrical necks, to which in each case the wide, straplike handle is joined with simulated cord lashing. A second alabaster pitcher—inspired, perhaps, by a Syrian prototype—is slenderly proportioned and exceedingly graceful, with elongated ovoid body, tall, thin neck, and long, looped handle. With a height of eight and a quarter inches, it is almost three inches taller than its mates.

Four long-necked little pottery ★jugs (fig. 123, foreground), coming from Theban burials of the earlier Thutmoside period, were almost certainly importations into Egypt, probably from Palestine-Syria. Of a type well known and widely distributed throughout the eastern Mediterranean world, they are made of a hard, fine-grained black ware not, apparently, indigenous to Egypt. The same ware was used in the manufacture of a slender ovoid ★vase without handles, also of non-Egyptian type. An exaggeratedly tall, thin ★jug of polished red ware is of undoubted Syrian inspiration, if not actually of Syrian origin. So also are two curious little red pottery ★jugs provided not only with vertical loop handles attached to the backs of their tall, tapered necks, but also with pierced lug handles projecting upward from the ends of their squat, oval bodies.

Among the more characteristic types of Egyptian household pottery produced at this period is the familiar footed jar with bulbous body and

FIGURE 122. Household vessels of bronze, copper, alabaster, serpentine, and faience. H. of inscribed bronze bottle 7 in.

cylindrical neck, usually made of a smooth buff or pink ware and decorated with simple linear patterns in black, red, and brown. Eight such jars in our collection had been adapted for use as large jugs by attaching to the neck of each a single vertical handle; while three others had been provided with a pair of stirruplike handles rising on either side of the shoulder of the vessel (see fig. 123). The ★jugs range in height from six and a quarter to ten and a half inches, while the ★two-handled jars are a little larger, reaching a maximum height of almost twelve inches. Nearly all are from well-dated Theban burials of early and middle Thutmoside times.

Another popular Eighteenth Dynasty form, the drop-shaped jar, or bottle, is represented by an example in bronze and three in white or pale yellow pottery. The whole of the ★bronze bottle (see fig. 122), including even the rim, was beaten to shape from a single sheet of metal. Not quite seven inches in height, it had been presented, as the engraved inscription on its shoulder tells us, by a man named Kheruef as a "god's offering to Amūn." It is probably from Upper Egypt, having been purchased in 1912 from a native of Asyūt. Two of the three ★pottery jars, including one with simple linear decoration in black and red (see fig. 123), are from the burial of Sen-ne-mūt's brother Amun-ḥotpe. The third jar comes from the well-known Theban tomb (No. 52) of the Astronomer(?) Nakhte, a contemporary of King Tḥutmosĕ IV. Adorned with broad bands of pale blue petals separated by groups of thin red lines, it is an early example of a class of fine decorated pottery which we find in gratifying profusion in the palaces and tombs of the late Eighteenth Dynasty (see pp. 187 f., 244, 247, 323).

The tomb of Sen-ne-mūt's younger brother also produced two high-necked ★cordiform jars of red pottery, whitewashed and attractively decorated with bands of geometric and floral ornament in black and red (see fig. 123). Here, too, was found a small ★brazier in greenish white *ḳulleh*-ware covered with a thick, creamy white slip. From the near-by tomb of Sen-ne-mūt's parents come two shallow brown pottery ★saucers, their interiors splashed with spots of red paint, their rims edged with thin red bands. With these may be compared a small, nicely made ★saucer of polished copper (see fig. 122), the style of which suggests that it, too, is to be dated to the early New Kingdom. Tombs of this period on the Dirāʿ Abu'n Naga yielded a larger ★dish made of fine gray pottery, a curious red pottery ★cup with a molded foot and a curved, bucket-type handle, and a small ★double jug of light-red ware, painted white and crudely decorated with vertical black and red stripes.

Three more or less well dated ★ring stands, two of faience and one of bronze, were designed to support relatively small vases or bowls of, presumably, the same materials. Though differently proportioned and ranging in diameter from four to six and three-quarters inches, the stands are all shaped like hollow spools, with flaring rims and incurved sides. Both faience stands are decorated in black line, one with a band of lotus petals, the other with an over-all scale pattern.

The big ★pottery jars used in Thutmoside households for the storage of supplies of food and drink show considerable variety in their forms. Besides great amphorae of the type found in the tomb of Raʿ-mosĕ and Ḥat-nūfer there are large cylindrical jars with rounded bottoms, high necks, and two or three handles, broad cordiform jars with or without necks but with two handles set high up on the shoulder of the vessel, and massive drop-shaped jars with wide mouths, bulging midsections, and capacities comparable to that of the modern beer keg. The heights of such jars range from sixteen and a half to twenty-seven inches and some of them are almost as broad as they are high. The favorite ware is a hard, medium-coarse, red pottery which is usually surfaced with a thin white slip or wash. One of the big drop-shaped jars, found reused in an embalmers' cache below the tomb of Sen-ne-mūt, still has around it the papyrus-rope ★sling by means of which it was carried to the cache. ★Fragments of the shoulders of two similar jars are inscribed with the word "Honey" neatly written in red hieroglyphs on a white rectangle framed in red.

A common method of sealing jars, both large

FIGURE 123. Pottery vessels of the Thutmoside period, including a number of foreign types. H. of tallest jar 14¼ in.

and small, was to place a pottery saucer, right side up or inverted, over the mouth of the vessel and lash it in place with a piece of linen cloth, knotting the latter about the neck of the jar and often securing the knot with a stamped mud or wax sealing. Another type of ★jar stopper, of which we possess half a dozen examples, is a thick disk or wad made from the pith and rind of the papyrus stalk. Several ★stoppers of pale, yellowish clay and dark gray Nile mud were evidently set in place while still soft and reproduce exactly the rim and mouth forms of the jars from which they came.

The ★sealings found on the jar coverings and on the cord lashings of boxes and baskets are small, circular or oval blobs of mud or, more rarely, wax, which while soft had been stamped one or more times with a scarab or with a rectangular or cartouche-shaped seal. Early Thutmoside tomb pits in the Seʿankh-ku-Rēʿ temple platform produced a series of sealings of the type referred to, including one in wax with the impression of a circular seal of the "Scribe Neb-mosĕ." The others had been stamped with scarabs bearing heraldic and decorative designs. The mud sealing on a knotted linen jar cover from the tomb (No. 121) of the Second Prophet of Amūn, Aʿḥ-mosĕ, bears a square seal impression with a device made up of lizards and intertwining uraei; while oval impressions on two sealings from Deir el Ballās show in one case the standing figure of a man and in the other a hieroglyph-and-scroll pattern. Remarkable for its clarity is the cartouche-shaped impression on a burnt clay sealing from Karnak(?) (ex Ward collection, No. 260). Here the cartouche, surmounted by the disk and plumes, contains the name of the god Amun Rēʿ, followed by the epithets "Lord of Thrones-of-the-Two-Lands" and "Resider in Most-select-of-places." The oval impression on an Eighteenth Dynasty sealing from the temple of Neb-ḥepet-Rēʿ Montu-ḥotpe at Deir el Baḥri is illegible; and thirteen small sealings from near the North Pyramid at el Lisht are probably of the Middle Kingdom, though they have been assigned somewhat loosely to "Dyn. XIV-XXII."

FIGURE 124. Brewer's vat (?). Wood. H. 27 in.

The big wooden jar, or ★vat, of figure 124 is one of a pair which had been broken up, packed in grass-rope donkey baskets, and deposited on the hill slope below Sen-ne-mūt's first tomb on the ʿIlwet esh Sheikh ʿAbd el Ḳurneh. Once identified as churns, the vessel and its mate are more likely to have been vats in which brewers prepared the mash used in the production of beer, an operation which was an almost daily occurrence in the average large Egyptian household. In both size and type they resemble the great mash tubs appearing in scenes of brewing preserved to us in tombs of the Middle and early New Kingdoms. Our vat, which stands twenty-seven inches in height, was made of two vertical segments, or staves, painstakingly carved from a sycamore log, tightly joined together with pegged tenons, and covered inside and out with a thick coat of varnish. The circular floor piece fitted snugly inside the staves and the whole had been caulked with linen rags, brown sizing matter, and grayish gum so that it would be capable of holding a liquid. The removable cover, made in two parts and having a broad slot left open down its middle, would permit a paddle or dasher to be worked both up and down and back and forth in the receptacle and, at the same time, would prevent the churned liquid from splashing out over the sides. It would also provide a rigid support for a sieve without interfering with the passage of the strained liquid into the container below.

A small alabaster ★mortar, probably designed for household use, is exactly like one found in an Eighteenth Dynasty tomb at Abydos. Shaped like a rimless flowerpot, to which has been added a pair of vertical lug handles, it is accompanied by an alabaster ★pestle of essentially "modern" form. The same type of pestle occurs in a ★mortar and pestle set of limestone, found near the North Pyramid at el Lisht, the mortar in this case being a roughly made, round-bottomed bowl six and a half inches in diameter. The rounded lower end of a large diorite ★pestle, also from el Lisht, has a diameter of over two inches.

To produce the characteristic design seen at this period on circular loaves of bread (see fig. 120), a circular wooden ★bread-stamp has projecting from its flat underside a convex boss surrounded by a ring of small, round-topped pegs. The top of the stamp is provided with a carved handle and has scratched upon it a mark of ownership(?) consisting apparently of a table ( ) surmounting a headrest ( ).

Another item of kitchen equipment of more than usual interest is a ★fire-making kit of the bow drill type, comprising the hardwood drill shaft, the granite drill cap, and the notched block of soft wood on which the drill was rotated—in short, all except the bow itself and the necessary tinder. Found in the ruins of workmen's huts in the Valley of the Tombs of the Kings, the kit had evidently been used repeatedly, the edges of its block showing the charred cavities acquired during the kindling of a number of fires.

The Eighteenth Dynasty coppersmith's hoard from el Lisht, previously described, contained, among multifarious other pieces of scrap metal, the blade of a curved bronze ★kitchen knife, a long, bronze ★spatula with rounded end, and a sheet-bronze ★chopper shaped like an axe blade, with a rounded edge and a straight back rolled to serve as a grip.

Still other items which one would be likely to find in a well-appointed New Kingdom house include a three-tufted ★broom made of a papyrus umbel lashed with cord, two crescent-shaped wooden objects identified as ★pack-holders (see pp. 413 f.), and a pierced wooden rod which, when threaded on the latchstring of a door, served as a sort of primitive ★key.

8. Weapons and Tools

Many factors, both psychological and material, contributed to the invincibility of the armies led by the Thutmoside pharaohs. Among the latter none was of greater importance than the maneuverability of the recently organized chariot divisions and the range and power of the New Kingdom bow.

For military purposes the Egyptian archer now favored a fairly long bow of recurved form, reflex action, and composite construction (see p. 29). Ṭhut-mosĕ I's Fanbearer Aʿḥ-mosĕ Pe'n-ḥat possessed three ★bows of this type, the fragments of which were recovered by our expedition from his tomb in western Thebes. Estimated to have had a length, when unstrung, of approximately five feet, each of these weapons is composed of two thin layers of antelope horn glued on either side of a flat or grooved wooden core, the whole covered with a thick coating of glue and enclosed within a smooth envelope of birch bark.

Two six-foot self ★bows of the recurved African type (⌣⌢; see fig. 125, bottom), found cached with a set of seventeen reed ★arrows below the hillside tomb of Sen-ne-mūt (No. 71), were undoubtedly hunting weapons made for the diversion of the great official, whose brief and undistinguished military career had evidently been confined to the days of his youth. With staves of lemonwood, circular in cross section and attaining at the centers a thickness of almost an inch and a half, these huge bows must have had a range comparable to that of the military weapons just discussed. Our two examples were apparently newly made and had never been strung, their plain, tapered tips showing no marks or other traces of

FIGURE 125. Theban weapons of the time of Ḥat-shepsūt: bows, arrows, javelins, throw-stick, club, dagger, and axe. L. of longer bow 70 ½ in.

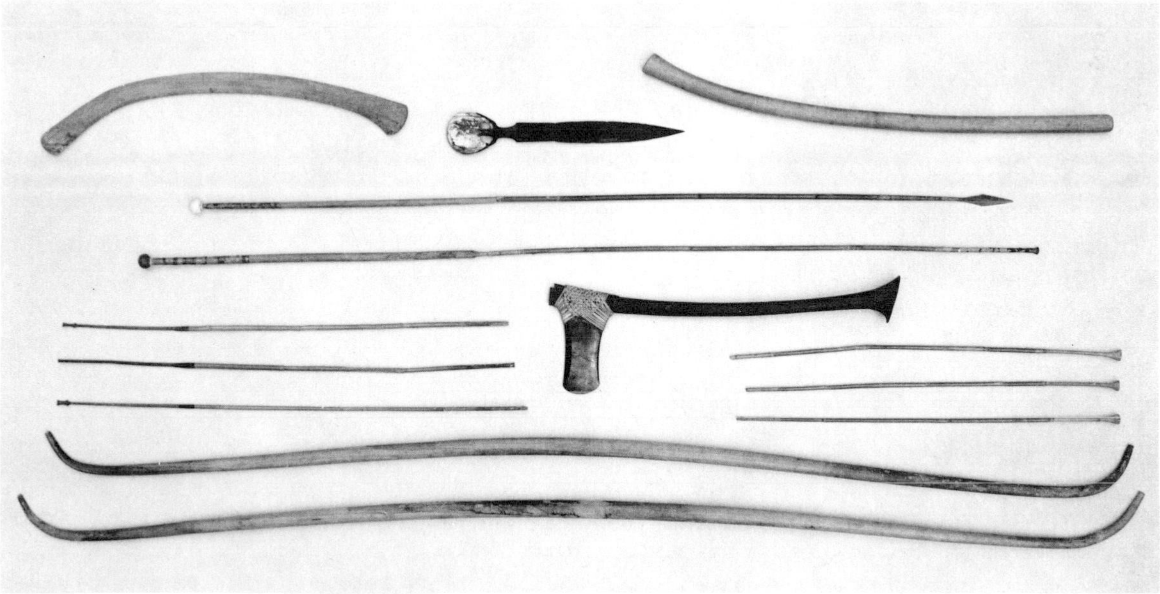

bowstrings. Their size and simple, sturdy construction invite comparison with the English longbow of the fourteenth to sixteenth centuries, though they could not have been drawn far enough to accommodate the latter's thirty-seven-inch clothyard arrows. The arrows found with our bows range, in point of fact, from twenty-eight and three-eighths to just under thirty inches. The shaft in each case is a length of glossy brown reed fitted with a tapered wooden tip, to the end of which a chisel-edged flake and two lateral barbs of quartz have been cemented with a resinous, brownish gray gum. At the other end of the arrow the base of the quarter-inch nock coincides with a natural joint in the reed and, immediately forward of this, three rounded feathers, symmetrically disposed around the shaft, were bound in place with strips of bark liberally coated with varnish. Both of the bows and some of the arrows had been deliberately broken, possibly to "kill" them and so render them harmless to their owner, or perhaps merely to allow them to be stowed more compactly. Unlike the bows and arrows used at this time in warfare, these hunting weapons hark back in their types to the Middle Kingdom, and in our collection can be duplicated almost exactly by examples found in tombs of the Eleventh and Twelfth Dynasties (see Part I, pp. 279 f.).

Another group of hunting arms recovered from the fill in front of the tomb of Sen-ne-mūt comprises three light reed ★arrows with blunt wooden tips for knocking down birds and small animals, two curved wooden ★throw-sticks used for much the same purpose, a curved hardwood ★club for dispatching the game so brought down, and two four-and-a-half-foot reed ★javelins with wooden shoulders and handles and bronze points, or piles (see fig. 125). The point of one of the javelins is of the elongated lozenge shape usual for weapons of this class (cf. fig. 36), while that of the other is a ridged bronze knob evidently designed for stunning rather than for piercing the quarry. The so-called handles of the weapons are finished at their butt ends with small ○-shaped knobs of ebony or ivory, and for a distance of six inches forward of the knobs they are wrapped with bands and lacings of red and yellow bark to serve as ornamental grips. The fact that the tapered forward ends of these handles fit only loosely into the hollow ends of the reed shafts suggests that they were not thrown with the javelins, but were used to launch them in the manner of spear throwers. Of seven similar javelins which had belonged to Sen-ne-mūt's contemporary, Nefer-khēwet, only the lozenge-shaped bronze ★points could be recovered, the reed shafts having been almost completely destroyed by dampness. Two leaf-shaped bronze ★javelin piles from el Lisht and another of unknown provenience have the same solid, tapered tangs as those we have been discussing. Part of a knobbed wooden rod taped with a strip of papyrus is probably a ★javelin handle rather than a walking stick as was once thought. Three ★knobs from the butt ends of similar javelin hafts are in two cases carved of indurated limestone and in one case of diorite. Miscellaneous fragments of New Kingdom ★arrows found near the pyramid of Amun-em-ḥēt I at el Lisht include a wooden nock and four long, tapered piles, two of hardwood, two of bone.

A leather-covered cartonnage ★quiver, purchased at Luxor and coming in all probability from a tomb in western Thebes, is decorated on the exterior with stitched ridges of leather arranged to form simple linear designs. Twenty-six inches in length, the slender, tubular sheath is open at the top and tapers slightly inward toward its rounded bottom.

In the center of figure 125 appears a ★battle axe which had belonged to Nefer-khēwet's son-in-law Baki, a tall, powerful man who probably served in the army of Tḥut-mosĕ III. The butt end of the ebony handle, partially eaten by termites, was recovered with the heavy bronze head, but most of the handle together with the rawhide lashing and its tightening wedge have been restored. The bronze ★heads of four similar axes range in length from three and a half to five and a half inches. The largest of these bears, at the center of the blade, an engraved figure of a falcon-headed god holding a *was*-scepter—probably the

insignia of the Corps of Rēʿ, one of the principal divisions of the Egyptian army. One of the other axe heads is engraved with a symbol which looks like the hieroglyph 𓋹.

Of archaic form and insufficiently sturdy to have been used in combat, the cast bronze ★parade axes of figure 126 show us five of the many attractive openwork designs which the ancient Egyptian metalworker devised for the adornment of these interesting ceremonial weapons.[6] At the top we see on the left the kneeling god of eternity holding in each of his outstretched hands the curved plant stem representing "years," and, on the right, the double bull symbolizing the two-valved door of heaven and its Januslike guardian. Below, the ever-popular cynocephalous ape appears alone, plucking papyrus plants, or facing a companion ape on the opposite side of a small papyrus column. The axe head with the two apes is inscribed with the titles and name of its former owner, the "Overseer of Prophets, the Guardian of Cattle, Khu-meḥ." It has been suggested that such axes as these were given to officers of the Egyptian armed forces as rewards for valor and were carried by them on state occasions.

FIGURE 126. Bronze parade axes. H. 3 3/8-4 in.

[6] These axe heads, dated on our accession cards to "Dyn. XVIII," probably belong to an earlier period. Dr. Henry G. Fischer has drawn our attention to a group of similar axe heads found at Dendereh in First Intermediate or early Middle Kingdom contexts.

The ★dagger shown at the top of figure 125 continues a Middle Kingdom type, but in its slender proportions and in the form of its long, ribbed blade it betrays its New Kingdom date. With an over-all length of fifteen inches, the handsome bronze weapon is provided with a smoothly finished pommel of ivory. A broad, almost flat ★dagger blade from the Seʿankh-ku-Rēʿ temple cemetery is also of bronze and also of a type which shows little advance over its predecessors of the Middle Kingdom. Having in its wide, upper end three rivet holes for the attachment of the handle, this blade has a length of just under eight inches.

Metal body armor, believed to have been first introduced in Hyksos times, was still extremely rare, the only actual piece of Thutmoside armor in our collection being a bronze ★corselet scale from the Lishti coppersmith's hoard. An inch wide and less than two inches in length, the scale is a pentagonal plate of heavy sheet metal strengthened by a vertical rib down its center and pierced with seven holes for attachment to a leather or cloth backing—presumably a shirt of some sort.

Beside the hunting weapons already referred to the Museum possesses a number of interesting items of equipment used by fishermen and fowlers of the earlier New Kingdom. The bronze ★head of a small harpoon, or fish-spear, from Deir el Ballās has a point with a single barb, while two similar ★heads in hardwood, coming from el Lisht, are in one instance single-barbed and, in the other, double-barbed. The points of two bronze ★fishhooks are also barbed and the tops of their shanks are flattened and bent forward to provide a means of attachment. Two barbless ★fishhooks, purchased at Deir el Ballās, have sharply bent shanks ending in each case in a small bulb or disk. The harpoon heads range in length from just over five to just over six inches, the fishhooks from one and an eighth to almost two inches.

Though fish-spearing and angling with hook and line were, then, popular New Kingdom pastimes, most of the serious fishing at this, as at other periods of Egyptian history, was done with nets. These were for the most part woven of linen cord and were of two general types: the light, circular casting net used by individual fishermen for catching small, minnowlike fish, and the big seines, or dragnets, operated by groups of men working from boats or from canal banks. One of our two Eighteenth Dynasty ★casting nets may be a funerary model since it measures only forty-three inches in diameter. Made up of linen cord knotted to form a fine, diamond mesh, it is provided around its perimeter with several dozen small lead weights and at its center with a braided drawstring. It comes from a tomb at Gebelein and may have belonged to the same man who owned the model beds and baskets described in the two preceding sections of this chapter. A full-size ★net of the same type is from Deir el Baḥri, having been found by our expedition "in the rubbish heap of the Ḥat-Ḥor shrine, near the south doors of the Montu-ḥotpe court."[7] Composed of a very light string mesh, the net had been rolled up into a ball ten and a quarter inches in diameter, in which, owing to its extreme fragility, it has been allowed to remain.

For sinking the lower edges of his seine the New Kingdom fisherman used specially designed ★net-weights of several different types. A favorite form was a semiovoid or semicylindrical weight, its flat top grooved longitudinally to fit snugly around the lower binding rope of the net, its convex underside notched near the ends for the cord lashings whereby it was fastened in place. Of this type we have three examples in limestone and two in alabaster, ranging in length from one and five-eighths to seven inches. A drop-shaped net-weight from a tomb at Abydos is pierced through its narrow upper end with a single suspension hole. Two semidiscoid weights of red pottery have in each case a pair of large holes just below their straight upper edges.

Besides the throw-sticks and the blunt-tipped arrows from below the tomb of Sen-ne-mūt, the activities of the ancient fowler and small-game

[7] See Winlock, *M. M. A. Bulletin*, XVII (1922), December, Part II, pp. 31-32. The quotation is taken from the accession card for this net.

hunter are represented in our collection by another ★throw-stick, in this instance from Deir el Baḥri, and by the ★central element, or backbone, of a small ivory bird trap, perhaps a toy (fig. 127). The trap, as can be seen, once comprised a miniature clapnet spread on two half hoops which, thanks to tension imparted by twisted cords, came together with a snap when released by means of a baited trigger pin. The element which we possess is an ornately carved rod of ivory providing at its broad end the mounting and anchor pegs for the curved frame and having a shaft in the form of the head of a spoonbill. The middle of the rod (the head of the spoonbill) is bored with a diagonal hole which serves as the housing for the trigger. Though they were not real, but only magical, weapons, mention should also be made of three fragmentary ★throw-sticks of blue and black faience decorated with *wedjat*-eyes, floral designs, and, in one case, a dwarflike figure (the demigod Bēs?) holding in either hand a large rabbit, grasped by the ears.

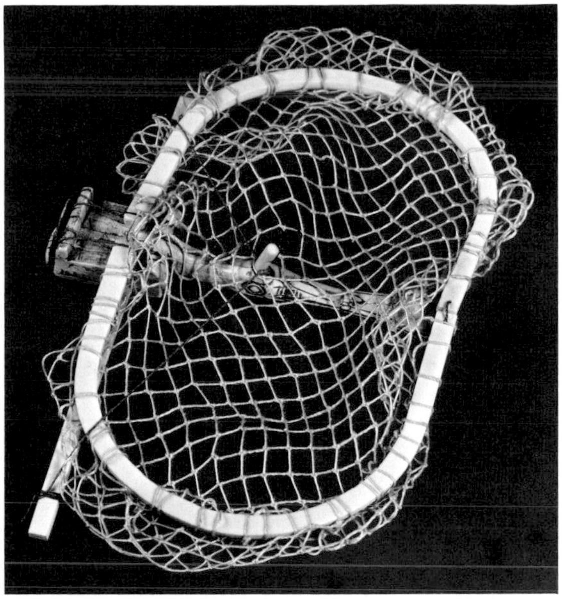

FIGURE 127. Ivory bird trap. The transverse bar, hoop, and net have been restored. L. 5 ¾ in.

Sharing the functions of both a weapon and a walking stick, the straight wooden staff, usually forked at the bottom and sometimes provided at the top with a bronze or leather ferrule, is found with great regularity in the burials of male contemporaries of the Thutmoside pharaohs. The eleven ★staves of this period in our collection are for the most part slender and in no case over five feet in length, a miniature example, made for Sen-ne-mūt's brother, the boy Amun-ḥotpe, measuring only two and a half feet from end to end. Three of the more ornate staves, unfortunately fragmentary, have their upper ends inlaid with bands of ivory or birch bark left white or stained black and red; and two of these are inscribed with the titles and names of their owners: the priest of (the) Amūn of Tḥut-mosě III, Montu (see also p. 118), and the "Scribe of the Ateliers of Pharaoh —may he live, prosper, and be well!—Ḳeny-Amūn, the justified." A light, whippy ★staff, forty-four inches long and slightly crooked at one end, is similar to the sticks carried nowadays by Sudanese camel drivers. Ornamental ★knobs, probably from the tops of walking sticks, include examples in limestone, alabaster, and colored glass.

Turning to the more workaday pursuits we find the implements of the Eighteenth Dynasty farmer hardly more numerous or more elaborate than those of his ancestors of the Old and Middle Kingdoms. A curved wooden ★sickle (), its sixteen-inch blade grooved to receive a row of small, serrated flint teeth, shows no notable advance in design over those of Egypt's earliest historic period. The wooden heads of two ★rakes—a model, under five inches wide, and a full-sized rake twenty-one and a half inches across—could scarcely be cruder, consisting in each case of a length of rough board with a saw-toothed edge, a rounded back, and a mortise or square notch near the center for the attachment of a handle. The hoe, or mattock (see fig. 128), one of Egypt's oldest implements, used by peasants and construction gangs alike, was still made of two pieces of wood—the blade and the handle—joined together at the apex of the  with a tenon-and-slot joint and held together by a transverse lashing of grass or palm-fiber rope. The

FIGURE 128. Wooden hoe, or mattock, from western Thebes. L. 19 in.

handles of the eleven New Kingdom ★hoes in our collection are carefully shaped for the maximum strength and effectiveness and are nearly always notched near the center for the rope binding. According to our standards they are short, their lengths running between seventeen and twenty-five inches, so that their users must have worked well bent over—as we know from tomb paintings and reliefs that they did. The paddlelike blades of the hoes, notched or slotted for the rope lashing, vary a good deal in shape, but most are short, broad, and rounded at the lower end. Considering the vast amount of tillage and excavation which was accomplished with digging implements of this sort, they must have been more efficient than they would appear.

The tools of the New Kingdom carpenter, stonemason, and metalworker are well represented by the often full-scale models placed in the royal and private foundation deposits already discussed (pp. 67 ff., 103). To these we may now add a few actual tools (see fig. 129) obtained from a variety of other sources and embodying a number of new types. The bronze and limestone ★heads of two small hammers have the shape of a modern blacksmith's hammer, with a blunt end and a wedge-shaped end. The hole for the circular handle is in each case drilled a little forward of the center of the head, toward the blunt, or heavier, end. Both heads are inscribed with hieroglyphic symbols, the bronze head with three [hieroglyph]-signs in relief, the limestone head with an incised 𓏁-sign. It has been suggested that these are the marks of the guilds or companies to which the owners of the hammers belonged. The bronze ★blade of a small carpenter's adze has a flanged head, a waisted neck, and an over-all length of five and a quarter inches; a narrow bronze ★chisel blade from a tomb at Abydos measures only three and three-eighths inches in length. A circular ★drill cap of alabaster is concave on the underside and slightly convex on top. One of two slate ★whetstones is triangular in shape while the other is a flat, irregularly shaped slab deeply scored on both sides with grooves made by a narrow-bitted tool such as a punch or drill head.

The carefully shaped ★head of a stonemason's maul, or hammer, has the form of the old rounded axe head (cf. fig. 126), but is made of hard stone (gabbro) and has a thickness at the middle of over two and a half inches. Two larger, oblong ★maul heads of indurated limestone were found at Ḳurneh by Sir Flinders Petrie. A heavy, tapered bronze ★chisel (fig. 129, left), seven and a half inches long, was evidently also a mason's tool and had seen a certain amount of service, its rounded head being dented and scratched by pounding. Of the pear-shaped, hardwood ★mallets used with such chisels two Eighteenth Dynasty examples from Deir el Baḥri have been retained for our permanent collection. Both measure a bit over ten inches in length, but whereas one is as good as new, the other is deeply gouged and bruised from prolonged use. Similar bruising appears on the head of a short, thick wooden ★wedge of a type clearly designed for splitting blocks of stone. Three flat-surfaced ★polishers, or grinders, one of serpentine, two of black granite, are believed to have been used for smoothing and finishing the surfaces of stone buildings or other monuments; and three pear-shaped chert ★borers, found in an alabaster quarry near Sheikh Said, were certainly employed in hollowing out the interiors of alabaster bowls and vases. A ★mason's float, used like a trowel for smoothing plastered surfaces, is a flat slab of wood eleven inches long, provided on the back with a horizontal handle rather like that of a modern suitcase. Purchased at Ḳurneh in 1911, our example of this implement is carefully carved from a single block of wood and is painted white. Three ★plummets, or plumb bobs, in alabaster, gray limestone, and haematite come in two instances from el Lisht and in the third from western Thebes. They vary somewhat in shape, but each is provided at the top with a flange pierced with a hole for the attachment of the plumb line.

Among the more interesting items of the New Kingdom mason's equipment are the so-called boning rods with which he checked the flatness of the stone surfaces he was in the process of dressing. A set of these comprised three short wooden rods of equal length, over the tops of two of which a cord was stretched from edge to edge of the surface being tested. The third rod, moved back and forth with its top always under the tightly stretched cord, served to locate high spots in the surface, which could then be dressed down. Our collection includes a ★set of boning rods (fig. 129, upper left), complete with cord, which was found in a workman's hut at Deir el Baḥri. The rods in this case are five and five-sixteenths inches long, the two stationary rods having holes for the cord drilled diagonally into their sides near the ends in such a manner as to come out at the centers of the ends. The movable rod is perfectly plain with slightly rounded ends. All three are nicely made and smoothly finished. Single ★boning rods, one

FIGURE 129. Tools and equipment of the New Kingdom craftsmen. L. of longer weaver's sword 25 5/8 in.

drilled, one plain, come, respectively, from the Valley of the Tombs of the Kings and from the forecourt of Ḥat-shepsūt's temple at Deir el Baḥri. The latter, which measures five and a half inches in length, had been used at one time as a paint stirrer and was found with a small red pottery ★bowl containing light blue paint.

One side of a metalworker's bipartite ★mold, carved of limestone (fig. 129, upper right), had been used for casting two small objects, probably of gold or silver: a little figure of a standing goddess(?) and an elaborate openwork necklace pendant embodying the tiny figure of a gazelle enclosed within a circular frame. Half of another ★mold, for producing a knobbed rod-shaped object, is made of gabbro and is provided with a pouring channel and four small holes by means of which it was aligned with the other side of the mold. An interesting type of ★metalsmith's burnisher, of which we possess two examples, is a pointed tip of bone or hard stone mounted in a tapered bronze sleeve which in turn appears to have been attached to a wooden handle. Other ★burnishers, apparently used also by workers in metal, are simply lumps or flakes of flint and agate, usually oval in shape and pointed at one end. Tubular clay ★crucibles found in the Ḥat-shepsūt and Sen-ne-mūt foundation deposits were probably models, their lengths in no case exceeding seven and a half inches. With them, as already noted on page 103, were found lumps of ★copper ore, ★lead ore, and ★charcoal for the smelting fires. Odd bits of worked and unworked metal include a length of bronze ★wire from an Eighteenth Dynasty burial at Thebes, a rough bronze ★casting from the Lishti coppersmith's hoard, and a lump of ★raw copper found in the Valley of the Tombs of the Kings.

Though leatherworking was a highly developed craft at all periods in Egypt, very few of the tools used in it have survived to the present day. Unusual interest therefore attaches to a ★leatherworker's cutter of bronze (fig. 129, top center) found in the Lisht hoard and comprising a crescent-shaped blade joined, like the top of a T, to the end of a tapered metal stock. With one tip of the blade broken off and an indeterminate amount missing from the upper end of the stock, the tool now measures five and three-quarters by three inches. It was beaten to shape from a single piece of bronze and the beveled cutting edge was produced by grinding the curved blade on both sides.

An elongated haematite pebble, pointed at the ends and shiny from prolonged use, has been identified, with considerable probability, as a ★burnisher used by a New Kingdom potter to impart a gloss to the surfaces of his vessels.

Not until we reach the later New Kingdom shall we have an opportunity to study the equipment and materials of another great Egyptian industry, that of the worker in glass, glaze, and faience (see pp. 254, 410 f.).

In contrast to its poverty in the implements of the potter, the leatherworker, and the Thutmoside glassmaker, our collection is rich in the equipment of the spinner and weaver of cloth. For this we have chiefly to thank the excavations of the Museum's Expedition in the New Kingdom village at el Lisht, the houses of which produced, besides spindles, reels, needles, and the like, numerous parts and appurtenances of both horizontal and vertical looms. Among the latter may be noted a number of big, specially shaped wooden ★pegs for setting out a horizontal loom, four heavy wooden ★heddle jacks, deeply notched on one side, ★weavers' "combs" of wood and ivory, and several sections of wood and ivory ★warp-spacers with narrow, closely spaced slots for aligning the warp threads. Three ★weavers' "swords" (see fig. 129, bottom) are indeed sword-shaped wands of wood, ten and a half to nineteen and a half inches long, provided in each case with a simple handle, or grip. Seven similar but much smaller implements, carved of bone, have been described as ★weavers' "daggers." A long flat ★stick with an accidental curvature, which once caused it to be classed as a bow, is probably a weaver's implement, perhaps a heddle bar or beater-in (see Part I, p. 265). Three ★loom weights, presumably from a vertical loom, are small, egg-shaped lumps of clay or limestone pierced near the top with a hole, through which in two cases a length of string or knotted linen strip is still looped. The example in limestone, two inches high, is roughly half the size of its mud companions, but probably of about the same weight and capable, therefore, of exerting almost exactly the same downward tension. The single ★shuttle of this period in our collection is a wooden rod under six inches long, tapering slightly toward the ends, which are rounded and slotted to receive the weft thread. ★Spindles show little or no advance over the Middle Kingdom models, each being made up, as before, of two parts: a slender, tapered wooden shaft, less than eight inches in length, and a discoid whorl with either a rounded back or a flat back and sloping sides. Made of wood, baked clay, limestone, or alabaster, the whorls have an average diameter of about two inches. ★Netting needles, four to seven inches long, are of bone or, more rarely, of bronze; and the flat ★reels, or bobbins, used with them are of wood, faience, or mud bound with strips of linen cloth.

Head and shoulders above the crafts and most of the other professions stood that of the scribes, from whose educated ranks the now greatly expanded civil service drew its candidates for the highest government offices. Pages could be devoted to the ever-growing importance and ever more varied activities of the New Kingdom scribe; but for the time being we shall content ourselves with inspecting briefly such items of his writing equipment as may be available for study in the Museum's collection. Chief among these are three long, narrow ★palettes, or pen cases, nine and a quarter to ten and a half inches in length, carefully carved from single pieces of fine-grained hardwood (cf. Part I, p. 292). Each is provided, down the center of the front, with a half-open slot for the scribe's writing rushes and, near the top, with a pair of circular wells for his black and red writing pigments. In two cases the lower half of the pen slot is fitted with a sliding cover, or slip, and in one instance the inkwells are framed by engraved *shenu*-loops. All show signs of use, with bits of caked pigment still visible in the inkwells and a frayed writing rush still in place in one of the pen slots. The cylindrical wooden ★base of a scribe's bag had apparently been attached to the cloth or leather tube which made up the rest of the bag by means of cords passed downward through rings projecting from its sides into holes drilled in its four stubby feet. To ensure a snug fit our cylinder is provided at its top and bottom with projecting flanges. The bag, which was evidently stiff enough to be stood upright on its wooden base, probably contained its owner's rolls of fresh papyrus and the other longer and bulkier items of his equipment. It was buried in a tomb in the Seʿankh-ku-Rēʿ cemetery in western Thebes during the reign of one of the earlier Thutmoside kings. For his seals, erasers, and the like another Theban scribe, who probably served under Ḥatshepsūt, had provided himself with a little cylindrical ★case carved entirely of wood. Found cached under a ★pottery bowl in the shale quarry surrounding Sen-ne-mūt's Deir el Baḥri tomb, the small tube is equipped with a flat wooden lid which swivels open on a single peg and is fastened shut by means of a cord passing from a knob on its top to another on the side of the case. A badly smudged hieratic inscription written in black ink on the top of the lid is perhaps to be read as the personal name "Montu-ḥotpe."

A curved bronze ★knife of the type used by scribes to trim brushes, cut papyrus, and the like suggests in its form the foreleg of an ox, and the tip of its handle is modeled to represent the hock and hoof of the animal. Seven and a quarter inches long, it had belonged to Nefer-khēwet's son, the Scribe Amun-em-ḥēt, a contemporary of King Tḥut-mosĕ III. Both the animal's leg and this particular shape of knife were called *khopesh*, the name being applied also to a scimitar of Asiatic origin recently adopted as a weapon by the Egyptian army. A ★burnisher, used to smooth the surfaces of papyri, especially at the joints where the strips overlap, is a small block of hardwood rounded at the top and provided with a short, rodlike handle. A similar ★burnisher from a tomb of the mid-Eighteenth Dynasty at Abydos has lost its handle, but is still inscribed with the title and name of its owner, the Scribe Mery-Maʿet. Since the length to which they were cut—nine inches—coincides with the width of the sheets of writing paper used at this period, it is probable that two ★sections of papyrus reed found in the forecourt of the Ḥat-shepsūt temple were destined for that purpose. Imitating in its form the large clamshells which Egyptian scribes had used from the earliest times as their inkwells, a handsome alabaster ★saucer of unknown provenience may without hesitation be added to our inventory of New Kingdom scribal equipment. Scarabs and other forms of seals employed by scribes have already been discussed in adequate, or even excessive, detail; but mention may be made of two oblong wooden ★seals engraved on their undersides with a hieroglyphic legend which appears to read: "Every god and goddess of the temples. . . ." With their backs carved to form pierced lug handles these seals, when complete, were over three inches long and were probably used to stamp large sealings, such as those on doors, boxes, jars, and the like.

In the first volume of this handbook (p. 297) we have discussed the scribe's use of weights and measures and have seen that during the Old and Middle Kingdoms the unit of weight used in the weighing of metals and other valuable commodities was the *deben* of 13 to 14 grams. Sometime between the end of the Twelfth Dynasty and the rise of the the New Kingdom a new unit, the *ḳidet*, or *kitĕ*, of 8 to 10 grams, was introduced and the *deben* was increased in value to equal 10 *ḳidet*, or about 91 grams. Some thirty stone ★weights from New Kingdom settlements at el Lisht and Meidūm conform to the new standard, their values including , ⅛ ¼, ⅓, ½, 1, 2, 4, 5, and 16 *ḳidet*, their actual weights ranging from 1 to 166 grams. They are of three general types—rectangular, almond-shaped, and domed—and of ten different materials: haematite, diorite, serpentine, gneiss, mica schist, limestone, alabaster, red porphyry, black porphyry, and bronze. The 16-*ḳidet* weight is inscribed with the numeral "8" (IIII/IIII), indicating that the unit used in this case was a double

FIGURE 130. Lead-filled bronze weight in the form of a recumbent calf. L. 2 7/16 in.

ḳidet. A 2-*ḳidet* weight of alabaster has engraved on its side the hieroglyph ⌓. The rest are uninscribed.

In the introduction to his catalogue of the weights and balances in the Cairo Museum Weigall, citing Ridgeway, notes that *pecunia*, the Latin word for "wealth," "is literally to be traced to *pecus* ["cattle"], an ox being the equivalent of money and all wealth being counted in units of oxen in the majority of early nations." "In Egypt," he goes on to say, "we have weights made in the form of oxen which well illustrate this subject."[8] Three such ★weights in the Metropolitan Museum are of bronze, hollow cast and subsequently filled with lead, poured in through small holes, to bring them up to the required weight. The largest and most carefully made of the three, weighing 84 grams, or 1 *deben* of 10 *ḳidet*, is in the form of a recumbent calf (fig. 130), while a 6-*ḳidet* weight of the same type (inscribed III/III) represents a short-horned bull in a similar pose. Though complete and of an equally well-known type, the third weight, with a value of 2 *ḳidet*, comprises only the head of an ox.

In her publication of our collection of Egyptian weights Bernice M. Cartland[9] points out that the "surprisingly wide" variation in weights of ostensibly the same values "depends upon three things: the impossibility of accurately accounting for the loss in weight caused by breakage, or the gain, in

[8] "Weights and Balances," *Catalogue général des antiquités égyptiennes du Musée du Caire*, Nos. 31271-31670, p. xv.

[9] *M. M. A. Bulletin*, XII (1917), p. 88.

the case of metals, caused by the accretion of oxides; a difference that might be expected in different localities in Egypt at the same time or at different dates; or a fraudulent tendency toward light weights which is also evident in coins of a later date."

9. Funerary Equipment

The reigns of Tḥut-mosĕ I to IV witnessed no very startling changes in Egyptian burial customs as they are known to us from private tombs of the Theban necropolis.

By Tḥut-mosĕ III's day, to be sure, the *rishi*, or "feathered," coffin had disappeared and the glossy black anthropoid coffin with yellow or gold bands of inscription had begun to replace its white predecessor. The Thutmoside coffins in our collection, however, happen to be of the earlier types. They include the lid of a modified *rishi* from the tomb of Aʿḥ-mosĕ Pe'n-ḥat (see p. 77) and two white anthropoids from below the hillside tomb of Sen-ne-mūt (see p. 111). The small ★*rishi* lid (fig. 131) is from the coffin of a child—apparently a young girl—who died at Thebes during the reign of Tḥut-mosĕ I. It is of unusual and to some extent transitional type, being neither a true *rishi* nor a conventional anthropoid form. Its colors are bright and attractive: the face and hands yellow, the headdress striped yellow and black, the great vulture wings green with red, white, and black details, and the inscription black on a band of yellow. Unhappily, when the wooden toe piece was broken away in some ancient accident it carried with it the name of the youthful owner. The rest of the inscription—a stereotyped offering formula calling upon "Osiris, the Great God, Lord of Abydos"—requires no special comment.

The white anthropoid ★coffin of Sen-ne-mūt's minstrel, Ḥar-mosĕ, is a somewhat simplified and streamlined version of the early Eighteenth Dynasty coffins which we met with in Chapter II

FIGURE 131. Lid of a child's coffin from western Thebes. L. 46 in.

(cf. fig. 38). Its eyes are inlaid (alabaster and obsidian in ebony rims) and its face, throat, and ears are covered with gold foil; but its painted decoration is confined to the blue and yellow striped headdress, the polychrome broad collar, and the blue and yellow bands of inscription. In these the "Singer Ḥar-mosĕ" is named as the beneficiary of an offering formula invoking Osiris, Ruler of Eternity, and is referred to as "one in honor with" the god Anubis and the Four Genii of the Dead. Almost seven feet long, the coffin is characterized in general by its slender proportions. It is an interesting piece of joinery, the box and lid together being made up of twenty-three intricately shaped pieces of one-and-a-half-inch plank fastened together with hardwood tenons and pegs.

The tenons and other fastenings used in such anthropoid cases are sometimes inscribed in ink with magical formulae which were clearly intended to increase their efficacy as binding elements not only of the man-shaped coffin, but also of the body of the man (or woman) contained in it. A ★coffin tenon from the tomb of Aʿḥ-mosĕ Pe'n-ḥat, for example, carries the words of a spell derived from the Pyramid Texts: "United for you are your bones in the West. It is Horus who unites you." The thought here seems to be that Horus holds together the bones of the deceased just as the tenons hold together the boards of the coffin.

The ★coffin of a woman buried only a few yards from Ḥar-mosĕ, though of the same type and date and decorated in the same manner as his, differs from it in several notable respects. Like the *rishi* coffins of the Seventeenth Dynasty (see pp. 29 f.) it is not a constructed coffin, but a dugout, its box and lid having been hewn in their entireties from two six-and-a-half-foot lengths of sycamore log. The hollowing-out and rough shaping was done chiefly with an adze, the marks of which are clearly visible on the unsmoothed and unpainted interior. Another difference lies in the proportions of this coffin, which is markedly shorter, broader, and thicker than that of Ḥar-mosĕ. Again the decoration of the white mummiform body is confined to longitudinal and transverse bands of yellow, but in this case they are not inscribed, suggesting that the coffin was a ready-made example purchased from stock and leaving us in doubt as to the identity of the woman to whom it belonged. Though the coffin itself is of mediocre quality, the other possessions of its owner and the manner of her burial indicate that she was a relatively important member of Sen-ne-mūt's household. We have therefore tentatively identified her as his sister, Aʿḥ-ḥotpe, whose figure appears in the reliefs of his tomb and whose mummiform statuette was found in front of it, not far from the burial in question (fig. 137).

The cartonnage mummy mask current during the Middle Kingdom was revived under the early Thutmosides, a notable example being the gilded ★mask found on the mummy of Sen-ne-mūt's mother, Ḥat-nūfer. Broader and shorter than its Middle Kingdom predecessors, it has the form of the head and shoulders of a woman wearing a long, striped headdress of traditional type and a huge broad collar, the curved bottom of which coincides with the curved bottom edge of the mask. The terminals of the collar are in the form of falcon heads with tie cords ending in half-open lotus flowers. The fabric of the mask consists of eleven layers of coarse linen cloth coated inside and out with fine white stucco and covered over the whole of the exterior with thin gold foil applied in overlapping sheets four and three-quarters inches square. Details of the headdress and broad collar were engraved in the surface of the outer layer of stucco and transferred to the foil by pressing the latter down into the incisions. With sockets of ebony, corneas of alabaster, and irises of obsidian the inlaid eyes give the carefully modeled but otherwise rather impassive face a touch of life. Massiveness is perhaps the outstanding characteristic of this mask, which measures almost twenty inches in height and almost eighteen inches in thickness from front to back.

In 1889 a similar ★mask, but with the gilding confined to the face, throat, and ears, was acquired by Theodore M. Davis in Luxor. It comes without much question from an important tomb in the Theban necropolis and is probably to be dated to the middle or later years of the Thutmoside period. The headdress in this case is painted black with yellow stripes, and on the tab at the back two Anubis animals, face to face on shrines, are drawn in heavy yellow outline. Blue, red, and green alternate in the bands of the broad collar, which as usual is provided with shoulder pieces in the form of painted falcon heads. The eyes are treated in exactly the same manner as on the Ḥat-nūfer mask and, in addition, the brows and corner markings are inlaid in ebony. Adhering to the front of the mask are bits of linen mummy wrappings and small sections of a papyrus Book of the Dead which had apparently been spread out over the head and breast of the mummy with the inscribed side up. It is difficult to be sure whether the bland and pleasant face is that of a man or a woman, but one's inclination is to identify the subject as a man.

With the example just described Mr. Davis acquired another cartonnage *mummy mask of an unusual and interesting type (fig. 132). In this instance the subject is without any doubt a woman, or, rather, a lady of fashion. Though her face and throat are gilded and her eyes inlaid like those of our other masks, she wears, not the traditional striped headdress and the funerary broad collar, but a wig and jewelry of the most up-to-date designs, seen on ladies of the court only from the second half of the Eighteenth Dynasty onward. The wig, a prodigious affair made up of innumerable crinkly black locks, is crowned by a floral fillet, most elaborately designed and painted in four or five colors. There is a broad collar, but, like the one shown in figure 71, it is made up of rows of gold *nefer*-signs against bands of green, blue, and red. Above the collar the lady wears a necklace composed of five rows of large ball beads, simulated here by hemispherical studs of polychrome faience glued to the surface of the mask. Gold, blue, and black pendants descending from the ends of this necklace and from a prominent lock on the front of the wig are also molded in faience and fastened in position with glue. Unhappily, the mask before it came into Mr. Davis's possession had suffered a good deal of damage: its back broken away and lost, the crown of its head and one of its sides crushed and warped out of shape.

FIGURE 132. Cartonnage mummy mask of an Eighteenth Dynasty lady, from western Thebes. H. 14 in.

In private tombs of the Eighteenth Dynasty, funerary jewelry—that is, jewelry designed and made to be worn only by the dead—is less common and less extensive than during the Middle Kingdom (see Part I, pp. 306 ff.). The early Thutmoside cemetery on the Seʿankh-ku-Rēʿ temple platform, however, yielded a pair of *collar terminals which, since they are made of fragile blue faience and are not provided with holes for suspension cords, can only have come from a funerary collar of the traditional type.

The most characteristic item of New Kingdom funerary jewelry is, of course, the heart scarab, the form and function of which we have already had occasion to discuss (pp. 37 f.). Of the many *heart scarabs in the Museum's collection thirteen are datable to Thutmoside times, but only three of these are of known provenience—in each instance a private tomb in western Thebes. They are distinguished from ordinary scarabs by their size (their lengths range from one to almost three inches) and by the fact that in nearly every case all or part of Chapter XXXB of the Book of the Dead is engraved on their undersides. The favorite material is a fine-grained, dark green stone usually called schist, but probably a type of graywacke. There are, however, two examples in serpentine and one in green jasper; it seems not to have mattered greatly so long as the stone was green or greenish and fairly durable. Five of the better scarabs are set in heavy gold mountings and four of these still retain the loop of gold wire or intricately plaited gold chain whereby they were suspended from the necks of their deceased owners. The example selected for illustration in figure 133 was found in position on the mummy of Sen-ne-mūt's mother, the House Mistress Ḥat-nūfer, and carries her name in the first line of its inscription. Another and even larger scarab, of serpentine, comes from the oft-mentioned burial of Ḥat-shepsūt's archivist, Nefer-khēwet, and a third is from an early Thutmoside tomb on the Dirāʿ Abu'n Naga, much of the contents of which was acquired by the Museum in 1925 through the generosity of Dr. and Mrs. Thomas H. Foulds. Though the owners of this tomb were apparently the Storekeeper of Amūn, Tety-nefer, and his wife Seni-sonbe (see also pp. 228 f.), our scarab is inscribed for a woman named Ima-Ba(?), who was presumably a member of their household. Eight of the remaining heart scarabs belonged, respectively, to "[the Temple Attendant?] of Amūn, Amun-em-ḥēt," the Mayor Nenu, the Craftsman Tutuy, the Singer Ruru, and four worthies named Tḥut-mosĕ, Seni-mosĕ, Pa-shed, and Peḳesh, the last clearly a foreigner. On two examples the names have been erased and on two others the spaces provided for them in the first lines of the inscriptions have been left blank.

From an unrecorded tomb somewhere on the Dirāʿ Abu'n Naga comes a ★heart pectoral in the form of a semicircular slab of schist pierced with holes for suspension and adorned on the outer side with an engraved broad collar framing the figure of a scarab beetle (𓆣) in high relief. A potent amuletic device in its own right (see Part I, p. 307), the collar, as frequently, has terminals in the shape of falcon heads. Drawn in outline on the inner side of the pectoral is a large heart sign (𓄣) inscribed with the usual spell, spoken in this instance by the "Transport Commander Ḥaty-ʿay." Though not very large (four and three-quarters inches wide), the pectoral would be much too heavy for ordinary, daily wear.

FIGURE 133. Heart scarab of the House Mistress Ḥat-nūfer. Green schist with gold mounting and chain. Front and back views. L. 2⅝ in.

It appears to have been under the first Thutmosides that funerary texts, which in earlier periods had been inscribed on the walls of burial chambers and coffins, began to be written on linen shrouds and rolls of papyrus and placed directly on the bandaged mummies of their deceased beneficiaries. The shrouds are usually long rectangular sheets of fine linen inscribed in ink with fifty or more columns of fairly large cursive hieroglyphs containing some of the more important spells, or chapters, from the Book of the Dead. Two fragmentary ★shrouds of this type from the tomb of Tḥut-mosĕ I's "Attendant and Fan-

bearer," Aʿḥ-mosĕ Pe'n-ḥat, carry between them parts of ten chapters of the Book of the Dead in which the title and name of the tomb owner are repeated over and over again, often followed by the name of his mother, the House Mistress Aʿḥ-ḥotpe. The surviving texts, drawn up in a dozen or so horizontal lines and thirty-two long vertical columns, comprise (in the order given) Chapters CXLIX and CXXXVIA and Chapters CXXIV, LXXXIII, LXXXIV, LXXXV, LXXXII, LXXVII, LXXXVI, and XCIX. The same selection of chapters arranged in the same order was evidently used on a similar ★shroud, a fragment of which was found by our expedition in the forecourt of the tomb of the well-known Eleventh Dynasty Chancellor Meket-Rēʿ. Here, on a piece of linen cloth measuring twenty by sixteen and a half inches, we have parts of seventeen columns of inscription with portions of Chapters CXXIV, LXXXIII, LXXXIV, and LXXXV of the Book of the Dead.

It is, however, in the large and often beautifully illustrated funerary papyri of the New Kingdom that the Book of the Dead comes into its own. Unfortunately, our collection, though rich in later Books of the Dead, includes only a few fragmentary examples of Eighteenth Dynasty date. One of these, acquired by Theodore M. Davis with the mummy masks described above, comprises two large ★sections of a roll of papyrus written and illustrated for the "Overseer of the Builders of Amūn, Amun-ḥotpe, begotten of Sen(en)a and born of the House Mistress Kem," a man already known to us from his funerary cones.[10] The papyrus, thirteen and a half inches high and originally perhaps fifteen to twenty feet in length, was inscribed with vertical columns of cursive hieroglyphs bordered at the top and bottom by horizontal bands of stars (𓇯-signs?) and interrupted here and there by small colored vignettes. In a horizontal line between the tops of the columns of text and the star-studded upper border the title of each successive spell, or chapter, was written in red ink. As frequently in papyri of this class, the texts are written retrogressively, with the columns of hieroglyphs facing to the right but reading from the left. The first ten columns of the left-hand section of our papyrus (length thirteen and a half inches) contain the second half of Chapter XLII of the Book of the Dead, "a spell for warding off the slaughter which is made in Herakleopolis." In Columns 11-21 we find most of Chapter LXIV, "a spell for going forth by day in the necropolis," including a small square vignette in which a mummiform figure labeled "Amun-ḥotpe" stands before some object from which descend two streams of liquid (?). The whole of the right-hand section, fourteen inches in length and comprising twenty columns of text, is taken up by the text and vignette of the popular Chapter LXXVIII—"a spell for assuming the form of a divine falcon." In the vignette Amun-ḥotpe, the owner of the papyrus, appears again as a mummiform figure wearing a pale blue headdress and standing behind a huge green falcon which, according to the accompanying label, he is in the process of becoming.

[10] Davies, *A Corpus of Inscribed Egyptian Funerary Cones*, No. 185.

Three ★funerary papyri were found in position on the fully wrapped mummy of Nefer-khēwet's son-in-law Baki, a contemporary of King Tḥutmosĕ III (see pp. 130, 212). An open sheet thirty-one inches long and just under ten inches wide, inscribed with groups of twenty lines of cursive hieroglyphic text, was spread out over the face and body of the mummy with its inscribed side up. Across the thighs lay a smaller sheet of papyrus folded twice lengthwise to form a flat packet eight and five-eighths by three and one-eighth inches. Finally, against the left shoulder of the mummy had been placed a roll of papyrus nine inches long and one and three-eighths inches in diameter. Unhappily, prolonged exposure to dampness had blackened the surfaces of these papyri, obliterated the bulk of the signs inscribed on them, and reduced their consistency to that of fine ash. It is unlikely that we shall ever be able positively to identify their contents; but three similar documents from the mummy of Sen-ne-mūt's mother, Ḥat-nūfer, (now in the Cairo Museum) contain nothing but chapters from the Book of the Dead.

On the mummy wrappings of an unidentified male member of Sen-ne-mūt's household are short ink ★inscriptions of a more workaday nature than those of the shrouds and funerary papyri. They are hieratic notations evidently written by the embalmers charged with preparing the mummy for burial, and constitute a sort of running record of the wrappings applied. The third layer of wrappings, for example, is composed of four sheets, each folded double, and in two places near the center of the outer sheet we find the docket "sheet wrapping of 8 folds." In the next layer out, a strip of cloth folded to form a pad over the chest bears the twice-repeated notation "bandage, linen." When, at length, the outermost sheet of all had been laid over the body and the embalmers had just completed stitching it together up the back, one of them wrote on the shoulder of the mummy as it lay face downward, completely wrapped, the words, "18 folds (layers?) of linen."

Much valuable information on the process of mummification and mummy wrapping can be obtained from the materials left over after the completion of the processes. Though such material was usually regarded as unsuitable for inclusion in the tombs themselves, it was frequently placed by the embalmers in big pottery jars and cached in the near vicinity of the tombs (see Part I, p. 166, and below, p. 302). Thus, on the hillside below the tomb of Sen-ne-mūt was found a huge drop-shaped ★jar of pink pottery whitewashed on the outside and containing three linen sheets with the fringes torn off, four wide bandages, three narrow bandages, and forty-three linen swabs, some soaked with an oily brown liquid, others twisted to form points and stained with a gray, crusty matter. One of the baskets placed in the burial chamber of Sen-ne-mūt's mother contained dirty, oil-stained linen which had almost certainly been used in the mummification of her body or that of her husband. It constitutes, then, a rare example of an embalmers' cache inside a tomb. The linen in this case consisted of seven bandages, eighteen feet long, rolled or twisted to form trussing ropes and occasionally split at the ends or knotted together to form loops. An ★embalmer's tool from a tomb pit in the Seʿankh-ku-Rēʿ temple platform is an adze-shaped scraper of hardwood with a rounded butt of the right size to have fitted comfortably into its user's hand. It is believed to have been employed in removing the viscera and cleaning out the body cavity preparatory to mummification.

After their removal from the body the viscera, as in previous periods, were mummified, wrapped in linen cloth, and placed in canopic jars of limestone or pottery which in turn were deposited in sets of four in the compartmented interiors of canopic chests. Though uninscribed and undecorated, Ḥat-nūfer's shrine-shaped ★canopic chest (fig. 134) is one of the more interesting and certainly one of the best preserved examples of its time. A cubical wooden box one royal cubit, or about twenty inches, on a side, it is mounted on sledge runners and is topped by a shallow cavetto-and-torus cornice. To carry out its resemblance to a shrine () the sides of the box slope very slightly inward and the lid has the rounded front

FIGURE 134. Canopic chest of Ḥat-nūfer, the mother of Sen-ne-mūt. H. 21 in.

and single pitch characteristic of shrine roofs. It is made throughout of heavy cypress planking and the corners of the box are dovetailed. Ostensibly the lid was held in place by lashing the knob on its top to a similar knob on the front of the box. Actually it was locked in position by a concealed device involving projecting battens on the underside of the lid, L-shaped sockets in the tops of the box walls, and a self-operating tumbler lock near the front edge of both. The removal of what proved to be the outer lid of the chest revealed an inner lid set two inches below the rim of the box and composed of two wooden valves, hinged vertically by means of cylindrical lugs projecting from their outer edges into holes in the inner surfaces of the box walls. These two "doors" rested on the two crossed partitions which divide the interior of the chest into four compartments, and were locked down by a boxwood bolt passed through wooden staples at the centers of their contiguous inner edges. The bolt is fitted with a small ebony tumbler which falls between the first and second staples when the bolt is shot home, thus preventing its removal. The chest is painted white inside and out, the paint on the exterior having been applied over a layer of fine linen cloth and stucco. Ḥat-nūfer's four pottery canopic jars, three with human-head stoppers, one with a jackal head, were retained in the division of finds by the Cairo Museum.

The ★canopic jars of Thutmoside date which form part of our collection are without exception of pottery and in the many instances where their stoppers are preserved these are in the form of a human head wearing a full, blue or blue and yellow striped headdress. The faces, painted red or yellow according to the sex of the owner, are more often than not beardless, though short, square-cut chin beards are by no means uncommon. Most of the jars have engraved or painted on their sides in three or four columns of hieroglyphs the regular canopic formula in which the human organ contained in the jar is identified not only with its deceased owner, but also with one of the Four Genii of the Dead, and is placed under the protection of one of the four great tutelary goddesses, Isis, Nephthys, Nit, and Serḳet. On one of the set of four *ḳulleh*-ware jars made for Nefer-khēwet's daughter, Ruyu, we read, for example: "Recitation: 'Isis, your arms embrace that which is in you and your protection is over the Imsety who is in you, the one in honor with Osiris, the House Mistress Ruyu, the justified.' " On the three other jars of the set the goddess Nephthys is paired with the genius Ḥapy, Nit with Dewau-mautef, and Serḳet with Ḳebeḥ-snēwef. Similar sets and individual jars, in most cases from private tombs in western Thebes, are inscribed for the King's Ornament Tet, the Familiar of the King,

Neny, the House Mistress Seni-sonbe, and the Storekeeper of Amūn, Tety-nefer. A jar bearing the name of the Foreman Tety is painted white with yellow and brown graining in imitation of alabaster (see fig. 135); and a rather squat jar on which a woman named Tḥūty is described as "one in honor with Imsety" is covered with a glossy dark red haematite slip. Also finished with a shiny dark red slip is an interesting set of four jars from Asyūt, on the sides of which pairs of human arms holding ☥-signs and 𓌀-scepters are modeled in relief. Wide horizontal bands of inscription encircling the mouths of these jars tell us that their owner was the "Singer Nofery," who, to judge from the feminine determinative following the name, was a woman. On the beardless stoppers which accompany Nofery's jars the details of the faces and wigs are drawn in heavy black line. Five unattached ★canopic jar stoppers, retained for our permanent collection because of their special interest or quality, include three examples in brownish red pottery, one in painted limestone, and one of wood covered with pitch—the last said to have come from the neighborhood of Medīnet Habu.

Another class of jar made solely as an item of tomb equipment is the dummy vase carved of solid wood and painted to imitate alabaster, breccia, or some other ornamental stone. We have already had occasion (pp. 154 f.) to discuss two ★jars of this class inscribed for Neb-seny, the First Prophet of Onuris under Tḥut-mosĕ IV. To these may now be added an uninscribed wooden ★beaker grained to represent calcite and a one-handled ★jug colored yellow and covered with elaborate red, black, and orange markings suggesting some form of agate (fig. 136). Similarly decorated ★jars, made of pottery, though usable as containers of commodities, bear inscriptions which mark them as funerary vessels. Thus, a long-necked cordiform vase painted to resemble red granite carries a panel of inscription in which its obviously deceased owner, the Storekeeper of Amūn, Mery, is described as "one in honor with Osiris"; and on a two-handled jar which still retains part of its linen and mud sealing the House Mistress Amun-em-weskhet is referred to as "the Osiris."

FIGURE 135. Canopic jars of the Eighteenth Dynasty. Painted pottery. H. 13½ and 14½ in.

Unlike the mass-produced *shawabty*-figures of later times those of the Eighteenth Dynasty still retain the salient characteristics of their predecessors of the Middle Kingdom and First Intermediate period (see Part I, pp. 326 ff., 350; and above, pp. 33 f.). Relatively large in size and, in private burials, still few in number, they have not yet entirely abandoned their original role as mummiform representations of their deceased owners. The spell written on them, however, makes it clear that their primary function was to substitute for their owners in the work gangs of the hereafter; and though this spell (Chapter VI of the Book of the Dead) had long since become a stereotype, the figures themselves display considerable individuality in their forms, style, and artistic pretensions. Some of the private ★*shawabty*-figures of Thutmoside date in our collection are certainly to be classed as miniature works of sculpture and could with perfect justification have been introduced as such at the beginning of this chapter. Others, especially the earlier examples, are so crude as to have value only as funerary symbols. In height they range from five inches to just under a foot, the smallest being a slender figure in painted limestone of an unnamed lady wearing a wig of developed Eighteenth Dynasty type, the largest a big limestone *shawabty* of the Mason of Amūn, Neb-waḥ-yeb, which came to us in 1937 as a gift of Mrs. Abbot Low Moffat. Four of the figures are carved of hardwood with their broad collars and bracelets in two cases overlaid with gold foil. They belonged, respectively, to the Scribe Tjay, the Guardian of Amūn, Meḥ, the House Mistress Wetjenet-tjesek-wenemty(?), and an unidentified individual, probably a man. Six others are of limestone with the signs in their inscriptions and other details usually painted. They include, besides those already mentioned, two figures of the Storekeeper of Amūn, Tety-nefer, from his tomb on the Dirāʿ Abu'n Naga, a double *shawabty* of the Controller Khaʿ-em-Wast and his wife Mesyet, a figure of the servant(?) of Montu, Ptaḥ-mosĕ, and one of the *Wēʿb*-priest of Onuris, Neṯer-mosĕ, of Abydos. One of two alabaster *shawabtys* bears

FIGURE 136. Dummy vases of painted wood. H. 7 and 7½ in.

the title and name of a certain Yey who, like Yuya and Ay of the later Eighteenth Dynasty (see p. 260), was a God's Father and Commander of Cavalry, but whose name, though similar in sound to the later dignitaries', is spelled differently. Crudely modeled pottery *shawabtys* from a tomb of the Eighteenth Dynasty at Rifeh are painted white with red and black bands. They are not inscribed, but are known to have belonged to a woman named Ta-roy.

In most instances the hands of the figures appear crossed over their chests, and in some of the more developed examples they hold hoes (𓌸) for digging or baskets for transporting the sand excavated in the work projects of the afterworld. When not suspended from the hands the baskets are sometimes worn slung over one or both shoulders. Frequently these and other implements used by the *shawabtys* are simply incised or carved in relief on the surfaces of the figures. Often, however, they are made separately—usually of metal—and inserted into holes in the clenched fists of their small owners. Besides a tiny copper ★axe, a copper ★mattock, and three bronze ★hoes, the *shawabty*-accessories in our collection include a model ★yoke and a pair of flat bags, or ★baskets, to go with it, all made of bronze. They come from a tomb of the earlier New Kingdom at Abydos.

Three almost identical mummiform ★statuettes of female members of Sen-ne-mūt's family were found loose in the chip heaps below his Sheikh ʿAbd el Ḳurneh tomb, near, but not in, the burial chambers of two of the ladies represented (fig. 137). Carved of wood with the headdress and eyes painted black, each of the little figures is mounted on a rectangular wooden base which brings its total height to seven inches. One of the statuettes has the name of Sen-ne-mūt's mother, the "one in honor with Osiris, Ḥat-nūfer," neatly written in black ink on its front; while on each of the other two the name of a sister(?) of the great man, in one case "Aʿḥ-ḥotpe," in the other "Iry," is inscribed on the top of the base block. Buried outside the tombs of their owners and evidently not to be classed as *shawabtys*, these statuettes are certainly Osirian in character and remind one of the wooden Osiris figures associated with the burials of later periods of Egyptian history.

Out of 370 stamped funerary cones from tombs in the Theban necropolis we have been able, in many cases, to recognize the owners as persons known to us from other sources and to assign them to the reigns of specific Thutmoside kings. There remain some ninety ★cones of this general period, the owners of which have not been so conclusively identified and dated—not, at least, by the compiler of this handbook. All except five of the people in question were men, and of these all save two bore official titles. In thirty-six cases the titles show that their holders were attached to that branch of the pharaonic government responsible for the administration of the temples and temple holdings of the state god Amūn, the offices including those of overseers of fields, gardens, oases, cattle, beekeepers, goldworkers, craftsmen, and boat crews of the god, and ranging downward from the First Prophet, or High Priest, of Amūn to ordinary *wēʿb*-priests, scribes, doorkeepers, and temple servants. Seventeen of our Theban tomb owners served in the national or provincial administration in such capacities as overseers or scribes of the treasury, overseers or scribes of the granary, accountants of grain and cattle, chiefs of merchants, and deputies of the Viceroy of Nubia. Thirteen others were attached to the service of the pharaoh and his family as stewards of the royal estates, chamberlains of the palace, tutors of the royal children, fanbearers "on the king's right hand," and the like. The army and navy claimed another thirteen, both as combat officers and military officials; and in this group we meet with commanders of soldiers and commanders of ships, lieutenant commanders, troop commanders, commanders of cavalry, chiefs of police (Medjay), and cadets of the royal household. Among the few priests and officials associated with deities other than Amūn may be mentioned a *wēʿb*-priest of the goddess Maʿet and an overseer of works of the god Montu, "Lord of Hermonthis." Four of the five women—all apparently wives or sisters of tomb owners—bear the title House Mistress, roughly the equivalent of our "housewife." The names of these people are for the most part of well-known Eighteenth Dynasty types, Amun-ḥotpe being the prime favorite, with ten examples, followed in order by Khonsu, Neb-seny, Aʿḥ-mosĕ, Amun-em-ḥēt, Amun-em-Opet, Woser-ḥēt, Pa-waḥ, Mery, Neb-waʿ, and Ḥeby, with fifty-nine less common names occurring only once each.

FIGURE 137. Funerary statuettes of Aʿḥ-ḥotpe and Ḥat-nūfer, the sister(?) and mother of Sen-ne-mūt. Painted wood. H. 7 in.

VI. The Reign of Amun-ḥotpe III

1. The King and His Monuments

THE MARRIAGE OF Tḥut-mosĕ IV to Mūt-em-weya, believed by some to have been a princess of Mitanni (see p. 147), must have taken place in the first year or two of his reign, for when, about 1397 B.C., King Neb-maʿet-Rēʿ Amun-ḥotpe III, the son of this union, succeeded his father as pharaoh he himself was not only of marriageable age but was probably already married to his own principal queen, Teye.

The young king's accession to the throne came at a moment in Egyptian history when, thanks to almost two centuries of unparalled achievement both at home and abroad, the country was at the pinnacle of its political power, economic prosperity, and cultural development. Moreover, the world was at peace and there was leisure for the ruler and the people of Egypt to enjoy the many pleasures and luxuries which life now had to offer them and to indulge to the full a truly oriental penchant for opulence and display.

Typical in every respect of the brilliant setting over which he presided, Amun-ḥotpe III contrived throughout his long reign to combine the unwavering pursuit of all manner of worldly pleasures with a program of self-glorification more elaborate and on a far grander scale than any previously undertaken.

The king's desire that his every action be made known to the world is attested by the extraordinary series of large commemorative scarabs which he caused to be issued during his first twelve years on the throne and which, like modern newsletters, were distributed throughout the country and even dispatched to the more distant outposts of the empire.

The first series of these scarabs, carved at the very beginning of the reign, announces the pharaoh's marriage to Teye, a woman of nonroyal birth; and with engaging frankness, which is repeated on many of the king's later monuments, gives the names of her untitled parents, Yuya and Tjuyu, adding, however, that "she is (now) the wife of a mighty king" whose empire extends from Karoy in the northern Sūdān to Naharīn in western Asia. Three *scarabs of this series, acquired by the Museum with the Ward, Murch, and Carnarvon collections, are made, as are most of their mates, of glazed steatite and measure between three and three and a half inches in length. Characteristically, the first five lines of the ten-line announcement inscribed on their undersides are taken up with the titulary of the king: "(Long) live the Horus, Strong-bull-appearing-in-truth, He of the Two Goddesses, Establisher-of-laws-(and-) pacifier-of-the-Two-Lands, the Horus of Gold, Great-of-valor-who-smites-the-Asiatics, the King of Upper and Lower Egypt, Neb-maʿet-Rēʿ, the Son of Reʿ, Amun-ḥotpe, Ruler of Thebes, given life!"

A great wild-cattle hunt held in Regnal Year 2 in the neighborhood of the Wādy Ḳeneh, in which the king, with the assistance of the officers and men of a near-by military colony, claims to have accounted for "96 wild bulls," is described in detail on a second series of scarabs; but of these our collection possesses no examples.

A third issue, of which more than forty specimens have survived to the present day, records the number of lions shot by Amun-ḥotpe III during the first ten years of his reign, the inscription ending in each case with the words "Statement of the lions which His Majesty brought (down) with his own arrows from Year 1 to Year 10: fierce lions, 102." Four ★scarabs of this type have been retained for our permanent collection because of the unusual care and skill with which they are carved and their almost perfect state of preservation. Three are of blue- or green-glazed steatite, while the fourth and largest of the lot is of limestone. With lengths ranging from just over two to three and a half inches, they show considerably more variation in size than the scarabs of the marriage series.

After the tenth year there is no further mention of hunting expeditions or of any activity involving physical exertion on the part of the king, who thenceforward appears to have given himself over to the pleasures of the ḥarīm and the banquet hall and to have devoted his attention chiefly to the rebuilding and beautification of Thebes and other favored sites in Egypt and Nubia.

In Year 10 itself Amun-ḥotpe III, following a lengthy correspondence with his uncle (?), King Shuttarna of Naharīn, arranged a marriage between himself and the king's daughter, Gilukhipa, whose arrival in Egypt with a retinue of 317 ladies and attendants was regarded as a "marvel" worthy of being recorded on a fourth set of commemorative scarabs. Even on these scarabs Teye and her parents occupy the place of honor after the king himself.

A fifth series of similar "bulletins" tells how at the end of the following year (Year 11) work was commenced on an artificial lake or harbor for Amun-ḥotpe's great queen in the district of Djaʿrukha, adjoining the royal palace in western Thebes. The excavation of the gigantic basin,[1] twelve hundred feet wide and over a mile in length, appears to have been completed in fifteen days, an estimated quarter million workmen being employed in the task. On the sixteenth day, early in Regnal Year 12, water was admitted to the lake through a broad canal from the Nile and the king sailed into it in the royal ship "Splendor-of-Aten."

Although our collection includes only a single ★scarab of the lake series (fig. 138), it is an exceptionally large and interesting example and is distinguished by the fact that it is of known provenience, coming apparently from the provincial locality to which it was originally issued. Acquired indirectly from a resident of the neighborhood of the ancient Nubian town of Buhen, near the Second Cataract of the Nile, the scarab bears on its back an inscription in which the "Good God, Neb-maʿet-Rēʿ," is designated as "one beloved of Horus, Lord of Buhen." The praenomen of the king, accompanied by the usual titles and epithets, is found again, on the right side of the scarab, in the triangular space between the legs of the beetle and the edge of the base.

On a related series of scarabs, smaller and more briefly inscribed than those of the great commemorative issues, we find the throne name Neb-maʿet-Rēʿ accompanied by elaborately worded epithets which seem at times to refer to specific events in the king's reign and are therefore of a semibiographical or even semihistorical nature. Unlike those of his predecessors (pp. 127, 144 f., 151 f.), the so-called minor historical scarabs of Amun-ḥotpe III conform for the most part to a single, well-defined type. The dozen or so ★scarabs of this class in our collection, for example, are all close to two inches in length and are almost without exception molded of blue or green faience. The legends which fill, but do not crowd, their oval fields, are made up in each case of a vertical cartouche and one or more groups of big, clear hi-

[1] The remains of which are still discernible in the present-day Birḳet Habu.

eroglyphs comprising the epithets. Among the latter some are commonplace—"beloved of Amūn," "image of Rēʿ"—while others describe Amun-ḥotpe III with more originality as "the sun of rulers," "enduring of monuments," and the like. Particularly common are expressions which reflect the king's real or alleged prowess in war, such as those in which he is called "lord of might and strength," "fighter of a hundred thousand," and "crusher of foreign countries."

Although the entire military career of the easy-going, luxury-loving pharaoh seems actually to have consisted of one relatively unimportant expedition into Nubia early in his reign and the sending of a few troops into Syria some years later, Amun-ḥotpe III lost no opportunity in his reliefs and inscriptions of representing himself as a mighty warrior and world conqueror. Florid accounts of the Nubian campaign of Year 5 are preserved to us in seven different inscriptions—at Thebes, Aswān, Konosso, and Semneh—and in these the king is described as a "fierce-eyed lion," a "lord of strength," and a "fire" which "rages" against his enemies. His southward advance probably did not carry him beyond the region of the Fourth Cataract, already subjugated by Tḥut-mosĕ III and Amun-ḥotpe II; but he characteristically claims on his Konosso stela that "there was no king in Egypt who did the like except His Majesty." His Golden Horus name, "Great-of-strength-who-smites-the-Asiatics," seems peculiarly inappropriate to a ruler whose indolent neglect of his Asiatic provinces paved the way for the collapse of Egypt's northern empire; and the epithets "smiter of Naharīn" and "captor of Shinar" certainly present an inaccurate picture of the peaceful relations which the king was always at pains to maintain with his powerful allies. Long rows of bound figures, personifying conquered foreign states, on temple walls and statue bases of Amun-ḥotpe III add to the illusion of world conquest; and in the great dedicatory inscription of the temple of Amun Rēʿ Montu at Karnak we are asked to believe that the building was constructed

FIGURE 138. Commemorative scarab of Amun-ḥotpe III in green-glazed steatite. L. 3 ¾ in.

FIGURE 139. King Amun-ḥotpe III. Colossal diorite statue from the temple of Amūn at Luxor. H. 8 ft. 4½ in.

from "the tribute of the chiefs of all foreign lands which His Majesty had taken in his victories as trophies of his strong arm."

It was as a builder and patron of the arts that Amun-ḥotpe III most truly earned the reputation for magnificence which to the present day is associated with his name. Superlatives fall thick and fast when one attempts to describe the vast size, the elegance of design, and the breath-taking richness which characterized his great temple to Amūn at Luxor, the impressive additions which he made to the principal shrine and precinct of the god at Karnak, his palace-city south of Medīnet Habu, his mortuary temple a mile and a half to the north, and the huge rock-cut tomb which he prepared for himself in the western branch of the Valley of the Tombs of the Kings.

The gigantic sandstone temple of Amūn, Mūt, and Khonsu at Luxor, a mile and a half south of Karnak, has the distinction of having been planned as a unit and three-quarters constructed by a single king. The first pylon and forecourt were added by Ramesses II, but the rest of the present temple, with the exception of a small shrine built by Tḥut-mosĕ III and some minor constructions of Tūt-ʿankh-Amūn and his immediate successors, is the work of Amun-ḥotpe III. From the sanctuary and complex of surrounding chambers at the southern end of the temple the processional way leads northward through two halls, a monumental pronaos and courtyard adorned with ninety-six magnificently proportioned papyriform columns of the clustered "bud" type, and thence between two rows of seven huge columns with spreading calyx capitals—representing perhaps the central aisle of a projected but never completed hypostyle hall. In size this great central colonnade surpasses any previously attempted, and in their proportions and spacing the towering shafts are as noble and impressive as anything which Egyptian architecture has produced. Known as the Southern Sanctuary—a name already current in the Middle Kingdom—the vast shrine was linked with the main temple of Amūn at Karnak by a paved avenue flanked on either side by a long row of ram-headed sphinxes, each having before it a small figure of Amun-ḥotpe III.

Two colossal seated ★statues of the king which once formed part of the sculptural adornment of this temple were appropriated, like many of his other monuments, by the Ramesside pharaoh Mery-en-Ptaḥ and bear the latter's unsightly cartouches on the arms and bodies of the figures and on the sides and fronts of the thrones (see figs. 139, 140). That these inscriptions were later additions to figures which appear to have been originally uninscribed but which from their style, proportions, facial type, and numerous significant details are clearly representations of Amun-ḥotpe III, has been demonstrated by Cyril Aldred and others, and since 1956 the statues have been restored to their rightful owner. Eight and a third and seven and a half feet in height, the great figures are carved with the utmost sensitivity and precision from single blocks of dark gray porphyritic diorite and are finished with what has been described as "a restrained surface polish." Both wear the goffered *shendyet*-kilt and the royal *nemes*, which in the case of the smaller statue was once surmounted by the towering Double Crown (𓋖). The sides of the throne of the larger statue (fig. 139) still retain, besides the inscriptions of the usurper, the more delicately carved elements of their original decoration—the eight-stripe block borders and the panels with the union of the emblematic plants of Upper and Lower Egypt.

Despite a high degree of idealization, which we have come to expect in the larger temple sculptures of this period, the face seen on our two statues is unmistakably that of Amun-ḥotpe III, with all the features familiar to us from his other portraits—the long, narrow eyes, prominent cheekbones, and full, sensuous mouth ever so slightly turned up at the corners. Designed to be looked up to from below, the figures appear a trifle top-heavy when brought down to eye level as in our photographs; but on the whole they are admirably proportioned and are endowed with a quality of monumental dignity and a sense of majesty rarely surpassed in the annals of ancient art. Above all, they show no break with the ancient traditions for royal temple sculpture as handed down from the Middle Kingdom and perpetuated under the pharaohs of the Eighteenth Dynasty—traditions which in less monumental works were already succumbing to new philosophical and artistic concepts of both domestic and foreign origin.

FIGURE 140. Colossus in dark gray diorite of King Amun-ḥotpe III from the Luxor temple. H. 7 ft. 5¾ in.

FIGURE 141. Sculptor's model for a relief head of Amun-ḥotpe III (?). L. 4¾ in.

One of the most striking portraits of Amun-ḥotpe III which has come down to us is a fragmentary quartzite ★head, slightly under life size, acquired by the Museum through purchase in the fall of 1956. Here with even greater clarity than on the Luxor statues we see again the king's long slanting eyes, massive cheekbones, full-lipped mouth, and thick, heavily muscled neck, modeled with extraordinary skill and assurance in the intensely hard, mottled brown stone. The peculiarly "oriental" quality of the eyes is accentuated by the double line of the upper eyelid, a stylistic detail found on other heads of Amun-ḥotpe III and his contemporaries. As frequently, the pharaoh is represented wearing the *kheperesh*, or Blue Crown, the top, back, and one side of which are unfortunately missing. Missing also are the king's nose and a portion of the left side of his face. In spite of these mishaps the head still retains much of the strength and beauty which must have made it one of the masterpieces of New Kingdom sculpture.

On a ★sculptor's model or trial piece carefully carved in limestone with the relief head of a king (fig. 141), we have without much doubt a profile portrait of Amun-ḥotpe III as a young man foppishly attired in an elaborately curled wig and *seshed*-circlet and wearing about his throat two strands of large lenticular beads. The soft and subtle modeling of the youthful face, the almost excessive interest in the details of the headdress, and the slightly feminine quality which pervades the work as a whole show us more accurately than do the big temple sculptures the direction in which Egyptian art is now tending. At the same time, the style of our relief does not exhibit the nervous sensibility, the exaggerated naturalism, and the other characteristic mannerisms of the only slightly later ʿAmārneh school.

These mannerisms, however, appear in unmistakable fashion in a headless ★statuette of Amun-ḥotpe III (fig. 142) carved in serpentine and said to have come from Thebes. Contrary to all previous tradition Egypt's king is here represented with unrestrained naturalism as a pathetically fat old man clad in a fringed and pleated overgarment of a type normally worn only by women (cf. fig. 161). The fringed robe worn by the pharaoh under this garment has been thought to be of Asiatic inspiration, and it has been pointed out that the position of the hands, unusual in Egyptian art, is common in Mesopotamia, appearing, for example, in the well-known statues of Gudea from Telloh. On his feet the king wears plaited rush sandals and about his throat an elaborate floral collar probably made of faience or of semiprecious stones. Two streamers hanging down the back of the figure indicate that the missing headdress was the Blue Crown. Both the back pilaster, which has the form of a *djed*-pillar, and the top of the base carry the names of Amun-ḥotpe III, the inscription on the former reading: "The Good God, the son of Amūn, whom he loved more than any (other) king, the King of Upper and Lower Egypt, the Lord of the Two Lands, Neb-maʿet-Rēʿ, given life forever." In both inscriptions the name of the god Amūn has been chiseled out, a defacement obviously perpetrated after the death of the old king and at the command of his "heretical" son Akh-en-Aten. The figure, however, belongs stylistically and iconographically to a school of art inaugurated under Akh-en-Aten and is, in fact, a three-dimensional version of a well-known relief portrait of Amun-ḥotpe III, accompanied by

Queen Teye, which was found in a house at Tell el ʿAmārneh. It must, then, have been carved at Thebes during the coregency of the two kings. During the same period works were apparently also being produced for Amun-ḥotpe III in the old, traditional style, so that for a brief interval there would seem to have been two schools of Theban artists functioning side by side, one reactionary, the other progressive.

Some of the more striking representatives of Amun-ḥotpe III and his family appear in the carved or painted tomb chapels of his Theban officials. A brilliant scene in Tomb 226 shows us the king enthroned under a triple baldachin of almost indescribable richness, attended by his mother, Queen Mūt-em-weya. In the chapel of his brother-in-law ʿA-nen (No. 120), we see the spendidly garbed pharaoh and Queen Teye seated together on a dais adorned with kneeling Nubian and Asiatic captives. A similar dais represented in the sculptured tomb of the Chief Steward Amun-em-ḥēt Surere (No. 48) is decorated with panels, in one of which the king, with upraised battle axe, is shown dispatching a bearded Asiatic chieftain. Among the statues of Theban rulers depicted in Tomb 19 (Nineteenth Dynasty) that of Amun-ḥotpe III occupies the third place in the second row. Thanks to the incomparable skill and patience of Nina de Garis Davies exact facsimile color ★copies of all four of these scenes may be studied in the Museum's Egyptian galleries.

At Karnak Amun-ḥotpe III added a new façade to the temple of Amūn in the form of the gigantic third pylon, a magnificent structure provided in front with an ornate vestibule and eight towering flag masts. In the foundations of this pylon his architects used hundreds of sculptured blocks taken from earlier royal buildings of both the Eighteenth Dynasty and the Middle Kingdom (see Part I, p. 181, and above, pp. 44, 47). Among the many other imposing structures which he contributed to the Karnak complex special interest attaches to the temple of Mūt, Amūn's divine consort, in the southern lake precinct called Ishru, and the temple of the ancient Theban god Montu (Amun Rēʿ Montu) in an enclosure of its own on the north of the precinct of Amūn.

For the courts of the Mūt temple the bountiful pharaoh provided almost six hundred colossal diorite statues of the goddess in the guise of the lioness-headed Sakhmet, "the terrible goddess of

FIGURE 142. Serpentine statuette of Amun-ḥotpe III. H. 9 in.

FIGURE 143. Statue of the goddess Sakhmet made under Amun-ḥotpe III, probably for the temple of Mūt at Karnak. Porphyritic diorite. H. 7 ft.

war and strife, who as the mother-goddess of the earlier Memphite triad had now seemingly become identified with Mut, the corresponding local Theban deity."[2] Many of these statues still stand in long, closely spaced rows around the scanty remains of the ruined temple; but many others have found their way into the Egyptian collections of Europe and America. Among the latter are eight big seated ★figures and the upper part of a ninth acquired by the Metropolitan Museum during the years 1907 and 1915, chiefly through the generosity of Henry Walters. Of these seven were formerly in the collections of Lord Amherst of Hackney and Dr. John Lee of Hartwell House, Aylesbury, and are believed to have been among those found by Giovanni Belzoni in 1817 in the western corridor of the Mūt temple enclosure. The two others were purchased in Cairo. All represent the goddess with the body of a slender young woman clad in a tight-fitting dress which extends from the ankles to just above the waist of the figure and is supported by straps ornamented with rosettes at the points where they pass over the breasts (see fig. 143). A broad collar and wide, banded bracelets and anklets complete the deity's archaic costume, and a long, striated wig of ancient type serves to conceal what would otherwise be an awkward transition between the human body and the magnificently modeled leonine head. In her left hand Sakhmet holds the symbol of "life" and on her head wears the disk of the sun fronted by an upreared uraeus. The sides of the throne on which she sits are in most cases adorned with panels and block borders exactly similar to those seen on our larger statue of Amun-ḥotpe III (fig. 139); and in two instances the fronts of the thrones bear inscriptions in which the "Good God, Lord of

[2] Lythgoe, *M. M. A. Bulletin*, XIV (1919), October, Part II, p. 3.

the Two Lands, Neb-maʿet-Rēʿ," and "the Son of Rēʿ, whom he loves, Amun-ḥotpe, Ruler of Thebes," is said to be "one beloved of Sakhmet, Mistress of ʿAget" and of the "Mound-of-the-face-of-Amūn." One of our statues is unfinished, its surfaces still bearing the marks of the stonemason's pick used in its shaping. In the case of this and three of the other figures the crowning solar disk, now missing, was carved from a separate block of stone and dovetailed in place; and in one instance the uraeus only had been made as a separate piece and let into a mortise on the front of the disk. Minor variations in style and proportions show that a number of different sculptors worked on the production of these statues, which, though designed primarily as oft-repeated accents in a grandiose religio-architectural scheme, are in individual instances monuments of great beauty, dignity, and technical excellence.

This is certainly true of a diorite ★cow's head (fig. 144) broken from a similar colossal statue of the goddess Ḥat-Ḥor and of a life-size ★head of the inundation god Ḥaʿpy, carved in the same dark gray porphyritic stone (fig. 145). Both heads were acquired at Luxor in 1919 and come in all likelihood from a single group of Theban temple statues, and both are almost certainly to be assigned to the reign of Amun-ḥotpe III. The face of the god, indeed, is to a great extent that of the king, with the arched brows, long narrow eyes, and sensitive, slightly smiling mouth which we have already seen on our portraits of the pharaoh. It has, moreover, the extraordinary delicacy and elegance which characterize the sculptured works of this slightly decadent, but enormously lively and attractive, phase of New Kingdom art. The Ḥat-Ḥor head, on the other hand, shows a masterly simplification and stylization of the animal form which compares favorably with that of the best of the Sakhmet heads. In each case the divinity of the subject is revealed by the long, archaic wig—somewhat incongruously combined with the animal head—and by other iconographical details, such as the solar disk between the towering horns of the Ḥat-Ḥor cow and Ḥaʿpy's narrow, braided chin

FIGURE 144. The goddess Ḥat-Ḥor. Porphyritic diorite. H. 20 in.

beard. A smaller ★head, broken away from a group of figures in mottled gray diorite, represents a beardless divinity (god or goddess) wearing the same wig, which in this case is fronted by a uraeus and had been surmounted by a cylindrical object —probably a crown of some sort or the base of a tall plumed or horned headdress. The handsome youthful face and the elegance of the style suggest a date in the reign of Amun-ḥotpe III, though a somewhat earlier dating, to late Thutmoside times, is by no means impossible.

A small but interesting monument from one of Amun-ḥotpe III's Karnak temples is a white faience ★box lid in the form of a cartouche, made apparently as a souvenir of his first jubilee in Regnal Year 30. Engraved on the top of the lid, inside

FIGURE 145. Ḥaʿpy, the god of the inundation. Porphyritic diorite. H. 12 in.

the frame of the cartouche, is one of the several "festival versions" of the king's titulary: "The Horus, Image-of-Rēʿ-before-the-Two-Lands, He of the Two Goddesses, Brilliant-of-appearances-and-great-of-dignity, the Horus of Gold, Fresh-of-*kus*-and-goodly-of-years, the Lord of *Sed*-festivals, the King of Upper and Lower Egypt, Neb-maʿet-Rēʿ Chosen-of-Rēʿ, the Son of Rēʿ, Amun-ḥotpe, Ruler of Thebes, given life, like Rēʿ." This is followed in the last two lines of the seven-line inscription by the words: "The appearance of the King at the first *sed*-festival is like (that of) Rēʿ when he rises."

Demolished in the Nineteenth Dynasty, the mortuary temple of Amun-ḥotpe III north of Medīnet Habu appears to have been the largest of its class ever constructed, and the two fifty-foot statues of the king which stood before it (long famous as the Colossi of Memnon) still dominate the plain of western Thebes. In the field behind the colossi lies the granite stela, once "wrought with gold and many costly stones," which marked the "Station of the King," and another stela from the same temple tells us that the building was "wrought with gold throughout, its floors adorned with silver and all its portals with fine gold." Called the "Mansion-of-Neb-maʿet-Rēʿ-on-the-west-of-Thebes," the temple appears to have been maintained in running order at least until the end of the Eighteenth Dynasty, our collection including a ★stela of that period (see also p. 306) belonging to a certain Woser-ḥēt who was both an "Accountant of All the Goodly Property in the Mansion of Neb-maʿet-Rēʿ" and the "First Prophet . . . in the Mansion of Neb-khepru-Rēʿ (Tūt-ʿankh-Amūn)."

Whereas every king of Egypt was in theory a god, there were few who interpreted this tradition so literally or emphasized their divinity with such insistence as did Amun-ḥotpe III. In the temple at Luxor a series of reliefs, similar to those of Ḥatshepsūt at Deir el Baḥri, portray in detail the divine birth of the king; and in his mortuary temple across the river the cult of the deified pharaoh ("Neb-maʿet-Rēʿ, Prince of Princes") was maintained side by side with that of "his father, Amūn." At Soleb, fifty-five miles below the Third Cataract of the Nile, Amun-ḥotpe III dedicated a handsome fortified temple to the worship of himself and of Amūn, several inscriptions from this building stating plainly that "He made (it) as his monument for his living image upon earth, Neb-maʿet-Rēʿ, Lord of Nubia in the Fortress Khaʿ-em-maʿet." Near by, at Sedeinga, the king erected a temple to his queen, Teye, who, in spite of her humble birth, appears also to have been deified and to have been worshiped, together with her husband, as a patron divinity of the region. In texts of the later New Kingdom Amun-ḥotpe III is named with Ptaḥ as one of the gods of Memphis and there is evidence that his "living image" was worshiped there in a great temple of his own building called the "House of Neb-maʿet-Rēʿ."

For the site of his tomb Amun-ḥotpe III selected the hitherto unoccupied western branch of the Valley of the Tombs of the Kings. Here his masons, tunneling down into the bedrock at the base of a cliff, hewed for him a great subterranean complex of stairways, passages, and chambers similar to that of Tḥut-mosĕ IV (see pp. 147 f.), but even larger and with the second bend in the plan reversing the direction of the first. Two suites of chambers opening off a corner of the sepulchral hall and not found in any other royal tomb are believed to have been provided for the burials of Queen Teye and Queen Sit-Amūn (see pp. 259 ff. and 262). Though only partially decorated and repeatedly plundered in ancient times the tomb has yielded, besides the granite lid of the king's massive sarcophagus, numerous small items of its original equipment.

The *shawabty*-figures of Amun-ḥotpe III, for example, have survived in fairly large numbers and in various materials, including wood, faience, and several kinds of ornamental stone. Most of them are fragmentary, and this is the case with three big ebony ★*shawabtys* acquired for the Museum in 1915 at the sale of the Rustafjael collection. The most complete of our three figures (fig. 146) lacks its headdress—evidently one of the crowns—which was probably made of faience or some similar material and doweled in place. The eyes, as can be seen, are inlaid in colored glass and the signs in the four-column inscription down the front of the figure are incised and filled with yellow paste. The inscription itself is a curiously expanded version of the *shawabty*-spell. Beginning with the title "(A spell for) causing the *shawabty* to perform labor in the necropolis in behalf of the honored one, the Osiris, King Neb-maʿet-Rēʿ, the justified," it runs on, "O gods who are at the side of the Lord of the Universe and who sit within his call, remember me when you pronounce his name. Give him[3] the offerings of the evening and hearken to his petitions in the district of Pōkĕ when he celebrates the *wag*-feast. Should it be (incumbent) upon the Osiris, King Amun-ḥotpe, Ruler of Thebes, the justified, to cultivate the fields, to irrigate the banks, to transport sand of the east to

[3] The deceased king, henceforward referred to in the third person.

FIGURE 146. *Shawabty*-figure of King Amun-ḥotpe III. Ebony. H. 15 ¾ in.

the west, ('I will do it! Behold, here am I!' [you shall say]). May the Osiris, King Neb-maʿet-Rēʿ, the justified, be remembered in the presence of Wen-nefer in order to receive food offerings in his presence."

A careful clearing of the tomb and its vicinity in February 1915 by the Earl of Carnarvon and Howard Carter resulted in the recovery of many other fine small objects associated with the king's burial; and of these a generous share came to the Metropolitan Museum in 1926 with the Carnarvon collection.

Best known—and deservedly so—is a group of five ★bracelet plaques of translucent carnelian and sard exquisitely carved in relief with miniature scenes and figures relating to the life of the king and his family. Three of the group, said to have been found in an ancient plunderers' dump outside the entrance of the tomb, were obtained with the Carnarvon collection (fig. 147). The others, formerly in the MacGregor and Walters collections, were acquired by purchase in 1926 and 1944. All had at one time been mounted in metal frames, not unlike the modern gold mountings in which the three Carnarvon gems are now exhibited,[4] and had been worn, perhaps by Queen Teye, in wide gold or silver bracelets similar to those found on the mummy of Amun-ḥotpe III's son(?), Tūt-ʿankh-Amūn. Both the front and back surfaces of the plaques follow the curve of the bracelets in which they were set, and in two instances they are notched at the ends or pierced with small holes for the studs by means of which they were anchored to their mountings.

In the scene on the largest of the four carnelian plaques we see the pharaoh participating in the culminating ceremonies of a *sed*-festival—probably his first. He is twice represented enthroned in full regalia in the twin festival pavilions, wearing, successively, the crown of Upper Egypt and the crown of Lower Egypt. In each case Teye stands before him wearing the tall double-plumed headdress of a queen and holding in one hand the symbol for "hundreds of thousands of years." Vertical columns of almost microscopic hieroglyphs at the ends of the cameo give the king's titulary in some detail. Two of the other plaques show us Amun-ḥotpe III and Teye enthroned together and attended by their daughters, Ḥenet-to-nēb and Iset. In one instance the king wears the Blue Crown and a dress kilt of elaborate design, in the other the Double Crown and the curious shirt of archaic type normally reserved for the *sed*-festival. The performance of a formal ceremony, probably associated with the royal jubilee, is further suggested by the action of the princesses, who function here as musician priestesses, rattling their sistrums () in the king's presence and bringing to him symbols of endless years and eternal life. A little man who appears behind Queen Teye on the Walters plaque, bending forward and holding over his shoulder a long-handled ostrich-plume fan (), is probably one of the great officials of the reign performing the highly honorable office of Fanbearer on the King's Right Hand. The presence of his figure in this august and otherwise royal company suggests that he was the donor of the bracelet and reminds us that, on the occasion of important festivals, bracelets and other valuable trinkets were, in fact, offered by prominent officials as gifts to the king and other members of the royal family.

The fragmentary fourth cameo preserves part of a coronation scene similar to those in Amun-ḥotpe III's temple at Luxor. On the right sits a falcon-headed divinity, labeled "Rēʿ Ḥor-akhty, the Great God," holding in his left hand the symbol for "years" and extending his right hand forward and upward to place a crown on the king's head. The latter, kneeling before his divine benefactor, is dressed in an elaborately decorated kilt and grasps in his hand the crook and *ladanisterion*. It is a reasonably safe guess that on the missing left half of the plaque there was, behind the figure of the king, a second seated divinity, facing to the right, and that this divinity was the great Lord of Karnak and King of the Gods, Amun Rēʿ.

In the openwork design of the sard plaque (fig.

[4] These were modeled on the silver bracelets of Queen Te-Wosret of the late Nineteenth Dynasty.

FIGURE 147. Bracelet plaques made during the reign of Amun-ḥotpe III, probably on the occasion of his first jubilee in Regnal Year 30. The two upper examples are of carnelian, the lower of sard. L. 2 1/8-2 1/4 in.

147, bottom) we see Queen Teye, represented as a winged female sphinx, holding in her extended hands the praenomen cartouche of her royal husband. Her strange floral headdress, springing from a piled-up coiffure bound with a ribbon, reminds us of that of the cataract goddess Anukis, and the generally Nubian appearance of the head is heightened by the massive earring and the dark, purplish brown color of the stone. It is perhaps a significant fact that a standing version of the sphinx of our bracelet gem occurs in the decoration of Teye's temple at Sedeinga in the northern Sūdān.

From unrecorded portions of the royal tomb come one complete and two fragmentary bangles, nineteen amulets, the butt end of an axe handle, parts of ten small vases, an inlay figure from a piece of furniture, and two uraeus heads from the cornice of a shrine—all of faience with the exception of one of the uraei which is of dark blue glass.

The complete ★bangle, a doughnut-shaped ornament of violet blue faience three and a half inches in diameter, carries on each of its sides a hieroglyphic titulary of Amun-ḥotpe III inlaid in pale blue glaze and running continuously around the circumference of the ring. Besides his more common titles and epithets the king is referred to in these texts as a Lord of Joy, Lord of Accomplishment, Lord of Diadems, Seizer of the White Crown, and as "one beloved of the Ennead of Gods." The fragmentary ★bangles were flat bands of dark blue faience curved around to form circular loops and inscribed on the outside with the pharaoh's names and titles, the hieroglyphs again inlaid in light blue glaze.

The ★amulets, all of blue or green faience, include, in addition to such common forms as the *wedjat*-eye, the *djed*-pillar, and the *nefer*-sign, two openwork cartouches with the king's throne name and three openwork designs in which a symbol of "life" grasps with a pair of human arms two *was*-scepters of "well-being." An interesting series of little openwork plaques are composed of groups of hieroglyphs which when strung together in rows made up continuous texts of an amuletic nature. Besides two examples of the preposition 𓅓 ("in," "from," "as") our amulets of this type preserve the phrases, ". . . (may) they make . . .," ". . . heaven, unite(d) . . .," and ". . . me on the throne

. . ." Most elaborate is an amulet comprising a kneeling figure of the god of eternity grasping in either hand the tall, curved symbol for "years," and supporting on his head a horizontal cartouche with the name and epithet "Neb-maʿet-Rēʿ Image-of-Rēʿ." Both the form of the praenomen and the composition as a whole are associated with the *sed*-festival and are paralleled almost exactly on a curious alabaster festival stela presently to be discussed (see p. 256). Finally, there is a little pendant representing the god Ptaḥ Sokar as a crouching child holding one hand to his mouth, a type particularly common during the kingship of Amun-ḥotpe III's son Akh-en-Aten. Since most of these amulets are duplicated by examples found in the ruins of the king's palace (see p. 252) it would seem that at this period no general differentiation existed between amulets designed to be worn by the living and those prepared for the dead.

Made of turquoise blue faience, the ★butt of the ceremonial axe handle is adorned with narrow black bands and has inscribed on its end, also in black, the praenomen cartouche of Amun-ḥotpe III resting upon a *neb*-sign and surmounted by a solar disk. A great variety of colors, shapes, and decorative signs appear in the faience ★vase fragments, the last including incised birds and lotus flowers, rows of little cornflowers in relief, and over-all scale patterns. Two of the fragments carry the king's praenomen and one his personal name accompanied by that of his eldest daughter and junior queen, Sit-Amūn. A fragment of faience ★inlay from a footstool, chest, or other article of furniture has the form of a kneeling figure clad in a long white garment adorned with a blue scale pattern. The ★uraeus heads, one of violet faience, the other of dark blue glass, come probably from rows of large wooden or metal uraei which at this period are frequently seen crowning the tops of shrines, screen walls, and other architectural elements. Two inches in length, each is deeply notched at the back to facilitate its attachment to the hooded neck of the emblematic serpent.

In the débris left by plunderers near the entrance of the tomb were found nineteen pieces of elaborately decorated chariot ★harness, made up of layers of pink, green, and white leather stitched together to form a variety of elements. Among these we can recognize parts of girths, chest bands, back pads, and blinkers, as well as a bridle strap of pink-dyed calfskin overlaid with green and white leather appliqués and adorned with a row of large, brightly gilded metal studs. Fragmentary as these elements are, they deserve our attention, for Egyptian horse harness of dynastic date is extremely rare and when found is usually in a hopelessly gummy condition.

Also from the Valley of the Tombs of the Kings and quite possibly from the tomb of Amun-ḥotpe III is a ★dish of fine buff pottery decorated on the interior with delicately painted palm and papyrus motifs symmetrically arranged around a central rosette. Both the style of the ornament and the prominence in the color scheme of an attractive shade of pale blue are peculiar to the decorated "palace" pottery produced in quantity under Amun-ḥotpe III and his immediate successors. It would, indeed, be difficult to assign this charming though, unhappily, fragmentary vessel to any other period.

The palace in western Thebes where the king seems to have lived during the greater part of his reign was not a single structure, but a vast complex of rambling one-story buildings covering an area of over eighty acres along the desert's edge south of Medīnet Habu. On the east it was connected with the Nile by the huge T-shaped lake already referred to and on the north was joined to the pharaoh's mortuary temple at Kōm el Ḥetān by a causeway, which continued running southward through the desert to a sun temple near Deir esh Shelwīt. Founded in or before the eleventh year of the reign in a locality then known as Djaʿrukha ("Searcher-of-the-evening"?), the palace itself appears to have been called the "House- (or Town) of-Neb-maʿet-Rēʿ-(is-)the-splendor-of-Aten." From the time of the celebration of the first *sed*-festival, in the thirtieth year, onward it was also called Per-ḥaʿy, the "House-of-rejoicing," and this is the name which is found on bricks and other inscribed objects from its buildings. Today the sprawling ruins, which are nowhere preserved above waist level, are known as *el malḳat*, or, more popularly, the "Malḳata," an Arabic expression meaning simply "the place where things are picked up."

The oldest and most important of its many buildings, the Palace of the King, occupies the southeast quarter of the great complex and is adjoined on the east by its kitchens, offices, and storerooms, and by a small royal dwelling (the South Palace), perhaps at one time the residence of Queen Teye. The rambling Middle Palace, with its big porticoed courtyard, was probably built for the pharaoh's son Akh-en-Aten and occupied by him previous to and during the first five years of his coregency with his father. Adjoining this palace on the west are two great houses, prepared presumably for two other members of Amun-ḥotpe III's extensive family, and three big villas, grouped together in a separate enclosure of their own and thought to have housed the three senior officials of the court—the vizier, the chancellor, and the king's chief steward. Rows of small, five-room houses farther to the west were clearly provided for minor officials or palace attendants. Similar rows of small houses, or servants' quarters, run parallel to the great North Palace, which appears to have been the residence of an extremely important royal lady, quite possibly Queen Sit-Amūn. The western end of this building is given over to magazines and workshops, and farther to the west are the remains of a workmen's village. North of the latter lies the royal Audience Pavilion, its floor elevated above the surrounding terrain, its northern façade provided with a balconylike projection jutting out into a deep, colonnaded courtyard. A much larger enclosure a hundred yards farther to the north comprises the forecourt, terrace, halls, sanctuaries, and magazines of a building identified by scores of stamped bricks and other inscribed objects found in it as the "Temple-of-Amūn-in-the-house-of-rejoicing." A Festival Hall prepared for the celebration of Amun-ḥotpe III's second *sed*-festival in Year 34 is probably one of the big colonnaded structures which extend along the northern side of the temple forecourt. Vast rubbish mounds in the open areas west of the palace buildings and along the embankments of the Birket Habu yielded quantities of inscribed jar fragments and other objects, as did also the South Village, a group of small factories and workmen's houses three hundred yards south of the main palace enclosure.

The whole of the area described was excavated during the years 1910-1920 by the Museum's Egyptian Expedition and, though little remained of the buildings and their furnishings, it was possible to salvage from their ruins sections of painted walls and ceilings, decorated vessels of pottery and other materials, hundreds of attractive small objects, and a considerable corpus of inscribed material, chiefly in the form of jar labels and sealings.

With the exception of the Temple of Amūn, where stone and tilework were employed to a limited extent, the palace seems to have been built throughout of sun-dried mud brick, faced inside and out with mud plaster and provided with roof beams, columns, door frames, and window grills of painted wood, the only stone elements found being the limestone column bases in the reception halls and an occasional doorsill, bathing slab, and catch basin.

In the columned halls, bedrooms, and dressing rooms the mud-plaster surfaces of the walls and ceilings were decorated with tempera paintings of great charm and vivacity. Though often employing conventional subjects and traditional motifs, the palace paintings display a more naturalistic trend and a much freer and looser treatment than do the more carefully executed tomb paintings of the period. They also show a freer use of elements and compositions borrowed from other nations of the eastern Mediterranean world—especially those derived from the art of the Helladic peoples of the islands and littorals of the Aegean area.

In a section of ★painted ceiling (fig. 148) from the Palace of the King, for example, we see the quadruple spiral combined with the ox head, or bucranium, both motifs of Aegean origin, though

FIGURE 148. Ceiling painting from the palace of Amun-ḥotpe III, partially restored. The background is red and blue, the spirals yellow, and the cows' heads red, white, and black. H. 55 in.

not necessarily of recent importation into Egypt. Actually what is employed in this version of the design would seem to be the cow's head of the goddess Ḥat-Ḥor, with the solar disk between the animal's horns here treated as a rosette. The lively action and free, over-all composition which we associate with the palace frescoes of Crete appear in two delightful ceiling ★paintings, where pigeons and pintail ducks with wings outspread fly hither and thither over a greenish yellow background. The rapidly executed ★painting of a red and white calf running through a pale green papyrus thicket (fig. 149), which was used to adorn the side of a brick bench in the royal ḥarīm, shows us the animal in the well-known Helladic posture known as the flying gallop. The end of the same bench was decorated with a ★panel enclosing a basket of fruit on a light wickerwork stand, a favorite motif of the New Kingdom mural painter, often used as a space filler (see fig. 211). Besides these originals our collection also comprises a number of facsimile color ★copies of palace paintings left *in situ*.

The contiguous S-spirals seen on our first section of painted ceiling appear again in the wall decoration of a series of rooms adjoining the palace's Temple of Amūn. Here, however, the design was not painted, but was molded in relief in gilded plaster and the squarish spaces between the spirals were inlaid with flat tiles of rich blue faience. Smaller, rectangular tiles of the same type were used to make up the block borders with which the wall areas were framed. At their tops the walls were crowned with cavetto cornices made of gilded wood, the leaves of the cavetto being inlaid with small scale-shaped tiles of blue and black faience. Little remained of either the wood or the plaster portions of the decoration, but more than enough ★tiles of the various types were recovered from the ruins to enable the Museum's technicians to restore a panel of the brilliant gold and blue wall surface and a section of the polychrome cornice.

Among the elements included in the decoration of the walls or doorways of these same rooms were gold and blue cartouches of Amun-ḥotpe III, each represented as resting on a ⌓-sign and surmounted by the sun's disk and double plume. One more or less intact ★cartouche of this type, containing the king's praenomen, "Neb-maʿet-Rēʿ," was brought to New York in 1917. Exclusive of the plumes and *neb*-sign it measures nine and a half inches in height and consists of a molded plaster frame into which is set a flat oval tile of bright blue faience, its surface provided with appropriately shaped hollows to take the backs of the gilded plaster hieroglyphs composing the king's name.

Portions of the palace, such as doorways, windows, and balconies, were adorned with friezes of small ★faience ornaments—bunches of dark blue grapes, green and white lotus flowers, and the like—and of these a dozen more or less complete examples have been retained for our collection. With flat or indented backs and dowel holes for attachment, these glossy, brightly colored incrustations must have added a gemlike glitter to the façades and interiors of the royal buildings. Two blue glass ★inlays, representing the ⌓-

hieroglyph and a clenched human hand, are probably from the decoration of elaborate door frames. A thick rectangular ★tile of dark blue faience, resembling a brick in its form and proportions, is adorned on its front and side edges with marsh scenes—clumps of reeds and papyrus and flying and sitting waterfowl—outlined in light gray glaze.

Stamped mud ★bricks from the palace structures maintain a ratio of approximately 3 : 1 ½ : 1 between their lengths, widths, and thicknesses, but range in length from eleven to fifteen inches, the larger sizes coming chiefly from the later buildings. The big rectangular and oval impressions on the tops of the bricks, probably made with hardwood stamps, contain the cartouches of Amun-ḥotpe III, sometimes accompanied by that of Queen Teye, sometimes followed by the name of the palace ("Per-ḥaʿy") or one of its parts the ("Temple-of-Amūn-in-Per-ḥaʿy").

Of the palace's movable furnishings those most closely linked in spirit and style with the decoration of the apartments for which they were made, and possessing, by the same token, probably the greatest charm and appeal of all the objects found in it, are its elaborately decorated vessels of painted pottery. Almost the only fine decorated pottery which had been produced in Egypt since prehistoric times, this justly famous ware is distinguished by the graceful shapes of its vessels, the preponderance of natural plant and animal forms in its decoration, and its characteristic "blond" color scheme, predominantly light blue on a buff ground with outlines and linear details in dark red and brownish black. Among the twenty-one complete or fragmentary items of ★palace pottery in our collection (see fig. 150) are tall ovoid and drop-shaped jars with long necks and flaring mouths, short-necked jars of medium size, both drop-shaped and ovoid, squat situlae with wide mouths, an enormous dish with a scalloped rim, and part of a flat dish with a low vertical edge. The decoration, derived from the wreaths with which jars were customarily draped at Egyptian banquets, consists chiefly of bands of leaves, petals, and other floral motifs. Lotus flowers, clumps of papyrus, flying birds, and running calves are also found, and several of the more elaborate vessels are adorned with Ḥat-Ḥor heads and rows of grape clusters modeled in relief. On the amphora of figure 150 (upper right) the body of the ibex on

FIGURE 149. Panel from a wardrobe room in the Theban palace of Amun-ḥotpe III. L. 19¼ in.

the shoulder of the jar is drawn in outline, while the head and neck of the animal are modeled in the round and are freestanding from the vessel except where the tips of the horns touch the rim.

The thousands of plain pottery jars—chiefly big amphorae—in which supplies of food, drink, and other commodities were brought to the palace storerooms bore in many cases hieratic labels written in black ink on the shoulders of the vessels (see fig. 151). Besides the name, quality, and source of the commodity contained in the jar these labels frequently give the date of bottling, expressed in terms of regnal years of Amun-ḥotpe III, a reference to the festival or other occasion for which the commodity was prepared, the name and title of the official who contributed the jar and its contents (either as a private donor or as a royal estate manager), and the name of the vintner, butcher, or other specialist who prepared the contents. The great majority of the fourteen hundred palace ★jar labels found by the Museum's Expedition are from jars of supplies which were prepared for one or another of the king's three *sed*-festivals, celebrated in Regnal Years 30, 34, and 37 respectively. The dates on our labels, however, include every one of the last eleven years of the reign (Years 28-38), with isolated examples extending back as far as Year 8. A "Regnal Year 1," occurring on the fragments of five wine jars from the Middle Palace, undoubtedly refers to the reign of Amun-ḥotpe III's son and coregent, Akhen-Aten, and is perhaps to be equated with Year 28 of the older pharaoh. According to their labels 375 of the jars had contained jerked meat; 298, ale; and 285, wine; with animal fat, vegetable oil, fowl, fruit, honey, and incense occurring in lesser quantities. The royal and temple domains which furnished the supplies included not only estates of Amun-ḥotpe III himself and his queens, Teye and Sit-Amūn, but others which had belonged to his father, Tḥut-mosĕ IV, to his mother, Queen Mūt-em-weya, to the national treasury, and to the gods Amūn and Rēʿ. Some of the beverages and foodstuffs had been shipped to Thebes from considerable distances. The best

FIGURE 150. Decorated pottery jars from the palace of Amun-ḥotpe III. H. 9⅝-27¼ in.

wines, for example, came from the region of Memphis, from three areas in the northern Delta, from Syria, and from the oases of the Libyan Desert. Among the seventy-three contributors listed by name and title in these inscriptions are some of the foremost officials of the reign—the King's Scribe Amun-ḥotpe, son of Ḥapu, the Viziers Raʿ-mosĕ and Amun-ḥotpe, the Chief Stewards Amun-ḥotpe of Memphis and Surere of Thebes, the well-known King's Scribes Khaʿ-em-ḥēt and Kheruef, the High Treasurer Ptaḥ-mosĕ, the Greatest of Seers Amun-em-ḥēt, the Treasurer Sobk-mosĕ, and many others. The label selected for illustration in figure 151 is from a fat-jar found in a great house adjoining the Middle Palace. It reads: "Regnal Year 38, the Five Epagomenal Days, the Birth(day) of Osiris.[5] Fat (of) breast meat of the cattle stable—a gift to His Majesty—may he live, prosper, and be well!—(from) the stockyards of the King's Scribe Aʿḥ-mosĕ. Prepared by the fat-renderer Yu-Amūn." Insignificant as such inscriptions may seem individually, collectively they constitute a corpus of material of no small historical importance. This label and fifteen others like it, for example, are the only evidence that we now possess that Amun-ḥotpe III reigned for as long as thirty-eight years.

Many of the jars had been sealed with heavy cylindrical stoppers of Nile mud bearing on their tops and sides oval seal impressions with abbreviated hieroglyphic versions of the labels on the shoulders of the jars. From the impressions on two palace ★jar sealings in the Museum's collection we learn, for example, that the contents of the jars had been, respectively, "*Ḥedebet*-beverage of the House of Amun-ḥotpe" and "Mutton fat of the Abode brought (for) the festival." As is often the case, the first of our sealings is painted in bright colors, its sides adorned with bands of white petals

[5] The 361st day of the Egyptian civil year. See Part I, p. 39.

FIGURE 151. Hieratic label on the shoulder of a pottery jar from the palace of Amun-ḥotpe III. H. 9 ¾ in.

on a blue ground, its top bearing, in two painted yellow ovals, the words "House of Amun-ḥotpe."

In West Villa "B" (the house of the vizier?), in the outbuildings of the Palace of the King, and in the southern rubbish mounds were found over eleven hundred small mud ★sealings from rolls of papyrus (▭), each bearing on its rounded back an average of eight seal impressions. A number of the impressions were probably made by scarabs and rectangular plaques—perhaps of glazed steatite—but the vast majority were evidently produced by gold, silver, or bronze signet rings of the massive, fixed-bezel type developed during the Eighteenth Dynasty and common from the reign of Amun-ḥotpe III onward (see fig. 180). This is indicated by the shapes of the impressions, which for the most part are long and perfectly symmetrical ovals, and by the elegance of the designs, the intricacy of the details, and the metallic clarity of the outlines of the forms. The very striking uniformity in style, quality, size, and shape displayed by the impressions, and the absence from their inscriptions of all personal names save only that of the king further indicate that the rings which produced them were standardized seals of royal authority issued by the pharaonic government for the use of its officials, and that the documents sealed with these rings were of an official nature. Here, as occasionally elsewhere, the praenomen of Amun-ḥotpe III is usually written with a monogram composed of the seated figure of the king 𓀭 ("Neb") holding the feather of truth 𓆄 ("maʿet") and surmounted by the sun's disk ☉ ("Rēʿ"). Frequently it is accompanied by titles and epithets, the latter sometimes of a semi-historical nature ("he who flooded Lower Egypt with his works," "he who has taken every foreign country," "the ichneumon [victorious] over [his] enemies"). More often the pharaoh is described as "one beloved of" the deity or deities of the localities where the sealings (and their documents) presumably originated ("Thōt, Lord of Hermopolis," "Horus, Lord of Ḥe-nēsu," Ḥar-shūf of Herakleopolis, and others). Some of the impressions contain only the names of divinities (Amun Rēʿ, Ptaḥ, Montu, Horus, Sētẖ) and some the names of rulers other than Amun-ḥotpe III. The latter include Tẖut-mosĕ III and IV, Amun-ḥotpe II, Akh-en-Aten, and ʿAnkhes-en-Amūn, the wife of Tūt-ʿankh-Amūn.

Among the more popular items of "costume" jewelry affected by the Egyptians of the late Eighteenth Dynasty were reproductions in glazed frit of the metal signet rings referred to in the preceding paragraph. Like their models, the faience rings are provided with oval, lozenge-shaped, or rectangular bezels fused to or molded in one piece with the rings proper. In many cases the molds used for the faience ring bezels appear to have been taken directly from actual signet rings—a fact which adds immeasurably to their interest and value. Cheaply and easily manufactured, the faience rings were equally easily broken; it is unlikely that they were intended as seals or even as real pieces of jewelry—more probably they were distributed as favors on the occasions of festivals, banquets, and the like and included among the funerary equipment buried in the tombs of the dead. Though almost always fragmentary, such rings have survived in enormous quantities and, since they frequently bear royal names and titles, often throw considerable light on the histories of the sites in which they occur.

Of the ★rings of this class, recovered intact or in fragments from the ruins of the palace of Amun-ḥotpe III, our own collection includes almost a thousand examples in blue, green, purple, or violet faience. Of these four hundred and fifty bear the names of the king ("Neb-maʿet-Rēʿ," "Neb-maʿet-Rēʿ Image-of-Rēʿ," or "Amun-ḥotpe, Ruler of Thebes"), thirty the name of Queen Teye, and one the name of Sit-Amūn. The bezels of several hundred others carry amuletic devices—figures of the goddess Thoueris and hieroglyphic symbols for "life," "goodness," "right," and the like—or purely decorative motifs, such as rosettes, palmettes, papyrus plants, and lotus flowers modeled in relief or combined in elaborate openwork designs. Rings with bezels molded in the form of the *wedjat*-eye were understandably popular, and of these we have many examples in various colors and combinations of glazes. The rarity of inscribed ring bezels with the name of Queen Sit-Amūn is explained by the fact that our rings come without exception from the older buildings of the palace group and may therefore be supposed to reflect an early period in the history of the palace—a period when Teye alone was the King's Great Wife and her daughter was only a senior princess.

Not all the finger rings picked up in the palace ruins were faience "party favors." The Middle Palace yielded a heavy copper ★signet ring with the throne name of Amun-ḥotpe III engraved on its long, oval bezel, and from the Palace of the King come two ★rings of the same type carved in carnelian and a silver ★ring with a rectangular bezel of brown and white agate. An attractive little ★ring made entirely of glass has an oval bezel of green glass and a finger loop composed of slender threads of polychrome glass twisted together in imitation of a wire or cord. The praenomen of Amun-ḥotpe III ("Neb-maʿet-[Rēʿ]") appears in the openwork design of a handsome, but unfortunately fragmentary, ★bracelet of bright blue faience (fig. 152), found during the season of 1910-1911 in one of the glass factories in the South Village.

A rich harvest of ★scarabs, ★cowroids, ★plaques, and other ★seal amulets of faience and glazed steatite yielded thirty examples with the names of the palace's royal owner, two with that of his great-grandfather, Tḥut-mosĕ III, and one with that of Queen Teye. Many of the uninscribed scarabs are adorned on their undersides with figures of animals (a hippopotamus, a crouching ibex, a crocodile on a shrine), while others carry decorative patterns, including S-spirals of Helladic type. A group composed of cowroids, *wedjat*-eyes, and seal amulets with backs in the shapes of human figures, mice, frogs, fish, grasshoppers, and scorpions, was found strung together with small faience ring beads to form a ★necklace almost three feet in length. Besides the name of the king several of the little seals of the group bear the names of divinities, the most interesting of which is that of the Syrian storm god Resheph.

FIGURE 152. Blue faience bracelet of Amun-ḥotpe III. Diam. 3⅛ in.

Fifty-five ★amulets, once worn by inmates of the palace, are without exception of faience or opaque glass, but vary considerably in their forms and colors, the latter including several shades of green, pale blue, indigo, violet, purple, red, brown, and white, as well as combinations of these colors in streaked or mottled patterns. The most popular types are the *wedjat*-eye and the figure of the dwarf god Bēs, who now appears not only in his truculent frontal pose, but also in side view, dancing and holding aloft a circular tambourine. Next come ten small figures of the almost equally popular hippopotamus goddess, Thoueris, and then a series of amulets of eighteen different varieties, represented by only one example each. Here we find, besides the usual symbols for "goodness," "well-being," "protection," "right," "favor," and the like, a figure of the god of eternity with his notched plant stems, a figure of the atmosphere god Shu, with arms upraised to support the heaven, and a figure of the goddess Maʿet perched upon a *neb*-sign—perhaps an abbreviated version of the king's throne name. A scarab beetle, a crocodile, a turtle, a Ḥat-Ḥor head of purple glass, and a heart amulet (♡) of variegated glass are all familiar forms; but a falcon with wings outspread, a pair of pigeons in black and red glass, a red faience crescent, and a star of blue faience are new or at least hitherto rare types. Two elaborate openwork amulets of blue faience representing the double *sed*-festival pavilion and a group of hieroglyphs forming the word *men*, "be firm," are paralleled almost exactly by examples from the tomb of Amun-ḥotpe III (see p. 243). Considering the fact that the average height of these little charms is under three-quarters of an inch, the amount of detail that some of them show is remarkable.

Also remarkable was the discovery in the Palace of the King of a section of a ★model throw-stick in blue faience, a type of amulet well known from tombs and temples of the Eighteenth Dynasty (see p. 149) but rarely found in the dwellings of the living. An inch and a quarter wide and oval in section, the fragment is inscribed in black with part of the nomen cartouche of Amun-ḥotpe III followed by the epithet "[beloved of] Amun Rēʿ, Lord of Heaven."

One of the rarest and most interesting objects recovered from the palace ruins is a ★*menyet*, or ceremonial necklace (fig. 153), of faience and glass beads, complete with its distinctively shaped bronze counterpoise. Worn or carried by priestesses or great ladies officiating as priestesses, such necklaces, as we have already had occasion to note, seem to have been associated particularly with the worship of the goddess Ḥat-Ḥor (see pp. 45 f.). In the present example the necklace proper is made up of innumerable strands of tiny blue faience disk beads, capped at the ends with large bronze disks and attached to the suspension rings of the counterpoise by strands of big ball and drop-shaped beads of stone, polychrome glass, and faience. Unlike the flimsy votive *menyets* found in great numbers at Deir el Baḥri and elsewhere, this example appears to have been designed for actual wear or use as a cult object. To its several points of interest may be added the fact that it comes from a house in the quarter of the palace believed to have been occupied by Queen Teye and her suite.

Necklace ★beads and ★pendants of faience, glass, and semiprecious stones were found in great profusion. Besides the types of pendants with which we are already familiar—drops, pomegranates, cornflowers, and bunches of grapes—a faience ★collar element in the form of a long, flat petal with a suspension ring at either end begins to make its appearance. Broad at the top and pointed at the lower end, the inverted petal represented is probably that of the white lotus (*Nymphaea lotus*). The element, in any case, is usually of white faience with spots of yellow at the tips, though examples in pale green and blue are by no means uncommon. Occasionally the front of the petal is adorned with the cartouche of the king outlined in dark blue glaze and surmounted by the sun's disk (red) and double plume. Another hitherto unencountered item of jewelry, the mushroom-shaped ★ear stud, is represented by two examples in grayish blue faience. This small ornament was evidently worn with its convex disk to the front and its slightly bulbous stem thrust through a perforation in its wearer's ear lobe.

Mirrors with handles in the form of a papyrus column were apparently still in fashion, for the ★tops of two such handles in dark blue and gray-blue faience were picked up in the ḥarīm section of the Palace of the King. In both cases the details of the papyrus umbels are outlined in a light green overglaze. The elongated figure of a leopard, extended in a flying gallop, with head turned and forepaw stretched out to grasp its prey, is seen upon close inspection to be the ★handle of a cosmetic spoon, the prey held in the jaws of the beast being, in fact, a portion of the bowl of the spoon. Executed in polished alabaster, the figure both in its proportions and its dynamic pose is strikingly similar to that of a panther appearing on a "Late Helladic I" dagger found in a shaft grave at Mycenae. The tiny alabaster ★head of a young girl, fitted with a black slate headdress and having a shallow circular tenon projecting downward from the base of the neck, comes without much doubt from a cosmetic spoon of the type shown in figure 162. Scarcely more than a child, the girl represented wears her hair "dressed in the fashionable 'bob' of the late XVIII Dynasty with . . . a side lock of braids reminiscent of the traditional Egyptian 'lock of youth.' "[6] Also from among the personal possessions of the occupants of the palace are five pairs of small bronze ★tweezers, a conical ★game piece in bright blue faience, and a minute strip of ebony ★inlay inscribed with the *nebty*-name of the king and probably once part of a jewel casket or cosmetic box.

Five fragmentary ★*koḥl*-tubes in yellow, white, and pale green faience imitate in their form a section of hollow reed. Three are inscribed in dark blue glaze with the titles and name of the king—the "Good God, Lord of the Two Lands, Neb-maʿet-Rēʿ, [given] life"—and a fourth bears the cartouche of Queen Teye and the wish "May she live!" One of the white faience tubes is uninscribed, but is adorned with an over-all scale pattern in blue line. A solitary ★*koḥl*-stick, six and a half inches long, is made of bronze.

[6] Phillips, *M. M. A. Bulletin*, XXXVI (1941), p. 174.

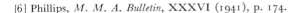

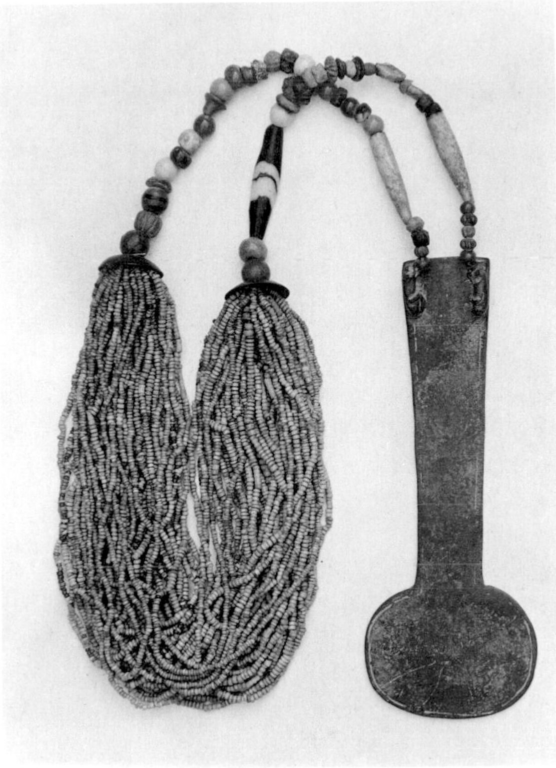

FIGURE 153. *Menyet* of faience, glass, and stone beads with a bronze counterpoise. L. of counterpoise 5 ¾ in.

The most interesting of the many ★faience vase fragments found in the palace ruins is a small piece from the side of a blue faience lotiform goblet engraved on the exterior with part of a *sed*-festival scene. At the right the king appears seated in a pavilion, wearing the crown of Lower Egypt and holding in his hands the crook and *ladanisterion*. At the left, above an arm holding the symbol of "many years" and having suspended from it one or more related symbols, can be made out the lower part of the cartouche with the name "[Amun]-ḥotpe, Ruler of Thebes." A fragmentary vase of white faience and another of yellow faience, both decorated and inscribed in dark blue, preserve on their sides parts of a rectangular panel with the names and titles of the king; and portions of the king's cartouche appear on fragments of three blue faience dishes. Pieces of a jar of blue faience and a saucer of gray faience carry the cartouche of Queen Teye, in the first instance accompanying that of the king. A globular vase of pale green paste, represented by a small fragment, had around its middle an incised band of hieroglyphs of which there remain only the words "stability, well-being, and joy"—obviously from a long royal titulary. Thirteen fragments of uninscribed vases are almost without exception of white faience decorated in blue and red, the patterns including scales, petals, fruits, lotus flowers, dots and lines. The handles of several faience jugs are adorned with inlaid chevrons and diamonds in contrasting colors. Two circular lids are in both cases of blue faience with radiating lotus petals drawn on their tops in heavy black line. From Newberry's excavations in the Palace of the King comes part of a white faience vase attractively decorated in violet outline with the figure of an ibex surrounded by flowering desert shrubs.

Though no complete vessels of glass were recovered in the course of the Museum's excavations, the palace area was found to be strewn with ★fragments of small glass vases and cups of many different shapes and of almost every conceivable color, shade, and combination of colors. Out of these it has been possible to restore three little vases of the common footed type and one equally small amphoralike vessel in mottled blue glass (cf. fig. 109). Pieces of two vases of purple and turquoise blue glass bear parts of engraved panels of inscription giving the names and titles of the pharaoh. The other hundred or so fragments in our collection are uninscribed, but many are decorated with designs and patterns of varied and elaborate types and all are of interest for the techniques involved in their production. Indeed, from this point of view they are particularly valuable because they *are* fragments and, above all, because they come from a known site and are securely dated to the reign of a single king. Of the lot only a dozen have been assigned accession numbers, but all are available for inspection in the Egyptian Department's study room.

Small ateliers in the South Village and elsewhere in the palace area still contained some of the ★materials and equipment used in the production of vessels, amulets, and other small objects of faience and glass. For study purposes several pieces of partially fired biscuit, a lump of unworked glass, pale green in color, a lump of blue frit coloring matter, and eight polychrome glass rods were brought back to the Museum. The rods are presumably those which, when incorporated in a molten state into the surfaces of glass vessels, produced the much admired striped and wavy bands of decoration seen in figure 109. Ninety-three small open ★molds of fine-grained, reddish brown pottery are the ones from which were cast many of the types of amulets, plaques, ring bezels, and appliqué ornaments which we have been discussing in the preceding pages. Among others we find here molds for turning out figures of Bēs and Thoueris, *wedjat*-eyes, rosettes, palmettes, drop- and leaf-shaped pendants, bunches of grapes, and cartouche-shaped plaques. The grape clusters produced from two of the molds were to have carried the praenomen of Amun-ḥotpe III vertical in the center of the ornament, and one type of cartouche plaque, to be issued probably on the occasion of a royal jubilee celebration, was to have contained the same name followed by the epithet "Lord of *Sed*-festivals." A limestone ★mold was designed for casting the figure of a roosting heron (), a hieroglyph used chiefly in the word for "inundation."

A small jar, a dish, and a cup of indurated limestone represent the sum total of the ★stone vessels acquired for our collection from the site of the palace. They are, however, an interesting trio, the vase decorated with vine patterns in relief below its two small handles, the dish having a large rosette carved in relief in the center of its interior, and the cup being of the low, two-ribbed type with gracefully incurved sides.

Since, as already inferred, the occupation of the Malkata palace seems to have been limited to the reigns of Amun-ḥotpe III and his two or three immediate successors, the discovery within its confines of a group of bronze ★corselet scales throws an interesting light on the use of metal body armor by the Egyptians of the New Kingdom. Four and a half inches in length, the large size of these scales reflects a primitive stage in the evolution of the scaled corselet, which in its trend toward greater flexibility and lightness naturally tends to decrease the size and increase the number of its elements. Each of our scales comprises a heavy bronze plate shaped rather like the sole of a pointed sandal and stiffened by an embossed ridge running longitudinally down its middle. Each is provided at the top and at the bottom with three or four holes by means of which it had been attached to the corselet. The latter we may suppose to have been made of leather or of padded cloth. It must have belonged to a member of the royal family or to a high-ranking officer of the palace guard, armor being at this time and for centuries to come quite out of the reach of the rank and file of the Egyptian army. The only other item of warlike equipment found on the site of Amun-ḥotpe III's pleasure city is a small ★arrow or javelin head having an elongated triangular point and a long, slender tang for insertion into the end of a wood or reed shaft. The chief interest of this otherwise insignificant weapon is that it is made of iron. It comes, incidentally, from the Middle Palace, thought to have been the residence of the peace-loving Akh-en-Aten.

The curved bronze ★blade of a large kitchen or butcher's knife, two small double-edged bronze ★knife blades of a type "almost peculiar to Egypt,"[7] two curved bronze ★cutting tools of the kind used by leatherworkers (see p. 218), a pair of bronze ★chisels, a bronze ★fishhook, and a palm-fiber ★paintbrush caked with red paint complete our inventory of the relatively few palace furnishings which have survived almost thirty-three centuries of incessant looting.

As if to belie our statement regarding the impermanence of faience finger rings, such a ★ring bearing the throne name of Amun-ḥotpe III was found on the hand of a Theban lady buried a century later. The lady in question, the House Mistress Iy-neferty, was the wife of Sen-nedjem, the well-known owner of Tomb No. 1 at Deir el Medīneh (see p. 414), probably to be dated to the early Nineteenth Dynasty.

Elsewhere than at Thebes the Egyptian Expedition, excavating around the pyramid of Amun-em-ḥēt I at el Lisht, turned up a blue faience ★ring with Amun-ḥotpe III's praenomen stamped on its long oval bezel.

A heavy gold ★signet ring (see fig. 180), formerly in the Amherst collection, was found at el ʿAmārneh by Sir Flinders Petrie during the winter of 1891-1892. Once ascribed to Akh-en-Aten and Nefret-ity, its beautifully engraved bezel is now seen to carry the monogrammatic praenomen of Amun-ḥotpe III, "Neb-maʿet-Rēʿ," followed by the epithet "beloved of Mūt(?)."

It is only natural that a number of attractive small objects bearing the name of Amun-ḥotpe III or otherwise associated with him should have come to the Museum as gifts or purchases unaccompanied by any record of their origins beyond the fact that they were formerly in the Carnarvon, Murch, Morgan, Ward, or other well-known private collection. Judging from the nature of the pieces themselves there is considerable likelihood that a fair percentage of them is either from the palace of the king or from his tomb. Appearances, however, are often misleading, and on the whole we shall be well advised to retain for these objects the designations, unsatisfying though they are, of "provenience unknown" or, at best, "provenience uncertain."

A case in point is the ivory ★water-color palette of figure 154, which, since it is inscribed with the name of Amun-ḥotpe III ("Neb-maʿet-Rēʿ, beloved of Rēʿ"), was once thought to have come from the king's own tomb, but which would appear in actuality to be from another source. The handsome object, carved from a single piece of ivory and delicately tinted with red and black stain, had seen considerable use at the hands of its

[7] Petrie, *Tools and Weapons*, p. 26.

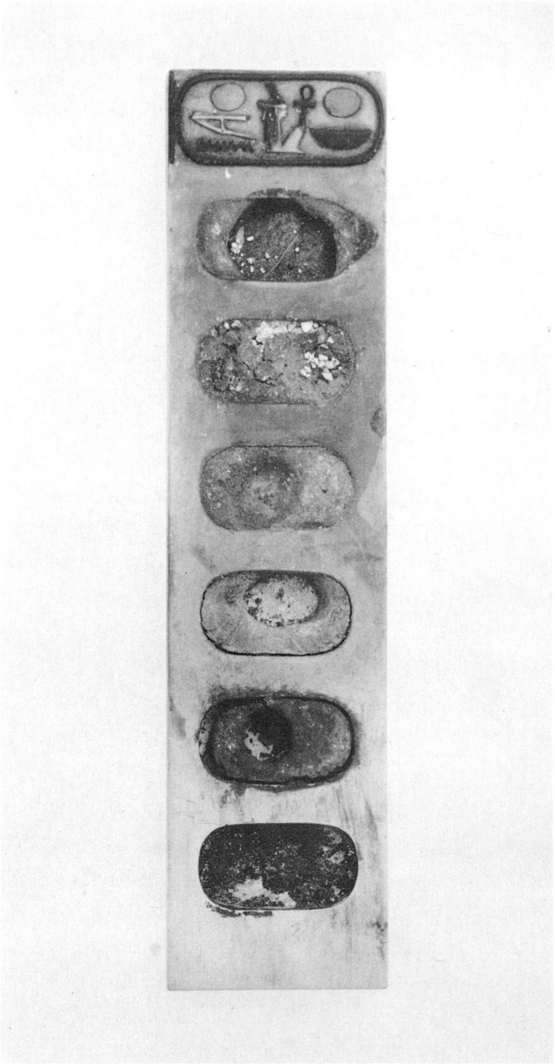

FIGURE 154. Ivory palette with the throne name of Amun-ḥotpe III. H. 7 in.

ancient owner, several of the cakes of mineral pigment contained in its six oval wells being almost used up. From top to bottom the colors of these pigments are blue, green, brown(?), yellow, red, and black, the gradual transition from cool to warm colors being no doubt intentional.

The upper part of a curious little trapezoidal ★stela of alabaster has carved on its front in very high relief a figure of the god of eternity holding in his extended hands the symbols for "many years" and carrying on his head the praenomen cartouche of Amun-ḥotpe III, including the epithet "image of Rēʿ." In the recessed spaces below the ends of the cartouche are engraved the groups "given life" and "like Rēʿ." With the figure of the god standing for the word "forever," the front of the little monument would then form a sort of rebus, reading "Neb-maʿet-Rēʿ, image of Rēʿ, given life, like Rēʿ, forever." The composition as a whole, including the particular form of the king's throne name used here, is one which we associate with the celebration of royal jubilee festivals, and, as if in confirmation of this, the lateral edges of the stela are inscribed in monumental hieroglyphs with the words "[very many] *sed*-festivals." On the top edge we find engraved "(Long) live the Son of Rēʿ, [Amun-ḥotpe, Ruler of Thebes]!" and on the back "all life and well-being to Neb-maʿet-Rēʿ," "all health to [Amun-ḥotpe, Ruler of Thebes]," "all joy to [Neb-]maʿet-Rēʿ," and "all strength to [Amun-ḥotpe . . .]." The fact that the king's personal name, embodying that of the god Amūn, was thrice erased by the Atenists suggests that the little monument stood in a fairly public place—perhaps the Festival Hall of the palace or one of the great temples. Long on the antiquities market and published at least twice between 1938 and 1952, this most interesting and unusual stela was acquired by the Metropolitan Museum in the fall of 1955.

Though of unrecorded provenience, nine ★faience finger rings of Amun-ḥotpe III, which came to the Museum as individual gifts or purchases, are in nearly perfect condition, unbroken, and with their glazes almost as bright as when they were made. Their colors include violet, turquoise blue, apple green, and yellow. The majority of their bezels, impressed or inlaid with the praenomen of the king, are oval; but there is one rectangular bezel in which the royal name is silhouetted in an intricate openwork design. A single example out of the nine carries the personal name of the pharaoh, "Amun-ḥotpe, Ruler of Thebes." One of the lot, acquired with a group of metal and faience rings of Akh-en-Aten (see p. 292), may well have come from Tell el ʿAmārneh.

Besides the big commemorative and minor historical scarabs of Amun-ḥotpe III and the miscellaneous seal amulets recovered from the ruins of his Malḳata palace, our corpus of ★scarabs, ★cowroids, ★plaques, and ★inscribed amulets includes over forty examples bearing the throne name Neb-maʿet-Rēʿ, the personal name Amun-ḥotpe, Ruler of Thebes, or, in a few instances, both names written in cartouches and preceded by the customary titles. On two large scarabs and an oval plaque the cartouche of the "King's Wife Teye" appears side by side with that of her husband. Two other outsize scarabs carry on their undersides large figures of the king wearing the Blue Crown and accompanied in each case by a hieroglyphic label giving his name and title. On one of these scarabs the pharaoh is shown standing and brandishing the crook scepter and a battle axe; on the other he sits enthroned, holding the *ladanisterion* and the symbol of "life." Not infrequently on his scarabs he appears in one of his favorite forms, as a sphinx or lion. The plaques are both oval and rectangular in shape, the latter including a hollow example with openwork ends. Besides the hemicylindrical type we find among the seals of Amun-ḥotpe III one faience cylinder seal, a form which by this time had become exceedingly rare. The inscribed amulets are without exception *wedjat*-eyes, chiefly of glazed steatite.

Comparable in style and quality to the carved carnelian bracelet plaques from the king's tomb (see p. 242) is a handsome necklace ★pendant of the same material, shaped like a festival pavilion ([hieroglyph]) flanked by uraei and having carved on its slightly convex front surface the monogrammatic version of Amun-ḥotpe III's praenomen (see p. 250), twice repeated and accompanied in each case by the epithet "Prince of Princes."

The names and titles of Amun-ḥotpe III, followed by those of the "King's Wife Teye," or, in one case, by those of the "King's Daughter and King's Great Wife Sit-Amūn," appear on a double ★*koḥl*-tube of wood and on two single ★*koḥl*-tubes of blue faience, which come, respectively, from the Carnarvon, Murch, and MacGregor collections. In length the three containers range from four and three-quarters to five and three-quarters inches, the well-known example with the name of Queen Sit-Amūn (fig. 155) being the longest of the lot. On the wooden tube the inscriptions are engraved and filled with blue pigment; on the faience tubes they are inlaid with black and dark blue glaze. All three imitate in their form sections of coarse reed and, though extremely fragile, all

FIGURE 155. Blue faience *koḥl*-tube inscribed in black with the names of Amun-ḥotpe III and Queen Sit-Amūn. H. 5¾ in.

three have come down to us in a well-nigh perfect state of preservation.

A squat drop-shaped little ★vase of white faience bears on its side a blue-inlaid panel of inscription in which the titulary of Amun-ḥotpe III is again followed by that of Queen Teye. Part of the same inscription is preserved on a fragment of white faience jar ★lid inlaid with purple glaze. Considerably more interesting are the inlaid panels on the sides of two larger but, unfortunately, fragmentary ★jars, one of white faience decorated in blue, the other of dark blue faience with white decoration. In the panel on the white jar the pharaoh's name, the "Good God, Lord of the Two Lands, [Neb-]maʿet-Rēʿ . . ." is accompanied by that of the "King's Daughter Ḥenet-[to-nēb] . . . born of the King's Great Wife Teye. . . ." Ḥenet-to-nēb, Amun-ḥotpe III's next oldest daughter after Sit-Amūn, we may remember as one of the two princesses appearing on the carnelian bracelet plaques from the king's tomb. The panel on the blue jar fragment shows us part of a scene in which the "Good God, Lord of the Two Lands, Neb-maʿet-Rēʿ, given life" stands with hands upraised in adoration before the lioness-headed goddess Weret-ḥekau, the divine personification of the pharaonic crown and uraeus. On her head the goddess, whose name means "Great-of-magic," wears the solar disk of her father, Rēʿ, and in her hands holds a slender papyriform scepter. Of the figure of the king only the top of the Blue Crown now remains. Scale and leaf patterns adorn the surfaces of the jars above and on either side of the inscribed panels.

The now familiar throne name of Amun-ḥotpe III appears twice again in our collection, inlaid in white glaze on the rounded top of a large blue faience ★knob, which comes either from the lid of a casket or from the top of a staff, and in green glaze on an elongated oval ★bead, also of blue faience.

In or about the twenty-eighth year of the reign (1370 B.C.) the pharaoh's son, Amun-ḥotpe IV, later known as Akh-en-Aten, appears to have been elevated to the kingship as his father's companion on the throne.[8] The move marked the beginning of the end for Amun-ḥotpe III and when, after a troubled coregency of four or five years, his son in 1365 B.C. transferred the capital and much of the court to Tell el ʿAmārneh, his authority as Egypt's ruler was virtually over.

Although, then, the last eleven years of the reign saw the youthful coregent taking matters more and more into his own hands and the elder pharaoh, now flabby, diseased, and probably senile, living in semiretirement in his palace at Thebes, there was no apparent letdown in the latter's building activities or in the luxurious splendor of his existence. His three jubilees, or *sed*-festivals, in Years 30, 34, and 37 respectively, were celebrated with elaborate ceremonies and lavish exchanges of gifts between the king and his court and were accompanied by the construction of such magnificent buildings as the temple at Soleb and a great Festival Hall adjoining the palace at Thebes. In addition to Queens Teye and Sit-Amūn most of the older courtiers remained with the king at Thebes, and on jars of food and drink contributed to his *sed*-festivals we have found the names of Amun-ḥotpe, son of Ḥapu, the Vizier Raʿ-mosě, the Chief Steward Surere, and many others (see p. 248). The procession of Asiatic princesses into the royal ḥarīm continued as before. Having earlier in his reign married the sister of King Tushratta of Naharīn and the sister of Kadashman-Enlil, the Kassite ruler of Babylon, Amun-ḥotpe III now requested and received as wives the daughters of these same kings, as well as the daughter of King Tarkhundaraush of Arzawa. That the aging pharaoh actually married Tushratta's daughter, Tadukhipa, is doubtful, since when we next hear of her it is as the wife of Amun-ḥotpe IV. It is not improbable that toward the end of his reign Amun-ḥotpe III accompanied

---

[8] This proposed coregency of the two kings, though suggested by existing evidence, is far from certain. It is not accepted by a number of modern scholars, who prefer to believe that Akh-en-Aten's reign of seventeen or more years commenced with the death of his father.

Teye on one of her visits to el ʿAmārneh, for the royal couple are represented, seated together as living persons, on several monuments found on that site, notably in the tomb of Ḥuya and on a painted limestone stela from the house of Pa-neḥesy.

During his thirty-sixth year[9] on the throne the pharaoh's infirmities, which included painful abscesses in his teeth, had become so acute that his "brother," King Tushratta, was prevailed upon to send him an image of the goddess Ishtar of Nineveh famous for its healing powers. The goddess's magic was apparently effective, for Amun-ḥotpe III was still alive two years later, as witnessed by a number of dated jar labels from his Theban palace. So far as is now known, he died at the age of about fifty-five in his thirty-eighth or thirty-ninth regnal year (Year 11 or 12 of Akh-en-Aten?) and was buried with characteristic magnificence in his great tomb in the western branch of the Valley of the Tombs of the Kings. The identity of his mummy, found cached in the tomb of Amun-ḥotpe II, has been questioned, but convincingly reaffirmed.

2. Queen Teye and Her Family

Prominent among those who molded the character of the reign was Queen Teye, whose portraits—especially a small head of green schist in the Cairo Museum—preserve her exotic appearance and reflect something of her shrewd mind and energetic nature. The king is rarely represented without her slender, erect figure by his side, and it is clear that throughout his entire life she enjoyed not only his deep affection but also his complete confidence in matters of state. Her detailed knowledge of his foreign policy and his relations with the rulers of neighboring lands is referred to in two letters written after the death of Amun-ḥotpe III by King Tushratta of Naharīn, requesting that these relations be maintained during the reign of her son, Amun-ḥotpe IV. Although, as queen mother, she seems to have furthered Amun-ḥotpe IV's political aspirations with the utmost devotion and to have constituted a great influence in his life, there is no evidence that she encouraged or even shared his radical religious views. Indeed, the maintenance of her cult after the collapse of the "Aten heresy" and the wholesale anathematization of its adherents indicates that, in the eyes of posterity at least, she was not associated with it. During the long coregency of her husband and son we see her maintaining liaison between the courts at Thebes and Tell el ʿAmārneh, her name and figure appearing in more or less contemporaneous inscriptions and reliefs at both places.

Aside from the many monuments in our collection which the King's Wife Teye shares with her husband or which, having come from his palace or tomb, have already been discussed, her name and title appear by themselves on three faience ★finger rings, on a steatite ★plaque mounted in a gold ring, and on four ★scarabs, four ★cowroids, and an ★eye amulet of glazed steatite. The largest of the scarabs bears on its underside a figure of the great queen enthroned and wearing on her head the vulture headdress surmounted, as frequently, by the towering double plume. In her hands she holds a fly-whisk and a symbol of "life" and before her we read in minute hieroglyphs: "The King's Great Wife Teye, may she live!"

There is considerable probability that it is the lower part of Queen Teye's face which is preserved to us in the wonderful ★yellow jasper fragment of figure 156. The pouting mouth and softly rounded chin, in any case, are like those seen on other portraits of Teye and in no way suggest the narrow, bony face of Akh-en-Aten's queen, Nefret-ity, with whom the piece was once identified. Stylistically the head shows some of the mannerisms of the ʿAmārneh school—notably, the parallel folds on the throat, here rendered by two crisply incised horizontal lines—and, though of unrecorded provenience, may even have come from Tell el ʿAmārneh itself. It evidently once formed part of

[9] The pertinent date has also been read—somewhat doubtfully, it would seem—as Year 39.

FIGURE 156. Queen Teye (?). Yellow jasper. Provenience unknown. H. 5 ½ in.

a life-size female statue, the exposed flesh parts of which were carved in yellow jasper, with the clothing, coiffure, and accessories made of other appropriate materials. This, too, points to ʿAmārneh as its probable source, most of the composite statues of this type and period being associated with the site of Akh-en-Aten's residence city. From the extent to which the left cheek and left side of the neck are carried back toward the rear of the head it is clear that the lady represented wore a short, close coiffure of the kind especially favored by Queen Teye (see fig. 157). The carving and finishing of the piece in the intensely hard, glass-like stone is scarcely short of miraculous. Our eyes are drawn primarily to the mouth, where the ancient sculptor has succeeded to a remarkable degree in reproducing the soft, fleshy quality of the human lips; but the same satiny surface and the same sophistication and sensitivity of modeling pervade the whole of the fragment, sharpening our regret that the upper half of this superb head seems to be irretrievably lost to us.

Teye's profile, familiar to us from many a monument of the period, is characterized by a delicate, retroussé nose, a small, firm chin, and a long, slender neck. Such a profile is seen in figure 157 on the tiny figure of a royal lady carved in *relief en creux* on what was once a small rectangular ★block of obsidian, adorned on at least two of its sides with sculptured scenes enclosed within wide, banded borders. The proximity of the figure to the immediately adjoining border suggests that it was standing and was preceded, near the center of the scene, by a larger figure of a king or god. The attire and attributes of the lady—the short, cap-like wig, the beribboned fillet with uraeus in front, the striated diadem above, and the gracefully drooping fly-whisk—are those of a queen rather than of a goddess, and are frequently found in representations of Teye herself. Even in our full-scale reproduction the fine details of the headdress and broad collar are difficult to see without a magnifying glass. Needless to say, the identification is not certain, and the little figure may well portray Teye's daughter Sit-Amūn, or another queen of the same general period and family.

Yuya and Tjuyu, the parents of Queen Teye, are introduced to us on Amun-ḥotpe III's earliest series of commemorative scarabs (see p. 231) and are met with frequently thereafter on monuments of the reign. They appear to have been residents of the town of Ipu (modern Akhmīm) in Upper Egypt where Yuya, the father, held the offices of Prophet and Overseer of Cattle of the local god, Mīn. It was probably as a result of his daughter's marriage that Yuya had bestowed upon him the title Father of the God, which seems to have been the regular designation of the pharaoh's father-in-law, and which Yuya shared with his predecessor(?), Yey (see p. 229), and his successor, Ay (see pp. 307 f.). Like them, too, he was also honored with the rank of Commander of Cavalry. The similarity of the names of Yey, Yuya, and Ay and the fact that at least two of them appear to have had ties with Akhmīm suggest that they belonged to the same family and may have been father, son, and grandson. This would mean that for three generations the kings of Egypt took as their wives girls from a single Upper Egyptian family who in the last two instances were their own first cousins. The

FIGURE 157. Fragment of a small obsidian block with a relief figure of a queen, possibly Teye. L. 1 ¼ in.

unusual physical characteristics of Yuya's mummy and the obvious difficulty encountered by Egyptian scribes in achieving a standard spelling of his name may indicate that the family was of foreign origin—probably Libyan or Nubian rather than Asiatic.

At their deaths Teye arranged to have her parents buried together in a small but richly endowed tomb in an isolated branch of the Valley of the Tombs of the Kings. Entered only once by ancient robbers, this tomb, when discovered by Theodore M. Davis in February 1905, still contained the greater part of its handsome furnishings, many inscribed with the names of the king and other members of the royal family. The bulk of these furnishings are in the Cairo Museum, but a few duplicates were brought to America by Mr. Davis and subsequently bequeathed by him to the Metropolitan Museum.

The objects thus acquired for our collection include three of Yuya's big wooden ★*shawabtys* (fig. 158), carved with consummate skill in beautifully grained hardwood and wisely left unpainted except for the hieroglyphs in their inscriptions and in two cases their faces, headdresses, and broad collars. The engraved texts, colored yellow on one figure, blue on another, and black on the third, consist throughout of the standard *shawabty*-spell, introduced by the words "Illuminating (instructing ?) the *shawabty:*" or "Illuminating (the Osiris) the Father of the God, Yuya, the justified." On the figure which holds in its hands the *djed* and *tyet*-symbols Yuya is referred to as "one favored by the Good God." The headdress and broad collar of this figure are painted blue and yellow, while the face, hands, collar, and headdress stripes of the more elaborate of its mates are overlaid with gold foil. The eyes of all three figures are outlined in black with white corneas. It is to be doubted that the pleasant, conventionally rendered faces bore more than the most superficial resemblance to that of Yuya, being, rather, the typical face of the reign of Amun-ḥotpe III (cf. fig. 145). Two of the figures had been enclosed within shrine-shaped ( ) ★*shawabty*-boxes of painted wood adorned in one case with red, blue, and green paneling and in the other with pictures of mummiform figures on the sides and a column of inscription down the front. This text, painted in dark green on a yellow ground, describes the owner of the box as "one in honor with Osiris, one favored by the Good God, Yuyu (*sic*), justified with the Great God." The figures hold no implements with which to perform their labors, but two ★model baskets, nicely made of sheet copper, a little wooden ★yoke, and a wooden ★hoe were found with them.

A pair of Yuya's ★sandals are woven of grass and light reeds and are provided with toe and instep straps of split papyrus rind. Eleven and a half inches in length, they differ from those shown in figure 104 in having pointed toes and being of somewhat finer weave. Two small scraps of ★linen cloth, a gift of Mrs. Emma B. Andrews, are said to be from the outer wrappings of the mummy of Tjuyu.

In a shallow pit at the western end of the tomb's burial chamber were found fifty-two big pottery jars containing packages of stained natron and other materials used in the embalming of the two mummies. Two of these ★jars, now in our collection, stand twenty-seven and twenty-one inches in height. Both are made of red pottery painted white on the outside, but the larger jar is drop-shaped, while the smaller is ovoid with a tall, slender neck. Their sealings, in one case a saucer lashed in place with a piece of cloth, in the other a domical mud stopper stamped all over with the seal of the Theban necropolis (see p. 303), are intact. The smaller jar had once been used for the transportation and storage of grain and bears on its shoulder a much faded hieratic label recording the amount of "barley brought on this day."

Lying on the rows of pots, where the plunderers had left it, was Yuya's chariot, its pole broken off short and the leather apron stripped from the front of its body, but otherwise complete and relatively undamaged. Needless to say, this most interesting object was retained in Cairo, but it may be studied in a large scale ★model made for us in 1921 by Andrea Altobello, at that time the head carpenter of the Cairo Museum.

Besides Queen Teye and perhaps the future king, Ay, Yuya and Tjuyu had at least one other child who rose to prominence, largely, we may suppose, as a result of his sister's marriage to the reigning pharaoh. This was ʿA-nen, Second Prophet of Amūn and Theban High Priest of Reʿ-Atūm, whose tomb chapel in western Thebes (No. 120) was cleared by the Museum's Expedition and copied for us by Mr. and Mrs. Davies.

Second only to Teye in Amun-ḥotpe III's favor was their eldest daughter, Sit-Amūn, whom her father seems to have married sometime before the thirty-first year of his reign and by whom he had several children, including apparently two future kings, Semenkh-ku-Rēʿ and Tūt-ʿankh-Amūn. We have almost no material on which to base a character study of Sit-Amūn, but if, as some think, she was the owner of a wonderful yew-wood portrait head in the Berlin Museum she was a person of very pronounced character, not all of it pleasant. Her name appears frequently in inscriptions both at Thebes and el ʿAmārneh and occurs on a number of small monuments in our own collection which we have already had occasion to discuss (see pp. 244, 251). The stewardship of her evidently large estates was entrusted to a man who was not only the outstanding official of her father's reign, but one of the truly great figures in New Kingdom history.

This was Amun-ḥotpe, son of Ḥapu, a native of Athribis in the Delta, whose family included also the Vizier Raʿ-mosě and another Amun-ḥotpe who was Chief Steward in Memphis. Following a brilliant career as King's Scribe, Scribe of Recruits, and Overseer of All Works of the King, Ḥapu's famous son was honored by his sovereign with a mortuary temple in western Thebes, comparable in magnificence to the near-by temples of the kings and endowed in perpetuity by special royal decree. By succeeding generations the King's Scribe Amun-ḥotpe (frequently also called Ḥuy) was revered as one of Egypt's great sages and proverbs attributed to him were translated into Greek twelve centuries after his death. Under Ramesses IV his mortuary cult was maintained together with those of the deified kings, and early in the Ptolemaic period he himself was worshiped as a god. In our collection he is represented by a single ★funerary cone from his Theban tomb, on which he is described as the "Hereditary Prince, Amun-ḥotpe, called Ḥuy. . . engendered of the worthy Ḥapu."

Sit-Amūn's younger sisters, all apparently children of Amun-ḥotpe III and Teye, included the Princesses Ḥenet-to-nēb and Iset, to whom we have already been introduced, Princess Nebet-ʿaḥ, represented with her parents in a colossal group statue from Medīnet Habu, and Princess Baket-Aten, the youngest of the lot, shown with her mother and father in the tomb of Ḥuya at el ʿAmārneh. A nonexistent sixth daughter of Amun-ḥotpe III, "Ḥenet-mer-ḥēb," was created in modern times through a miscopying of the name Ḥenet-to-nēb.

A limestone ★canopic jar, inscribed for the King's Daughter Iny, is one of many belonging to otherwise unidentified members of the family and ḥarīm of Amun-ḥotpe III who were buried together in a tomb or group of tombs in the cliffs west of Deir el Baḥri. Similar in most respects to those of Tḥut-mosě III's three Syrian wives (see p. 137), the present jar is stylistically and technically of very much higher quality, the beardless human head which serves as its stopper being, indeed, a first-class example of New Kingdom

FIGURE 158. *Shawabtys* and *shawabty*-boxes of Yuya, the father of Queen Teye. Painted and gilded wood. Pedestals modern. H. of figures 9-10⅝ in.

sculpture. A well-cut inscription on the side of the jar associates its contents with the genius Ḥapy and places it under the protection of the goddess Nephthys.

It is possible that a King's Eldest Son Tḥutmosĕ, known to us chiefly from monuments found in or near the Serapeum at Memphis, was in actuality a son of Amun-ḥotpe III who died prematurely. Foremost among the king's other sons are to be counted his three successors—Amun-ḥotpe IV (Akh-en-Aten), whose mother was Teye, and Semenkh-ku-Rēʿ and Tūt-ʿankh-Aten (Tūt-ʿankh-Amūn), apparently the offspring of Sit-Amūn.

3. The Contemporaries of Amun-ḥotpe III and Their Possessions

Side by side with the fanfare and magnificence for which the reign of Amun-ḥotpe III is famous, we find in the sculpture and painting of the period, in the housefurnishings and personal possessions of the court, and in the graceful and elaborate costumes which were fashionable at this time the sophistication and elegance, the lively imagination and love of novelty, the aristocratic taste and high standard of technical excellence demanded by a people accustomed to the utmost in luxury and graceful living. These qualities appear with compelling clarity in the statues, tomb reliefs, and other superb works of art and craftsmanship produced for the officials of the pharaoh's government, their families, and households.

FIGURE 159. A high official of the reign of Amun-ḥotpe III. Porphyritic diorite. H. 11 ¼ in.

Beauty and elegance are combined in the ★head of a life-size statue (fig. 159) faultlessly carved in porphyritic diorite and representing without much doubt one of the high officials of the reign. Who this official was is difficult to say. The individual portrait quality of the head is not strong, and some of its salient features, such as the full, sensitive mouth, the heavily rimmed almond-shaped eyes, and the prominent, arched eyebrows remind us as much of Amun-ḥotpe III himself as of any of his contemporaries. It bears scarcely any resemblance to the known portraits of Amun-ḥotpe, son of Ḥapu; but could conceivably represent the king's brother-in-law, ʿA-nen, whose well-known statue in Turin shows the same rather long, narrow face and the same extraordinarily long and slender neck. The elaborate double wig with the vertical underpanel of curls descending from behind the ears was affected by almost every fashionably dressed gentleman of the period and, though known earlier, was particularly characteristic of the time with which we are dealing. The head, formerly in the collection of Paul Mallon, is of unrecorded provenience. It was presented to the Museum in 1925 by Mrs. Philip J. Mosenthal in memory of her husband.

The ★face of a similar statue, in this case slightly under life size and carved of indurated limestone, is from the Museum's Theban excavations of 1934-1935. Among the more notable characteristics which mark the official represented as a contemporary of Amun-ḥotpe III is the double line of the upper eyelids, often seen on portraits of the pharaoh himself. A modified version of the same wig and much the same type of face appear on a tiny alabaster ★head, formerly in the Murch collection. Here the sensitively modeled, though now somewhat battered, little face is characterized especially by its very long, slanting eyes.

During the reign of Amun-ḥotpe III, more perhaps than at any other period in Egyptian history, it was the fashion for high-ranking officials to have themselves represented as scribes, seated cross-legged on the ground and writing in a papyrus roll held half open on the lap. A small ★figure of this class (fig. 160) exquisitely carved in serpentine and still mounted on its original alabaster base shows all the salient characteristics of its type and period. The heavy thighs and the rolls of fat about the mid-section of the body bespeak the prosperous official, well fed and exempt from hard physical labor. The face is dreamy and pensive as becomes a scholar in the act of composing or assimilating the written word. The head, as often at this time, is inclined forward and downward to suggest not only concentration on the task at hand but also, perhaps, humility in the presence of a divine patron. It is, indeed, not unlikely that, like a well-known little group in the Berlin Museum, our scribe once sat at the end of an oblong wooden base facing a somewhat larger figure of the god Tḥōt in the form of a cynocephalous ape. For some reason an inscription carved on the open portion of the papyrus roll was erased in ancient times. The figure, an anonymous gift, was acquired at Thebes.

A large wooden ★statuette representing a young man with shaven head and short, flaring kilt which stands upright upon a wooden base was once a work of the very highest quality. The youthful face, long, interestingly shaped head, and softly modeled body are carved with the utmost skill and sensitivity in a fine, dark wood, probably a kind of ebony. The eyes are inlaid with metal rims, cornea pieces of alabaster, and irises of obsidian; the kilt was stuccoed and painted a creamy white; and, as often, the forward portions of the

FIGURE 160. Serpentine statuette of a Theban scribe. The base is alabaster. H. 5 in.

feet were made of separate pieces of wood and tenoned in place. Over seventeen inches in height, the figure still retains much of the peculiarly gracious quality which we associate with the reign of Amun-ḥotpe III. Unhappily, it has been seriously damaged by termites, one arm, half of the head, and areas of the shoulders and kilt having been disfigured or completely devoured by the destructive insects.

Charmingly characteristic of the lighter and more frivolous side of the period embraced by the coregency of Amun-ḥotpe III and IV is a much smaller ebony *statuette of a young lady (fig. 161), which, unlike the example just discussed, came to us in 1941 in an almost perfect state of preservation. Students of Egyptian art will recognize it as one of five little wooden figures of women which were found about 1900 in a tomb near Kōm Medīnet Ghurāb in the Fayyūm together with objects bearing the names of Amun-ḥotpe III, Queen Teye, and Amun-ḥotpe IV.[10] The inscription engraved on the top of its base is an offering formula invoking the goddess Mūt, "Mistress of Heaven," in behalf of the "spirit of the Chief of Weavers Teye." The figure, then, was a funerary statuette, a fact in no way suggested by the impish face, the informal pose, and the ultrafashionable attire. In keeping with the prevailing style Teye's soft, diaphanous robe is worn gathered over one shoulder and completely off the other, leaving her right side bare down to the waist. Every detail of her wondrously elaborate wig, including three long braids dangling down the center of the back, is rendered with meticulous care. Both the headdress and the chubby, snub-nosed face which it frames are disproportionately large and, as is often the case with figures of this class, the curves of the body are a trifle overemphasized. A final touch is added by the lady's necklace, which is made up of real beads—gold, carnelian, and other semiprecious stones. The small clenched hands, now empty, may at one time have held a bird or cat and a

FIGURE 161. The Lady Teye. Ebony. H. 9½ in.

lotus flower or perhaps a *menyet*-necklace and some other trinket.

A similar *statuette, also carved of wood and standing nine and three-quarters inches in height without its base, represents a comely, slenderly proportioned young woman wearing a long, crinkly wig and a simple, tight-fitting robe. The flesh tints and such details as the embroidered edges of the garment had been added in paint, only traces of which are now visible. In addition, the figure is lacking its right arm and is so worn and battered that much of its original beauty has been lost. Once part of the Farman collection, it came to the Museum in 1904 as a gift of Darius Ogden Mills.

To a different category belongs the *figure of a woman, nude except for a long braided wig and massive ear studs, represented lying on a bed with the usual high footboard, the whole carved from a block of limestone and measuring slightly over fourteen inches in length (cf. fig. 117). The wig, bound with a fillet of floral ornaments and surmounted by a cone of perfumed ointment, has been gathered on one side of the girl's head and hangs in a heavy cascade of braids over her right shoulder, leaving her left shoulder and the left side of her neck exposed. Such figures, as we have seen on page 16, are presumed to have been placed in tombs, not as portraits of individual women, but as a magical means of restoring the procreative powers of the deceased tomb owner. Our present example, well-proportioned and carefully modeled, is an unusually large and attractive example of its class.

To the figures of frivolous young women produced during the reign of Amun-ḥotpe III may be added an alabaster *cosmetic spoon (fig. 162) in the form of a swimming girl being towed through the water by a gazelle, the body of which is hollowed out to form the bowl of the spoon. The heads of both the girl and her pet were carved as separate pieces and cemented in place, the circular tenon descending from the latter serving also as a

[10] Of the four other statuettes two are in the Brooklyn Museum and two are in private collections in France.

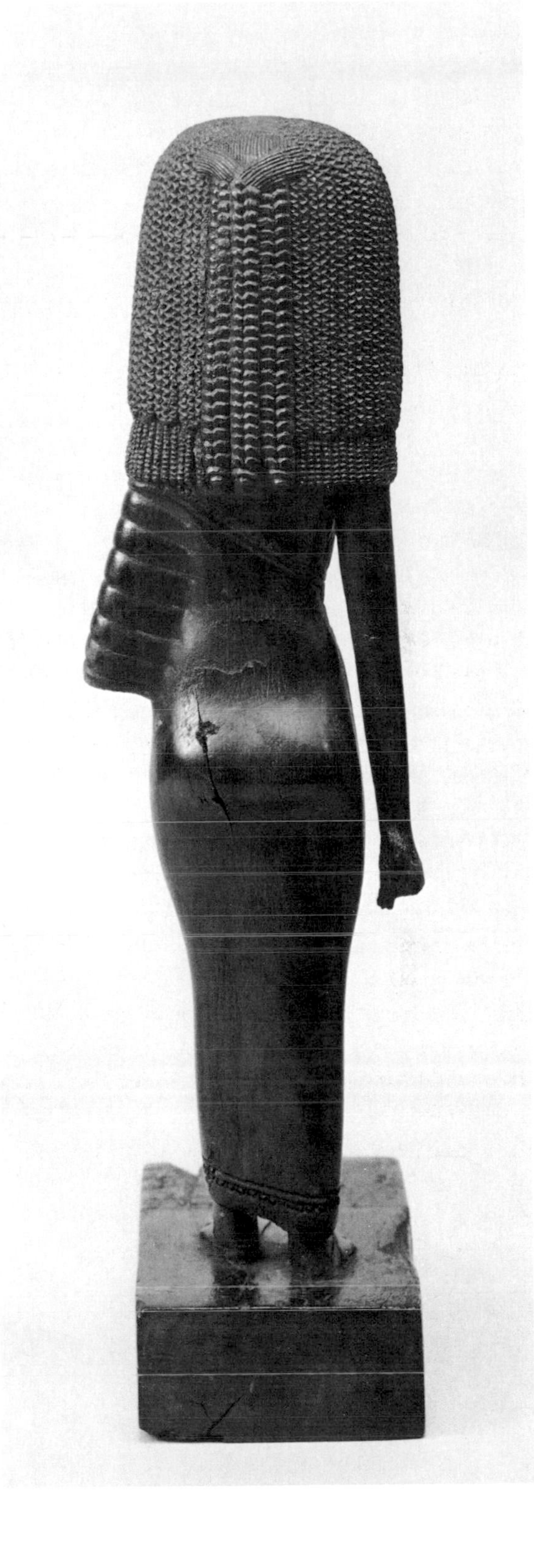

FIGURE 162. Cosmetic spoon of alabaster with slate overlays. L. 9 in.

pivot for the lid of the container. The maiden's intricate coiffure and the narrow girdle which is her only article of attire are made of black slate and cunningly fitted in place. Except for the length of the braids hanging down the right side of the head the hair of the figure is dressed in the same manner as that of a similar head (see p. 253) found in the ruins of the Malḳata palace. The remarkable little ★head of figure 163, in this case delicately carved in a fine, hard wood, is evidently also from a cosmetic spoon. Here, however, the swimming lady has "piled her tightly crimped locks on top of her head to keep them from getting wet."[11] The resulting coiffure and the strangely "oriental" facial type are more immediately reminiscent of Gandharan than of Egyptian art, but find parallels in cosmetic spoons and other works of pre-ʿAmārneh and ʿAmārneh times.

Three small, but exceptionally fine, examples of animal sculpture attributable to the period of Amun-ḥotpe III include a rock crystal ★figure of the hippopotamus goddess Thoueris, four inches in height, a small ★bull's head molded in violet glass, and a blue faience ★seal in the form of a crouching ibex. The Thoueris figure with gaping mouth and pendulous human breasts stands ponderously upright holding before it a squat ☥-sign. In the top of its head is a dowel hole for the attachment of a now missing headdress. The bull's head, apparently broken away from a complete figure of the animal, is hollow cast, the wrinkle lines around its eyes and muzzle being added with a graver's tool. Aesthetically and stylistically the best of the three, the little ibex seal has engraved on its oval underside the figures of a crocodile and a *bolti*-fish.

By way of transition from figure sculpture in the round to the two-dimensional world of tomb reliefs and paintings we may consider briefly two delightful small products of the metalworkers' ateliers in which the figures and other elements represented are silhouetted in delicate openwork designs (fig. 164). The little bronze figure of a Nubian dancing and playing on his lute is found upon close inspection to be the handle of a ★razor, the blade of which with its curved cutting edge can be seen extending downward beneath the feet of the figure. Both the facial type and the dress of our lute player bespeak his African origin, the latter comprising a loincloth, probably of slit leather, a shaggy or kinky mop of hair into which has been thrust an ostrich feather, enormous annular earrings, and a heavy bead collar, bracelets, and anklets. His lute is an ornate little instrument with a small, lozenge-shaped soundbox and a long, carved neck topped by a reversed duck's

[11] Phillips, *M. M. A. Bulletin*, XXXVI (1941), p. 173.

FIGURE 163. Head of a girl from a cosmetic spoon. Hardwood. H. 1 ¾ in.

head. An openwork bronze ★counterpoise from a ceremonial necklace, or *menyet*, seems to have been conceived of as a symbolic representation of the goddess Ḥat-Ḥor, with whose cult the *menyet* was especially associated. Its top, in any case, has the form of the head of the goddess, exquisitely molded and chased and crowned with the customary solar disk and cow's horns. The deity's face could well have been borrowed from one of Amun-ḥotpe III's queens, Teye or Sit-Amūn, and the extraordinary delicacy and virtuosity of the workmanship as a whole point strongly to a date in his reign. In the openwork designs below, Ḥat-Ḥor is twice again represented, once as a standing female figure and once as a cow gliding on a papyrus boat through a thicket of gigantic papyrus reeds.

In 1908 the Metropolitan Museum purchased from the Egyptian Government the decorated sandstone lining of the burial chamber of the Treasurer Sobk-mosĕ, an official of Amun-ḥotpe III who made his home at Sumenu (modern Rizeiḳat), some twelve and a half miles upriver from Thebes. In 1954 the north and west walls of the chamber, with scenes showing Sobk-mosĕ's funeral procession and his presentation to the gods of the Underworld, were transferred to the Museum of Fine Arts in Boston in exchange for the granite sarcophagus of Prince Min-djedef of the Fourth Dynasty. Retained for our own collection were the massive ★ceiling slabs of the chamber, inscribed, like the lid of a coffin, with a prayer to the sky goddess Nūt and with dedications of Sobk-mosĕ to eight other divinities; the ★east, or entrance, wall of the little room with scenes showing the ritual lustrations of the deceased official; and the long ★south wall (fig. 165) inscribed with the text of seven prayers addressed to various deities and preserving, at its east end, a figure of Sobk-mosĕ or of some member of his family in the act of burning incense and pouring a libation. Owing largely to the intractable nature of the gritty brown stone the figures are carved throughout in *relief en creux* with a minimum of interior detail and the hieroglyphs are incised in simple silhouette. Much faded patches of red, blue, and black paint on the figures, in the hieroglyphic signs, in the *ḫekeru*-ornaments (see Part I, pp. 162 f.) of the friezes crowning the walls, and on the uncarved lower portions of the walls bear witness to the fact that the interior of the chamber, now the dingy brown of the bare stone, was once brightly colored.

The seven prayers on the south wall of the room are addressed, respectively, to the sun and the moon, to Ptaḥ "south of his wall," to Ḥa, god of

FIGURE 164. Bronze razor and *menyet* counterpoise. H. 4 and 6 ⅜ in.

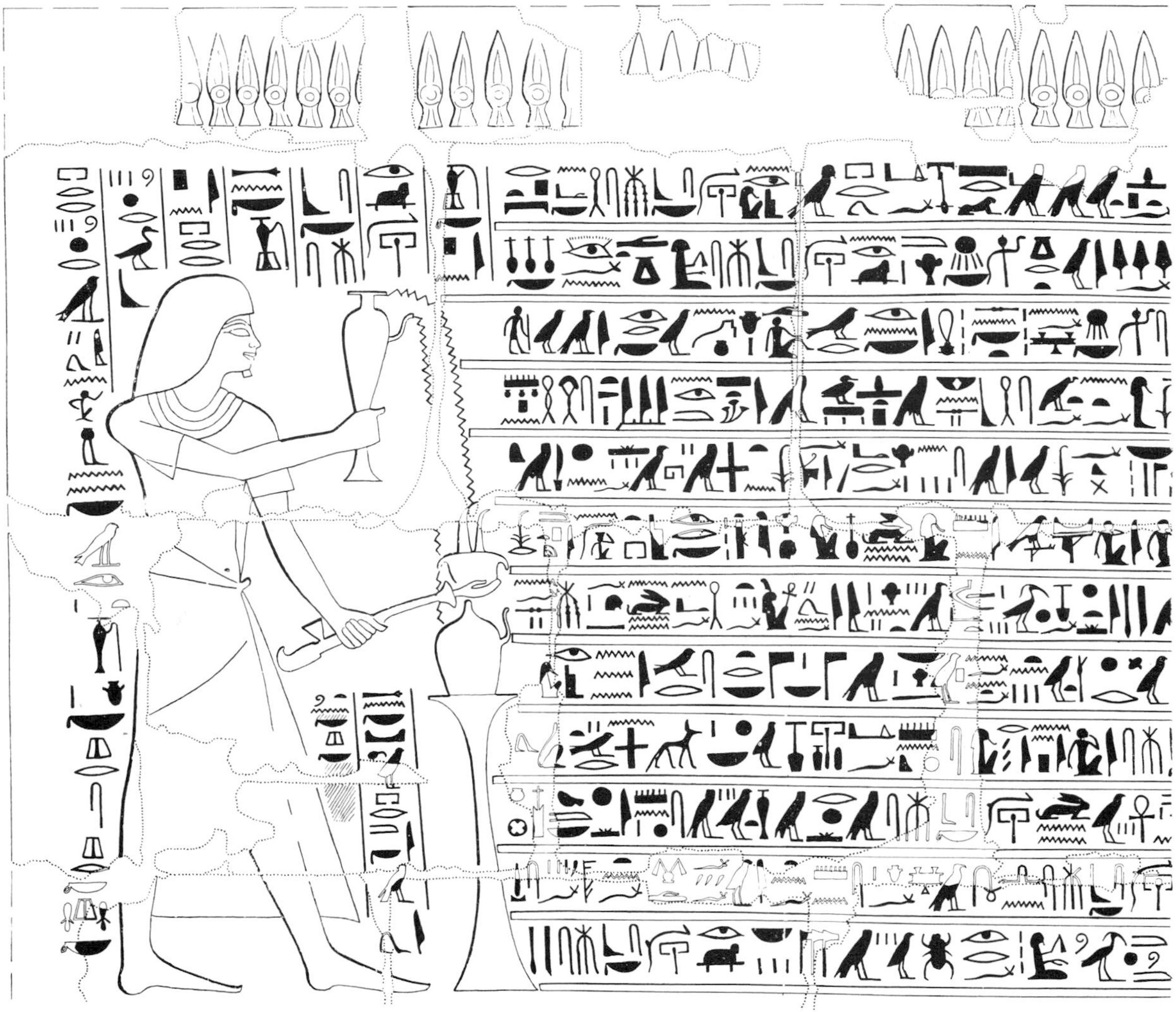

FIGURE 165. South wall of the burial chamber of the Treasurer Sobk-mosĕ. L. 10 ft. 5 in.

the Western Desert, to Amūn and Wen-nefer, to the Nile and the Primaeval Waters, to the grain god Nepri, and to Merḥet, the goddess of the embalming oil used in the preparation of Sobk-mosĕ's mummy. The prayer to the moon (lines 2-5), which is known also from the Theban tomb (No. 57) of Sobk-mosĕ's fellow official Khaʿ-emḥēt, and which is more or less typical of the series, runs as follows: "O Moon, who are in the day of (your) first appearance, brilliant of luster, be bright in the face of the Osiris, the Overseer of the House of Silver, Sobk-mosĕ, that he may gaze upon your beauty, that he may rejoice over you, that he may worship your beams. Raise up the mummy of the Osiris, the Overseer of the House of Silver, Sobk-mosĕ—let him not be laid upon his side—that he may stretch out his arms to you in welcome. Make light for him dark roads, as you did (for) Weary-of-heart (Osiris). See you that old age has come to the accurate accountant, the possessor of insight into the hearts of the people, the Osiris, the Overseer of the House of Silver, Sobk-mosĕ. He has built his tomb chapel, which he founded in your province. He has furnished it with (representations of) great gods and with images of his father and mother. Make it festive with offerings of food and with supplies which are

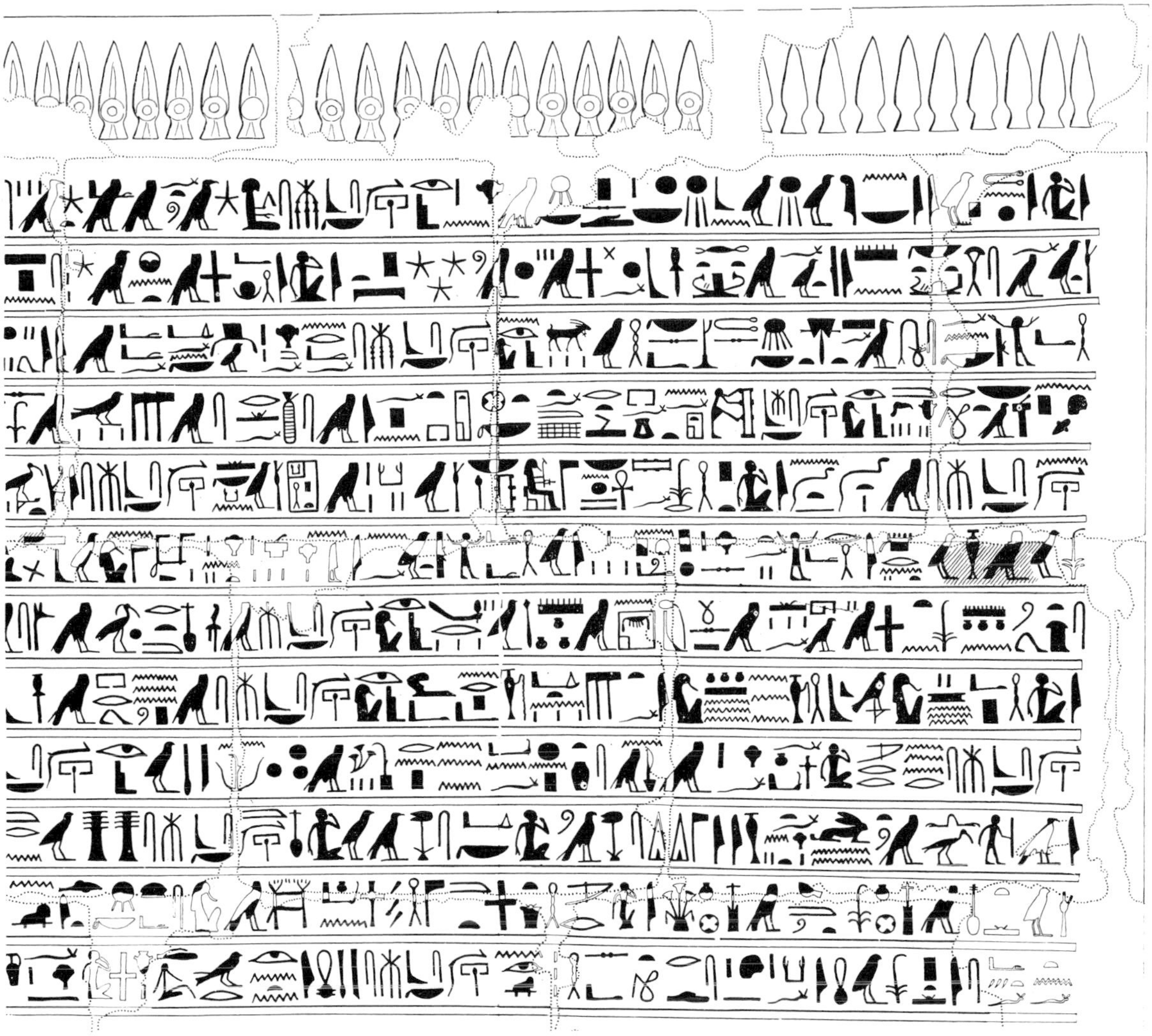

produced in the field. Cause this monument of the Overseer of the House of Silver, Sobk-mosĕ, to endure throughout the whole of eternity." In the prayer to Ḥa, Amūn, and Wen-nefer (lines 6-7) Sobk-mosĕ, who served also as one of Amun-ḥotpe III's architects, is referred to as the "Overseer of Works [in] Southern Opet (Luxor), who drew forth monuments for the King of his time from the pure alabaster of Ḥat-nūb."[12] Aside from his tomb he and his family are known to us from a number of inscriptions datable to the reign of Amun-ḥotpe III, including, we may recall, two jar labels (see p. 248) of Regnal Year 30 from the pharaoh's Theban palace.

Two sections of ★painted mud-plaster ceiling from Tomb 226 at Thebes comprise parts of large rectangular panels decorated with rows of S-spirals and rosettes and bounded by red and white zigzag borders and wide bands of yellow intended to receive inscriptions. On a third fragment of ★ceiling from the same tomb the over-all design is made up of large contiguous rosettes with small crosses in the diagonal interstices between the circles. The same pattern occurs also on a small piece of ★ceiling painting from the so-called Tomb of the Two Sculptors (No. 181). The medium, as usual, is

[12] The principal alabaster quarry used by the ancient Egyptians, situated in the desert about fifteen miles east of Tell el ʿAmārneh (see Part I, p. 65).

FIGURE 166. The Mayor of Memphis, Men-kheper, as represented on a limestone doorjamb from his tomb at Thebes. H. of figure 11 in.

tempera or, perhaps more properly, gouache, the colors including red, yellow, buff, blue, black, and white. Among the fragmentary scenes preserved in Tomb 226 is one in which Amun-ḥotpe III is represented with his mother, Queen Mūt-em-weya. In another scene he appears as one of four children of Tḥut-mosĕ IV held on the lap of the owner of the tomb, a King's Scribe, Steward, and Overseer of Royal Tutors whose name unfortunately has not been preserved.

Typical of the elegance and sophistication which we have come to expect in the private tomb sculpture of the reign of Amun-ḥotpe III is a small seated figure of the Mayor of Memphis, Men-kheper (fig. 166), carved in delicate sunk relief on an indurated limestone ★doorjamb from the Theban necropolis. His fashionable wig and clothing, his handsome chair and heart amulet, and his staff and scepter of authority mark our youthful official as a man of both taste and substance; and the accompanying inscription tells us that, in addition to being the headman, or mayor, of the great city of Memphis, Men-kheper was a King's Scribe and Liegeman of the King. The massive bracelet which he wears on his right wrist is similar to one in our own collection made of faience and inscribed with the titulary of Amun-ḥotpe III (see p. 243). Above the figure an offering formula written in two long vertical columns invokes the sun god Rēʿ Ḥor-akhty Atūm in behalf of the owner of the doorjamb, who is described as a son of the Scribe Amun-ḥotpe and the House Mistress Ḥenwet. The jamb itself, the left of a pair, measures six feet five inches in height. It was found by the Museum's Expedition reused as a doorsill in a great Saïte tomb at the foot of the ʿAsāsīf valley. Elsewhere this same Men-kheper is known to us from a headless sandstone statue discovered at Deir el Baḥri by the Egypt Exploration Fund.

From Tūneh in Middle Egypt, the site of the cemetery of ancient Hermopolis, come two big limestone ★stelae (fig. 167) of another important and obviously well-to-do official—the King's Scribe, Scribe of the Recruits, and King's First Herald Senu, whose facial type and elaborate attire no less than the gemlike style in which his stelae are carved mark him as a contemporary of Amun-ḥotpe III. On the taller of the two monuments Senu stands in adoration before two of the so-called Genii of the Dead, the human-headed Imsety and the ape-headed Ḥapy, while in the register below, the Lector Priest Pa-waḥy calls upon the gods of the region of Hermopolis to safeguard and provide for the soul of the deceased official. The second stela shows us Senu worshiping a statue of the Abydene god, (Osiris) Khenty-Amentiu, who wears on his head the *atef*-crown and whose body is covered with an over-all feather or scale pattern. The Lector Priest Pa-waḥ(y), assisted by his son Khaʿ, again officiates in the lower register, purifying Senu's food offerings with water and saying the while: "Osiris, King's Scribe

Senu, you are purified like Horus, you are fumigated like Sēth. Your adversary is beneath your feet and your enemies are overthrown as if they had never existed." Students of ancient costume will find much to interest them in the wigs, kilts, and broad collars worn by the owner of our stelae and in the leopard-skin mantle and pleated sash seen on the figures of his lector priest. Confronted by these products of a provincial atelier, students of Egyptian art can hardly fail to be impressed by the uniformly high standard maintained at this period not only at Thebes and Memphis, but apparently throughout the whole of the country. From three stelae in the Louvre and a statue in Bologna we learn that our Hermopolitan dignitary was also a Scribe of the Army of the Lord of

FIGURE 167. Stelae of the King's Scribe Senu, from Tūneh. Limestone. H. 29 ½ and 24 ⅝ in.

the Two Lands and that he had a similarly titled son named Si-Amūn.

A fragment of a large limestone ★stela on which the Overseer of the Royal Ḥarīm Pay is seen standing with hands upraised in adoration before the falcon-headed sun god Rēʿ Ḥor-akhty is closely similar in style to the stelae of Senu, but is carved in true low relief characterized by great delicacy and wealth of detail. Pay wears the somewhat foppish costume of the period with flaring sleeves and pleated over- and under-kilts. The god, who stands erect facing him over a small libation stand, holds a *was*-scepter and is clad in a short, half-goffered kilt and a scaled corselet. His falcon head is crowned by a big solar disk with pendent uraeus and above him is the down-curving right wing of another sun's disk. The fragment, which measures twenty-five by sixteen inches, comprises only part of the lunette of the great stela.

Three small votive ★stelae, on which a statue of the god Ptaḥ is shown receiving offerings from the donors of the little monuments, were found, with scores of others of the same type, in the ruins of the great temple of Ptaḥ at Memphis. On one of the stelae Ptaḥ shares his honors with Amun Rēʿ, Lord of Karnak, the figures of the two deities facing one another across a libation stand while their worshipers, two men named Ḳen and Mery-en-Ptaḥ, kneel with hands upraised in a lower register. On each of the other two stelae the mummiform figure of Ptaḥ stands alone in its little pavilion confronted by a single worshiper. A pair of human ears carved before the figure of the deity is probably intended to ensure that the prayers of the supplicant will be heard (see pp. 173 f.). In the lunettes of two of the stelae a winged sun's disk hovers over the heads of the gods, while the figure of a mortal is surmounted by a *wedjat*-eye. Somewhat roughly executed, the stelae range in height from seven and a quarter to thirteen and three-eighths inches.

From the same part of the Ptaḥ temple—the so-called West Hall—comes a limestone ★altar slab, or "grill," inscribed in behalf of the King's Scribe and Chief Steward in Memphis, Amun-ḥotpe, a brother of the Vizier Raʿ-mosĕ and one of Amun-ḥotpe III's top officials, known to us from a score of other monuments scattered throughout the museums of the world. Two feet square and three inches thick, the slab has carved on its top a row of four hemicylindrical ridges, or bars, clearly intended to enable offerings to be burned or, rather, cooked upon it. The ribbed upper surfaces of similar slabs found in New Kingdom houses at Deir el Medīneh are charred and grease-stained from cooked meat offerings, which in these instances would appear to have been small fowls such as pigeons and ducks. The inscriptions, which are confined to the edges of our slab, are offering formulae invoking the great Memphite god Ptaḥ and his consort the goddess Sakhmet. In one of them Ptaḥ, who, like Amūn at Thebes, is called King of the Gods, is asked to grant "a happy lifetime beholding his countenance daily, without ceasing, to the *ku* of the Hereditary Prince and Count, the Chancellor of the King of Lower Egypt, the Sole Companion, the real Scribe of the King, whom he loved, the Chief Steward in Memphis, Amun-ḥotpe."

A full-size funerary model in "alabaster" of a ★scribe's palette, or pen case, is one of three found in 1822 in the tomb of the same Chief Steward Amun-ḥotpe, at Saḳḳāreh. A slab of milky white calcite, seventeen and a half inches long, its back and edges are quite plain, but on its front are carved the salient features of the average writing palette: the open upper end of the pen slot, with the tops of the rush pens appearing in it, and above this two circular inkwells, here merely suggested by two ○-signs incised in outline on the surface of the stone. Down each side of the front of the palette runs a column of incised hieroglyphic inscription containing an offering formula enlisting the aid of Osiris and ending in each case with the now familiar titles and name of the great Memphite steward.

Also from northern Egypt and datable to the latter part of the Eighteenth Dynasty is another ★model writing palette (fig. 168), similar to the foregoing, but smaller and carved of green slate.

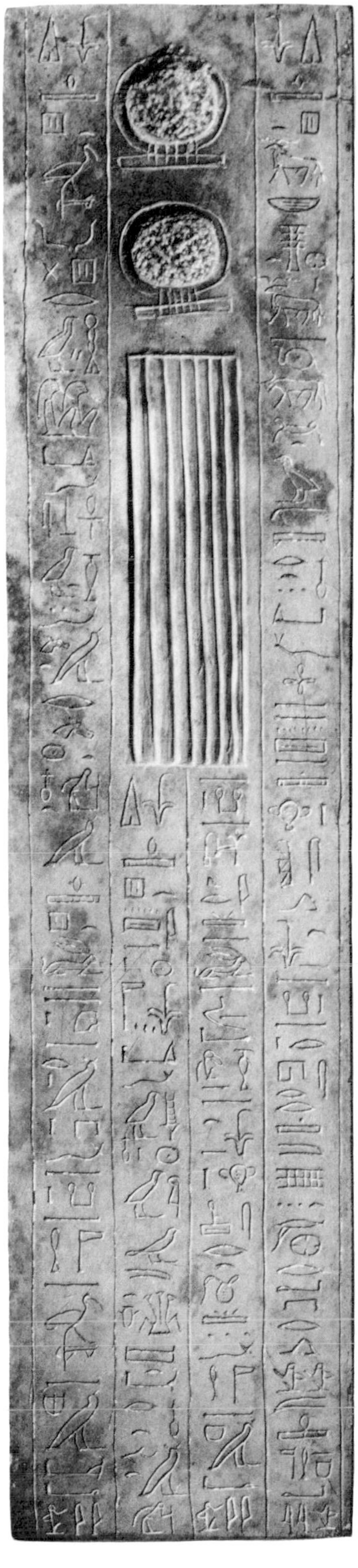

FIGURE 168. Funerary model of a scribe's palette. Slate. H. 11 13/16 in.

Three offering formulae engraved on the front of the palette invoke, respectively, Tḥōt, "who judged the two parties (Horus and Sētḫ)," Amun Rēʿ, King of the Gods, and Ba-neb-Dēdet, the ram god of the Delta town of Mendes, in behalf of the Prophet of Tḥōt, Neḥem-ʿay, who is called "the mouth which gives satisfaction in the nomes of the Northland." Five columns of enigmatic, or cryptographic, inscription on the back of the slab have been interpreted by Dr. Étienne Drioton as a hymn to Tḥōt, the divine patron of the palette's priestly owner and of all Egyptian scribes.

Such monuments as these reflect the gradual shift of Egypt's political, economic, and social centers of gravity back to the northern part of the country, whither broader lands, a more temperate climate, and a more central position in the Egyptian empire tended to draw the pharaoh and his court away from their recently established capital and cult center at Thebes. This trend, already discernible under Tḥut-mosĕ III and Amun-ḥotpe II, gained momentum as the end of the dynasty was approached. So it was that during the second half of the Eighteenth Dynasty there grew up west of the city of Memphis an important upper-class cemetery which extends along the desert's edge for a distance of almost a mile and includes the tombs of such well-known dignitaries of the reign of Amun-ḥotpe III as the Chief Steward Amun-ḥotpe and the High Priest Ptaḥ-mosĕ. Since the desert here is flat and open the burial shafts are deep vertical pits and the tomb chapels were freestanding structures of brick and limestone surmounted by small pyramids with pinnacles of limestone or granite. Many of these chapels were adorned with painted reliefs of great interest and beauty and were provided with one or more fine stelae of limestone or quartzite.

It is, however, in western Thebes that we find the tombs of the majority of Amun-ḥotpe III's key officials. That of Mery-mosĕ, his Viceroy of Nubia, situated on the southeastern slope of the Ḳurnet

Mura‘i, has been identified by two handsome anthropoid sarcophagi and a number of other inscribed objects found in it. Among the latter is certainly to be counted a small oval ★plaque of serpentine inscribed in tiny hieroglyphs with Chapter XXXA of the Book of the Dead, "a spell for preventing the heart of . . . from creating opposition against him in the necropolis." The plaque was without much doubt once inlaid in a pectoral which was worn, like a heart scarab, over the breast of the deceased official. In the first line of its inscription, as occasionally elsewhere, Mery-mosĕ's name is preceded by the title King's Son, an elliptical writing of the Viceroy's title King's Son of Kush (see p. 42). Exactly two inches in length, this handsome and historically interesting little monument was presented to the Museum in 1948 by Mr. and Mrs. Nasli Heeramaneck.

Besides the inlay from his heart pectoral the "King's Son of Kush, Mery-mosĕ," is represented in our collection by seven pottery ★funerary cones from his Theban tomb. Single ★cones of other officials, priests, and soldiers of Amun-ḥotpe III include those of the Overseer of the (Residence) City and Vizier Ra‘-mosĕ (Tomb 55); the Vizier and First Prophet of Amūn, Ptaḥ-mosĕ; the King's Scribe and Fanbearer Surere (Tomb 48); the Overseer of the King's Ḥarīm Woser-ḥēt (Tomb 47); the Steward of Amūn, Nakht-Sobk; the Keeper of the Royal Treasury Meḥ; the Chief *Wēb*-priest Sobk-mosĕ; the Standard-bearer Amun-mosĕ (Tomb 89); the Standard-bearer of the King's Ship "Appearing-in-truth" Si-Iset; and the Purveyor of Dates Nefer-renpowet (Tomb 249). Of the First Prophet of Amūn, Mery-Ptaḥ, we possess three stamped mud ★bricks measuring fourteen by six and three-quarters by three and a half inches. ★Cones of the Steward of the King's Wife, Mery, and the Under Steward of the King's Wife, the Scribe Iḥuy, may well belong to this period, Teye being the King's Wife most frequently referred to by her title alone. So also may an inscribed and painted pottery ★jug which formed part of the burial equipment of a Chantress of Amūn and House Mistress named Tuy.

Though uninscribed, a set of four painted limestone ★vases (fig. 169) are thought to have belonged to the Sculptor(?) of Amūn, Ḥuy, a contemporary of Amun-ḥotpe III whose tomb on the Dirā‘ Abu'n Naga yielded also a number of *shawabty*-figures and other inscribed objects. The vases themselves are near-duplicates of a set found in the tomb of the parents of Queen Teye and inscribed with the name of her father, Yuya. Like the Yuya vases ours are funerary dummies, solid stone except for shallow cavities below their elaborately decorated lids. The latter, as can be seen, are surmounted by a head of the dwarf god Bēs, an ox head, a recumbent calf, and a frog, skillfully carved and naturalistically colored. The significance of these devices is not apparent. It is conceivable that they are merely amusing ornamental motifs chosen more or less at random. Like canopic jars, vases of this class seem to have been provided in sets of four. The known sets, however, are confined to the time of Amun-ḥotpe III and are too few in number to warrant any general conclusions regarding their meaning and purpose.

An interesting little ★double vase of fine buff pottery is painted white with black splotches, probably in imitation of breccia or some similar black and white stone (fig. 169, foreground). A second ★vase of the same type, formerly in the Theodore M. Davis collection, is made of *ḳulleh*-ware with a glossy greenish white slip, but is not painted. Here the small drop-shaped jar which forms the second element of the painted example is replaced by a graceful two-handled flask of a type recently introduced into Egypt. Similar specimens of the double vase have been found in association with objects bearing the name of Amun-ḥotpe III, whose reign, as we have seen, was productive of just such elaborately playful knickknacks.

Four perfectly preserved ★glass vessels from western Thebes and the region of Tūneh in Middle Egypt are datable to the reign of Amun-ḥotpe III on the basis of fragments of similar vessels found in his Theban palace (see p. 254). Included are two small two-handled flasks like the example in pottery just discussed, one in polychrome glass with

the familiar wavy ornamentation (cf. fig. 109), the other of milky white glass with a black and white striped rim. A slender, footed vase with a long, graceful neck and four small loop handles rising from its shoulder is made of dark blue glass with zigzag stripes of light blue, yellow, and white. The three-ribbed cup of figure 170, easily one of the most beautiful objects in our collection, is a wonderful shade of bright turquoise blue. Formerly in the Carnaarvon and Hood collections, it is said to have been acquired originally from a native of Ḳurneh. The same type and quality of glass is seen in a tiny ★ornament having the form of a baby in a shawl, which must once have been resting on its mother's back.

A variant form of the two-handled ★flask in alabaster is from a tomb of the time of Amun-ḥotpe III at Abydos, and from an adjacent and apparently contemporary tomb comes a delicate silver ★earring supporting a little silver pendant in the shape of a cornflower. A tomb of one of the king's Theban officials on the hill called el Khōkheh yielded a red jasper ★earring of the plain penannular type (cf. fig. 102) and a blue faience ★finger

FIGURE 169. Set of funerary vases of painted limestone and two double vases of painted pottery. H. 4 3/8-12 in.

ring with a uraeus engraved on its bezel. ★Parts of floral collars in white and pale green faience include two lotiform terminal plates, a score of long, petal-shaped pendants, and a quantity of small rosettes. These are of unrecorded provenience, but are similar to elements recovered from the ruins of the Malḳata palace.

Among the many beautiful small objects which made up the Carnarvon, Murch, Morgan, and Ward collections are thirty ★finger rings of gold, silver, bronze, quartz, rock crystal, carnelian, feldspar, glazed steatite, and faience. These too, though datable typologically to the general period of Amun-ḥotpe III, are without documentation. Only three are inscribed: a carnelian signet ring with the title the "King's Great Wife whom he loves," and two faience rings with the name of the god Amun Rēʿ, followed in one instance by the epithet "Lord of Upper and Lower Egypt." A massive gold signet ring has engraved upon its

FIGURE 170. Cup of turquoise blue glass from western Thebes. Diam. 4 ½ in.

long oval bezel a decorative design composed of a clump of papyrus plants flanked by frogs on *neb*-signs, while a second example, also of gold, carries the figures of two rather elongated fish, side by side, and a bronze ring has a single *bolti*-fish flanked by *nefer*-signs (see fig. 180). The design on a similar ring carved entirely of white quartz consists of a solar barque surmounted by a disk and crescent and a seated figure of the sun god Rēʿ. A *wedjat*-eye and a crescent moon, both incised, adorn the bezels of two polished stone rings shaped, respectively, of carnelian and green feldspar. Other bezel devices, chiefly on faience rings, include single and grouped hieroglyphs, sistrums with pendent uraei, an upright figure of the hippopotamus goddess Thoueris, a running ibex with head turned back, a squatting ape, and a cow standing in a papyrus barque. The bezel of a rock crystal ring is not a flat oval plaque, but is carved in the round in the shape of an openwork *wedjat*-eye. So too are the bezels of five similar rings in blue, green, violet, and white faience. Another faience ring has a bezel in the form of two opposed lotus flowers with oval bead shapes between, the whole molded in the round and colored yellow, red, and blue. Two rings made entirely of faience imitate in their forms the earlier metal rings with swiveled scarabs and cowroids. A heavily oxidized ★mass of silver ornaments, acquired with the Davis collection, includes an openwork silver *wedjat*-eye and a silver ring with rectangular faience fish bezel of a type copiously represented in the palace of Amun-ḥotpe III.

Thirty-two small open ★molds of fine-grained reddish brown pottery are similar to those found in the ruins of the palace and, in the absence of evidence to the contrary, may be assigned to the period with which we are now concerned. Intended chiefly for the production of amulets and small ornaments of faience and glass, these molds preserve, in reverse, a great variety of different forms: scarab backs, *wedjat*-eyes, symbols of "stability," *ḥes*-vases, uraei, cornflowers, rosettes, bunches of grapes, figures of Bēs and Thoueris, crowned vultures, groups of hieroglyphs, and the so-called aegis of Sakhmet or Bastet. Of unknown provenience, twenty-three of the molds were presented to the Museum by Miss Lily Place and nine by Mrs. Lucy W. Drexel.

Three cylindrical ★wooden containers, one fluted, the others carved with broad friezes of animals and plants, are now thought to be of doubtful authenticity, but are mentioned here so that those who are familiar with our collection will not think they have been overlooked. They belong to a class of object characteristic of the late Eighteenth Dynasty and well represented in the Louvre and other great European collections, but which, unhappily, are easily and convincingly reproduced by the facile wood-carvers of modern Egypt. A cylindrical ★ivory vessel with the same type of ornament, though said to have come from Heliopolis, near Cairo, was probably made in Syria by Phoenician craftsmen. Carved from a single section of elephant tusk, it represents a small, two-handled bowl resting on a tall, cylindrical stand, the latter decorated in relief with trees flanked by upreared ibexes. The iconography and style of the carving suggests a date not far removed from the reign of Amun-ḥotpe III, a period when the flood of Asiatic imports into Egypt must have been nearing its all-time peak.

4. The Rise of the Aten

Thanks largely to the close relations maintained with the Mediterranean and Asiatic nations to the north and east, to the steady influx of foreigners into the Valley of the Nile itself, and to the inevitable intermarriages which had taken place between these foreigners and the native Egyptians, we find under Amun-ḥotpe III a highly cosmopolitan society, acutely conscious of its place in world civilization and endowed with both the desire and the ability to think in terms of the universal and to cope with problems of world-wide significance. In the religion this new point of view resulted in a return to the universal principles inherent in the worship of the sun as embodied especially in the god Rēʿ Ḥor-akhty of Heliopolis and in a related form of the solar deity recently risen to prominence and called quite simply (*pa*) *Aten*, "the Disk." It also led to the intensified "solarization" of the state god Amūn, whose functions as a bringer of victory in war and as the special patron of the Theban dynasts had already begun to be overshadowed by his new role as a cosmic creator god and ruler of the universe. Precisely this concept of the god is expressed in a hymn composed in the reign of Amun-ḥotpe III for the king's architects, Suti and Ḥōr, and here also we meet with ideas and phraseology closely similar to those found in the famous hymns to the Aten compiled under the "heretic," Akh-en-Aten.

The emergence of the Aten as a recognized member of the Egyptian pantheon probably occurred during the period of imperial expansion under Tḥut-mosĕ III and Amun-ḥotpe II. A royal commemorative scarab carved a few years later has been interpreted as providing "definite proof, not only that the Aten was already regarded as a separate and distinct form of the sun-god by Tuthmosis IV, but that he was actually worshiped as a god of battles who gave victory to Pharaoh and ensured his pre-eminence over the rest of the world, making all mankind the subjects of the Disk."[13] It is not, however, until the reign of Amun-ḥotpe III that we hear of temples erected in behalf of the new god, both at Heliopolis, the ancient stronghold of the solar religion, and at Karnak in the sacred precinct of Amūn, and find him officially honored in the nomenclature of such important items as the king's flagship, "Splendor-of-Aten," and a royal palace of the same name, not to mention the names of two of the king's children, Baket-Aten and Tūt-ʿankh-Aten. Whether Amun-ḥotpe III himself actively promoted or merely tolerated the rapidly expanding cult of the Disk is a moot question. The king's devotion to Amūn and the munificence with which throughout his life he supported the temples and priesthoods of the state god suggest, however, that the growth of the Aten worship was sponsored by other and more restless minds than his.

---

[13] Shorter, *The Journal of Egyptian Archaeology*, XVII, 24.

VII. The ʿAmārneh Period and Its Aftermath

1. Akh-en-Aten

THE EXTRAORDINARY EPISODE in Egyptian history generally referred to as the ʿAmārneh period may be said to have begun about 1370 B.C. with the coronation at Thebes of King Nefer-khepru-Rēʿ, Amun-ḥotpe IV, and to have ended two decades later, following the death of the royal "heretic," with the abandonment of the site in Middle Egypt which had served as his residence city and which has come to be known in modern times as Tell el ʿAmārneh. Though Amun-ḥotpe III seems to have survived his son's elevation to the throne by as much as ten or a dozen years it was the younger man who now controlled the destiny of the country and whose strange and complex personality is reflected in almost every historical and cultural development of his time.

Physically weak and unprepossessing, with a frail, effeminate body and an emaciated, lantern-jawed face, the new king had in him nothing of either the soldier or the statesman. As time went on he concerned himself less and less with the affairs of the nation and the empire and more and more with matters of the mind and the spirit—chiefly, be it said, of his own mind and spirit. Exulting in the epithet "he who lives on truth (*maʿet*)," he sought in his life an ever closer and more harmonious relationship with nature and in his religion a more direct and rational relationship with his deity.

The inconsistencies and artificialities which he found in the state religion were disturbing to his eager, sensitive mind, and early in his life he became a zealous adherent of the cult of the Aten, not only adopting the life-giving disk as his personal divinity but turning his back upon Egypt's old gods and upon many of the traditions which had grown up under them. His proscription of the state god Amūn and his fellow divinities seems to have been primarily an act of religious fanatacism and not, as is sometimes suggested, a political move designed to check the temporal power of the priesthoods, for at this period, as Edgerton has pointed out, "the priests and other temple functionaries were as truly the Pharaoh's agents as the army officers or the tax-collectors"[1] and were appointed and removed at will by the pharaoh himself. Nor is the monotheistic aspect of the remodeled sun cult of great significance to the history of world religion, since the worship of the Aten appears, in fact, to have been confined to the pharaoh and his immediate family, the courtiers addressing their devotions to the deified king himself and the people of Egypt, as usual, remaining outside the pale of the theologically initiated. With little or no ethical content it is difficult to see how

[1] *Journal of Near Eastern Studies*, VI (1947), p. 156.

the Aten cult can be presumed to have been a forerunner of Judaism and Christianity. The longer Aten hymn, beautiful as it is, is hardly more than a lyrical meditation on the manifestation of God in nature, resembling the Psalms in this respect and in some of its verbal imagery but in very little else.

It is probable that Amun-ḥotpe IV came to the throne at the age of about sixteen, already a devotee of the "living Aten," and shortly thereafter married his gracious and beautiful cousin, Nefret-ity, thought to have been a daughter of Queen Teye's brother, the Troop Commander Ay. For a few years he continued to reside in his father's palace at Thebes and to preserve, at least outwardly, the conventional attitude of respect for the state god Amūn and his divine associates, retaining his given name, "Amūn-is-content," and permitting himself to be represented offering to Amūn and adoring, among other deities, the goddess Nekhābet of el Kāb. During this period, however, his principal activity was the construction at Karnak of a temple to the Aten, lavishly adorned with painted reliefs and provided with a solar obelisk, or *benben*, of sandstone and with colossal figures of the king executed in the exaggeratedly naturalistic style characteristic of the earlier stage of the religious and cultural "revolution." It must have been an uncomfortable period for both Amun-ḥotpe IV and his evidently orthodox father, and in the fourth year of the coregency, following an open clash with the priesthood of Amūn, the younger pharaoh decided or, more likely, was induced to leave Thebes and establish his residence elsewhere.

By the sixth year of his reign he and his family, together with a considerable retinue of officials, priests, soldiers, and craftsmen, had moved to Tell el ʿAmārneh, two hundred and sixty miles downriver from Thebes, and there, in a great semicircular bay of the eastern cliffs, had founded a new residence city called Akhet-Aten, the "Horizon-of-Aten." Spread out along the river for a distance of almost eight miles, the city comprised temples to the Aten with open altar courts for the worship of the solar disk, palaces and gardens for the king and his family, villas for the courtiers, a Hall of Foreign Tribute, a records office, a military barracks, a workmen's village, and, in the cliffs to the east, rows of rock-cut tombs for the more important officials. It is the sculptured scenes and inscriptions in these tombs and on fourteen big rock-cut stelae marking the boundaries of the city which have provided us with much of our information on life at Akhet-Aten and on the activities of the pharaoh and his family. For the burial of the royal family, including apparently the king, a large and elaborately decorated tomb was hewn in a desert valley some five miles east of the city and there was actually buried the little Princess Meket-Aten, the second of six daughters born to Nefret-ity and her husband.

The pharaoh meanwhile had changed his name to Akh-en-Aten, "He-who-is-serviceable-to-Aten," and had conferred upon his queen the throne name Nefer-nefru-Aten, "Beautiful-in-beauty-is-Aten." In the fifth year of his reign he had celebrated a *sed*-festival marking, it has been thought, the thirtieth anniversary of the "birth" of the Aten. A second *sed*-festival was observed some four years later. The king's three elder daughters, Meryet-Aten, Meket-Aten, and ʿAnkhes-en-pa-Aten, appear to have been born before Year 6; Nefer-nefru-Aten, junior, between Years 6 and 9; and Nefer-nefru-Rēʿ and Sotep-en-Rēʿ, the babies of the family, between Years 9 and 12.

The last half decade of Akh-en-Aten's reign witnessed the death of his father Amun-ḥotpe III and the estrangement of his wife Nefret-ity. As his coregent during his last three or four years the pharaoh appointed his youthful half brother Semenkh-ku-Rēʿ (see p. 297 ff.), and transferred to this evidently highly esteemed young man Nefret-ity's throne name, Nefer-nefru-Aten. Akh-en-Aten himself did not long survive his seventeenth year on the throne, dying apparently at el ʿAmārneh in 1353 B.C. Contrary probably to his own wishes, his body was transferred to Thebes and was buried there in a small, undecorated tomb in the Valley of the Tombs of the Kings, the

FIGURE 171. Sculptors' studies for heads of King Akh-en-Aten, from el ʿAmārneh. Sandstone and limestone. H. 3 5/8-8 5/8 in.

funerary equipment buried with it including items prepared originally for his mother, Queen Teye, and his eldest daughter, Meryet-Aten (see pp. 294, 297 f).

The influence which during his brief period of ascendancy this remarkable man exerted on almost every phase of Egyptian culture is nowhere so manifest as in two closely related media of expression, the written language and the art. Consistent with the ideals exhibited in his short-lived religious reforms we find in the inscriptions and in the works of sculpture and painting produced at this time the tendency to shake off existing traditions and to reproduce more closely the language as actually spoken by living persons and the images as actually seen by living artists. In the language this change had a lasting effect, resulting in the more extensive colloquialization of the "classical" idiom, Middle Egyptian, and the evolution therefrom of a stage in the written language which we call Late, or New, Egyptian.

In the art one of the most striking manifestations of the new naturalism was the candid representation not only of the king's curious physique, but also of the more intimate and tender moments in his family life. From the former, at first exaggerated to the point of caricature, later rendered with more restraint, was developed the typical "ʿAmārneh" figure adopted by the king's followers in their statues and tomb reliefs and characterized by an elongated face and head, bulbous thighs and abdomen, and a spindly neck, arms, and lower legs. From the latter were evolved livelier, more dramatic, and better integrated compositions in which, as Aldred has pointed out, "the emphasis is now upon a unity of the whole in place of the former assemblage of parts."[2] As we should expect, natural plant and animal forms occur in greater profusion than ever before and are rendered with a vivacity and charm unsurpassed in the long history of Egyptian art. The technical ineptitude apparent in some of the earlier works of the ʿAmārneh school is attributable in part to the experimental nature of the works themselves and in part to Akh-en-Aten's initial lack of thoroughly trained artists, most of whom were absorbed in the grandiose artistic and architectural projects sponsored by his father. With time and with the death of the

[2] *New Kingdom Art in Ancient Egypt*, p. 26.

older king this deficiency was corrected, and many of the later products of the ʿAmārneh ateliers are, technically speaking, above criticism. Thanks to the proclivity for standardization which seems to have been inbred in the Egyptian artist, the extraordinary mannerisms of the ʿAmārneh style soon became fixed conventions, repeated over and over again and identifying with unmistakable clarity the products of this most distinctive phase of New Kingdom art.

To the earlier, more revolutionary stage of ʿArmārneh art belong seventeen ★sculptors' studies, or trial pieces, coming from workshops in the town of Akhet-Aten where they were found by Flinders Petrie and Howard Carter during the winter of 1891-1892. All except one were formerly in the collection of Lord Amherst of Hackney and were acquired either directly or indirectly from this collection. There are eight studies for heads of Akh-en-Aten, three in the half round, one in low relief, and four in *relief en creux* (see fig. 171). Each shows us a more or less exaggerated version of the king's long, bony face, emphasizing in particular the narrow, slanting eyes, retroussé nose, sullen, fleshy mouth, pointed chin, and scrawny neck of this ruler who in his devotion to "truth" encouraged his court artists to caricature his own physical peculiarities. The grotesque sandstone head at the left of our illustration could well have served as a model for the heads of Akh-en-Aten's Karnak colossi (see p. 281), though it comes in fact from el ʿAmārneh and probably postdates the Karnak figures by two or three years. All our sketches represent the pharaoh's ear lobes as pierced for rings, studs, or other ornaments, a concession to fashion or to realism in art not found in earlier royal portrait heads. Akh-en-Aten's headdresses include the softly rounded *khat*, or bagwig, the more formal *nemes*, and the Blue Crown, only the lower edges of which are actually shown. On the back of the second slab of figure 171 the head of a horse has been roughly, but expertly, sketched in relief, and below the head on the panel at the extreme right the sculptor has made a second study of the pharaoh's thick-lipped mouth. Another trial piece carries, besides a small head of the king in left profile, two sketches of a clenched human hand and wrist, the latter adorned in each case with a wide, banded bracelet. So conditioned had Akh-en-Aten's sculptors become to reproducing his portrait that we find it even in a large and detailed version of the hieroglyph ♡ carved with a number of other signs on a limestone slab of our present series. Here, though seen in full front view, the small head is unmistakably that of the king, even to the pierced ear lobes.

FIGURE 172. Head of a Nubian. A sculptor's study in limestone from el ʿAmārneh. H. 4 in.

Two studies in *relief en creux* for heads of Nefret-ity caricature the queen's thin, delicate face and long, slender neck with the same unrestrained exaggeration seen in the portraits of her husband. In both sketches Nefret-ity wears a short, shingled wig, bobbed at the back but descending on either side of the face in a graceful point—an extremely attractive headdress found at this period chiefly on royal ladies and on soldiers of the palace guard. In one instance a coiled uraeus rises from the brow of the headdress and in the other a large earring appears half hidden behind the locks which frame the face of the queen. Well under life size, the two portraits are somewhat hastily carved on rough slabs of limestone.

One of the younger royal princesses is sketched in relief as a small nude figure with grotesquely elongated skull, clad only in the same short, cap-like wig worn by her mother. A much battered little limestone figure, carved in the round but preserved only from the shoulders to the thighs, is thought to represent another of Nefret-ity's daughters, wearing in this case a diaphanous mantle of pleated linen and displaying the wasp-waisted, full-hipped form characteristic of the period.

The five remaining trial pieces, all executed in *relief en creux*, are taken up with a variety of male heads and figures, including two Nubians (see fig. 172), an elderly peasant, and an Egyptian official with head bowed slightly forward—types which we meet with in the tomb and temple reliefs of el ʿAmārneh. The head of the Nubian selected for illustration shows the same mannerisms and exaggerations in the treatment of the racial type that we have found at this period in the individual portraits of the king and his family. In the tombs of Akh-en-Aten's courtiers Nubians and other foreigners appear in the great scenes representing the reception by the pharaoh of foreign tribute and embassies from neighboring lands. A particularly successful example of the new naturalistic trend is the study of the old peasant with his shaggy, balding head, hard-bitten, wrinkled face, bent body, and stringy arms extended forward in an awkward gesture of address. A small ★slab of limestone found by the Egypt Exploration Society in the so-called Royal Estate bears a hastily executed profile head of one of the king's daughters in which the sculptor has experimented with the position of the eye.

To the same period but to a somewhat different category belongs a small ★fragment of quartzite stela or parapet with the upper part of a figure of Queen Nefret-ity executed in sunk relief. Here the queen, whose arms are raised in adoration and whose figure was probably preceded by that of her husband in similar pose, wears on her head a long, curled wig adorned near the top with a fillet and uraeus surmounted apparently by the sun's disk and horns. The ear lobes of the royal lady are pierced with prominent circular holes and on her upper arms and breast she wears pairs of small cartouche-shaped ornaments containing (when represented in greater detail than here) the so-called "didactic names" of the Aten (see p. 292). Though it is a far cry from this scrawny caricature to the beautiful limestone bust of Nefret-ity in Berlin, there are enough features in common to show that both heads represent the same person—a slender, long-necked woman with a pointed chin, sloping forehead, and fine straight nose very slightly bulbed at the tip.

Since the Sanctuary of the Great Temple of the Aten at Akhet-Aten, one of the first buildings erected on the new site, seems to have been built and furnished with its sculptured decoration before the ninth year of the reign, the statues and reliefs with which it was adorned belong also to the earlier stage of the ʿAmārneh movement and show in their style the closest affinities with the pieces which we have been discussing. The difference between the two groups is chiefly one of finish and technique, our studies being for the most part hasty sketches by student sculptors, while the temple sculptures are the finished products of ʿAmārneh's leading artists.

With the destruction of Akh-en-Aten's city, which followed the death of its founder by only a few years, the Great Temple was razed to the ground and its statues and reliefs smashed to bits and piled up in heaps outside the temple's southern enclosure wall. One of the heaps of statue fragments, often referred to nowadays as the favissa of the temple, was found by Petrie and Carter during the winter of 1891-1892, most of the pieces from it passing forthwith into the collection of Lord Amherst and, with the sale of this collection in 1921, into the possession of several different purchasers, including the Earl of Carnarvon and the Metropolitan Museum of Art. Our share of the find, including the subsequently acquired Carnarvon and Altoumian pieces, comprises 375 ★fragments of statues, statuettes, and altars in hard and soft limestone, alabaster, quartzite, and diorite. Ranging in size from eighteen-inch statuettes to colossi which must have been nine or ten feet in height, the majority of the statues appear to have been standing figures of the king and queen holding before them trays for offerings or tablets with the cartouches of the Aten. The two "marble" torsos of figure 173 are from statues of this type which in these instances were about two-thirds life size Akh-en-Aten's figure, nude above the belt line of

FIGURE 173. Nefret-ity and Akh-en-Aten. Parts of two indurated limestone statues from the Great Temple of the Aten at el ʿAmārneh. H. 11 ¼ and 13 ⅛ in.

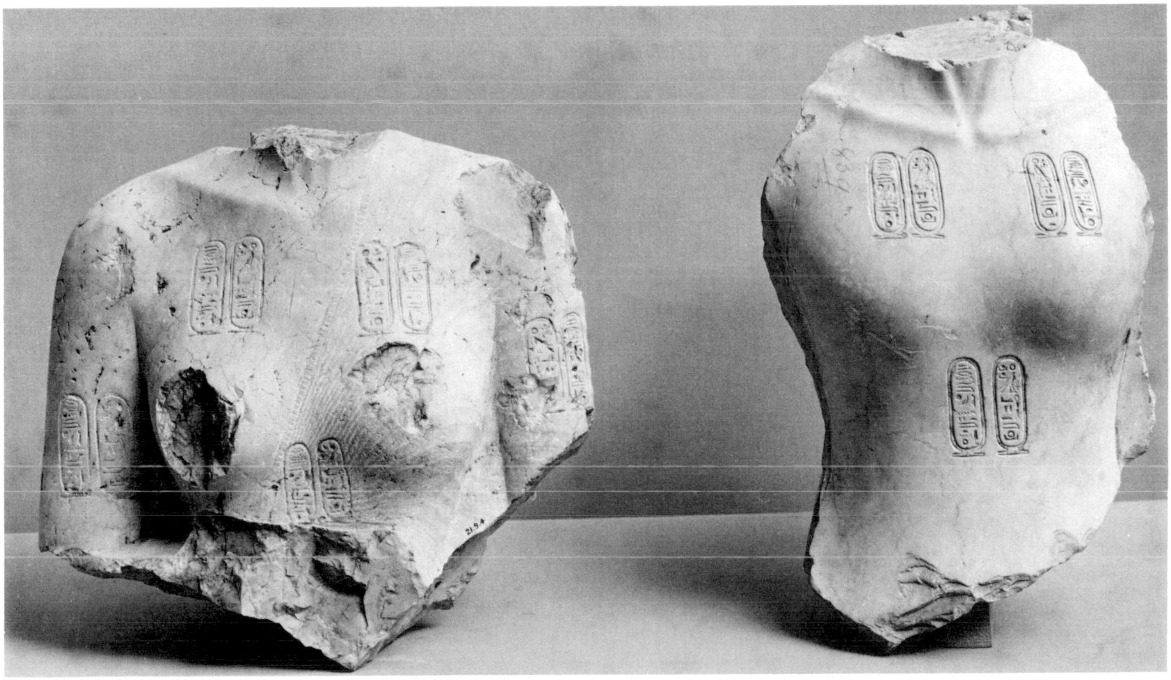

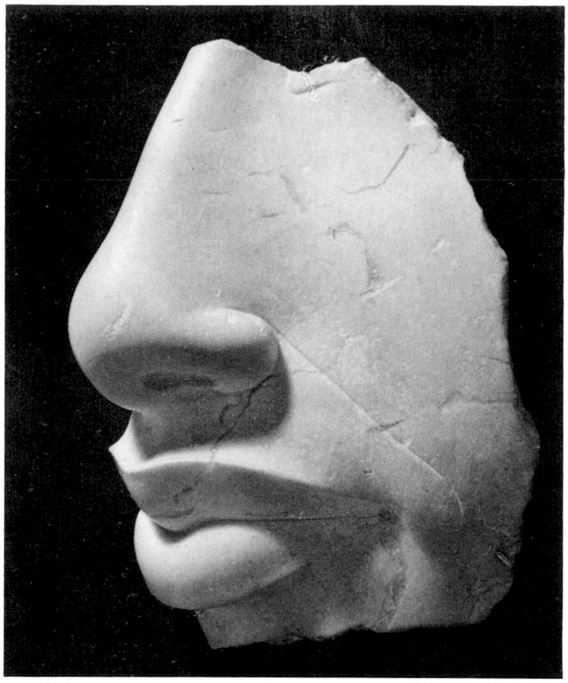

FIGURE 174. The nose and mouth of King Akh-en-Aten. Fragment of a hard limestone statue from el ʿAmārneh. H. 3 ¼ in.

his rippled kilt, is almost as effeminate as that of his wife, who wears beneath her fringed and pleated mantle a perfectly plain, tight-fitting undergarment. The pairs of cartouches liberally strewn over the bodies and arms of both figures and forming an ornamental band at the top of the king's kilt contain the names of the sun god in the form current until late in Akh-en-Aten's eighth regnal year—"Rēʿ lives, Ḥor-akhty who rejoices on the horizon in his name: Shu who is Aten." The same cartouches appear one above the other on the back pilasters of the figures, followed, like the names of an earthly king, by the expression "given life forever and ever." Besides the names of the god the back pilaster of the female figure carries on one of its sides the name of the queen, ". . . Nefret-ity, may she live forever and ever!"

The wonderfully sensitive modeling and surface finish which characterize these figures are seen to even greater advantage in the nose and mouth of what must have been a superb statue of the king carved in the same hard, marblelike limestone (fig. 174). Five fragmentary heads of Akh-en-Aten, their elongated faces almost completely battered away, wear a variety of royal headdresses, the *khat*, the *nemes*, and in two cases the Blue Crown. A number of the trays, basins, and cartouche tablets held by the figures have been partially reassembled from small fragments, and on these, beside or below the names of the Aten, we find portions of the titularies of the king and queen. Here, as elsewhere, the pharaoh is called the "King of Upper and Lower Egypt, living on truth, the Lord of the Two Lands, Nefer-khepru-Rēʿ, Sole-one-of-Rēʿ, the Son of Rēʿ, Living-on-truth, the Lord of Crowns, Akh-en-Aten, whose life's span is long"; and the queen, the "King's Great Wife, whom he loves, Mistress of [the Two Lands], Nefer-nefru-Aten Nefret-ity, may she live forever and ever!" All told, Akh-en-Aten's name is preserved on twenty-one of our fragments and Nefret-ity's on twenty, with one doubtful mention of the Princess ʿAnkhes-en-pa-Aten. One or two over life-size seated statues are represented chiefly by small fragments of their thrones. Several pieces of altar railing in indurated limestone include bits of the molded coping of a parapet (a larger section of which is in the Brooklyn Museum) and the top of what appears to have been a newel post, adorned with the double cartouches of the Aten. A fine red quartzite stela or parapet, of which we possess a small fragment, was decorated in deeply cut *relief en creux* with a more or less stereotyped scene showing Akh-en-Aten and his family in the act of worshiping their god. Our piece of this once handsome monument preserves only the mid-section of the figure of the king and, to his left, the upraised hand of the queen offering a cartouche-shaped ornament(?) with the names of the Aten.

Of the painted limestone reliefs which decorated the walls of Aten's Sanctuary very little has been recovered, but our own collection is fortunate in including four admirably carved ★blocks of this relief coming apparently from three different scenes. Since the subjects represented appear also in the private tombs of el ʿAmārneh their identification presents no difficulty. Two of our blocks are evidently from the top of a scene in which Akh-en-

Aten and his family were shown taking their ease in a vine-clad arbor, a subject which at any other period would have been regarded as unsuitably intimate and informal for use in a temple. Preserved are the tops of columns of hieroglyphs with the titles of the king, the queen, and their two eldest daughters and, above these, part of the leafy vine (convolvulus or woodbine) which shaded the royal heads from the heat of the sun. A third block permits us a glimpse into one of the outer courts of the temple, where two rows of little altars carry their burdens of food and drink and in the foreground a line of trussed sacrificial oxen await their doom. It is characteristic of the lively naturalism of ʿAmārneh art that the bound animals are not treated as repetitions of a stereotyped element, but that each is given an individuality of its own, twisting its head and bellowing in discomfort or lying exhausted with lolling tongue.

The block illustrated in figure 175 was recovered from the temple ruins in 1927 and is described by Dr. Henri Frankfort of the Egypt Exploration Society's expedition as belonging "to the best relief-work known from ʿAmarnah."[3] On it we see two of the royal chariots attended by kowtowing grooms or charioteers standing waiting for their owners, who were evidently represented off to the left participating in a ceremony of some sort. The restless prancing of the pair of spirited little horses has been admirably caught by the Egyptian sculptor, who has also provided us with a number of interesting details of the harness and adornments of the steeds and of the form and equipment of the light, two-wheeled chariots. Especially to be noted are the trimming of the horses' manes to form decorative crests above their heads, the solar disk ornament surmounting the forward end of the chariot pole, the six-spoked chariot wheel, the bow case and quiver strapped to the right side of the chariot body, and the light, long-lashed whips held by the grooms. As almost always in Egyptian art, the horses as well as the men were colored a dark red, now somewhat faded. In addition to the pair of sandals which he carries slung on his arm the groom on the right is shown, perhaps inadvertently, wearing a second pair on his feet. Below are seen soldiers of the king's bodyguard, including apparently three Nubians, a group of musicians comprising a lute player and two flautists, and a cluster of singers or temple attendants, all bowing low in the presence of the deified pharaoh and his heavenly counterpart the sun god. Though the royal chariots and royal retainers appear

[3] *The Journal of Egyptian Archaeology*, XIII (1927), p. 210.

FIGURE 175. Chariots of the royal retinue awaiting their owners. Painted limestone relief from the Great Temple of the Aten at el ʿAmārneh. L. 21 ¼ in.

FIGURE 176. Head of King Akh-en-Aten in dark red quartzite. From a sculptor's atelier at el ʿAmārneh. H. 4 5/16 in.

here in a moment of relative immobility, we are reminded of the scenes in the tombs of the courtiers in which Akh-en-Aten, Nefret-ity, and their daughters are shown driving at breakneck speed through the streets of Akhet-Aten with their military escorts racing along beside them at a dead run. Like most temple reliefs of the ʿAmārneh period, our four blocks are uniform in size and relatively small, measuring one royal cubit (twenty-one inches) in length and three palms (nine inches) in height.

Eight small sculptured fragments in the earlier ʿAmārneh style include a broken quartzite ★inlay in the form of a profile head of the king, a ★forearm and hand from a quartzite statuette of one of the princesses, and a ★sculptor's model in plaster of an elongated human foot, all from the so-called "Mansion of Aten" (*Ḥat-Aten*) and all from the Egypt Exploration Society's excavations of 1931-1933. Two small ★bits of sandstone statues, inscribed in one case with the praenomen of the king and in the other with the names of the Aten, are said to have come from el ʿAmārneh or its immediate vicinity. Two other fragments, though of unrecorded provenience, are almost certainly also from el ʿAmārneh. One is a beautifully modeled ★hand broken from a large statuette in indurated limestone. The other is the bent right ★arm of an ebony statuette of about the same scale, inscribed below the shoulder with the cartouches of the Aten surmounting those of the king. A ★fragment of plaster *relief en creux*, on which is preserved a large cartouche of Nefret-ity, is perhaps from one of the tombs at el ʿAmārneh.

With the dark red quartzite ★head of Akh-en-Aten shown in figure 176 we have left behind the violent initial phase of ʿAmārneh art and entered its second stage, when good taste and superior technical ability had combined with the zeal for naturalism to produce portraits of great discernment and sensitivity and often of great beauty. Here, in spite of the disconcertingly dark shadows left by the missing eye inlays, we have a wholly believable likeness of the king, which, though showing all the features so cruelly caricatured in the earlier heads, has managed at the same time to retrieve some of the dignity and nobility associated with Egyptian kingship. The statue, or large statuette, to which this head belonged was probably made of several materials, only the exposed flesh portions being of red quartzite, while the clothing may have been of limestone or alabaster and the missing headdress of faience or some similar substance. The cuttings on the top and sides of the head indicate pretty clearly that the headdress in this case was the royal *nemes*. Other details which we note in passing are the pierced ear lobes and the lines which descend from the sides of the king's nose past the corners of his mouth, adding to his generally bitter expression a touch of weariness.

The same "somewhat idealised naturalism"[4] is

[4] Aldred, *New Kingdom Art in Ancient Egypt*, p. 29.

FIGURE 177. The Princess ʿAnkhes-en-pa-Aten (?). Head of a painted limestone statuette from el ʿAmārneh. H. 1 3/8 in.

seen in a delightful little painted limestone ★head (fig. 177) found by the Egypt Exploration Society in a private house in the southwest quarter of Akhet-Aten and acquired for the Metropolitan Museum through the generosity of Mrs. John Hubbard. For many years this small portrait has been described as that of a young man, but Cyril Aldred's recent reassessment of the evidence provided by the wig and the facial type has led us to return to John Pendlebury's original identification of the subject as one of Akh-en-Aten's daughters, probably his highly favored third daughter, the Princess ʿAnkhes-en-pa-Aten.

Though many of Egypt's traditional funerary beliefs and customs, especially those associated with the ancient Underworld god Osiris, seem to have been abandoned by Akh-en-Aten in favor of a doctrine of immortality based on the life-giving properties of the solar disk, he retained, among others, the practice of providing his tomb with scores of small mummiform figures carved in his own likeness and probably intended to perform much the same functions as the *shawabtys* of his predecessors and successors. The upper part of a fine quartzite ★figure of this type (fig. 178), found with many others near the Royal Tomb at el ʿAmārneh, is, however, somewhat noncommittal in this regard. Like many royal *shawabtys* it is inscribed only with the king's names and titles written in a vertical column down the front, holds in its hands a pair of ʿ*ankh*-signs, and, in place of the curved Osirian beard, wears on its chin the square-cut pharaonic goatee. The headdress of this particular example is of the long, archaic type worn by divinities, but it too has been "modernized" by the addition of the royal uraeus. The most striking characteristic of these small and more or less mass-produced figures is the extraordinary individuality of their tiny faces, which in some cases deserve to be counted among the more accurate and lifelike portraits of the pharaoh now in existence.

Also from the Royal Tomb and formerly in the Ward collection are what appear to be three small ★fragments of Akh-en-Aten's alabaster canopic chest. As restored from other fragments in the Cairo Museum this chest is seen to have been a cubical box adorned on the corners with winged falcons in high relief and inscribed on the sides with

FIGURE 178. Quartzite *shawabty* of the pharaoh Akh-en-Aten. H. of fragment 5 3/4 in.

the cartouches of the king and of the Aten. Our pieces are sections from the sides of such a box. One of them preserves portions of the Aten cartouches, and another, part of a bird's wing in fairly bold relief. The third fragment shows a perfectly plain, flat surface, three and a half inches across.

Turning from figure sculpture and relief to the justly famous mural painting of Akhet-Aten we find in the painted walls and pavements of the royal palaces and private villas of Akh-en-Aten's pleasure city the most attractive of all the manifestations of ʿAmārneh art. Like the murals in the palace of Amun-ḥotpe III at Thebes the ʿAmārneh paintings are executed in gouache on a stucco-covered mud-plaster or concrete base. Stylistically they have much in common with the approximately contemporary Theban paintings, retaining the old conventional treatment of details, but showing in general an even greater freedom, naturalism, and feeling for space, and a subtler and more harmonious palette of colors. Their predilection for pure landscape, influenced perhaps by the palace frescoes of Crete, is well exemplified in the wonderful marsh scenes which adorned the pavements of Akh-en-Aten's principal palace. Discovered by Sir Flinders Petrie in 1891-1892, these pavements subsequently suffered severe damage and were taken to Cairo for reconstruction. One of the ★pieces of painted pavement thus salvaged (fig. 179) was not used in the reconstruction and in 1920 was acquired in Cairo for the Metropolitan Museum. In it we see a stretch of green, blue, and yellow marsh with a widgeon, accurately drawn and naturalistically colored, perched on a flowering shrub, while on the right a clump of papyrus thrusts its green and dark red umbels into the scene. At the bottom is the banded, polychrome border of the panel. Two similar ★fragments of painted pavement, with ducks rising in flight out of clumps of papyrus plants, are from the Water Court of the so-called Precinct of the Southern Pool (*Maru-Aten*), near the south end of the ʿAmārneh plain.

Besides these original fragments our collection permits a study of some of the masterpieces of ʿAmārneh painting in a series of facsimile color ★copies brilliantly executed by Nina and Norman de Garis Davies. Included are a fourteen-foot copy of the great marsh scene in the so-called Green Room of the North Palace and a copy of the well-known painting from a private house showing the little Princesses Nefer-nefru-Aten and Nefer-nefru-Rēʿ seated on a cushion at the feet of their parents.

★Tiles and ★inlays of polychrome faience were used extensively in the decoration of the ʿAmārneh palaces, chiefly in the form of small, sometimes interlocking elements encrusted into stone door or window frames or balcony railings or arranged in rows to form ornamental friezes and dadoes at the tops and bottoms of wall surfaces. Floral motifs predominate, and among these the most popular are flat triangular inlays, engraved and colored to represent the flowers of the blue and white lotus, and elongated lotus bud inlays with convex surfaces. Parts of birds are also found, particularly the wings of birds in flight, and portions of human figures including, in our own collection, a complete little head of red faience with a black wig and black and white eyes. Rectangular tiles with marsh plants and flowering shrubs drawn on their surfaces in delicately colored polychrome glazes may have been fitted together to form scenes, but the examples so far recovered are too few and too fragmentary for us to be certain of this. Inlays carved in various colored stones were also used, and of these we possess ★part of a bird's wing in a light greenish "marble" with the outlines of the feathers engraved to take additional inlays.

Numerous pieces of jewelry and other items of personal adornment, some from el ʿAmārneh itself, others of unknown origin, are either associated directly with Akh-en-Aten and his family or show in one way or another the influence of his all-pervading personality. Among these none is perhaps more characteristic of the period than a type of openwork faience amulet in the form of a figure of the king, portrayed with unrelenting realism but represented as seated on the ground like a child with his knees drawn up and one finger held to his mouth in a traditionally infantile gesture. Though

FIGURE 179. Section of pavement from the Great Palace at el ʿAmārneh. Gouache on stucco and concrete. L. 20 ½ in.

he wears his customary pleated kilt and sometimes the Blue Crown or other royal headdress, there is no doubt that the pharaoh is meant to appear here as a child or, rather, as a child deity. An identification with the Child Horus (Harpokrates) has been suggested; but it seems more likely that what is intended is a representation of Akh-en-Aten as the "child of the Aten" and, thus, as a symbol of the life-giving power of the solar disk. Seven ★amulets of this type in our collection range in height from just under half an inch to just over an inch and an eighth. They are without exception of blue faience and are, also without exception, of unrecorded provenience. Two came to us as a gift of David Dows, together with a miscellany of more commonplace ★amulets, ★pendants, and necklace ★beads which are probably also to be dated to the ʿAmārneh period. The same curious little seated figure of the king, usually surmounted by the solar disk, is found engraved on the underside of a ★scarab in our own collection and on two small mud ★sealings from the Theban palace of Amun-ḥotpe III. Two faience ★amulets of closely related type have the form of the queen or of one of the ʿAmārneh princesses, shown seated on a throne and holding in one hand a lotiform fly-whisk. Akh-en-Aten's favorite epithet "Living-on-truth," combined with the titles "King of Upper and Lower Egypt" and "Son of Rēʿ," make up the openwork designs of three large ★amulets in blue faience, while three others of the same series comprise groups of amuletic hieroglyphs and, in one case, an elaborate palmette motif. A pair of little ★amuletic figures of the dwarf god Bēs, dancing and playing a tambourine, are said to have come from el ʿAmārneh itself. Not quite an inch and a half in height, one is of glossy bright green faience, the other of dark blue faience with touches of green on the arms and tambourine.

Small faience and sheet-metal ★cartouches with the names of the Aten and, less frequently, of the king were worn by devotees of the solar disk as dress ornaments (see fig. 173) and perhaps also as amuletic pendants in necklaces, bracelets, and the like. Each of the tiny plaquelike ornaments is provided with two or three points of attachment, which are either little rings projecting above and below the ends of the cartouche or small holes pierced through them near the edges. Their lengths range from five-eighths of an inch to two and a half inches, the last dimension being, however, exceptional. A single double cartouche of this class is of thin sheet gold. The rest of our twenty-one examples are of faience, the most popular colors being turquoise blue, bright yellow, violet, and white. On these little monuments the names of the Aten appear most frequently in their earlier form: "Rēʿ lives, Ḥor-akhty, who rejoices on the horizon in his name: Shu who is Aten." Four of our cartouches, however, carry the later version, in use only from the ninth year of the reign onward: "Rēʿ lives, Ruler of the Horizon, who rejoices on the horizon in his name: Rēʿ the Father, who has returned as Aten." Three of the smaller plaques contain the praenomen of Akh-en-Aten, "Nefer-khepru-Rēʿ, Sole-one-of-Rēʿ," and one the name of his queen, "Nefer-nefru-Aten Nefretity." The upper part of a ★uraeus in blue faience, also apparently an amulet, bears the second of the earlier Aten cartouches molded in relief on the breast of the royal serpent. A blue faience ★bead, purchased in New York in 1945, has the form of a double cartouche with Akh-en-Aten's throne and personal names.

Though of unrecorded provenience, a group of thirteen metal ★signet rings (fig. 180) of the heavy late Eighteenth Dynasty type are almost certainly from Tell el ʿAmārneh. In twelve cases their flat, oval bezels are engraved with the praenomen of Akh-en-Aten, who is invariably referred to as the "Sole-one-of-Rēʿ" and is sometimes also said to be "beloved" of Aten or of Rēʿ Ḥor-akhty. The thirteenth ring bears the king's personal name accompanied by the epithet "child of the Aten," written here, as elsewhere, with the figure of the pharaoh seated in the childish pose discussed above. Most of the rings are of copper, but there is a single example each of gold, electrum, and bronze. There is also a ★signet ring of the older type comprising a bronze scarab with Akh-en-Aten's throne name, swiveled on a tapered copper finger loop. The bezel of a massive bronze ★ring, found by the Egypt Exploration Society at el ʿAmārneh, carries a row of five engraved *nefer*-signs; and an elaborate gold ★ring, said also to be from el ʿAmārneh, has a bezel in the form of two cartouches side by side, each surmounted by the sun's disk and double plume and each containing a dancing figure of the god Bēs. The praenomen of Akh-en-Aten is found on the bezels of six fragile little ★finger rings of blue, red, and apple green faience, his personal name appears on two others, and a ninth carries the name of the Aten, followed by the expression "all beauty and life."

The scarabs and other seal amulets of this reign are not nearly as numerous as those of Akh-en-Aten's predecessors and successors, possibly because the scarab was associated with the ancient sun god Khepri, a theriomorphic deity not in tune with the doctrines of Atenism. In our collection only twelve ★scarabs, three ★cowroids, a ★cartouche plaque, and a ★*wedjat*-eye plaque bear the names of the royal "heretic"—in almost every instance his praenomen, Nefer-khepru-Rēʿ Wʿa-en-Rēʿ. The titles and epithets which on these seals sometimes accompany the king's name are an interesting and rather mixed lot. They include "Lord of Accomplishment," "appearing like Rēʿ," "beloved of (the goddess) Weret-ḥekau," "contented (with) truth," and "rich in posses-

FIGURE 180. Royal and other signet rings of the late Eighteenth Dynasty. Gold, silver, bronze, chalcedony, and faience. Diam. ¾-1 ⅛ in.

sions." Glazed steatite, as usual, is the favorite material, but one small scarab, engraved on the underside with the nomen Akh-en-Aten, is made of gold. A steatite scarab, formerly in the Carnarvon collection, was evidently carved at the beginning of the reign, for on it the king is called the "Good God, Nefer-khepru-Rēʿ, the Son of (Rēʿ), Amun-ḥotpe, Ruler of Thebes." Among hundreds of document *sealings from the palace of Amun-ḥotpe III at Thebes, one is stamped in several places with the throne name Nefer-khepru-Rēʿ, and two others carry seal impressions in which the king is referred to as the "child of Aten."

Small pottery *molds for the production of almost every type of faience element described above—amulets, plaques, rings, and seals—were found in the ruins of the workshops of Akhet-Aten. Well over two hundred examples were acquired by the Museum from the Amherst and Murch collections. Of these eighteen are molds for single and double cartouche plaques of Akh-en-Aten (praenomen and nomen), Nefret-ity, and the god Aten, whose names are invariably given in the earlier of the two forms. From the rest the glaziers of el ʿAmārneh produced little pendants of many different floral and vegetable designs, lotiform collar terminals, rosettes and rings for use as dress ornaments, the bezels and loops of finger rings, scarabs and cowroids, inlays and beads, individual hieroglyphic signs, *wedjat*-eyes and amuletic figures of the deities Bēs, Thoueris, and Ptaḥ Sokar, heads of the goddess Ḥat-Ḥor, and, as already noted, seated figures of the king in his role as the child of the Aten.

The graceful alabaster drinking *goblet of figure 181 was evidently carved early in the reign. In the engraved panel on its side we find the cartouches of the Aten given in their earlier form, the king referred to in his second cartouche as "Amun-ḥotpe, the God, Ruler of Thebes," and the name of the King's Great Wife, Nefret-ity, written without her Atenist praenomen. The cup itself is an object of great beauty, delicately carved in the form of an open flower of the white lotus, with walls of translucent thinness. It is said to have come, not from Tell el ʿAmārneh, but from a tomb "somewhere else in Upper Egypt,"[5] together with a handsome decanter in dark green

[5] Winlock, *M. M. A. Bulletin*, XVII (1922), p. 171.

FIGURE 181. Alabaster goblet with the names of Amun-ḥotpe IV and Queen Nefret-ity. H. 5 ½ in.

faience, a double *shawabty*-figure of a couple named Khaʿ-em-Wast and Mesyet (see p. 229), and a gold signet ring of Tūt-ʿankh-Amūn (see p. 300). The ★decanter, a long-necked globular vessel almost ten inches in height, also has a panel of inscription on its side, in this case molded in low relief and containing only the cartouches of the king and queen surmounted by plumes and resting on 𓋞-signs. The fact that here the pharaoh is called Akh-en-Aten and Nefret-ity has adopted the throne name Nefer-nefru-Aten suggests a date somewhat later in the reign than that assigned to the goblet. The two types of vessel, however, are not infrequently represented together in drinking scenes preserved to us in the tombs of the ʿAmārneh courtiers. Though only four and a half inches high, a little drop-shaped unguent ★jar of alabaster is elaborately inscribed, a panel of incised and blue-filled hieroglyphs on its side giving the names of the Aten, the titles and names of the king, and, following these, the titulary of an apparently hitherto unknown member of the latter's ḥarīm. In the three columns of text to the right of Akh-en-Aten's cartouches this woman, whose name suggests a foreign origin, is described as the "greatly beloved Wife of the King of Upper and Lower Egypt, Living-on-truth, Nefer-khepru-Rēʿ, the goodly child of the living Aten who shall live forever and ever, Keya."

Akh-en-Aten's burial place at Thebes (see p. 281) was discovered by Theodore M. Davis in the winter of 1907 and, on the strength of some of the larger inscribed objects found in it, was promptly —and mistakenly—called the tomb of Queen Tîyi.[6] An oblong wooden box in the southwest corner of the burial chamber of this tomb contained a quantity of small objects, chiefly funerary models of vessels and implements in faience and stone. A selection of the faience pieces brought to America by Mr. Davis includes a ★miniature bangle (◎) under an inch and a quarter in diameter, a ★model club of the type used by fullers (𓌉), two small ★bowls (▽) and a squat little ★situla, a ★miniature chest or jewel casket with a sloping lid, and a ★pendent ornament in the form of a bunch of grapes. Obviously mass produced and with their glazes now faded and discolored by dampness, these objects do not make a very brave show, but they are not untypical of the smaller items of funerary equipment found in other royal tombs of the late Eighteenth Dynasty. With them is a ★model of a butcher's knife (𓌪) carved of limestone and measuring six and three-quarters inches in length—less than a third the size of an actual knife of this class.

Six rectangular and trapezoidal sheets of heavy ★gold foil, fallen from the underside of the lid of the coffin, were found spread out over the mummy of the king. With the exception of a small piece engraved with a feather design they are quite plain. In size they range from seven and a half by six and an eighth inches to seventeen by seven

[6] Davis, *The Tomb of Queen Tîyi.*

and a quarter inches. The coffin itself, a magnificent anthropoid case heavily gilded and inlaid with colored glass, appears to have been designed originally for a woman.

One of the most curious and interesting monuments of Akh-en-Aten in our collection is a small L-shaped *pedestal of ivory with the upright arm of the L carved in the form of a round-topped stela. The top of the plinth behind the stela (the horizontal arm of the L) is grooved to receive the base of a little statuette of the king(?), who was probably represented as kneeling with hands upraised in an attitude of adoration. The front of the stela is engraved with the cartouches of Akh-en-Aten surmounted by the Aten disk with hands reaching downward from the ends of its life-giving rays. Below the cartouches and again on the opposite end of the plinth are the interlaced plants symbolizing the union of Upper and Lower Egypt. On the sides of the plinth tiny figures of foreigners—Nubians, Libyans, and Asiatics—kneel beside trays of offerings with hands extended in supplication to the pharaoh. We are reminded again of the great scenes in the tombs of the courtiers at el ʿAmārneh in which Akh-en-Aten, following the death of his father in the twelfth year of his reign, is shown receiving the tribute-bearing representatives of the nations of Africa and western Asia.

A less favorable and undoubtedly more accurate picture of the pharaoh's relations with his Asiatic contemporaries is provided for us by the famous ʿAmārneh Letters, a file of more than three hundred and sixty cuneiform tablets found in the ruins of the Records Office at Tell el ʿAmārneh and consisting chiefly of communications addressed to Amun-ḥotpe III and Akh-en-Aten by the kings of Hatti, Arzawa, Mitanni, Assyria, Babylonia, and Cyprus and by the city rulers and tribal chieftains of Palestine and Syria. Many of the letters contain pleas for help from the pharaoh's loyal vassals and allies—which in the case of those addressed to Amun-ḥotpe III at Thebes may never have reached their destination, and in the case of those addressed to Akh-en-Aten evidently did not receive the attention they deserved. In them we can follow the rapid decline of Egyptian power in hither Asia and the growth of a new Asiatic empire, that of the Hatti, or Hittites. Before the end of Akh-en-Aten's reign it would appear that all of Syria and Palestine had been lost, the former to the Hittite king, Suppiluliumas, the latter to local rebels and to bands of roving Bedawīn, among them the much discussed Habiru. The situation, more grave than any which had confronted Egypt since the days of the Hyksos, was too much for a man of Akh-en-Aten's unwarlike nature to cope with. As two ʿAmārneh Letters[7] in our own collection show, however, he continued for a while at least to command the respect of his Asiatic neighbors and on occasion sent, or planned to send, troops to the aid of his Syrian vassals.

Written in Akkadian, the diplomatic language of the period, the first of our two *letters (fig. 182) reads as follows: "To the king of Egypt thus speaks Ashur-uballit, king of Assyria: May it be well with you, your house, your wives, your chariots, and your warriors! I have sent my messenger to you in order to see you and to see your land. That which my father did not send have I now sent to you. One splendid chariot, two horses, and one . . . of beautiful lapis lazuli have I sent to you as a gift. The messenger whom I have sent to you to see . . . let him see and then go. Let him learn your desire and the desire of your land and then go." Our second tablet carries a letter from Abi-milki, prince of Tyre: "To the king my lord, thus Abi-milki your servant: Seven and seven times I fall down at your feet. What the king my lord has said, that I am carrying out. The whole land is afraid before the warriors of the king my lord. I have caused my people to man ships for the use of the warriors of the king my lord; and he who does not obey—his house is no more nor his strength. Behold I am protecting the city of the king my lord. And . . . the king my lord for his servant who is with him."

---

[7] Nos. 15 and 153 of Knudtzon, *Die el-Amarna-Tafeln.*

In Nubia, despite some building activity by Akh-en-Aten at Sesebi near the Third Cataract of the Nile, there seems also to have been a slackening of Egyptian control and a resulting decrease in the production of the all-important gold mines. In Egypt itself the king's preoccupation with his personal religion and his personal design for living had not only made him many enemies, but had led him to neglect his administrative responsibilities, so that outside of el ʿAmārneh itself disorder and corrupt practices by military and civil officials were added to the woes of a population already suffering from widespread unemployment and economic distress.

FIGURE 182. Clay tablet with a letter in Akkadian cuneiform from King Ashur-uballit I of Assyria to King Akh-en-Aten. H. 3 1/16 in.

Toward the end of his reign the pharaoh, ill and disillusioned, seems to have attempted, through his coregent Semenkh-ku-Rēʿ, a reconciliation with the adherents of the old state god Amūn, and in so doing to have offended Queen Nefret-ity to the extent that she withdrew, with her religious convictions and her youthful brother-in-law Tūtʿankh-Aten, to the extreme northern quarter of the residence city. There, presumably, she remained until the death of her husband, an event believed to have taken place in the eighteenth year of the reign, or, as has been estimated, about 1353 B.C. The manner and time of Nefret-ity's own demise and the place of her burial are unknown.

Each of Akh-en-Aten's three eldest daughters was, in her own way, a historical figure. Meryet-Aten and ʿAnkhes-en-pa-Aten, as we shall see presently, played important roles in the drama which followed their father's death. Meket-Aten, the second daughter, whose own death occurred when she was still a child, is remembered chiefly for the love borne her by her parents and for the uncontrolled and unabashed grief which they exhibit in the reliefs of her burial chamber. Of the many toys which this beloved little girl must have owned two have found their way into our collection. One is a minute gold *situla, neatly inscribed on the side with the title and name of the "King's Daughter, Meket-Aten." Only an inch and three-quarters high, it could have served as a drinking cup for one of the princess's dolls. The other toy, a miniature *palette of the type used by scribes and water-colorists, is carved of ivory (fig. 183). Its four oval inkwells contain cakes of different colored pigments—black, blue, and green(?)—and its tiny pen slot holds three carefully pointed writing rushes. Engraved in almost microscopic hieroglyphs on the slip of ivory which covers the lower half of this slot are the words "The King's own beloved daughter, Meket-Aten, born of the King's Great Wife Nefer-nefru-Aten Nefret-ity." They are followed by the in this case rather pathetic formula "May she live forever and ever!"

2. Semenkh-ku-Rēʿ and Meryet-Aten

Semenkh-ku-Rēʿ, the frail and ascetic-looking young man whom Akh-en-Aten selected as his coregent and successor, was apparently a son of Amun-ḥotpe III and the latter's daughter Sit-Amūn, and therefore both a half brother and nephew of the "heretic" king. The relationship was further enhanced and the young king's right to the throne strengthened by his marriage to Akh-en-Aten's eldest daughter, the Princess Meryet-Aten. About 1355 B.C. he was elevated to the coregency with the throne name ʿAnkh-khepru-Rēʿ and the epithets "holy of forms" and "beloved of Wʿa-en-Rēʿ" or "of Nefer-khepru-Rēʿ" (i.e., Akh-en-Aten). He also had conferred upon him the cognomen Nefer-nefru-Aten, formerly borne by Akh-en-Aten's estranged consort Nefret-ity, and in several of his inscriptions he uses this as his personal name in place of Semenkh-ku-Rēʿ. After a year or two at el ʿAmārneh he was apparently sent to Thebes as Akh-en-Aten's representative, and there, though he retained his Atenist names and epithets, he permitted the worship of the old gods to be resumed and in the mortuary temple which he built for himself at Thebes established an endowment to provide offerings for Amūn. The evidence for this is a Theban graffito dated to Semenkh-ku-Rēʿ's third regnal year and containing a prayer to Amūn recited by a "Priest and Scribe of the God's Offering of Amūn in the Mansion of ʿAnkh-khepru-Rēʿ at Thebes." In the same year or shortly thereafter the young pharaoh died, having outlived his older coregent by probably not more than a few months. His tomb has not been found and, curiously enough, a gilt shrine, a set of canopic coffins, and other funerary objects designed and executed specifically for his burial were not used in it but were appropriated by his successor, Tūt-ʿankh-Amūn.

Among the objects associated with the Theban burial of Akh-en-Aten (see p. 281) which Mr. Davis was allowed to retain for himself and which subsequently came with his collection to the Metropolitan Museum, is an alabaster ★canopic jar with a stopper carved in the form of the head of an ʿAmārneh princess (fig. 184). Though the panel of inscription on the side of the jar was carefully removed to conceal the identity of its original owner, there is considerable likelihood that the princess here portrayed was Semenkh-ku-Rēʿ's wife and Akh-en-Aten's eldest daughter, Meryet-Aten. It would also seem that the head was carved before Meryet-Aten became queen, for originally it carried no royal insignia, the hole on the brow for the uraeus and the body of the serpent outlined on the top of the headdress having been added

FIGURE 183.
Toy writing palette of the Princess Meket-Aten. Ivory. H. $5\frac{5}{16}$ in.

when the stopper was adapted for use by Akh-en-Aten. As Aldred has pointed out, "the refined idealism"[8] of this and Meryet-Aten's three other canopic heads, now in the Cairo Museum, "shows that they were made at a time when the excesses of the early Amarna style were already on the wane." This, in turn, suggests that the set to which our jar and stopper belong was executed at el ʿAmārneh between the ninth and fourteenth years, 1362-1357 B.C., of the reign of Akh-en-Aten. Here the liveliness of the charming little portrait was heightened by inlaying the rims and brows of the eyes with dark blue glass and the irises with obsidian. The graceful valanced wig affected by the royal ladies of el ʿAmārneh is reproduced in exceptional detail and, as on other royal canopic jars of this general period, the shoulder of the stopper is adorned with an elaborate broad collar.

The Museum possesses no inscribed objects of Meryet-Aten, either as a queen or a princess, but two copper ★signet rings from el ʿAmārneh and four blue faience ★rings of unknown origin carry Semenkh-ku-Rēʿ's throne name followed by the epithet "holy of forms," or by the expression "beloved of Nefer-khepru-Rēʿ."

A large openwork ★amulet of green-glazed steatite representing an infant pharaoh being suckled by a queen or goddess belongs stylistically to the ʿAmārneh period, and the emaciated features of the young king are so like the existing portraits of Semenkh-ku-Rēʿ that there is rather more than a possibility that the piece was carved during his reign. On his head the pharaoh of our amulet wears the Double Crown and the single braided side lock which betokens his boyhood. He is nude except for a broad collar, armlets, and bracelets, and his figure with its broad hips and skinny arms is of the ʿAmārneh type. The larger figure of his human or divine nurse (the goddess Isis?) is clad in a long, tight-fitting dress and a full, curly wig with a uraeus rising from the brow and, above, a cylindrical tiara drilled on top to receive a pair of gold(?) plumes. Formerly in the MacGregor collection, this interesting little monument is illustrated by Henry Wallis in his *Egyptian Ceramic Art* (1898), figure 24.

[8] *New Kingdom Art in Ancient Egypt,* p. 84.

3. Tūt-ʿankh-Aten Becomes Tūt-ʿankh-Amūn

With the death of Semenkh-ku-Rēʿ the throne of Egypt passed to his younger brother, Tūt-ʿankh-Aten, a boy of nine or ten who seems to have remained at el ʿAmārneh with the dowager queen Nefret-ity and to have been married to her second surviving daughter, the Princess ʿAnkhes-en-pa-Aten. With them no doubt was Nefret-ity's father, the elderly army officer Ay, who had been one of Akh-en-Aten's most favored courtiers and who evidently still exercised a strong influence on the affairs of the dynasty and of the nation. This was the group which had remained loyal to the Aten in the face of Akh-en-Aten's and Semenkh-ku-Rēʿ's relapse into orthodoxy, but which was itself soon to recognize the advisability of returning to the old religion and to the traditions under which Egypt had attained greatness. For perhaps three years Tūt-ʿankh-Aten ruled from el ʿAmārneh and then, guided by his older advisers, he transferred his residence to Thebes and, shortly before or shortly after doing so, changed his name to Tūt-ʿankh-Amūn and that of his queen to ʿAnkhes-en-Amūn. The steps which he took to re-establish order in the land and to restore the temple images and temple properties of Amūn and his fellow divinities are described on a big quartzite stela set up at Karnak, and the newly revived ceremonies honoring Amūn on the occasion of the great Feast of Opet were recorded during his reign in a series of wonderful reliefs in the Luxor temple. One of the more important monuments testifying to Tūt-ʿankh-Amūn's devotion to Amūn is a magnificent diorite group in the Louvre in which the god appears as an over life-size seated figure with hands extended forward to grasp in a protective gesture the shoulders of a much smaller, standing figure of the pharaoh.

FIGURE 184. Princess Meryet-Aten (?). Alabaster canopic jar stopper adapted for use in the burial of King Akh-en-Aten. H. 7 in.

FIGURE 185. Head of the god Amūn with the features of King Tūt-ʿankh-Amūn. Diorite. Provenience unknown. H. 17 in.

From similar groups, one in porphyritic diorite, the other in indurated limestone, come two heads (figs. 185, 186) in our collection, both of which have the round boyish face inherited by Tūt-ʿankh-Amūn from his father, Amun-ḥotpe III. Both heads are executed in a style derived unmistakably from the art of el ʿAmārneh in its later, more moderate phase (cf. fig. 176) and show at the same time a degree of idealization and refinement which we associate with earlier temple statues. The diorite ★head is from a figure of the god Amūn somewhat larger in scale than that of the Louvre group, but otherwise very like it. The god is readily identified by his slender, braided chin beard and his distinctive cap from the top of which once towered two tall stone plumes. The back pilaster, from which the head is thrust forward on a long, sloping neck, is uninscribed, which suggests that the figure was designed to stand with its back against a wall or pier of the temple.

The group to which our limestone ★head belonged represented the symbolic coronation of the king by an anthropomorphic deity, again in all probability the state god Amūn. In this group the pharaoh appeared at much reduced scale, standing before a life-size figure of the god, whose right hand was stretched out to set the Blue Crown on the king's head (fig. 186). Despite the fact that it is only about half life size our head is among the more sensitive and lifelike portraits of Tūt-ʿankh-Amūn which have survived. Rich in detail, it shows us the piercing of the king's ear lobes and all the minor characteristics of the Blue Crown, including the ribbed streamers which descend from its back. Not many three-dimensional coronation groups have survived, but representations of the pharaoh receiving his crown from a divinity are fairly common in reliefs and paintings of the New Kingdom —notably in the Luxor temple reliefs of Tūt-ʿankh-Amūn's father, Amun-ḥotpe III. Though its subject matter suggests a Theban origin, it is not impossible that the group of which our small head once formed a part was carved at el ʿAmārneh, both its style and the hard marblelike stone of which it is made being compatible with such a provenience.

The bezel of a massive gold ★signet ring, believed to have come from the tomb of an important Upper Egyptian official (see p. 294), is engraved with Tūt-ʿankh-Amūn's praenomen, "Neb-khepru-Rēʿ," surrounded in the oval field by the words "beloved of Amun Rēʿ, Lord of Eternity" (fig. 180, bottom right). It is amusing to note that in the word for "eternity," even though it occurs in an epithet of the god Amūn, the engraver had not yet broken himself of the habit of using the Aten disk with the pendent sign for "life." The ring itself weighs 73.2 grams, or "as much as four or five large modern signet rings." Winlock has estimated that in antiquity the gold contained in this single ring would have purchased "at least nine or ten acres of good

FIGURE 186. King Tūt-ʿankh-Amūn. Head of the pharaoh from a coronation group in indurated limestone. H. 6 in.

farming land," or "enough to support a fairly prosperous family."[9]

Elsewhere in our collection the king's throne name, Neb-khepru-Rēʿ, is found on two faience ★finger rings, three faience ★cartouche plaques and five small pottery ★molds from el ʿAmārneh, a green glass(?) ★scarab where it is flanked by kneeling figures, and a glazed steatite ★scarab on which the pharaoh is represented as a sphinx trampling on a fallen enemy. It occurs also on a mud ★sealing used to secure the cloth wrapping of a hoard of scrap metal found at el Lisht (see p. 190), on a second ★sealing where it again accompanies the figure of the victorious royal sphinx, and, inlaid in brown and white glaze, on a small blue faience ★knob from the end of a staff or scepter. The personal name, "Tūt-ʿankh-Amūn, Ruler of On of Upper Egypt," is molded in the bezels of three faience ★finger rings, one of which is from a private tomb at Abydos. Here, as elsewhere, "On of Upper Egypt" is an expression for Thebes. Two other faience ★rings, one from the excavations of the Egypt Exploration Fund at Sedment, carry the name of Queen ʿAnkhes-en-Amūn, as does also a small mud document ★sealing from the Theban palace of Amun-ḥotpe III.

[9] *M. M. A. Bulletin*, XVII (1922), p. 172.

When in the ninth or tenth year of his reign Tūt-ʿankh-Amūn died before having reached his twentieth birthday, his tomb in the western branch of the Valley of the Tombs of the Kings was apparently not yet ready for occupancy and he was buried in the main valley in a small tomb which had probably been prepared for the queen's grandfather, Ay, the old soldier who had recently had added to his long list of honors the office of Vizier. It was here in the autumn of 1922 that the Earl of Carnarvon and Howard Carter found the young pharaoh encased in his gold and inlaid coffins and surrounded by his incredibly rich funerary equipment and personal belongings. Those who have not visited the suite of galleries in the Cairo Museum where the contents of Tūt-ʿankh-Amūn's tomb are exhibited may acquire an idea of the sheer bulk of material involved in this find from the fact that in our files Harry Burton's photographic record of this material alone comprises almost fourteen hundred negatives. It is an astounding testimonial to the splendor of the period and to the skill and productivity of the royal ateliers that during his brief reign this relatively unimportant pharaoh could have amassed such a wealth of beautiful and costly objects, and it speaks well for the devotion and integrity of those who laid him to rest that he was able to carry this breath-taking treasure with him into the hereafter.

In preparation for burial the body of the king was elaborately mummified, loaded with jewelry, and swathed in fine linen wrappings, and as one of the final rites in the burial service a funerary banquet in which at least eight persons participated was served in or near the tomb. At the completion of the rites the materials and equipment left over from the embalming process and the vessels and other objects used at the funerary meal were carefully packed in big pottery jars and deposited in a rock-cut pit more than a hundred yards to the southeast of the mouth of the tomb. Here in 1908 they were found by Theodore Davis, and in the following year were contributed by him to the Museum's then small and struggling Egyptian Department. For our permanent collection we have retained one of the huge whitewashed ★jars in which the cache was stowed and fourteen pottery ★dishes, ★bowls, and ★vases from the table service used at the funerary banquet, including an elegant long-necked wine bottle (fig. 187) finished

FIGURE 187. Pottery wine jar from a funerary cache of King Tūt-ʿankh-Amūn. H. 14½ in.

with a polished dark red slip and decorated with bands of floral ornaments in pale blue, red, and black. A dozen ★stoppers from the larger food and beverage jars are made of strips of papyrus pith folded back and forth to form flat, circular plugs. Two big mud ★sealings are painted blue and stamped in several places with the official seal of the royal necropolis—the canine animal of Anubis crouching above nine bound enemies. Smaller mud ★sealings from boxes, baskets, or jars bear the names of Tūt-ʿankh-Amūn and the epithets "son of Ptaḥ," "beloved of Chnūm," and "rich in favors." Three of the floral ★broad collars worn by guests at the banquet are made up of real leaves and flowers—the collar shown in figure 188, for example, being composed of olive leaves, cornflowers, and berries of the woody nightshade interspersed with thin blue faience disk beads, the whole strung on strips of palm leaf and sewed to a backing of papyrus.

FIGURE 188. Floral broad collar worn by a guest at King Tūt-ʿankh-Amūn's funerary banquet. Diam. 18 ½ in.

The mass of linen cloth left over from the embalming and wrapping of the king's mummy included three semicircular ★kerchiefs, or wig covers, each made up of two thicknesses of cloth sewn together around the edges and provided with a binding tape, the ends of which were carried back from the sides of the straight forehead band and tied together at the back of the wearer's head. A woven linen ★bandage, or tape, two and three-eighths inches wide and over five feet in length, is one of fifty found in the cache. Unlike the usual Egyptian mummy bandages, which are simply strips torn from sheets, it has a finished selvage along both its edges. Two of the many ★sheets found are inscribed in black ink with the titles and throne name of Tūt-ʿankh-Amūn and are dated, respectively, to Regnal Years 6 and 8, the latter having been apparently the next to last year of the young pharaoh's life.

In the mouth of the first of the big jars opened Mr. Davis found an attractive little cartonnage ★mask of the type placed over bundles containing the viscera of the deceased so that they resembled miniature mummies (see fig. 189). The stucco-covered surface of the mask, including the beardless face, is painted yellow with the stripes of the headdress and the details of the jewelry added in blue. Red is used only on one of the bands of the broad collar and on the lotiform ends of its tie cords. The nose had apparently been broken in antiquity—perhaps before the mask was placed in the jar. It is difficult to see what connection this single canopic mask could have had with the mummification or burial of Tūt-ʿankh-Amūn, whose viscera were found in his canopic chest encased in four miniature gold coffins.

During the reign of the youthful pharaoh the man who seems actually to have controlled the affairs of the nation and what remained of the empire was the Commander in Chief of the Army Ḥor-em-ḥēb. Having, presumably, served with distinction under Amun-ḥotpe III and Akh-en-Aten, Ḥor-em-ḥēb was now able to refer to himself, probably quite accurately, as the "Deputy of the King in Front of the Two Lands." For Tūt-ʿankh-Amūn he led at least one successful expedition into Palestine and another into Nubia, restoring Egyptian prestige in these areas at least to the extent that African and Asiatic tribute once

FIGURE 189. Miniature mask of linen and plaster from a funerary cache of Tūt-ʿankh-Amūn. H. 6 in.

again flowed into the pharaonic treasury in appreciable quantities. Though a native of Ḥe-nēsu in Middle Egypt he appears to have made his headquarters at Memphis, and it is from the superb reliefs which once adorned his tomb at Saḳḳāreh that most of our knowledge of this phase of his career is derived.

To the same period in the life of this future king belongs a well-known diorite *statue in our collection (fig. 190) which is believed to have come from the temple of Ptaḥ at Memphis and in which Ḥor-em-ḥēb, like other great men of his time, chose to have himself represented as a scribe. Here we see him seated cross-legged on the ground, looking up from a half-open roll of papyrus in which he has just finished writing a long and rather turgid hymn to the god Tḥōt. His right hand which held the writing rush is broken away, but on his left knee is his ink shell with its two cakes of writing pigment, and carved in low relief on the chest and back of his figure are the scribe's palette, bowl, and pen case in their traditional, or hieroglyphic, form ([hieroglyph]). A small figure of the god Amūn engraved on the general's right forearm may have been an amulet or just possibly a tattoo. Like the reliefs from Ḥor-em-ḥēb's Saḳḳāreh tomb, to which it is very closely related, our statue belongs to a late, typically Memphite phase of the ʿAmārneh style, its delicate, intellectual face and soft, effeminate form harking back to an ideal established years earlier under Akh-en-Aten. The adjective "Buddhalike" has been not ineptly applied to the figure, the mood of which is serene, contemplative, and a trifle melancholy. Great technical skill has been expended by the sculptor in reproducing the details of the general's foppish attire—his long, wavy wig, the flaring sleeves of his diaphanous shirt, and his intricately pleated kilt with the flouncelike apron in front. In keeping with his unwarlike appearance Ḥor-em-ḥēb's titles as given on the present statue (and elsewhere) indicate that he was primarily a military official rather than a combat, or front line, officer. They include Hereditary Prince and Count, Fanbearer on the King's Right Hand, Commander in Chief of the Army, King's Scribe, and Deputy of the King in Front of the Two Lands. The inscriptions around the base of the statue are offering formulae invoking Tḥōt, Lord of Hieroglyphs and Lord of Hermopolis, Ptaḥ south of his wall, Sakhmet beloved of Ptaḥ, Ptaḥ Sokar, Lord of Shetyet, and Osiris, Lord of Ro-setau—the last four being deities local to the region of Memphis. In one of the brief speeches which follow the invocations proper, Ḥor-em-ḥēb boasts of his punctiliousness in suppressing crime and lawlessness, in a manner anticipatory of the decree which he later issued as king and of the reforms which he introduced at that time (see p. 309).

The activities of another of Tūt-ʿankh-Amūn's great officials, the Viceroy of Nubia Ḥuy, are known to us chiefly from the intensely interesting paintings in his tomb chapel (No. 40) on the eastern slope of the Ḳurnet Muraʿi in western Thebes.

FIGURE 190. General Ḥor-em-ḥēb portrayed as a scribe. H. 46 in.

FIGURE 191. Woser-ḥēt and his wife, Nefret-iry, on a limestone votive stela from Deir el Baḥri. L. 19 in.

A tempera ★copy over seventeen feet in length executed by Charles K. Wilkinson reproduces for us at full scale and in full color the great scene in the forehall of this tomb in which Ḥuy presents to Tūt-ʿankh-Amūn the princes of northern and southern Nubia with their families, followers, and tribute. Three other color ★copies, also by Mr. Wilkinson, show us the Viceroy's luxuriously appointed Nile ship, or dahabīyeh, two tribute-laden ships of the Nubian princes, and a pair of freight boats being hauled over a sand bar. Of these and other tomb paintings of the period Norman de Garis Davies has said: "The tomb of Ḥuy is a strange blend of dullness and brilliancy, of features derived from the revolutionary era and others which forecast the tasteless and lifeless Ramesside style. These tombs therefore bear witness to the bewildered hesitancy in which Theban art stood for a while before it subsided into the long monotony of the later sepulchral art."[10]

Since, despite his return to orthodoxy, Tūt-ʿankh-Amūn was regarded by his successors as an Atenist interloper not entitled to be included in the official lists of Egypt's rulers, it is unlikely that his mortuary temple near Medīnet Habu was maintained for any length of time after his death. Indeed, two quartzite colossi of the young pharaoh made for this temple were inscribed for his immediate successor, Ay, and shortly thereafter were usurped by Ḥor-em-ḥēb. It would seem, therefore, that a High Priest of Tūt-ʿankh-Amūn's mortuary temple named Woser-ḥēt, who appears with his wife on a fragmentary ★stela (fig. 191) from Deir el Baḥri, must have been a contemporary or near contemporary of Tūt-ʿankh-Amūn himself. On the stela Woser-ḥēt and his wife, Nefret-iry, are represented kneeling side by side with hands upraised in prayer, their delicately modeled faces and slender figures retaining much that is reminiscent of the art of el ʿAmārneh. Except that he wears no wig and has adorned his neck with a broad collar and a double-stranded necklace of lenticular beads, the man's elaborate attire is closely similar to that which we have just seen on the diorite statue of Ḥor-em-ḥēb. Nefret-iry has topped off the fashionable costume of a lady of the late Eighteenth Dynasty with a lotus flower and a cone of perfumed ointment of the kind worn at banquets and on other festive occasions. In the columns of inscription immediately in front of his figure Woser-ḥēt calls himself the "Accountant of All the Goodly Property in the Mansion (i.e., mortuary temple) of Neb-maʿet-Rēʿ (Amun-ḥotpe III) and the First Prophet of [Amūn(?) . . .] in the Mansion of Neb-khepru-Rēʿ (Tūt-ʿankh-Amūn)." He then goes on to say with refreshing (and unusual) modesty: "I was one calm and . . . [of lo]ve, one patient and careful in my language. I was one content with [his] lot [and not] rapacious. I went on my way without deviating from it. I put my trust in my god and he was responsive." The columns of text above the figure of Nefret-iry tell us that besides being the Mistress of a House and a Favorite of Ḥat-Ḥor she was, like many of her well-to-do contemporaries, a Chantress in the temple choir of the god Amūn.

[10] Davies and Gardiner, *The Tomb of Ḥuy*, p. 3.

4. The God's Father Ay

Tūt-ᶜankh-Amūn was the last male descendant of the Thutmoside pharaohs, and when he died without having produced an heir the throne of Egypt suddenly became a prize for anyone who could successfully lay claim to it. The first to try was the widowed queen, ᶜAnkhes-en-Amūn, who, realizing that her chances of ruling in her own right were small, induced Suppiluliumas, the king of the Hittites, to send her his son, Prince Zannanza, to be her consort and share the crown with her. Fortunately for Egypt's future autonomy the Hittite prince was assassinated while en route to his wedding—probably by agents of the omniscient and omnipotent Ḥor-em-ḥēb. ᶜAnkhes-en-Amūn, however, was not long to remain unwed. With Ḥor-em-ḥēb's undoubted connivance she became the official queen of her own grandfather, the Vizier Ay, who, with his claims thus reinforced by a marriage to an heiress of the royal line, was enabled to assume the throne in time to officiate as king at Tūt-ᶜankh-Amūn's funeral.

For his throne name Ay adopted the conventional form Kheper-khepru-Rēᶜ, adding to it his favorite epithet "doer of right"; but in his nomen cartouche he retained his old title, Father of the God, which he had acquired as Akh-en-Aten's father-in-law, thereby reminding his subjects of his long-standing relationship with the royal family. On the lintel blocks of a colonnade which he erected at Karnak he was at pains to emphasize his close association with his predecessor, setting Tūt-ᶜankh-Amūn's titulary below his own on one side of the lintel and referring to the young king as his "son." The principal monuments of Ay's brief reign are a rock-cut shrine in the cliffs behind his home town of Akhmīm and the imposing mortuary temple which he built for himself immediately to the north of Medīnet Habu. Far up the Nubian Nile at Shatawi, above Abu Simbel, he is represented in another rock shrine making offering to a group of divinities.

FIGURE 192. A king of the late Eighteenth Dynasty, perhaps Ay. Red granite. H. 10 in.

In the Museum's collection Ay's kingly praenomen, "Kheper-khepru-Rēᶜ Iry-maᶜet," is found on a glazed steatite ★scarab from the northern cemetery at el Lisht and, inlaid in light blue glaze, on a large ★knob in violet faience coming either from the top of a cane or from an article of furniture. On the knob the cartouche is flanked by crowned uraei, rests upon a *nebu*-sign, and is surmounted by a solar disk. In the cartouche on an altogether similar ★knob we read "The God's Father, Ay, the God, Ruler of Thebes," and this occurs also on the bezel of a bright green faience ★finger ring from a private tomb at Abydos.

The few existing portraits of Ay, including perhaps a plaster mask from el ᶜAmārneh, show us a narrow, bony face with rather small, squinty eyes and a long, slender nose. Such a face is seen on a red granite royal ★head (fig. 192) found by our Egyptian Expedition in the forecourt of Ḥatshepsūt's temple at Deir el Baḥri. The king represented wears a *nemes* and uraeus of late Eighteenth

Dynasty type, and the carving of the face—notably the treatment of the expressive, thick-lipped mouth—has in it more than a little of the ʿAmārneh tradition. The identification, which of course is far from certain, was suggested, with strong reservations, by Cyril Aldred.

A representation of King Ay at the window of his palace is found in the tomb chapel of one of his Theban contemporaries, the Chief Scribe of Amūn, Nefer-ḥotep (Tomb 49). Other scenes in this tomb show its owner and his wife on a visit to the temple of Amūn at Karnak, the same couple offering to the deified King Amun-ḥotpe I, and Nile boats laden with mourners on their way to Nefer-ḥotep's funeral. In 1933 the tomb was published in behalf of the Metropolitan Museum by Norman de Garis Davies and our collection was enriched by ★copies of these three scenes prepared in color by Mrs. Davies. One of Nefer-ḥotep's ★funerary cones is also in the Museum's collection, having been acquired in 1909 as a gift of Herbert E. Winlock.

As Ḥor-em-ḥēb had no doubt anticipated, the reign of his old companion in arms was not a long one. Within four or five years Ay was dead and laid to rest in the western branch of the Valley of the Tombs of the Kings in a tomb (No. 23) which scholars now believe had been prepared originally for Tūt-ʿankh-Amūn (see p. 302). Here were found Ay's handsome granite sarcophagus and, on the walls of the burial chamber, paintings in which he is accompanied not by ʿAnkhes-en-Amūn but by his older wife Ty, her name enclosed within a cartouche and preceded by the titles of queen. The fact that the sarcophagus was smashed and the names and faces of the king and his wife were erased from the wall paintings has led to speculation as to whether Ay actually was buried in this tomb or in a secret cache somewhere in the vicinity.

5. Ḥor-em-ḥēb and the Restoration

At Ay's death in 1339 B.C. the throne, to the surprise of no one, passed to Ḥor-em-ḥēb. Thus the man who, in the words of a text describing his coronation, had "acted as viceregent of" Egypt "over a period of many years"[11] became at last its king. The coronation itself was performed at Thebes, with Ḥor-em-ḥēb making a dramatic entrance into the temple of Amūn at the time of the great Feast of Opet and receiving from the god his crowns and his pharaonic titulary, including his throne name as King of Upper and Lower Egypt, "Djeser-khepru-Rēʿ Chosen-of-Rēʿ."

In our collection this name is preserved on a faience ★finger ring from a private tomb at Abydos, on a small ★cartouche plaque in green-glazed steatite, and on three ★scarabs, one of red jasper, the two others of blue-glazed steatite. On the steatite scarab it is surmounted by a winged sun's disk and by the name of the god Ptaḥ flanked by falcons and is accompanied by the expressions "beloved of Ptaḥ, Lord of Heaven," and "beloved of Amūn, Lord of Eternity." More common is the king's personal name, "Ḥor-em-ḥēb Mery-Amūn," which occurs on seven faience ★rings, one from near the South Pyramid at el Lisht, on two ★cartouche plaques, and on three ★scarabs, all of glazed steatite. This name is found also on four pottery ★molds for ring bezels and, inlaid in gold, on the shaft of a large bronze ★*tyet*-symbol where it is followed by the words "beloved of Sobk." Part of the ★shaft of a divine standard in gray basalt comes evidently from a large standing statuette of the king. It is inscribed for ". . . the Son of [Rēʿ], Ḥor-em-ḥēb Mery-Amūn, beloved of Tḥōt, Lord of Hermopolis, he who is in the midst of the Hare Nome."

Though he had risen to power in the service of the Atenist pharaohs, Ḥor-em-ḥēb, upon becoming king himself, directed a portion of his very considerable energies toward obliterating the memory of his four predecessors, from Akh-en-Aten to Ay inclusive, and destroying every trace of their god. The city of Akhet-Aten, which was

---

[11] Inscription on a statue of Ḥor-em-ḥēb and Queen Mūt-nedjemet in Turin as translated by Gardiner in *The Journal of Egyptian Archaeology*, XXXIX (1953), p. 14.

perhaps still inhabited at the beginning of his reign, he razed to the ground, methodically smashing every piece of sculpture which had adorned the temples of the no longer "living" Aten. At Karnak he dismantled Akh-en-Aten's temple and used the sculptured blocks from it for the foundations and fill of the three great pylons (Pylons II, IX, and X) which he added to the temple of Amūn.

Beside the tenth pylon was set up a huge stela with the copy of a decree issued by Ḥor-em-ḥēb as part of a more constructive program, aimed at restoring to the country the order and prosperity which it had enjoyed previous to the ʿAmārneh debacle. The decree in question contains regulations intended to expedite the collection of national revenues and at the same time alleviate the suffering of the citizenry by abolishing graft and corruption among military and civil officials and by "packing" the courts of the land with men "of good character," chiefly priests and "lay officials of the residence."

Engrossed during most of his long and conscientious reign with internal problems, the ex-general had little opportunity for large-scale military operations abroad. A single campaign or tour of inspection into Kush and a trading expedition to Pwēnet served to maintain Egypt's ascendancy over Nubia and the lands to the south; and a treaty which is believed to have been concluded at this time with the Hittites helped to safeguard the pharaoh's holdings in Palestine.

Probably the activity which most effectively strengthened Ḥor-em-ḥēb's hold on the throne and ensured his acceptance by his successors was his rehabilitation of the temples, temple properties, and priesthoods of Amūn and other leading divinities. Some historians have felt that in this he went too far and purchased the recognition of later generations "by an abdication of the traditional supremacy of the pharaoh, surrendering much of his over-all authority to the priesthood and the civil courts."[12]

However that may be, he was certainly regarded by posterity as the first legitimate successor of Amun-ḥotpe III, and in the official lists of the Ramesside period his name follows immediately after that of the earlier pharaoh. In the oft-cited scene in Tomb 19 at Thebes, preserved to us in Charles Wilkinson's color ★copy, his statue occupies the fourth place in the second row, between those of Amun-ḥotpe III and Ramesses I. A "Regnal Year 59" attributed to him in a court record of the Nineteenth Dynasty indicates that in official documents of the later New Kingdom the years of his reign were counted from the moment when Akh-en-Aten first came to power. Actually, Ḥor-em-ḥēb seems to have ruled for a total of thirty-five or thirty-six years, dying at an advanced age in or about 1304 B.C.

His tomb (No. 57) in the Valley of the Tombs of the Kings has the long, straight plan inaugurated by his Atenist predecessors and adopted by his Ramesside successors. From the rock-cut entrance of the tomb a series of stairways and sloping passages lead downward over a protective well to a columned sepulchral hall and sunken crypt in which rests the pharaoh's magnificent granite sarcophagus, its corners adorned in high relief with figures of winged goddesses. Of the sarcophagus and the carved and painted decoration of the hall and the preceding chambers we have, besides Harry Burton's complete photographic record, eight color ★copies made for Theodore M. Davis, the discoverer of the tomb, by Lancelot Crane. ★Fragments of two pottery wine jars, found by Mr. Davis in the vicinity of the tomb, are inscribed in hieratic with the name of a funerary foundation of "Ḥor-em-ḥēb Beloved-of-Amūn . . . in the House of Amūn."

For his mortuary temple Ḥor-em-ḥēb simply took over and completed the temple of Ay at Medīnet Habu, substituting his name for that of his predecessor on portions of the building which already existed and on a pair of colossal quartzite statues which Ay himself had "borrowed" from Tūt-ʿankh-Amūn. Among the antiquities recovered from the ruins of this temple is a ★sculptor's

[12] Wilson, *The Culture of Ancient Egypt*, p. 239.

trial piece—a slab of limestone six and three-quarters inches long, with studies in relief for two male heads in left profile, a small standing figure of a king, a large human hand, and a group of crinkly locks from a long headdress. The more complete of the two heads shows us a thin, youthful face of ʿAmārneh type with slanting eyes, a slightly retroussé nose, and a small, sulky mouth. The lobes of the ears are represented as pierced for studs or earrings. The headdress, a perfectly plain, long wig cover, is noncommittal as to the rank of the person portrayed. Possibly a portrait of either Ay or Ḥor-em-ḥēb was intended. The upper part of the small standing figure is missing, but the elaborate kilt with pendent bull's tail and inlaid metal apron is of the type worn by pharaohs of the later New Kingdom.

Among the few private tomb chapels in the Theban necropolis datable to the reign of Ḥor-em-ḥēb, that of the God's Father of Amun Rēʿ, Nefer-ḥotep (No. 50), is notable for the songs of the harpers who participate in its principal banquet scene and for its remarkable painted ceilings. Of the latter Charles Wilkinson has given us two fine color ★copies (one a restored version) of a section of ceiling on which spirals, palmettes, grasshoppers, and cows' heads are effectively combined in an unusual over-all pattern. Three ★funerary cones inscribed for a Fourth Prophet of Amūn named Nefer-ḥotep may or may not have come from this tomb.

The fragments of a papyrus ★Book of the Dead of late Eighteenth Dynasty style suffice to show that it was a manuscript of the highest quality written in a beautiful hieroglyphic hand and illustrated with large and harmoniously colored scenes and figures. The few remaining scraps of this once fine roll preserve portions of Chapter I of the Book of the Dead and of several other long spells of the same type. It bears the name of the "Scribe Roy" and comes from the Dirāʿ Abu'n Naga in western Thebes, not far from the tomb (No. 255) of the King's Scribe Roy who was also a Steward in the Estate of Ḥor-em-ḥēb and probably one of the king's contemporaries.

As his right-hand man and successor on the throne Ḥor-em-ḥēb chose an old comrade in arms, Pa-Ramesses, son of the Troop Commander Sēthy, whose family resided in the northeast Delta and worshiped the god Sēth of Avaris. During the reign of his friend and patron Pa-Ramesses, later known to us as King Ramesses I, the founder of the Nineteenth Dynasty, served not only as a top-ranking military officer and as a royal emissary to foreign lands, but also as Vizier, Chief Justice, Overseer of Priests, and "Vice-regent of His Majesty in Upper and Lower Egypt." The offices of Vizier and Troop Commander were likewise held by Pa-Ramesses's son, Sēthy, another of Ḥor-em-ḥēb's ranking officials and Egypt's future kings. It was apparently as an official of Ḥor-em-ḥēb that Sēthy, on the four hundredth anniversary of the occupation of Avaris by the Hyksos, made the visit to the temple of Sēth which is recorded on the Stela of the Year 400 (see p. 4), a monument erected on the site of Avaris during the reign of Ramesses II.

6. The Late Eighteenth Dynasty in Art and Craftsmanship

The Museum's collection is rich in attractive small objects produced during the reigns of the ʿAmārneh and post-ʿAmārneh pharaohs. The imagination, sense of design, and great technical skill exhibited by some of these pieces suggest that they were products of the royal ateliers and that they came originally from royal tombs or palaces. Since, however, they bear no kings' names and in most cases are insufficiently complex to be datable stylistically to one or another individual reign, they are best considered as a group and assigned en masse to the late Eighteenth Dynasty. This is true also of bits of relief, *shawabty*-figures, and the like which had belonged to officials and other well-to-do citizens of the same general period whose association with any particular pharaoh cannot be established. These nonhistorical and occasionally frivolous works of art and craftsmanship are sometimes characterized by an elegance, taste, and technical virtuosity reminiscent of the court ateliers of Amun-ḥotpe III, sometimes by the informality and mannered naturalism of the ʿAmārneh school, and sometimes—in works which were perhaps produced in the time of Tūt-ʿankh-Amūn and Ay and during the early years of the reign of Ḥor-em-ḥēb—by a rather pleasant combination of both styles. A few of the obviously later pieces are beginning to exhibit the stereotyped formality or empty fussiness which heralds the approach of the Ramesside period.

FIGURE 193. The god Amūn. Dark gray diorite. H. 20 ½ in.

A handsome diorite ★head of the god Amūn (fig. 193), though tending toward the cold conventionality of Ramesside temple sculpture, still retains the clean, crisp modeling which we associate with the earlier New Kingdom and shows just a trace of the ʿAmārneh type in its pleasant, youthful face. It has been dated, probably quite correctly, to the last years of the Eighteenth or the very beginning of the Nineteenth Dynasty. The perfect preservation of Amūn's tall, plumed cap provides us with a rare opportunity of studying this strange and interesting headdress in a detailed three-dimensional representation. The head, purchased in Cairo in 1907, is about two-thirds life size.

To the late Eighteenth or early Nineteenth Dynasty is probably also to be dated the upper half of a large slate ★statuette representing an unidentified king holding before him a naos (𓉴), on the front of which are carved figures of the god Amūn and his consort the goddess Mūt. Most of the king's crown has been broken away and the inlays are missing from his eyes and eyebrows. So also is his long pharaonic beard, which was attached to the upper part of his chest with a stout dowel. In a shallow recess on the front of the little shrine the figures of the two deities stand hand in hand, Amūn wearing his towering plumes and Mūt the Double Crown above a long, striated headdress.

A fine, but woefully fragmentary, serpentine ★statuette found in the tomb of King Amun-ḥotpe I and once thought to represent Queen Aʿḥ-mosĕ Nefret-iry comes almost certainly from a secondary, or "intrusive," occupation of the tomb. The figure is that of a woman clad in an elaborately pleated and fringed robe of a type unknown before the latter part of the Eighteenth Dynasty and wearing on her head a massive wig composed of innumerable fine, wavy locks bound near the top of the head with a fillet of leaf-shaped beads(?). The details of the wig and dress are so meticulously carved that, in spite of their battered condition, the fragments of this statuette will repay inspection by students of ancient costume. The ★head of another dark stone figure, in this case a man with shaven head, has the broad and exaggeratedly elongated skull form which characterizes the ʿAmārneh type. The figure, which was about one-third life size and rather summarily carved, was supported up the back by a heavy rectangular pilaster.

The little painted limestone ★group of figure 194, though said to have come from Gebelein, is

FIGURE 194. Two men and a boy. Painted limestone. H. 7 7/8 in.

completely in the ʿAmārneh tradition, not only typologically and stylistically but also in the frankly affectionate relationship which is seen to exist between the two men and the boy. It must, however, have been carved during the latter part of Akh-en-Aten's reign, when under the growing influence of Memphis the exaggerated mannerisms and extreme sentimentality of the earliest ʿAmārneh style were beginning to capitulate to a feeling of dignity and monumentality handed down perhaps from the days of the Old Kingdom. The group has been thought to depict some ceremony in the life of the boy, on the right, and his father or elder brother, on the left, with the figure in the middle representing an officiating priest. However that may be, its points of interest are many, not the least being the light which it throws on the costumes and coiffures of its period.

It is altogether in keeping with the warm and lighthearted spirit which pervaded the life of the court during the last half century of the Eighteenth Dynasty that this period should have been particularly productive of little figures of dwarfs, animals, birds, and the like, carved of wood, ivory, or stone and evidently intended for no more serious purpose than to delight and amuse their owners. That the latter were often children and not infrequently royal children may be deduced from the nature and quality of the figures themselves.

It is to this period, then, rather than to an earlier time that one is inclined to assign the painted wooden ★horse and rider of figure 195. Indeed, the wig and facial type of the man and the proportions and style of his figure and that of his mount would seem to point quite clearly to an ʿAmārneh or post-ʿAmārneh date for the group. Though one of the rare representations of an Egyptian riding on the back of a horse (in this case a mare), our statuette is by no means the only one, a soldier astride a very similar steed appearing in a well-known relief from the Memphite tomb of Ḥor-em-ḥēb, which, as we have seen, dates from the reign of Tūt-ʿankh-Amūn. Normally, to be sure, the Egyptians used these small, lightly built animals only in pairs to draw their flimsy two-wheeled

FIGURE 195. Equestrian group of the late Eighteenth Dynasty. Painted wood. H. 12 in.

chariots (see fig. 175 and cover design). We are not, however, justified in assuming that every mounted Egyptian was necessarily a groom, many of those shown in later battle reliefs being clearly archers, spearmen, and mounted scouts. The man in our present group may well be a soldier availing himself of a ride. The curious white markings of his little black mare have been taken by some to be natural piebald markings. Winlock, however, has suggested that they "may represent chalking or painting somewhat like that still practiced on donkeys and camels in Egypt."[13]

A charming series of little ivory carvings portray in lively, sensitive, and sympathetic fashion the animals most familiar to and beloved by the people of ʿAmārneh and early post-ʿAmārneh times. The lithe ★figure of a gazelle (fig. 196) with brown-tinted muzzle, eyes, and hooves stands on a wooden base painted brown to suggest a desert crag and inlaid in blue pigment with flowering shrubs of the sort found in the rocky valleys of the Eastern

[13] *M. M. A. Bulletin*, XI (1916), p. 86.

Desert. The ears of the little animal have been broken off and its horns, evidently made of a different material, such as silver, are now missing. The ivory ★handle of a light whip is carved with the figure of a running or prancing horse (fig. 197) painted reddish brown with a black mane and a black stripe down the middle of the gracefully arched back. The eyes, one of which has fallen out, were inlaid with garnet. A lop-eared ★hound, also carved with fore and hind legs spread far apart in a flying gallop, has a movable lower jaw operated by a rod passing down under the breast of the figure. The hound's tail is missing, but its other characteristics are carved with such liveliness and accuracy that it is easily recognizable as an ancient forerunner of the modern Salūki. A minute ★figure of a Salūki puppy cast in black bronze and provided with an inlaid gold collar shows the animal seated on its haunches with its head turned back over its left shoulder. Though modeled in extraordinary detail this most engaging little figure stands only five-eighths of an inch in height. A comical ★group in blue- and black-glazed faience, not quite four inches high, shows us a large monkey plucking at a lozenge-shaped stringed instrument while perched on the shoulders of a man who plays the double clarinet. Though provided with a suspension ring so that it could be worn as a pendent ornament, it is unlikely that this humorous duet could have been thought of as an amulet.

To the same general category of small sculptured knickknacks belongs an alabaster ★cosmetic container in the form of a household dwarf waddling along under the weight of a great wide-mouthed storage jar which he carries on his left shoulder and steadies with his two upraised hands (fig. 198). With his shaven head bent over to the right and his arms and hips swung out to the left to bring them under the center of the load, the small figure completely defies the much touted Egyptian "law of frontality." Details worth noting are the stylish cut and pleating of the little man's stubby but fashionable kilt and the ornamental band of petals around the top of his jar. Another ★figure of a dwarf, in this case a nude Negro cast in bronze, stands with his hands at his sides upon an ornate bronze tripod and supports on his head a small bronze cup in the form of a lotus flower. The legs of the tripod are topped by papyrus umbels and end below in leopard heads. Only five and a quarter inches high over all, this elaborate little object is thought to have been a censer. It was once assigned to the Ptolemaic period, but Winlock has argued convincingly for a date toward the end of the Eighteenth Dynasty.

An alabaster ★perfume bottle has borrowed its slender form from the very ancient *ḥes*-vase (𓏀), the conical stopper in this case being carved in one piece with the jar itself (fig. 199, center). Because its tiny "eye-dropper" mouth would have been too small to permit the insertion of a boring tool, the bottle was made in two vertical halves, hollowed out and neatly cemented together with a resinous, orange-colored glue. The polychrome appliqué

FIGURE 196. Ivory gazelle mounted on a carved and inlaid wooden base. From western Thebes. H. 4 5/16 in.

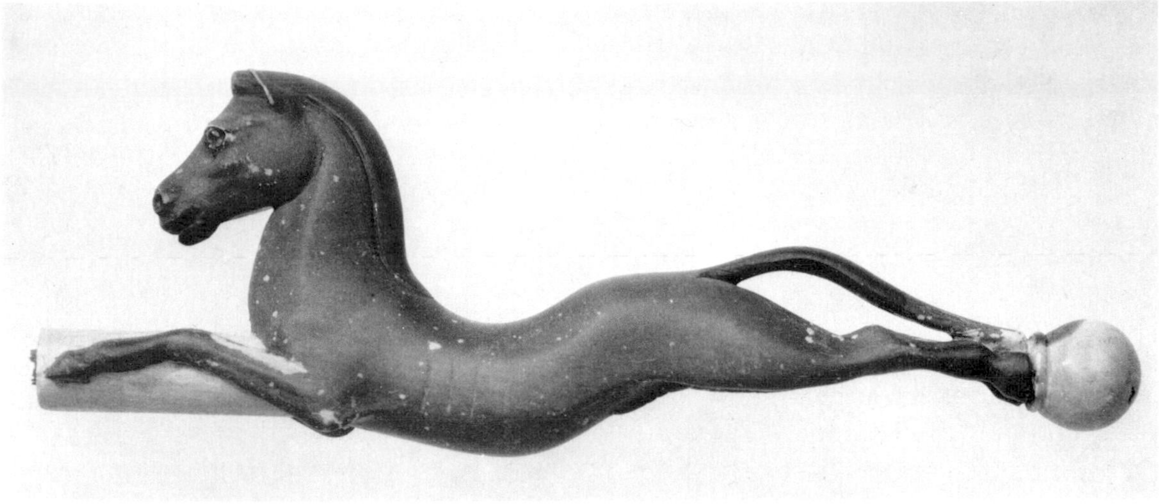

FIGURE 197. Tinted ivory whip handle from a tomb(?) in western Thebes. L. 6 in.

design on the side of the vase is a marvel of the lapidary's art. The nude figure of the girl—who seems to have stepped directly from one of the scenes preserved in relief at Tell el ʿAmārneh—is delicately carved from a thin flake of carnelian, the back of which has been hollow ground to fit the curved surface of the vase exactly. The hair of the figure, dressed in the characteristic long, heavy side lock, is a nicely worked and dexterously fitted piece of polished obsidian or black glass. Minute spears and triangles of purple glass (imitating lapis lazuli), light blue glass (imitating turquoise), and polished carnelian have been joined together to form the lotus flower on which the figure stands, and at the base of the flower a spot of sparkling yellow has been supplied by a piece of thin gold plate. The cementing agent is the same orange glue referred to above, so sparingly used that a jeweler's glass is required to detect its presence.

Two ivory ★duck-shaped boxes (fig. 199, sides) were evidently intended to hold rouge or other cosmetic pastes which could be scooped out and applied with a fingertip. Imitating the larger boxes of wood or stone which, in tombs from the Old Kingdom onward, were used to contain actual trussed fowls (see p. 52), the shallow, spoonlike receptacles are equipped with lids which swivel open but which, thanks to an ingenious hinge arrangement, are not otherwise removable. The form of the dressed duck is reproduced in full, each box, as our illustration shows, being carved with equal detail on all sides. A touch of color and realism was added by tinting the heads, throats, wing joints, and feet of the birds with a thin, brownish black stain. The familiar and attractive motif of a *bolti*-fish nibbling at the stems of symmetrically composed lotus flowers, buds, and pads is adapted for use as a lacy, openwork ★ointment spoon carved of translucent white alabaster. Seven inches long and comprising when complete six little basins for salves or cosmetics, this fanciful and extremely fragile container is said to have come from the "district" of Tell el ʿAmārneh.

The figures of a fashionably dressed man and woman are executed in bold relief on the front of a ★triple *koḥl*-tube carved from a single piece of ivory in a style which in its heaviness heralds the approach of the Ramesside period. The couple are in festive attire, their elaborate wigs surmounted by long-stemmed lotus flowers, and the man is in the act of holding a small drinking cup to his wife's (?) lips. Behind the figures the simulated binding of the three vertical tubes is decorated at the top and bottom with a band of geometric ornament—blocks, straight lines, and wavy lines. A small ivory pin driven into the front of each tube near the top was evidently for a cord from the now missing stopper. Of unknown provenience, the container measures five and three-eighths inches in height. A handsome haematite ★*koḥl*-stick, its handle covered with sheet silver, is from the Egypt Exploration Society's excavations at el ʿAmārneh and is therefore securely dated between the sixth year of Akh-en-Aten and the beginning of the reign of Ḥor-em-ḥēb.

From the same excavations comes a pair of curved ivory ★castanets having the form of human hands and forearms and carved from a single hippopotamus tusk sawn in two down the middle. A string-hole is provided near the top of each castanet and a group of five incised lines around the wrist undoubtedly represents a bracelet. In a similar pair of ★castanets, also of ivory but of unknown provenience, the hands spring from heads of the goddess Ḥat-Ḥor carved, respectively, in right and left profile so as to form a single head when the clappers are held together. Here the goddess appears as a woman, wearing her characteristic heavy wig, bound with ribbons and ending in front in spirals, and about her throat a deep, many-tiered broad collar. A full-face ★head of Ḥat-Ḥor, carved of ebony and surmounted by a small temple façade flanked by figures of cats, is perhaps also from the end of an elaborate castanet. The goddess in this case has the ears of a cow and her wig is fronted and crowned by uraei. In the doorway of the little shrine is a figure of a cobra goddess and on the jambs on either side the words "beloved of Mūt, Lady of Ishru."

A type of plastic ornament of which the ʿAmārneh and post-ʿAmārneh age was particularly productive was the small inlay figure or decorative element molded in glass or faience or carved in various colored stones. A group of gracefully proportioned and admirably modeled ★inlay figures (fig. 200) from a royal footstool or similar piece of furniture represent captive and suppliant Nubians of several different tribes, distinguished from one another by differences in costume and facial types. They are made for the most part of opaque black glass and show their subjects kneeling in obeisance before the king, kneeling with arms pinioned behind the body, and arched backward with both arms and legs trussed. One figure is completely nude, one wears a long mantle of turquoise blue glass, and a third was clad in a short kilt which

FIGURE 198. Cosmetic container of the late Eighteenth Dynasty, said to be from the neighborhood of el ʿAmārneh. Alabaster. H. 7 ¾ in.

was made in a separate piece from some light-colored material and is now missing. All wear heavy annular earrings in their ears and have their woolly hair cut short in a caplike trim. With the same group of inlays the Museum acquired parts of two ★figures of standing Egyptians in red glass and a small black glass ★Anubis animal in crouched position. Late Eighteenth Dynasty inlays obtained with the Murch collection include a small profile ★head in glazed limestone, an ★arm of black glass, a ★hand of red glass, and a ★lotus flower of green- and white-glazed faience. From Bashford Dean we received as a gift twenty-five small ★chevron-shaped plaques of carnelian and colored glass of the type used to inlay the feather pattern on, for example, the coffin used in the burial of King Akh-en-Aten (see pp. 294 f.). A dark blue glass ★trefoil inlay from the Valley of the Tombs of the Kings has been ingeniously identified as one of the piebald markings from a figure of the cow of Ḥat-Ḥor. Near Deir el Ballās Mr. Lythgoe in 1917 acquired a handsome piece of beryl inlay carved in the form of the ★owl hieroglyph (𓅓).

FIGURE 199. Alabaster perfume vase and ivory cosmetic boxes of the late Eighteenth Dynasty. H. of vase 4¼ in.

It is likely that a number of these elements were inlaid in the sides of ornate wooden shrines. From the cornices of the same or similar shrines come five ★uraeus heads in blue and green faience and two large bronze ★uraei, their hoods recessed for colored inlays. Both of the bronze uraei are provided at the bottom with tenons for attachment to the cornices and the head of the larger of the two is surmounted by a solar disk with a ring at the back.

Aside from the examples already discussed, the relief sculpture of the late Eighteenth Dynasty is represented in our collection by three ★blocks of limestone relief, two from private tombs in the Memphite necropolis, the third from an unrecorded source. All three blocks are executed in *relief en creux* and all three betray close typological and stylistic affinities with the art of el ʿAmārneh in its later, more mature phase. One of the two

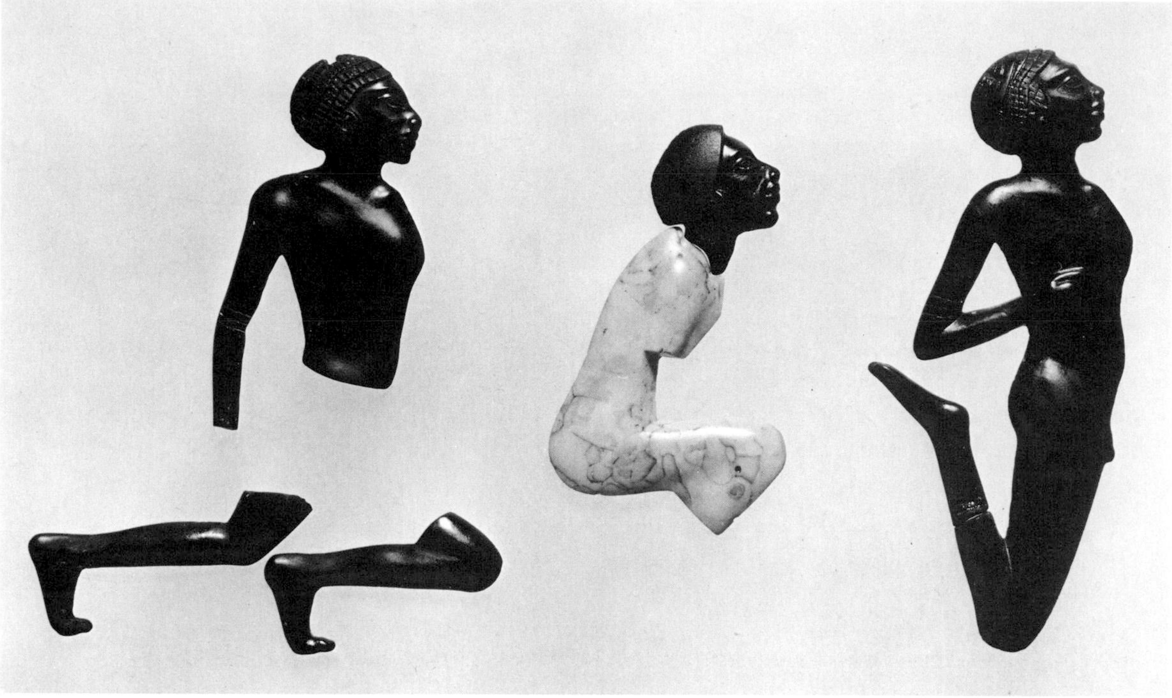

FIGURE 200. Inlay figures from an article of furniture. Black and turquoise blue glass. H. of right-hand figure 5 ½ in.

Memphite reliefs (fig. 201) portrays in lively fashion activities on the riverside estate of an evidently rich and powerful official. In an upper scene the owner of the estate, accompanied by a fashionably dressed retinue, inspects his cattle stables, where monstrously fat steers are being hand fed by squatting herdsmen. Below, grain ships under sail approach the riverbank where their cargoes are unloaded, measured into heaps, and carried off by a line of porters. In the second relief we see the God's Father Ḥatiay, followed by his son, the *Wēʿb*-priest Ptaḥ-mosĕ, and preceded by his *In-mūtef*, or funerary, priest with side lock and leopard skin, kneeling in adoration before "Sokar Osiris," the god of the Memphite necropolis. The god is not shown, but he is twice named in a long offering text written in vertical columns of hieroglyphs over and between the figures of his worshipers. Both Ḥatiay and his son are unmistakable ʿAmārneh types, with elongated heads, scrawny necks and arms, and diaphanous, intricately pleated garments. In his left hand the former holds a censer and libation vase, while his son carries a long-stemmed floral bouquet. Our third relief, a fragment six inches square, preserves the figures of two goddesses(?) standing and facing to the right. Their heads above their long, archaic wigs were surmounted by emblems on standards, of which very little now remains. The goddess on the right has her arms extended in a way that suggests that she may be holding the figure of an infant king—perhaps in a scene depicting the divine birth of one of Egypt's pharaohs. In their faces and in their bodily forms both figures show the very strong influence of the ʿAmārneh tradition.

Nine small paintings and drawings datable to the time of Akh-en-Aten and his successors are not only charming and interesting in themselves, but exemplify better than any of the other media studied the free compositions, curvilinear forms, and flowing line which distinguish the art of this period. A ★scrap of painted mud plaster on which is preserved the head and shoulders of a man with hands upraised before his face in an attitude of adoration is said to be from a tomb at Tell el ʿAmārneh but is more likely to have come from western Thebes, where the painted tomb chapel was still in high favor. Drawn in heavy red outline and subsequently filled in with dark red, black, and white, the figure stands out sharply against the chalky white background which had now replaced the bluish gray or golden yellow of earlier periods. White is also used as the background color of a ★panel of painted linen (fig. 202) on which a well-to-do Theban named Ḥori is seen seated beside a table of offerings, his head surmounted by a cone of perfumed ointment. Other panels of this type have been found in some quantity at Deir el Medīneh, sewn on the breasts of fully wrapped mummies or the linen palls which were once laid over their coffins. Few, however, can equal the present example in the quality of its draughtsmanship, the brilliance of its colors, and its exceptional state of preservation.

A fragmentary ★toy chariot of painted wood has on the outside of its body an extraordinary little painting of a Negro astride a prancing horse which was either stained or clipped in a zebralike design of black and white stripes. Not to be outdone by his mount, the Negro wears a red and white striped shirt, a bright red cap, and a floral garland about his neck. This gaily colored miniature, only two inches high, can without hesitation be dated stylistically to the ʿAmārneh period.

The most elaborate and most interesting of four ★drawings on flakes of limestone found by Theodore Davis in the Valley of the Tombs of the Kings is a colored sketch of a youthful princess holding in her arms an infant girl almost as large as herself. The royalty of the young mother is proclaimed by a uraeus which rears itself from her forehead, and her extreme youth is indicated by the fact that she still wears her hair in a single long side lock, bound with a clasp over her right ear and streaming down over her shoulders and back. The exact form and arrangement of the side lock seen here occurs apparently only during the ʿAmārneh period (see fig. 199). There is, then, considerable probability that the girl represented was one of Akh-en-Aten's daughters, the most likely candidate being ʿAnkhes-en-pa-Aten (later the wife of Tūt-ʿankh-Amūn), who, it would appear, gave birth to a daughter when she herself was still in her early teens. The three other drawings show us, respectively, the nude figure of an ʿAmārneh princess squatting on a cushion with one hand to her mouth, the profile head of a bearded Asiatic drawn in very heavy outline, and a colored sketch of an elaborate palmette ornament with flowers and tall, pointed leaves springing from its top.

The jewelry of the ʿAmārneh age, both royal and private, is characterized by an increased use of floral and vegetable elements—flowers, rosettes, palmettes, leaves, petals, and small fruits and berries—reproduced in faience, glass, or more valuable materials and effectively combined to form attractive and often elaborate ornaments. The faience ★collar of figure 203 is an excellent example of what the jewelers of the period were capable of producing in the field of inexpensive "costume" jewelry. It is made up of five rows of polychrome

FIGURE 201. An estate by the river bank. A Memphite tomb relief of the late ʿAmārneh period. Limestone. L. 52 in.

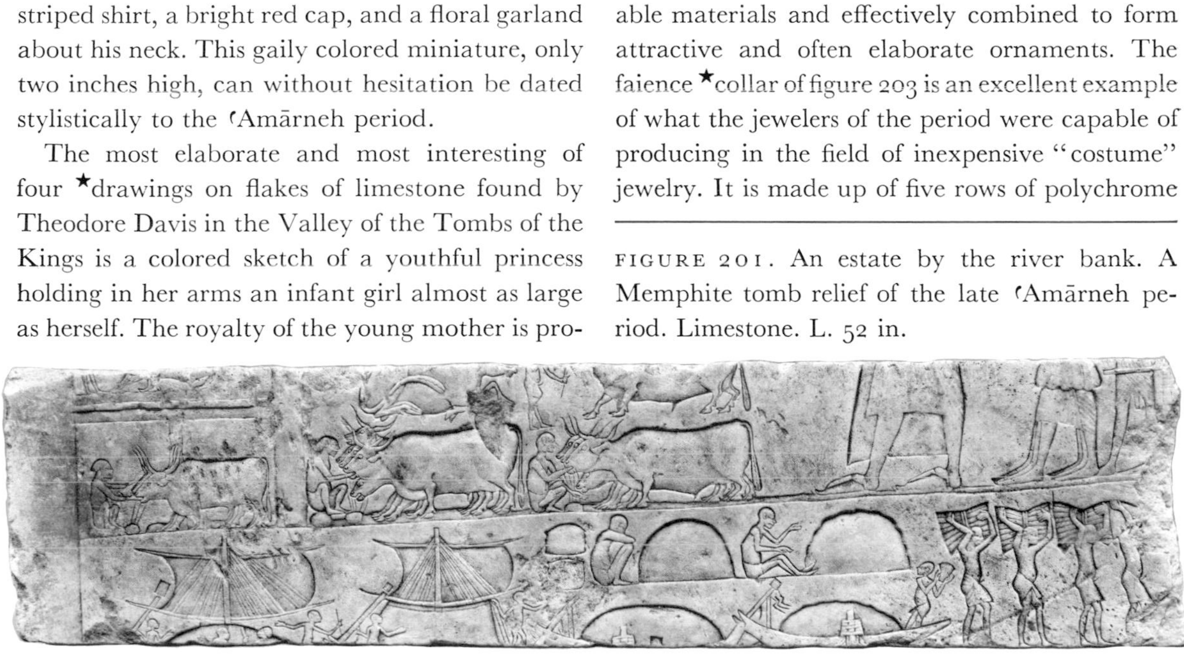

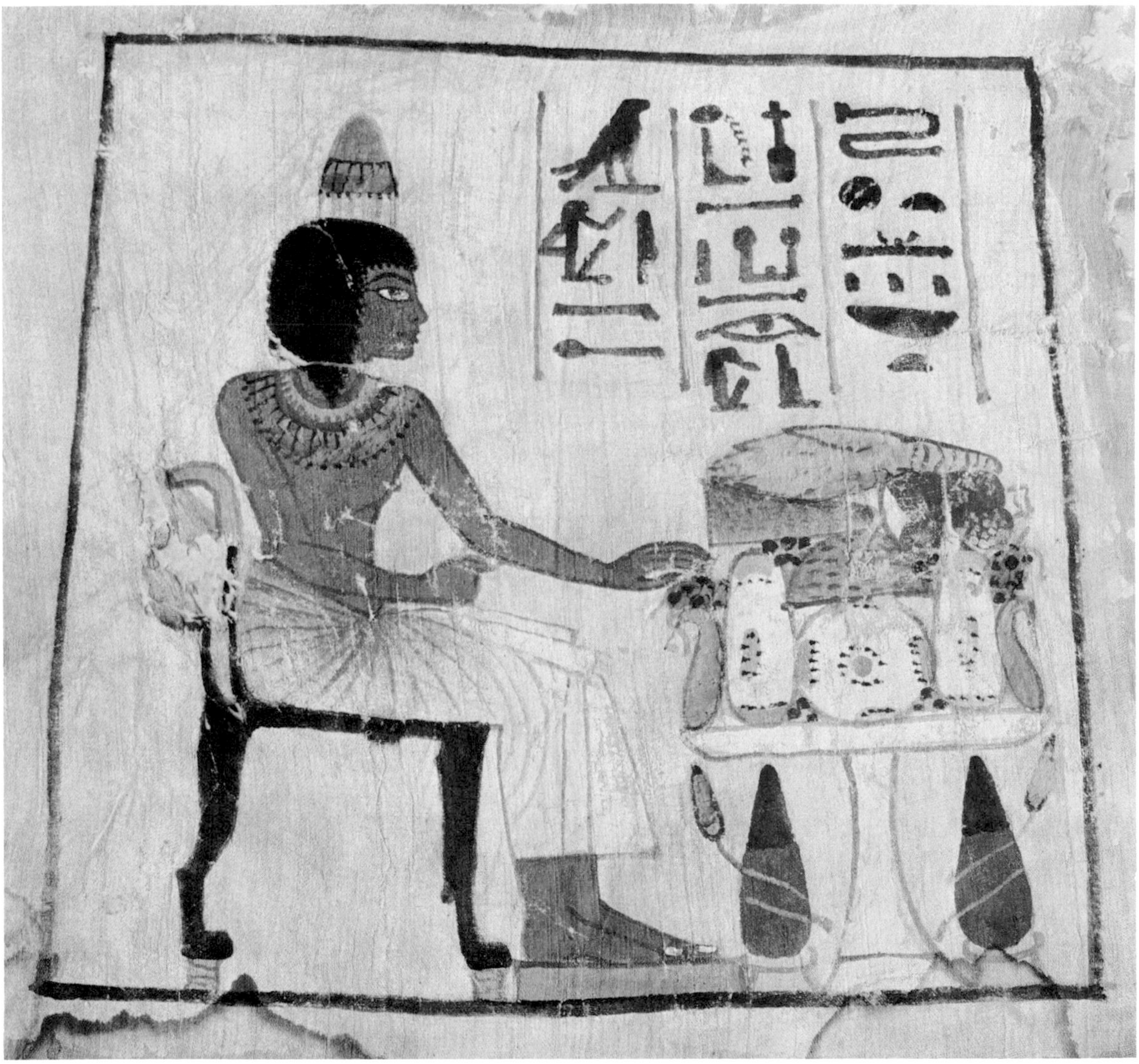

FIGURE 202. "An offering of all things good and pure for the spirit of the Osiris, Ḥori, the justified." Painted linen shroud, probably from Deir el Medīneh. H. 15 in.

elements (blue, green, red, yellow, and white) having the forms of cornflowers (innermost row), dates (next three rows), and lotus petals (outermost row) joined together with lines of tiny ring beads and ending in two white faience terminals adorned with lotus flowers, buds, and petals, and with poppy petals and persea fruits. The cylindrical pendants dangling from the broad ends of these terminal plates may represent tassels finishing off the ends of the main stringing threads of the collar. The color tones of the glazes are light and cheerful and the whole collar has about it a feeling of festival gaiety. A comparison with the natural floral collar of figure 188 shows us how accurately the jeweler has been able to capture the spirit of the original. A less complete ★collar of the same type, but with terminals in the form of lotus flowers, comes from the excavations of the Egypt Exploration Society at el ʿAmārneh. Parts of two other

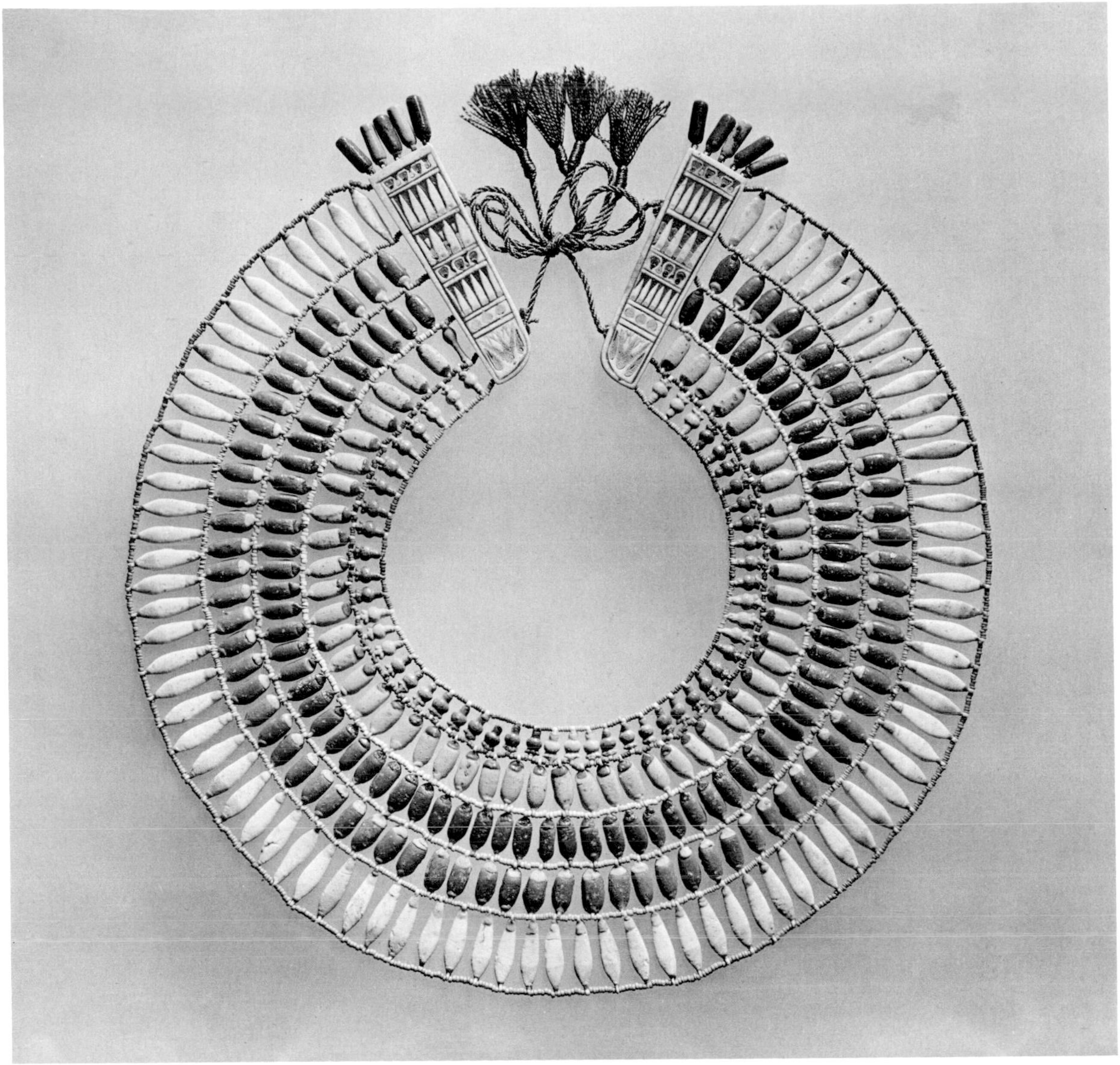

FIGURE 203. Floral collar of polychrome faience. Late Eighteenth Dynasty. Diam. 12 ½ in.

★collars include not only the cornflower, date, and lotus-petal elements, but also little faience daisies, or rosettes, grape clusters in purple faience, and small white faience end pieces in the form of the conventional "lily" flower. One of a dozen lotiform collar ★terminals is of bright blue faience; the eleven others, probably from el ʿAmārneh, are glazed in two colors—light green and white.

Three attractive ★necklaces found in the ruins of private houses at el ʿAmārneh are composed of little cornflower, lily, and lotus-flower pendants of blue and yellow faience strung at intervals on slender strands of blue, red, yellow, and white disk beads. The threads on which these necklaces were strung have been replaced, but the beads themselves have been kept in their original order as found. A single blue faience ★necklace pendant in the form of a composite lily and lotus flower is also from el ʿAmārneh, but from an unspecified part of the site. A string of carnelian ★necklace elements comprising forty-four cornflower pendants separated by groups of small spherical beads is of unknown origin, but probably of the same period as the ʿAmārneh necklaces. So also is a similar ★string of beads and pendants, in this case, however, of polychrome glass and faience. The date of an interesting ★string of carnelian amulets and ball beads is indicated by the fact that one of the amulets is a figure of Akh-en-Aten represented as a seated child (see pp. 290 f.). The other amulets, all carefully carved in the hard, translucent red stone, include figures of Rēʿ, Atūm, Bēs, and Thoueris, the falcon of Horus and the ape of Tḥōt, the scarab beetle, the uraeus, and the *bolti*-fish, the heart, the human hand, and two or three plain drop-shaped pendants.

A pair of penannular ★earrings of light blue glass are stated in the manuscript catalogue of the Carnarvon collection to be "from El Amarna." The outside of each ring is decorated with a ridge-like molding of white glass, and a pair of minute loops of dark blue glass project upward on either side of the opening in the main ring, obviously to take a pin or bar which passed through the wearer's ear lobe.

Only a few of the finger rings in our collection which do not bear royal names can be assigned on stylistic or other grounds to the late Eighteenth Dynasty. A blue faience ★ring from a private tomb at Abydos, with the legend "To Amun Rēʿ belongs the breath of life," is probably of this period. So also is a similar faience ★ring on the bezel of which a kneeling figure of the air god Shu, with arms upraised to support the heaven, is molded in low relief. Shu appears again on the bezel of a ★signet ring carved of some hard black stone. A symbol of "life" adorns the bezel of a very similar ★ring molded of dark blue glass, and a single sedge plant that of a little gold ★ring of the same general type. The bezels of two red jasper ★rings have the form of double cartouches, side by side, each containing a hieroglyphic sign meaning in one case "power" and in the other "good." Far and away the most attractive of the lot is a ★ring bezel of polychrome faience, the openwork design of which consists of a figure of the cow of the goddess Ḥat-Hor couchant beneath an enormous lotus flower.

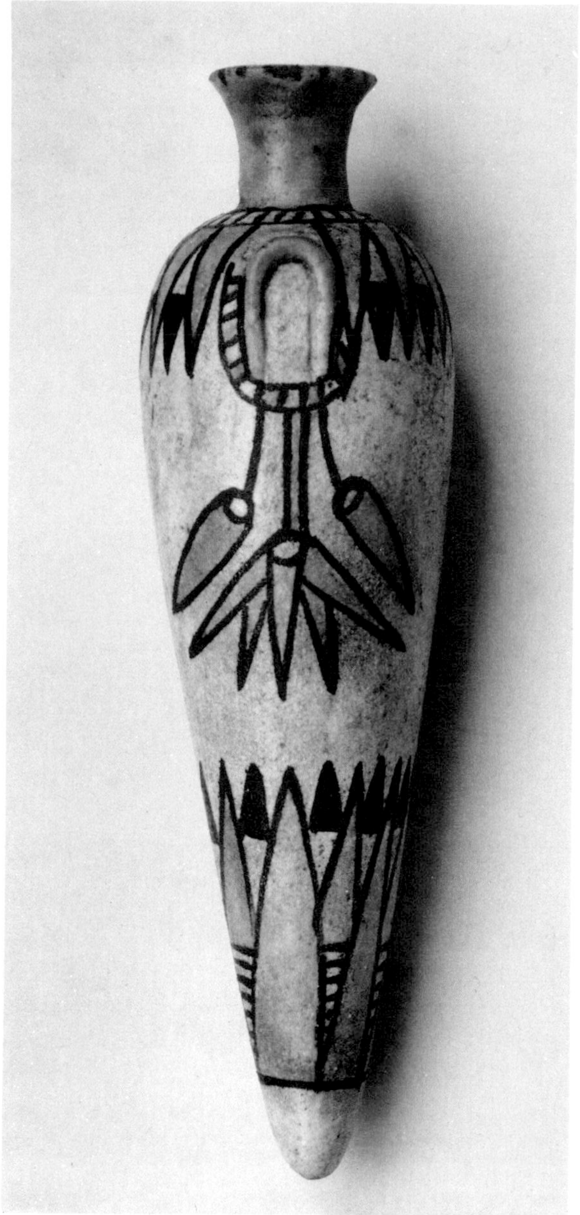

FIGURE 204. A small vase of white faience with blue and black decoration. H. 6 in.

Here mention may be made of a pair of gray steatite ★scarabs of developed Eighteenth Dynasty type inscribed, respectively, for the King's Son Amun-em-ḥēb and the King's Daughter Meryet-Nūb, both, so far as can be discovered, unknown from any other source. The scarabs, formerly the property of the Earl of Carnarvon, were acquired by him from the Timins collection. To this period may belong also a gold ★finger ring mounting a scarab of lapis lazuli inscribed for the Prophet of Onuris, Ptaḥ-mosĕ.

A small gold ★tube adorned with an over-all feather or scale pattern inlaid with carnelian, lapis lazuli, and green feldspar was probably part of a richly decorated fan or mirror handle. From the top of a staff or from a cosmetic box or similar small article of furniture comes a ★knob of blue glass with band and dot patterns encrusted in yellow and black glass. A ★miniature amphora of white faience (fig. 204), probably designed as a perfume vase, is charmingly decorated with friezes of blue lotus petals outlined in black and, below each of its two small handles, with a lotus flower and buds also colored blue with black details. A vase exactly like it was found at Sesebi in the northern Sūdān in association with inscribed objects of the late Eighteenth and early Nineteenth Dynasty.

One of two small pottery ★rattles—perhaps children's toys—is very like an example found over thirty years ago in the ruins of a house at Tell el ʿAmārneh. It consists of a drop-shaped hollow bulb of red pottery with a closed top in the form of the head of a horned animal, the horns in this case curved back to form a complete loop. A similar ★rattle, also of red pottery, is more naturalistically modeled to represent a recumbent cow or ox, the tail of the animal curled over the right flank, the head turned engagingly back over the right shoulder. Both contain loose pebbles or other small, hard objects which produce a mild rustling sound when the rattles are shaken. An attractive little ★model or toy which reproduces the form of a deep two-handled basket is carefully shaped in fine buff pottery and shows all the details of a real basket, including the stitching on the handles.

An enormous, wide-mouthed ★pottery jar (fig. 205), decorated with bands of floral ornament in light blue, red, and black and finished above and below the bands of decoration with a shiny dark red slip, is the type of vessel from which wine or beer was served at banquets. Both the color scheme of the jar and the details of its decoration, which include wavy "water" lines, bunches of grapes, and rows of lotus, mandrake, and poppy petals, are paralleled almost exactly on a wine bottle used at the funerary feast of King Tūt-ʿankh-Amūn (fig. 187). Only slightly earlier in date, since they come from private villas at el ʿAmārneh, are a two-handled ★flask, or "pilgrim's bottle," made of smooth reddish buff pottery, and a squat little two-handled ★jar of the same ware, covered with an inverted red pottery saucer.

In 1939 the Museum received as a bequest from Howard Carter two very handsome funerary ★broad collars in violet blue faience, one of which

FIGURE 205. Wine or beer jar of the late Eighteenth Dynasty. Painted pottery. H. 27 1/4 in.

FIGURE 206. *Shawabty*-figure of Mery-Rēʿ, perhaps the owner of a well-known tomb at el ʿAmārneh. Serpentine. H. 8 ½ in.

has been expertly restrung by Miss Charlotte R. Clark. Except for their color, which seems to have been an innovation developed during the Eighteenth Dynasty, perhaps in imitation of lapis lazuli, these collars differ in no essential respect from the Middle Kingdom example illustrated in figure 198 of the first volume of this handbook. Minor variations on the ancient model include slight changes in the proportions of the collar itself and its rounded terminal plates and an increase in the number of drop-shaped pendants in its outermost row.

As the New Kingdom passed into its later phase the *shawabty*-figure, while retaining the traditional mummylike pose, began to abandon the simple mummy shape and to show its deceased owner wearing the often elaborate clothing and coiffure of his day. In the big serpentine **shawabty* of figure 206, for example, Mery-Rēʿ, the man represented, is clad in the curly wig and pleated shirt and kilt which were fashionable in the late Eighteenth Dynasty. We note, however, that his feet are still shown wrapped together like those of a mummy and that his hands, holding symbols of "stability" and "protection," are crossed over his breast in the old Osirian position. Furthermore, the knoblike object above his wrists would seem to be the end of a long Osirian beard which must have added an incongruous touch to his otherwise up-to-date costume. Since there is no suitable space on the front of the figure for the *shawabty*-spell, this is engraved in ten lines of hieroglyphs around the sides and back of the kilt. A large alabaster **shawabty*, which, like that of Mery-Rēʿ, is said to have come from el ʿAmārneh, is similar to it in size and in the kind of kilt represented, but wears on its head a long, simple wig of archaic type and holds in its hands a pair of hoes (𓌸). Down the front of the figure is a much abridged version of the *shawabty*-spell, recited in behalf of "Ro-sandj, son of Sēth-er-ḥēt."

A somewhat smaller **shawabty*-figure, in this case carved of black steatite, is also very like that of Mery-Rēʿ, but is more elaborate in its details and, at the same time, distinctly inferior in its style. Here the owner, a certain My-Ptaḥ, holds both the hoes and the amuletic symbols, has a *ba*-bird (i.e., a human-headed bird representing the soul of the deceased) with spread wings carved on his breast, a basket (for carrying sand in the hereafter) engraved on his left shoulder, and stands on his two sandaled feet. Besides the Chapter of the *Shawabty* inscribed on the back and sides of My-Ptaḥ's kilt, a panel on the front of the garment bears the words "Illuminating the Osiris." A pair of painted limestone ★*shawabtys*, almost nine inches high, represent a well-to-do Egyptian and his wife, neither of whose names is preserved in the badly faded inscriptions on the backs of the figures. The man's costume is practically a duplicate of that shown in figure 206, but his hands, open with the palms turned inward, rest on his thighs and his sandaled feet are represented below the triangular apron of his long kilt. The woman's figure, on the other hand, is completely mummiform, the only touch of modernity being her crinkled and filleted wig. Her hands are crossed over her breast and in each of them she holds a Ḥat-Ḥor-headed sistrum. A mummiform ★*shawabty* inscribed with the masculine name Nakht-Mīn is of the effeminate ʿAmārneh type with the broad hips, slender arms, and prominent breasts borrowed by Akh-en-Aten's courtiers from the figure of their king. Six and three-eighths inches in height, it is cast in solid bronze, a material rarely used for figures of this class and period.

In view of the political and cultural resurgence of northern Egypt during the latter half of the Eighteenth Dynasty (see p. 275) it is not surprising to find a falling-off in the number of government officials buried in the Theban necropolis and a corresponding sparsity of stamped funerary cones of ʿAmārneh and post-ʿAmārneh times. Only six ★cones in our own collection can reasonably be attributed to this period and it is not unlikely that one or two of them belong to the early years of the Nineteenth Dynasty rather than to the last decades of the Eighteenth. The stamp impressions on the ends of these cones give the titles and names of four men: the Scribe of the Granary Te-pa-Aten; the Chief of Police, Overseer of the Countries of Syria, and First Charioteer of His Majesty, Pe'n-Rēʿ; the God's Father, First Fanbearer of the Lord of the Two Lands, and King's Great Herald Mey; and the Skipper of the First Prophet of Amūn, Neb-ʿan-su. Two other ★cones of Eighteenth Dynasty type, but otherwise undated, belonged, respectively, to the Page Ny-Amūn, and the Chief Page and *Wēʿb*-priest of Amūn, Neta-way-ref.

VIII. The Nineteenth Dynasty[1]

1. Ramesses I and Sēthy I

When, about 1304 b.c., General Pa-Ramesses of Avaris ascended the throne of Egypt as King Men-peḥty-Rēʿ Ramesses I, the founder of the Nineteenth Dynasty, he was too old a man to bear alone the burdens of kingship and seems almost from the outset to have shared the duties of the pharaonic office with his middle-aged son, the Upper Egyptian Vizier and Troop Commander Sēthy. It was a wise policy, for the old soldier survived his accession by only a year and four months. Like his predecessors of the Eighteenth Dynasty and his successors down to the end of the New Kingdom, he was buried at Thebes, in a small but handsomely decorated tomb (No. 16) in the Valley of the Tombs of the Kings, the haste with which this tomb was made ready for its royal occupant being evidenced by the fact that the decoration of both the sepulchral hall and the pharaoh's massive red granite sarcophagus is not carved, but merely drawn and painted. Though Thebes, then, remained the site of the royal necropolis and its god, Amūn, retained his exalted status as Egypt's state deity, the residence of the king and the capital of the empire had been transferred to the northeastern Delta, the home district of the new dynasty, and the deities of that region, including the ancient god Sēth, had been elevated to positions of primary importance in the Egyptian pantheon.

The sixteen-month reign of the first Ramesses, understandably enough, produced no events of major historical importance and not many inscribed monuments, the latter including, besides the royal tomb and sarcophagus, some reliefs on the second pylon at Karnak and a stela from Wādy Ḥalfa dated to the beginning of the king's second regnal year. A sanctuary provided for the cult of Ramesses I in the funerary temple of Sēthy I at Ḳurneh belongs, naturally, to the reign of the latter king, as do also the ★reliefs from a little chapel which Sēthy built for his father next to his own magnificent temple at Abydos. Aside from these reliefs, a discussion of which will follow shortly, the only objects in our collection inscribed with the name (in every case the throne name) of Ramesses I are a glazed steatite ★scarab, a green faience ★plaque, and a faience ★seal in the form of a crouching ibex. Among the statues of New Kingdom pharaohs represented in Tomb 19 at Thebes that of Ramesses I occupies the next to last place in the second row and is followed by that of Sēthy I, in whose time the tomb appears to have been decorated. In Mr. Wilkinson's color ★copy of this most interesting scene we see, at the left, the owner of the tomb, the First Prophet of Amun-ḥotpe of the Forecourt, Amun-mosĕ, presenting offerings to the figures of the deified pharaohs.

Despite its brevity the reign of King Men-maʿet-

[1] For a list of kings see Chronological Table.

Rēʿ Sētẖy I, which began with the death of his father in 1303 B.C. and lasted for little more than a dozen years, was one of the most brilliant in New Kingdom history. Like the reign of Amun-em-ḥēt I of the Twelfth Dynasty it was hailed in official texts of its time as the dawn of a new era, a "Repeating of Births," and in many respects it does indeed deserve to be regarded as a period of renaissance. In view, however, of the recently established and generally accepted chronology for the early Nineteenth Dynasty it seems doubtful that either Sētẖy ("Menephtah") or his father (Men-peḥty-Rēʿ) is to be associated with an era described by Theon of Alexandria as *apo Menophreōs*, which began in 1321-1317 B.C. and has been identified as the last pre-Christian Sothic cycle (see Part I, p. 40).

It is evident that for some time previous to his accession Sētẖy had been making preparations for a re-expansion of Egyptian power in southwestern Asia, and in his first year as king he achieved promising results. Marching out of the border fortress of Tjel at the head of three divisions of the newly reorganized army, the warlike pharaoh overran Palestine and Syria as far north as the Lebanon, reoccupying a chain of strategic fortified towns en route and returning to Egypt with droves of prisoners and other rich booty. The campaign is recorded in a series of imposing reliefs on the north wall of the hypostyle hall in the temple of Amūn at Karnak. Our collection is fortunate in including a ★cast of one of the most stirring of these scenes, in which Sētẖy appears in his chariot leading the attack against a walled city of Canaan, perhaps Gaza. In subsequent campaigns the warrior king advanced up the Amorite coastlands, captured the key city of Ḳadesh on the Orontes, and somewhere to the north of Ḳadesh defeated an army of the powerful and ever-dangerous Hittites. Unable to crush his formidable foe or to consolidate his position in northern Syria, Sētẖy seems to have come to terms with the Hittite king, Muwatallis; the terms included, however, the cession to Egypt of the whole of Palestine and the Syrian coastal region northward to the river Litāny. Meanwhile the pharaoh had been forced to deal with an incursion of Libyan tribesmen into the western Delta, driving back the invaders in two pitched battles and warding off a menace which under his successors was seriously to threaten the security of the land. Far to the south, at ʿAmāreh West, midway between the Second and Third Cataracts of the Nile, Sētẖy founded an important fortified town which was to serve as the seat of the Deputy Viceroy of Kush. In the temple at ʿAmāreh a stela, now in Brooklyn, recorded a campaign conducted in the fourth year of the reign against the Nubian land of Irem. Still further to the south, near the Fourth Cataract, a stela dated to Sētẖy's eleventh regnal year describes the additions which he made at that time to the great temple of Amūn at Napəta (Gebel Barkal).

At Karnak Sētẖy, in conjunction with his son and coregent Ramesses II, carried out the plan of his father, Ramesses I, for the conversion of the court between the second and third pylons of the temple of Amūn into a vast hypostyle hall, 6000 square feet in area, its lofty roofs supported by 134 tremendous sandstone columns, its wall and column surfaces adorned with six acres of painted reliefs. One of the seven wonders of the ancient plifies this stupendous structure perfectly exem-world, the flair for the colossal which is a dominant characteristic of Ramesside temple architecture.

Equally amazing in its own way and infinitely superior in the quality of its sculptured decoration is Sētẖy's huge rock-cut tomb (No. 17) in the Valley of the Tombs of the Kings. Here a series of passages and chambers, adorned with painted reliefs of great beauty and delicacy, leads gradually downward for a distance of more than three hundred feet to a pillared sepulchral hall and vaulted crypt, where, under a painted astronomical ceiling, the king's body once rested in a magnificent alabaster sarcophagus. Prominent among the texts with which the walls of this and other royal tombs of the Nineteenth and Twentieth Dynasties are inscribed are excerpts from or complete versions of a number of funerary "books"—the Book of Him Who Is in the Underworld (*Imy-Dēt*), the

Book of the Gates, the Book of the Caverns, the Book of the Day, the Book of the Night, and the Book of the Cow of Heaven. In the tomb of Sēthy I we find also the longer Litany of the Sun and our earliest copy of an ancient text describing the Deliverance of Mankind from Destruction. Sēthy's mummy, that of an extremely handsome man in his sixties, was recovered in 1881 from the Cache of Royal Mummies at Deir el Baḥri.

Over seven hundred of the king's *shawabty*-figures were found in and near his tomb, and of these the Museum acquired between 1909 and 1950 two complete and five fragmentary examples in blue and green faience, green-glazed steatite, and wood. The big ★*shawabty* of figure 207 is of rich deep blue faience with the stripes of the pharaoh's *nemes*, the mattocks which he holds in his hands, and the details of his eyes and jewelry picked out in a glossy black overglaze. Black is used also for the hieroglyphs of the conventional *shawabty*-spell (Chapter VI of the Book of the Dead) which covers the lower half of the figure and which begins with the words "Illuminating the Osiris, the King, the Lord of the Two Lands, this Men-maʿet-Rēʿ, the justified, who says, 'O you *shawabty*, if the Osiris, the Son of Rēʿ, Sēthy Mery-en-Ptaḥ, the justified, is called to do work. . . .' " Our six other ★*shawabtys* of Sēthy I are somewhat smaller in scale, a complete wooden example, acquired in 1950 as a gift of Mrs. Minda Moore, measuring just over seven inches in height.

A mile to the southwest of his own tomb, in a rocky amphitheater similar to the Valley of the Tombs of the Kings, Sēthy prepared a tomb for his mother, Queen Sit-Rēʿ. In doing so he set a precedent which was destined to be followed by his successors for generation after generation until, by the end of the Twentieth Dynasty, this particular bay of the western cliffs contained over seventy tombs of wives and children of the Ramesside pharaohs, many of them decorated with reliefs and paintings comparable to those in the kings' own

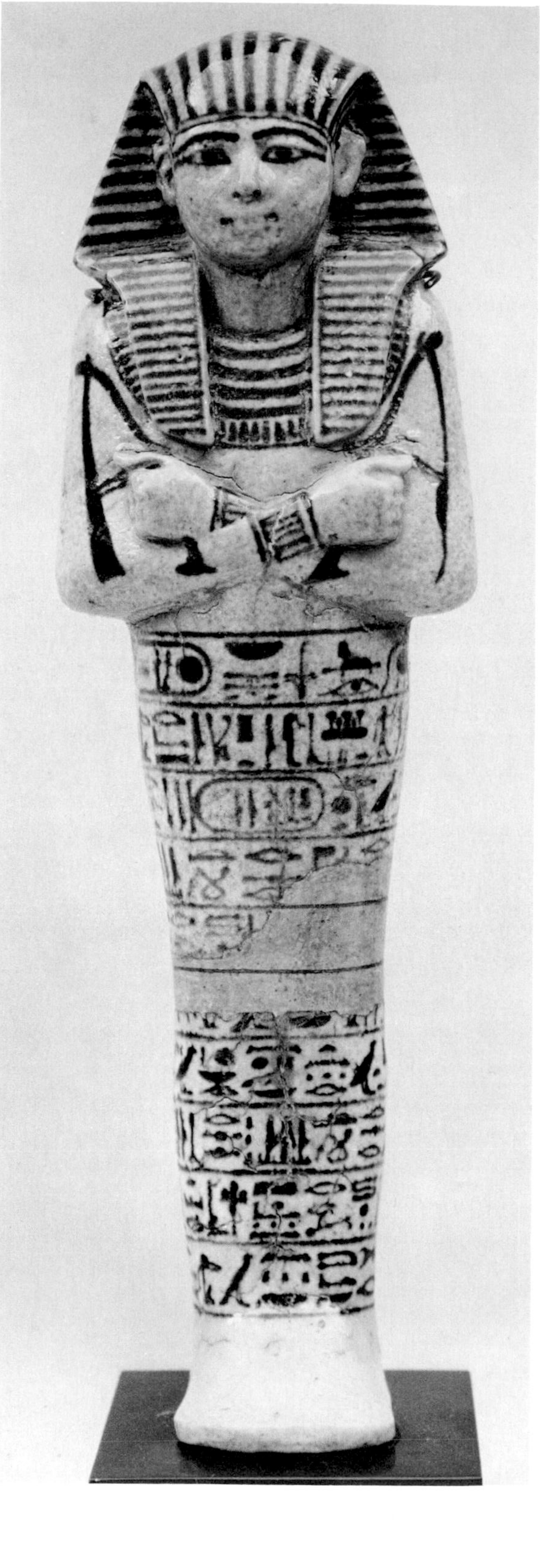

FIGURE 207. *Shawabty*-figure of King Sēthy I. Blue faience. H. 11 ⅞ in.

tombs. Today it is known as the Valley of the Tombs of the Queens or, in Arabic—somewhat more accurately—as el Wādy el Bibān el Ḥarīm.

At Abydos, near the "tomb" of the god Osiris and the cenotaphs of Egypt's earliest kings, Sēthy built for himself a remarkable subterranean cenotaph, the so-called Osireion, and immediately to the east of it an even more remarkable L-shaped temple, dedicated to the service of the deified pharaoh and six of his fellow divinities and containing in one of its many galleries a list of the kings of Egypt from the beginning of the First Dynasty onward. Breasted has called this temple "perhaps the noblest monument of Egyptian art still surviving in the land,"[2] and his fellow historian Vandier has noted in its wonderful painted reliefs "the purity of line, the elegance of movement, the technical perfection, and the sensibility"[3] which, while reflecting the influence of the ʿAmārneh school, seem to hark back beyond it to the artistic traditions of the reign of Amunḥotpe III.

Despite the damage wrought by prolonged exposure to dampness and resulting salt action, these qualities are evident also in the ★reliefs with which Sēthy adorned the interior of a small limestone chapel dedicated by him to his father, Ramesses I, and erected just outside the northeast corner of his own temple enclosure at Abydos. The relief of figure 208 is from the rear, or west, wall of the chapel's central room. In it we see Ramesses I presenting a tray of food and floral offerings to the Abydene symbol of Osiris, which was apparently a long wig mounted on a pole and surmounted by two tall plumes.[4] The elaborate stand supporting the symbol is provided with carrying poles and sledge runners and is adorned with small figures of the king, the "Souls" of Buto and Nekhen (see Part I, p. 189), the canine animal of Anubis, the uraeus serpent, and, at the base of the pole, with mummiform figures of the twin lion deities Shu and Tefēnet. In front and back, symbols of "life" with human arms hold standards with figures of the ram god of Mendes(?). Beside the symbol of her husband stands the goddess Isis, her head surmounted by an elaborate plumed headdress, her hand upraised in a gesture of adoration or protection. The scene is repeated on the left half of the same wall, but in this case it is Sēthy I, wearing a caplike crown and holding an elaborate ointment container, who makes the offering, and the falcon-headed Horus who stands protectively beside the symbol of his divine father. The columns of delicately carved hieroglyphs overhead give the names, titles, and epithets of the participants in the scenes and record the speeches of appreciation addressed by the god Osiris to his royal devotees.

In the reliefs from the south wall of the little chapel Ramesses I, followed by his queen, Sit-Rēʿ(?), and other members of his family, makes offering to a mummiform statue of Osiris which stands upright in a small shrine and is attended by the goddesses Isis and Ḥat-Ḥor. Ḥat-Ḥor, who appears in her funerary role, as Mistress of the West, holds in her right hand a *menyet*-necklace and a loop sistrum, while the queen, who stands facing the divine trio behind the figure of the king, brandishes before her face a pair of shrine-shaped sistrums of more elaborate form. The queen's long, diaphanous robe is most intricately draped and pleated and her short wig below her towering headdress is adorned with a *seshed*-circlet evidently of metal and semiprecious stones. The king, wearing the Blue Crown and short dress kilt with pendent bull's tail, is in the act of burning incense and pouring a libation over a prodigious pile of food offerings which separates the shrine of the god from the figures of the pharaoh and his family. Of the latter there are preserved in whole or in part the tall, graceful figures of three women and two men, each holding a long-stemmed bouquet

[2] *A History of Egypt*, p. 415.

[3] Drioton-Vandier, *L'Égypte*, p. 482.

[4] The symbol may be studied in three dimensions in a painted wooden funerary ★model of uncertain date. Here the emblem (*ab*) is mounted on a -sign (*dju*) apparently to form a monogrammatic rendering of the Egyptian place name *Abdju*, "Abydos."

and each dressed in the very height of early Nineteenth Dynasty fashion.

Our largest panel of relief, from the north wall of Ramesses I's Abydene chapel, shows in gratifying detail the preparation and serving of the king's funerary banquet, a more or less stereotyped scene familiar to us from tomb and temple reliefs of earlier periods (see, e. g., Part I, pp. 92 f., 98, 146, 187 f.). Here, as usual, the composition is dominated by a large figure of the deceased banqueter, in this case King Ramesses I, who sits enthroned at the left, wearing on his head the kingly *nemes* and holding in his right hand the symbol of eternal "life." The columnar table toward which he extends his other hand is stacked with vertical slices of bread and beyond it are meats, vegetables, fruits, and beverages destined for the feast. All these and many other items are named in the tabulated list of offerings spread out before the face of the deceased king and extending across a now missing upper register. Below the list, in thirty-four or more columns of incised hieroglyphs, are the words of an ancient spell handed down from the Pyramid Texts (§§ 118-133) and designed to ensure to the deceased person not only an uninterrupted supply of food and drink offerings, but also the ability to assimilate and enjoy them. A somewhat longer version of the same spell is found in New Kingdom Books of the Dead (Chapter CLXXVIII). The names of the king, "Men-peḥty-Rēʿ" and "Ramesses," are repeated again and again throughout this text, preceded by such titles as King, King of Upper and Lower Egypt, Lord of the Two Lands, Lord of Crowns, Lord of Achievement, and Son of Rēʿ. In the register below, several different classes of priests—prophets, lector priests, a *setem*-priest, and an embalmer—prepare the tables for the banquet, perform the preliminary purifications and fumigations, and recite the "numerous beatific spells," while the last officiant at the extreme right drags behind him a bundle of *heden*-plant in a rite called "bringing the foot," apparently intended to ward off evil spirits or demons. Below the throne of the king, fat nature gods of the North and South (fig. 209) bind together the heraldic plants of Upper and Lower Egypt and approach from both sides bearing offering mats and other beneficent symbols. Of the procession of regular offering bearers in the lowest register there now remains only the lead figure, a lector priest carrying a foreleg of beef. It is probable that the missing right end of the wall was taken up by a large standing figure of Sēthy I functioning as his father's chief offering priest.

With the exception of a large section of the north wall, all the foregoing blocks of chapel relief were acquired in 1911 as a gift of J. Pierpont Morgan. The section referred to was presented to the Museum in 1912 by Dikran G. Kelekian, together with a block from the left jamb of the chapel doorway on which is preserved the upper part of a large figure of Sēthy I wearing the *atef*-crown. Other portions of the chapel, not in the Museum's collection, include a great limestone stela with Sēthy's dedication of the little building (called a "mansion of eternity") to his father and to Osiris Wen-nefer.

From Abydos also comes a handsome, if somewhat battered, diorite ★statue (fig. 210) in which Sēthy, wearing the traditional kilt, *nemes*, and chin beard of his exalted station, is represented as kneeling and holding before him an offering slab and what was once a large ⊔-sign (for *ka*, "food"?) mounted on a papyrus column. An inscription engraved on the pilaster running up the back of the figure tells us that he is "one clean of hands bringing an offering to his father, Osiris, Lord of the Abydene Nome—the King of Upper and Lower Egypt, Men-maʿet-Rēʿ"; and texts on the sides of the flange which supports the offering slab describe him as the "Good God, rich in provisions, who brings food (*ka*) to the Lords of the Abydene Nome" and as the "Good God, clean of hands, who contents the gods of the Abydene Nome, the Son of Rēʿ, Lord of Crowns, Sēthy Mery-en-Ptaḥ." The cartouches of the king, topped by double plumes and flanking the word *enḥeḥ*, "eternity," are inscribed on the vertical surface between the arms of the *ka*-sign, and part of the expression "horizon of eternity," referring

FIGURE 208. Ramesses I offers to the Osiris symbol. Limestone relief from a chapel at Abydos. H. 44 in.

presumably to a temple or chapel, is preserved on the bracket which supported the spout of the offering slab above. The almost totally destroyed forward edge of the slab was also inscribed and its top is carved in low relief with representations of food and drink offerings. The statue, like Sēthy's tomb and temple reliefs, is a work of great elegance and refinement, impeccable in its modeling and finish and undeniably beautiful in its own formal way. It is lacking, however, in vigor and feeling, and in this lack it presages the spiritual and emotional emptiness characteristic of so many works of later Ramesside art.

Four wooden builders' ★cramps inscribed with the names of Sēthy I are said to have come from the Abydos temple. As usual, they are double-ended dovetails of some hard, dark wood (acacia?) and measure twelve to seventeen and a quarter inches in length. In three cases the praenomen cartouche of the king, preceded by the title the Good God or the Lord of the Two Lands, is carefully incised on the upper surface of the cramp. The fourth cramp carries on one of its edges the title Son of Rēʿ, followed by the pharaoh's personal name, Sēthy Mery-en-Ptaḥ.

To protect the property and personnel of the Nubian estates of his temple at Abydos from being commandeered by government officials and from other acts prejudicial to their independence, the king issued a long, detailed, and harshly worded decree, a copy of which has been preserved to us on a cliff at Nauri, some fifty-five miles below the

Third Cataract of the Nile. The inhumanly cruel punishments with which, in this decree, Sētẖy threatens his subjects and the fact that now and again magic is invoked to support the king's laws indicate a sorry letdown in both the power and the dignity of the pharaonic office and a widespread lack of discipline among the officials of the pharaonic government. Here again, as in the art of the period, we have a foretaste of the general decline which was soon to follow.

More constructive were the steps taken by Sētẖy, also in behalf of his Abydene temple, to resume exploitation of the desert gold mines east of Edfu and to facilitate delivery of the gold by improving traveling conditions to and from the mines. The road to the mines ran through a rocky valley known today as the Wādy Miāḥ. Here, at a spot thirty-seven miles from the Nile, the king established (or re-established) a well and a small settlement, and near by in the face of a sandstone cliff excavated a little temple with inscriptions describing these activities, one of which is dated to the ninth year of his reign.

With the statue of Sētẖy I described above the Museum acquired a black diorite ★offering table dedicated by the king to his patron divinity the god Sētẖ of Ombos, and the latter's wife the goddess Nephthys. It comes in all probability from the temple of Sētẖ at Ombos (modern Ṭūkh) on the west side of the Nile some seventy-five miles upriver from Abydos. Exactly two royal cubits (41 ⅜ inches) in length and just over a cubit in width, the table is an oblong rectangular slab of stone with the usual offering mat, loaves of bread, and libations vases carved in low relief on its broad upper surface. In one of two little panels on the front edge of the slab Sētẖy is seen prostrating himself in adoration before a seated figure of "Sētẖ, the Ombite, Lord of the Southland." The figure of the god, topped by the head of Sētẖ's curious, long-nosed animal, has been hacked out at some subsequent period of Egyptian history when Sētẖ was no longer revered as the god of the ruling dynasty but was once again abhorred as the traditional enemy of Osiris and the personification of evil. The other panel contains a pendent figure of Nephthys also seated and receiving the attentions of the prostrate Sētẖy, who in this case holds a libation vase and a burning censer. It is one of the few records of a cult of Nephthys which has been preserved to us. A band of inscription running horizontally around the four edges of the slab contains two complete and, in part, variant titularies of the king. From the Nephthys panel clockwise we read: "(Long) live the Horus, Appearing-in-Thebes-who-causes-the-Two-Lands-to-live, He of the Two Goddesses, Repeating-births, powerful of arm who repels the Nine Bows, Horus of Gold, Repeating-appearances-in-glory, rich in archers in all lands, the King of Upper and Lower Egypt, Men-maʿet-Rēʿ, the Son of Rēʿ, Sētẖy Mery-en-Ptaḥ, beloved of Nephthys, Mistress of the Gods, and given life"; and from the Sētẖ panel counterclockwise: "(Long) live the Horus, Strong-bull-contented-with-truth, He of the Two-Goddesses, Great-of-splendor-in-the-heart(s)-of-mankind, Horus of Gold, Contented-with-strength-and-beloved-of-Rēʿ, the King of Upper and Lower Egypt, Men-maʿet-Rēʿ, the Son of Rēʿ, Sētẖy Mery-en-Ptaḥ, beloved of [Sētẖ], the son of Nūt, may he live forever!" In the second of these texts the hieroglyph , "Sētẖ," has been intentionally erased. The Cairo Museum possesses a smaller version of this offering table dedicated by the same pharaoh to the sun god Atūm Khepri at Heliopolis.

A cartouche-shaped ★plaque three and an eighth inches in length comes probably from a foundation deposit of a building erected by Sētẖy I in the great temple enclosure of Ptaḥ at Memphis. On the front of the plaque, inlaid in white glaze, is the name of the king, "Men-maʿet-Rēʿ, Ruler of Heliopolis," and on the back, the name of the building, "the temple (called) Sētẖy-Mery-en-Ptaḥ-is-serviceable-in-the-House-of-Ptaḥ." Except for the concluding phrase the name is similar to those which Sētẖy bestowed on the hypostyle hall at Karnak and on his cenotaph at Abydos.

Tile inlays from palace doorways of Sētẖy I have been found in some quantity near the modern

FIGURE 209. Nature gods of Upper and Lower Egypt on the north wall of the Abydene chapel of King Ramesses I. L. of panel 39 ½ in.

village of Ḳantīr, in the eastern Delta sixty miles northeast of Cairo. It is evident from the scale and richness of these inlays that the palace in question was a large and extremely handsome building, magnificent enough to have been the pharaoh's principal residence. The finest groups of Ḳantīr tiles bearing Sēthy's titulary are in the Cairo Museum and the Louvre, our own collection including only a single fragmentary ★inlay plaque of yellowish faience with the upper half of the nomen "Sēthy [Mery-en-Ptaḥ]" encrusted in dark gray glaze. The ancient town occupied today by the villages of Ḳantīr and Khataʿneh now appears to have been both extensive and important and it is perhaps here rather than at Ṣān el Ḥagar, or Tanis, twelve miles to the north, that we should place the official residence and capital of the kings of the Nineteenth and Twentieth Dynasties.

A bronze ★signet ring, two faience ★cartouche plaques, and fourteen steatite ★scarabs in the Museum's collection carry one or another of the names of Sēthy I, sometimes accompanied by appropriate titles and epithets, sometimes in association with the name of Sēthy's much admired predecessor Thut-mosĕ III. An unusually large scarab of glazed steatite, found near the North Pyramid at el Lisht, is inscribed at the top of its oval field with the name of the god Ptaḥ, below this with two horizontal lines of text containing short titularies of Sēthy I, and at the bottom with a row of amuletic hieroglyphs. The titles used here and on some of the other scarabs are the Good God, King of Upper and Lower Egypt, and Lord of the Two Lands. The epithets include "image of Rēʿ, twice firm," "chosen of Rēʿ," "Lord of Strength," "beloved of Montu," "beloved of Ptaḥ," and "beloved of all lands." The personal name Sēthy, alone or accompanied by the expressions "beloved of Ptaḥ" or "beloved of Amūn," is found on one of the plaques and on three of the scarabs.

Two prominent Thebans, the Vizier Pa-sēr and his father the High Priest of Amūn, Neb-enteru, held office under both Sēthy I and Ramesses II. Of the former we possess, besides an inscribed faience ★bead and two steatite plaques, four stamped mud ★bricks and a handsome blue faience ★*shawabty*-figure from his tomb (No. 106) in western Thebes. The *shawabty*, which is almost six inches in height, wears a long striped headdress and an enormous broad collar and is inscribed in black with Chapter VI of the Book of the Dead written in six horizontal lines around the lower half of the figure. On these objects Pa-sēr bears the titles Hereditary Prince, Count, God's Father Beloved of the God, Overseer of the City, and

Vizier; and on one of the bricks he is designated as the son of the "First Prophet of Amūn, Neb-enteru, called Tēr." A fragment of limestone relief from the tomb of the Eleventh Dynasty Chancellor Achtoy at Deir el Baḥri carries an ink *graffito dedicated by the "First Prophet of Amūn, Neb-enteru, to his ancestor, Achtoy," and dated to "Regnal Year 17 of the King of Upper and Lower Egypt, User-maʿet-Rēʿ" (Ramesses II).[5]

On a stamped *funerary cone from Tomb 41 at Thebes another of Sēthy's key officials, the Chief Steward Amun-em-Opet, bears, in addition to his principal title, the not uncommon designation "Leader of the Festivals of Amūn." Twelve color *copies by Norman de Garis Davies, Charles Wilkinson, and Norman Hardy reproduce at full scale and with meticulous exactitude the paintings in one of the finest Theban tomb chapels of the reign, that of the royal mortuary priest Woser-ḥēt (No. 51). To the reigns of Sēthy I and Ramesses II are probably to be assigned the tombs of the Servitor in the Place-of-truth Sen-nedjem, and his family, at Deir el Medīneh (see pp. 387, 414).

2. Ramesses "the Great"

With the death of Sēthy I in 1290 B.C. his son Ramesses, who for some years had shared with him the administration of the country and the leadership of its armed forces, assumed the throne as King User-maʿet-Rēʿ Ramesses II and entered upon a reign which was destined to last for two-thirds of a century. A brash young man of about twenty, not overburdened with intelligence and singularly lacking in taste, the new pharaoh brought to the now arduous task of holding together the Egyptian empire tremendous energy and personal magnetism and a consuming desire to be known by his own and by future generations as a great and good ruler. Though his victories on the field of battle were sometimes inconclusive, his achievements in the field of diplomacy of transient value, and the works of architecture and sculpture with which he flooded the land more notable for their size and quantity than for their beauty, Egypt prospered in his time and the empire survived in the midst of dangers as serious as any which it had had to face.

At the outset of his reign Ramesses exhibited his piety and filial devotion by carrying to completion a number of his father's more important buildings, including Sēthy's temple at Abydos, his mortuary temple in western Thebes, and the great hypostyle hall at Karnak.

The palace which Sēthy seems to have founded at Ḳantīr in the northeastern Delta was taken over and enlarged by his son, the doorways, balconies, throne rooms, and private compartments of the new palace buildings being adorned with faience tiles and statues of a size and richness unequaled in the annals of Egyptian art. In 1922 and in 1928-1929 the Museum acquired by purchase 240 fragments of these tiles and statues, from which we have been able not only to restore a number of the individual units used in the decoration of the palace, but also to reconstruct portions of some of the architectural elements to which they had been applied.

It is evident, for example, that the faience *statues of lions and most of the larger and heavier *tiles pieced together from our fragments once formed the ornamental revetments of several richly decorated throne daises. Included in this category are tiles in the form of individual steps, tiles from stairway balustrades and from the sides of elevated platforms, tiles from a paneled dado, tiles from a cavetto cornice, and floor tiles from the tops of the daises. The tiles which made up the sloping stairway balustrades and those from the sides of the dais platforms are decorated with figures of prone and kneeling foreigners—Nubians, Libyans, and Asiatics—offering tribute (see fig. 211); the steps carry on their treads bound foreign captives; and

[5] See Part I, p. 164. Neb-enteru is mistakenly referred to there as a "scribe."

FIGURE 210. Sēthy I offering to Osiris. Porphyritic diorite. H. 45 in.

FIGURE 211. A Nubian chieftain. Tiles from a throne dais of King Ramesses II. H. 21 ¼ in.

each of the floor tiles displays on its surface one of the "Nine Bows"—emblems of the subdued foreign enemies of Egypt. On the blue and white dado tiles, palace-façade panels alternate with clumps of the heraldic plants of Upper and Lower Egypt. The backs of the remarkable faience figures of lions are flat and unglazed and it is probable that they were attached as ornaments to the newel posts at the bottoms of the dais stairways. Each statue showed the royal beast sitting upright on its haunches and biting the head of a kneeling foreign chieftain whom it holds between its forepaws. In the example of figure 212 the head of the foreigner, together with the lower jaw of the lion, is missing; but the man is identified by his distinctive clothing (cf. fig. 211) and by a hieroglyphic inscription down the front of his figure in which we read: "Says the wretched [fallen] chief of Kush, 'The breath of life!' " The captive's robe is blue with the decoration of the garment and the inscriptions, including the praenomen cartouche of Ramesses II on the right side of the breast, encrusted in pale green glaze. The lion, which by contrast is pale green with black details, bears the cartouches of the king on its shoulders, the praenomen User-maʿet-Rēʿ Sotep-en-Rēʿ on the right shoulder, the nomen Raʿ-mesē-se Mery-Amūn on the left shoulder. The ground color of all the other tiles from the throne daises is gray with the figures and other elements in the decoration overlaid or encrusted in a remarkably wide range of attractive and harmonious polychrome glazes—pale bluish green, yellow, light brown, red, dark brown, black, and white.

The same colors are found in a series of big rectangular ★tiles with relief figures of foreigners offering tribute, which were probably used to decorate the bases of the walls of the throne rooms or other public chambers of the palace. A cubit (20.5 inches) in height, each of these panels carried, when complete, the figure of a Nubian, Syrian, Libyan, or Mediterranean islander standing with hands upraised beside a light table supporting a basket of fruit or other offering.

A third group of our Ḳantīr ★tiles comes evidently from the ornate window and balcony of the palace where the pharaoh periodically presented himself before his subjects—the so-called "window of appearances"—and from the adornment of other great windows and doorways of state. Of this group some seventy-five fragments belonged to tiles in the form of large cutout figures of bound foreigners which seem to have been inlaid in rows in the fronts of balcony balustrades. Numerous other fragments are from the frames of doorways and windows. They include faience headdress pieces from relief figures of the king, fragments of tiles in the form of *rekhyet*-birds (𓅨) with hands upraised on *neb*-signs ("all the people in adoration"), parts of narrow upright panels with bound foreign captives, and several types and sizes of inlay tiles with the names and titles of Ramesses II.

One lot of the inscribed inlays—small white tiles with hieroglyphs encrusted in a dark purplish gray glaze—are sufficiently numerous to allow us to restore in part the text which they formed: "Shines the Good God, Smiter of [Retenu?] . . . Lord of the Two Lands, Lord of Achievement, User-maʿet-Rēʿ [Sotep-en-Rēʿ], the Son of Rēʿ, Raʿ-[mesēse Mery]-Amūn, like Rēʿ forev[er]."

The foreigners appearing on the tiles and statues from the semipublic portions of the palace are represented in considerable detail and probably with more care than the average run of portrayals of foreign types by Egyptian artists. Unfortunately, the general standard of accuracy and consistency in such ancient racial portraits is seldom so high as to make the identifications of the types matters of certainty. Among our fragmentary figures we can, however, distinguish six general groups of peoples: dark-skinned, woolly-haired Kushites of Nubia and the Sūdān, blond Tjemeḥu and brown-skinned Teḥenu Libyans from the desert regions west of the Nile, hook-nosed, long-haired Hittites of Asia Minor, yellow-skinned Syrians of several different tribes, bearded Mesopotamians dressed in colorful woolen robes, and red-skinned "Sea Peoples" of the islands and littorals of the Aegean and other Mediterranean areas. The appearance of the last group, which included Philistines, Dardanians, Lycians, Sardinians, and Sicilians, is particularly significant, for these were the pre-Greek peoples of Indo-European origin whose expansion throughout the Near East was soon to undermine its ancient powers and alter extensively its ancient character.

It will have been noted that the figures of foreigners preserved on the tiles and statues from Ḳantīr are used exclusively on elements which occupied inferior positions in the decorative scheme of the palace (bottoms of doorjambs, treads of steps, floor plaques, sides of low platforms, bases of walls, etc.) and that, in almost every case, the foreigner is represented either as a bound enemy or as a groveling vassal. This is typical of the arrogant, unfriendly, and obviously apprehensive spirit with which the Egyptians of the Ramesside period regarded their foreign neighbors, the same bullying attitude being expressed with great consistency throughout the art of the period. It is especially striking when compared with the feeling toward foreigners displayed in paintings and reliefs of the earlier dynasties, wherein we frequently see a friendly and dignified intercourse taking place between the Egyptians and the representatives of

FIGURE 212. Faience lion of Ramesses II holding a bound Nubian chieftain. H. 27½ in.

outlying nations, the visiting and gift-bearing foreigners often on a practically equal footing with their Egyptian hosts.

In sharp contrast to the figures of conquered enemies, formal inscriptions, official emblems, and highly conventionalized decorative motifs appearing on the tiles of the three preceding groups is the subject matter of our fourth group of Ḳantīr ★tiles. Here we find depicted only the lighter, the more attractive, and the more intimate of the pharaoh's surroundings: parts of canal or lakeside scenes with the luxuriant floral growth which fringed and filled the waterways of the royal gardens or estates, together with the abundant fish and bird life found therein; ladies of the royal ḥarīm at play in equally idyllic surroundings; and figures of the ugly, but much beloved, little household god Bēs. The assumption, based on the general character of their decoration, that these tiles are from the living quarters of the various palace suites is borne out by the fact that altogether similar subjects and compositions adorned the painted walls of the private rooms and passages of the palaces of Amun-ḥotpe III at Thebes and Akh-en-Aten at el ʿAmārneh (pp. 245 ff. and 290).

The intricate and subtle polychromy of the Ḳantīr tiles is well exemplified in the aquatic scene of figure 213. The ground color here is gray, the banks and water ripples black. The lotus flowers and buds are pale green and yellow, the pads pale green. The bank grasses and flowers are pale green and pale blue, the spiny plants displaying red flowers at the tops of their stalks. The fish is cream-colored, with pale purplish patches over its body, the details of the fins, scales, tail, etc., being outlined in dark brown or black. The duck appearing in the second fragment has a pale brown breast and throat, with bluish gray and white back and wings, the plumage being picked out in black and dark brown.

A considerable quantity of disk-shaped ★rosettes, also from Ḳantīr, are of fine-grained white, gray, and bluish green faience with the petals encrusted in glazes of contrasting colors. Ranging in diameter from one and an eighth to four and a quarter inches, they cannot be localized to any one part of the palace decoration or to any one variety of architectural element. They were probably employed freely wherever space fillers were needed or where there were surfaces to be decorated which required flexible patterns composed of small units or units evenly graduated in size. A rosette motif was used, for example, in the border patterns of the floors of the throne daises.

With the palace tiles the Museum acquired a handsome, but woefully fragmentary, ★draughtboard of bright blue and white faience inscribed on the top and side with the names of Ramesses II.

Two large faience ★bricks, more than fourteen inches in length, come almost certainly from foundation deposits of an important building erected by Ramesses II at Ḳantīr—possibly from those of his palace. They are made of the same coarse, sandy material used in the statues and the larger tiles from the palace, the glaze being a greenish blue with the names and titles of the king drawn on it in black outline. The more simply inscribed of the two bricks bears on its front "The Lord of the Two Lands, User-maʿet-Rēʿ Sotep-en-Rēʿ"; while the other example has on both the front and the back surface the praenomen of the king and his nomen, "Raʿ-mesē-se Mery-Amūn," each of the cartouches being set over the sign for gold (*nebu*) and being surmounted by the double plume. Around the edges of the latter brick are written two longer, nearly identical inscriptions, in each of which we read: "(Long) live the Horus, Strong-bull-loving-truth, King of Upper and Lower Egypt, Ruler of the Nine Bows, Lord of the Two Lands, User-maʿet-Rēʿ Sotep-en-Rēʿ, Lord of Crowns, Raʿ-mesē-se Mery-Amūn, given life." On the top or rear edge the praenomen and nomen of the king are repeated, preceded by the titles Lord of the Two Lands and Lord of Crowns respectively.

Under Ramesses II the royal residence and administrative center in the northeast Delta was expanded into a vast and magnificently endowed domain and was renamed in honor of the young king Per-Raʿ-mesē-se Mery-Amūn ʿA-nakhtu, "House-of-Ramesses-beloved-of-Amūn-great-of-

FIGURE 213. A pool or canal with birds, fish, and plants. Tiles from a palace of Ramesses II at Ḳantīr. L. 23 ½ in.

victories." It came also to be known more briefly as Per-Raʿ-mesē-se, or Pi-Raʿmesse (the Biblical Raamses?), and was sometimes referred to elliptically as the "Great-of-victories." Texts of the Nineteenth and Twentieth Dynasties indicate that the domain so called comprised a city with a royal palace, private dwellings, and temples to the gods, a military base suitable for the marshaling of large bodies of infantry and chariotry, a harbor for ships on a branch of the Nile, and landed estates with gardens, vineyards, and orchards. Per-Raʿ-mesē-se appears to have been distinct from the town of Djaʿnet, or Tanis (modern Ṣān el Ḥagar), where an accumulation of Ramesside temple monuments[6] combined with other considerations has led a number of our foremost Egyptologists to place it. A more likely location seems to be the neighborhood of the modern villages of Khatāʿneh and Ḳantīr, where, as we have just seen, copious traces of a palace of Ramesses II have been found and where an extensive townsite of Ramesside and earlier times has only recently begun to be explored.

It was in all probability from Per-Raʿ-mesē-se that Ramesses II in the fifth year of his reign (1286 B.C.) set out at the head of four army divisions to smash a powerful coalition of Asiatic peoples assembled by the Hittite king Muwatallis and to continue his father's attempts to regain for Egypt her erstwhile holdings in northern Syria. Though in a famous battle near Ḳadesh on the river Orontes he led the van of his forces into an enemy trap, saw one of his divisions routed by the Hittite chariotry, and had to fight his own way out of a desperate situation, he managed in the end to rally his troops and convert what might have been a disastrous defeat into a somewhat questionable victory. Detailed representations and accounts of this battle and of some of the more successful campaigns in Palestine and Syria which preceded and followed it were carved on the walls of Ramesses II's great rock-cut temples at Abu Simbel and Derr in Nubia, in his temple to the north of that of Sēthy I at Abydos, in the forecourt and on the outer of the two pylons which he added to the temple of Amūn at Luxor, in the Amūn temple at Karnak, and in the so-called Ramesseum, the huge and imposing mortuary temple which he erected for himself in western Thebes.

Two *blocks of painted sandstone temple relief, with the colors in one case almost perfectly preserved, show us parts of one of Ramesses II's great Asiatic battle scenes. On the larger block (fig. 214) we see a welter of dead and dying Syrians, laid low by the pharaoh's arrows, sprawled about in one of the free, over-all compositions which from the time of Tḥut-mosĕ IV onward characterize such

[6] Apparently for the most part transported thither during the Twenty-First and succeeding dynasties.

FIGURE 214. Painted sandstone relief from a temple of Ramesses II at Thebes. L. 45 ¼ in.

scenes. The red and yellow of the men's flesh, the black of their hair and beards, and the blue and yellow decoration of their garments and accouterments stand out sharply against the white background of the block and give us an idea of how brilliant the interiors of New Kingdom temples, now the dingy brown of the bare sandstone, must once have been. Over the heads of the pharaoh's stricken foes we can see the bellies and forelegs of his chariot horses, surging ahead in a flying gallop. The more fragmentary of the two blocks preserves parts of the figures of four white-clad Syrians standing apparently on the wall of a city and clinging to one another in terror before the onslaughts of the king. These blocks were recovered by our Egyptian Expedition from the foundations of a temple of Ramesses IV at the foot of the ʿAsāsīf valley in western Thebes, whither they had been taken in the Twentieth Dynasty and reused as ordinary building stones.

With them, re-employed in the same manner, were found the two lower courses of a gigantic red granite temple ★doorjamb (fig. 215) inscribed with the names and titles of Ramesses II and adorned on the front with superimposed panels showing the king offering to the gods Ptaḥ Ta-tenen, Amun Rēʿ Ka-mūtef, and another. In the short horizontal texts between the panels the pharaoh is described as "one beloved of" Montu and Ḥat-Ḥor, both of whom present "life to (his) nostrils." The second line of inscription below the bottom panel gives the name of the door to which the jamb belonged: "the great door (of) Raʿmesē-se Mery-Amūn (called) Amūn-rejoices-in-his-monuments." This was the name of the doorway in the center of the west wall of Ramesses II's forecourt in the Luxor temple—a doorway which faced west and would have had on its left, or southern, jamb figures of the king wearing, as here, the crown of Upper Egypt. Another point in favor of the identification is the prominence accorded on our jamb to the ithyphallic deity Ka-mūtef, a Theban version of the fertility god Mīn, and to the Memphite creator god Ta-tenen, both of whom, as forms of Amūn, had important cults in the Luxor temple. On the other hand, there may well have been a doorway of this name in the Ramesseum, where Mīn Ka-mūtef and Ta-tenen were also revered and which is less than half a mile from the site where the jamb was found. Wherever it was, the doorway was still standing in the reign of Ramesses III, who at that time caused his own cartouches to be added in lightly engraved bands around the bases of its jambs. The contrast in style between these cartouches and the admirably executed original decoration of our jamb shows how rapid was the decline of Egyptian art during the latter half of the Nineteenth Dynasty.

A large ★slab of limestone purchased in Luxor in 1910 and presented to the Museum in 1954 by Mrs. Constantine Johnston Beach bears part of an act of endowment drawn up under Ramesses II in behalf of one of his Theban temples—probably the Ramesseum. Preserved are most of the last eleven lines of a well-cut hieroglyphic text listing the daily allowances of food, drink, and clothing allotted to the temple personnel and citing the king's instructions ("what was said in the Majesty of the Palace on this day") regarding certain crown properties assigned to the support of the "temple of User-maʿet-Rēʿ, given life." Among the latter are a tract of land apparently once attached to the Theban palace (see p. 244) of Amun-ḥotpe III and called the "district of He-of-Tekhenu-Aten" and fields belonging to the "House of the Adoratress (of Amūn)," an important landowning institution mentioned from time to time in administrative texts of the Ramesside period.

From one of the vaulted brick store chambers surrounding the Ramesseum comes the ★shoulder of a large pottery amphora bearing a hieratic label in black ink which identified the contents of the jar as "[wine of the vi]neyard of the Mansion of Millions of Years of the King of Upper and Lower Egypt, User-maʿet-Rēʿ Sotep-en-Rēʿ . . . Raʿ-mesē-se Mery-Amūn, which is on the west of the northern (?) river arm," and gave the name of the "master vintner" under whose supervision the wine was prepared. Though "Mansion of Millions of Years" refers to the king's mortuary temple in western Thebes, the vineyard in question was without much doubt in the northern Delta.

The painted quartzite ★head of figure 216, which represents a youthful pharaoh wearing the *kheperesh*-helmet, or Blue Crown, is thought to have come from Karnak. In the belief that it closely resembles the head of a famous statue in Turin it has been identified as a portrait of Ramesses II. The validity of the identification suffers somewhat from the fact that several competent

FIGURE 215. Red granite doorjamb from a temple of Ramesses II at Thebes. Lower block. H. 9 ft. 6 in.

FIGURE 216. King Ramesses II (?). Painted quartzite. H. 17½ in.

students of Egyptian art believe the Turin statue to have been made for Sēthy I and subsequently appropriated by his son. In our head the inconsistency between the highly accomplished modeling of most of the face and the surprisingly crude handling of the eyes has even led some connoisseurs to cast doubt upon its authenticity. While, in the absence of any really cogent evidence, one hesitates to throw out so handsome and, in many respects, so characteristic a piece of sculpture, we shall perhaps be wise to regard this royal head as one of our not completely solved problems.

No problem except that of provenience attaches itself to the ★mid-section of a life-size statue of Ramesses II delicately carved in dark gray diorite and representing the king standing and holding against his side a tall staff, or pole, once surmounted by the ram's-head emblem of the god Amūn. The staff, which with others of the same type the pharaoh is presumably in the act of presenting to a temple of the state god, was inscribed over most of its length. What remains of the inscription tells us that its donor was the "King of Upper and Lower Egypt, Lord of the Two Lands, Lord of Achievements, User-maʿet-Rēʿ Sotep-en-Rēʿ," and that "he made (it) as his monument to his father, Amun Rēʿ, Lord of Karnak, making for him a noble staff of" some precious material, the name of which is lost. For the occasion Ramesses II wears an intricately draped and pleated kilt and an elaborate beadwork(?) apron fronted by six uraei, and carries in his clenched right hand a horizontal rodlike object, perhaps the handle of a scepter. His oval belt clasp contains his praenomen, and his titles and names are repeated on the sturdy pilaster which is carved in one piece with the back of the figure. Statues of this type, though known from the time of Amun-ḥotpe III onward, are relatively rare, none of the extant examples equaling the present fragmentary figure in the gracefulness of its proportions and the beauty of its workmanship.

The end of a large ★spool-shaped object of red granite with the praenomen of Ramesses II engraved on its flat forward surface comes from the hand of a colossal standing statue of the king similar to those now to be seen in the forecourt of the Luxor temple. The object is believed to represent a rolled-up document called in Egyptian an *imyet-per*, corresponding roughly to our deed of title to property.

Outside of Thebes there is hardly a site of any consequence from one end of the empire to the other which does not possess a temple or other building constructed or enlarged by Ramesses II or which has not produced some monument, large or small, bearing his familiar and ubiquitous cartouches. From Petrie's excavations at Ahnāsyeh, the site of ancient Herakleopolis, on the southeastern fringe of the Fayyūm, our collection acquired a large ★block of limestone temple relief on which the king is represented enthroned within a uraeus-crowned pavilion, wearing on his head the crown of Lower Egypt and holding in his hands the Osirian crook and *ladanisterion*. Despite the pharaoh's youthful appearance there can be little doubt that he is here shown celebrating one of his numerous *sed*-festivals. Executed in Rameses II's favorite medium, *relief en creux*, the carving of the figure is a little hard and metallic and the incised hieroglyphs in the accompanying inscriptions are lacking in grace and attention to detail.

Forty miles north of Herakleopolis, near the pyramid of King Se'n-Wosret I at el Lisht, our own expedition turned up a limestone ★ostrakon inscribed in hieratic with the cartouche of "Raᶜ-mesē-se Mery-Amūn—may he live, prosper, and be well!" and the name of a certain Mery, son of Beder, whose father's name suggests that he was of the seafaring Tjeker people. A pylon-shaped ★stela of limestone, on which Ramesses II is described as "one beloved of Ḥat-Ḥor, Mistress of the Southern Sycamore," comes probably from a suburb of the city of Memphis where the goddess referred to had her temple. The trapezoidal field of the stela, evidently a votive, bears only the two cartouches of the king, flanked on the left by the epithet already quoted and on the right by the words "one beloved of Ḥat-Ḥor, Mistress of the West." Though of unrecorded provenience, a big ★commemorative scarab of Ramesses II, formerly in the Carnarvon collection, is inscribed not only with the titles and names of the pharaoh, but also with the name of a royal domain called the "Mansion-of-Raᶜ-mesē-se-Mery-Amūn-beloved-like-Atūm-on-the-Western-Waters." Since the "Western Waters" are believed to have been the Canopic arm of the Nile, the place mentioned was probably in the northwestern Delta. The scarab, a fairly well-known monument, is of pale greenish blue faience and measures three and an eighth inches in length.

Another Delta town, Hurbeiṭ, in the east central section of the great alluvial plain, yielded a block of early Ramesside temple ★relief with the head and shoulders of a bearded Asiatic—Syrian or Mesopotamian—admirably rendered in deep *relief en creux*. The man, his hands uplifted in an attitude of supplication, was one of a procession of foreigners, the shoulder and part of the head of another figure being visible at the right edge of the block. Except for the fact that it is of limestone this piece shows marked affinities with the portraits of foreigners preserved in the great sandstone temple reliefs of Ramesses II and is in all probability to be assigned to his reign.

The activities of the king's working parties in the copper and turquoise mines of Sinai are attested by the official inscriptions and inscribed votive offerings which they left in the temple of Ḥat-Ḥor at Serābīt el Khādim. Of the latter the Museum in 1909 received as a gift from the Egypt Exploration Fund thirty-six ★fragments of blue faience bangles inscribed in black with the titles and names of Ramesses II. Of the three types of inscription found on these bangles, one reads: "The King of Upper and Lower Egypt, Lord of the Two Lands, User-maᶜet-Rēᶜ Sotep-en-Rēᶜ, given life"; another: "The Son of Rēᶜ, Lord of Crowns, Raᶜ-mesē-se Mery-Amūn, beloved of Ḥat-Ḥor, [Lady of Turqu]oise"; while the third consists only of the king's nomen cartouche surmounting a "gold"-sign.

The upper part of a small seated ★statue in dark gray diorite has been identified by Cyril Aldred on stylistic and iconographical grounds as a representation of Ramesses II "or his successor." A little over twelve inches in height from crown of head to solar plexus, the figure wears the long, kingly chin beard and the banded *nemes* with double-looped uraeus over the brow. The youthful, half-smiling face is not unattractive, but the work as a whole is stiff, mechanical, and lacking in liveliness. Neither the ancient provenience nor the more recent source of the piece is known.

The small objects of the reign which bear the names of the king and his family are many and various and, so far as the Museum's collection is concerned, usually of unrecorded provenience. With the Carnarvon collection we acquired an attractive little circular ★cosmetic box of ivory and ebony, its swivel lid engraved with the cartouches of Ramesses II and his queen "Nefret-iry

Beloved-of-Mūt," and adorned with the ivory figure of a crouching sheeplike animal. Part of a ★ceremonial cubit rod, carved of mudstone, was obtained by purchase in 1955. It is quasi-rectangular in section, one upper edge being beveled back and marked with a division of two fingers' width. The three other surfaces of the rod are inscribed with the names, titles, and epithets of Ramesses II, including the Golden Horus name, "Rich-in-years-(and-)great-of-victories," which he favored especially in his temple at Abydos. On one side of the rod the pharaoh is appropriately compared with the god Tḥōt, the divine exponent of exactitude, and on the top he is called the "sovereign who celebrates a million *sed*-festivals."

The king's praenomen preceded by the title Lord of the Two Lands is engraved on the side of a ★heart amulet of opaque red glass and, without a title, on a large ball ★bead of the same material. It is found also on three ★cartouche-shaped necklace pendants or dress ornaments molded of blue faience, and on a fourth of carnelian, the cartouche in each case being surmounted by the solar disk and double plume. On a long oval ★bead of pale blue faience the royal name is encrusted in dark blue glaze and is here accompanied by the title the Good God. A similar ★bead, but with the color scheme reversed, bears the nomen, Raʿmesē-se Beloved-of-Amūn, and the title Son of Rēʿ. A variant writing of the same name appears on a small ★plaque of blue faience in the form of a cartouche, which, since it is without suspension rings, is evidently not a pendant, but comes in all probability from a foundation deposit. Two blue faience ★finger rings carry the praenomen and a third the nomen, while the bezel of a handsome little double ★ring, carved of carnelian, comprises both of the pharaoh's cartouches, set side by side and topped in each instance by the sun's disk and double plume (cf. fig. 180, second row, right end).

Among fifty-four ★seal amulets of Ramesses II (see fig. 217) the scarab, as usual, predominates, with forty-three examples, as against three rectangular plaques, three oval plaques, four animal seals (a lion, a baboon, and two monkeys), and one hemicylindrical seal. In forty-five instances the material is gray steatite, usually coated with a greenish blue glaze, the other materials including faience, red jasper, carnelian, crystal, white quartz, green feldspar, and pink limestone. In many cases the designs engraved on the undersides of the scarabs and seals and on both sides of the plaques are miniature scenes in which the king appears in full regalia, slaying his enemies with axe or spear or driving his chariot over their prostrate forms. On a particularly elaborate little plaque, said to have been found at Carchemish on the Euphrates, the pharaoh is assisted in the slaughter by a lion which runs along beside him for all the world like a great dog and which may have been the prototype for the faience lions of Ḳantīr (fig. 212). Divinities are frequently represented, alone or attended by the king, and among these the most common are the mummiform god Ptaḥ, the ape of the moon god Tḥōt, the ram of Amūn, and the falcon-headed figure or sphinx of the sun god Rēʿ. On one scarab we find an amusing monogrammatic writing of the king's personal name, in which a solar disk with pendent uraei ("Raʿ") surmounts the figure of a royal child ("mes") holding his hand to his mouth and seated above a double "s"-sign. The hemicylindrical seal and several of the scarabs (including one with a human face) have the royal cartouche and other devices engraved on their backs (see fig. 217). Three scarabs are mounted in finger rings of silver or bronze and one is set in a gold funda, the ring for which has been lost. A limestone ★mold was used for producing small faience or glass cartouches with the throne name User-maʿet-Rēʿ Sotep-en-Rēʿ.

Following two decades of intermittent warfare in which neither side gained a decisive advantage, Ramesses II and Hattusilis, who had with some difficulty succeeded his father, Muwatallis, as king of the Hittites, concluded a treaty of peace and formed a defensive alliance against the rising power of Assyria and the inroads of the Sea Peoples. The treaty, drawn up in Ramesses II's twenty-first regnal year (1270 B.C.), was engraved in duplicate on tablets of silver. Copies of it in cuneiform and

FIGURE 217. Scarabs, plaques, and seals of King Ramesses II. Glazed steatite. L. ⅝-1 in.

hieroglyphic are preserved to us, respectively, on clay tablets from the archives of the Hittite capital at Boghaz Keui and in temple inscriptions at Karnak and in the Ramesseum. Thereafter cordial relations were maintained between the two powers, letters passed back and forth between the pharaoh and the Hittite royal family, and in the thirty-fourth year of his reign (1257 B.C.) Ramesses married the eldest daughter of Hattusilis in a ceremony widely publicized as a symbol of "peace and brotherhood."

This marriage seems to have marked the end of Ramesses II's career as a warrior and as a diplomat. Like Amun-ḥotpe III before him, he whiled away the last decades of his long life in idleness and self-indulgence, dwelling contentedly amid the beauty and luxury of Per-Raᶜ-mesē-se, basking in the unrestrained adulation of his court, and continuing the seemingly endless quest for new wall and column surfaces on which to inscribe his name and extol his virtues.

To these decades belong three ★inscribed wine jars in our collection, one of unknown provenience, the others from the well-known Theban tomb (No. 217) of the Sculptor Ipy. The hieratic labels on their shoulders date them—or, rather, their contents—to the thirty-ninth, forty-ninth, and fifty-fifth years of the reign; and the last of the three labels goes on to tell us that the contents of its jar was "[sweet] wine of the vineyard of the Chief of the Estate, which is on(?) the river arm." Though the very high year dates alone are sufficient to identify the reign in question, the titles and names of the king were actually given in the first label, the second line of which begins with the words: "The King of Upper and Lower Egypt, User-[maᶜet]-Rēᶜ. . . ."

In the fifty-third year of his reign the now aged pharaoh celebrated his ninth *sed*-festival, and in the sixty-seventh year (1223 B.C.) he died in his middle eighties and was buried in the Valley of the Tombs of the Kings in a tomb (No. 7) almost as elaborate as that of his father, but less well preserved and far less well known to modern visitors. A ★cup of turquoise blue faience and the corner of a blue faience ★offering slab(?), inscribed in each case with the names and titles of Ramesses II, may well have come from this tomb. Both are objects of a funerary nature and both are from western Thebes, the fragment of offering slab having been found by Theodore Davis in the Valley of the Tombs of the Kings. The mummy of the king, recovered in good condition from the Royal Cache near Deir el Baḥri, is that of a white-haired old man five feet eight inches in height, with a long, narrow face, low, sloping forehead, massive jaw, and prominent aquiline nose.

The tomb (No. 66) of the King's Great Wife Nefret-iry is one of the largest and most elaborate in the Valley of the Tombs of the Queens and the paintings adorning its walls are among the finest which Ramesside art produced. A series of remarkable color ★copies of these paintings, prepared for the Museum by Nina de Garis Davies and Charles K. Wilkinson, are doubly valuable, since in several instances the originals have suffered severely from natural causes "which are in large measure beyond repair."[7]

The fame of Ramesses II and probably also the fact that he was popularly known as Sēse—a short form of Raʿ-mesē-se—caused him to be assimilated by writers of Graeco-Roman times with the legendary hero Sesostris, or Sesoōsis, a figure derived primarily from the great Twelfth Dynasty pharaoh, Se'n-Wosret III. In more recent times, under a somewhat distorted version of his throne name User-maʿet-Rēʿ, he has, thanks to Percy Bysshe Shelley, become familiar to English readers as "Ozymandias, king of kings."

3. Contemporaries of Ramesses II and Their Monuments

Considering the multitude of officials, priests, soldiers, craftsmen, and other well-to-do citizens whose lifetimes fell within the sixty-seven-year reign of Ramesses II, it is not surprising to find that in our collection alone there are enough private works of art and craftsmanship datable to this reign to warrant their being treated under a heading of their own. Several of these works carry the cartouches and occasionally the figure of the king as well as the names and titles of their owners, and in some instances their inscriptions throw light on the national and local administrative systems, on the relationship between the pharaoh and his officials, on the ideals which governed the Ramesside official class, and other matters of a historical or semihistorical nature. From the art historian's point of view they are typical of their period, combining much that is still striking and graceful with a growing dullness of content, an increasingly mechanical style, and a slovenliness in the handling of detail which is particularly apparent in the carving of the inscriptions. As is often the case with material of great antiquity, the survival of which has been more or less a matter of chance, some of the foremost works which have come down to us belonged to persons of secondary importance, while the greatest men of their time are represented by the smallest and least impressive of their possessions. Of the well-known Vizier Pa-sēr, for example, we possess only the few small monuments already described in the section devoted to King Sēthy I.

Three of the eight First Prophets, or High Priests, of Amūn who served under Ramesses II are represented by equally unimpressive, though not altogether uninteresting, objects. The earliest of the three, Neb-wenenef, received his appointment to office in Ramesses II's first regnal year on an occasion vividly recorded in an inscription in his Theban tomb (No. 157). A little temple which Neb-wenenef built for himself(?) on the edge of the cultivated land in western Thebes lies just to the south of the mortuary temple of Sēthy I, under whom he had served as First Prophet of Ḥat-Ḥor and Onuris. The largely ruined building was identified by two foundation deposits, part of the contents of which came to the Museum in 1909 as a gift of the Egyptian Research Account. Included among the objects so acquired are a limestone ★"brick" engraved with the cartouches of

[7] Davies, *M. M. A. Bulletin*, XVII (1922), December, Part II, pp. 51-52.

Ramesses II and the name and title of the "First Prophet of Amūn, Neb-wenenef, the justified," two small ★cartouches of faience with the names of the king, a rectangular faience ★plaque with the title and name of the High Priest, and sixteen little faience ★models of meat offerings in the forms of whole trussed steers and the heads, *khopesh*-joints, and rib cuts of similar animals. A Theban ★graffito referred to on page 334 tells us that in Year 17 of Ramesses II the First Prophet of Amūn was Neb-enteru, the father of the Vizier Pa-sēr, who is also mentioned on one of the latter's stamped mud ★bricks. In Year 46 the office was held by the celebrated Bak-en-Khonsu, known to us from a Theban court record of that date formerly in the Berlin Museum (Papyrus 3047), from two remarkable biographical inscriptions on statues in Munich and Cairo, and from any number of other inscribed monuments. A rectangular faience ★plaque in our collection bears on one of its sides the name and title of Bak-en-Khonsu and on the other those of his father, the Overseer of Recruits of the House of Amūn, Amun-em-Opet. In the Berlin papyrus Bak-en-Khonsu is named as the senior member of a council of nine judges (all priests!) appointed to hear a civil case involving the income from landed property.

The second member of the council, the Prophet of Amūn, Woser-Montu, was without much doubt the owner of a red granite ★sarcophagus which came to the Museum in 1917 as a gift of J. P. Morgan. Like others of its class and period this monument is a large and somewhat coarsely executed anthropoid case, having the form of a colossal bandaged mummy and comprising a hollowed-out box and lid, each carved from a single block of stone and each measuring seven feet eight inches in length. On its chin the figure represented wears the long Osirian beard and on its head the long, striped headdress of archaic type bound with a floral fillet, while its clenched hands, crossed over its breast, hold the *djed*-symbol of "stability" and the *tyet*-symbol of "protection." The rest of the decoration follows the usual scheme for anthropoid coffins of the New Kingdom (see pp. 69 f., 221), but includes a number of elements not found on the earlier coffins. On the lid, for example, the prayer to the sky goddess Nūt, which descends in vertical columns from below the kneeling and winged figure of the goddess, is flanked on either side by an Anubis animal couched upon a shrine (), and further down, on the insteps of the mummiform figure, is a pair of human-headed *ba*-birds () with hands upraised, facing one another from each side of the central columns of text. Kneeling figures of the goddesses Nephthys and Isis occupy their customary stations on the head and foot ends of the lid, and below the Isis figure the foot end of the box is adorned with large *djed*- and *tyet*-symbols. Besides the *wedjat*-eyes and the panels with the figures and speeches of Anubis and the Four Genii of the Dead, the sides of the box carry at each of their ends an extra panel with a figure of the Ibis-headed Thōt and a "recitation" made by him. Of the Four Genii only Imsety is human-headed, Ḥapy having the head of an ape, Dewau-mautef the head of a prick-eared dog or jackal, and Ḳebeḥ-snēwef the head of a peregrine falcon. On the interior the floor of the box is adorned with a full-length figure of Nūt, whose outstretched arms extend up its sides so as to embrace, as it were, the body of the deceased once contained in the sarcophagus. Like those on the coffins and some of the sarcophagi of the Eighteenth Dynasty, the majority of the texts will be found incorporated in a version of Chapter CLI of the Book of the Dead. Besides being a prophet of the state god Amūn, Woser-Montu was also the First Prophet of Montu, Lord of Hermonthis, and is frequently so referred to in the texts on his sarcophagus. That he was identical with a similarly named First Prophet of Montu, Lord of Thebes, who was the owner of a big Ramesside tomb on the southeastern slope of the Ḳurnet Muraʿi, seems probable, though not absolutely certain. If the identification is correct our sarcophagus, of course, would have come from this tomb.

During the early Nineteenth Dynasty the ancient Upper Egyptian town of Si'ūt (modern Asyūt) was the home not only of several well-to-do officials of the national administration, but also of an accomplished atelier of sculptors, to whose able

FIGURE 218.
Up-wawet and Isis Ḥat-Ḥor, a limestone group dedicated by the Granary Overseer Si-Iset of Si'ūt. H. 51 in.

hands we owe three admirable pieces of private tomb statuary datable to the reign of Ramesses II. They come from two evidently adjacent tombs in the cliffs near Deir Durunka, two and a half miles south of Asyūt, where they were found in 1913 in excavations conducted in behalf of the late Sayed Pasha Khashaba.

A limestone ★group (fig. 218) representing Up-wawet, the god of Si'ūt, and his mother, Isis Ḥat-Ḥor, Mistress of Medjedny, is from the tomb of the King's Scribe and Overseer of the Granaries of Upper and Lower Egypt Si-Iset. Besides the name, titles, and parentage of its owner it bears, high up on the front of the back pilaster, between the heads of the deities, the titles and cartouches of King Ramesses II. The wolf-headed Up-wawet, whose name means "Opener-of-the-ways," wears a long, striated headdress and a short goffered kilt, both of Old Kingdom type, and holds in his hands the *was*-scepter and a flat object evidently not completely carved. His mother's costume, except for her fashionable sash, is equally archaic. She holds the symbol of "life" and the long, slender papyrus scepter affected by goddesses, and her head is surmounted by the sun's disk nestled between the horns of the cow of heaven. The column of inscription between the figures gives their names and epithets, and the line of hieroglyphs on the front and sides of the base contain two offering formulae in which each of the two deities is invoked in turn in behalf of the tomb owner and dedicator of the group. In six long columns of hieroglyphic text on the broad rear surface of the back pilaster Si-Iset prays to Osiris Wen-nefer that his soul may not only achieve divinity in the necropolis and "in the land of the righteous," but may also go forth and "take pleasure on earth in all the forms it desires," and that he himself may "go forth from heaven, descending to earth without being turned back on the way." He asks these favors in return for having served Osiris in various ways, fixing "the double plume on the fetish of Abydos within the sarcophagus" and binding the bandage on the body of the god, while the heart of the latter's enemy is placed beneath his feet. The last column is taken up with the titles and names of Si-Iset's father, Ḳeny, and his grandfather, Si-Iset, both of whom had also been King's Scribes and Overseers of the Granaries of Upper and Lower Egypt.

The other fine New Kingdom tomb at Deir Durunka had belonged to a King's Scribe, Chief Lector Priest, and Chief Physician named Amun-ḥotpe, evidently a near contemporary of Si-Iset. In this tomb were found two extraordinary limestone statues of Amun-ḥotpe's son Yūny, who was a Chief Scribe of the King, Chief Lector Priest, Overseer of *Wēʿb*-priests, and Royal Steward. In the larger of the two statues (fig. 219) Yūny appears alone, a life-size figure kneeling and holding before him a small shrine containing a mummiform statuette of the god Osiris. "He is dressed in the costume of an influential personage of his time, with an intricately curled wig, full and billowing linen garments, finely pleated, and a most elaborately woven pair of papyrus sandals upon his feet. On his right wrist he wears a massive bracelet and around his neck an amulet and a collar of large beads. Two unusual holes in the back of the statue, at the nape of the neck, are obviously intended for the attachment of some other ornament, perhaps a necklace of real flowers to be renewed with fresh garlands on each festival day. The eyes and eyebrows were originally inlaid with copper, and the only important mutilation in the whole statue was caused by the carelessness of the ancient thief who chiseled them out for the metal and in doing so broke away the nose and part of the face. Paint was used but sparingly—black on the wig, red inside the shrine and green and red on the winged disk over its door, and blue in the hieroglyphic inscriptions. The rest of the surface was left in the pure white of the limestone from which the statue was carved."[8] Graceful standing figures of Yūny's wife, Renūtet, holding in her hand a ceremonial necklace (*menyet*) and wearing on her head a cone of perfumed ointment, are carved in bold relief on the sides of the back

[8] Winlock, *M. M. A. Bulletin*, XXIX (1934), pp. 184 f.

pilaster. The rear surface of the pilaster carries the statue's two principal inscriptions—offering formulae calling upon the gods Tḥōt, Chnūm, and Upwawet to provide Yūny with funerary offerings and prerogatives of a variety of types. A three-line text on the front of the base is an appeal for prayers addressed to priests, scribes, and other literate passers-by, while the sides and back of the base are taken up with an elaborate titulary of Yūny, which ends with the words, "(this) statue was made for him to receive life and to rest in his tomb chapel by his assistant, the Scribe of Holy Writ. . . ." The ornate shrine, as can be seen, is covered with symbols, figures, and texts relating to the service of Osiris Wen-nefer and the benefits which Yūny may expect to derive therefrom. Among the deities mentioned in the texts who are associated with localities in the vicinity of Asyūt and Deir Durunka are Ḥat-Ḥor, Lady of Medjedny, Chnūm, Lord of Shas-ḥotep (Hypsēlē), and the Lords of Dju-fyet (the Cerastes Mountain or Twelfth Nome of Upper Egypt).

About half life size, the painted limestone ★group of figure 220 represents Yūny and Renūtet, his wife, seated side by side on a pair of high-backed, lion-legged chairs here treated like a single chair or bench, their elaborate headdresses, jewelry, and clothing treated with the same minute attention to detail seen on the larger statue. As a priestess of Ḥat-Ḥor Renūtet is again shown with her *menyet*, which she holds by its counterpoise, allowing the necklace proper to dangle over her knees. Her husband contents himself with a long handkerchief, the blocked-out ends of which may be seen descending from his clenched left hand. The inscription on the front of his pleated kilt speaks of "everything which comes forth from upon the offering table of Atūm, Lord of the Two Lands (and) of Heliopolis, and the pure food which comes forth from the Great Mansion for the King's Chief Scribe and Royal Secretary Yūny, the justified." In a long text engraved on the top of the base before the feet of the figures he is called the "Hereditary Prince and Count, the Sole Companion, the Province Administrator, the mouthpiece of the King throughout the Two Banks (Egypt), one high of office and great of wealth, a magnate in front of the people, whom the King exalted throughout the land, one who filled the ears of the Horus with truth, at whose sayings one was satisfied, the possessor of the plummet of his heart, who did not seize upon what was brought(?), the actual Scribe of the King, whom he loved, the *Setem*-priest of the King, the Chief of . . . He Who Is Over the Secrets in the House of the Morning, the King's Scribe, the Chief Lector Priest, the Overseer of *Wēʿb*-priests, the Steward and Overseer of Estates of the Lord of the Two Lands, the Secretary of the Good God, Yūny, engendered of the worthy Chief Physician Amun-ḥotpe, the justified." The edges of the broad back pilaster against which the figures sit are inscribed with more titles and epithets of Yūny and his wife, the latter referred to as "his beloved companion (possessed) of his affection, one favored by the Mistress of Heaven, the possessor of grace with everyone, the Chief of the Ḥarīm of Ḥat-Ḥor, Lady of Medjedny." The rear surface of the pilaster is treated like a stela with two registers of delicately carved reliefs, in each of which a couple is shown seated behind a table of offerings receiving the ministrations of one of their offspring. In the upper register a son of Yūny and Renūtet pours a libation and burns incense to his father and mother. Below, Renūtet, accompanied by "her maidservant, Ḥat-Ḥor," sprinkles with a libation vase the offerings heaped up before her parents, the King's Scribe Tjay and "his sister" the House Mistress Yia.

Stylistically the Yūny statues are far above the average run of Ramesside tomb figures and in both their faces and figures retain much that is characteristic of the late Eighteenth Dynasty. May we attribute this maintenance of the high artistic standards of a recently bygone age to the fact that

FIGURE 219. The King's Scribe Yūny, offering an enshrined statuette to Osiris. Indurated limestone. H. 51 in.

our statues were produced by provincial sculptors who had not yet fallen into the habits of slovenliness and bad taste which were beginning to be exhibited by their contemporaries at Thebes, Memphis, and Per-Raʿ-mesē-se? The figures, in any case, are to be dated to the early years of the reign of Ramesses II, removed by only a few decades from the period to which stylistically they seem to belong. Not the least of their virtues is the very considerable contribution which their careful, three-dimensional treatment of every detail of their owners' clothing and accessories makes to our knowledge of ancient Egyptian costume.

More typical of the products of the Ramesside ateliers is ★part of a large and brightly painted limestone statue which represented one of Ramesses II's officials kneeling and holding before him a shrine surmounted by the ram's head of the god Amūn and fronted by a standing figure of the king. All that we possess of this statue is the figure of the pharaoh, the upper part of the shrine with the names of Ramesses II carved on its sides above the outstretched hands of the donor, and, above this, the bottom of the striped headdress worn by Amūn's ram. From the shins to the crown of the head of the royal figure our fragment measures just under twenty-three inches in height. Here the king is represented wearing a green and yellow striped *nemes*, a broad collar of polychrome beadwork, and a dress kilt colored yellow, to imitate gold, and adorned in front with an elaborate polychrome pendant. The royal flesh was painted dark red and the royal eyes white with black irises, rims, and brows. On the sides of the shrine the cartouches of Ramesses II are carved in considerable detail and were once gaudily colored—blue, green, red, yellow, black, and white. They are preceded by the usual titles (Lord of the Two Lands, Lord of Crowns) and followed by the epithets "beloved of Amun Rēʿ, King of the Gods," and "beloved of Amun Rēʿ, Presider over the West." A pretentious but uninspired piece of work, the statue is characterized particularly by an emptiness of content and a consistent coarseness in the handling of details. It came to the Museum in 1890 as a gift of James Douglas, but its original provenience is unknown.

A crude little ★offering slab of black diorite, inscribed for a woman named Ḥetep-nefret, has carved in relief on its upper surface eight circular loaves of bread and two tall libations vases, the latter engraved in each case with the nomen cartouche of Ramesses II. On a tiny rectangular ★plaque of green-glazed steatite we see the "Scribe of the Granary of the God's Offering of Every God, Pa-sēr," standing in adoration before a small altar on which rests the cartouche with the king's praenomen, "User-maʿet-Rēʿ Sotep-(en-Rēʿ)," preceded by the titles "Lord of the Two Lands" and "Lord of Crowns." From Tomb 324 at Thebes comes a pottery ★funerary cone stamped with the titles and name of another of Ramesses II's contemporaries, the "First Prophet of Horus, Sobk, Anubis, and Khonsu, the Scribe of the First Prophet of Montu, Lord of Hermonthis, Ḥatiay."

Painted scenes from seven of the more notable private tombs of the reign in the Theban necropolis may be studied in the Museum's fine series of color ★copies by Nina and Norman de Garis Davies, Charles Wilkinson, and others. The tombs referred to are those of the Prophet of Amun-ḥotpe of the Forecourt, Pa-neḥesy (No. 16); the Chief Linen-maker of Amūn, Tḥōt-em-ḥēb (No. 45); the Scribe of the God's Offering of Amūn, Ḥor-em-ḥēb (No. 207); the Sculptor Ipy (No. 217); the Priest Amun-em-ōnet (No. 277); the Herdsman of Amun Rēʿ, Amun-em-ḥēb (No. 278); and the Chief of the Altar in the Ramesseum, Nakht-Amūn (No. 341).

4. Mery-en-Ptaḥ Averts Disaster

It has often been remarked that when Ramesses II finally died in 1223 B.C. he had outlived not only his own generation, but also most of the succeeding generation. Thirteen of his innumerable sons, including the highly regarded Khaʿ-em-Wast, had predeceased him; and when Prince Mery-en-Ptaḥ, his fourteenth son, took over the reins of government, first as regent for his senile father and shortly thereafter as king, he himself was a man already in his late fifties.

The situation which the new ruler inherited was a difficult one. Decades of idleness and extravagance on the part of the once warlike Ramesses had weakened Egypt's prestige abroad and undermined her internal economy. Though friendly relations seem still to have existed between the pharaoh and the king of the Hittites, the latter was now too beset with troubles of his own to be a useful ally, and at least once during Mery-en-Ptaḥ's reign he had to call upon Egypt to bolster his inadequate food supplies. Meanwhile, great numbers of the warlike Sea Peoples—Achaeans, Tyrsenians, Lycians, Sardinians, and Sicilians—had moved into the coastal region to the west of the Delta and, in alliance with the Libyan population of that area, now threatened Egypt with the first serious, large-scale invasion since the time of the Hyksos. In Mery-en-Ptaḥ's fifth year on the throne (1219 B.C.) the invasion was actually attempted. Thanks, however, to the courage and energy of the elderly pharaoh and the murderous effectiveness of his Egyptian archers the attackers were checked with great slaughter in a six-hour battle near the border settlement of Per-yeru and the remnants of their forces were routed and dispersed. One of the several accounts of this engagement which has come down to us, the so-called Hymn of Victory, from the king's mortuary temple, refers also to Mery-en-Ptaḥ's real or imaginary military activities in Syro-Palestine and lists a number of conquered cities and small states including Canaan, Askalon, Gezer, Yenoam, and Israel—the last mentioned here for the first and only time in Egyptian records.

The low state of the national resources is reflected in Mery-en-Ptaḥ's monuments, many of which seem to have been either usurped directly from his predecessors or, in the case of buildings, to have been constructed of materials plundered from earlier structures. Examples of the first of these two procedures are our two big diorite statues of Amun-ḥotpe III, which the Nineteenth Dynasty pharaoh adopted as his own by simply carving his cartouches on their arms and bodies and covering their bases and thrones with his coarsely executed and tediously repetitious titulary. Eliminating the repetitions, we find this titulary to be made up of the following elements: "The Horus Strong-bull-rejoicing-in-truth, the Good God, Son of Amūn, King of Upper and Lower Egypt, Prince of Joy, Lord of the Two Lands, Lord of Achievements, Ba-en-Rēʿ Mery-Amūn, the Son of Rēʿ, the Lord of Crowns, Mery-en-Ptaḥ Ḥetep-ḥer-Maʿet, beloved of Amun Rēʿ, King of the Gods, and given life, like Rēʿ, forever." At the time of their usurpation the statues were removed from their original positions in the Luxor temple and, though they are by no means a pair, were set up on either side of the eastern doorway leading into Ramesses II's forecourt.

The second method employed by Mery-en-Ptaḥ in achieving imposing monuments at relatively small outlay is illustrated by his mortuary temple

FIGURE 220. Yūny and his wife, the priestess of Ḥat-Ḥor, Renūtet. Painted limestone. H. 33 ¼ in.

in western Thebes, which seems to have been built in its entirety from the wreckage of the adjacent temple of Amun-ḥotpe III. Even the bricks used in Mery-en-Ptaḥ's temple were filched from the earlier structure and the text of the Hymn of Victory, referred to above, was carved on the back of one of Amun-ḥotpe III's big hard-stone stelae. The name of the temple, the "Mansion-of-Ba-en-Rēʿ-Mery-Amūn-in-the-estate-of-Amūn-on-the-west-of-Thebes," is preserved in the titulary of one of its priests, a man named Nedjem who lived in the time of Ramesses III of the Twentieth Dynasty and is known from a diorite ★statue in our collection found in 1906 by Naville at Deir el Baḥri. Much the same procedure was probably followed elsewhere, as, for example, at Hermopolis, where a long stela inscription of Mery-en-Ptaḥ describes in glowing words the temple to Amūn which he caused to be built in the enclosure of the local god Tḥōt.

On the other hand, the palace of Mery-en-Ptaḥ which adjoins the great temple of Ptaḥ at Memphis (Mit Rahīneh) appears to have been constructed anew from the ground up. Inlaid limestone columns, doorways, and other elements from this large and brilliantly decorated building may be seen today in the University Museum in Philadelphia.

The king's tomb (No. 8) is one of the largest and most interesting in the Wādy el Bibān el Molūk. It is excavated under the northern cliffs of the rocky amphitheater, a hundred yards west of the tomb of Ramesses II; and contains, in addition to the usual painted wall reliefs and texts, the lids of Mery-en-Ptaḥ's two granite sarcophagi, the cartouche-shaped inner lid adorned in high relief with a colossal mummiform figure of the pharaoh.

Of the furnishings of the royal tomb the Museum is fortunate in possessing a large alabaster ★jar (fig. 221) which was found with twelve others just outside the tomb entranceway. As can be seen, the jar is provided with handles in the form of heads of the slim-horned Nubian ibex which were probably fitted at one time with ears made of silver or gold. Somewhat crudely engraved on the broad cylindrical neck are the cartouches of Mery-en-Ptaḥ surmounted by a winged sun's disk, and beside these is a faded ink inscription giving the capacity of the vessel as "22 *hin*-measures." Since the actual capacity of the jar, when filled to the top, is just under eleven quarts, the *hin*-measure used here would have been almost exactly equal to a pint, a value very slightly under that computed for this measure from other sources.

The limestone ★figure of the king shown in figure 222 does not come from his tomb or its vicinity, but is said to have been found miles away, cached under a boulder in the Wādy Gabbānet el Ḳurūd, a desert valley west and a little south of Deir el Baḥri. The incised and blue-filled inscription down the front of the figure gives only the royal names and titles (the "Lord of the Two Lands, Ba-en-Rēʿ Mery-Amūn, [the Lord of] Crowns, Mery-en-Ptaḥ Ḥetep-ḥer-Maʿet") followed by the epithets "beloved of Sokar in Shetyet, the Lord of Ro-setau" and "given life." The figure, then, was probably not a *shawabty* in the

FIGURE 221. Alabaster jar of King Mery-en-Ptaḥ. Gift of Almina, Countess of Carnarvon. H. 15¼ in.

strict sense, but simply a small mummiform or Osiride(?) representation of the king. Considering its minute size it is surprising how accurately the carefully modeled face seen here agrees with the other known portraits of this strikingly handsome ruler. Among the details not overlooked by the sculptor of our figure is the piercing of the king's ear lobes.

Our only other inscribed monuments of this pharaoh are two ★cartouche-shaped plaques of faience stamped with his throne name and in one case with the words "House of Amūn," and a faience ★scarab on which the cartouche of Ṭhut-mosĕ III of the Eighteenth Dynasty is accompanied by Mery-en-Ptaḥ's well-known epithet "Ḥetep-ḥer-Maʿet." Nineteen terra-cotta ★molds come, however, from a courtyard added by Mery-en-Ptaḥ to the temple of Ptaḥ at Memphis and in all probability date from his time. Included are molds for a variety of amulets and small ornaments—figures of Sakhmet and Bēs, heads of Bēs, the aegis of Bastet, *wedjat*-eyes, scarabs, cornflower pendants, and several types of rosettes.

Though Manetho gives Mery-en-Ptaḥ a reign of nineteen and a half to twenty years, his highest known date, preserved in Papyrus Sallier I, is Regnal Year 10. His principal queen was his half sister Iset-nefret, and by her he appears to have had a son, Sēthy Mery-en-Ptaḥ, who, following an apparent interruption in the dynastic succession, occupied the throne for a brief time as King Sēthy II. Mery-en-Ptaḥ himself must have been over seventy at the time of his death. His mummy, that of a corpulent, bald-headed old man, five feet seven and a half inches in height, was found cached in the tomb of Amun-ḥotpe II (No. 35) together with those of Ṭhut-mosĕ IV, Amun-ḥotpe III, Sēthy II, and others.

FIGURE 222. Osiride figure of King Mery-en-Ptaḥ wearing the royal *nemes*. Limestone. H. 7 ¼ in.

5. The End of the Dynasty

The seventeen years which followed the death of Mery-en-Ptaḥ saw the throne of Egypt occupied by four somewhat ephemeral rulers whose order and relationship one to another is not yet established beyond a reasonable doubt.

Most students of Egyptian history, however, agree that Mery-en-Ptaḥ's immediate successor was a nephew named Amun-messĕ, or Amenmesses, who assumed the throne name Men-mi-Rēʿ and reigned for something over four years. Before his disappearance from the scene he was able to prepare for himself a good-sized tomb (No. 10) in the Valley of the Tombs of the Kings, the decoration of which was subsequently obliterated by one of his successors. The inscribed monuments of this king are not numerous, and in our own collection, as in many others, he is not represented at all.

Amun-messĕ appears to have been succeeded by his cousin, King User-khepru-Rēʿ Sēthy II, and he, in turn, by his widow, Queen Te-Wosret, and his son(?), King Akh-en-Rēʿ Mery-en-Ptaḥ Si-Ptaḥ, perhaps the offspring of a Syrian inmate of the royal ḥarīm. It now seems certain that Si-Ptaḥ, as he is commonly called, was identical with "Ramesses Si-Ptaḥ" in whom some scholars were once inclined to recognize a different ruler. Si-Ptaḥ's reign of at least five years has left us a number of interesting monuments.

When cleared by Theodore Davis in 1912 the lower chamber of the king's tomb yielded a handsome cartouche-shaped sarcophagus of red granite and a considerable quantity of funerary and other objects which had belonged to Si-Ptaḥ himself, to Queen Te-Wosret, and to other members of the pharaoh's household. Most of the objects which Mr. Davis was allowed to retain in the division of finds were presented by him to the Metropolitan Museum in 1913 or were acquired with his collection in 1930. Included in this most generous gift were eleven complete and numerous fragmentary *shawabty*-figures of the king, fragments of three royal sarcophagi and two canopic chests carved of alabaster, and two mud jar stoppers bearing the impression of royal seals.

King Si-Ptaḥ's ★*shawabtys* are without exception of alabaster and, as can be seen from the example illustrated in figure 223, are rather summarily and in some cases even roughly carved. They range in height from eight to eleven and a half inches and show considerable variation in their proportions, some being broad and squat, some elongated and slender. All wear the royal *nemes* and uraeus and show the hands clenched and crossed over the breast. Black ink is used to accent the eyebrows, eyes, and mouth and for writing the inscriptions which cover the lower parts of the figures. These normally consist of a vertical column down the front, with the words "Illuminating the Osiris, King Akh-en-Rēʿ, the Son of Rēʿ, Mery-en-Ptaḥ Si-Ptaḥ, the justified," and four or five horizontal bands running around the figure and containing the usual spell exhorting the *shawabty* to substitute for the king in the work gangs of the afterlife. In style and execution many of these royal figures are of a surprising crudity—well below the standard of good private *shawabtys* of the earlier New Kingdom (cf. figs. 158, 241).

The ★fragments of the alabaster sarcophagi and canopic chests, though amounting to several hundred pieces, are too small and too incomplete to allow any one of the five monuments to be actually restored. It can be seen, however, that one of the sarcophagi was rectangular and that it was engraved inside and out with small-scale figures and texts taken from popular funerary "books" of the period (see pp. 327 f.). The two others were colossal anthropoid cases and the larger of them, which wore the pharaonic *nemes*, was presumably that of King Si-Ptaḥ himself, though his name does not happen to be preserved on any of the existing fragments. This was probably also the case with one of the two canopic chests, which was decorated in relief with figures of four winged goddesses standing at the corners of the chest and crossing their wings protectively over its sides. Between the figures the lower part of the chest was adorned with a dado of conventionalized palace-façade paneling. Inside, the block had been provided with four deep cylindrical cavities to receive the king's viscera or the containers to which they had been consigned.

Less fragmentary than its companion, the second canopic chest is seen to have consisted of a cubical box, one royal cubit (20.6 inches) on a side, hewn from a single block of alabaster. The edges of its thick lid were carved in the form of a

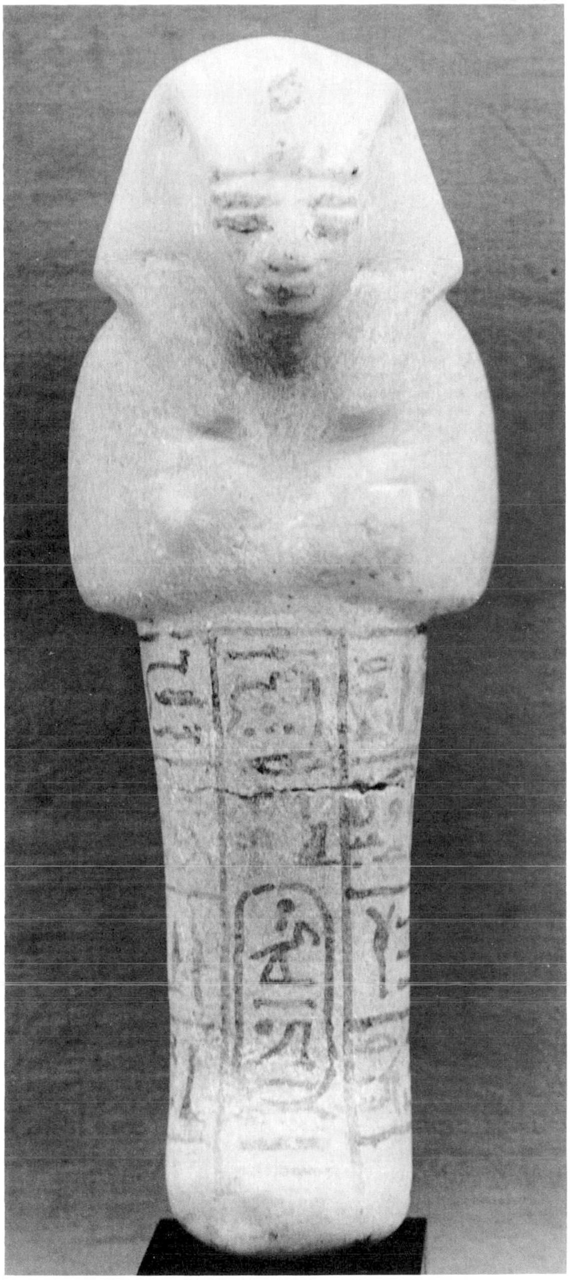

FIGURE 223. Alabaster *shawabty* of King Si-Ptaḥ. H. 8¼ in.

cavetto-and-torus cornice and above this rose a shrine roof engraved on the sides with serpents (𓆓) and around the edges of its upper surface with block borders. Standing figures of the goddesses Isis, Nephthys, Nit, and Serḳet appeared in panels on the sides of the box, flanked by the usual canopic texts written in vertical columns. In these the owner of the chest is identified as the "King's Wife Ti-ʿa," and her viscera are said to be associated with the Four Genii of the Dead and taken under the protection of the Four Goddesses. Ti-ʿa appears to have been one of the more important members of Si-Ptaḥ's ḥarīm, but is not mentioned in extant documents of the late Nineteenth Dynasty. Her name (written in a cartouche) is the same as that of Amun-ḥotpe II's well-known consort, but both the style and the finding place of the canopic chest make it impossible that it could have belonged to the Eighteenth Dynasty queen.

The ★jar stoppers from the tomb are circular plugs of Nile mud nine inches in diameter and slightly domed on top. They bear, respectively, eight and ten deep but illegible impressions of a cartouche-shaped seal which probably contained the name of the king. After being stamped and allowed to dry the stoppers were given a coat of thin white paint.

A pair of gray steatite ★scarabs of Si-Ptaḥ, formerly in the Carnarvon collection, are of unknown provenience. One bears on its underside the king's throne name, Akh-en-Rēʿ Sotep-en-Rēʿ, the other his personal name, Mery-en-Ptaḥ Si-Ptaḥ.

It was probably shortly after the death of her husband, Sēthy II, that Te-Wosret, like Ḥatshepsūt before her, discarded the title King's Great Wife and assumed the full titulary of a reigning pharaoh. As "King" Sit-Rēʿ Meryet-Amūn Te-Wosret Sotepet-en-Mūt she had prepared for herself a handsome tomb (No. 14) in the Valley of the Kings and a mortuary temple on the edge of the cultivated land in western Thebes.

Among the objects recovered from the foundation deposits of this temple and subsequently acquired by the Museum are three ★inscribed "bricks," two of limestone, one of sandstone; several small rectangular and cartouche-shaped ★plaques of faience, a faience ★scarab, and sixteen small faience ★models of food offerings—whole trussed oxen, heads and legs of beef, ducks and

FIGURE 224. Part of the silver and gold temple service of the goddess Bastet of Bubastis. Reign of Te-Wosret and Sēthy II. Diam. of bowl 8 in.

pigeons, and a head of romaine lettuce. The two limestone bricks measure roughly twelve by six by three inches and are engraved with the names of the female ruler incorporated into that of her temple: "The Mansion of Millions of Years of the King of Upper and Lower Egypt, Sit-Rēʿ Meryet-Amūn, the Son (*sic*) of Rēʿ, Te-Wosret Sotepet-en-Mūt, in the Estate of Amūn." Smaller than its companions, the sandstone brick carries only Te-Wosret's two cartouches preceded by the titles Lord of the Two Lands and Lord of Crowns. The plaques and the scarab bear only the names, without titles, and one of the tiny faience *khopesh*-joints has a single cartouche written upon it in black.

The cartouches of Te-Wosret occur also on one of a rich hoard of vessels of silver and gold discovered in 1906 in an ancient cache near the temple of the goddess Bastet at Bubastis (modern Tell Basta) in the eastern Delta. The names of both Te-Wosret and Sēthy II appear on vessels from the same find, now in the Cairo and Berlin Museums. Since these are the only royal names preserved in this particular hoard and since the pieces found form stylistically and technically a homogeneous group, there is every probability that the whole lot was produced during the period with which we are dealing, that is, the late Nineteenth Dynasty. Our share of the Tell Basta treasure, as this famous find is now generally known, comprises nine more or less complete ★vases and ★bowls and ★fragments of perhaps fifteen others, ten beverage ★strainers, including four complete examples, a small silver ★jewel casket, an ornamental ★boss for the center of a bowl, a ★buckle (?), and several ★handles from vases and strainers (see figs. 224-226). The vast majority of the vessels are of silver or silver alloy, but there are three of gold and a number of others adorned with gold rims and decorated with gold bands or bosses. Predominant among the types are the slender, drop-shaped situla and the squat jug with high, cylindrical neck and occasionally an ornamental handle. We find also the small, cordiform vase with long neck and flaring lip, an elongated ovoid jar with cylindrical neck, and a shallow bowl with a low foot on the outside and a conical boss on the interior. Most of the strainers are shallow metal saucers with perforated bottoms and single handles shaped and decorated in imitation of a lotus flower and its curving stem. One, however, is a deep,

FIGURE 225. Neck of a silver vase adorned with an embossed gold band. Diam. 1 ¾ in.

cuplike little vessel with a flaring rim and a perforated bottom. The jewel casket is a small circular box with slightly flaring sides and a domical lid pierced with a circle of paired drop-shaped perforations and decorated around the edge with an engraved ray pattern. It contained, when found, a light mesh *chain woven of fine silver wire and supporting two pendant amulets.

Many of the vessels carry embossed or engraved decoration and it is this, rather than their forms, which is perhaps their major interest. The necks and bottoms of the little situlae are often adorned with bands of lotus petals and the necks of some of the jugs are banded with friezes of continuous spirals, lotus flowers, grape clusters, rosettes, and floral motifs. Between these there are occasionally broad bands containing little scenes in the marshes, or deserts with lions and hounds running down antelope, and herds of horses with their foals galloping through tall papyrus thickets from which pintail ducks rise in flight. The body of one of the silver jugs (fig. 224, left) is fluted and its handle ends at the top in the head of a lion, the jaws of the beast clamped upon the rim of the vessel. On a heavily embossed gold band at the top of the neck of a slender silver vase (fig. 225) we see a pair of heraldic lions (Shu and Tefēnet?) flanking an elaborately chased head of the goddess Ḥat-Ḥor, a deity closely related to Bastet, the owner of our temple service. The disk-shaped flange of a gold boss from the interior of a bowl is richly adorned with filigree work of Syrian type—concentric bands of beads, running spirals, braids, and guilloches.

The most lavishly decorated and far and away the most interesting vessel of the group is the embossed silver bowl shown at the center of figure 224 and in detail in figure 226. Around a large central rosette composed of radiating lotus petals and leaves, the outside of the bowl is decorated with four concentric bands, or registers, containing little scenes evidently borrowed in part from contemporary or earlier tomb paintings. The innermost band, surrounding the floral centerpiece, is given over to agricultural and pastoral scenes, the harvesting and treading of grapes, the gathering of papyrus, and the breeding of farm animals. Parts of what appears to have been a hunting scene along the fringes of the Nile Valley take up the next register, and here we see groups of huntsmen, a lion, antelope, ostriches, quail, and other wild birds amid date palms and large palmettolike trees. In the third band (fig. 226) fowlers are closing a big clapnet on a flight of ducks and geese, while on the opposite side of the bowl boatmen engage in real or mock combat. A boat appears

FIGURE 226. Detail of the silver bowl shown at the center of figure 224.

also in the outermost register, which, however, is occupied chiefly with scenes showing the herding of cattle, the lassoing of horses, and the netting and cleaning of fish, all of these activities taking place in a marshland setting, against a background of tall papyrus plants. Though lacking the precision and clean draughtsmanship of earlier New Kingdom work, the tiny scenes are represented in an attractive and lively manner and, thanks to overall chasing with an engraver's tool, with a surprising amount of detail.

At least two of our Tell Basta vessels were dedicated by private contemporaries of Te-Wosret and Sēthy II. The fluted jug with the lion-headed handle which appears in the left background of figure 224 is inscribed "for the spirit of the uniquely excellent one, the witness true of heart, the King's Butler, clean of hands, Atum-em-to-neb." The same Atum-em-to-neb was the donor of two silver vases in Cairo, and additional fragments of one of these are now divided between the Berlin Museum and our own collection. In panels engraved on the sides of the elongated ovoid jar referred to above, we see a fashionably dressed lady, the "Chantress Mery(et)-Ptaḥ," shaking a sistrum before the goddess "Bastet, Mistress of Bubastis." The cat-headed deity, whose head is here surmounted by a sun's disk and uraeus, sits on a throne and holds in her hands an *ʿankh*-sign and a slender papyrus scepter. A short offering formula, engraved in a vertical column behind her back, calls upon her to "give life to the nose of her daughter."

The names of Te-Wosret were embossed on the neck of a silver jug of which we possess only a fragment with the tops of the two cartouches and the titles Lord of the Two Lands and Lord of Crowns. Mistakenly read as those of Ramesses II, these cartouches led at one time to some confusion concerning the dating of the treasure.

A silver ★statuette of a king in the guise of the god Horus the Child (Harpokrates), once thought to belong to this treasure, comes probably from a cache of the Ptolemaic period.

Te-Wosret's tomb (No. 14) is one of the most elaborate in the Valley of the Tombs of the Kings. In the decoration of this tomb the female ruler appears alone or in company with Si-Ptaḥ, whose name was subsequently replaced by that of Sēthy II. Later still the whole tomb was appropriated and enlarged for his own use by Sēth-nakhte, the founder of the Twentieth Dynasty. In its final form it comprises in all twenty-seven chambers and passages, including two large rectangular halls, their ceilings supported in each case by eight square piers.

In a small uninscribed tomb (No. 56) not far from that of Si-Ptaḥ, Theodore Davis found a cache of Nineteenth Dynasty objects, including a quantity of gold jewelry which had belonged to Te-Wosret or some member of her court. From this find the Museum received a very handsome gold filigree ★necklace (fig. 227) composed of seventy-seven openwork spherical beads and twenty-six delicately worked filigree pendants in the form of cornflowers. Strung up, the necklace measures twenty-four inches in length and is as light and attractive a piece of jewelry as one could find. The same cache also produced a pair of carnelian ★pendants in the form of a scarab with wings outspread in such a manner as to form a circular openwork frame around the body of the beetle.

There is some probability that a fragment of limestone temple ★relief, acquired in 1948 as a gift of Mr. and Mrs. George D. Pratt, carries a portrait head of Te-Wosret herself (fig. 228). Both the style and the facial type remind us of the relief portraits of Sēthy II, but the long wig and the tall headdress with the sun's disk and cow's horns mark the subject as either a queen or a goddess. Despite the refinement of the face itself we see the characteristic Ramesside coarseness in the handling of details and the finish of the surfaces. The line of chisel cuts near the top of the fragment reflects an unsuccessful attempt on the part of a later builder to convert the slab of relief into a square building block or paving stone.

FIGURE 227. Gold filigree necklace of the time of Queen Te-Wosret from the Valley of the Tombs of the Kings. L. 24 in.

The accession date of Sēthy II was recorded on a limestone ★ostrakon from the Valley of the Tombs of the Kings which is now in our collection. Unfortunately, the initial groups which gave the regnal year and the month number have been broken away, but the rest of the text on the recto of the ostrakon is well preserved. Its first three lines read as follows: "[Regnal Year . . . Month . . . of Prō]yet, Day 16. The Scribe Pa-sēr came with the pleasant news that User-khepru-Rēʿ Sotep-en-Rēʿ (Sēthy II) had arisen as ruler . . . ." The rest of the entries on the recto, comprising nine additional lines, are dated from Month 3 of Akhet, Day 12 to Day 22, and are accounts concerned chiefly with a certain Neb-nakhte and with the Gang Foreman Nefer-ḥotep, a man prominent among the workers in the Theban necropolis from the time of Ramesses II to that of Sēthy II. The entries appear to have been continued on the verso, but here they are so rubbed and faded as to be legible only in parts. The activity in which Nefer-ḥotep and his companions were at the time engaged was probably the excavation of the king's tomb (No. 15) in the Wādy el Bibān el Molūk.

This tomb, far less elaborate in plan than that of Te-Wosret, consists of four corridors in series, an antechamber, a four-piered sepulchral hall, and a small innermost chamber. It is, however, handsomely decorated with painted inscriptions and reliefs, including several fine portrait heads of

FIGURE 228. Relief head of a goddess or queen, possibly Te-Wosret. Limestone. H. 14½ in.

the good-looking young pharaoh. A ★sketch for one of these portraits is quite possibly preserved to us on a flake of limestone (fig. 229) found by Theodore Davis in the Valley of the Tombs of the Kings. Drawn in fine, sensitive black outline, the royal head is seen in left profile wearing a graceful medium-length wig with a fillet and uraeus. It is accompanied on the same ostrakon by sketches of another king's head wearing the *khat* headdress, by the figure of a charging bull, and by a human ear with the now characteristic slit for an earring in the lobe.

Besides the remains of the cover of his sarcophagus and other pieces of his funerary furniture the tomb of Sēthy II yielded a number of his ★*shawabtys*. Of the latter we possess two insignificant fragments in blue faience with the cartouches of the king and a portion of the *shawabty*-spell written on them in black glaze.

Our other monuments of Sēthy II consist entirely of small faience ★tiles, or plaques, from foundation deposits of the king's buildings, ten green- and white-glazed steatite ★scarabs, and a bronze ★signet ring with the nomen Sēthy Mery-en-Ptaḥ. The tiles, of which there are eight, are of three types. The most common is a rectangular plaque of white faience, three and a half inches in length, carrying on its front a slightly raised cartouche in which the two names of Sēthy are encrusted in a grayish blue glaze. The second type is similar, but the cartouche contains only the praenomen, User-khepru-Rēʿ [Sotep-en-Rēʿ], and is surmounted by the solar disk and double plume. In the third class of tile the names and, in one instance, the titles of the king are engraved in the surface of a plain rectangular slab of greenish blue faience. The largest of these measures four and three-eighths inches in length.

One of the scarabs carries on its underside a little scene showing the king in his chariot drawing his bow against a bearded enemy. It reminds us of the designs on similar scarabs of Ramesses II (see fig. 217), but is less skillfully drawn and engraved. The nine other scarabs bear the praenomen, User-khepru-Rēʿ Sotep-en-Rēʿ or, more frequently, User-khepru-Rēʿ Mery-Amūn, and in one case the personal name Sēthy Mery-en-Ptaḥ.

Considering the relative brevity of his reign and the uncertainty of the times, the monuments of Sēthy II are surprisingly numerous, including not only his tomb and mortuary temple in western Thebes, but also a temple, sphinxes, statues, and stelae at Karnak, architectural elements at Memphis and Heliopolis, a King's House near Faḳūs in the eastern Delta, two inscriptions at Sinai, and enormous cartouches cut on the face of the cliffs near Manfalūt in Middle Egypt.

Sēthy II, as we have seen, was succeeded, at the end of the dynasty, by a king who called himself Sekhaʿ-en-Rēʿ Ramesses Si-Ptaḥ; but modern scholars are now inclined to see in the names of this alleged king simply a variant writing of the titulary of (Mery-en-Ptaḥ) Si-Ptaḥ. According to a passage in the Great Harris Papyrus, which purports to describe events leading up to the reign of Ramesses III, the Nineteenth Dynasty ended in a period of anarchy ("empty years"), "when 'Ir-su,' a Syrian, was among their chieftains and made the whole land tributary to himself." The picture here presented is probably exaggeratedly dismal, for this portion of the Harris Papyrus is largely propaganda intended to magnify the achievements of the founders of the Twentieth Dynasty by presenting the period preceding them in as unfavorable a light as possible. It is not unlikely that "Ir-su" was either an epithet ("the Self-made"?) for one of the last rulers of the Nineteenth Dynasty, who may have had a Syrian mother, or was one of several Syrian Chancellors who in Ramesside times achieved considerable power and importance.

FIGURE 229. Limestone ostrakon with the head of a late Nineteenth Dynasty king, possibly Sēthy II, and other sketches. H. 12 ¼ in.

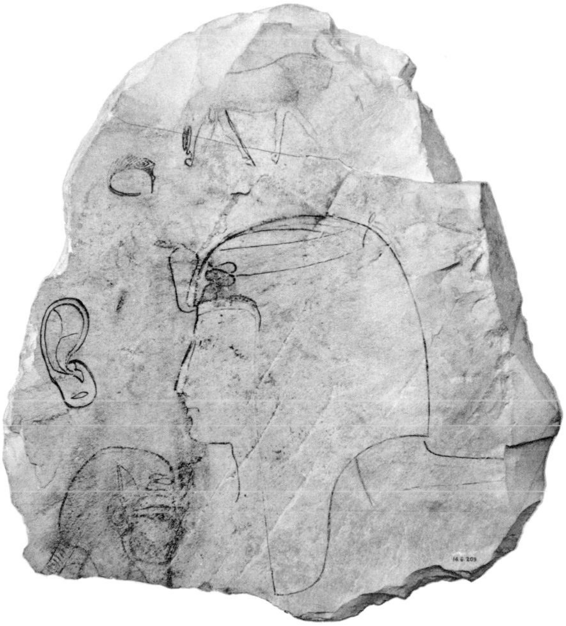

IX. The Later Ramessides

1. The Rise of the Twentieth Dynasty

THE ORIGINS OF King User-khaʿu-Rēʿ Sētḫ-nakhte, the founder of the Twentieth Dynasty, are unknown. His personal name, compounded with that of Sētḫ, the family god of the Nineteenth Dynasty, was a fairly common one at this time. His brief reign produced no foreign conquests, but was characterized, according to the extremely favorable testimony of the Harris Papyrus, by the re-establishment of order in the land and the return to the temples of their revenues. He started a tomb for himself (No. 11) in the Valley of the Kings, but at his early death this was abandoned unfinished and he was buried in the tomb of Te-Wosret (No. 14), the plan of which was somewhat enlarged and the inscriptions and reliefs of which were altered where necessary. His mortuary temple, if one existed, has not been found or at least not identified. In our collection he is represented by two ★scarabs, one of glazed steatite found near the North Pyramid at el Lisht, the other, of faience, of unknown origin. Both have somewhat coarsely engraved on their undersides the nomen Sētḫ-nakhte Merery-Rēʿ Mery-Amūn.

Like Ramesses I, the founder of the Nineteenth Dynasty, Sētḫ-nakhte was evidently well along in years at the time of his accession and, like the earlier ruler, he seems almost from the beginning of his reign to have shared the burdens of kingship with his capable and energetic son. At his death, in or about 1192 B.C., this son acceded to the throne as Ramesses III and in a reign of over thirty-one years did as much as could be done at this late stage to revive the glories of the New Kingdom.

2. The Last Great Pharaoh of the New Kingdom

In an evident desire to emulate his famous namesake and predecessor Ramesses II, the new king adopted the latter's praenomen, User-maʿet-Rēʿ, followed, however, by the distinguishing epithet Mery-Amūn, "Beloved-of-Amūn." Unfortunately, he also imitated the earlier pharaoh's cumbersome style of temple architecture and his irritatingly bombastic manner of reporting his achievements. Like Ramesses II, he concentrated his military activity in the first decade or so of his reign, allowing the advantages gained at that time to be dissipated by long years of pleasure-filled ease which, he boasts, were enjoyed not only by himself but by all the members of his armed forces.

Happily for Egypt, internally decadent and beset by dangers from all sides, Ramesses III was a far more able general and strategist than his vainglorious model. In his fifth and eleventh years he decisively defeated invading hordes of western Libyans, spearheaded by the now dominant Meshwesh, and in his eighth year beat back a coordinated mass invasion by land and by sea of the Sea Peoples, the pre-Greek inhabitants of the islands and littorals of the Mediterranean. Among these we find named and represented the Peleset, or Philistines, the Tjeker, or Teucrians, the Shekelesh, or Sicilians, the Danuna, and the Weshesh. It is a significant fact that all three of these wars were defensive actions fought, except for the land operation against the Sea Peoples, on or even inside Egypt's own borders. The loss of any one of them would have meant the end of Egypt's history as a nation, for these were not merely military assaults aimed at plunder or political domination, but attempted occupations of the rich Delta and Valley of the Nile by whole nations of land-hungry peoples including not only the fighting men of the groups involved, but their families, herds and other chattels. It is also significant that Ramesses III's victorious armies were themselves extensively made up of foreign troops, Sardinians, Kahak, Philistines, Teucrians, Tyrsenians, Nubians, and even Libyans, the last becoming with the advancing years an ever more important part of the armed forces on which Egypt now depended for her safety.

The pharaoh seems to have followed his rout of the Sea Peoples by one or more Asiatic campaigns designed to re-establish Egypt's hold over Palestine and portions of Syria. In the course of these campaigns he claims to have captured five fortified cities, including Tunip, Arzawa, and Ḳadesh (?), but failed to dislodge the warlike Philistines and the piratical Teucrians from the Palestinian coastal areas, where they remained, a menace alike to coastwise shipping and to the adjoining hill tribes of the interior. With his death Egypt appears to have abandoned all her holdings in Asia and a few years later stopped sending expeditions to the mines of Sinai.

In dealing with the internal ills which were now besetting his country Ramesses III was less successful than he had been in defending it against its foreign enemies. His much cited reclassification of the population into court officials, provincial magnates, four different military groups, and the laboring class seems singularly arbitrary and uninspired. A deeply religious man, his immense annual donations to the temples of Amun Rēʿ and other leading divinities are recorded with pride in the Great Harris Papyrus; but during his twenty-ninth year government workmen employed in the Theban necropolis often found themselves weeks in arrears on their monthly rations and were forced to strike to prevent themselves and their families from starving. Respect for the pharaonic office and for official authority in general was on the decline. Caricatures in which the king is represented as a mouse or other animal and his most heroic deeds lampooned are found in papyri and on ostraka of the period. At Athribis one of Ramesses III's viziers revolted against him and had to be removed from office. Finally, at the end of his reign a palace conspiracy organized allegedly by the king's wife, Teye, her son, Prince (Ramesses) Pe'n-ta-weret, and other members of the royal household and entourage brought to an end the old pharaoh's life. Accounts of the trial and punishment of the conspirators, drawn up probably under his son and successor Ramesses IV, are preserved to us in at least four different documents, chief among which is the so-called Judicial Papyrus of Turin.

Meanwhile, however, Ramesses III had succeeded in maintaining or reinaugurating many of the public enterprises which we associate with the earlier reigns of the New Kingdom. Tribute still seems to have been collected from Nubia and Palestine, a successful trading expedition was sent to Pwēnet via the Koptos Road and the Red Sea, a huge new gallery was opened in the limestone quarries near Tureh, the mines of Sinai were worked, and new copper mines were opened in the Gebel ʿAtaḳa, east of Cairo. Shade trees were planted throughout the land and the policing of highways was made so efficient that even unescorted women might walk abroad without fear of molestation. Among the king's numerous buildings the most interesting and the best preserved are the three relatively small temples which he founded at Karnak in behalf of the Theban triad and, of course, his great mortuary temple at Medīnet Habu in western Thebes.

FIGURE 230. Sandstone window grill from the palace of Ramesses III at Medīnet Habu. H. 40 ½ in.

The three Karnak shrines, dedicated, respectively, to Amūn, Mūt, and Khonsu, are similar to one another in plan and are wholly typical examples of the small processional temple of the New Kingdom, the Amūn and Khonsu temples being frequently used as such in courses on Egyptian architecture because of their completeness and remarkable state of preservation. Each comprises a pylon, a colonnaded forecourt, a raised vestibule, a hypostyle hall and a sanctuary surrounded by small subsidiary chambers. The temple of Amūn is decorated throughout with statues, reliefs, and inscriptions of Ramesses III himself including, on its exterior walls, copies of decrees issued by him in behalf of his religious foundations; but in the Khonsu temple we find his reliefs only in the little rooms at the extreme rear of the building, the rest of the decoration and probably much of the forward part of the structure itself having been added by Ramesses IV, Ramesses XI, and Ḥery-Ḥōr.

The king's mortuary temple at Medīnet Habu is closely modeled on that of his idol, Ramesses II, having not only essentially the same plan as the Ramesseum, but also many of the same scenes and texts, lifted bodily from the earlier building. The great battle and hunting scenes on the pylons and outer walls of the temple, however, seem for the most part to have been original with Ramesses III and, though often awkwardly composed, badly drawn, and indifferently executed, they are colorful, naturalistic, and full of life, movement, and excitement. Access was gained to the temple precinct through lofty fortified gateways in the east and west sides of the massive girdle wall. These structures, the famous High Gates of Medīnet Habu, are characterized by pairs of tall crenelated towers, the upper chambers of which, to judge from their decoration, were evidently used as pleasure pavilions by the king and members of his ḥarīm.

As in the Ramesseum, the forecourt of the temple proper was adjoined on its southern side by a small brick palace, or royal resthouse, the colonnaded sandstone façade of which was formed by the south wall of the temple court. The façade is pierced with three doorways and, at its center, with an ornate "window of royal appearances," transformed, with the remodeling of the palace late in the reign of Ramesses III, into a projecting balcony. Back of its façade the little building in its second and final form is seen to have consisted of anterooms, a columned audience hall, a small throne room, and modest living apartments for the king and members of his family or ḥarīm. Many of its architectural elements, such as column bases, throne daises, door frames, and window grills were of stone. Of the last named we are fortunate in possessing an almost complete example found in the ruins of the palace by Harry Burton while conducting excavations on behalf of Theodore M. Davis.

The ★grill, as can be seen in figure 230, is a square slab of sandstone carved with an elaborate openwork design divided into two registers. At the top two solar falcons extend their wings in a protective gesture toward a pair of disk-crowned cartouches containing in both instances the praenomen of Ramesses III. Below, cartouches with the king's personal name, Raʿ-mesē-se, Ruler of Heliopolis, are worked into a row of large amuletic hieroglyphs, the symbols for "life," "stability," and "well-being." The carving of the grill is mechanical and lacking in refinement, but the general effect of its symmetrically arranged and sharply silhouetted elements is both striking and attractive.

From the decoration of the sandstone door frames of the Medīnet Habu palace come a number of polychrome faience ★inlay plaques, or, as they are more often called, tiles. One such plaque (fig. 231) bears the praenomen and nomen cartouches of Ramesses III, mounted side by side upon "gold"-signs, and preceded by the titles Lord of the Two Lands and Lord of Crowns. The plaque itself is of white faience while the hieroglyphs, raised slightly in relief, are overlaid with bright blue, green, and red glaze. The upper part of a narrow rectangular tile, of the type for which Medīnet Habu is famous, preserves in relief the head and shoulders of a bearded, long-haired Asiatic captive, seen in full front view, the arms crossed and lashed together over the top of the head in a most extraordinary position. This tile, like its more complete mates in Cairo, Boston, and elsewhere, is notable for the many and varied colors of its glazes—the yellow of the man's skin, the black of his hair and beard, and the bright reds, blues, and whites of his elaborate robe and cap. Fragments of small square plaques carry figures of *rekhyet*-birds perched on blue and buff checkered *neb*-signs and provided with human arms upraised in an attitude of worship. They come probably from the lower part of a doorjamb and symbolize the common conception of "all the people in adoration" before the king (see also p. 336). The blue checks in the *neb*-signs are inlaid and the spaces around the figures of the birds are filled with thin flakes of faience held in place by mortar. Part of a green faience tile from a floral frieze is inlaid with a row of slender white petals carved of alabaster, and there are, in addition, ninety similar alabaster ★inlay pieces in the forms of petals, scales, lozenges, squares, rectangles, and chevrons. Two other objects in our collection, a drop-shaped faience ★bead and a red pottery ★mold for a rosette, also came from the Davis-Burton excavations of 1912-1913 at Medīnet Habu.

FIGURE 231. Faience inlay plaque with the names of King Ramesses III. H. 3 ¾ in.

Besides this royal resthouse in western Thebes and his principal residence at Per-Raʿ-mesē-se in the Delta, Ramesses III seems to have possessed a richly decorated palace at Leontopolis (modern Tell el Yahudīyeh), some twenty miles northeast of Cairo. Little now remains of the building itself, which appears, as at Medīnet Habu, to have been attached to a temple, but much of its glazed tile decoration has been recovered, including twenty pieces acquired by the Museum with the Douglas, Drexel, and Morgan collections.

The ★tiles from Tell el Yahudīyeh are generally similar to those from Medīnet Habu, but show individual characteristics and a few individual types of their own. The narrow vertical plaques with figures of bound enemies occur in some quantity, and of these we possess a fragment with the head and shoulders of a Nubian, identified by his facial type, his brown skin, his gaily patterned garment,

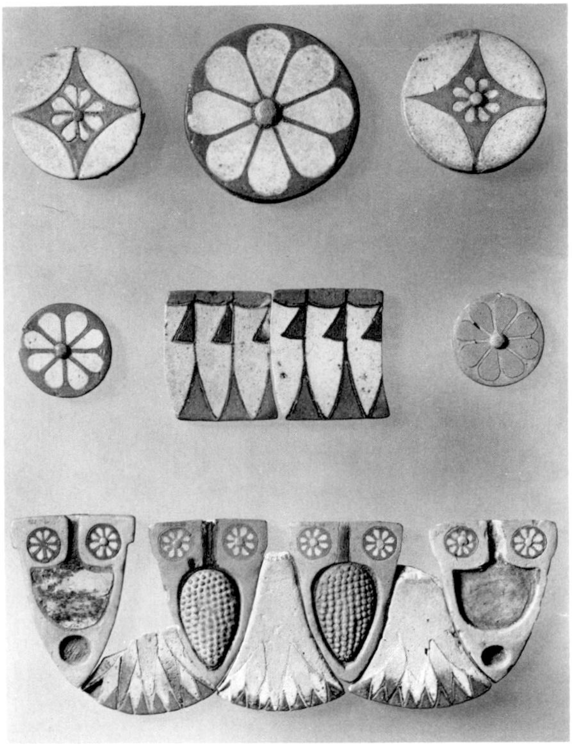

FIGURE 232. Tiles from a palace of Ramesses III at Tell el Yahudīyeh. H. of lotus frieze 2 ¾ in.

and the feather projecting from his short, kinky hair. The upper end of a rope, looped about the captive's neck, is ornamented with what appears to be the emblematic plant of Upper Egypt. Two square tiles of gray faience carry relief figures of the now familiar *rekhyet*-birds in the act of adoration, in one case surrounded by background fillers of blue faience, in the other mounted on blue, red, and white checkered *neb*-signs. Flat faience elements from a lotus frieze, once inlaid along the top of one of the palace walls, include three yellow lotus flowers with lavender, purple, greenish blue, and white details and five lotus-bud plaques of yellow faience which fitted between the flowers and are themselves inlaid with clusters of purple faience grapes, mushroom-shaped ornaments of greenish blue, and small polychrome rosettes (see fig. 232). A selection of similar rosettes—faience disks with central bosses or bronze nailheads and in each case eight radiating petals inlaid in contrasting colors—are graduated in diameter from one to one and three-quarters inches. In several the circle of white petals is enclosed within a four-pointed star of dark gray faience. Another of the palace friezes was made up of small squarish faience plaques carrying in each case a row of three slender white petals notched with red triangles and outlined in heavy black line against a green background. The tiles of this type, of which we possess two complete examples, have their lateral edges curved in such a way that they could be fitted snugly together to form a long, continuous band of petals. A large white hieroglyph representing a seated figure of the god Ptaḥ holding a *was*-scepter and wearing on his head the ram's horns and double plume is molded in relief on a fragment of dark gray faience tile. It is adjoined on the right by the border line of what was evidently a monumental column of inscription. Part of a similar tile preserves the top of a large uraeus, elaborately executed in raised white outline and probably at one time inlaid with paste or bits of colored faience. A section of a rodlike object projecting from the hood of the serpent suggests that it represented the goddess Udōt of Lower Egypt extending an amuletic symbol to the falcon atop the king's Horus name. From Tell el Yahudīyeh also comes a fragmentary alabaster ★inlay figure from one of the palace balconies. The portion preserved is the right shoulder of an elaborately garbed Asiatic with the praenomen cartouche of Ramesses III engraved upon it.

An irregularly shaped ★fragment of hieratic papyrus, torn from one of the big rolls characteristic of late Ramesside times, measures almost sixteen inches in height and fourteen inches in its maximum width. It is inscribed on both sides with parts of four different and apparently unrelated texts written at various times during the reign of Ramesses III. The most interesting text occurs on the back, or verso, of the fragment—that is, the side on which the vertical fibers of the papyrus lie uppermost. It is written in nine horizontal lines in a bold and stylish hand not unlike that of the Great Harris Papyrus and was dated to a year in the reign of the "Lord of the Two Lands, User-maʿet-Rēʿ Mery-Amūn—may he live, prosper, and be healthy!—the Son of Rēʿ, Lord of Crowns, like Amun Rēʿ, King of the Gods. . . ." The laudatory phrases which follow the names of the king include references to the "House of Sēth ʿA-peḥty, son of Nūt," and "he who illuminates Heliopolis," and end with the wish that the "House of the King—may he live, prosper, and be well—may be strong and powerful forever." The body of the text lists a series of high-ranking army officers ("[Commanders] of the Army, Leaders of the Armed Forces," etc.) in connection with the "cultivation of the great *Khato*-lands of the pharaoh—may he live, prosper, and be well!" and, in addition, names several military officials associated in some way with the mortuary temples of Ramesses II (". . .y of [?] the Mansion of Millions of Years of the King of Upper and Lower Egypt, User-maʿet-Rēʿ . . .") and Sēthy I (the "Scribe of the Army Na-ḥer-ḥu, of the Mansion of Men-maʿet-Rēʿ . . ."). Above this, written in a smaller, more cursive, and more businesslike hand is a five-line report recording, among other matters, the arrival of a cargo ship laden with supplies—baskets, fruit, salt, and large plants or trees called "wolf sandals." On the recto of the papyrus the principal text is a copy of a real or model letter addressed by one Fanbearer on the King's Right Hand to another and written in much the same big, florid hand as that which covers most of the verso. The letter is largely taken up with an elaborate formula of greeting, but toward the end the writer acknowledges the receipt of an earlier message and refers to affairs having to do with the Stablemasters Ḥat-nūfer and Yay and a man named Amun-em-weya. Alongside the letter, but written upside down in relation to it, are a series of short reports on the progress of work "in the tomb"—perhaps the king's tomb. They are dated to Regnal Year 16, Months 2 and 3 of Akhet, and mention "cutting stone" and "boring through," presumably from one subterranean chamber to another. These sadly damaged texts are set down in the same unaffected handwriting as the report on the verso of our papyrus and may have been written by the same scribe.

FIGURE 233. Sculptor's unfinished sketch of a temple relief showing the pharaoh smiting his enemies. L. 4 3/8 in.

A monument which can with some probability be associated with Ramesses III is a small, partially completed ★sculptor's sketch (fig. 233) of one of the great symbolic scenes in which the king slaughters his enemies in the presence of a god. During the New Kingdom scenes like this occur with some frequency in temple reliefs from the time of Tḥut-mosĕ III onward, but in the details of its iconography our sketch resembles most closely those carved at gigantic scale on the pylons and the wall surfaces at Medīnet Habu. With his left hand the victorious pharaoh grasps by their top-knots a cluster of twenty-seven foreigners, some facing left and some right, while the three at the center of the group are seen in full front view. In his upraised hand he brandishes the traditional mace, here fitted with a blade, and on his head wears the double plume flanked by uraei. Like Ramesses II, he is accompanied by a lion who strides along beside him assisting in the carnage. The figure of the god is only blocked out, but we can see that he is in the act of extending toward the pharaoh the curved scimitar, or *khopesh*, symbolizing warlike might. Above and to the left are the projecting blocks in which the names and epithets of the deity and the king were to have been carved, including one which we recognize from its outlines as that for the Horus name of the ruler. The style of the piece, in particular the modeling of the king's torso, suggests that our sketch may have been produced at a much later period, but the original from which it was copied can almost certainly be attributed to the late New Kingdom and probably to the reign of Ramesses III.

Three pairs of Ramesses III's cartouches (praenomen and nomen) were lightly engraved in a row across the base of our big granite doorjamb of Ramesses II (fig. 215), obviously while the monument was still standing in its original position. It is worth noting that the cartouches are merely an unobtrusive addition to the decoration of the monument which, out of reverence for its owner, was left otherwise untouched.

Two rectangular faience ★plaques, two blue faience ★scarabs, and seven plain faience ★rings are from foundation deposits laid down by Ramesses III during his reconstruction of a portion of the ancient temple at Abydos. The plaques are similar to those of Ramesses IV shown in figure 234 and, like a third ★plaque, of unknown origin, each bears the throne name of Ramesses III on one side and his personal name on the other. The same two names—User-maʿet-Rēʿ Mery-Amūn and Raʿmesē-se, Ruler of Heliopolis—occur either singly or, in two cases, together on six ★scarabs and two ★seal plaques in our collection. Three of the scarabs are somewhat roughly molded of faience, two are of glazed steatite, and the sixth is of bronze with lugs for attachment to a finger ring. On the back of one of the plaques, which is rectangular, there is engraved the mummiform figure of the god Ptaḥ confronted by two other mummiform deities, their heads surmounted by disks. The other plaque is oval and its back is carved in relief with a figure of the pharaoh brandishing a *khopesh*-scimitar. With this Asiatic weapon he is about to slay an Asiatic enemy in the form of a human-headed lion held upside down by its tail in a manner reminiscent of Assyro-Babylonian seals and reliefs. The edges of the plaque are decorated with the figures of four bound captives and on its underside the cartouches of the king are held aloft by a kneeling figure of the god Shu.

The tomb of Ramesses III is one of the largest and most elaborate in the Valley of the Tombs of the Kings, comparing in size and intricacy, though not in the beauty of its decoration, with that of King Sēthy I. Thither, not long after the beginning of the thirty-second year of his reign, the old king's body was brought from his Theban palace, where he chanced at the time to be staying, and buried with all pomp and ceremony in a massive red granite sarcophagus. A few decades later, in the Twenty-First Dynasty, it was removed to the Deir el Baḥri cache where it was found in modern times encased in the coffin of Queen Aʿḥ-mosĕ Nefret-iry of the early Eighteenth Dynasty.

Four of the six known sons of Ramesses III had died in their youth and were buried in handsomely decorated tombs in the Valley of the Tombs of the Queens. A scene in the tomb (No. 55) of the second of these, Prince Amun-ḥir-khepeshef, may be studied in the Museum in a facsimile color ★copy by Nina de Garis Davies. In it we see the resplendent figure of the king standing hand in hand with the goddess Ḥat-Ḥor, followed by the young prince, who functions here as his father's fanbearer.

Ramesses III's fifth son, Pe'n-ta-weret, having failed to make himself king through the attempted assassination of his aged father (see p. 365), the throne passed to the next prince in line, the loyal and able Ramesses, better known to us as King Ḥiḳ-maʿet-Rēʿ Ramesses IV. His accession was evidently recognized as having taken place on the day of his father's death—Month 3 of Shōmu, Day 15, in the old pharaoh's thirty-second regnal year (1160 B.C.).

3. The Aspirations of Ramesses IV

Though already in his middle forties Ramesses IV came to the throne hoping and apparently expecting to rival in achievement and length of reign not only his father but also his father's famous predecessor Ramesses II. To strengthen his hold on the kingship and to assure himself of the continued support of the influential priesthood of Amūn and the other gods, he caused to be drawn up Papyrus Harris I, or, as it is generally called, the Great Harris Papyrus. Here, as we have seen, Ramesses III's donations to the temple estates are listed and confirmed, Egypt's salvation at the hands of Sēth-nakhte is described, and the deceased Ramesses III is repeatedly made to call down the blessings of the gods on his allegedly chosen successor. Similar phrases are found in a hymn addressed by Ramesses IV to Amun Rēʿ, preserved to us in a papyrus in Turin, and on a stela which in the fourth year of his reign the new king caused to be set up in the temple of Osiris at Abydos. In his prayer to Osiris the pharaoh asks for a reign twice as long as that of Ramesses II, claiming that in four years he has showered more offerings and other benefits upon the deity than were contributed by Ramesses II during his sixty-seven years on the throne.

Some two dozen localities, from the mining regions of Sinai to the Second Cataract of the Nile, have produced inscribed monuments of Ramesses IV. A scarab with his name found at Tell Fārʿa and a statuette base from Megiddo of the time of Ramesses VI are not sufficient evidence to prove that he and his equally unwarlike successors retained control over Palestine, which, as already noted, seems with the death of Ramesses III to have been irretrievably lost. Nubia, on the other hand, was by now so thoroughly Egyptianized that it was to all intents and purposes a part of Egypt itself and no military campaigns were required to keep it in hand. It was administered on behalf of Ramesses IV by the Viceroy Ḥori (II), a native of the Delta city of Bubastis.

Ten rock-cut stela inscriptions in the Wādy el Hammāmāt attest the king's vigorous exploitation of the ancient graywacke quarries. The most interesting of these texts records in detail a great expedition sent out in Regnal Year 3 under the leadership of the First Prophet of Amūn, Ramesses-nakhte, and comprising no less than 8,368 men, including a fully organized division of the Egyptian army.

Unhappily for Egypt, the plans and ambitions of Ramesses IV were cut short by his death in the sixth year of his reign (1154 B.C.). He had, however, been able to complete and decorate his tomb (No. 2) in the Valley of the Tombs of the Kings and to provide it with a handsomely carved sarcophagus and lid of red granite. The plan of the tomb is relatively simple, comprising an entrance ramp, three corridors, an antechamber, a sepulchral hall, compartments for *shawabtys* and statues of divinities, and finally an innermost "treasury." Aside from the monument itself the plan of the royal tomb is preserved to us in a carefully annotated drawing made by one of the king's architects on a papyrus now in Turin. The mummy of the pharaoh, that of a bald-headed little man in his early fifties, was found cached in the tomb of Amun-ḥotpe II in a cheap sycamore coffin which had been hastily reinscribed in the Twenty-First Dynasty.

At the foot of the ʿAsāsīf valley in western Thebes Ramesses IV founded a gigantic processional temple, its axis coinciding with that of the southernmost of the three avenues (see p. 119) leading down from Deir el Baḥri. The huge building, designed to be half again as big as his father's temple at Medīnet Habu, seems to have been still in an early stage of construction at the time of the king's death; but in 1912-1913 our Egyptian Expedition was able to trace the outlines of its pylons and first two courts and in 1934-1935 we found under the mid-section of the temple plan seven intact foundation deposits containing literally hundreds of plaques and other objects inscribed with the names of Ramesses IV.

Of the contents of these deposits, which included pottery vessels with food and drink offerings, the Museum was allowed to retain in the division of finds 251 objects, a small selection of which is shown in figure 234. Specifically, our share of the find comprises one semicircular ★tablet of alabaster, two gold and eleven bronze ★plaques, 113 rectangular, oval, and cartouche-shaped ★plaques of faience and blue and violet glass, a blue faience ★scarab, 44 small faience ★models of food offerings and 79 unworked ★samples of green feldspar and red jasper. Engraved cartouches on the alabaster tablet contain the names of the pharaoh in their simplest forms, Ḥiḳ-maʿet-Rēʿ and Raʿ-mesē-se. The same two names occur on opposite sides of each of the faience plaques, while the glass plaques, which are molded on one side only, carry either the throne name or the personal name and the scarab only the former. On the bronze plaques the cartouches are engraved, but on the gold plaques they are stamped in the thin sheet metal. Two faience plaques from a deposit under the south wall of the temple bear on one side an early form of the king's praenomen, User-maʿet-Rēʿ Sotep-en-Amūn, and on the other side his more usual praenomen written in a single cartouche with his personal name, Raʿ-mesē-se Mery-Amūn. The offerings represented, either in relief or in the half round, in our little faience models are trussed oxen, calves' heads, legs, sides, and other cuts of beef, a head of lettuce, a double roll, a lotus flower, and a bird surmounted by a snake. There were also plaques with relief figures of running, falling, or crouching ibexes and metal name plaques of electrum or silver, but these remained in Egypt and must be seen in the Cairo Museum (see, however, the second paragraph below).

The western portions of the temple site yielded over seven hundred fragments of painted limestone and sandstone relief, including many blocks pilfered from the adjacent Valley Temple of Ḥatshepsūt and from a temple of Ramesses II (see pp. 339 f.). These reliefs were not brought to New York but were stored in the magazines of the Museum's expedition house, not far from the temple area. Eighty-four fragments, chiefly limestone, actually bear the cartouches of Ramesses II. Many carry the names of Ramesses III, three the names of Tḥut-mosĕ III, two those of Amun-ḥotpe II, one that of Mery-en-Ptaḥ, and one the upper part of the cartouche with the throne name of Amun-ḥotpe I. In addition, there are half a dozen fragments with parts of the cartouches of Ramesses V and 160 which either bear the names of Ramesses VI or are carved and painted in exactly the same coarse style as the ones on which his name actually occurs. The last include parts of columns and their capitals. Not a single fragment of relief from the temple can be assigned with certainty to its founder. It would appear, then, that the structure, in so far as it was completed at all, was completed under Ramesses V and VI, with the latter providing the bulk of its extant decoration. On the other hand, there is every probability that the great building was planned by Ramesses IV as his mortuary temple, but was abandoned toward the end of his reign in favor of a more modest temple north of Medīnet Habu, much of which now lies under the garden of the local resthouse of the Service des Antiquités. In any case, the "Mansion of the King of Upper and Lower Egypt, Ḥiḳ-maʿet-Rēʿ Sotep-en-Amūn in the Estate of Amūn," as the mortuary temple of Ramesses IV was called, is mentioned as a going concern in two papyri of a slightly later period.

Two more foundation deposits of Ramesses IV were discovered by the Earl of Carnarvon and by our own expedition under the foundations of small temple colonnades a hundred yards north of the great temple at the foot of the Montu-ḥotpe avenue. The ★plaques, ★model offerings, and ★samples of feldspar and jasper acquired by the Museum from these two deposits amount to 243 pieces. They are similar to those from our seven more southerly deposits, but include one electrum and two silver plaques with the names of the king and nineteen faience offering plaques with figures of ibexes. The praenomen User-maʿet-Rēʿ Sotep-en-Amūn, which Ramesses IV seems to have used only during his first year on the throne, occurs more frequently than in our other groups, as do also the more elaborate version of his personal name and the combination of both the praenomen and nomen in a single cartouche.

Perhaps from still another foundation deposit comes a small oblong ★plaque of alabaster painted on one side to resemble a scribe's writing palette,

with inkwells and brushes, and inscribed on the other side with the cartouches of Ramesses IV in their earlier form. The praenomen User-maʿet-Rēʿ Sotep-en-Amūn is found also in our collection on three glazed steatite ★scarabs, one from Aswān and two from near the North Pyramid at el Lisht. It must be pointed out, however, that besides Ramesses IV, at least nine kings of the Late Dynastic period also bore this praenomen. While the scarabs seem from their type and style to belong to the Twentieth Dynasty, a steatite ★plaque with the same cartouche elaborately carved in relief on one of its sides is probably of much later date. On a glazed steatite ★scarab, formerly in the Farman

FIGURE 234. Objects from foundation deposits of Ramesses IV. L. of alabaster tablet 2 ¾ in.

collection, the king, who is here labeled "Ḥikmaʿet-Rēʿ" is represented—somewhat unrealistically—driving his chariot over a prostrate Asiatic.

4. Disintegration under Ramesses V – X

The causes which led eventually to the collapse of the New Kingdom, though many and various, were more or less interrelated. Egypt, possessing no native source of iron ore, had remained to all intents and purposes in the Bronze Age, while other nations of the ancient world had for centuries been producing weapons and implements of iron and had stepped up their methods of warfare and their agricultural and industrial processes accordingly. No longer able to maintain her empire against these formidable rivals or to compete with them successfully on an economic basis, Egypt had been forced to abandon her holdings in western Asia and with them not only her prestige as a world power but also an important part of her national income. Moreover, an inordinate proportion of the property and income which still did accrue to the pharaonic government from other sources was now being diverted to the temple treasuries of the god Amūn and his fellow divinities, where it was used, among other things, to entice more and more of the nation's young men into the priesthood and away from economically or otherwise useful pursuits. While there has been in the past a tendency among modern writers to overemphasize the political importance of the priesthood of Amūn, there can be no doubt that it was a very real menace to the prosperity of the country and to the authority of the kings who with misguided piety continued to nurture it.

Influenced no doubt by the torrent of propaganda originating in the government schools, another large sector of Egypt's manhood had also abandoned the careers of craftsman and soldier for the comparatively easy life of a clerk or minor official in an administrative system which by now probably had more personnel than it had assets to administer. As a result the arts and crafts continued their steady march downward toward mediocrity, and the armed forces, as we have seen, came to be made up more and more of foreign mercenaries with little or no feeling of loyalty toward the land of which they were now the principal defense. It was not long before these detachments of Libyans and other foreign troops, finding themselves without regular pay and without wars to occupy and enrich them, began to plunder the inhabitants of Egypt itself, apparently with more or less complete impunity. As in many periods of acute distress, robbery and other forms of lawlessness increased among the rank and file of the people and corruption and embezzlement among the officials of their government.

More damaging perhaps than any of these material evils was Egypt's loss of her belief in the divinity of her kings, a belief which throughout the Old, Middle, and earlier New Kingdoms had been the basis of the system of government under which the country had developed and achieved greatness. Two centuries earlier, in the studied informality of the court at el ʿAmārneh the ancient concept of the god-king, ruling by divine right from a level far above that of ordinary mortals, had been dealt a blow from which it had never recovered. By the middle of the twelfth century B.C. it was dead and the civilization which for the preceding two millenniums had grown up believing in it was slowly but surely dying.

At this sorry stage of her affairs it was Egypt's misfortune to have the throne occupied by a succession of seven pious nonentities, who, lacking the energy or ingenuity to invent names for themselves, retained throughout the personal name Ramesses and borrowed their throne names from their more distinguished predecessors. The chief concern of these kings seems to have been the preparation of their often large and elaborately decorated tombs in the Wādy el Bibān el Molūk, and in this five of them were in varying degrees successful, the tombs of Ramesses VI (No. 9), Ramesses VIII (No. 1), Ramesses IX (No. 6), Ramesses X (No. 18), and Ramesses XI (No. 4) being the principal surviving royal monuments of this phase of Egyptian history.

All seven of the last Ramesside rulers appear to have been descended from Ramesses III through one or another of his numerous sons.

Ramesses V is generally considered to have been a son of Ramesses IV. He reigned for not much more than four years, succumbing in the thirty-fifth year of his life to a virulent case of smallpox. If, as seems probable, there was an epidemic of the then uncontrollable disease, it would have carried off also most of his immediate family and other intimates. His tomb at the time was unfinished and was promptly appropriated and completed by his successor, Ramesses VI. As we have seen, he apparently contributed sculptured chambers to the great temple founded by his father at the foot of the ʿAsāsīf valley, but here too his work was superseded and engulfed by that of Ramesses VI. His mortuary temple, whether here or elsewhere, is listed as a landowning institution in the Wilbour Papyrus, now in the Brooklyn Museum. This great administrative document, the most important of its kind which has come down to us, records tax assessments and measurements of landed property taken in Middle Egypt during the summer of the king's fourth (and last?) year on the throne. Aside from his tomb (No. 9; usurped by Ramesses VI), the largest surviving monument of Ramesses V is a stela in the sandstone quarries at Gebel Silsileh, the text of which contains little but florid and meaningless phrases of self-adulation. In our collection the king's cartouches are preserved on a long, tapered wooden ★peg, perhaps from one of his coffins, since it was found by Theodore Davis in the Valley of the Tombs of the Kings. At the beginning of the ink inscription which runs vertically down the length of the peg and which appears to be a short protective spell of the type normally found on coffin fastenings, we read: "[The King of Upper and Lower Egypt,] User-maʿet-Rēʿ Sekheper-en-Rēʿ, the Son of Rēʿ, Raʿ-mesē-se Amun-ḥer-khepeshef Mery-Amūn." The same rather elaborate, if completely eclectic, personal name occurs also on a steatite ★scarab acquired in 1905 with the Ward collection.

The age of Ramesses VI at the time of succession and the hostility which he exhibited toward the monuments and memory of Ramesses IV suggests that he was a son of the latter's older brother, Pe'n-ta-weret, whose death at the hands of Ramesses IV had followed hard upon his attempt to assassinate their father, Ramesses III. Though Ramesses VI usurped the tomb and perhaps the mortuary temple of his cousin and immediate predecessor Ramesses V, he permitted services for the deceased Ramesses V to be maintained in the

FIGURE 235. Gold and bronze signet rings of Ramesses VI and faience cup of Ramesses VIII. H. of cup 4 in.

temple at Derr in Nubia and probably elsewhere. A stela which he caused to be set up at Koptos in honor of his daughter, the Adoratress of the God (Amūn), Iset, gives also the names and titles of his queen, the King's Great Wife Nūbet-khesdebet. Following an uneventful reign of not more than five years he died, as his mummy shows, at the age of about forty. In the Museum's collection the names of Ramesses VI are found engraved on the bezels of three handsome metal ★signet rings, one of gold and two of bronze (fig. 235, foreground). The gold ring, which is of the heavy fixed-bezel type, carries the king's elaborate nomen, Raʿ-mesē-se Amun-ḥer-khepeshef, the God, Ruler of Heliopolis. It was purchased in Luxor and is believed to have belonged to an important Theban official of the reign. One of the other rings is of the same type, but of bronze, while the third example is composed of a bronze scarab attached by the usual swivel mounting to a bronze finger loop. Both of the bronze rings are engraved with the praenomen Neb-maʿet-Rēʿ, which Ramesses VI borrowed from the Eighteenth Dynasty pharaoh

FIGURE 236. Sketch in black ink of King Ramesses IX. Limestone ostrakon from the Valley of the Tombs of the Kings. L. 6 in.

Amun-ḥotpe III, but which is here written in typical Ramesside fashion and followed by the epithet Mery-Amūn.

Ramesses VII[1] is known chiefly for having carved his name beside the figure of one of the sons of Ramesses III on the temple walls at Medīnet Habu. His reign, usually placed at less than a single year, produced a few small monuments, among them a cartouche-shaped ★plaque of green faience which bears a slightly garbled version of the nomen, "Raʿ-mesē-se Sēth-ḥer-khepeshef Mery-Amūn." Acquired in 1914 with the Altman collection, the little cartouche is exactly an inch in length.

In the background of figure 235 is one of a set of four green faience ★cups inscribed for Ramesses VIII, a king who reigned for at least seven years and has left us a number of monuments, including a modest tomb (Bibān el Molūk, No. 1), but about whom almost nothing of a historical nature is known. In the panels on the sides of three of our cups, as elsewhere, he is called the "Lord of the Two Lands, User-maʿet-Rēʿ Mery-Amūn Sotep-en-Rēʿ, the Lord of Crowns, Raʿ-mesē-se It-Amūn, the God, Ruler of Heliopolis," and is described as one beloved of Amun Rēʿ, King of the Gods, of Mūt the Great, Mistress of Ishru, and of Khonsu Nefer-ḥotep. The inscriptions are drawn in black, as are also the bands of petal ornaments below the rims of the little vessels and the rows of diagonal strokes on their lips. The fourth cup is not inscribed, but is decorated a short distance below the rim with a band of triangles or zigzags. Since the mummy of Ramesses VIII has not been recovered it is interesting to note that this set of cups, perhaps originally from his tomb, was found in the débris near the Cache of Royal Mummies at Deir el Baḥri.

Toward its end the nineteen-year reign of Ramesses IX was enlivened by an outbreak of tomb robbery in the Theban necropolis, during which the pyramid of King Sobk-em-saf II of the Seventeenth Dynasty was broken into, other royal tombs were damaged, and numerous private burials were plundered. Despite a series of somewhat perfunctory investigations and inquests, the records of which are preserved to us in a group of well-known papyri in London, Liverpool, and Brussels, the robberies continued under Ramesses X and XI, and by the middle of the Twenty-First Dynasty almost every important tomb in the necropolis, royal and private, had been pillaged. It would seem, indeed, that some of the Theban officials charged with the protection of the tombs were in league with the robbers, and that the gold and other precious substances which the latter stripped from the deified dead and returned to circulation constituted a welcome contribution to the country's foundering economy. Though their own great tombs stood waiting for them in the Valley of the Kings it is questionable whether Ramesses IX and his two successors, hundreds of miles away in their Delta residence, were aware of the depths to which their Theban representatives had sunk or, being

[1] On the identities of Ramesses VII and VIII see Nims, *Bibliotheca Orientalis*, XIV (1957), p. 138.

aware, could have done anything about it. In a remarkable relief between the seventh and eighth pylons at Karnak Ramesses IX is shown bestowing rewards on the High Priest of Amūn, Amun-ḥotpe, whose figure is not only the same size as that of his sovereign, but in this scene is decidedly more eye-catching.

The limestone ★ostrakon of figure 236 carries an ink sketch of Ramesses IX wearing the Blue Crown and holding in his extended right hand a figure of the goddess Maʿet, symbolizing "right" or "justice." Since the accompanying inscription speaks of presenting incense it is not unlikely that the little figure of the goddess was molded in some aromatic substance. Above are the cartouches with the pharaoh's praenomen, Nefer-ku-Rēʿ Sotep-en-Rēʿ—borrowed in part from King Pepy II of the Sixth Dynasty—and his nomen, Raʿ-mesē-se Khaʿ-em-Wast Merery-Amūn. The drawing was found by Theodore Davis in the Wādy el Bibān el Molūk and is probably a preliminary sketch for a scene in the king's lavishly decorated tomb (No. 6). Thanks to Nina de Garis Davies we possess color ★copies of two scenes in another richly decorated Theban tomb of the period (No. 65)—that of the Chief of the Temple Scribes of Amūn, I-mi-sība. In both scenes Ramesses IX burns incense before the barque of Amūn, which in one case rests in a pavilion upon an altarlike support and in the other is being borne forth in procession upon the shoulders of its priests.

The first and third years of King Kheper-maʿet-Rēʿ Ramesses X are recorded in papyri and ostraka having to do, respectively, with the trials of tomb robbers and a new strike by the unpaid and hungry workmen of the Theban necropolis. His names are found on small objects from Ḳantīr in the Delta and occasionally at Karnak, notably in the small Twentieth Dynasty temple of Khonsu. He has left us a tomb (No. 18) in the Valley of the Tombs of the Kings which never progressed beyond the cutting of its entrance passageways. Otherwise, characteristically little is known of this next to last ruler of a line which by now was obviously moribund.

5. Ramesses XI and the End of the New Kingdom

Though the last of the Ramesside pharaohs occupied the throne for at least twenty-eight years, the rulership of both Upper and Lower Egypt was taken out of his hands long before he himself finally passed into oblivion.

In Upper Egypt the transfer of power seems to have commenced at Thebes with an uprising directed against the High Priest of Amūn, Amun-ḥotpe, in which bands of Libyans and other foreigners played an important role. Order was restored by the Viceroy of Nubia, Pa-neḥesy, who appeared in Upper Egypt at the head of a strong contingent of troops, ousted Amun-ḥotpe from office, and returned to his post in Nubia leaving an officer named Ḥery-Ḥōr in charge at Thebes. Ḥery-Ḥōr, though apparently without any priestly background or training, promptly had himself appointed High Priest of Amūn. A few years later, while retaining both the high priesthood and the command of the southern army, he replaced Pa-neḥesy as Viceroy of Nubia and also took over the office of Upper Egyptian Vizier. By this time he was virtually the ruler of the whole of the Southland and proceeded to make additions to the temple of Khonsu at Karnak in his own name with only an incidental mention of the pharaoh to whom he theoretically owed allegiance.

The rise to power of Ḥery-Ḥōr is believed to have been the occasion for the inauguration of a new "era" called the Repeating of Births, or the Renaissance. Year 1 of this era is known to have coincided with Regnal Year 22 of Ramesses XI and we have additional dates running through to Year 7 of the so-called Renaissance, the latter date corresponding to the twenty-eighth year of the reign.

Meanwhile, control of Lower Egypt had been taken over by the northern Vizier and High Priest of Amūn, Nesy-Ba-neb-Dēdet, more commonly known as Smendes, an elliptical Greek version of his name. This man, who had apparently started life as a well-to-do merchant of the eastern Delta town of Tanis, was destined to be the founder of the principal, or Tanite, branch of the Twenty-First Dynasty. In Ramesses XI's twenty-sixth year (Year 5 of the Renaissance) it was to Smendes, rather than to the king, that Ḥery-Ḥōr's envoy Wen-Amūn presented his credentials, and it was from Smendes that he received his passage to Byblos and some much needed assistance later on his mission (see p. 431).

Thus the last pharaoh of the Twentieth Dynasty appears to have finished out his reign as a shadow king, living on in his palace at Per-Raʿ-mesē-se bereft of power and unnoticed except by a few faithful officials and the few religious institutions to which he had contributed. It was not, however, until his death, about 1080 B.C., that Smendes in the North and Ḥery-Ḥōr in the South allocated, each to himself, the titles and insignia of kingship, thereby bringing the New Kingdom to a definite end and plunging Egypt into the final tumultuous phases of her dynastic history.

X. The Art and Culture of the Ramesside Period

IN THE TWO PRECEDING chapters we have concentrated our attention on the historical development of the Nineteenth and Twentieth Dynasties and on the monuments in the Museum's collection which, because they are associated with individual kings or their courts, may be regarded as contributing to our knowledge of that development. The in many cases similar objects to which we now turn are either of unknown ownership or belonged to persons whose historical significance, if any, has not yet been established. Frequently it is difficult if not impossible to determine whether an individual piece was produced under the Nineteenth or the Twentieth Dynasty. Typological, iconographical, and stylistic details, often reinforced by circumstances of discovery, however, have combined to earmark as Ramesside the many works of art and craftsmanship in question. Conversely, the works themselves, though historically uninformative, have much to tell us of the life, tastes, and credos of Egypt's people during the two and a quarter centuries which witnessed the death throes of the last of her three great "kingdoms."

1. Figure Sculpture

The base of a large diorite ★statuette, which represented a Ramesside pharaoh standing and holding before him a small shrine or offering table, came to the Museum in 1956 as a gift of Albert Gallatin. Beneath the king's sandaled feet are engraved the traditional "Nine Bows" and across the top of the base is a line of well-cut hieroglyphic inscription which states that "all lands and all foreign countries are at the feet of this Good God, whom the people worship that they may live." A short vertical text running forward from the right foot wishes the unnamed ruler "all life and well-being, all health, and all joy," and on the stump of the statuette's back pilaster is preserved the final sign in the word "forever."

Fifty-two years earlier, in 1904, we received as a gift of Darius Ogden Mills the limestone plinth of a large private statuette of the same period. The plinth is a thick, rectangular block of stone, twelve inches in length, its upper surface rebated and provided with horizontal peg holes to receive the base of the now missing figure. A band of deeply engraved hieroglyphic inscription which runs horizontally around the block an inch or so below its top consists of two short offering formulae invoking the god Osiris in behalf of two Troop Commanders of the Garrison Troops of Ptaḥ named ʿAḥa-ʿa and Khaʿy. Since ʿAḥa-ʿa ("The-fighter-is-great") is named again in a short line of text across the front of the top of the plinth, we may suppose that the lost figure was his funerary statuette, dedicated perhaps by his son (?) and successor Khaʿy. The garrison troops of Ptaḥ we should expect to have found stationed at Memphis.

FIGURE 237. Statuette of a scribe in dark gray diorite. H. 8 5/8 in.

With these two not very notable exceptions our larger pieces of Ramesside sculpture, both royal and private, have already been discussed in Chapters VIII and IX (see especially pp. 347 ff.). There remain, however, a number of minor works which in several instances make up in interest or attractiveness what they lack in importance.

In the diorite ★statuette of figure 237 we see the familiar figure of the well-fed scribe or government official looking up from a roll of papyrus which he holds open on his lap and on which, to judge from the position of his damaged right hand, he has been writing. Inspiration in this case is provided by the god Tḥōt's cynocephalous ape, the symbol and source of learning, which squats on the writer's shoulders and clasps his head with its forepaws. The shingled wig and the diaphanous shirt with pleated sleeves could easily belong to the late Eighteenth Dynasty, but the squat proportions and summary modeling of the figure, the lack of expression in the broad, flaccid face, and a characteristic coarseness of finish point to a date well down in Ramesside times. Purchased in 1928 from a native of Luxor, the statuette is said to have come from Ḳurneh in western Thebes. It is not inscribed.

Nor is there an inscription on the charming serpentine ★pair statuette of figure 238, so that the identity of the modishly dressed couple here portrayed remains unknown. The little group was probably carved during the earlier decades of the Nineteenth Dynasty. It is very similar to its Eighteenth Dynasty prototypes (cf. fig. 87), but there is a mechanical quality in the handling of the forms and the intricately pleated garments which suggests a Ramesside dating. Understandably enough, this pair of small figures has long attracted the interest of students not only of ancient costume but also of ancient furniture, for the chairs on which the couple sit are represented in almost as great detail as their clothing and coiffures. The group was acquired in Luxor and, like the scribe, is probably of Theban origin.

Almost the identical costume worn by the lady of our group is seen on a ★statuette carved of quartzite and representing a young woman standing in rigid frontal pose with her hands at her sides. Here, however, the long, braided wig is less full and the pleated over-mantle is draped in such a way as to leave the right breast exposed. The figure with its uninscribed rectangular base stands eight and a half inches in height. It is provided to the height of the shoulders with a flat back pilaster which also was left uninscribed. Though for its period a piece of exceptionally high quality, the statuette is, unhappily, not in the best of condition, having suffered the loss of its nose, its right arm, and much of the forward part of its base. It, too, was purchased in Luxor.

An extraordinary little bronze ★figure (fig. 239) of a slender, foppishly dressed young man kneeling with hands raised in adoration is typical both in style and costume of the late New Kingdom. Particularly characteristic are the graceful, rather effeminate wig, the exaggeratedly flaring sleeves, and the pleated kilt with its balloonlike apron in front (cf. fig. 219). Our statuette is solid cast and is provided on the underside with a bronze tenon an inch in length. It comes undoubtedly from one of the familiar groups made up of a figure of a divinity confronted on a common pedestal by that of his worshiper. Another small bronze *statuette, from a perhaps more elaborate group of the same type, represents a "priest" with shaven head and long, pleated skirt standing and holding in his extended hands a *ḥes*-vase (𓏀) and an ornate rod-like censer with a butt in the form of a falcon head. The man, then, is in the act of burning incense and pouring a libation, two of the principal rites performed daily in the presence of a god or his symbol. This figure, too, is a solid casting, but its arms, together with the objects which they hold, were made as separate pieces and attached to the shoulders by bronze tenons. Both the censer and the libation vase were at one time overlaid with gold foil. The height of the statuette, exclusive of the lugs which project downward from the soles of its feet, is four and a half inches. Aside from the individual interest which each may have these two little figures are notable as being among the few examples of New Kingdom sculpture in bronze which have survived to the present day.

A somewhat less convincing addition to this select company is a small bronze *head, formerly in the Carnarvon collection, which since before 1926 has carried the date "Dyn. XVIII-XIX," but which may well belong to a much later period. It is apparently the head of a man or beardless male divinity wearing a close, caplike headdress once surmounted by an object or device of some sort. The handsome little face is admirably modeled and the whites of the eyes are overlaid with sheet gold. The height, from collarbone to crown of head, is one and three-eighths inches.

Though *shawabty*-figures are normally treated not as works of sculpture but as items of funerary equipment, at least four of our Nineteenth and Twentieth Dynasty *shawabtys* are of a quality which entitles them to be separated from their more commonplace mates and elevated to the status of portrait statuettes. This is certainly true of the remarkable little limestone *statuette of figure 240 in which we see the "Scribe of Recruits Ḥuy" dressed in the elaborate costume of his period and wearing suspended from his neck an amulet in the form of a Ḥat-Ḥor-headed sistrum. The rather distinctive face and the way in which the head is bent slightly forward suggest that the sculptor was here attempting to portray an individual. Only the pose, with the feet together and the hands crossed over the breast (holding hastily sketched mattocks?), reminds us that this is a funerary

FIGURE 238. A man and wife of the early Nineteenth Dynasty. Serpentine. H. 6 ¼ in.

FIGURE 239. A Nineteenth Dynasty (?) dandy kneeling in adoration before a god. Bronze. H. 2 7/8 in.

figure and in all probability a *shawabty*. It was purchased in Cairo and may come from a tomb in the Memphite area. A painted limestone ★*shawabty* from Deir el Medīneh in western Thebes is similar in that it represents its owner, the Guardian Amun-em-Opet, as a living person, standing on his two feet and clad in the curly wig and foppishly elaborate garments which he wore, or would like to have worn, on earth. It would appear, however, to be later in date than the figure of Ḥuy and, though almost twice its size, is more coarsely modeled and colored. In this case the hands hang down in front of the figure, resting on the thighs. The whole surface of the statuette is painted, the clothing white, the flesh brown, the wig and inscription black, and a funerary broad collar, which has been incongruously added to the late New Kingdom costume, striped brown and yellow.

Most of our Ramesside ★*shawabtys* are of the more usual mummiform type inscribed in horizontal bands with Chapter VI of the Book of the Dead. Among these an exceptionally fine example in slate (fig. 241), made for a man named Tjebu-Rēʿ, shows the hands of the mummy open on the thighs and has carved over its breast the "soul" (*ba*) of the deceased in the form of a human-headed bird with outspread wings.

The hollow-cast bronze ★head of what was apparently a large and handsome *shawabty* is said to have been found under a boulder in the Wādy Gabbānet el Ḳurūd, a desert valley west of Deir el Baḥri where many of the wives and daughters of New Kingdom pharaohs had their tombs (see pp. 130 f.). It was perhaps under the same boulder that a mummiform statuette of King Mery-en-Ptaḥ was found (see pp. 354 f.), but this is altogether uncertain. The head, which is provided with three bronze tenons for attachment to its figure, is made in two interlocking parts, the rather thin, beardless face (including the throat) and the long, full headdress, once apparently coated with blue paste.

FIGURE 240. *Shawabty*-figure of the early Nineteenth Dynasty. Limestone, with wig, eyes, and inscription painted black. H. 3 5/16 in.

The eyes and eyebrows are inlaid with obsidian and artificial glass. The over-all height of this admirable example of New Kingdom sculpture in metal is just two inches.

Another class of funerary figure, the nude female "doll," placed in the tomb apparently to restore the procreative powers of the deceased, is represented by a red pottery *statuette five inches high, which, unlike the hideous productions of earlier times (see fig. 6), portrays a slender and exceedingly attractive young woman. The hair of the girl is arranged, in characteristically elaborate fashion, in two great masses on the sides of her head, and around her hips she wears a narrow bead girdle. A comparison with similar figures found at Deir el Medīneh tends to date our figure to the latter half of the Ramesside era.

The ruins of the ancient village which grew up around the North Pyramid at el Lisht yielded a quantity of small and for the most part crude *statuettes of men and animals carved of limestone or wood or molded in faience, pottery, and Nile mud. Among the examples which the staff of our Egyptian Expedition have dated to the Twentieth Dynasty are a limestone head of a man with a curiously rounded face, several small faience heads with or without chin beards, two extremely crude red pottery "idols," roughly human in form, a very primitive carved wooden crocodile, and a number of little mud figures of hippopotami and oxen, the latter decorated with minute blue faience ring beads which had been pressed into the surface of the mud while it was still soft.

2. Stelae and Other Forms of Relief Sculpture

A study of the Museum's fairly extensive collection of private stelae of the New Kingdom discloses the surprising fact that only four of them, all of limestone and all from western Thebes, are datable to the Nineteenth or Twentieth Dynasty. These four small monuments, however, show a wide range of different types and each is unusual and interesting in its own way.

FIGURE 241. Slate *shawabty* of Tjebu-Rēʿ. Nineteenth Dynasty. H. 7 ½ in.

The largest of the stelae, a round-topped ★slab of fine white stone fourteen and a half inches high, carries in the upper of its two registers figures of the mummiform god Osiris and the deified King Amun-ḥotpe I, the former preceded at the right by a tall stand laden with food offerings. Osiris, here described as the "Lord of Everlastingness and Ruler of Eternity," wears the *atef*-crown and, in the hands which emerge from the front of his mummy wrappings, holds the crook, *ladanisterion*, and *was*-scepter. Amun-ḥotpe I, whose cult as a patron divinity of the Theban necropolis and its activities reached its height during the later New Kingdom, is labeled the "Lord of the Two Lands, Djeser-ku-Rēʿ," but is anachronistically decked out in the elaborate kilt and headdress of a Ramesside pharaoh. He too holds the crook and *ladanisterion* and, in his pendent right hand, the symbol of "life." In the lower register Pe'n-Amūn, the dedicator of the stela, and an unnamed male relative (son or brother?) kneel side by side, each with his hands raised before him in a gesture of worship. The stela was found by Theodore Davis in the Valley of the Tombs of the Kings. Its figures are carved in shallow *relief en creux* in an accomplished but rather lifeless manner. Its inscriptions are incised.

This is true also of a smaller but more elaborately inscribed and decorated ★stela acquired in 1928 from a native of Ḳurneh. Here we see again the tall mummiform figure of Osiris standing at the left of the scene which occupies the upper half of the stela, accompanied in this case by his consort Isis. Before him the Magnate of the Seal of the Treasury of the House of Amūn, Pa-nakht-(em-)Opet, and his wife, the Chantress of Amūn, Akhet-ibḳet-Mūt(?), kneel facing one another and receive in their cupped hands streams of water poured from a *ḥes*-vase by a goddess who stands on an object or structure of some sort at the extreme right of the scene. The head of this goddess, who is identified in the text above as "Nūt the Great, Mother of the Gods," is surmounted by what appears to be a bowl for incense with smoke rising from it (𓊮). The bulk of the text referred to is an "Offering which the King gives" formula invoking Osiris, Isis, and Wen-nefer in that order. Above, in the curve of the lunette, is a sun's disk with down-sweeping wings. The lower half of the stela is taken up by a longer offering formula composed in seven horizontal lines of relatively large hieroglyphs. Here the deities called upon are Rēʿ Atūm, Ptaḥ Sokar, Osiris, and Djeser-ku-Rēʿ Amun-ḥotpe (I), the "Cult Image of Amūn." The boons asked for seem to have been inspired by Chapter CLXVIII of the Book of the Dead and include "goings and comings with Rēʿ, unhampered progress like the Lords of Eternity," "a going forth with the spirits of Onet," and "a following of Sokar . . . and Osiris." At the end we are told that it was Nesy-pa-ḥer-ḥat, Pa-nakht-(em-)Opet's son and the inheritor of his office, "who causes his name to live." The personal names as well as the style of the work permit us to date this most interesting little monument to the Twentieth Dynasty.

A miniature ★stela, only four and a half inches in height, has the upper part of its field taken up by the figure of a sphinx crouched upon a shrine and representing in all probability the Great Sphinx at Gīzeh, revered during the New Kingdom and later times as the sun god (Ḥaurūn) Harmakhis. Below is a table of food offerings and kneeling beside it with hands upraised in an attitude of prayer a man named Pery-Amūn, for whom or by whom the stela is said to have been made. A pair of human ears floating in space above the back of the sphinx is to ensure Pery-Amūn's prayers being heard by the deity. Except for the brief inscription, which is incised, the decoration of the small slab is executed in bold and rather coarse relief of characteristic Ramesside type. The piece was acquired in Luxor and comes probably from that general neighborhood.

Much the same style of relief is seen on a curious little ★stela (fig. 242) from the artisans' village at Deir el Medīneh, where it had probably once been set up in a household or local shrine as a votive offering to the two great mother goddesses represented on it. Its inscriptions tell us that the large

FIGURE 242. Limestone votive stela from Deir el Medīneh. H. 7 in.

female head mounted on an altarlike pedestal at the right is that of "Mūt the Great, Mistress of Ishru," the principal goddess of Thebes and the consort of the god Amūn; and that the hippopotamus deity who stands facing her in front of an acacia tree is "Ta-weret (the Great One), Mistress of Heaven." In the latter case we may suspect that "Ta-weret" is used here as an epithet rather than as a name and that a representation of the local hippopotamus goddess Ipet is actually intended. The association of either Ipet or Thoueris with an acacia tree (clearly identified by its long, indented pods) seems to be otherwise unrecorded. The head of Mūt reminds us of those adorning the bow and stern of the sacred barque of the goddess and may perhaps be thought of as a symbol for the barque, which normally rests on a pedestal of the type shown. Both deities wear the sun's disk and cow's horns, which tend to assimilate them with the other leading mother goddesses, Isis and Ḥat-Ḥor, and this helps to explain Ipet's appearance as a tree goddess. Between them a slender stand supports a libation vase garnished with lotus flowers. This, in theory, would have been contributed by the dedicator of the stela, the Sculptor (?) of Amūn, Khonsu, whose title and name were hastily scratched on the band provided for that purpose at the base of the slab. Clearly we have here a stock ex-voto sold ready made to devotees of Mūt and Ipet and not a monument designed and executed for an individual worshiper.

A ★fragment of limestone tomb relief, fifteen and a quarter inches in length, preserves the figures of a man named Pa-shed and his wife paying their respects to Osiris, whose figure, except for his *ladanisterion*, has been broken away and lost. Pa-shed's upraised hands are empty, but his wife holds a small jug in one of hers and has looped over the same arm a long-stemmed lotus flower and two buds. Despite the pretentious intricacy of their clothing and accessories the figures are hastily and carelessly carved and their rather birdlike faces are coarse and unattractive. The medium is shallow *relief en creux*. Though the provenience of the piece is uncertain (Theban Tomb No. 292 or 339?) its style is beyond any question of the Ramesside period.

An earlier piece of Ramesside tomb ★relief was found by Petrie at Memphis incorporated into the wall of a building erected apparently under Ramesses II. On it we see the head of a massive long-horned bull with a boy seated between the great spreading horns and grasping them with his outstretched hands. Any doubt regarding the age of the lad is removed when we note that he is still wearing the braided side lock of youth. The fragment is thought to have formed part of a scene showing the funeral sacrifice of a bull by the sons of the deceased tomb owner. Stylistically the relief is not far removed from those of the ʿAmārneh period and could, indeed, be assigned to the very end of the Eighteenth Dynasty.

New Kingdom tomb chapels, as we have seen, were frequently topped by small, sharp-angled brick pyramids painted white and capped with pyramidia of limestone. One such ★pyramidion, formerly in the Amherst collection but otherwise of unknown origin, bears on two of its sides a solar barque above a pair of adoring cynocephalous apes, and on its other two sides a kneeling figure of the tomb owner with hands upraised, surmounted by an Anubis animal on a shrine. The figures are knowingly but carelessly carved in shallow *relief en creux* and were once painted in a few simple colors—red, blue, white, and black. In the longest of the hastily engraved inscriptions the owner, the Mortuary Priest Yūf-ʿau, hails Rēʿ Ḥor-akhty, the "Great God, Lord of Heaven," that the latter may in turn supply the usual funerary benefits. The other texts place Yūf-ʿau under the protection of Osiris and in one case give the name of his father, the Mortuary Priest Iy-ḥēr. The personal names and the rough finish and generally sketchy workmanship confirm Winlock's dating of the monument to the Twentieth Dynasty. With a height of fourteen and one-eighth inches and a base of ten and a quarter inches the pyramidion—and the pyramid from which it came—slopes steeply upward at an angle of 70°.

Two of four limestone ★sculptors' studies, or, as they are also called, trial pieces, come from the Valley of the Tombs of the Kings and carry in one case the profile head of a youthful pharaoh of the late Nineteenth Dynasty wearing the *seshed*-circlet with uraei over a short, caplike wig. The outlines of the head are lightly incised and its details sketched in very shallow sunk relief. In a larger but less detailed sketch we see the disk-crowned falcon of Rēʿ Ḥor-akhty accompanied by a symbol of "life" and by a pendent uraeus, which descends from the broken left-hand edge of the flake. The relief figure of a Ramesside pharaoh spearing a fallen Libyan whom he grasps by the topknot is carved with care and with a good deal of spirit on a small, round-topped slab of limestone said to be from Tanis in the northeastern Delta. On the back the head of a hook-nosed and bearded foreigner with a serpent(?) issuing from his mouth is drawn with deeply incised outlines. The fourth study, found by the Egypt Exploration Fund in the temenos of Osiris at Abydos, comprises four hieroglyphic signs—the uraeus, the goose, the falcon, and the vulture—carefully and expertly carved in low relief. In height the four slabs range from three and three-eighths inches (the king and the Libyan) to eleven and three-eighths inches (the falcon of Rēʿ Ḥor-akhty).

3. Paintings and Drawings

Under the Ramesside pharaohs the tendencies which we observed in the private tomb paintings of the later Eighteenth Dynasty (see pp. 163 f.) became increasingly pronounced. In the Theban tomb chapels funerary and religious subjects had now largely replaced the earlier scenes of daily life, and large, integrated compositions had taken the place of the successions of isolated episodes seen in the chapels of the Thutmoside era. The draughtsmanship, though often stylish in its fluency, is generally less clean and precise and the colors, against the chalky white backgrounds, are less clear and bright. A good deal of the work is of mediocre quality and the subject matter, from our point of view, is frequently dull and repetitious. There are, however, some notable exceptions, and it is chiefly these exceptions which Nina de Garis Davies and Charles Wilkinson have selected as the subjects of an attractive series of color copies now on exhibition in the Museum's galleries and study areas. Some of the more important tomb chapels copied could be used to fill out our knowledge of the reigns of individual kings and have already been referred to in Chapters VIII and IX. Among those less securely dated and at the same time represented in our color ★copies are the justly famous tomb of Sen-nedjem at Deir el Medīneh (No. 1, early Nineteenth Dynasty), the chapels of Nefer-sekheru (No. 296, Ramesside) and Ḥiḳ-maʿet-Reʿ-nakhte (No. 222, Twentieth Dynasty), and the portions of the tomb of Ḥuy (No. 54) usurped by the priest and storehouse director Kenro, of the early Nineteenth Dynasty. Outstanding is Wilkinson's copy of the wonderful scene in Tomb No. 1 showing Sen-nedjem and his wife Iy-neferty in the blessed fields of the afterworld, worshiping the gods, harvesting grain and flax, and driving a plow yoked to a team of piebald cows. Here the small scale of the scenes and a miniaturelike delicacy in the handling of the figures remind us of the colored vignettes in more or less contemporary funerary papyri.

To make the comparison we may turn to a large and handsomely illustrated ★papyrus of the early Nineteenth Dynasty which was acquired in 1935 as a gift of Edward S. Harkness. Thirteen feet in length and over a foot in height, the papyrus was prepared for a steward named Sētẖ-nakhte, who is thrice portrayed in its vignettes dressed in the height of late New Kingdom fashion and whose name, titles, and epithets are repeated countless times in the cursive hieroglyphic text. The latter, drawn up in vertical columns and carefully written in black and red ink, consists in its entirety of Chapter CLXVIII of the Book of the Dead, the so-called Chapter of the Offerings (see also p. 384). In the body of this spell prayers are addressed to forty-one Underworld deities and each prayer is accompanied by a small, square vignette representing the deity in question and is followed by an oft-repeated refrain stating that "a bowl is offered to them on (earth) by . . . the Steward Sētẖ-nakhte." At the beginning, or right-hand end, of the roll Sētẖ-nakhte kneels in adoration before a large symbol of the West (𓋀), which is protected above by winged *wedjat*-eyes and is attended by a row of cynocephalous apes and two rows of kneeling and chanting divinities. Next we see our well-to-do steward in his graceful wig and long, flowing garments standing and saluting Osiris, whose tall mummiform figure is most elaborately drawn and colored and is here supported on either side by

FIGURE 243. Funerary papyrus of the Steward Sēth-nakhte. Last or left-hand section. L. 31 in.

smaller figures of the goddesses Isis and Nephthys. Then follow the forty-one prayers and refrains and the forty-one small vignettes with figures of the miscellaneous deities, demigods, and daemons invoked—sphinxes, male and female beings, mummiform figures, bull gods, a hoopoe perched on a papyrus umbel, and a gateway enclosing a solar disk with down-streaming rays. At the end of the papyrus (fig. 243) Sēth-nakhte again worships Osiris, raising his right hand toward the deity and holding high in his left hand a little figure of the goddess of truth or justice (Maʿet). Here Osiris appears as the falcon-headed Khenty-Amentet, the "Foremost-of-the-West," and both he and his worshiper stand in a sort of small kiosk topped by a frieze of *maʿet*-plumes and uraei. Though not the finest of its kind in existence, Sēth-nakhte's papyrus displays the elegant draughtsmanship and the wide range of harmonious colors which we find in the better examples of late New Kingdom manuscript illustration.

The fluency and extraordinary virtuosity of the trained Ramesside draughtsman is seen to equal advantage on the uncarved limestone votive ★stela of figure 244. Here, in accordance with the usual practice, the design was first rapidly sketched in fine red outline and then redrawn in its final form in firmer and slightly heavier black line. The stela, now ready for the sculptor's chisel, shows us two brothers, Amun-nakhte and Amun-em-Opet, and the former's son Pe'n-ta-weret, singing a hymn to Amun Rēʿ, whose barque is seen in the upper register being borne in procession on the shoulders of its priests. The vessel, characterized by its ram's-head bow and stern ornaments, is carried on five long poles by twenty *wēʿb*-priests of Amūn, here aligned in four rows. Beside it walks the First(?) Prophet Amun-em-Opet wearing a leopard skin and having his head shaved like those of his companions. Five of the bearers are identified by name (Amun-em-Opet, Nefer-ḥotep, Pa-ḥery-pedjet, Amun-mosĕ, and Raʿ-mesē-se Mery-. . .), a fact which suggests that they were relatives of the three men by whom the monument was dedicated. Of the latter, Amun-nakhte and his son were Scribes in the Place-of-truth (i.e., the necropolis at Thebes), while the brother, Amun-em-Opet, was a Chief Artificer of the Lord of the Two Lands.

The admirably executed ink drawings on a smaller limestone ★stela from the Wādy el Bibān el Molūk show us the ram of Amūn with proudly

FIGURE 244. Unfinished stela from Thebes. Limestone, with drawings and inscriptions in red and black ink. H. 16 ¾ in.

FIGURE 245. A Ramesside pharaoh spearing a lion. Limestone ostrakon from the Valley of the Tombs of the Kings. L. 5 ½ in.

arched neck feeding from an offering table, and above, in the semicircular lunette, Meres-ger, the cobra goddess of the Theban necropolis, followed by a smaller serpent, approaching a large basket of fruit. Both deities are labeled and a short hieroglyphic inscription over the back of the ram states that the little monument (height five and five-eighths inches) was dedicated by the "*Wēʿb* and Lector Priest of All the Gods of the West, Nefer-ḥotep, the justified."

One of the richest sources of our knowledge of the art and culture of the Ramesside period is the vast number of practice drawings and preliminary sketches made, for the most part, on flakes of limestone by the scribes and "outline draughtsmen" of the Theban necropolis. Thirty-one such ★ostraka in the Museum's collection have come to us from the excavations of Theodore Davis and the Earl of Carnarvon in the Valley of the Tombs of the Kings (fourteen examples), from the courtyard of an abandoned Middle Kingdom tomb near Deir el Baḥri (Tomb 312), and from the artisans' village and cemetery at Deir el Medīneh. Only two of the lot are of unrecorded provenience and since one of these is from the Davis collection and the other was purchased in Luxor the presumption is that they also are of Theban origin. The drawings, which range from hasty sketches to carefully finished little pictures, are executed entirely in black and/or red ink, the two colors normally found on the ordinary scribe's palette. The majority seem to be preliminary studies of figures and groups to be used in the decoration of the walls and furnishings of royal and private tombs; but a few preserve for us the more frivolous themes which we may suppose went to make up the mural decoration of dwelling houses, villas, and palaces. Still others, also few in number, would appear to have been drawn solely for the amusement of the artist and his friends.

Among the studies devoted to the heads and figures of Ramesside kings is a flake (fig. 245) on which a pharaoh, accompanied by a lop-eared hound,[1] is shown spearing a lion already wounded by the royal arrows. The king's flesh and the crown of Lower Egypt which he wears are tinted with diluted red ink, as are also portions of the dog and the disproportionately small, but ferocious, lion. Above, in a florid hieratic script characteristic of the period, are written the words "The slaughterer of every foreign country, the pharaoh—may he live, prosper, and be well!" On the back of the flake a four-line text in the same handwriting contains a laudatory address to the king: "My good lord—may he live, prosper, and be well!—the sun of every land, the ruler—may he live, prosper, and be well!" and so on. On three other ostraka the necropolis draughtsmen have practiced drawing portrait heads in profile of Nineteenth or Twentieth Dynasty kings wearing in two cases the Blue Crown. One of the royal heads is partially overlapped by an amusing sketch of a tall thin priest(?) named Pay and his Nubian wife, Meres-ger, a slatternly fuzzy-haired creature naked except for a bead girdle about her bulging mid-section. A childishly crude little drawing of a royal prince standing and holding in his hand an ostrich-plume fan exaggerates the size of the young

[1] Probably a Salūki. Compare the ivory hound described on p. 314.

man's braided side lock, the length of the fringe on his kilt, and the curl of the toes of his sandals. By contrast, the charming figure of a scantily clad queen or princess brandishing in her hands a pair of large sistrums is drawn with the utmost sophistication in the light, sure line of the professional artist. A male head interestingly rendered in full front view wears a flaring, shingled wig and a short chin beard and shows the ear lobes pierced with prominent horizontal slits. The same experimental spirit is found in a little sketch of a blind and hunchbacked harper kneeling on the ground with his great bow harp tucked in against his shoulder and his feet awkwardly splayed out to the sides.

Figures of divinities include, on one ostrakon, the Theban triad, Amūn, Mūt, and Khonsu, lined up one behind the other, and on another, Amūn by himself wearing, as usual, his tall plumed headdress and surmounted by a hieratic label which announces, quite unnecessarily, that this is "Amun Rēʿ, King of the Gods." Horizontal guide lines were used in establishing the proportions of a mummiform figure of the god Ptaḥ, which was outlined first in red ink and then corrected in black. The end of a vertical hieroglyphic text in front of the figure preserves the words "in his good name of Sokar," and below, in a horizontal line, mention is made of the Draughtsman Amun-ḥotpe and a Scribe of the Lord of the Two Lands whose name is lost. The god Sobk appears on a flake of limestone from Deir el Medīneh as a crocodile-headed figure attired in a kilt and corselet and wearing on his head the sun's disk, ram's horns, and double plume. He stands in front of a large palm branch and holds in his hands a symbol of "life" and a *was*-scepter twined with lotus flowers. On a fragmentary ostrakon from the same site we see a goddess standing behind an upright mummy and protecting it with her great down-sweeping wings.

A massive flake of stone (fig. 246), found in 1913 by Theodore Davis, carries an elaborate sketch for the decoration of a wall of a king's tomb. In the upper of two registers, below a frieze of *ḫekeru*-ornaments, the mummiform god Osiris stands within a light pavilion confronted by a fetish in the form of an animal skin suspended from a papyrus plant. In the text before him he is described as "Osiris Khenty-Amentet, the Great God who is in the necropolis," and in the text behind he endows the royal tomb owner with "all protection,

FIGURE 246. Limestone ostrakon from the Valley of the Tombs of the Kings. H. 16 ½ in.

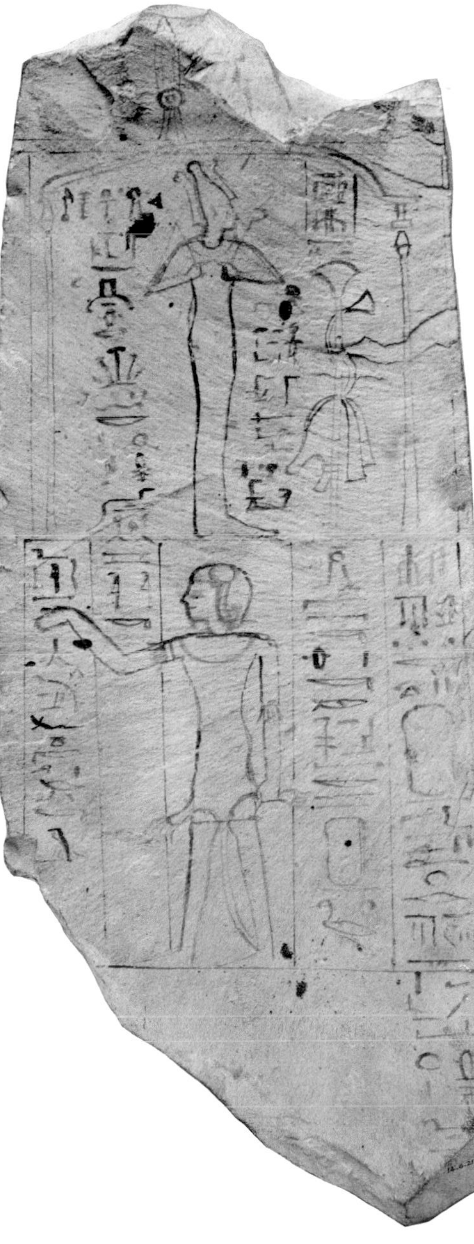

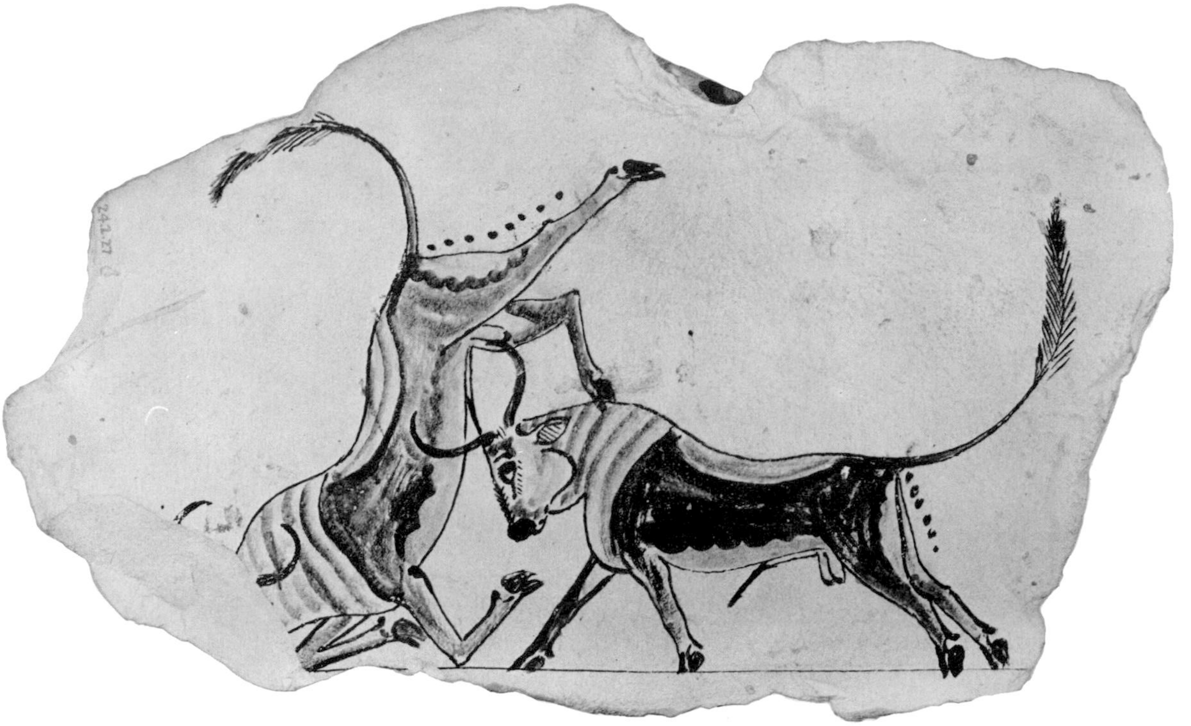

FIGURE 247. Colored drawing in black and red ink on a flake of limestone from Deir el Medīneh. L. 7¼ in.

life, stability, well-being, and health and all joy . . . like Rēʿ, forever and ever." Below, a *setem*-priest, clad in his leopard skin and cap with side lock, extends his hand in a ceremonial gesture. The text here is a speech addressed to the king by the genius Dewau-mautef: "I am your beloved son, Horus. I bring to you your heart, Osiris, King, Lord of the Two Lands . . . (blank cartouche), Son of Rēʿ, begetter of all gods, Lord of Crowns . . . (blank cartouche), justified with all the gods of the Holy Land, like Rēʿ, forever." On the back of the huge flake the wolf god Up-wawet appears upon his standard accompanied by a speech of assurance which he addresses to the deceased king.

The seminude corpse of a man lying extended in an open anthropoid coffin is carefully drawn in red ink on an ostrakon from the Valley of the Kings. It may have been intended for use in one of the elaborate tomb plans current at this period (see p. 371), but differs from the designs for the lids of sarcophagi in that the body is not mummiform but is represented with feet apart and in considerable anatomical detail. From Deir el Medīneh comes an ostrakon on which the hieroglyphic texts used on New Kingdom coffin lids have been laid out diagrammatically in their proper relative positions, with blanks left in the columns of inscription for the name of the deceased. On the back of the same flake are parts of the texts normally found on the sides of coffins and sarcophagi. In a humorous caricature of a funerary subject rapidly sketched in black and red ink we see a funeral barque proceeding westward but bearing beneath its canopy a recumbent donkey in place of the usual mummy.

Eight spirited sketches of animals include a pair of bulls fighting (fig. 247), a horse rubbing its nose on its foreleg (fig. 248), a charging lion, a gazelle feeding, a running calf with turned-back head, several crocodiles, cobras, and falcons, and a scene in which various birds and their nests appear in the midst of flowering marsh plants. An eagle owl (𓅓) and a *sūt*-plant (𓇓), conventionally rendered in heavy black outline, are evidently hieroglyphs.

A final group of five small ostraka is taken up

with preliminary sketches of architectural and decorative elements—two floral capitals carefully drawn in red ink on grids of proportion squares, an elaborate palmette border, a composite tree or plant of perhaps Syrian inspiration, and a crude drawing of a door (▯) with an unidentified symbol (?) scrawled on it.

Some of the most accomplished and most attractive paintings of the period have come down to us on coffins, canopic chests, *shawabty*-boxes, and other pieces of funerary equipment. These are discussed and a small selection is illustrated in the next to last section of this chapter.

4. Ostraka with Inscriptions

One hundred and thirty inscribed ★ostraka of Ramesside date, acquired by the Museum between the years 1909 and 1932, come with one exception from the Theban necropolis and deal with or reflect in some way the activities of that vast and intensely busy institution. Ninety are from the excavations of Theodore Davis in the Valley of the Tombs of the Kings, nine are from the village and cemetery area at Deir el Medîneh, and nineteen are from the vicinity of the mortuary temple of Ramesses III at Medînet Habu. One ostrakon, purchased in 1921 from a native of Ḳurneh, is almost certainly from western Thebes, as are also ten others obtained in the same year at the sale of the Amherst collection. The remaining ostrakon, a potsherd with a Nineteenth Dynasty copy of part of the "instruction" addressed by King Amun-em-ḥēt I to his son Se'n-Wosret I,[2] was found by our expedition near the latter's pyramid at el Lisht.

Nine of our Theban ostraka, bearing vertical columns or horizontal lines of cursive hieroglyphs, are clearly studies of the ways in which texts destined to be used in the decoration of royal or private tombs could be composed to fit the wall or ceiling spaces available for them. The texts themselves are what we should expect: excerpts from the Book of the Dead and other funerary writings, portions of hymns to Amūn and his fellow divinities, offering formulae, royal and private titularies, and symmetrically grouped symbols for "life," "well-being," and the like. In one of these texts an unnamed pharaoh is described as the "image of Rēʿ before the Two Lands, the one chosen of Amūn to function as king forever and ever." Another inscription, drawn up in three or more horizontal lines below a large sketch of a broad collar, lists by name and title a number of draughtsmen and "servitors" in the Place-of-truth, including two men named Khaʿu and Neb-maʿet.

Similar texts occur also among the hieratic ostraka, but these, as usual, are concerned chiefly with the daily business of the necropolis and the activities and requirements of its personnel. A report dated to "Regnal Year 25" records the progress of the "work in the tomb" and another refers to the "Mansion of King . . .-Rēʿ Mery-[Amūn]," perhaps Ramesses III. Visits of inspection "to the tomb of the pharaoh—may he live, prosper, and be well" by a scribe and by a chief of police named Neb-semen are recorded on two other ostraka, and there are a number of brief letters or, perhaps better, memoranda which were exchanged between scribes and other local officials. One of the last, dated simply to "Day 10," is introduced by an elaborate formula of greeting in which the writer "inquires concerning the condition" of the addressee and calls down upon him

FIGURE 248. Limestone ostrakon from Tomb 312 in western Thebes. L. 8 ½ in.

[2] See Part I, p. 179. The excerpt preserved on our ostrakon corresponds to Papyrus Sallier II 2, 4-7.

the favor of various deities. Unhappily, the body of this particular communication is not preserved, but one of the other notes is a request for a loan of grain and a third deals with a situation involving a workman and a "witness."

Most numerous are the rosters of workmen and their supervisors and the records of supplies issued to or received by them. The former include gang foremen, builders, draughtsmen, "servitors," rowers, and Nubians. The latter comprise, in addition to beverages and foodstuffs, clothes, cedarwood, plaster, carrying poles, mats, and, again and again, lamps or torches. Among the personal names preserved in these lists or inscribed singly on individual ostraka we find Amun-em-ōnet, Amun-ḥotpe, Amun-nakhte, Baki, Ḥōr, Ḥor-nefer, It-nefer, Iy-iy, Kay, Ḳeḥ, Ḳen, Khaʿ-em-ḥēt, Khonsu-nakhte, Mery-Rēʿ, Mey, Nakht-Amūn, Neb-nefer, Nefer-ḥēr, Nesu-Iset, Pa-nefer, Pay, Pe'n-ʿarḳu, Sen-nedjem, and Tja-tjay.

Several ostraka were used for simple arithmetical computations, a typical example being a small but complete flake of limestone on which the numbers 64, 68, 66, and 11 have been successfully added together to produce a total of 209. Columns of crudely drawn hieroglyphic signs followed by numbers are perhaps marks used by artisans such as potters or tilemakers, accompanied by tallies of the daily output of the individual craftsmen.

Three fragmentary and badly faded literary excerpts show the red punctuation dots characteristic of school copies of such texts. Two of these preserve part of the Instruction Composed by a Man for his Son, known to us elsewhere from a leather roll in the British Museum, a papyrus in the Louvre, and a number of ostraka, including an earlier example in our own collection (see p. 177). Four ostraka inscribed in vertical columns in an archaizing handwriting carry portions of a popular miscellany of the early Middle Kingdom or First Intermediate period called the Book of Kemyet. A few groups from a medical or magical text include the Egyptian word for pyemia, a form of blood poisoning. Scribbles, made up of meaningless groups of ill-formed hieroglyphic or hieratic signs, are probably to be attributed to beginners in the courses in writing offered by the necropolis scribes during their leisure hours.

The majority of our ostraka inscriptions are on flakes of limestone, but a score or so are written on potsherds. Mixed in with the latter are three ★jar labels from the shoulders of big amphorae which at one time had contained wine. One of these is dated to "Regnal Year 2" of an unspecified king, and among the ostraka we find dates in Years 1, 2, 5, 6, 10, 21, and 48, the last referring without much question to the reign of Ramesses II.

5. Jewelry

The jewelry worn by private citizens of the Ramesside age shows no very notable advances in types, techniques, and materials over that current during the Eighteenth Dynasty.

Light necklaces and bracelets made up of strings of beads either graduated in size or supporting one or more pendant amulets still predominate and are found alike on the bodies of the dead and among the jewelry which they had owned and worn as living persons. The ★beads and pendants employed are for the most part of familiar types. Among the former we find, for example, the ever-popular tubular bead, slenderly proportioned and usually made of faience, the ball bead, more often than not roughly shaped and slightly flattened on the ends, large and small disk beads, coarse lenticular beads strung up into short, heavy chokers, and barrel beads of various shapes and proportions. The grooved spherical bead resembling a nasturtium seed also occurs, as does the thickset tubular bead adorned with an incised grid pattern. New forms include the carinated barrel bead, a short, thick version of this popular shape with a distinct ridge, or keel, running around its middle, and the frosted barrel bead of black or dark blue faience with chips of white and yellow glass encrusted in a band around its mid-section. Three beads have the form of tiny rosettes with the petals indicated in low relief. A series of seven cylindrical beads of blue faience carry cartouches in black line containing what appear to be garbled versions of the throne names of three famous kings of bygone eras, Pepy II, Tḥut-mosĕ III, and Amunḥotpe III. A large openwork barrel bead, a flat lozenge-shaped bead of polychrome glass, a square plaque with an incised X on either side, a semidiscoid bead with serrated edges, and a yellow glass bead shaped like a spool are represented by single examples only, in no case very securely dated.

The forms of the *pendants are as varied as those of the beads with which they were combined. Besides such simple shapes as the drop, bulla, lozenge, pear, disk, clamshell, petal, leaf, and inverted knob we find at this period necklace and bracelet pendants in the form of inverted lotus flowers, lilies, and palmettes, cornflowers, rosettes, bunches of grapes, small vases, and *posesh-kef* implements and what are believed to be girdle pendants reproducing the *sūt*-plant of Upper Egypt.

Faience is more than ever the favorite material for beads, pendants, and other types of amulets and, in addition to the ever-popular turquoise blue, is found in dark blue, purple, green, red, yellow, gray, white, and black. Garnet occurs as the material of a string of graduated barrel beads formerly in the Murch collection and carnelian as that of a string of small ball beads supporting pendants in the shape of cornflowers. The only other stone beads of the late New Kingdom in our collection are thirty-six unfinished lumps of garnet, carnelian, haematite, and rock crystal from a jeweler's workshop near the North Pyramid at el Lisht, dated by Mace to the Twentieth Dynasty. On the other hand, beads and pendants made of colored glass in imitation of garnet, haematite, amethyst, lapis lazuli, turquoise, agate, onyx, and other semiprecious stones are becoming more and more common and are beginning to include polychrome examples with variegated bands and "eyes" of the kind which we find in such profusion in later periods of Egyptian history. A string of tubular beads and a necklace of graduated lenticular beads, both from el Lisht, are in the first instance of blue paste and in the second of unglazed clay and bone.

Aside from those already mentioned only nine of our scores of strings of Nineteenth and Twentieth Dynasty beads have retained their original order of stringing and can properly be called *necklaces. One such necklace, found in position on the mummy of Iy-neferty of Theban Tomb No. 1, comprises a long double strand of blue faience tubular beads strung together with short double tubes and globular beads of blue, yellow, and red faience and supporting an openwork rectangular pendant of dark blue faience on which the kneeling god Eternity is seen holding in each hand the symbol for "years." The length of this necklace, forty-five inches, would permit it to have been looped two or more times around its wearer's neck. Forty small circular pendants of yellow glass with white faces and black "eyes" and rims are strung together with matching discoid beads of blue and yellow glass to form a very pretty little necklace thirteen and a half inches in length. Our seven remaining necklaces are made up in each case of beads which increase gradually in size toward the middle of the string, allowing little room for doubt on the order of the stringing. Ranging in length from eleven and a half to over sixteen inches, these necklaces are composed, respectively, of carinated barrel beads, nasturtium-seed beads, and large disk beads of blue faience, ordinary barrel beads of lavender glass, and ball beads of blue and black glass.

It is probable that some of our shorter strings of late New Kingdom beads were worn as bracelets. In no instance, however, can we be sure that this was the case, since there is no certainty that the strings are complete or in their original arrangement. A very simple *bracelet composed of a glazed steatite scarab mounted on a loop of cord comes from a tomb of the Nineteenth Dynasty near Deir el Baḥri. The scarab bears a motto which is apparently to be read "The eye of Rēᶜ is behind them." An ivory *divider bar from a bracelet or anklet, with holes for ten parallel strands of beads, was found in the ruins of the

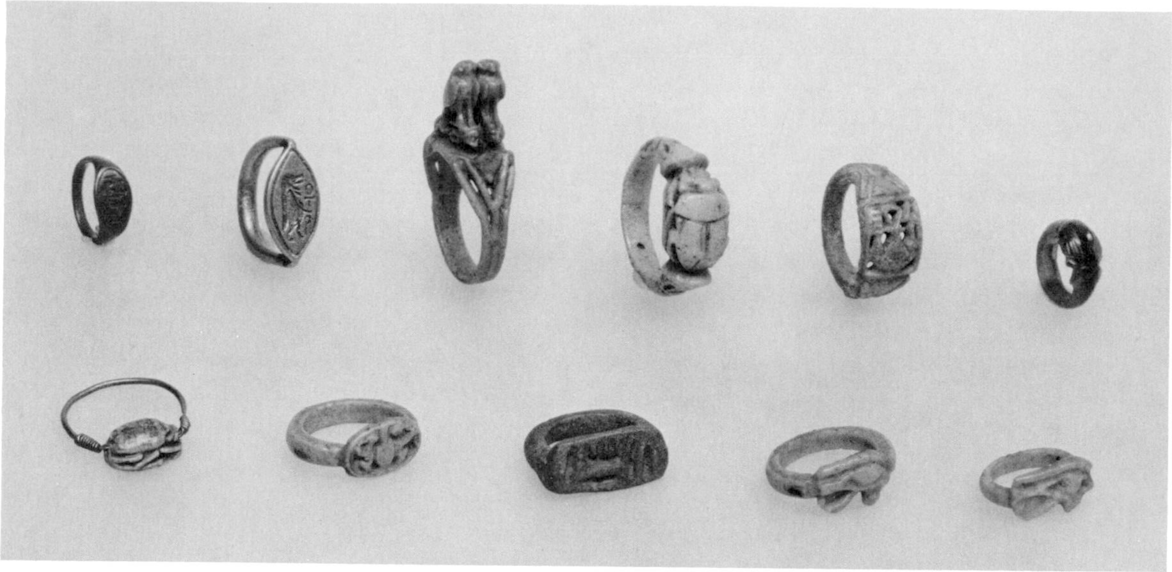

FIGURE 249. Finger rings of the later New Kingdom. Gold, bronze, carnelian, and faience. Diam. of largest ring 1 ⅛ in.

New Kingdom village at el Lisht and has been dated to the Twentieth Dynasty.

Though the finger ring appears to have remained in high favor throughout Ramesside times, relatively few well-dated examples in materials other than faience have survived to the present day. Our own collection includes only sixteen such ★rings which can be assigned to the Nineteenth or Twentieth Dynasty (see fig. 249). Among these are three small but extremely handsome gold signet rings, their bezels exquisitely engraved with the personal name Khenty-echtay-sai, with a figure of the hippopotamus goddess Thoueris, and in the third instance with a seated female figure, probably also a goddess. One of two bronze rings has a cartouche-shaped bezel containing a group of amuletic hieroglyphs, while the oval bezel of its mate is engraved with the title Sealer(?) of All Cattle. The bezel of a similar signet ring carved of black steatite carries a kneeling figure of the god Shu with arms upraised supporting the sun's disk between the hills of the horizon. The device on a heavily oxidized bronze ring of the same class from el Lisht is no longer clearly discernible. Three signet rings of the older type consist of glazed steatite scarabs mounted on loops of gold and bronze wire in such a manner that they can be rotated and their engraved undersides used as seals. Two of the scarabs bear mottoes praising the beneficence of the deities Ptaḥ and Maʿet; the third carries the figure of a lion crouched above a *neb*-sign. In three other rings of this type the scarab in each case is set in a rotating gold frame, or funda, and in a seventh both the scarab and the finger loop are of bronze. The designs on these last four rings are a standing figure of the god Amūn, a pair of winged scarab beetles, the emblematic union of the plants of Upper and Lower Egypt, and an unidentified symbol or figure. A carnelian ring with a bezel in the form of a trussed duck is expertly carved from a single piece of the glossy, translucent red stone.

Festival and funerary rings molded of blue or green faience are as numerous as ever, but tend now to be carelessly made and for the most part less attractive than their predecessors of the Eighteenth Dynasty. Two of our ★faience rings, both turquoise blue, came from the hands of the mummy of the lady Iy-neferty, the wife of the owner of Theban Tomb No. 1, who, as we shall see on page 414, was laid to rest in the time of Sēthy I or early in the reign of Ramesses II. One of these (see p.

255), perhaps an heirloom, bears the throne name of King Amun-ḥotpe III. The other, its long straight-sided bezel stamped in crude hieroglyphs with what appears to be the name Amūn, is typical of its class and period. It is coarsely molded and the ring proper, made as a separate piece, is carelessly fused to the back of the bezel. Forty-seven similar rings from the New Kingdom village site at el Lisht carry on their bezels inept attempts to reproduce the throne names of Tḥut-mosĕ III (Men-kheper-Rēʿ) and Ramesses II, the title King of Upper and Lower Egypt, the name Amūn, standing figures of several divinities (Tḥōt, Horus?), a cartouche containing a figure of the goddess Maʿet, an openwork cartouche with pendent uraei, a group of unidentified animals, and a symmetrical design composed of rectangles, circles, and dots. Ten other rings from the same site are without bezels altogether, consisting simply of crudely shaped loops of faience, square in cross section and more or less circular in outline. They are similar to the plain faience rings present in royal foundation deposits of the Twentieth Dynasty (see p. 370) and may, indeed, have come from such a deposit. With them was found an elaborate and—for its period—unusually handsome faience ring with a square openwork bezel mounted between molded lotus flowers (see fig. 249). The design in the bezel—a familiar one—consists of the hieroglyphic monogram meaning "all life, stability, and well-being."

A similar ring, formerly in the Murch collection, has a bezel in the form of a scarab molded in the round and suspended between a pair of lotus flowers, also in the round. Even more elaborate is a blue faience ring acquired with the Carnarvon collection. Here an openwork bezel is surmounted by the freestanding figures of two little falcons holding beneath their talons a pair of prostrate human "enemies." Four other faience rings from the same collection are said to have come from a foundation deposit of the Nineteenth Dynasty. *Wedjat*-eyes and a rampant uraeus form the bezels of three of these rings, while the fourth has a flat rectangular bezel impressed with what may have been a *nefer*-sign. The oval bezel of another Carnarvon ring, reputedly from the Dirāʿ Abu'n Naga in western Thebes, bears the words "Amun Rēʿ, Lord of Upper and Lower Egypt." It is of bright blue faience and, like most of its mates, measures a little under an inch in outside diameter. A similar ring purchased by Mr. Lythgoe near Deir el Ballās bears the figure of a falcon-headed(?) god holding a *was*-scepter. The bezel of a double ring from the same neighborhood is in the form of a head of the goddess Ḥat-Ḥor. An engraved figure of the Syrian god Resheph, wearing his tall, pointed headdress with pendent streamer, appears on a ring from the Murch collection, while the bezel of another ring acquired with it is molded in the form of a rampant uraeus.

FIGURE 250.
Signet ring of blue faience.
Late Twentieth Dynasty.
L. of bezel 2 3/8 in.

Toward the end of the Twentieth Dynasty a new type of faience ★signet ring with a very long and elaborately inscribed bezel begins to put in its appearance. In the example of figure 250 the bezel is cartouche-shaped and its surface is slightly curved from end to end, allowing it to be used with a rocking action. The engraved text asks Tḥōt, Lord of Hieroglyphs, and Maʿet, the "scribe of the Ennead itself," to grant the owner of the ring "a long and happy old age (in) Karnak and (in) the following of the King." Rings of this class are particularly common during the so-called Third Intermediate period, remaining popular until the end of the Twenty-Third Dynasty.

By Ramesside times the earring, scarcely known in Egypt before the Seventeenth Dynasty, had become a standard article of personal adornment, affected alike by men and women and by kings and commoners. The size and intricacy achieved by such ornaments are exemplified by two incredibly elaborate gold earrings in the Cairo Museum inscribed, respectively, with the names of Sēthy II and Ramesses XI. Our own relatively small series of Nineteenth and Twentieth Dynasty ★earrings are all of the annular or penannular type designed to be worn clipped to the ear lobe or passed through a hole pierced in it. An especially attractive example in pale blue glass banded with darker blue, yellow, and white, is provided with two little suspension rings of yellow glass and has fused to its outer perimeter a twisted cord of black and white glass. A bright blue glass earring with a scalloped outer edge comes from the Museum's excavations at el Lisht, as do also two thick little rings of brownish red glass and a circular loop of tapered silver wire.

Ten roughly molded little rosettes of blue, violet, yellow, and brown faience, each with a circular hole through its middle, are probably ★dress ornaments (see pp. 186 f.). All ten are from the New Kingdom rubbish heaps around the North Pyramid at el Lisht.

As with other objects worn or used by the people of ancient Egypt, fashions in amulets are seen to change from one period to another, some of the older types passing out of use and new forms being constantly developed. Thus, a critical appraisal of the hundreds of ★amulets in our collection discovers only forty-eight types which can be assigned to the Ramesside age. Animal forms are still popular, and among these we find the squatting cynocephalous ape, the cat, the crocodile, the falcon, the ibex, the ibis, the lion, the ram, the frog, the fly, the cobra and other serpents, the vulture, the scarab beetle, and a crouching antelope identified as a klipspringer. Animal-headed and completely anthropomorphic divinities, though not as common as in later periods, are becoming somewhat more numerous and include now little standing or seated figures of the falcon-headed Horus, the youthful Harpokrates (fig. 251), the kneeling atmosphere god Shu, and Ḥeḥ, the god of eternity, the dwarf gods Bēs and Ptaḥ Sokar, the goddesses Bastet, Sakhmet, Thoueris (many examples), Isis, Nūt, Maʿet, and the head of the goddess Ḥat-Ḥor. Old stand-bys such as the *wedjat*-eye, the heart amulet, the red *tyet*-knot symbolizing the "blood of Isis," the *posesh-kef* implement, the papyrus column, and the symbols of "life" (*ʿankh*) and "stability" (*djed*) occur, as always, in great numbers and in a considerable variety of materials. On the other hand, parts of the human body, so common during the late Old Kingdom and First Intermediate period, are relatively rare, comprising now only the eye, the hand, and the face seen in full front view. Knots, shells, stars, and crescents are still found, but they, too, are becoming rare. New forms introduced during the Nineteenth or late Eighteenth Dynasty are the double plume and the sun god in his barque, the latter having the form of a flat, boat-shaped plaque with the hull, occupants, and details of the sacred vessel carved or molded in low relief. A most elaborate amulet in the shape of a cowrie shell (fig. 252) carries an openwork design in the center of which an ape is seen squatting upon a shrine in an attitude of adoration, flanked on either side by an upreared uraeus. Seven strings of faience amulets from the North Pyramid village area at el Lisht are made up of *wedjat*-eyes, flies, human hands, figures of the god Bēs, and figures of the hippopotamus goddess Thoueris.

FIGURE 251.
The Child Horus.
Lapis lazuli amulet
of the late New Kingdom.
H. 1 5/8 in.

Well over half of our Nineteenth and Twentieth Dynasty amulets are modeled or molded of blue, green, yellow, or reddish brown faience, with the balance carved for the most part of semiprecious stones. Among the latter green feldspar, lapis lazuli, carnelian, and agate are the top favorites, with a few examples occurring in beryl, red jasper, serpentine, crystal, and porphyry as well as in syenite, diorite, graywacke, slate, glazed steatite, as well as blackened limestone. Ten amulets are molded of blue, green, red, or white glass, but this material is relatively uncommon, the heyday of the glass amulet not yet having arrived. Blue paste, with only three examples, is meagerly represented, and for each of the remaining materials—gold, electrum, and wood—we possess only a single amulet of nonroyal ownership and Ramesside date.

Though they are not amulets, properly speaking, mention may be made here of forty-three small faience ★models of food offerings which come from two unidentified foundation deposits in the general neighborhood of Thebes. Molded of blue, green, red, and gray faience, they are similar to the models found in the temple deposits of Rameses IV (fig. 234). The types include running and crouching ibexes, birds, trussed steers, calves' heads, *khopesh*-joints and other cuts of beef, and what appear to be heads of lettuce.

The seal amulet, with an engraved inscription or distinctive design on its underside, seems to have lost little or none of its popularity, the Museum's collection comprising more than five hundred ★scarabs, ★scaraboids, ★cowroids, ★plaques, and other forms of ★seals which, though without identifiable royal names, are datable by type and content to the Ramesside age. As usual, the scarabs are many times more numerous than all the other types combined, and include now two new forms of back, one with an enlarged base and spreading legs around a small body, the other plain with an elongated head, lateral notches, and stilted legs. During this period, too, the human-headed scarab makes its reappearance (see fig. 217). The backs of many of the oval seals are provided with a longitudinal handle pierced transversely for a suspension cord and splaying out toward each end of the seal where it is adorned with a flower or palmette in low relief. Other forms assumed by the carved backs of our Ramesside seals—depending to some degree on their shapes—are the *bolti*-fish, the hedgehog, the baboon, the frog, a sphinx, a pair of crocodiles, one or a pair of grotesque human faces, the head of the goddess Ḥat-Ḥor, the head of a lion, the *wedjat*-eye, several varieties of rosette, and a rounded cone with a band of decoration around its base. Many of these were by now traditional forms handed down from the earlier centuries of the New Kingdom (see p. 126). The backs of two of our plaques (one rectangular, one oval) are decorated with a little openwork design showing the goddess Isis nursing her son Horus in the papyrus thickets of Chemmis (see p. 403). An exceptionally handsome steatite plaque acquired with the Carnarvon collection carries on

FIGURE 252.
Amulet of blue and yellow faience. L. 1 3/16 in.

its back two registers of figures carved in low relief and separated by a band of incised inscription. In the upper register the gods Amūn and Rēʿ sit watching Horus and Tḥōt standing with hands upraised on either side of a *wedjat*-eye; below we see a Ramesside pharaoh slaying one foreign chieftain in the presence of a goddess and driving his chariot over the prostrate form of another. Most of the plaques are rectangular and are engraved on both sides with inscriptions and designs similar to and in several instances duplicating those found on the undersides of scarabs. Scaraboids, cowroids, button seals, and seals with plain, hemicylindrical backs occur, but are exceedingly rare. Blue- or green-glazed steatite is still the favorite material for all types of seal amulets, but examples in faience are more numerous than heretofore, the colors of the latter including turquoise and dark blue, light and dark green, red, and black. A few scarabs, plaques, and seals are molded of blue, green, or black paste and an even smaller number of blue, green, and amethyst glass. Carved stone seal amulets include isolated examples in carnelian, green and red jasper, lapis lazuli, diorite, haematite, crystal quartz, unglazed steatite, and blackened limestone.

As always, the major interest of these little monuments is the seemingly endless variety of legends engraved on their undersides or, in the case of the flat plaques, on both sides. Perhaps the most striking feature of the Ramesside seal inscriptions is the absence of the names and titles of private individuals. The royal names Sēthy and Ramesses appear alone on three of our scarabs and the name of the Old Kingdom Vizier Ptaḥ-ḥotpe is inscribed on three others—probably as a magical means of evoking for the owners of the scarabs some of the wisdom of the famous sage.

By contrast, the names and figures of deities and the slogans or spells associated with them are more numerous and more varied than ever before. Over a hundred scarabs and seals bear the name and/or figure of the state god Amūn, who appears on them in human form wearing his tall plumed headdress, as a standing or crouching ram, or as one of his temple obelisks. Frequently the great god is shown receiving the adoration of a standing or kneeling pharaoh. More often than not he is referred to as Amun Rēʿ and his name is followed by such epithets as "King of the Gods," "Lord of the Two Lands," "beautiful of breath," "giver of life and speech," and "establisher of the peace of Egypt." His name is also incorporated into what are usually called mottoes but seem in many instances to be short spells. Examples are: "Goodness is in the House of Amūn," "The favor of Amūn is in Thebes," "Amūn causes the heaven of Thebes to shine." As we have seen (pp. 182 f.), some of the same mottoes or spells occur also on scarabs of the earlier New Kingdom.

Even more numerous are the seal amulets which place their wearers under the protection of the sun god, whose presence is indicated either by his name, Rēʿ, or by his barque with the disk of the sun floating above it. The short texts in which Rēʿ is invoked include New Year's wishes ("May Rēʿ grant a happy New Year"); spells to reassure the timid ("When Rēʿ is behind [one] there is no fear"); spells in behalf of the king ("Rēʿ is satisfied with the Ruler of Thebes") and the owner's home town ("The city which Rēʿ loves is stable"); and incantations of a generally beneficent nature ("The eye of Rēʿ is behind them," "The eye of Rēʿ is life and protection"). Other deities who are named, represented, or invoked in similar fashion are Anubis, Bastet, Bēs, Demedj (a name of the sun god), Ḥat-Ḥor, Horus, Isis, Khonsu, Maʿet, Montu, Mūt, Nephthys, Nekenyet (an Underworld goddess), Nit, Onuris, Osiris, Ptaḥ, Sakhmet, Serḳet, Sēth, the ape and ibis of Tḥōt, the hippopotamus Ipet or Thoueris, Wen-nefer, the *bennu*-heron, or phoenix, a serpent goddess, and the fat nature gods of Upper and Lower Egypt. Bēs, whose squat, bandy-legged figure appears frequently, is sometimes accompanied by one or more monkeys, and on a scarab formerly in the Ward collection he and a monkey friend are seen drinking through tubes from an enormous jar which stands between them. Khonsu is not represented, but his name occurs often in the slogans or spells ("Khonsu establishes [my] name," "Khonsu is [my] stability"). Ptaḥ is described as the "Lord of Truth and the begetter of mankind" and is said to be "good in my sight because he gives strength," and the little text on one of our blue paste scarabs tells us that "endurance is for him who follows Tḥōt."

All told, our scarab inscriptions assure their owners of more than fifteen different boons, starting with a wish for a single happy New Year and ending with the gift of "millions of years." Among the hoped-for benefits are freedom from fear, good eyesight, love, protection, favor, stability, endurance, honor, virtue or beauty, breath (i.e., life), truth or justice, fluency of speech, and a lasting remembrance. Many of the texts do not include the names of divinities, and among these we may note especially a group devoted to well-known cities—"The guardian of Thebes is my protection," "It is Thebes where the God shines on every servant," "Memphis is mighty forever, the Mistress of Truth," "How beautiful is Aphroditopolis!" Of a somewhat more practical nature are "The inundation is food," "A real doer is pleasing to the god."

Another class of legend consists of royal or priestly titles (the Good God, Ruler of the Two Lands, the King's Daughter, the Prophet of Khonsu), which are incorporated occasionally into short sentences ("The King is in his counting house,"[3] "The King's son endures"). As usual, a good many scarabs bear single hieroglyphs with amuletic significance ("life," "goodness," "truth," "stability," and so on), while on others the same signs are grouped symmetrically to form ornamental designs. Other decorative motifs are made up of uraei, sistrums, lotus and papyrus plants, looped cords, twisted cords, cross patterns, and linear designs of a purely geometric nature.

A large group of uninscribed scarabs and plaques are taken up entirely with figures of the king. They show us the pharaoh variously crowned and attired, standing between emblems of the East and West, seated on his throne, drawing his bow, driving his chariot, and dispatching his enemies with upraised axe or mace. Not infrequently the ruler appears as a sphinx wearing the royal *nemes* or the Double Crown and holding before him a figure of the goddess of truth or other appropriate symbol. In one instance a pair of winged royal sphinxes stand face to face, each trampling on a fallen enemy. Human figures, unidentified by any kind of insignia, also appear on the undersides of our Ramesside seal amulets, sometimes in pairs, sometimes in association with various animals and birds—lions, antelopes, crocodiles, giraffes, serpents, falcons, and geese.

Animal forms, alone or in groups, are as popular as ever, and among these we recognize without difficulty antelopes, beetles, bulls, crocodiles, dogs, ducks, falcons, fish, hares, hippopotami, horses (eleven examples), ibexes, lions, monkeys, ostriches, rhinoceri, scorpions, spoonbills, and storks. The groups occasionally show animals in naturalistic associations or contexts, such as a lion springing on an oryx and monkeys swarming up a palm tree. Griffins and sphinxes with the heads of rams and jackals(?) occur in small numbers, as do also designs in which the rampant or coiled uraeus is the dominant motif. Needless to say, there is a residue of unidentified animals, just as there is a number of illegible (or at least unread) inscriptions and designs. There are also a dozen or more faience and hard stone scarabs, the undersides of which are plain, blank ovals.

Some of our late New Kingdom seal amulets are from the Museum's excavations at Thebes and el Lisht, but the great majority were acquired between 1904 and 1930 with the Farman, Ward, Murch, Carnarvon, and Davis collections, many of the Carnarvon scarabs, in turn, having once formed part of the Timins collection. All have been drawn and catalogued by Nora E. Scott and it is from her catalogue that the foregoing paragraphs have been largely derived.

Considering the wealth of information to be obtained from these hundreds of little documents on the life, religion, and decorative art of their period, it is clear that they deserve a far more thoroughgoing and detailed treatment than the relatively brief and cursive survey they have received here.

Before taking our leave of the Museum's collection of late New Kingdom jewelry, mention should be made of an extremely handsome series of ★gold amulets which were formerly assigned to this period, but which belong almost certainly to later phases of Egyptian history—the Twenty-Second to Twenty-Sixth Dynasties and the age of the Ptolemies. Included are two sets of hollow gold rams' heads, strung in one case with oval gold beads to form a necklace, six gold pendants in the form of the aegis of the cat goddess Bastet, three inlaid gold *bolti*-fish with exaggeratedly large fins and tails, five little gold sistrums of the Hathorian type, three gold and inlaid *ba*-birds with outspread wings, a hollow gold figure of a falcon wearing the Double Crown, two hollow gold beads in the shape

[3] With apologies to the old nursery rhyme. The word actually is *per-ḥedj*, "treasury."

of trussed ducks, and a score of tiny gold figures of the deities Tḥōt, Anubis, Chnūm, Harpokrates, Isis, Nephthys, Sakhmet, and Thoueris.

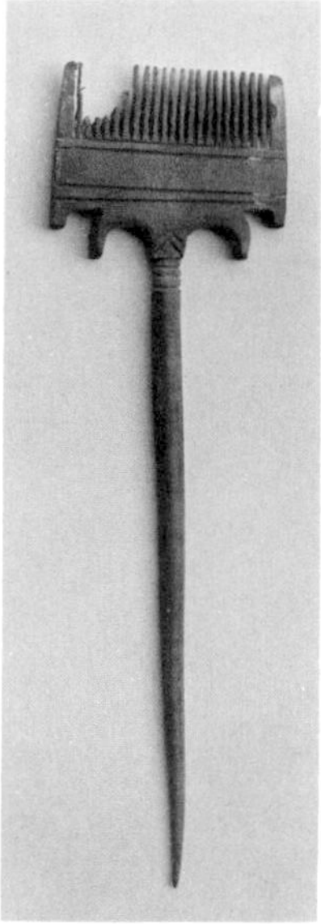

FIGURE 253.
Hairpin and comb combined.
Hardwood. L. 6 ¾ in.

6. Coiffure, Make-up, and Games

Considering the size and intricacy of the coiffures affected by fashionable Egyptians of the later New Kingdom it is surprising to find that the combs of the period remained for the most part small and of simple design. Three ★combs of bone and hardwood found by Arthur C. Mace at el Lisht and dated by him to the Twentieth Dynasty are all close to two and three-quarters inches in length. Two have short, coarse teeth and plain, slightly rounded backs, in one instance adorned just above the teeth with incised horizontal lines. The third is a double comb with fine and coarse teeth back to back on either side of a central grip. The top of an even smaller ivory ★comb, formerly in the Carnarvon collection, is ornamented with the figure of a horse feeding at a trough. A similar comb from Ghurāb, at the entrance of the Fayyūm, is dated to the reign of Ramesses II. The combined ★comb and hairpin of figure 253 was found in a tomb in the "Tety Pyramid Cemeteries" at Saḳḳāreh together with a scarab of King Sēthy I. A graceful juncture between the two elements is achieved here by means of the spreading papyrus umbel at the top of the pin.

Nine bone or ivory ★hairpins from near the North Pyramid at el Lisht are also dated by Mace to the Twentieth Dynasty. Most of them are plain, tapered pins averaging three and three-quarters inches in length; but two were at one time surmounted by little carved ornaments and one still retains a band of striated lines around its top.

The make-up kits of the late New Kingdom villagers of el Lisht included multiple ★*koḥl*-tubes of blue faience, a bronze ★tube with a haematite ★*koḥl*-stick still in it, a ★*koḥl*-stick of wood with a flat point at the end of its handle, two bone ★cosmetic sticks, each having a flat, spoonlike end, a tapered stone ★spatula, a pair of bronze ★tweezers, and a tiny, circular ★cosmetic box of wood. Despite the fact that the little box is under two inches in diameter both it and its low, domical lid were fitted with knobs so that they could be lashed together with cord and perhaps sealed. The tweezers differ from our earlier examples in that they are pinched together a short distance below the top to provide a suspension loop and a waisted grip.

Among the many interesting objects acquired by the Museum in 1886 from the tomb of Sen-nedjem at Deir el Medīneh (see pp. 414 ff.) are two painted wooden ★cosmetic boxes, one of which is inscribed for Sen-nedjem's wife, the House Mistress Iy-(nefer)ty. Each box is a little over a foot square, rests on four short wooden legs, and has its interior divided into four small compartments. Both are painted white on the exterior and are decorated with floral and geometric designs in black and red, the decoration of the uninscribed box (fig. 254) being the more elaborate and interesting of the two. The flat lids, in one case double valved, in the other single, open upward on horizontal pivots and are provided with the usual pairs of opposed knobs whereby they could be tied shut and sealed. Attractive as they are, the two caskets seem to have been somewhat hastily made and finished and are perhaps to be classed as funerary objects rather than as containers used throughout the lifetime of their owner. This impression is borne out by the inscriptions on the first casket wherein Iy-(nefer)ty is described as "the Osiris" and is referred to as one "justified," that is, deceased.

The fragmentary ★lid of a small oval or cartouche-shaped cosmetic box of glazed steatite is elaborately carved with a figure of the goddess Isis nursing the infant Horus in the midst of a conventionally rendered papyrus thicket. The locale of the little scene is, presumably, the island of Chemmis in the marshes near Buto (or Beḥdet?) where Isis is reputed to have borne her son in secret in order to save him from his father's slayer, the malevolent Sētẖ. The headdress of the goddess and other portions of the design were once inlaid with colored pastes. When complete the width of the richly decorated little container was about two inches.

Two small ★cosmetic dishes carved of hardwood are adorned with little rams' heads projecting in four places from the sides of their rims and serving as rudimentary handles. Roughly four inches in diameter, both dishes are from the New Kingdom village site at el Lisht.

During the later New Kingdom the popularity of small perfume and cosmetic vessels of colored glass continued unabated, and new forms and new color schemes begin to appear side by side with the old favorites. Our nineteen complete or nearly complete ★glass vessels of this period include, besides the shapes illustrated in figure 109, the "pilgrim bottle" with a pair of little loop handles flanking the neck, the slender drop- or pomegranate-shaped flask, and a squat, thickset version of the footed vase with broad, cylindrical neck (see fig. 255). Attractive monochrome vases and bowls of white, yellow, green, and gray glass, their rims, shoulders, and feet sometimes accented with narrow spiral moldings of blue and white glass, are now almost as common as the popular but, to our taste, somewhat gaudy dark and light blue vessels banded with waves or zigzags of rainbow-like color. A hemispherical bowl of blue glass with a yellow rim and eight of our vases are from a glass factory of the Twentieth Dynasty discovered in

FIGURE 254. Cosmetic box from the tomb of Sennedjem. Painted wood. L. 13 in.

1912 near el Menshīyeh, on the east bank of the Nile between Girgeh and Akhmīm in Upper Egypt. The others are of Theban or unknown origin and include pieces donated to the Museum by Miss Helen Miller Gould, J. Pierpont Morgan, and Henry G. Marquand. The area surrounding the pyramid of King Amun-em-ḥēt I at el Lisht and, in particular, the remains of a glass factory of the late Ramesside period in the New Kingdom village yielded 184 ★fragments of glass vessels, many with portions of the sandy cores still adhering to their inner surfaces. In this rich and rewarding study collection we find parts of nearly all the shapes shown in figures 109, 170 and 255, executed in light and deep blue, lavender, green, yellow, white, and black glass and decorated with a great variety of designs and patterns—waves, zigzags, bands, lines, and piebald mottling in two or more contrasting colors. Fragments of green, white, and deep blue vases, undecorated except for their slender blue and white rim moldings, are especially numerous. Four ★fragments of a piebald vase of black and white glass with a blue rim were acquired with the Carnarvon collection.

Nine very small ★vessels of blue faience decorated with linear designs in black or violet overglaze can hardly have been used for any other purpose than to contain minute quantities of valuable cosmetic oils, pastes, and perfumes. The largest of the series, a slender, drop-shaped little

FIGURE 255. Glass vessels of the Nineteenth and Twentieth Dynasties. H. of tallest vase 7 ¾ in.

flask adorned with lotus flowers and buds, is scarcely five inches high, while the height of a companion vase of the same type is just over three inches. A third vase, which imitates in its form a tiny basket complete with cover, is decorated with geometric patterns of the sort found on New Kingdom basketry, and a rather squat little beaker, or oil jar, is covered with an over-all scale pattern. The slightly convex discoid lid of a similar beaker measures only an inch and three-eighths in diameter. A shallow saucer about the size of a silver dollar has a black rim folded in to form four rudimentary little spouts. An even smaller cup of bright blue faience was found near the North Pyramid at el Lisht, as were also three fragments of vases decorated, respectively, with a small portion of a royal cartouche, a flying dove or pigeon, and lotus flowers drawn with the greatest attention to detail. Two squat little ★jugs of green faience are adorned with bands of petals inlaid in blue glaze and, in one instance, with a semicircular design resembling a highly conventionalized winged sun's disk. The larger of the two, once provided with a pair of handles, stands four and five-sixteenths inches in height. The smaller jug has only one handle. Three small ribbed ★jugs of blue faience, which were once included with this late New Kingdom group, evidently belong to a much later period in Egyptian history; and a tiny ★lotiform cup of ivory, found at Lampsacus on the Hellespont, is almost certainly of post-New Kingdom date and probably not of Egyptian manufacture.

A polished black pottery ★vase in the form of a *bolti*-fish (cf. fig. 65) may at one time have contained some type of cosmetic, as may also a red pottery ★jar somewhat crudely modeled in the shape of a monkey with its paw to its mouth. A small footed ★vase of polished serpentine and an even smaller footed ★cup of alabaster complete our list of privately owned cosmetic vessels of Ramesside date. Both are excavated pieces, dated to the Nineteenth Dynasty, the vase coming from a tomb at Sedment near Herakleopolis, the cup from a tomb cleared by the Egypt Exploration Fund at Abydos. Their heights are, respectively, four and three inches.

Evidence for the continued popularity of games, especially board games such as *senet* and *tjau*, is provided in our collection by a ★game board and a score of playing pieces, or ★draughtsmen, from tombs and houses of Ramesside date at el Lisht. The board in this case is simply a small rectangular slab of limestone marked off with incised lines into fifteen squares (three rows of five each) and carrying on its back a crude sketch of the mummiform god Ptaḥ. The draughtsmen, for the most part, are of the usual conical and spool-shaped types, but show a good deal of variation in their forms, the tall pieces being either true or waisted cones, the spools sometimes broad and low, sometimes high and narrow with conical tops. There are several thick, disk-shaped pieces, rather like our modern checker men, and one pyramidal piece. The materials include blue, green, brown, black, and white faience, pottery, clay, and wood. Two slender peg-shaped ★playing pieces of bone and alabaster are probably from a board game similar to the ancient "hounds and jackals."

Though dice do not appear to have been common in Egypt until Graeco-Roman times, isolated examples of New Kingdom date have been found by Howard Carter at Thebes and by the Egypt Exploration Society at el ʿAmārneh. There is, then, some probability that a blue faience ★die from our own excavations in the village area at el Lisht has been correctly dated to the Twentieth Dynasty. It is a cube of faience, nine-sixteenths of an inch on a side, carrying on each of its surfaces from one to six incised dots. The arrangement of the dots differs from that seen on our modern dice, the numbers one, two, three, and five following one another in succession on the four sides of the cube, with the four and six opposed to one another on its top and bottom. Since the Theban and ʿAmārneh dice just referred to show still other arrangements of their dots, it is clear that no standard scheme had as yet been adopted.

7. Household Furnishings

Of the sparse, primitive, and usually fragmentary furnishings of the mud-brick hovels which composed the late New Kingdom village at el Lisht, only a few representative pieces have been retained for our permanent collection. A crudely shaped wooden ★headrest, found in one of the houses, is made up of two elements, the usual long oval base and the curved pillow which in this case extends like the branch of a tree from one side of the upright column and is carved in one piece with it. Another house yielded a ring-shaped ★pad of split reeds, bound with two-ply grass cord, of the type used nowadays by Egyptian peasant women for carrying water jars on their heads. From a third house we obtained a rectangular wooden ★dish, or platter, with sharply in-sloping ends, roughly carved from a block of coarse-grained local wood. A blue faience ★serving dish with vertical sides and flat, slightly projecting rim is a characteristically sturdy piece of rural village crockery. It is decorated on the exterior with a simple geometric pattern made up of alternating vertical black bands and large dots. A cylindrical ★spout with a flanged pouring end comes evidently from a household ewer of glossy white and brown faience.

Two lotiform faience drinking ★goblets, formerly in the Gréau collection, are of a shape midway between that of the wide, short-stemmed cups of this class seen in Eighteenth Dynasty tomb paintings and the tall, slender lotiform goblets produced in great numbers under the Twenty-Second Dynasty. Of the latter the Museum possesses a fine series, including a number of well-known examples adorned with elaborate little scenes in low relief. Our two small Ramesside cups are both of blue faience with the petals of the lotus flower drawn upon their outsides in heavy black line. A third ★goblet of the same period, though also made of blue faience, has the wider, more open form of the white lotus and a stem somewhat longer in proportion to the height of the cup (cf. fig. 181). In this case the rim of the little vessel has been given the natural undulations of the top of the flower and the details of the petals have been engraved upon its sides. Like others of its class a shallow ★drinking bowl of greenish blue faience (fig. 256) carries on its interior a small circular picture rapidly but deftly sketched in black line. Here, appropriately enough, we see the figure of a butler at a banquet bearing in one hand a slender wine jar and in the other a cone of perfumed ointment, while a convolvulus, or morning-glory, vine and another type of vine hang from his arms in graceful cascades.

FIGURE 256. Faience drinking bowl of the Nineteenth Dynasty. Interior. Diam. 4 7/8 in.

By Ramesside times bronze drinking and serving vessels had become commonplace in even the more modest Egyptian households. The fact that relatively few such vessels have survived to the present day is attributable in part to the melting-down and reuse of the metal by intervening generations and in part to its destruction through oxidation and other forms of corrosion. The Museum's ten small but complete ★bronze vessels of late New Kingdom date represent more than forty years of collecting coupled with the generosity of three private donors, Miss Helen Miller Gould, Dr. Bashford Dean, and Mr. W. Gedney Beatty. Seven of the vessels are small bowls or drinking cups and include both the shallow, round-bottomed form and the shouldered, or carinated, type with projecting lip, the history of which extends back to the time of the Old Kingdom. One of the shallow bowls is provided with a plate for the attachment of a handle, riveted to its side just below the rim, and one of the carinated bowls has a lotus-flower motif engraved on its bottom. Squat little bronze jugs, their single handles expanding at the top into openwork bronze lotus flowers, are probably to be equated with the tiny metal pitchers used during the Eighteenth Dynasty to contain flavoring for wine (see p. 207). Our two examples, the larger of which is only four and three-quarters inches high, were found by the Egypt Exploration Fund in private tombs of the Nineteenth and Twentieth Dynasties at Abydos. The smallest of our bronze vessels, a minute drop-shaped situla fitted at the top with two rings for its handle, may also have been a container for a liquid flavoring of some sort. A ★cup-shaped bronze object found in the village area at el Lisht is probably not a vessel, as was once thought, but a metal sheathing or ferrule from the end of a staff, the leg of a chair, or the like. It is only an inch and three-quarters in diameter and is pierced below its rim with thirteen circular holes.

Though perhaps to be classed as funerary vessels, a pair of brightly painted ★pottery jars from the tomb of Sen-nedjem at Deir el Medîneh are of a type (see fig. 257) used in households of the early Nineteenth Dynasty for serving wine and other beverages. Both are medium-sized cordiform jars with two horizontal handles and tall necks widening slightly toward the top. They are made of fine-grained red pottery, covered with a buff slip, and are adorned on the necks and shoulders with bands and festival garlands somewhat carelessly applied in red, blue, and black paint.

Sixty-five complete and fragmentary flint ★knives found in the ruins of the Twentieth Dynasty houses at el Lisht testify to the continued use of this inexpensive and readily available material for household and industrial implements throughout the dynastic period. The knives, which average five to six inches in length, are of the usual household type with straight backs and curved cutting edges.

8. The Professions and Crafts

The weapons of the Ramesside soldier and huntsman are not as well represented in our collection as those of their Thutmoside predecessors (see pp. 211 ff.), but the village site at el Lisht and tombs of the late New Kingdom at Thebes and Abydos between them have contributed three bronze ★spear heads and a ★spear butt, a bronze ★javelin head, two bronze ★arrow heads and five hardwood ★arrow tips, a charioteer's ★whip, and the ★head of a staff carved of alabaster. The spear, javelin, and arrow heads differ from those of the Middle and earlier New Kingdom in having tapered tubular sockets which fitted around the ends of the wooden shafts and extended forward along the axis lines of the slender, leaf-shaped, triangular, or lozenge-shaped blades to form reinforcing midribs. The design, a relatively recent innovation in dynastic Egypt, not only added rigidity to the spear blade itself, but also provided a much stronger union with the shaft than was possible with the one-piece tanged heads of earlier times. Our classification of the heads is largely a matter of size, the spear heads averaging over a foot in length, the arrow heads around two inches, and the javelin head falling between, with a length of just under five inches. The spear butt, which is socketed like the heads, is simply a plain tapered point, circular in cross section and ten inches in length. Much the same type of simple point is seen in the wooden arrow tips, which range in length from two and a half to six and a half inches. It is clear, however, that the tanged ends of these points were inserted into the ends of the reed shafts of the arrows in a manner current since the dawn of Egyptian history.

FIGURE 257. Painted pottery jar from a Ramesside tomb in western Thebes. H. 12 in.

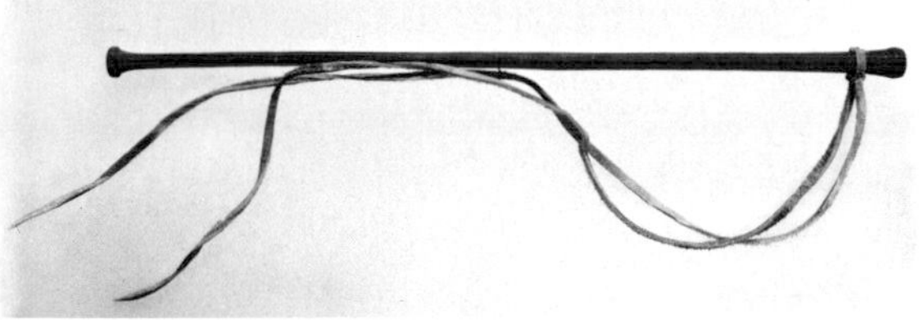

FIGURE 258. Charioteer's whip of the late Twentieth or early Twenty-First Dynasty. L. 20¼ in.

The charioteer's whip (fig. 258) consists of a slender, tapered handle nicely carved of some fine, dark wood and provided with two light leather lashes each about the breadth of a lead pencil. It was found at Thebes in the coffin of a man named Yoty-Amūn who was a "Shield-bearer of the General" and, to judge from his full and bushy beard, an Asiatic. Winlock has contrasted the lightness of this whip with the massiveness of the one (fig. 59) carried, as an overseer of rowers or workmen, by Sen-ne-mūt's boat captain Neb-iry, adding by way of explanation that "a maddened horse could kick a flimsy Egyptian chariot to pieces, while the patient fellāh learned to take his blows in silence."[4] It is interesting to note that before being placed in the coffin the whip was deliberately "killed"—that is, rendered harmless to its deceased owner—by being broken into three pieces. A small alabaster object curving to a blunt point at the top and provided with an oval, ear-like projection on either side has been taken to be

[4] *Excavations at Deir el Baḥri*, p. 77.

the head of a staff or, perhaps, the butt of a javelin or whip handle. It is socketed at the bottom and provided with two small holes, for a pin or rivet, running laterally through the socket. Four ★model axe heads, two of limestone, two of red pottery (imitating bronze?), are of the deep, waisted type used on battle axes (see figs. 36, 125). With lengths of two to two and five-eighths inches, they come from the general rubbish surrounding the North Pyramid at el Lisht.

To judge from the number of harpoons, fish-hooks, and net-weights found in their houses, fishing was one of the principal occupations of the late New Kingdom villagers of el Lisht. Fourteen small bronze ★harpoon heads from the village ruins are, with one exception, single barbed, the exception having not only a double-barbed point but also a spur projecting laterally from the side of its tang. The tangs are rectangular in cross section and taper slightly for easy insertion into the end of a wooden shaft. The average length of the heads is about four inches. Of eleven bronze ★fishhooks the six larger examples, with lengths from one and three-sixteenths to one and five-eighths inches, are barbed like our modern hooks, but in place of the eye the end of the shaft in each case is coiled to form a small circular knob around which the line could be made fast. The smaller hooks, which range in length from less than half an inch to just under an inch, are barbless. The ★net-weights, or sinkers, include ten examples in limestone, alabaster, and pottery of the types described on page 214. Besides these there are two ovoid weights of limestone grooved longitudinally for a cord lashing, a rectangular weight with both longitudinal and transverse grooves, and three cylindrical weights with a single groove around the middle of the cylinder or near one of its ends. Most interesting are eight lead ★sinkers consisting of small, roughly rectangular sheets of the soft metal which had been folded once lengthwise and their edges pressed together around the perimeter of a light casting net (see p. 214). Of the nets themselves all that has survived is a ★fragment of a medium-fine diamond mesh woven of two-ply linen string with a netting knot similar to that used in our modern fishing nets.

Evidences of the agricultural activities of the Lishti villagers consist chiefly of a great number of ★sickle flints, several with the resinous black gum whereby they were fastened in place in the grooved wooden sickle blades still adhering to their backs. All of these flints have serrated cutting edges and many are slightly curved to coincide with the arc of the sickle. For purposes of illustration a series of the flints have been set into a reconstructed wooden sickle modeled on those found by Petrie at el Lāhūn and Hauwāreh (fig. 259). A full-sized basketwork ★sieve, over sixteen inches in diameter, is similar to the models included in the foundation deposits of the earlier New Kingdom (fig. 47). Like them it consists of a coiled basketry rim, sewn with Ḥalfa-grass strip, and a central mesh woven of narrow strips of a stiffer rush or reed. Such sieves appear to have been used alike by farmers and housewives for sifting grain and flour, by brewers for straining their mash, and by masons for sifting sand and gravel. A socketed bronze ★hoe blade, also from el Lisht, has been dated by its finders to "Dyn. XIX or later," but is of a type which is not common in Egypt until Graeco-Roman times. On the other hand, several massive flint ★hoe or mattock blades turned up in the houses of the North Pyramid village are probably contemporary with the Ramesside occupation of the site.

Tools and other equipment which had belonged to the village carpenters include four very small bronze ★chisels, a bronze ★bit from a bow drill, two diorite ★drill caps, four small bronze ★nails, two quartzite ★hones, and what was either a cylindrical wooden carpenter's ★mallet or the leg of a heavy wooden stool. The chisels, one of which is double-ended, have blades that fan out to more than twice the widths of their shanks. In two cases the latter were formed by turning in the edges of the blade at the top, thus narrowing and thickening the tool at this point. The drill bit is a slender tool with an elongated lozenge-shaped point and a long, tapered tang. It measures exactly five inches in length. The drill caps are of the usual hemispherical type with the sockets in their undersides showing ample evidence of use. Two of the nails have well-developed disk-shaped heads and shafts which are either circular or square in cross section. The other two have rudimentary heads, rather like modern finishing nails, and short, thick shafts, cylindrical at the tops and four-sided at the points. Both hones are so small as to be properly called slipstones. Neither, however, is wedge-shaped, one being a rod of quartzite, oval in cross section, the other a flat, nearly square slab with one rounded edge. The latter, which is the larger of the two, measures only four and three-eighths inches in its greatest dimension. Shaped rather like a one-handled rolling pin, the mallet—if that, indeed, is what it is—has an over-all length of eleven and five-eighths inches. One diorite ★axe head, three flint ★axe heads, and a considerable quantity of flint ★scrapers and ★flakes, though of types hardly distinguishable from their prehistoric forerunners, may also have been used by our peasant carpenters of the Twentieth Dynasty.

A stonemason's ★chisel from the ʿAsāsīf valley in western Thebes is a massive bronze tool eight and a quarter inches long with the cylindrical shank and tapered cutting edge seen on our modern cape chisels. With it were found four of the heavy, pear-shaped ★mallets employed by Egyptian masons, each whittled to shape from a single section of acacia log and showing in all cases evidence of more or less prolonged use. The village area at el Lisht yielded a set of three wooden ★boning rods and five stone ★plumb bobs, the former certainly, the latter probably having formed part of the equipment of the local stonemasons. The boning rods, with a uniform length of five and three-quarters inches, are a trifle longer than the Eighteenth Dynasty examples described on page 217. All the plummets are more or less cordiform, with horizontally drilled knobs or lugs at their tops for the attachment of the plumb lines. One is of alabaster, two of limestone, and two of a hard, brownish stone not yet identified. Cylindrical ★cores made by a three-quarter-inch tubular drill boring into blocks of graywacke and obsidian testify to the speed and efficiency of this type of drill even when working in stones of the utmost hardness. The cores, which are only about two inches in length, have been catalogued as coming from stone vases; while this is possible, it is anything but certain.

FIGURE 259. Ancient sickle flints mounted in a restored wooden sickle. L. 14 in.

Two pointed quartzite ★burnishers of the type used by metalworkers were found at el Lisht in association with material generally datable to the Twentieth Dynasty. Near by was found a three-inch ★section of hollow reed packed with small fragments of gold foil and plugged at the open end with a wad of linen. It has been identified with some probability as part of a goldsmith's supply of scrap metal.

A painter's ★palette of hard glazed paste (fig. 260), nicely carved in the form of a human hand holding a shell, still contains traces of red paint of the kind used by Egyptian draughtsmen for their preliminary sketches and in laying out the decoration of tomb and temple walls. Other paraphernalia of the painter's craft include two quartzite ★grinding slabs and nine stone ★grinders for pulverizing pigments, a small alabaster ★mortar and pestle, not unlike those in present use, and ★lumps of ocher and malachite employed, respectively, in the manufacture of red and green pigments. The grinders are for the most part of the waisted conical type with rounded top and flat, circular grinding surfaces, smaller versions of which were used

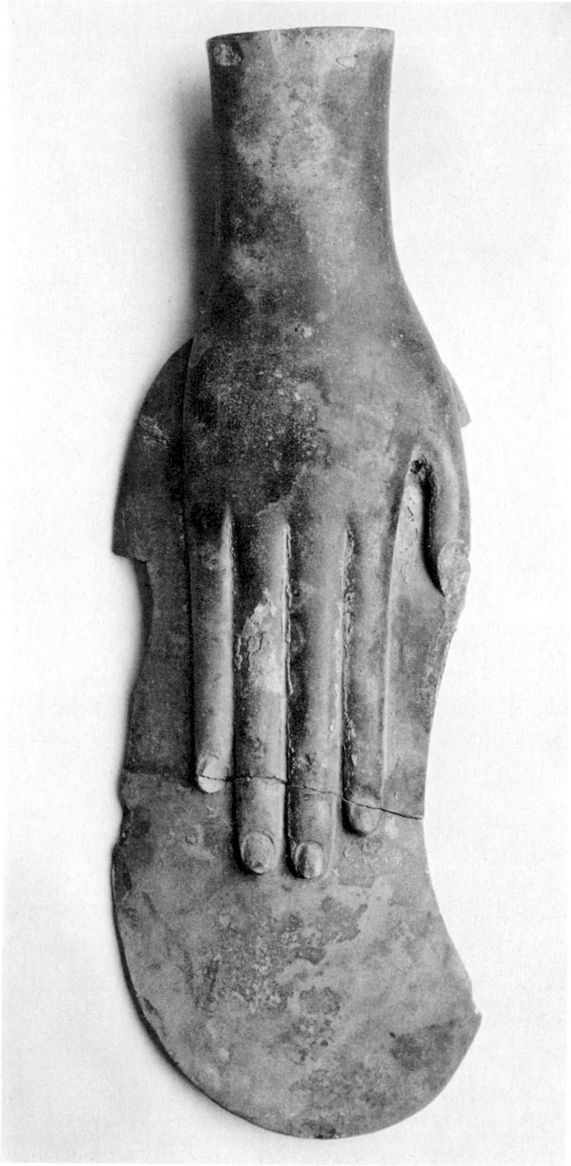

FIGURE 260. Painter's palette of fine glazed paste. L. 7 ½ in.

by Egyptian scribes for grinding their writing pigments. Three are of quartzite, two of diorite, and two of serpentine. Besides these there are two small oval grinders (or polishers?) carved of limestone and provided with handles like that of a mason's float or modern tailor's flatiron.

A house in the New Kingdom village at el Lisht had evidently been used during the Twentieth Dynasty as a faience and glass factory. It was found to contain a great quantity of equipment and materials used in the production of glazed objects, as well as numerous examples of the objects themselves in partially finished states. Among the samples brought home for our study collection are ★fragments of biscuit forming parts of the necks and bodies of faience vases, cylindrical ★sections of vases in a more advanced stage of manufacture, and unfinished blue and white faience ★beads embedded in lumps of clay or strung on slender reeds in readiness for firing. Also found were well over a hundred slender rods, or ★"canes," of blue, lavender, green, yellow, red, brown, black, and white glass, seventeen partly worked ★lumps of colored glass including deep blue, violet, and grayish lavender, numerous fragments of clay ★crucibles coated on the inside and streaked on the outside with films of glass, small bricklike and conical pottery ★supports for crucibles and for glass and faience objects in the process of being fired, bits of the sandy clay ★cores around which glass vessels had been formed, and chunks of ★slag, blue and green ★coloring matter, pink ★paste, and ★charcoal. An unfinished spherical ★bead is seen to be composed of a slender rod of blue glass wound round and round a tiny lead bar. From the same factory site come two roughly rectangular plaques of glazed frit, which, to judge from their worn edges, were used as ★rubbers in the shaping of faience and glass vessels. They measure, respectively, three and a quarter by two and a quarter and three by one and a half inches. A small pottery ★mold picked up in the débris of the workshop was used in the production of a pendant amulet of faience or glass in the form of a rectangular plaque with a relief figure of the goddess Nit.

Two rodlike ★ingots of light turquoise blue glass, just under seven inches long, are objects of unusual rarity and interest for the student of ancient glass manufacture. Though acquired at Thebes, it is not unlikely, as Newberry has suggested, that they were produced in "glass works in the northwestern Delta, where the necessary materials for glass-making are to be found"[5] and which remained Egypt's most important center of glass production down into Graeco-Roman times. With these ingots we may study a large ★lump of unfinished dark blue glass found by Naville at Deir el Baḥri.

Since the production of linen cloth for use as clothing, bedding, and ultimately as funerary wrappings was one of the major activities of most well-ordered Egyptian households it is not surprising to find the late New Kingdom houses at el Lisht well provided with the tools and accessories of the weaver's craft. Among the more interesting accessories are two heavy limestone bowls, or ★tension buckets (see fig. 261), used for holding and paying out the sliver, or rove, of flax fibers from which thread was spun. Each of the buckets is large enough to have contained two balls of the rove and each is provided on its interior with two small limestone rings through which the rove was passed on its way to the spinner (see Part I, p. 265). Thanks to these rings the balls remained in place in the buckets and sufficient tension was maintained on the rove to keep it from becoming tangled en route to the spindles. The spinners of ancient Egypt, usually women, are sometimes shown in paintings and tomb models using two spindles at a time, drawing the rove for both from a single tension bucket. Two of our four more or less complete ★spindles of Ramesside date have thick, disk-shaped whorls of wood, while the other two have heavy, conical whorls of limestone and clay. Besides those provided with whorls there is an extra spindle ★shaft with a narrow spiral groove around its upper end. ★Spindle whorls found without their shafts, or sticks, include five disk-shaped examples of pottery, bone, and wood, a barrel-shaped whorl of wood, and two conical whorls of limestone decorated with incised linear patterns of simple types. Two small ★balls of fine linen thread measure two and a half and one and three-quarters inches in diameter. Thread seems also to have been

FIGURE 261. A spinner's tension bucket. Limestone. Diam. 9 in.

wound on little ★reels, or bobbins, of which we possess fourteen examples carved of wood or limestone or modeled in pottery, clay, and faience. Fifteen ★loom weights of limestone, clay, and pottery show a surprising variety of forms. Some are disk-shaped, some ovoid, some rectangular, while others are pear- or drop-shaped and a few consist simply of potsherds pierced with holes for suspension. In a cylindrical weight of red pottery the suspension hole runs longitudinally through the cylinder. Some of the discoid weights are drilled with multiple holes, usually two or three but in one case eight. Several of the weights still retain parts of their suspension cords.

Two long, pointed bone objects, one flat and one round in cross section, have been identified as ★netting needles, and a waisted rod of ivory with one end flattened, pointed, and perforated as a ★netting bobbin. Three tapered bronze ★sewing needles, with circular or oval eyes drilled through their thick ends, are much larger and coarser than our modern needles, running in length from three and eleven-sixteenths to six inches. A small, thick slab of hard, gray stone (fig. 262) concave on one side and grooved on the other is without much doubt an ancient Egyptian equivalent of our ★thimble. With a length of one and thirteen-sixteenths and a width of one and three-eighths inches

[5] *The Journal of Egyptian Archaeology*, VI (1920), p. 157.

FIGURE 262. "Thimble" of hard gray stone. L. 1 13/16 in.

it was apparently worn over the middle finger of the hand and was held in place by the index and third fingers. Long wear had turned a small circular socket provided near one end of the groove for the head of the needle into a hole running clean through the little slab.

Despite its small size and isolated position the late New Kingdom village at el Lisht seems to have boasted one or more scribes, parts of whose equipment was recovered by the Museum's Expedition during the seasons of 1910-1911 and 1914-1915. Two very small but nicely made bronze ★knives come without much doubt from a scribe's kit. The smaller of the two is of the familiar *khopesh*-scimitar type with a bent back and a curved cutting edge. The larger, four inches in length, has a straight, double-edged blade shaped like an elongated laurel leaf and a bronze handle in the form of a duck's head turned back upon the bird's neck. Implements for pulverizing the scribe's black and red writing pigments include a nicely made rectangular ★grinding slab of dark gray diorite and three small conical ★grinders of diorite and serpentine. Fourteen small limestone ★stamps (or burnishers?) with rectangular, circular, oval, or shield-shaped undersides and stubby, perforated handles may also have been scribal accessories. A few are engraved with what may have been intended as cursive hieroglyphs, but the majority are either blank or carry simply grids of incised lines.

Among the units of measure with which the Egyptian scribe was required to be familiar one of the most important was the royal cubit of seven palms (20 9/16 inches) and its various divisions and subunits including the small, or short, cubit of six palms (17 3/4 inches). Our own knowledge of this standard unit of linear measure stems not from the relatively simple wooden cubit rods actually used to record and lay out measurements, but from the elaborately inscribed ceremonial cubit rods of stone, some of which seem to have been kept in the temples of the gods while others were buried in the tombs of royal architects and other prominent officials of the New Kingdom. Two such ★cubit rods, carved, respectively, of chert and green slate, are each represented in our collection by a single fragment (see fig. 263) comprising less than one-sixth of the original rod but sufficing to show the character of the monument and the nature of its texts. Both rods belonged to a type which carried, in addition to all the duly labeled divisions and subdivisions of the cubit, "such a bewildering amount of assorted information that 'almanac' seems a better word than 'cubit rod' by which to describe them."[6] The fragment illustrated, for example, preserves on the front edge of the rod the first and second "digits" of the cubit subdivided, respectively, into two halves and three thirds, on the bevel the names of the corresponding nomes of Upper Egypt (Elephantine and Edfu), and on the top of the rod the names of the deities associated with the individual digits (in this case Rēʿ and Shu). On the bottom of the rod the first line of text starts off with the words "The hour according to the cubit: a jar(?) of copper filled with water . . ." which have been thought to refer to a water clock and the manner of reading it. The second line, the mid-section of which probably contained the names and title of a king, begins: "This is a communication for those who shall be introduced [into Mendes] . . . ." The third line would seem to have given the relative heights of the annual inundation at different places along the Nile Valley. On the back of the rod the list

[6] Scott, *M. M. A. Bulletin*, n. s. I (1942), p. 72.

of nomes is resumed with the names of the Seventh and Eighth Nomes of Lower Egypt (Metelis and Pithom). The little text on the end of the rod tells us that "The cubit is life, prosperity, and health, the repeller of the rebel, the . . . going forth of Chnūm, who is in Es[neh] (?)." The piece is of unknown provenience, having come to the Museum in 1941 as part of the bequest of W. Gedney Beatty. The fragment of the slate rod, acquired in 1925 as a gift of Dr. and Mrs. Thomas Foulds, comprises the third to seventh digits of the cubit and bears additional portions of the texts already referred to, including, in the first line on the bottom, "measurements in cubits and palms according to the months of the year," "possibly a table by which readings of a sun-dial might be interpreted."[7]

Six stone and two pottery ★weights, chiefly from el Lisht, are a rather mixed lot and can in only two cases be related to the *ḳidet* standard of the New Kingdom (see p. 220). A small domical, or muffin-shaped, weight made of haematite and weighing at present 19 grams, is readily identified as a 2-*ḳidet* weight. Less certainty exists regarding a little oblong rectangular block of sandstone with a gabled top, which bears the Egyptian numeral for 40, but weighs only 301 grams (i.e., 7.5 grams per unit). Two limestone weights, inscribed "40" and "4" and weighing, respectively, 1449 and 544 grams, give us unit values of 36.2 (a quadruple *ḳidet*?) and 136 grams; while two alabaster weights of "30" and "5[0]" units work out at 36.2 and 28 grams per unit. Two smooth red pottery disks, which have been identified only with some question as weights, have diameters of two and eleven-sixteenths and two and three-quarters inches. Arthur C. Mace has dated the stone weights without exception to the Twentieth Dynasty and the pottery disks to "Dyn. XX-XXII."

There remain to be mentioned a few objects from our excavations in the late New Kingdom village at el Lisht which are not associated with any particular craft or occupation. A roughly

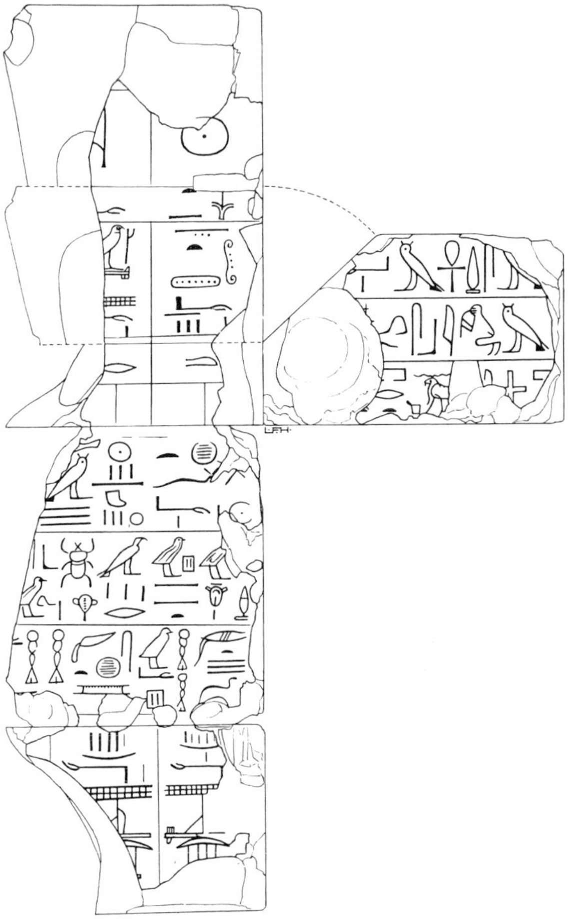

FIGURE 263. Fragment of a ceremonial cubit rod. Chert. End view and orthographic projection. L. of fragment 1 13/16 in.

made V-shaped ★fork of wood with a loop of palm-fiber rope lashed to its notched ends comes probably from a donkey's packsaddle where it was used as a primitive form of block, or pulley, for tightening the rope girth of the saddle or the lashing of its pack. Four other ★forks of the same type include two with a small triangular or trapezoidal spur of wood left projecting upward on the inside of the apex of the V so as to form double notches here for two strands of rope. In almost every case the notches, whether single or double, are grooved and worn smooth from the friction of the tautly drawn girth ropes. These so-called pack-holders,

[7] *Ibid.*, p. 73.

which continued in use well down into the Christian Era, average about six inches in width across the ends. A slightly curved ★rod of wood, also with notched ends, was probably used for much the same purpose. It was once thought to be a yoke, but its length, which is only twelve and three-eighths inches, is hardly sufficient for that. A thick, disk-shaped block of hardwood with a groove around the outside and a large, smooth hole through its center is almost certainly a ★dead-eye, a rudimentary form of block used until fairly recent times for setting up and tautening the stays of masts and particularly the shrouds on sailing ships. The diameter of this interesting and extremely rare piece of ancient tackle is six and one-eighth inches.

9. Funerary Art

Though the Ramesside era produced no important innovations in the burial practices current during the earlier New Kingdom, the tomb furnishings of the period show marked developments in their forms, decoration, and color schemes. The tendency is now toward greater type standardization in each of the various classes of funerary objects—a tendency which in the period immediately following the end of the New Kingdom was to lead to the mass production of coffins, *shawabtys*, and other items of tomb equipment of monotonously uniform types.

For private burials the anthropoid, or mummiform, coffin had entirely supplanted its rectangular predecessor. Though intricately constructed and elaborately decorated such coffins were apparently relatively inexpensive, so that even a moderately well-to-do citizen could afford a set of two or more nested one within another and often, from the early Nineteenth Dynasty onward, containing a decorated inner cover laid over the top of the mummy and, underneath this, a painted cartonnage mask covering its head and shoulders. Built usually of sycamore or some similar coarse-grained native Egyptian wood, the coffins are surfaced with a layer of fine white gesso and are decorated inside and out with a multiplicity of small panel pictures, figures of Underworld deities, ornamental elements, and hieroglyphic texts. From mid-Ramesside times until the end of the Twenty-First Dynasty the prevailing ground color is yellow, usually darkened to a yellowish brown by a coating of glossy, resinous varnish which with age has lost much of its original transparency. The other colors—blue, green, red, black, and white—are often so thickly applied that the figures and hieroglyphs painted with them stand out in relief above the surrounding surfaces (see fig. 267).

The coffin, inner cover, and mask of the House Mistress Iy-neferty, wife of the Servitor in the Place-of-truth Sen-nedjem, are from the latter's well-known tomb (No. 1) at Deir el Medīneh. Sen-nedjem, an evidently prosperous member of the staff of the Theban necropolis, appears to have died early in the Nineteenth Dynasty, leaving behind him a number of sons, among them Khonsu and Khaᶜ-bekhenet (of Tomb No. 2), whose life spans must have extended into the reign of Ramesses II. The tomb of Sen-nedjem, found with its decoration and contents intact, was opened on February 6, 1886, under the supervision of Gaston Maspero, at that time director of the Egyptian antiquities service. Most of the tomb furnishings were installed in the old Bulaḳ Museum in Cairo, but in May 1886 twenty-nine items, including the coffins of Iy-neferty and her son Khonsu, were purchased from the Egyptian Government by the Metropolitan Museum and added to its embryonic Egyptian collection.

Iy-neferty's ★coffin (fig. 264, left), just over six feet in length, represents her as a slender mummiform figure with forearms crossed below small but clearly indicated breasts. On its head the coffin effigy wears the long wig fashionable at this period, bound at the top with a wide floral fillet and at the sides with intricately patterned ribbons; and

FIGURE 264. Coffin, lid, and inner cover of Iy-neferty, the wife of Sen-nedjem (Tomb No. 1). L. of coffin 74 in.

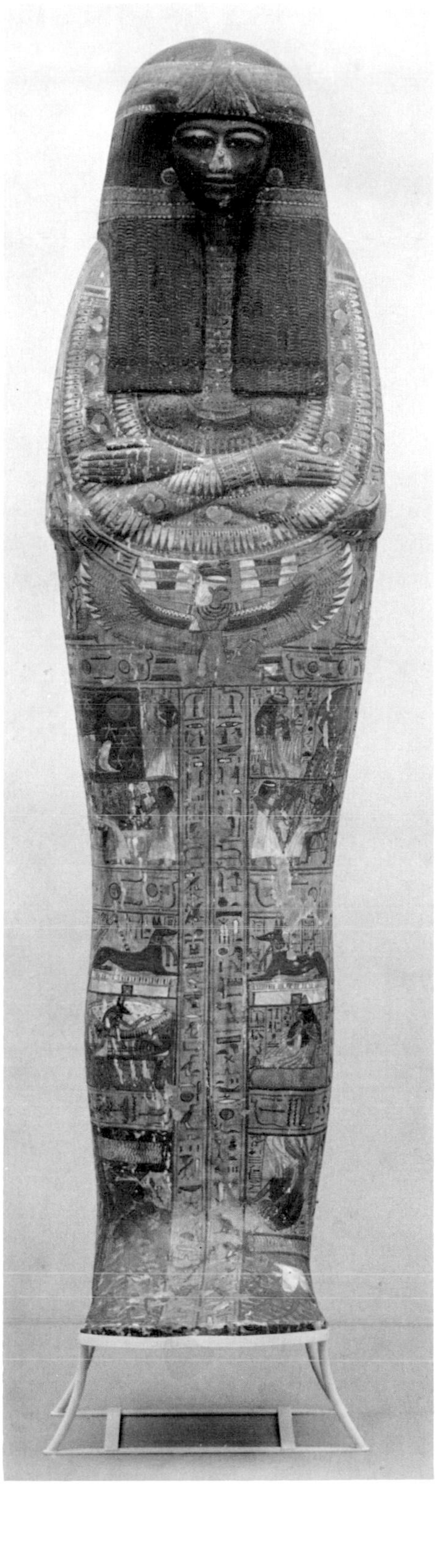

over its breast an enormous floral collar with lotus terminals. Below the collar a kneeling figure of the sky goddess Nūt with wings outspread is flanked by a pair of solar barques, and down the center of the lid, in two long columns of polychrome hieroglyphs, are the usual prayers for protection addressed by the deceased to the goddess (see p. 70). Four small panels over the thighs of the figure show Iy-neferty worshiping the solar disk and a group of star gods and receiving, in turn, the attentions of her sons Khonsu and Raʿ-mosĕ, one of whom pours out a libation before his seated mother while the other reads from an open roll of papyrus. Next come a pair of Anubis animals crouched upon their shrines, and then another series of panels in one of which the deceased lady appears as a mummy lying on a bier and having its mouth ceremonially "opened" by the canine-headed Anubis. On the lower legs and instep of the coffin lid Iy-neferty is represented three more times, once as a human-headed *ba*-bird drinking from a stream of water poured out by a goddess. The head and foot ends of the coffin are protected, as usual, by the goddesses Nephthys and Isis, and on the sides of the case Anubis, Tḥōt, and the Four Genii of the Dead appear in their customary panels accompanied by the traditional texts. The underside of the lid is also decorated; here we find a representation of the deceased worshiping a disk-crowned deity, and nine columns of funerary text[8] rather hastily inscribed in yellow paint.

On her carved and painted ★inner cover (fig. 264, right) we see Iy-neferty, not as a bandaged mummy, but as she appeared in life, standing on her two feet and clad in a long, white pleated robe from which her arms project in naturalistic fashion. The left arm with clenched fist is carried across the front of the body as if holding a fold of the robe in place, while the right arm, laden with bracelets, is allowed to hang down over the right thigh. A funerary touch is added by mourning figures of two of the deceased woman's daughters painted on the flat undersurface of the feet of the effigy.

Iy-neferty's cartonnage ★funerary mask is practically a replica of the upper third of her coffin, but its headdress, here fronted by a pair of prominent forelocks, is of necessity narrower and more close-fitting than that of the outer case. In front the rim of the mask coincides with the rounded outer edge of the deep floral collar. Behind, a short rectangular flap projects downward only slightly below the level of the nape of the neck. The over-all height of the mask is nineteen and three-quarters inches.

The mummy of Iy-neferty was found in her coffin wrapped in a palm-stick mat and four layers of linen pads, sheets, and bandages.[9] It is the body of a woman seventy-five years of age or older at the time of her death, an event which, we may suppose, occurred early in the reign of Ramesses II.

It was, presumably, some years later that the Servitor in the Place-of-truth Khonsu, a son of Sen-nedjem and Iy-neferty, died at the age of sixty and was buried with his parents in their tomb at Deir el Medīneh. For his burial he was provided with a funerary mask and a set of two anthropoid coffins similar in style to those of his mother and of equally fine quality. Almost six feet seven inches in length, Khonsu's ★outer coffin is larger than Iy-neferty's, more heavily proportioned, and somewhat simpler and more traditional in its decoration. On its head the figure wears a modified version of the long, striped headdress of ancient type, and on its chin the long, braided Osirian beard. The clenched hands, crossed over the breast, hold a wooden *tyet*-symbol, for "protection," and a *djed*-symbol, for "stability." Below a winged figure of the sky goddess transverse bands of ins ription divide the lower half of the lid into eight panels, four on either side of the central columns of text. These are taken up by a pair of Anubis animals, kneeling figures of the goddesses

[8] Chapter CLXXX of the Book of the Dead: "A spell for going forth by day and worshiping Rēʿ in the necropolis."

[9] After unwrapping, the mummies of both Iy-neferty and Khonsu were transferred in 1933 to the Peabody Museum in Cambridge, Massachusetts.

Isis and Nephthys, a standing figure of Khonsu worshiping a mummiform figure of Osiris, and, on the instep, a tree goddess pouring out water for the "souls" of Khonsu and his wife, Ta-meket. Isis and Nephthys guard the ends of the coffin and Tḥōt, Anubis, and the Four Genii its sides.

Khonsu's ★inner coffin (fig. 265) is to a great extent a smaller and more slenderly proportioned version of his outer case, differing from it chiefly in the form of the headdress and beard and in the arrangement and subject matter of the painted panels on the lower half of the lid. On this coffin the wig is of the graceful shawl type worn by gentlemen of the mid-Nineteenth Dynasty and the beard is the short goatee fashionable at the period. Four of the six lid panels show us Khonsu and his wife kneeling in adoration below seated figures of Osiris, Anubis, Isis, and Nephthys. In the two others the solar disk is seen supported in one case by the arms of the sky goddess Nūt and in the other by the scarab beetle of the sun god Khepri. The ★mask, found in position on Khonsu's mummy, reproduces in painted cartonnage the head and broad collar of the inner coffin. Its face, however, is beardless, and the lobes of its ears, visible between the upper and lower elements of the wig, are pierced with small circular holes.

With Khonsu's mask and coffins we also acquired his ★canopic chest (fig. 266), a cubical box seventeen and a half inches on a side, mounted on sledge runners and topped by a frieze of *ḫekeru*-ornaments and a gaily colored cavetto cornice. A large knob on the front of the chest and another above it on the low shrine-type lid served as a means of lashing the latter securely in place. Beneath a two-valved inner lid, crossed partitions divide the interior into four deep compartments for the now missing canopic jars. The decoration of the chest, which is painted yellow and varnished to match its owner's coffins, consists of standing figures of the goddesses Isis, Nephthys, Nit, and Serḳet, paired back to back on the front and back

FIGURE 265. Inner coffin of Khonsu, son of Sennedjem. L. 74 in.

FIGURE 266. Canopic chest of Khonsu. Wood, stuccoed, painted, and varnished. H. 17½ in.

of the box, and figures of the Four Genii of the Dead similarly grouped on its sides. Each figure is accompanied by a text in which "the Osiris, Khonsu, the justified," is assured of the deity's protection. The lid is adorned with Anubis animals crouched on shrines above symbols of "protection" and "stability." The texts here are speeches addressed to the deceased by Anubis and Nūt. In one of these Khonsu's title is given in its full form, the "Servitor in the Place-of-truth on the west of Thebes."

Our remaining New Kingdom coffins date from the last years of the Twentieth Dynasty and probably to the period when virtual control of the country had been taken over by Smendes in the North and Ḥery-Ḥor in the South. Outstanding is a set of two large and exceptionally handsome anthropoid cases made for a man named Amun-em-Opet, whose father, I-mi-sība, served under Ramesses IX and has left us a decorated tomb chapel (No. 65) in the Theban necropolis (see p. 377). Like I-mi-sība, Amun-em-Opet was a God's Father of Amun Rēʿ and a Scribe of the Double Treasury of the Lord of the Two Lands and the House of Amūn. Both his ★coffin effigies wear the long, archaic headdress, the Osirian chin beard, and a gilded pectoral supported on suspenderlike bands over a deep floral collar, and both hold in their hands wooden replicas of a rolled-up document called an *imyet-per*, or title to property. Their decoration (see fig. 267) is characterized by a reduction in scale and a multiplication in the number of panels, figures, texts, and other elements which cover their cases and lids inside and out and from top to bottom. Down the center of the lids, below various winged deities, the panels take the forms of naos-shaped pectorals containing in each case a central symbol (the solar disk, the *tyet*-symbol, the *djed*-column) flanked by falcons, seated divinities, *wedjat*-eyes, and the like. Elsewhere the deceased appears again and again, making offering to a host of different deities, and twice he is seen being presented to Osiris by the Sovereign or Mistress of the West. On the interiors of the coffins brightly colored paintings show us, in one of the many panels, the deified king, Amun-ḥotpe I, attended by the nature gods of Upper and Lower Egypt and surmounted by his cartouche, which in turn is protected by hovering falcons. In the panels above, below, and on both sides are solar barques, winged sun disks, mummiform deities, amuletic symbols, and a seemingly infinite variety of protective figures and devices. These coffins, indeed, are practically illustrated guidebooks to the mythology and funerary beliefs of the period. They are also excellent, though often neglected, examples of the art of the late New Kingdom painter, and could profitably have been considered in the third section of this chapter together with the tomb paintings, illustrated papyri, and drawings on ostraka.

Especially fine are the paintings on the interior of a lidless ★coffin of the late Twentieth or early Twenty-First Dynasty which was acquired in 1911 from the Egyptian Government and is said to be from western Thebes. Here the dominant feature is a great Osiride figure of King Amun-ḥotpe I, the royal patron of the Theban necropolis, painted on the floor of the coffin in brilliant, unvarnished colors. A green and yellow striped *nemes* graces the head of the deified pharaoh and the whiteness of his tall mummiform figure is relieved by a polychrome shoulder ornament and a dark green network pattern. His identity—for other deified kings are also represented on the floors of coffins—is established by the cartouche painted in the panel above him.

In praiseworthy efforts to remedy in part the ravages wrought by the tomb robbers of the late New Kingdom, the officials of the Theban necropolis rewrapped and reburied the plundered mummies of bygone kings and their families, using for the purpose linen, coffins, and other funerary equipment of their own period (see, e. g., pp. 44, 51). So it was that the body of the infant King Amun-em-ḥēt (see p. 52), believed to have been the son and nominal coregent of Amun-ḥotpe I, came finally to be laid to rest in the cliffs near Deir el Baḥri by a Servitor in the Place-of-truth named Pay-nedjem, who is known to have lived and been active at the end of the Twentieth Dynasty.

The ★coffin used for the reburial of the royal child is a roughly made little anthropoid case, forty-one inches in length, stuccoed and painted brownish yellow. The lid appears to be a discarded inner cover from the coffin of an adult, shortened to the required length by cutting out a foot or so from the middle of the figure and joining together the remaining body and leg sections. It, too, is yellow, with the beardless face, crossed hands, and exposed feet colored dark red and the plain shawl wig painted black. A blue and white collar and bracelets and a prayer to the goddess Nūt written in blue hieroglyphs down the center line of the lid complete the decoration of the makeshift little monument. As we have already noted in Chapter II, the mid-section of the inscription, with the name of the original owner, has been erased and the kingly titles and name of Amun-em-ḥēt have been inserted in a hieratic script typical of the very late New Kingdom. Inside the coffin the robbed and badly damaged ★mummy of the child was found neatly rewrapped in linen ★bandages and ★scraps of linen sheeting and covered over with flowers, long-stemmed lotus buds, and garlands of persea leaves. Near by had been placed a red pottery ★bowl containing sixteen dates.

The most attractive and interesting object recovered from this rather pathetic burial is a painted wooden ★pectoral (fig. 268) found suspended on a loop of cord over the breast of the fully wrapped little mummy. In its form the pectoral imitates a parade shield of the type found in the tomb of Tūt-ʿankh-Amūn and frequently represented in New Kingdom reliefs and paintings. Even the black and white bull's-hide edging of the shield is faithfully, if somewhat conventionally, reproduced. The brightly colored openwork design shows us Amun-em-ḥēt's father(?), King Amun-ḥotpe I, about to slay with his battle axe an Asiatic and a Nubian chieftain—a military theme appropriate to the decoration of a shield, but lacking, it would seem, in any direct funerary connotation. Though the inscribed panel in the upper right-hand corner of the field tells us clearly that this is the "Lord of the Two Lands, Djeser-ku-Rēʿ, the Lord of Crowns, Amun-ḥotpe," both the king's fussily elaborate costume and the whole style of the work indicate clearly that the pectoral was a product of the late Ramesside period, not far removed in date from the Twenty-First Dynasty. This dating is supported by a hieratic docket written on the back of the inscribed panel by the "Servitor in the Place-of-truth Pay-nedjem, son of the Chief of the Gang of the Place-of-truth, Baki-mūt."

Nine other funerary ★pectorals of Ramesside date are of the more common pylon or naos type designed in most cases to act as a setting or as a substitute for the heart scarab. The materials of which they are made include glazed steatite (four examples), blue faience (three examples), painted

FIGURE 267. Detail of the lid of the inner coffin of Amun-em-Opet. Wingspread of winged sun disk 9 ½ in.

wood, and painted stucco. The form, as can be seen in figure 269, is that of a simple cavetto-crowned structure with battered, or sloping, sides. The interior of the building, appropriately framed by block borders, is apparently thought of as exposed to our view together with the figures and amuletic devices enshrined in it. In five instances the central element on the front of the pectoral is a large scarab beetle riding on a sacred barque and flanked by the goddesses Isis and Nephthys, by a pair of cynocephalous apes, or by figures of the tomb owner in an attitude of worship. Here the beetle apparently serves a double function, as a heart scarab and as the *ba* of the sun god lighting the way to the Underworld. Four of the beetles are, or were, actual heart scarabs of stone or faience mounted in openings in the centers of the pectorals or in shallow cavities in their fronts. On the backs the center of the design is taken up by the flat underside of the scarab, inscribed with Chapter XXX of the Book of the Dead, or by a facsimile of it drawn on the surface of the pectoral. In the instance illustrated, the inscribed oval rests on a barque between twin *djed*-pillars; in another it emerges in the middle of a little scene showing the owner of the pectoral worshiping Osiris. One of two small steatite pectorals, said to have come from a tomb near Edfu, carries on its back a similar scene in which the Prophet of Amūn, Ḥuy-nefer, kneels with hands upraised before a seated figure of Osiris. On the front of his second pectoral Ḥuy-nefer worships the Mnevis bull (the "Herald of Rēʿ") and on its back the canine animal of the god Anubis. Both pectorals are inlaid with bits of faience and colored glass and are adorned at the bottom with a frieze of pendent lotus flowers. A painted wooden pectoral inscribed for the Servitor in the Place-of-truth Si-Basty is decorated on the front with a representation of its owner in the form of a human-headed *ba*-bird and on the back with a winged figure of the goddess Isis. Two handsome

FIGURE 268. King Amun-ḥotpe I on a painted wooden pectoral of the late Twentieth Dynasty. Colors: red, green, yellow, black, and white. H. 4 5/16 in.

pectorals of bright blue faience, formerly in the Carnarvon collection, belonged, respectively, to the Engraver of the Monuments of Amūn, Yūnero, and the House Mistress Mūt-nefret (fig. 269), while an inlaid and gilded steatite pectoral from the Morgan collection was made for a man whose name seems to have been either Dja or Wedja-Ḥōr. Several examples are provided near their tops with rows of holes whereby they could be sewn to the wrappings over the breasts of their owners' mummies. None are large, the widths of the seven complete pectorals ranging from two and a half to five and a quarter inches.

Throughout the Ramesside period and well down into the later dynasties the heart scarab, made of the traditional green stone and inscribed with Chapter XXX of the Book of the Dead, remained the most common and the most important amulet placed by the Egyptians upon the bodies of their dead. Unlike the pectoral, it is now usually found under the outer wrappings of the mummy, on or next to the body itself. Since it was held firmly in place by the wrappings it required no mounting and is not at this period normally provided with one.

The eighteen ★heart scarabs in our collection which can be assigned typologically to the Nineteenth and Twentieth Dynasties are with one exception of unrecorded origin, coming chiefly from the Murch, Timins (per Carnarvon), and Davis collections. The exception, acquired in 1889, is known to be from Thebes. Ten of the scarabs are carved of graywacke, serpentine, green feldspar, emerald matrix, and other kinds of green stone, but there are also examples in black stone, steatite, limestone, blue and gray faience, and green glass. In size they vary considerably, the largest measuring three and nine-sixteenths inches in length, the smallest only an inch and seven-sixteenths. The back of the beetle is usually rendered with a minimum of detail, but in two instances the wing cases are striated longitudinally, and on one faience scarab the back is inlaid in dark glaze with figures of two *ba*-birds (𓅡 and 𓅽) face to face. When present, the heart spell is invariably engraved in horizontal lines on the undersides of the scarabs. Three scarabs, however, are uninscribed. On a number of others—obviously purchased ready made from an undertaker's stock—the space provided at the beginning of the spell for the name of the beneficiary has been left blank. In nine cases the names of the owners are preserved, and these include the First Prophet of Tḥōt, Amun-em-Opet; the Priests of Amūn, Amun-em-ḥēt and Pa-di-Mūt; the Chantress of Amun Rēʿ, Ikay; the Guardian (?) Ptaḥ-em-weya; and five men named Yay, Pa-shed, Raʿ-mosě, Ḥesy-ʿA-khopesh, and Tḥōt-em-ḥēb.

A large, black stone ★heart amulet (𓄣) was obviously designed and used in place of a heart scarab. Its back is flat like the underside of a scarab and is inscribed with Chapter XXX of the Book of the Dead. The last two lines of the text run over onto the rounded front of the amulet where they are engraved above the figure of a winged goddess kneeling on a "gold"-sign. On the other hand, a big serpentine ★scarab, formerly in the Carnarvon collection, is probably not to be classed as a heart scarab. It is without a text, its underside being engraved simply with a figure of Osiris ("Lord of the Holy Land") flanked by winged figures of Isis and Nephthys. On the back is a solar disk between *wedjat*-eyes and on the wing cases seated figures of Rēʿ Ḥor-akhty (?) and Osiris.

The canopic jars of the late New Kingdom are characterized by a change in the shape and proportions of the jars themselves, which now tend to be tall, slender, and without the pronounced shoulder seen on their Eighteenth Dynasty predecessors, and by the use of a different type of stopper for each of the Four Genii represented—a human head for Imsety, the head of a cynocephalous ape for Ḥapy, a dog or jackal head for Dewau-mautef, and the head of a peregrine falcon for Ḳebeḥ-snēwef.

The change in proportions is not yet apparent in the earliest ★canopic jar of our Ramesside series, possibly because it is made of bright turquoise blue faience, an unusual and fragile material; but the sides of the vessel are nearly parallel and the break at the shoulder is already much reduced (see fig. 270, cf. fig. 39). The panel on the side of the jar, hastily but skillfully drawn in heavy black line, shows us the Overseer of the King's House of Adoration Sētẖ-em-ḥēb, saying his prayers to the falcon-headed Rēʿ Ḥor-akhty, who sits enthroned, holding a cluster of symbols and attended by the goddess Isis and another female, probably Sētẖ-em-ḥēb's wife. In the inscription below the panel Sētẖ-em-ḥēb is associated with Imsety, the "son of Osiris," the only one of the Four Genii still represented with a human head. The pieces of the jar were found, together with the fragments of two others of the same set, in a tomb on the hill known as el Khōkheh, in western Thebes. Two fragmentary faience ★stoppers were also found and one of these, with the black canine snout of the genius Dewau-mautef projecting from a blue and yellow striped wig, has been restored for our collection.

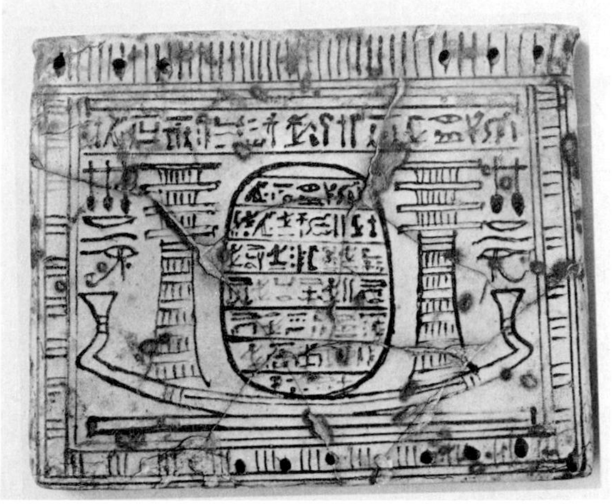

FIGURE 269. Blue faience pectoral of the Lady Mūt-nefret. Back. L. 5¼ in.

From Tūneh in Middle Egypt comes a slenderly proportioned ★canopic jar (see fig. 270) of fine translucent alabaster adorned on the side with an engraved and colored panel showing the fashionably attired but unnamed owner of the jar offering a bowl to Osiris. The man's head is shaven and his billowing white garments reach downward to his ankles. The god, as usual, is mummiform with red plumes on his tall headdress. Between the figures three columns of hieroglyphic text contain the traditional canopic formula, spoken in this case by Nephthys who extends her protection over the genius Imsety and over "the one in honor with Imsety." Above, a green and black lotus flower hangs downward from the collar of the now missing human-headed stopper. A second ★jar from the same site, though acquired with the one just described and almost identical with it in size, is from a different set. It is undecorated except for three columns of inscription engraved on its side in which the genius Ḥapy and his deceased protégé are assured of the usual divine protection. The jars came to the Museum accompanied by two carved and painted alabaster ★stoppers, one in the form of the ape head of Ḥapy, the other with the bewigged falcon head of Ḳebeḥ-snēwef. The stoppers seem to belong to a single set and the ape-headed example fits well (and appropriately) on the second of our jars, bringing its over-all height to eighteen inches.

An alabaster ★canopic jar and human-headed ★stopper, acquired with the Murch collection, were made for an Overseer of Cattle of the House of Ptaḥ named Ḥuy, and may come from a tomb in the Memphite area. Though probably from one and the same set, they do not belong together, the inscription on the jar identifying its contents with the ape-headed Ḥapy who, as often, is said to be embraced and protected by the goddess Nephthys. The jar, thirteen and three-eighths inches in height, is of mediocre workmanship. The beardless head which forms the stopper is somewhat more carefully carved and its mouth and the alternate bands of its broad collar are colored red.

An effectively simplified version of the head of Ḥapy's ape is preserved to us on a limestone ★stopper found by the Egypt Exploration Fund in a tomb of the Nineteenth Dynasty at Abydos. The head seems at one time to have been painted yellow and it is not unlikely that some of the details omitted by the sculptor were added in paint.

Toward the end of the New Kingdom the Egyptians evolved an alternate method of preserving and magically safeguarding the viscera of the dead. As before, each organ was removed and individually mummified; but instead of being deposited in a canopic jar stoppered with a carved

FIGURE 270. Canopic jars of the late New Kingdom from Thebes and Tūneh. Alabaster and blue faience. H. 13¼-17½ in.

head of the appropriate Genius of the Dead, it was wrapped around a small wax figure of the genius and replaced in the body of its deceased owner. Two such ★figures in our collection (fig. 271) represent the human-headed Imsety and the canine-headed Dewau-mautef, both in the form of mummies wearing long headdresses and having the hands crossed or held together over the breast. Four and a half inches in height, they are larger and more carefully modeled than others of their class and are probably to be dated to the last years of the Twentieth Dynasty. The procedure described, however, is particularly characteristic of private burials of the Twenty-First Dynasty, where for the time being it all but eliminated the use of canopic jars.

In the development and use of the *shawabty*-figure the later New Kingdom was a period of transition. The funerary figures of this class found with private burials of the Eighteenth Dynasty are usually large, few in number, and carved with the same care devoted to other types of tomb statuettes. More often than not they were made expressly for their individual owners, and not infrequently each figure was enclosed in a shrine-shaped case, or box, of its own (see fig. 158). By contrast, the *shawabtys* of the Twenty-First Dynasty and succeeding periods are for the most part small molded figures of faience or clay turned out by the thousands in accordance with a few standard designs, one man's *shawabtys* being distinguishable from another's only by the names of the owners inscribed upon them. Well-to-do persons were often provided with four hundred or more of the little figures—one worker for every day of the year plus what is assumed to be a foreman, with whip and flaring kilt, for every ten workmen. During the Ramesside age we find both types, the big custom-made figure of stone or wood surviving in modified form into the Twentieth Dynasty[10] but being gradually replaced by the mass-produced *shawabty* modeled or molded of faience or pottery. At this time also we find two forms of *shawabty* coexisting side by side—the traditional mummiform figure and the recently developed small standing statuette, dressed according to the fashion of the day, but posed, equipped, and inscribed so as to leave no doubt as to its function.

FIGURE 271. Wax figures of two Genii of the Dead. H. 4 1/2 and 4 3/8 in.

Among the sixty or so ★*shawabty*-figures of Ramesside date in our own collection, special interest attaches to a series of thirteen found in the tomb of Sen-nedjem at Deir el Medîneh and belonging therefore to the earlier part of the Nineteenth Dynasty. The largest and most elaborate of the group is a painted limestone figure made and inscribed for Sen-nedjem himself (fig. 272). Carved with considerably less finesse than its Eighteenth Dynasty prototypes, the stocky mummiform statuette is brightly and attractively colored, its blue wig, dark red flesh color, and black inscription standing out sharply against the pure white of the

[10] See the four *shawabtys* discussed in the first section of this chapter.

figure proper. In readiness for the labors described in the spell written upon it, the little worker holds in its crossed hands a pair of mattocks and carries on its left shoulder a basket for "transporting sand." A slender wooden *shawabty* of Sen-nedjem's wife, the House Mistress Iy-neferty, is similar in style and general color scheme, but the wig in this case is black, the broad collar yellow, and the inscription is not carved but merely painted on. Three unpainted figures carved of limestone bear short ink inscriptions giving in one instance the name of Iy-neferty (shortened to "Iy-ty"), and in the two others that of the Harpooner(?) of the Temple, Mosĕ, probably a son or grandson of Sen-nedjem. They are in the form of small mummies with beardless faces, long headdresses, and crossed arms, but on the larger *shawabty* of Mosĕ (height seven and a quarter inches) the feet are represented as if projecting from the bottom of a long, tight garment. A fourth figure of the same type is engraved with the title and name of the Sculptor Nefer-renpowet (the owner of Tomb 336 ?) followed in five horizontal lines of text by an abridged version of the *shawabty*-spell. Another limestone *shawabty*, standing almost nine inches in height, is neither painted nor inscribed, but may, as Maspero supposed, have been one of Sen-nedjem's own. Two of a group of four brightly painted pottery *shawabtys*, all about seven inches high, are inscribed for Sen-nedjem's son Khonsu, who is represented as a standing figure clad in the costume of his period, but holding in his crossed hands a pair of painted mattocks. The other pair, made for Khonsu's wife Ta-meket, are both mummiform, but one is painted white with red and black details and one black with yellow details. Two painted limestone figures of Khaʿ-bekhenet, another of Sen-nedjem's sons and the owner of Theban Tomb No. 2, were appropriated for his mother, Iy-neferty, and bear her name hastily added in ink beside his own. Eight and a quarter and six and a half inches high, they reproduce the two forms seen in the unpainted *shawabtys* of Mosĕ, one having a pair of dark red feet emerging from under its long white wrappings.

FIGURE 272. *Shawabty*-figure of the Servitor in the Place-of-truth Sen-nedjem. From Theban Tomb No. 1. Painted limestone. H. 10 5/8 in.

The majority of our remaining Nineteenth and Twentieth Dynasty *shawabtys* are of turquoise blue or creamy white faience with wig stripes, eye outlines, inscriptions, mattocks, baskets, and other linear details added in a black or dark brown overglaze. Most of them are of the conventional mummiform type, slenderly proportioned and ranging in height from three to ten and a quarter inches. Many are inscribed with Chapter VI of the Book of the Dead written in horizontal bands around the lower half of the figure, but an almost equal number bear only the names and titles of their owners preceded by the epithet "the Osiris," or by the expression "illuminating the Osiris." A few wear a kilt with projecting apron in front and hold a two-lashed whip in place of a mattock, and these we may recognize as the foremen of the work gangs of the hereafter. The largest and finest of our faience *shawabtys* is a big polychrome figure from the "Tety Pyramid Cemeteries" at Saḳḳâreh, made and inscribed for the Scribe of the Treasury of the Lord of the Two Lands, Woser. Among the more or less distinguished owners of the others are the King's Wife Nesy-Iset; the King's Son of Kush, Khaʿ; the First Prophet of Amūn, Pa-neḥesy; the Prophet of Amūn, Iret-Ḥōr; the God's Father of Amūn, Nesy-pa-per-nūb; the Chantress of Amūn, Kamaʿ; the Scribes of the Treasury Woser-ḥēt-mosĕ and Pa-Rēʿ-em-ḥēb; the Scribe of the Offering Table of the Lord of the Two Lands, Yuw-Amūn; the Overseer of the Prison(?) Sēth-em-ḥēb; the Department Head Piyay; the Shepherd Amun-khaʿu; the House Mistress Nebet-iry; a woman named Meket, and two men named Roy and Ḥori.

A gracefully proportioned and carefully painted wooden *shawabty*, seven and a half inches high, belonged to a sculptor, or inscription carver, named Ipy, who, to judge from the style of the figure, lived during the early part of the Nineteenth Dynasty, but whose title differs from that of his better-known fellow practitioner and namesake, the owner of Theban Tomb No. 217 (p. 345). Five other figures, also of wood, are coarsely carved and garishly colored in a style suggestive of later Ramesside times. They bear the names of the *Wēʿb*-priest of Amūn, Bak-en-Khonsu, the *Wēʿb*-priest Bak-en-Mūt, the Lady Ḥetepy, and an untitled worthy named Mery-Sēth. One of three painted pottery *shawabtys*, inscribed in black ink for "the Osiris, Pa-tjau-medy-Amūn," has the form of a kilted foreman carrying in his right hand a painted whip. The two others are mummiform, with the name in one case obliterated and in the other not filled in in the space provided for it after the words "illuminating the Osiris." Fragments of a handsome steatite *shawabty* with a well-cut inscription were found by Theodore Davis at Medînet Habu and have been dated—somewhat questionably, it would seem—to the Twentieth Dynasty. The upper two-thirds of an unusually large and skillfully carved figure of painted limestone is so battered and salt-ridden that its black and red ink inscription is no longer legible.

The bronze ★head, forearms, and *ba*-bird pectoral of a composite *shawabty*-figure made for a Nineteenth Dynasty lady are shown in figure 273 mounted on a modern wooden body. The head, which was hollow cast and cemented to the top of the figure, is that of an attractive young woman

FIGURE 273. Bronze mountings for a *shawabty* of a lady. The wooden figure is restored. H. 7 in.

wearing a long wig with a lotus flower over the forehead, a pair of massive discoid ear studs, and two necklaces of lenticular beads. The slender arms are solid bronze and are held in place by tapered tenons projecting upward from the elbows. From similarly elaborate and nicely made figures come a small red faience ★face with the rims and brows of the eyes inlaid in blue paste and a beautifully modeled little ★face of dark red glass similarly inlaid and accompanied by a pair of clenched hands, also of red glass.

Five painted wooden ★*shawabty*-boxes, designed in each case to contain a pair of figures, have the form of a single or double shrine of Lower Egypt () mounted on sledge runners. The sides and lids of the little shrines are decorated with conventionalized paneling appropriate to such archaic structures, painted in blue, green, and red on a yellow ground. Knobs on the boxes and their lids permitted the latter to be tied in place with cord and perhaps sealed. Two of three perfectly preserved boxes from the tomb of Sen-nedjem are adorned with paneling only, but carry on their lids the titles and names of two of Sen-nedjem's sons, Khaʿ-bekhenet and Raʿ-mosĕ. On the front of the third box (fig. 274) two fully bandaged mummies are represented standing side by side, their masks surmounted by cones of perfume. The accompanying inscription tells us that the box was made for the Servitor in the Place-of-truth Pa-Rēʿ-em-nekhu, a son or grandson of Sen-nedjem who appears to have died at an early age. It is probable that the painted figures represent, not the *shawabtys* contained in the box, but the actual mummy of Pa-Rēʿ-em-nekhu.

This conclusion is supported by the decoration of the front of our fourth *shawabty*-box (fig. 275), which also carries a representation of its owner, here protrayed as a living person seated side by side with his wife as if at a banquet or other festive occasion. From the inscription we learn that the man is the Sculptor in the Place-of-truth Nakht-Amūn, the owner of Tomb 335 at Deir el Medīneh, and that his wife (called his "sister" or "female companion") is the House Mistress Nūb-sha'es. In this most attractive and skillfully executed little painting Nakht-Amūn holds a lotus flower to his nose, while his wife, her head topped by a cone of festival scent, rests her hands affectionately on her husband's arm and shoulder. The white background and the figures with their sharp faces, crinkly wigs, and diaphanous garments, stained here and there with brown ointment(?), seem lifted directly from a tomb painting of the period in which the couple lived—the early or middle decades of the Nineteenth Dynasty.

The largest and most elaborately decorated of the five *shawabty*-boxes comes from Tūneh el Gebel, the cemetery of ancient Hermopolis. Over seventeen inches in height, it is painted white and is adorned with figures on each of its four sides. On the front we see the owner, a lady dressed in long, flowing garments and an exceptionally long wig, holding in her extended left hand a tall floral bouquet. Facing her, on the left side of the box, is a mummiform figure of Osiris wearing the *atef*-crown. A similar figure on the right side wears on its head the ram's horns and double plume flanked by large uraei. On the back of the little shrine Osiris appears again, this time receiving "life" from the falcon-headed Harendotes (Horus, Avenger-of-his-father). The scenes are well drawn and attractively colored in red, green, yellow, and black; but unfortunately both the box and its decoration have suffered considerable damage. The lid which came with it but which is not its own is inscribed for a Chantress of Tḥōt named Mi.

In the same lot of antiquities from Tūneh the Museum acquired a wide-mouthed pottery ★jar sealed with a clay stopper and containing eleven large pottery ★*shawabtys*. The sides of the jar are decorated with seated figures of the Four Genii of the Dead rapidly sketched in black outline, and between two of the figures is a column of inscription with the words "illuminating the Osiris, Burero." The same inscription is written in black on the front of each of the *shawabtys*. These average seven and a half inches in height and comprise a gang of ten mummiform workers and a foreman wearing a kilt with a flaring apron. As with some of the Twentieth Dynasty *shawabtys* already discussed, the feet of the figures are clearly represented emerging from the bottoms of the tight mummiform sheaths—a treatment evidently intended to enable them to move about and perform their allotted tasks.

During the Eighteenth Dynasty it became the custom to place in the tombs of the dead a bed on which a silhouette of the mummiform god Osiris had been formed with a coating of rich earth enclosed within a light wooden frame. Shortly before the tomb was closed the earth was planted with barley seeds and repeatedly watered so that in the course of the ensuing weeks the seeds sprouted and formed for a short while a green and living figure of the god, whose resurrection, together with that of the deceased tomb owner, was thus strikingly symbolized. It is probably these "Osiris beds," or "germinated Osiris figures," which have led in recent times to the absurd belief that seeds found in ancient tombs can still be made to grow.

A later variation of the Osiris bed is a pottery ★brick with a recessed upper surface in which has been cut a shallow cavity in the shape of a figure of Osiris wearing the *atef*-crown and holding the crook and *ladanisterion*. Clearly this cavity was to contain the earth for a germinating Osiris figure which, thanks to the rebated surface of the brick, could be kept soaked with water until the seeds planted in it had sprouted. Much smaller, of course, than the earlier beds, our pottery model measures nine and a half inches in length by four and an eighth inches in width. It was purchased from a native of Thebes during the season of 1919-1920. From Thebes also come a bright blue faience ★tile inscribed on both sides with offering formulae invoking Osiris and Amun Rēʿ and a group of ★model fruits similar to those found in tombs of the Middle Kingdom (see Part I, fig. 225).

In a tomb on the northern slope of the ʿIlwet esh Sheik ʿAbd el Ḳurneh the Museum's Expedition found ★scraps of a once fine illustrated papyrus of Ramesside date. Preserved are parts of a large and elaborately colored vignette representing the sun god Rēʿ Ḥor-akhty, and small sections of funerary texts in a good hieratic hand of the Nineteenth Dynasty. The papyrus was probably a Book of the Dead, but not enough of it remains to make the identification certain.

FIGURE 274. *Shawabty*-box of Pa-Reʿ-em-nekhu, from the tomb of Sen-nedjem at Deir el Medīneh. Painted wood. H. 11 ¼ in.

At Thebes the Ramesside age witnessed a sharp falling-off in the production and use of stamped pottery funerary cones. Our own collection includes the ★cones of scarcely a dozen different tomb owners whose careers are datable to the Nineteenth and Twentieth Dynasties. Among these we meet the Commander of Cavalry and Overseer of the Cattle of Amūn, Piyay, the owner of Tomb 344; the Overseer of Ships, Scribe of the Cavalry, and Scribe of the Army Nenay; the Royal Steward and Overseer of Crafts Tjet; the Chief Merchant(?) Tjay; the Lieutenant Commander of Police Si-Mūt; the Chief of Henchmen and Troop Commander Pa-sēr; the Chief of Servants of the House of His Majesty, Pa-su; the Accountant of Bread

FIGURE 275.
Painted wooden *shawabty*-box of the Sculptor Nakht-Amūn. Nineteenth Dynasty. H. 12 ½ in.

and Overseer of the Cattle of Amun Rēʿ, Woser-ḥēt (tomb on the Dirāʿ Abu'n Naga); the Accountant of Grain and Overseer of the Fields of Amūn, Amun-em-Opet, called Tja-nefer; and the Cultivator of Amūn, Pa-shed.

Looking back over this brief series of names and titles we are struck with the preponderance of army officers and military officials among the prominent and well-to-do men of the time. The age, as we have seen, was warlike, and, for a while at least, the armed forces offered riches, rapid promotions, and other tempting inducements to the young men of the country, luring them away from the learned professions and from the schools for embryonic civil officials. It was to offset these temptations that much of the so-called school literature of the period was composed.

10. The Literature of the Later New Kingdom

Aside from its invaluable, though often faulty, copies of the classics of the older periods of Egyptian history,[11] the Ramesside age produced a rich and varied literature of its own, written for the most part in the recently accepted colloquial language which we call New Egyptian and characterized by a new liveliness, informality, and penchant for satirical humor. The stories, poems, precepts, letters, magical and religious texts, and other forms of literary output to which this most prolific age gave birth are preserved to us in several remarkable groups of hieratic papyri, chiefly from Thebes and Memphis, and on hundreds of hieratic ostraka, the majority of which come from Deir el Medīneh and adjoining areas of the Theban necropolis. The lion's share of the papyri, including the great Harris, Anastasi, Sallier, and Beatty series, are, appropriately enough, in the British Museum, but manuscripts of major importance are found also in the museums of Turin, Bologna, Leiden, Moscow, and Cairo.

As before, the short story, usually with a historical or mythological background and often with a symbolic or didactic content, remained in high favor. Now, however, the tales are lighter and spicier in tone and are more simply and informally told than their carefully studied predecessors of the Middle Kingdom. Such stories are the popular folk legend which we call the Tale of the Two Brothers, the rather bawdy and often ludicrous Contendings of Horus and Sēth, the almost equally irreverent Outwitting of Rēʿ by Isis, the fairy tale of the Doomed Prince, the allegorical Blinding of Truth by Falsehood, the legend of Apopy and Seḳen-en-Rēʿ (see p. 7), a fragmentary myth concerning the Insatiable Sea and the Goddess Astarte, the Taking of Joppa, a diverting episode in one of the Palestinian campaigns of Tḥut-mosĕ III, and the incomparable Travels of Wen-Amūn, in which are described the half-comical, half-pathetic misadventures of an Egyptian emissary to Syria in the days of Ramesses XI (see p. 378). Fragments of similar narratives include a romantic account of another episode in Tḥut-mosĕ III's Asiatic wars, a Ghost Story in which the High Priest Khonsu-em-ḥēb encounters in a dream the spirit of King Rēʿ-ḥotpe's treasurer, the Quarrel of Harsaphes with a goddess, two versions of a mythical tale involving a goddess and a king, and the record of a highly edifying Dispute between the Head and the Body.

In the field of narrative poetry the outstanding works of the period are the long poem describing Ramesses II's heroism at the Battle of Ḳadesh (see p. 339) and that commemorating the great victory of Mery-en-Ptaḥ over the Libyans (see p. 353). Shorter poems are devoted to the joy attendant upon the accessions of Mery-en-Ptaḥ and Ramesses IV and to the enumeration of the Parts of the Pharaoh's War Chariot, the names of which are used in puns redounding to the glory of the vehicle's royal owner. Poems in Praise of the Delta Residence of the Ramesside kings picture in glowing terms the beauty and richness of the royal do-

[11] Notably, the Story of Si-nuhet, the Satire on the Trades, the Instruction of King Amun-em-ḥēt I, the Hymn to the Nile, and the Book of Kemyet (see Part I, pp. 122, 179).

main (see pp. 338 f.). Among the poems extolling in general terms the godlike power and beneficence of the kings are a fine Hymn to Ramesses II, preserved on a number of stelae from his rock temple at Abu Simbel, an elaborate Encomium to Ramesses IV, copied down for us in a papyrus now in Turin, and a hymn to Ramesses V written on the back of the Beatty papyrus with the Contendings of Horus and Sēth.

Many of the hymns composed during the Ramesside period in honor of Amun Rēʿ and other leading divinities were clearly influenced both in concept and phraseology by the solar hymns of the late Eighteenth Dynasty (pp. 279, 281). In the Thousand Songs praising Thebes and its god, set down during the reign of Ramesses II on a papyrus now in Leiden, stress is laid upon the natural phenomena in which the deity manifests himself and upon his role as a universal creator god in whom, by a process of syncretism, the forms and powers of all other gods are combined. Shorter hymns and prayers to Amūn, known to us chiefly from papyri in the British Museum, reflect the same point of view, but, in common with similar hymns and prayers to Thōt, Osiris, and Rēʿ Ḥorakhty, are notable for their variety of approach and the richness of their metaphor.

Far more appealing to our modern taste are the love songs of the time, in which young lovers pine romantically for one another or are united in the midst of charming natural settings—orchards and gardens bright with trees, flowers, and pools or streams of water. Half a dozen collections of such lyrics, evidently intended to be sung to the accompaniment of musical instruments, have come down to us in papyri and on ostraka of the late New Kingdom, a period which seems, indeed, to have been the golden age of this class of poetry.

Though unstinting in its admiration for the "wisdom literature" of bygone eras the Ramesside age produced relatively little of its own, no complete *sbōyet*, or "teaching," of the traditional type being attributable to this time. For the Eighteenth Dynasty we have the Maxims of Any and the Instruction of Amun-nakhte and for the Late Dynastic period Amun-em-Opet's rather cautious Precepts for Living; but from the Nineteenth and Twentieth Dynasties only a few sections of unidentified teachings, made up mostly of interdictions against foolhardy and unbridled behavior, have been preserved.

On the other hand, the schools for scribes, to which the majority of our surviving Ramesside manuscripts owe their existence, compelled their students to cover many pages of papyrus and scores of ostraka with copies of model letters and other compositions exhorting them to be diligent in their studies and to set their hearts on becoming clerks and, eventually, officials in the government service. These "school writings"—also called "anthologies" or "miscellanies"—harp endlessly upon the advantages of the scribal profession and, like the earlier Satire on the Trades, draw amusingly exaggerated pictures of the miseries of such rival callings as that of the soldier, the farmer, the baker, and even the priest. They point out that only the learned are sure of immortality, and in support of this view mention some of the well-remembered writers and sages of long ago—Ḥordjedef, I-em-ḥotep, Achtoy, and Ptaḥ-ḥotpe. The other letters, real or fictitious, used by the schoolboys as their models include communications on many different subjects, official and otherwise—the tracking down of runaway slaves, work orders, protests against unjust taxation, congratulations on government appointments, preparations for a royal jubilee, the activities and hardships of frontier officials, family matters, and so on, practically ad infinitum. Needless to say, these documents, copied mainly for their forms and as exercises in calligraphy, are a golden source of information on the life of the times. Most admired and most copied of the lot is the so-called Satirical Letter, in which one government official sarcastically berates another for his ignorance and incompetence, at the same time displaying his own knowledge of the manifold subjects which a well-trained scribe was required to know.

Another aid to instruction used in the Egyptian schools was a composition to which modern writers have applied the Greek term onomastikon. This was simply a list, or catalogue, of the names of every natural phenomenon, person, locality, or object with which a government scribe was expected to be cognizant, arranged according to subject and carefully spelled out in the approved orthography of the day. Our most complete onomastikon of Ramesside times was compiled by a Scribe of Holy Scripture named Amun-em-Opet who lived toward the end of the Twentieth Dynasty. As preserved to us in a papyrus in Moscow known as the Golénischeff Glossary, it comprises 610 entries ranging from heavenly bodies to cuts of meat. Partial copies of the same vocabulary are found in two papyri and a fragmentary leather roll in the British Museum, on several scraps of papyrus from the Ramesseum, and on a few ostraka.

The magical "books" of the late New Kingdom are numerous and diversified in their formats. The majority of such writings were intended primarily to exorcise sickness-bringing demons, ward off noxious creatures such as snakes and scorpions, and offset the effects of their poisons in persons already stricken. They take the form either of collections of spells pure and simple or of prayers, litanies, hymns, and ancient myths arranged so as to perform the functions of spells. Examples are the myth concerning Rēʿ and Isis, referred to on page 431, which was used as an incantation against scorpion venom, and an earlier myth describing the Deliverance of Mankind from Destruction, which was inscribed in the tombs of Sēthy I, Ramesses II, and Ramesses III as a charm to protect the body of the king from harm. Two special types of magical books which are represented at this period are the Calendars of Lucky and Unlucky Days (Papyrus Sallier IV and Papyrus Cairo 86637) and a book devoted to the Interpretation of Dreams (Papyrus Beatty III). Here also may be mentioned numerous small pieces of pottery and limestone from Deir el Medîneh inscribed with questions apparently to be addressed to oracles.

The principal funerary "books" of the Ramesside era have already been mentioned (pp. 327 f.), and we have had occasion to refer to the famous tomb-robbery papyri (p. 376), the records of the trial of the participants in the conspiracy against Ramesses III (p. 365), the accounts of the workmen's strikes in the Theban necropolis (p. 365), and the two great administrative documents of the age, Papyrus Harris I and the Wilbour Papyrus. We have still to speak of the many other "non-literary" writings of the period, the series of late Ramesside letters and the juridical, legal, and administrative texts which have done so much to fill out our picture of life in Egypt during the latter part of the New Kingdom. Here we find, set down on papyri and ostraka and occasionally on tomb walls, the records of civil lawsuits between private citizens, one or two wills, a marriage settlement, and an unusual deed of adoption; a variety of texts dealing with the taxation and transport of grain, protests against unjust taxes, records of wages and of prices paid for commodities in terms of gold, silver, and copper; account books, work reports, and, from the Theban necropolis, innumerable lists of workmen, their rations and their supplies (see pp. 393 f.). It will be recalled, moreover, that our most important single document on the course of Egyptian history, the Turin Canon of Kings, was drawn up at Memphis in the reign of Ramesses II and that three of our other lists of kings are also dated to the Nineteenth Dynasty.

It has been truly said that the literature of the Ramesside period is a far more accurate and honest reflection of the eventful, many-faceted age which produced it than is the often spiritless and to an increasing degree fossilized art of the time. Students of the period are also agreed that, aside from the influence exerted on the literary output by a much expanded school system, the most striking innovation present in the writings of the later New Kingdom is an enormously increased interest in and knowledge of the lands, peoples, and cultures lying beyond Egypt's own borders. "The texts express an awareness of foreign countries as places where an Egyptian might live, rather than as regions of lonely exile. The stories of the Two

Brothers, the Enchanted Prince, and Astarte and the Sea, as well as the long Satirical Letter all show an acclimatization to Syria as an essential of the text. Many of the texts display a relish for foreign words and phrases, as exhibiting the cosmopolitan learning of the scribe . . . . The free interplay of ideas had already broken down the sacred barriers around the Nile Valley."[12]

Less than a century and a half after the end of the New Kingdom Egypt began acquiring an even more intimate knowledge of her foreign contemporaries, for thenceforward, with only a few brief intervals of autonomy, she was destined to be ruled by a long succession of alien dynasties—Libyans, Kushites, Assyrians, Persians, Macedonians, and Romans. This final phase of ancient Egyptian history is too important and too richly represented in the Museum's collection to be summarized in a postscript to the present book, and can, it is hoped, be presented in a volume of its own.

[12] Wilson, *The Culture of Ancient Egypt*, p. 261.

BIBLIOGRAPHY

Abbreviations

For the nineteen periodicals and series most frequently cited the following conventional abbreviations are used:

Abh. Berlin = *Abhandlungen der (königlich) preussischen Akademie der Wissenschaften* [Berlin], Jahrgang . . . Philosophisch-historische Klasse.

AJSLL = *The American Journal of Semitic Languages and Literatures.*

ASAE = *Annales du Service des antiquités de l'Égypte.*

BIFAO = *Bulletin de l'Institut français d'archéologie orientale du Caire.*

BMFA = *Bulletin of the Museum of Fine Arts* [Boston].

BMMA = *Bulletin of the Metropolitan Museum of Art.*

CCG = *Catalogue général des antiquités égyptiennes du Musée du Caire.*

FIFAO = *Fouilles de l'Institut français d'archéologie orientale du Caire.*

JEA = *The Journal of Egyptian Archaeology.*

JNES = *Journal of Near Eastern Studies.*

Mitt. Kairo = *Mitteilungen des deutschen Instituts für ägyptische Altertumskunde in Kairo* (I-XIII), *Mitteilungen des deutschen archäologischen Instituts, Abteilung Kairo* (XIV-XV).

MIFAO = *Mémoires publiés par les membres de l'Institut français d'archéologie orientale du Caire.*

MMAF = *Mémoires publiés par les membres de la Mission archéologique française au Caire.*

PSBA = *Proceedings of the Society of Biblical Archaeology.*

Rec. trav. = *Recueil de travaux relatifs à la philologie et à l'archéologie égyptiennes et assyriennes.*

Sb. Berlin = *Sitzungsberichte der (königlich) preussischen Akademie der Wissenschaften* [Berlin]. Philosophisch-historische Klasse.

Unters. = *Untersuchungen zur Geschichte und Altertumskunde Aegyptens*, edited by Kurt Sethe and Hermann Kees.

ZAS = *Zeitschrift für ägyptische Sprache und Altertumskunde.*

ZDMG = *Zeitschrift der deutschen morgenländischen Gesellschaft.*

Bibliography[1]

20. General Works on the Fifteenth to Twentieth Dynasties

ARKELL, A. J. *A History of The Sudan from the Earliest Times to 1821*. London, 1955.

BARGUET, P., AND LECLANT, J. *Karnak-Nord IV, 1949-1951. Fouilles conduites par Cl. Robichon* (*FIFAO*, XXV). Cairo, 1954.

VON BECKERATH, J. *Tanis und Theban. Historische Grundlagen der Ramessidenzeit in Ägypten* (*Ägyptologische Forschungen*, XVI). Glückstadt, 1951.

BISSON DE LA ROQUE, F., AND OTHERS. *Rapport[s] sur les fouilles de Médamoud, 1925-1935* (*FIFAO*, III-IX, XIII). Cairo, 1926-1936.

BREASTED, J. H. *Ancient Records of Egypt: Historical Documents*, II-IV: *The Eighteenth Dynasty*, *The Nineteenth Dynasty*, and *The Twentieth to Twenty-sixth Dynasties* (*Ancient Records*, 2nd series). Chicago, 1906.

BRUYÈRE, B. *Rapport[s] sur les fouilles de Deir el Médineh, 1922-1951* (*FIFAO*, I-VIII, X, XIV-XVI, XX, XXI, XXVI). Cairo, 1924-1953.

CAPART, J., AND WERBROUCK, M. *Thebes, the Glory of a Great Past*. English translation by W. E. Caldwell. Brussels, 1926.

CARNARVON, THE EARL OF, AND CARTER, H. *Five Years' Explorations at Thebes: A Record of Work Done 1907-1911*. London, 1912.

ČERNÝ, J. *The Inscriptions of Sinai by Alan H. Gardiner and T. Eric Peet. Second Edition Revised and Augmented. Part I. Introduction and Plates* (*The Egypt Exploration Society*, 45th Memoir). London, 1952.

——— *The Inscriptions of Sinai from Manuscripts of Alan H. Gardiner and T. Eric Peet edited and completed. Part II. Translations and Commentary* (*The Egypt Exploration Society*, 45th Memoir). London, 1955.

——— *Graffiti hiéroglyphiques et hiératiques de la nécropole thébaine* (*Documents de FIFAO*, IX). Cairo, 1956.

———, BRUYÈRE, B., AND CLÈRE, J. J. *Répertoire onomastique de Deir el-Médineh* (*Ibid.*, XII). Cairo, 1949.

CHEVRIER, H. "Rapport[s] sur les travaux de Karnak," 1926-1939, 1947-1954, *ASAE*, XXVI-XXXIX (1926-1939) and XLVI-LIII (1947-1955), *passim*.

CHRISTOPHE, L. A. *Karnak-Nord III, 1945-1949. Fouilles conduites par C. Robichon* (*FIFAO*, XXIII). Cairo, 1951.

DARESSY, G. *Recueil de cones funéraires* (*MIFAO*, VIII, pp. 269-352). Cairo, 1892.

——— *Cercueils des cachettes royales* (*CCG*, nos. 61001-61044). Cairo, 1909.

——— "Inscriptions des carrières de Tourah et Mâsarah," *ASAE*, XI (1911), pp. 267-268.

[1] Continued from *The Scepter of Egypt, Part I, From the Earliest Times to the Middle Kingdom*. Compiled in April, 1958. The views expressed in the publications cited are not, in many cases, those adopted in the present book.

DAVIES, N. DE G. *A Corpus of Inscribed Egyptian Funerary Cones*. Edited by M. F. Laming Macadam. Oxford, 1957.

VON DEINES, H. "Die Nachrichten über das Pferd und den Wagen in den ägyptischen Texten," *Mitteilungen des Instituts für Orientforschung*, I (1953), pp. 3-15.

DESROCHES-NOBLECOURT, C. "Matériaux pour l'étude des relations entre Ugarit et l'Égypte," in Schaeffer, C. F.-A., *Ugaritica III* (*Mission de Ras Shamra*, VIII). Paris, 1956.

DRIOTON, É., AND VANDIER, J. *L'Égypte* (*"Clio": Introduction aux études historiques. Les peuples de l'Orient méditerranéen*, II). 3rd edition. Paris, 1952.

EDGERTON, W. F. "The Government and the Governed in the Egyptian Empire," *JNES*, VI (1947), pp. 152-160.

FAULKNER, R. O. "Egyptian Military Organisation," *JEA*, XXXIX (1953), pp. 32-47.

GAUTHIER, H. *Le Livre des rois d'Égypte*, II, III (*MIFAO*, XVIII, XIX). Cairo, 1912, 1914.

——— "Les 'Fils royaux de Kouch' et le personnel administratif de l'Éthiopie," *Rec. trav.*, XXXIX (1921), pp. 179-238.

GILLETT, C. R. "The Ward Collection of Egyptian Scarabs," *BMMA*, I (1906), pp. 43-45.

GOYON, G. *Nouvelles Inscriptions rupestres du Wadi Hammamat*. Paris, 1957.

HELCK, W. *Untersuchungen zu Manetho und den ägyptischen Königslisten* (*Unters.*, XVIII). Berlin, 1956.

——— AND OTTO, E. *Kleines Wörterbuch der Ägyptologie*. Wiesbaden, 1956.

HITTI, P. K. *History of Syria, Including Lebanon and Palestine*. London, 1951.

——— *Lebanon in History, from the Earliest Times to the Present*. London, 1957.

KEES, H. *Das Priestertum im ägyptischen Staat vom Neuen Reich bis zur Spätzeit* (*Probleme der Ägyptologie*, I). Leiden and Cologne, 1953.

LACAU, P. *Stèles du Nouvel Empire* (*CCG*, nos. 34001-34189). Cairo, 1909-1957.

LECLANT, J. "Fouilles et travaux en Égypte," 1951-1957, *Orientalia* XX-XXVII (1951-1958), *passim*.

LEFEBVRE, G. *Histoire des grands prêtres d'Amon de Karnak jusqu'à la XXIe Dynastie*. Paris, 1929.

LEGRAIN, G. "Rapport[s] sur les travaux exécutés à Karnak," 1899-1903, *ASAE*, I, II (1900, 1901) and IV, V (1903, 1904), *passim*.

——— *Répertoire généalogique et onomastique du Musée du Caire: Monuments de la XVIIe et de la XVIIIe Dynastie* (*Service des antiquités de l'Égypte*). Geneva, 1908.

——— "Fouilles et travaux en Soudan," 1948-1954, *Ibid.*, XX-XXIV (1951-1955), *passim*.

LEPSIUS, C. R. *Denkmaeler aus Aegypten und Aethiopien*, parts 1 and 2. 6 parts. Berlin, 1849-1859.

MASPERO, G. *Les Momies royales de Déir el-Baharî* (*MMAF*, I). Cairo, 1889.
MEYER, E. *Geschichte des Altertums*, II, parts 1 and 2. 2nd editions. Stuttgart and Berlin, 1928, 1931.
MONTET, P. *Le Drame d'Avaris: Essai sur la pénétration des Sémites en Égypte*. Paris, 1941.
NELSON, H. H. *Key Plans Showing Locations of Theban Temple Decorations* (*The University of Chicago Oriental Institute Publications*, LVI). Chicago, 1941.
NEWBERRY, P. E. *The Timins Collection of Ancient Egyptian Scarabs and Cylinder Seals*. London, 1907.
——— *Funerary Statuettes and Model Sarcophagi* (*CCG*, nos. 46530-48575). Cairo, 1930-1957.
NIMS, C. F. "Places about Thebes," *JNES*, XIV (1955), pp. 110-123.
NORTHAMPTON, THE MARQUIS OF, SPIEGELBERG, W., AND NEWBERRY, P. E. *Report on Some Excavations in the Theban Necropolis during the Winter of 1898-9*. London, 1908.
OTTO, E. *Topographie des thebanischen Gaues* (*Unters.*, XVI). Berlin, 1952.
——— *Ägypten. Der Weg des Pharaonen-Reiches* (*Urban-Bucher*, V). Stuttgart, [1953].
PETRIE, W. M. F. *Researches in Sinai*. New York, 1906.
——— *Qurneh* (*British School of Archaeology in Egypt and Egyptian Research Account*, 15th Year). London, 1909.
——— *A History of Egypt*, II, 7th edition; III, 3rd edition. London, 1924, 1925.
PILLET, M. "Rapport[s] sur les travaux de Karnak," 1921-1925, *ASAE*, XXII-XXV (1922-1925), *passim*.
REISNER, G. A. "The Viceroys of Ethiopia," *JEA*, VI (1920), pp. 28-55, 73-88.
SAUNERON, S. *Les Prêtres de l'ancienne Égypte* ("*Les Temps qui Court.*" Éditions du Seuil). Bourges, 1957.
SÄVE-SÖDERBERGH, T. *Ägypten und Nubien: Ein Beitrag zur Geschichte altägyptischer Aussenpolitik*. Lund, 1941.
SEIDL, K. *Einführung in die ägyptische Rechtsgeschichte bis zum Ende des neuen Reiches*, I: *Juristischer Teil* (*Ägyptologische Forschungen*, X). Glückstadt, 1939.
SETHE, K. *Urkunden der 18. Dynastie* (*Urkunden des aegyptischen Altertums*, IV). 4 parts. Leipzig, 1906-1909.
SMITH, G. E. *The Royal Mummies* (*CCG*, nos. 61051-61100). Cairo, 1912.
SPIEGELBERG, W. *Studien und Materialen zum Rechtswesen des Pharaonenreiches der Dynast. XVIII-XXI*. Hannover, 1892.
——— *Ägyptische und andere Graffiti* (*Inschriften und Zeichnungen*) *aus der thebanischen Nekropolis*. 2 vols. Heidelberg, 1921
STEINDORFF, G., AND SEELE, K. C. *When Egypt Ruled the East*. 2nd edition revised by Keith C. Seele. Chicago, 1957.
VANDIER, J. *Manuel d'archéologie égyptienne*, II. 6 parts. Paris, 1954-1955.
VARILLE, A. *Karnak I* (*FIFAO*, XIX). Cairo, 1943.
VERCOUTTER, J. *L'Égypte et le monde égéen préhellénique. Étude critique des sources égyptiennes* (*Du Début de la XVIIIe à la fin de la XIXe Dynastie*) (*Institut français d'archéologie orientale, Bibliothèque d'étude*, XXII). Cairo, 1956.
——— "New Egyptian Texts from the Sudan," *Kush: Journal of the Sudan Antiquities Service*, IV (1956), pp. 66-82.
WARD, J. *The Sacred Beetle: A Popular Treatise on Egyptian Scarabs in Art and History*. London, 1902.
WEIL, A. *Die Veziere des Pharaonenreiches chronologisch angeordnet*, part III. Strassburg, 1908.
WILSON, J. A. "Egyptian Texts," in Pritchard, James B. (ed.), *Ancient Near Eastern Texts Relating to the Old Testament*. Princeton, 1950.
——— *The Culture of Ancient Egypt*. Chicago, 1956.
WINLOCK, H. E. *Excavations at Deir el Baḥri, 1911-1931*. New York, 1942.
WOLF, W. *Die Welt der Ägypter* (*Grosse Kulturen der Frühzeit*, III, edited by H. T. Bossert). Stuttgart, 1955.
WRESZINSKI, W. *Atlas zur altaegyptischen Kulturgeschichte*, parts I and II. Leipzig, 1923, 1935.
YOYOTTE, J. "Égypte ancienne," in *Histoire universelle I: Des Origines à l'Islam* (*Encyclopédie de la Pléiade*). Paris, 1956.

21. The Hyksos

ALBRIGHT, W. F. "Palestine in the Earliest Historical Period," *Journal of the Palestine Oriental Society*, XV (1935), pp. 193-234.
——— "The Excavations of Tell Beit Mirsim, Volume II: The Bronze Age," *Annual of the American Schools of Oriental Research*, XVII (1938). See pp. 28 n. 2, 44 ff.
——— "The Role of the Canaanites in the History of Civilization," in *Studies of the History of Culture Presented to Waldo G. Leland*. New York, 1942.
ALT, A. *Die Herkunft der Hyksos in neuer sicht* (*Berichte über die Verhandlungen der Sächsischen Akademie der Wissenschaften zu Leipzig*, Philologisch-historische Klasse, CI, 6). Berlin, 1954.
VON BISSING, F. W. "Das angebliche Weltreich der Hyksos," *Archiv für Orientforschung*, XI (1936-1937), pp. 325-335.
——— "Zur Geschichte der Hyksos," *Orientalische Literaturzeitung*, XLVII (1944), pp. 85-92.
BRÖGELMANN, E. "Noch einmal: Die Hyksosfrage," *ZDMG*, XC (n. s. XV) (1936), pp. 441-443.
CARTER, H. "Report on the Tomb of Zeser-ka-Ra Amenhetep I" etc., *JEA*, III (1916), pp. 147-154. See p. 152, pl. XXXI, 1.
CHACE, A. B., MANNING, H. P., AND BULL, L. *The Rhind Mathematical Papyrus. British Museum 10057 and 10058*. 2 vols. Oberlin, 1927, 1929. See p. 49, photo 1, pl. 1.
CZERMAK, W. "Über den Seth der Hyksoszeit," *MIFAO*, LXVI (1935-1938), pp. 721-738.
DARESSY, G. "Un Poignard du temps des rois pasteurs," *ASAE*, VII (1906), pp. 115-120.
DAWSON, W. R. "A Bronze Dagger of the Hyksos Period," *JEA*, XI (1925), pp. 216-217.
DONNER, H. "Die Herkunft des ägyptischen Wortes [*ssmt*] = Pferd," *ZAS*, LXXX (1955), pp. 97-103.
DUSSAUD, R. "Quelques Précisions touchant les Hyksos," *Revue de l'histoire des religions*, CIX (1934), pp. 113-128.
ENGBERG, R. M. *The Hyksos Reconsidered* (*The University of Chicago Oriental Institute Studies in Ancient Oriental Civilization*, No. 18). Chicago, 1939.
FRASER, G. W. "Notes on Scarabs," *PSBA*, XXI (1899), pp. 148-157.
GALLING, K. "Hyksosherrschaft und Hyksoskultur," *Zeitschrift des Deutschen Palästina-Vereins*, LXII (1939), pp. 89-115.
GARDINER, A. H. "The Defeat of the Hyksos by Kamōse: The Carnarvon Tablet, No. 1," *JEA*, III (1916), pp. 95-110.
——— "Davies's Copy of the Great Speos Artemidos Inscription," *Ibid.*, XXXII (1946), pp. 43-56. See pp. 47-48, cols. 37-41.

GUNN, B., AND GARDINER, A. H. "New Renderings of Egyptian Texts. II. The Expulsion of the Hyksos," *JEA*, V (1918), pp. 36-56.

HABACHI, L. "La Libération de l'Égypte de l'occupation Hyksos. A propos de la découverte de la stèle de Kamosé à Karnak," pp. 52-58 in *Les Grandes Découvertes archéologiques de 1954*. Cairo, 1955.

JIRKU, A. "Aufstieg und Untergang der Hyksos," *Journal of the Palestine Oriental Society*, XII (1932), pp. 51-61.

JUNKER, H. "Pḥrnfr: 3. Die Verehrung des Seth im Nordostdelta," *ZAS*, LXXV (1939), pp. 77-84.

KANTOR, H. J. "The Chronology of Egypt and its Correlation with That of Other Parts of the Near East in the Periods Before the Late Bronze Age," in Ehrich, Robert W. (ed.), *Relative Chronologies in Old World Archaeology*. Chicago, 1954. See pp. 12-15, figs. 1 and 4.

KOENIG, J. "Aperçus nouveaux sur les Hyksôs (À propos de publications récentes)," *Revue d'assyriologie et d'archéologie orientale*, L (1956), pp. 191-199.

LABIB, P. C. *Die Herrschaft der Hyksos in Ägypten und ihr Sturz*. Glückstadt, Hamburg, New York, 1936.

LANCZKOWSKI, G. "Zur Herkunft der Hyksos," *Orientalische Literaturzeitung*, LI (1956), pp. 389-393.

MACE, A. C. "The Murch Collection of Egyptian Antiquities," *BMMA*, VI (1911), January, Supplement.

——— "The Egyptian Expedition, 1920-1921: Excavations at Lisht," *Ibid.*, XVI (1921), November, part II, pp. 5-18.

——— "A Group of Hitherto Unpublished Scarabs in the Metropolitan Museum," *JEA*, VII (1921), pp. 36-38.

MAYANI, Z. *Les Hyksos et le monde de la Bible* (*Bibliothèque historique*). Paris, 1956.

MONTET, P. "La Stèle de l'an 400 rétrouvée," *Kêmi*, IV (1931 [1933]), pp. 191-215.

NEWBERRY, P. E. "Notes on the Carnarvon Tablet No. 1," *PSBA*, XXXV (1913), pp. 117-122.

OLMSTEAD, A. T. *History of Palestine and Syria to the Macedonian Conquest*. New York, 1931. See pp. 115-130.

PETRIE, W. M. F. *Hyksos and Israelite Cities* (*British School of Archaeology in Egypt and Egyptian Research Account*, 12th Year). London, 1906. See pp. 3-16.

——— *Beth-Pelet I* (*Tell Fara*) (*Ibid.*). London, 1930.

REISNER, G. A. "A Garrison which held the Northern Sudan in the Hyksos Period, about 1700 B.C.," *BMFA*, XII (1914), pp. 9-24.

——— *Excavations at Kerma*. Parts I-VI (*Harvard African Studies*, V, VI). Cambridge (Mass.), 1923. See in parts I-III pp. 28; 38 f.; in parts IV-VI pp. 75 f.

RICKE, H. "Der 'Hohe Sand in Heliopolis,' " *ZAS*, LXXI (1935), pp. 107-111.

ROWE, A. *A Catalogue of Egyptian Scarabs, Scaraboids, Seals and Amulets in the Palestine Archaeological Museum* (*Government of Palestine Department of Antiquities*). Cairo, 1936.

——— "Addendum No. 1 on Egypto-Canaanite Contacts (*A Catalogue of Egyptian Scarabs, etc. in the Palestine Archaeological Museum, 1936*)," *The Quarterly of the Department of Antiquities in Palestine*, VIII (1938), pp. 72-76.

SÄVE-SÖDERBERGH, T. Review of H. E. Winlock, *The Rise and Fall of the Middle Kingdom in Thebes* (New York, 1947), in *Bibliotheca Orientalis*, VI (1949), pp. 85-90.

——— "The Hyksos Rule in Egypt," *JEA*, XXXVII (1951), pp. 53-71.

SCHAEFFER, C. F.-A. "À Propos de la Chronologie de la XIIe Dynastie égyptienne et des Hyksos," *Chronique d'Égypte*, XXII (1947), pp. 225-229.

SETHE, K. "Neue Spuren der Hyksos in Inschriften der 18. Dynastie," *ZAS*, XLVII (1910), pp. 73-86.

——— "Der Denkstein mit dem Datum des Jahres 400 der Ära von Tanis," *Ibid.*, LXV (1930), pp. 85-89.

SPEISER, E. A. "Ethnic Movements in the Near East in the Second Millennium B.C.: The Hurrians and Their Connections with the Ḫabiru and the Hyksos," *Annual of the American Schools of Oriental Research*, XIII (1933), pp. 13-54.

STOCK, H. *Studien zur Geschichte und Archäologie der 13. bis 17. Dynastie Ägyptens unter besonderer Berücksichtigung der Skarabäen dieser Zwischenzeit* (*Ägyptologische Forschungen*, XII). Glückstadt, 1942. See pp. 42-48, 63-75.

VANDIER, J. "Quelques Nouvelles Hypothèses sur la fin du Moyen Empire égyptien," *Journal des Savants*, October-December, 1944, pp. 154-168.

VAN DE WALLE, B. "Hyksos," *Dictionnaire de la Bible*. Supplément (edited by A. Robin), IV (18) (1941), pp. 146-168.

WEILL, R. *La Fin du moyen empire égyptien*. 2 vols. Paris, 1918.

——— "Compléments pour 'La Fin du moyen empire égyptien,' " *BIFAO*, XXXII (1932), pp. 7-52.

WINLOCK, H. E. *The Rise and Fall of the Middle Kingdom in Thebes*. New York, 1947. (See pp. 96-103, 150-170.

WOLF, W. *Die Bewaffnung des altägyptischen Heeres*. Leipzig, 1926. See pp. 29-59.

YADIN, Y. "Hyksos Fortifications and the Battering Ram," *Bulletin of the American Schools of Oriental Research*, 137 (February, 1955), pp. 23-32.

22. The Seventeenth Dynasty[1]

VON BISSING, F. W. "Die älteste Darstellung des Königs im 'Kriegshelm,' " *ZAS*, XLI (1904), p. 87.

BREASTED, J. H. *The Edwin Smith Surgical Papyrus* (*The University of Chicago Oriental Institute Publications*, III, IV). 2 vols. Chicago, 1930. See Vol. I, pp. 18, 28, 29.

BRUNTON, G. "Two Faience Statuettes," *ASAE*, XXXIX (1939), pp. 101-103.

BRUYÈRE, B. "Figurines féminines de l'Hathor nue égyptienne," pp. 109-150 in *Rapport sur les fouilles de Deir el Médineh, 1934-1935* (*FIFAO*, XVI). Cairo, 1939.

CAPART, J. *Recueil de monuments égyptiens*, 2nd series. Brussels, 1905. See pl. LXXXVI.

———, GARDINER, A. H., AND VAN DE WALLE, B. "New Light on the Ramesside Tomb-Robberies," *JEA*, XXII (1936), pp. 169-193.

DARESSY, G. "Le cercueil du roi Kamès," *ASAE*, IX (1908), pp. 61-63.

——— "Les Listes des princes du commencement de la XVIIIe Dynastie à Deir el-Médineh," pp. 283-296 in *Recueil d'études égyptologiques dédiés à la mémoire de Champollion*. Paris, 1922.

DESROCHES-NOBLECOURT, C. " 'Concubines du mort' et mères de famille au Moyen Empire," *BIFAO*, LIII (1953), pp. 7-47.

ERMAN, A. "Historische Nachlese: 2. Der König *Ḏḥwti*," *ZAS*, XXX (1892), pp. 46-47.

——— *The Literature of the Ancient Egyptians*. Translated into English by Aylward M. Blackman. London, 1927. See pp. 52-54, 132-134, 165-167, 170-172.

[1] See also the works of Gardiner, Gunn, Mace, Newberry, Säve-Söderbergh, Stock, Vandier, Weill, and Winlock listed in the preceding section.

GARDINER, A. H. "A Monument of Antef V from Coptos," *PSBA*, XXIV (1902), pp. 204-205.
GAUTHIER, H. "Deux Sphinx du moyen empire originaires d'Edfou," *ASAE*, XXXI (1931), pp. 1-6.
HABACHI, L. "Preliminary Report on the Kamose Stela and Other Inscribed Blocks Found Reused in the Foundations of Two Statues at Karnak," *ASAE*, LIII (1955), pp. 195-202.
HAMMAD, M. "Découverte d'une stèle du roi Kamose," *Chronique d'Egypte*, XXX (1955), pp. 198-208.
HARARI, I. "Portée de la stèle juridique de Karnak," *ASAE*, LI (1951), pp. 273-297.
KAMAL, M. "Gift of His Majesty King Farouk 1st (1937) to the Egyptian Museum," *ASAE*, XXXVIII (1938), pp. 1-20. See pp. 19, 20.
KEES, H. "Zu einigen Fachausdrücken der altägyptischen Provinzialverwaltung," *ZAS*, LXX (1934), pp. 83-91. See pp. 86-91.
LACAU, P. "Le roi [*Swḏd-n-rʿ Nb-ỉry-r-ȝw*]," *BIFAO*, XXX (1931), pp. 881-896.
——— "Une Stèle du roi 'Kamosis' [*Kȝ-ms*]," *ASAE*, XXXIX (1939), pp. 245-271.
——— *Une Stèle juridique de Karnak* (*Supplément aux ASAE, Cahier No. 13*). Cairo, 1949.
LANSING, A. "Excavations in the Assasîf at Thebes," *BMMA*, XII (1917), May, Supplement, pp. 7-26.
——— "Excavations in the Asasif at Thebes, Season of 1918-19," *Ibid.*, XV (1920), July, part II, pp. 11-24.
——— "Egyptian Acquisitions," *Ibid.*, XXXIII (1938), pp. 85-86.
LEFEBVRE, G. *Romans et contes égyptiens de l'époque pharaonique. Traduction avec introduction, notices et commentaire.* Paris, 1949. See pp. 131 ff.
LEIBOVITCH, J. "Description of the Scarabs Found in a Cemetery Near Tel Aviv," *ʿAtiqot: Journal of the Israel Department of Antiquities*, I (1955), pp. 13-18.
LICHTHEIM, M. "The Songs of the Harpers," *JNES*, IV (1945), pp. 178-212. See pp. 191-195.
MONTET, P. "La Stèle du roi Kamose," *Comptes rendus de l'Académie des inscriptions et belles lettres*, 1956, pp. 112-120.
MURRAY, M. A. "Queen Tety-shery," *Ancient Egypt*, 1934, pp. 6, 65-69.
NEWBERRY, P. E. "The Parentage of Queen Aah-hetep," *PSBA*, XXIV (1902), pp. 285-289.
PETRIE, W. M. F. *Koptos*. London, 1896. See pp. 9, 10, 12, 13.
——— *Diospolis Parva: The Cemeteries of Abadiyeh and Hu, 1898-9* (*The Egypt Exploration Fund*, 20th Memoir). London, 1901. See p. 52, pl. XXXII, 17.
PIRENNE, J., AND STRACMANS, M. "La Portée historique et juridique de la stèle de Karnak datée du règne de Souadj-en-Rê," *Revue internationale des droits de l'antiquité*, II (1953), pp. 25-44.
ROEDER, G. *Aegyptische Inschriften aus den Königlichen Museen zu Berlin*, II. Leipzig, 1913. See pp. 190-192, no. 1625.
SÄVE-SÖDERBERGH, T. "The Nubian Kingdom of the Second Intermediate Period," *Kush: Journal of the Sudan Antiquities Service*, IV (1956), pp. 54-61.
SEIDL, E. "Eine neue Urkunde aus Ägypten zum Prinzip der notwendigen Entgeltlichkeit," *Studi in onore di Vincenzo Arangio Ruiz* [Naples], I (1952), pp. 47-56.
SMITHER, P. C. "The Report Concerning the Slave-Girl Senbet," *JEA*, XXXIV (1948), pp. 31-34.
WAINRIGHT, G. A. "A Dagger of the Early New Kingdom," *ASAE*, XXV (1925), pp. 135-143.
WINLOCK, H. E. "On Queen Tetisheri, Grandmother of Ahmose I," *Ancient Egypt*, 1921, pp. 14-16.
——— "The Tombs of the Kings of the Seventeenth Dynasty at Thebes," *JEA*, X (1924), pp. 217-277.

23. The Pan-Grave People

BARGUET, P. "Quelques Tombes du massif nord de la nécropole de Tôd," *BIFAO*, L (1952), pp. 17-31.
BRUNTON, G. *Qau and Badari*, III (*British School of Archaeology in Egypt*, 1926). London, 1930. See pp. 3-7.
——— *Mostagedda and the Tasian Culture* (*British Museum Expedition to Middle Egypt*, 1st and 2nd Years, 1928, 1929). London, 1937. See pp. 114-133.
FIRTH, C. M. *The Archaeological Survey of Nubia Report for 1908-1909*, I. (*Ministry of Finance, Egypt: Survey of Egypt*). Cairo, 1912. See pp. 3, 15-19, 27.
GARSTANG, J. "An Ivory Sphinx from Abydos," *JEA*, XIV (1928), pp. 46-47.
JUNKER, H. *Bericht über die Grabungen der Akademie der Wissenschaften in Wien auf den Friedhöfen von el-Kubanieh-Nord, Winter 1910-1911* (*Denkschriften der Akademie der Wissenschaften in Wien*, Philologisch-historische Klasse, LXIV). Vienna and Leipzig, 1920. See pp. 30-35, 109 ff.
——— *Toschke. Bericht über die Grabungen der Akademie der Wissenschaften in Wien auf dem Friedhof von Toschke (Nubien) im Winter 1911-1912* (*Ibid.*, LXVIII). Vienna and Leipzig, 1926. See pp. 11, 12, 14, 59 n. 1, 70.
KIRWAN, L. P. Review of G. Brunton, *Mostagedda and the Tasian Culture*, in *JEA*, XXV (1939), pp. 107-109.
LEFÉBURE, E. "Le Bucrâne," *Sphinx*, X (1906), pp. 67-129.
PETRIE, W. M. F. *Diospolis Parva: The Cemeteries of Abadiyeh and Hu, 1898-9* (*The Egypt Exploration Fund*, 20th Memoir). London, 1901. See pp. 45-49, 51.
——— *Gizeh and Rifeh* (*British School of Archaeology in Egypt and Egyptian Research Account*, 13th Year). London, 1907. See pp. 20-21.
REISNER, G. A. *The Archaeological Survey of Nubia, Bulletin No. 4*. Cairo, 1909.
SÄVE-SÖDERBERGH, T. *Ägypten und Nubien: Ein Beitrag zur Geschichte altägyptischer Aussenpolitik*. Lund, 1941. See pp. 51, 130, 135-140.
WAINWRIGHT, G. A. *Balabish* (*The Egypt Exploration Society*, 37th Memoir). London, 1920.
WEIGALL, A. E. P. *A Report on the Antiquities of Lower Nubia* (*The First Cataract to the Sudan Frontier*) *and Their Condition in 1906-7* (*Egypt: Department of Antiquities*). Oxford, 1907. See pp. 25-32.

24. The Early Eighteenth Dynasty

AYRTON, E. R., CURRELLY, C. T., AND WEIGALL, A. E. P. *Abydos*, part III (*The Egypt Exploration Fund*, 25th Memoir). London, 1904. See pp. 29-38, 43-45, 54.
BARGUET, P. "L'Origine et la signification du contrepoids de collier-menat," *BIFAO*, LII (1953), pp. 103-111.
VON BISSING, F. W. *Ein thebanischer Grabfund aus dem Anfang des neuen Reichs*. Berlin, 1900.
BOTHMER, B. V. "Scarabaeus Venerabilis," *BMFA*, XLVIII (1950), pp. 86-87.
BOUSSAC, H. *Tombeaux thébains: Le tombeau d'Anna* (*MMAF*, XVIII). Paris, 1896.

BRUNTON, G. "Syrian Connections of a Composite Bow," *ASAE*, XXXVIII (1938), pp. 251-252.

CAPART, J. "La Statue d'Aménophis Ier à Turin," *Chronique d'Égypte*, XIX (1944), pp. 212-213.

——— AND OTHERS. *Fouilles de El Kab*, III. (*Fondation égyptologique Reine Élisabeth*). Brussels, 1954.

CARTER, H. "Report on the Tomb of Zeser-ka-Ra Amenhetep I, Discovered by the Earl of Carnarvon in 1914," *JEA* III (1916), pp. 147-154.

ČERNÝ, J. "Le Culte d'Aménophis Ier chez les ouvriers de la nécropole thébaine," *BIFAO*, XXVII (1927), pp. 159-203.

VON DEINES, H. " 'Das Gold der Tapferkeit,' eine militärische Auszeichnung," *ZAS*, LXXIX (1954), pp. 83-86.

DERRY, D. E. "An X-ray Examination of the Mummy of King Amenophis I," *ASAE*, XXXIV (1934), pp. 47-48.

DRIOTON, É. "Un Document sur la vie chère à Thèbes au début de la XVIIIe dynastie," *Bulletin de la Société française d'égyptologie*, 12 (February, 1953), pp. 10-19.

EBERS, G. *Papyros Ebers: Das hermetische Buch über die Arzeneimittel der alten Ägypter in hieratischer Schrift*. 2 vols. Leipzig, 1875. For other works on the medical Papyrus Ebers see *The Scepter of Egypt*, Part I, p. 371.

EDGERTON, W. F. "Critical Note on the Chronology of the Early Eighteenth Dynasty (Amenhotep I to Thutmose III)," *AJSLL*, LIII (1937), pp. 188-197.

ERMAN, A. "Zwei Aktenstücke aus der thebanischen Gräberstadt," *Sb. Berlin*, 1910, pp. 330-347. See pp. 344-347.

GARDINER, A. H. *Notes on the Story of Sinuhe*. Paris, 1916. See pp. 100-102.

HAYES, W. C. "Portrait of King Amen-ḥotpe I," *BMMA*, n. s. IV (1946-1947), pp. 140-142.

HICKMANN, H. "La Menat," *Kêmi*, XIII (1954), pp. 99-102.

KEES, H. *Die Königin Ahmes-Nefretere als Amonspriester* (*Nachrichten von der Gesellschaft der Wissenschaften zu Göttingen*, Philologisch-historische Klasse, Fachgruppe I: *Altertumswissenschaft*, n. s. II, 6). Göttingen, 1937.

——— "Das Gottesweib Ahmes-Nofretere als Amonspriester," *Orientalia*, XXIII (1954), pp. 57-63.

LANSING, A. "Excavations in the Assasîf at Thebes, *BMMA*, XII (1917), May, Supplement, pp. 6-26.

——— "Excavations at Thebes 1918-19," *Ibid.*, XV (1920), December, part II, pp. 4-12.

LEGRAIN, G. "Notes d'inspection," *ASAE*, IX (1908), pp. 54-60.

——— "Un Miracle d'Ahmès Ier à Abydos sous la règne de Ramsès II," *Ibid.*, XVI (1916), pp. 161-170.

LEIBOVITCH, J. *Le Griffon* (*Trois Communications faites à l'Institut d'Égypte*). Cairo, 1946.

——— "Le Griffon dans le Moyen-Orient antique," *ʿAtiqot: Journal of the Israel Department of Antiquities*, I (1955) pp. 75-88.

MUSTAKI, E. "An Unpublished Copper Adze-head of Ahmosis I," *ASAE*, XLV (1947), pp. 121-122.

NAVILLE, E. *The XIth Dynasty Temple at Deir el-Bahari* parts I and III (*The Egypt Exploration Fund*, 28th and 32nd Memoirs). London, 1907, 1913. See part I, pp. 60-61; part III, p. 23.

NELSON, H. H. "Certain Reliefs at Karnak and Medinet Habu and the Ritual of Amenophis I," *JNES*, VIII (1949), pp. 201-229, 310-345.

PARKER, R. A. *The Calendars of Ancient Egypt* (*The University of Chicago Oriental Institute Studies in Ancient Oriental Civilization*, No. 26). Chicago, 1950. See pp. 37 ff., §§ 188 ff.

RANDALL-MACIVER, D., AND MACE, A. C. *El Amrah and Abydos, 1899-1901* (*The Egypt Exploration Fund*, 23rd Memoir). London, 1902. See pp. 75, 76, 84.

SAUNERON, S. "La Tradition officielle relative à la XVIIIe dynastie d'après un ostracon de la Vallée des Rois," *Chronique d'Égypte*, XXVI (1951), pp. 46-49.

SCHÄFER, H. "Zwei Heldentaten des Ahmase, des Sohnes des Ebene aus Elkab," *ZAS*, LII (1914), pp. 100-103.

SETHE, K. "Das Jubiläumsbild aus dem Totentempel Amenophis' I.," *Nachrichten der Königliche Gesellschaft der Wissenschaften zu Göttingen*, Philologisch-historische Klasse, 1921, pp. 31-35.

SPIEGELBERG, W. *Zwei Beiträge zur Geschichte und Topographie der thebanischen Necropolis im neuen Reich*. Strassburg, 1898.

——— "Eine Inschrift aus dem Tempel der Ahmes-Nefret-ere," *ZAS*, XLV (1908), pp. 87-88.

WINLOCK, H. E. "A Restoration of the Reliefs from the Mortuary Temple of Amenhotep I," *JEA*, IV (1917), pp. 11-15.

——— *The Tomb of Queen Meryet-Amūn at Thebes* (*The Metropolitan Museum of Art Egyptian Expedition Publications*, VI). New York, 1932.

25. Tḥut-mosĕ I, Tḥut-mosĕ II, and Ḥat-shepsūt

ALLEN, T. G. A. "A Unique Statue of Senmut," *AJSLL*, XLIV (1927), pp. 49-55.

BALLARD, G. A. "The Egyptian Obelisk Lighter," *The Mariner's Mirror*, XXXIII (1947), pp. 158-164. See also *Ibid.*, XXVII (1941), pp. 290-306.

BARAIZE, E. "Rapport sur l'enlèvement et le transport du sarcophage de la reine Hatchopsitou," *ASAE*, XXI (1921), pp. 175-182.

BARGUET, P. "Une Statuette de Senenmout au Musée du Louvre," *Chronique d'Égypte*, XXVIII (1953), pp. 23-27.

VON BISSING, F. W. *Die Baugeschichte des südlichen Tempels von Buhen (bei Wadi Halfa)* (*Sitzungsberichte der Bayerischen Akademie der Wissenschaften*, Philologisch-historische Klasse, 1942, IX). Munich, 1942.

——— "Pyene (Punt) und die Seefahrten der Ägypter," *Die Welt des Orients*, III (1948), pp. 146-157.

——— "Baumeister und Bauten aus dem Beginn des Neuen Reichs," *Studi scritti in onore di Ippolito Rosellini* [Pisa], I (1949), pp. 127-234.

BORCHARDT, L. *Zur Baugeschichte des Amonstempels von Karnak* (*Unters.*, V, 1). Leipzig, 1912.

BRUYÈRE, B. *Deir el Médineh, année 1926: Sondage au temple funéraire de Thotmès II (Hat Ankh Shesept)* (*Rapport sur les FIFAO*, IV, 4). Cairo, 1952.

BULL, L. "A Group of Egyptian Antiquities," *BMMA*, XXVII (1932), pp. 130-134.

CARTER, H. "Report upon the Tomb of Sen-nefer Found at Biban el-Molouk near that of Thotmes III No. 34," *ASAE*, II (1901), pp. 196-200.

——— "A Tomb prepared for Queen Hatshepsuit and Other Recent Discoveries at Thebes," *JEA*, IV (1917), pp. 107-118.

DARESSY, G. "La Chapelle d'Uazmès," *ASAE*, I (1900), pp. 97-108.

Davies, N. de G. "The Tomb of Senmen, Brother of Senmut," *PSBA*, XXXV (1913), pp. 282-285.

Davis, T. M., Naville, E., and Carter, H. *The Tomb of Hâtshopsîtû* (*Theodore M. Davis' Excavations: Bibân el Molûk*). London, 1906.

Drioton, É. "Deux Cryptogrammes de Senenmout," *ASAE*, XXXVIII (1938), pp. 231-246.

Edgerton, W. F. *The Thutmosid Succession* (*The University of Chicago Oriental Institute Studies in Ancient Oriental Civilization*, No. 8). Chicago, 1933.

Engelbach, R. *The Problem of the Obelisks; from a Study of the Unfinished Obelisk at Aswan*. New York, 1923.

Fairman, H. W., and Grdseloff, B. "Texts of Ḥatshepsut and Sethos I inside Speos Artemidos," *JEA*, XXXIII (1947), pp. 12-33.

Fakhry, A. "A New Speos from the Reign of Hatshepsut and Tuthmosis III at Beni-Ḥasan," *ASAE*, XXXIX (1939), pp. 709-723.

Faulkner, R. O. "Egyptian Seagoing Ships," *JEA*, XXVI (1940), pp. 3-9.

Gardiner, A. H. "Davies's Copy of the Great Speos Artemidos Inscription," *JEA*, XXXII (1946), pp. 43-56.

Gilbert, P. "Le Sens des portraits intacts d'Hatshepsout à Deir-el-Bahari," *Chronique d'Egypte*, XXVIII (1953), pp. 219-222.

Grébaut, E. *Le Musée égyptien: Recueil de monuments et de notices sur les fouilles d'Egypte*, I (*Ministère des travaux publiques*). Cairo, 1890-1900.

Habachi, L. "Two Graffiti at Sehēl from the Reign of Queen Hatshepsut," *JNES*, XVI (1957), pp. 88-104.

Hall, H. R. "The Statues of Sennemut and Menkheperrēʿsenb in the British Museum," *JEA*, XIV (1928), pp. 1-2.

Hayes, W. C. *Royal Sarcophagi of the XVIII Dynasty* (*Princeton Monographs in Art and Archaeology:* Quarto Series XIX). Princeton, 1935.

—— "The Tomb of Nefer-khēwet and His Family," *BMMA*, XXX (1935), November, sect. II, pp. 17-36.

—— *Ostraka and Name Stones from the Tomb of Sen-mūt* (*No. 71*) *at Thebes* (*The Metropolitan Museum of Art Egyptian Expedition Publications*, XV). New York, 1942.

—— "Recent Additions to the Egyptian Collection," *BMMA*, n. s. VII (1948-1949), pp. 60-63.

—— "The Sarcophagus of Sennemūt," *JEA*, XXXVI (1950), pp. 19-23.

—— "Varia from the Time of Hatshepsut," *Mitt. Kairo*, XV (1957), pp. 78-90.

Helck, H. W. *Der Einfluss der Militärführer in der 18. ägyptischen Dynastie* (*Unters.*, XIV). Leipzig, 1939.

—— "Die Berufung des Vezirs *Wśr*," pp. 107-117 in *Ägyptologische Studien Hermann Grapow zum 70. Geburtstag gewidmet* (*Deutsche Akademie der Wissenschaften zu Berlin, Institut für Orientforschung, Veröffentlichung* 29). Berlin, 1955.

Hölscher, U., and Anthes, R. *The Excavations of Medinet Habu*, II: *The Temples of the Eighteenth Dynasty* (*The University of Chicago Oriental Institute Publications*, XLI). Chicago, 1939.

Kuentz, C. *Obélisques* (*CCG*, nos. 1308-1315, 17001-17036). Cairo, 1932.

Lacau, P. "Sur un des Blocs de la reine [*Mɜʿt-kɜ-Rʿ*] provenant du IIIe pylône de Karnak," *ASAE*, XXVI (1926), pp. 131-138.

Lacau, P., *continued*

—— "La Chapelle rouge d'Hatshepsowet (Sanctuaire de la Barque) au temple de Karnak," *Annuaire du Collège de France*, XL (1943), pp. 79-81, 99-102.

—— "Deux Magasins à encens du temple de Karnak," *ASAE*, LII (1952), pp. 185-198.

—— "Sur la reine Hatshepsēwe," *Revue de l'histoire des religions*, CXLIII (1953), pp. 1-7.

Lansing, A., and Hayes, W. C. "The Museum's Excavations at Thebes," *BMMA*, XXXII (1937), January, sect. II, pp. 4-39.

Legrain, G., and Naville, É. "L'Aile nord du pylône d'Aménophis III à Karnak," *Annales du Musée Guimet*, XXX (1902), pp. 1-22.

Marx, E. "Egyptian Shipping of the Eighteenth and Nineteenth Dynasties," *The Mariner's Mirror*, XXXII (1946), pp. 21-34.

Mond, Sir Robert, and Myers, O. H. *Temples of Armant: A Preliminary Survey*. 2 vols. London, 1940.

Naville, E. *The Temple of Deir el Bahari* (*The Egypt Exploration Fund*, 12th-14th, 16th, 19th, 27th, 29th Memoirs) 7 vols. London, 1894-1908.

—— *The XIth Dynasty Temple at Deir el-Bahari* (*Ibid.*, 28th, 30th, and 32nd Memoirs). 3 vols. London, 1907-1913.

Newberry, P. E. "Extracts from My Notebooks," nos. 6, 9, 18, 32, 33, 60, *PSBA*, XXII (1900), XXIV (1902), XXVII (1905), *passim*.

—— "A Statue of Hapu-seneb: Vezîr of Thothmes II," *Ibid.*, XXII (1900), pp. 31-36.

—— "Notes on Seagoing Ships," *JEA*, XXVIII (1942), pp. 64-66.

Randall-MacIver, D., and Woolley, C. L. *Buhen* (*University of Pennsylvania. Egyptian Department of the University Museum. Eckley B. Coxe Junior Expedition to Nubia*, VII, VIII). Philadelphia, 1911.

Ricke, H. "Ein Tempel mit Pfeilerumgang Thutmoses' III und Hatschepsuts in Karnak," *ASAE*, XXXVII (1937), pp. 71-78.

—— "Der Tempel 'Lepsius 16' in Karnak: Grabungsvorbericht," *Ibid.*, XXXVIII (1938), pp. 357-368.

—— *Das Kamutef-Heiligtum Hatschepsut's und Thutmoses' III in Karnak: Bericht über eine Ausgrabung vor dem Muttempelbezirk* (*Beiträge zur ägyptischen Bauforschung und Altertumskunde*, III, 2). Cairo, 1954.

Säve-Söderbergh, T. *The Navy of the Eighteenth Egyptian Dynasty* (*Uppsala Universitets Årsskrift* 1946: 6). Uppsala, 1946.

Scharff, A. "Zwei Rundbildwerke der Königin Hatschepsut," *Berliner Museen, Berichte aus den preussischen Kunstsammlungen*, LII (1931), pp. 28-34.

Schott, S. "Zum Krönungstag der Königin Hatschepsût," *Nachrichten der Akademie der Wissenschaften in Göttingen*, I, Philologisch-historische Klasse, 1955, No. 6, pp. 195-219.

Schweinfurth, G. "Neue thebanische Gräberfunde," *Sphinx*, III (1900), pp. 103-107.

Sethe, K. "Ein bisher unbeachtet gebliebene Episode der Puntexpedition der Königin Hatschepsowet," *ZÄS*, XLII (1905), pp. 91-99.

—— *Das Hatschepsut-Problem noch einmal untersucht*, (*Abh. Berlin*, 1932, No. 4). Berlin, 1932.

Smith, W. S. "Two Fragments from Hatshepsut's Karnak Obelisk," *BMFA*, XL (1942), pp. 45-48.

Sølver, C. V. "The Egyptian Obelisk-Ships," *The Mari-*

ner's Mirror, XXVI (1940), pp. 237-256; XXXIII (1947), pp. 39-43.

TYLOR, J. J. *Wall Drawings and Monuments of El Kab. The Tomb of Paheri* (*The Egypt Exploration Fund*). London, 1895.

VARILLE, A. "Quelques Notes sur le sanctuaire axial du grand temple d'Amon à Karnak," *ASAE*, L (1950), pp. 127-135.

——— "Description sommaire du sanctuaire oriental d'Amon-Rê à Karnak," *Ibid.*, pp. 137-172.

——— AND ROBICHON, C. "Quatre Nouveaux Temples thébains," *Chronique d'Égypte*, X (1935), pp. 237-242.

WERBROUCK, M. *Le Temple d'Hatshepsout à Deir el Bahari* (*Fondation égyptologique Reine Élisabeth*). Brussels, 1949.

——— "Une Tête royale égyptienne: Hatshepsout," p. 81 in *Actes du XXIe Congrès international des orientalistes*, July 23-31, 1948. Paris, 1949.

WINLOCK, H. E. "Excavations at Thebes," *BMMA*, XVII (1922), December, part II, pp. 19-49.

——— "The Egyptian Expedition," 1925-1931, *Ibid.*, XXIII-XXVI (1928-1932), *passim*.

——— "A Granite Sphinx of Ḥat-shepsūt," *Ibid.*, XXX (1935), pp. 159-160.

——— "Notes on the Reburial of Tuthmosis I," *JEA*, XV (1929), pp. 56-68.

26. Thut-mosĕ III, Amun-ḥotpe II, and Thut-mosĕ IV

ALT, A. "Das Stützpunktsystem der Pharaonen an der phönikischen Küste und im syrischen Binnenland," *Beiträge zur biblischen Landes- und Altertumskunde*, LXVIII, 2 (1950), pp. 97-133.

——— "Neue Berichte über Feldzüge des Neuen Reiches nach Palästina," *Zeitschrift des Deutschen Palästina-Vereins*, LXX (1954), pp. 33-75.

BADAWI, A. M. "Die neue historische Stele Amenophis' II," *ASAE*, XLII (1943), pp. 1-23.

——— *Memphis als zweite Landeshauptstadt im Neuen Reich*. Cairo, 1947.

BADAWY, A. "A Collection of Foundation-Deposits of Tuthmosis III," *ASAE*, XLVII (1947), pp. 145-156.

BANNISTER, F. A., AND PLENDERLEITH, H. J. "Physico-chemical Examination of a Scarab of Tuthmosis IV bearing the Name of the God Aten," *JEA*, XXII (1936), pp. 3-6.

BARGUET, P. "L'Obélisque de Saint-Jean-de-Latran dans le temple de Ramsès II à Karnak," *ASAE*, L (1950), pp. 269-280.

——— "La Structure du temple Ipet-sout d'Amon à Karnak du Moyen-Empire à Aménophis II," *BIFAO*, LII (1953), pp. 145-155.

BOTHMER, B. V. "Membra dispersa. King Amenhotep II Making an Offering," *BMFA* LII (1954), 287, pp. 11-20.

BREASTED, J. H. *A New Chapter in the Life of Thutmose III* (*Unters.*, II, 2). Leipzig, 1900.

BUCHER, P. *Les Textes des tombes de Thoutmosis III et d'Aménophis II* (*MIFAO*, LX). Cairo, 1932.

BULL, L. "Two Egyptian Osirid Figures," *BMMA*, XXV (1930), pp. 164-166.

CARTER, H. "Report on the Robbery of the Tomb of Amenothes II, Biban el Moluk," *ASAE*, III (1902), pp. 115-120.

———, AND NEWBERRY, P. E. *The Tomb of Thoutmôsis IV* (*CCG*, nos. 46001-46529). London, 1904.

———, NEWBERRY, P. E., AND MASPERO, G. *The Tomb of Thoutmôsis IV* (*Theodore M. Davis' Excavations: Bibân el Molûk*). London, 1904.

C[ARTLAND], B. M. "The Dress of the Ancient Egyptians. II. In the Empire," *BMMA*, XI (1916), pp. 211-214.

CHRISTOPHE, L.-A. "Notes géographiques à propos des campagnes de Thoutmosis III," *Revue d'égyptologie*, VI (1950), pp. 89-114.

DARESSY, G. *Fouilles de la Vallée des Rois (1898-1899)* (*CCG*, nos. 24001-24990). Cairo, 1902.

DAVIES, N. DE G. "The King as Sportsman," *BMMA*, XXX (1935), November, sect. II, pp. 49-53.

——— *The Tomb of Rekh-mi-Rēʿ at Thebes* (*The Metropolitan Museum of Art Egyptian Expedition Publications*, XI). 2 vols. New York, 1943.

DESROCHES-NOBLECOURT, C. "Nouveaux Commentaires sur l'obélisque de Saint-Jean de Latran," *Revue archéologique*, XXXVII (1951), pp. 5-13.

DRIOTON, É. "Voeux inscrits sur des scarabées," *Mitt. Kairo*, XIV (1956), pp. 34-41.

DUNHAM, D. "A Fragment from the Mummy Wrappings of Tuthmosis III," *JEA*, XVII (1931), pp. 209-210.

EDEL, E. "Die Stelen Amenophis' II. aus Karnak und Memphis mit dem Bericht über die asiatischen Feldzüge des Königs," *Zeitschrift des Deutschen Palästina-Vereins*, LXIX (1953), pp. 97-176.

ENGELBACH, R. "The Obelisks of Pylon VII at Karnak," *Ancient Egypt*, 1923, pp. 60-62.

ERMAN, A. "Die Sphinxstele," *Sb. Berlin*, 1904, pp. 428-444.

FAIRMAN, H. W. "Preliminary Report[s] on the Excavations at ʿAmārah West, Anglo-Egyptian Sudan," 1938-1939 and 1947-1948, *JEA*, XXV (1939), pp. 139-144; XXXIV (1948), pp. 3-11.

FAKHRY, A. "The Funerary Temple of Tuthmosis III," *ASAE*, XXXVII (1937), pp. 27-30.

FAULKNER, R. O. "Egyptian Military Standards," *JEA*, XXVII (1941), pp. 12-18.

——— "The Battle of Megiddo," *Ibid.*, XXVIII (1942), pp. 2-15.

——— "The Euphrates Campaign of Tuthmosis III," *Ibid.*, XXXII (1946), pp. 39-42.

——— "The Installation of the Vizier," *Ibid.*, XLI (1955), pp. 18-29.

GARDINER, A. H. "The Installation of a Vizier," *Rec. trav.*, XXVI (1904), pp. 1-19.

——— "The Autobiography of Rekhmerēʿ," *ZAS*, LX (1925), pp. 62-76.

——— "Tuthmosis III Returns Thanks to Amūn," *JEA*, XXXVIII (1952), pp. 6-23.

——— "Blocks from the Temple of Tuthmosis III at Armant," *Studi scritti in onore di Ippolito Rosellini* [Pisa], II (1955), pp. 91-98.

GAUTHIER, H. *Le Temple d'Amada* (*Service des antiquités de l'Égypte. Les Temples immergés de la Nubie*). Cairo, 1913.

GILBERT, P. "Le Temple d'Aménophis II à Karnak," *Chronique d'Égypte*, X (1935), pp. 233-236.

GLANVILLE, S. R. K. "Records of a Royal Dockyard of the Time of Tuthmosis III: Papyrus British Museum 10056," *ZAS*, LXVI (1931), pp. 105-121; LXVIII (1932), pp. 7-41.

Grapow, H. *Studien zu den Annalen Thutmosis des Dritten und zu ihnen verwandten historischen Berichten des Neuen Reiches* (*Abhandlungen der Deutschen Akademie der Wissenschaften*, Philologisch-historische Klasse, 1947, 2). Berlin, 1949.

Habachi, L. "An Inscription at Aswān Referring to Six Obelisks," *JEA*, XXXVI (1950), pp. 13-18.

Hassan, S. "The Great Limestone Stela of Amenḥotep II," *ASAE*, XXXVII (1937), pp. 129-134.

——— "A Representation of the Solar Disk with Human Hands and Arms and the Form of Horus of Beḥdet, as Seen on the Stela of Amenhetep IInd in the Mud-brick Temple at Giza," *Ibid.*, XXXVIII (1938), pp. 53-61.

Hayes, W. C. "A Statue of the Herald Yamu-nedjeḥ in the Egyptian Museum, Cairo, and Some Biographical Notes on Its Owner," *ASAE*, XXXIII (1933), pp. 6-16.

——— *Royal Sarcophagi of the XVIII Dynasty* (*Princeton Monographs in Art and Archaeology:* Quarto Series, XIX). Princeton, 1935.

Helck, W. "Eine Stele des Vizekönigs *Wśr-Śt·t*," *JNES*, XIV (1955), pp. 22-31.

——— *Urkunden der 18. Dynastie*, 17-19 (*Urkunden des ägyptischen Altertums*, IV). Berlin, 1955-1957.

Junker, H. "The First Appearance of the Negroes in History," *JEA*, VII (1921), pp. 121-132.

Komorzynski, E. "Über die soziale Stellung des altägyptischen Soldaten," *ASAE*, LI (1951), pp. 111-112.

Lansing, A. "Two Imitation Stone Vases of the XVIII Dynasty," *BMMA*, XXXVI (1941), pp. 140-141.

Loret, V. "Le Tombeau de Thoutmès III à Biban-el-Molouk," *Bulletin de l'Institut égyptien*, 3rd Series, IX (1899), pp. 91-97.

——— "Le Tombeau d'Aménophis II et la cachette royale de Biban-el-Molouk," *Ibid.*, pp. 98-112.

Mond, R., and Myers, O. H. *Temples of Armant: A Preliminary Survey* (*The Egypt Exploration Society*). 2 vols. London, 1940.

Müller, H. W. "Ein ägyptischer Königskopf des 15. Jahrhunderts v. Chr.: Ein Beitrag zur Stilentwicklung der Plastik der 18. Dynastie," *Münchner Jahrbuch der bildenden Kunst*, 3rd series, III/IV (1952/53), pp. 67-84.

Nagel, G. "Le Linceul de Thoutmès III. Cairo, Cat. No. 40.001," *ASAE*, XLIX (1949), pp. 317-329.

Nelson, H. H. *The Battle of Megiddo*. Chicago, 1913.

Newberry, P. E. "Extracts from My Notebooks," nos. 4, 5, 19, 20, 32 (c) (g), 35, 40, 48, 53, 54, *PSBA*, XXI, XXII, XXIV, XXV (1899, 1900, 1902, 1903), *passim*.

——— "A Glass Chalice of Tuthmosis III," *JEA*, VI (1920), pp. 155-160.

Noth, M. "Die Wege der Pharaonenheere in Palästina und Syrien: Untersuchungen zu den hieroglyphischen Listen palästinscher und syrischer Städte, III. Der Aufbau der Palästinaliste Thutmoses III," *Zeitschrift des Deutschen Palästina-Vereins*, LXI (1938), pp. 26-65.

——— "Die Annalen Thutmoses III als Geschichtsquelle," *Ibid.*, LXVI (1943), pp. 156-174.

Parker, R. A. "The Lunar Dates of Thutmose III and Ramesses II," *JNES*, XVI (1957), pp. 39-43.

Peet, T. E. "Egypt, the Imperialism of the Eighteenth Dynasty," pp. 21-81 in *Great Events in History*. London, 1934.

Petrie, W. M. F. *Six Temples at Thebes*. London, 1897.

Phillips, D. W. "Fish Tales and Fancies," *BMMA*, n. s. II (1944-1945), pp. 184-189.

R[ansom], C. L. "A Commemorative Scarab of Thutmose III," *BMMA*, X (1915), pp. 46-47.

Reisner, G. A. "The Barkal Temples in 1916," *JEA*, IV (1917), pp. 213-227; V (1918), pp. 99-112; VI (1920), pp. 247-264.

——— and Reisner, M. B. "Inscribed Monuments from Gebel Barkal. Part 2. The Granite Stela of Thutmosis III," *ZAS*, LXIX (1933), pp. 24-39.

Ricke, H. *Der Totentempel Thutmoses' III. Baugeschichtliche Untersuchungen* (*Beiträge zur ägyptischen Bauforschung und Altertumskunde*, III, 1). Cairo, 1939.

Säve-Söderbergh, T. *Four Eighteenth Dynasty Tombs* (*Private Tombs at Thebes*, I). Oxford, 1957.

Schäfer, H. "König Amenophis II als Meisterschütz," *Orientalische Literaturzeitung*, XXXII (1929), cols. 233-244.

Scott, N. E. "Egyptian Accessions," *BMMA*, n. s. VI (1947-1948), pp. 62-65.

Sethe, K. "Eine ägyptische Expedition nach dem Libanon im 15. Jahrhundert v. Chr.," *Sb. Berlin*, 1906, pp. 356-363.

——— *Die Einsetzung des Veziers unter der 18. Dynastie. Inschrift im Grabe des Rēch-mi-reʿ zu Schech Abd el Gurna* (*Unters.*, V, 2). Leipzig, 1909.

——— "Zur ältesten Geschichte des ägyptischen Seeverkehrs mit Byblos und dem Libanongebiet," *ZAS*, XLV (1908), pp. 7-14.

Shorter, A. W. "Historical Scarabs of Tuthmosis IV and Amenophis III," *JEA*, XVII (1931), pp. 23-25.

Spiegelberg, W. "Ein Gerichtsprotokoll aus der Zeit Thutmosis' IV," *ZAS*, LXIII (1928), pp. 105-115.

Varille, A. "La Grande Stèle d'Aménophis II à Giza," *BIFAO*, XLI (1942), pp. 31-38.

Virollaud, C. "L'Egypte et la Syrie au temps de la XVIIIe dynastie pharaonique (1580-1320)," *L'Ethnographie*, n. s. 45 (1947-1950) [Paris, 1952], pp. 3-16.

van de Walle, B. "Les Rois sportifs de l'ancienne Égypte," *Chronique d'Égypte*, XIII (1938), pp. 234-257.

Weigall, A. E. P. "A Report on the Excavation of the Funeral Temple of Thoutmosis III at Gourneh," *ASAE*, VII (1906), pp. 121-141; VIII (1907), p. 286.

Winlock, H. E. *The Treasure of Three Egyptian Princesses* (*The Metropolitan Museum of Art. Publications of the Department of Egyptian Art*, X). New York, 1948.

——— "Ancient Egyptian Kerchiefs," *BMMA*, XI (1916), pp. 238-242.

Wolf, W. "Zwei Beiträge zur Geschichte der 18. Dynastie," *ZAS*, LXV (1930), pp. 98-102.

Yeivin, S. "Canaanite and Hittite Strategy in the Second Half of the Second Millennium B.C.," *JNES*, IX (1950), pp. 101-107.

Yoyotte, J. "Un Porche doré: La Porte du IVe pylône au grand temple de Karnak," *Chronique d'Égypte*, XXVIII (1953), pp. 28-38.

27. The Reign of Amun-ḥotpe III

Aldred, C. "Amenophis Redivivus," *BMMA*, n. s. XIV (1955-1956), pp. 114-121.

Barguet, P. "La Reconstitution par Cl. Robichon d'une statue d'Aménophis III à Karnak-Nord," *Bulletin de la Société française d'égyptologie*, 12 (February, 1953), pp. 41-42.

von Bissing, F. W. "Die blauäugige Königin Teje," *ZAS*, LXXIII (1937), pp. 123-124.

Borchardt, L. "Zur Geschichte des Luqsortempels," *ZAS*, XXXIV (1896), pp. 122-138.

BORCHARDT, L., *continued*

——— *Der Porträtkopf der Königin Teje. Ausgrabungen der Deutschen Orient-Gesellschaft in Tell el-Amarna*, I (*18. Wissenschaftliche Veröffentlichung der Deutschen Orient-Gesellschaft*). Leipzig, 1911.

BOSSE-GRIFFITHS, K. "The Memphite Stela of Merptaḥ and Ptaḥmosĕ," *JEA*, XLI (1955), pp. 56-63.

BOTHMER, B. V. "Two Heads of the New Kingdom," *BMFA*, XLVII (1949), pp. 42-49.

BULL, L. "A Group of Egyptian Antiquities," *BMMA*, XXVII (1932), pp. 130-134.

CAPART, J. "Statuettes funéraires égyptiennes," *Chronique d'Égypte*, XVI (1941), pp. 196-204.

CASSIRER, M. "A *ḥb-sd* Stela of Amenophis III," *JEA*, XXXVIII (1952), pp. 128-130.

CHASSINAT, É. "Une Tombe inviolée de la XVIIIe Dynastie découverte aux environs de Médinet el-Gorab dans le Fayoûm," *BIFAO*, I (1901), pp. 225-234.

——— "Une Statuette d'Aménothès III," *Ibid.*, VII (1910), pp. 169-172.

CLARK, C. R. "Costume Jewelry in Egypt in the XVIII Dynasty," *BMMA*, n. s. VIII (1949-1950), pp. 154-156.

DARESSY, G. "Le Palais d'Aménophis III et le Birket Habou," *ASAE*, IV (1903), pp. 165-170.

——— "Les Costumes d'Aménôthès III," *BIFAO*, XI (1914), pp. 25-28.

DAVIES, N. DE G. *The Tomb of the Vizier Ramose* (*Mond Excavations at Thebes*, I). London, 1941.

DAVIS, T. M., MASPERO, G., AND NEWBERRY, P. E. *The Tomb of Iouiya and Touiyou* (*Theodore M. Davis' Excavations: Bibân el Molûk*). London, 1907.

DORESSE, M. AND J. "Le Culte d'Aton sous la XVIIIe dynastie avant le schisme amarnien," *Journal asiatique*, CCXXXIII (1941-1942), pp. 181-199.

DRIOTON, E. "Notes diverses. 15. Deux scarabées commémoratifs d'Aménophis III," *ASAE*, XLV (1947), pp. 85-92.

EDWARDS, I. E. S. "The Prudhoe Lions," *Annals of Archaeology and Anthropology* (*University of Liverpool*), XXVI (1939), pp. 3-9.

ENGELBACH, R. "Material for a Revision of the History of the Heresy Period of the XVIIIth Dynasty," *ASAE*, XL (1940), pp. 133-165.

——— "A 'Kirgipa' Commemorative Scarab of Amenophis III presented by His Majesty King Farouk I to the Cairo Museum," *Ibid.*, XL (1941), pp. 659-661.

——— AND MACALDIN, J. W. "The Great Lake of Amenophis III at Medînet Habu," *Bulletin de l'Institut d'Égypte*, XX (1938), pp. 51-61.

ERMAN, A. "Neues aus den Tafeln von el Amarna," *ZÄS*, XXVIII (1890), p. 112.

FAKHRY, A. "A Note on the Tomb of Kheruef at Thebes," *ASAE*, XLII (1943), pp. 447-508.

FAULKNER, R. O. "A Possible Royal Visit to Punt," *Studi scritti in onore di Ippolito Rosellini* [Pisa], II (1955), pp. 84-90.

GARDINER, A. H. "Four Papyri of the 18th Dynasty from Kahun," *ZÄS*, XLIII (1906), pp. 27-47.

——— "Three Engraved Plaques in the Collection of the Earl of Carnarvon," *JEA*, III (1916), pp. 73-75.

GARNOT, J. STE.-F. "Notes on the Inscriptions of Suty and Ḥor (British Museum Stela No. 826)," *JEA*, XXXV (1949), pp. 63-68.

GAUTHIER, H. "Les Statues thébaines de la déesse Sakhmet," *ASAE*, XIX (1920), pp. 177-207; XXVI (1926), pp. 95-96.

GAYET, A. *Le Temple de Louxor. Constructions d'Aménophis III* (*MMAF*, XV, 1). Paris, 1894.

GLANVILLE, S. R. K. "Amenophis III and His Successors in the XVIIIth Dynasty," pp. 105-139 in Brunton, W., *Great Ones of Ancient Egypt*. London, 1929.

——— "Some Notes on Material for the Reign of Amenophis III," *JEA*, XV (1929), pp. 2-8.

GRIFFITH, F. LL. "Stela in Honour of Amenophis III and Taya from Tell el-ʿAmarnah," *JEA*, XII (1926), pp. 1-2.

GUENTCH-OGLOUEFF, M. "Le Culte solaire sous la XVIIIe dynastie avant le schisme amarnien," *Journal asiatique*, CCXXXIV (1943-1945), pp. 414-415.

HAYES, W. C. "A Writing-palette of the Chief Steward Amenḥotpe and Some Notes on Its Owner," *JEA*, XXIV (1938), pp. 9-24.

——— *The Burial Chamber of the Treasurer Sobk-mosĕ from er Rizeiḳât* (*The Metropolitan Museum of Art, Papers*, No. 9). New York, 1939.

——— "Minor Art and Family History in the Reign of Amun-ḥotpe III," *BMMA*, n. s. VI (1947-1948), pp. 272-279.

——— "La 37e et la 38e Année de règne d'Aménophis III," *Chronique d'Égypte*, XXIV (1949), p. 96.

——— "Inscriptions from the Palace of Amenhotep III," *JNES*, X (1951), pp. 35-56, 82-111, 156-183, 231-242.

HELCK, H.-W. *Der Einfluss der Militärführer in der 18. ägyptischen Dynastie* (*Unters.*, XIV). Leipzig, 1939.

——— "Die Sinai-Inschrift des Amenmose," *Mitteilungen des Instituts für Orientforschung*, II (1954), pp. 189-207.

——— "Inhaber und Bauleiter des thebanischen Grabs 107," *Ibid.*, IV (1956), pp. 11-26.

——— *Urkunden der 18. Dynastie*, 20, 21 (*Urkunden des ägyptischen Altertums*). *Historische Inschriften Amenophis' III.* Berlin, 1957, 1958.

KEES, H. "Ein Onkel Amenophis' IV. Hoherpriester von Heliopolis?" *ZÄS*, LIII (1917), pp. 81-83.

KNUDTZON, J. A. *Die el-Amarna-Tafeln* (*Vorderasiatische Bibliothek*). 2 vols. Leipzig, 1908, 1915.

KOMORZYNSKI, E. "Eine ḥb-sd-Stele Amenophis' III," *Archiv für ägyptische Archäologie*, I (1938), p. 170; *Archiv für Orientforschung*, XVII (1954-1955), p. 48.

LACAU, P. "Le plan du temple de Louxor," *Mémoires de l'Institut national de France* (*Académie des inscriptions et belles-lettres*), XLIII, 2 (1951), pp. 77-92.

LANSING, A. "Excavations at the Palace of Amenhotep III at Thebes," *BMMA*, XIII (1918), March, Supplement, pp. 8-14.

——— "Accessions to the Egyptian Collection," *Ibid.*, XXIII (1928), pp. 158-160.

——— "A Commemorative Scarab of Amen-ḥotpe III," *Ibid.*, XXXI (1936), pp. 12-14.

——— "An Eighteenth Dynasty Lady," *Ibid.*, n. s. I (1942-1943), pp. 266-270.

LEIBOVITCH, J. "Une Nouvelle Représentation d'une sphinge de la reine Tiy," *ASAE*, XLII (1943), pp. 93-105.

——— La Sphinge (*Deux Communications faites à l'Institut d'Égypte*). Cairo, 1947.

LYTHGOE, A. M. "Statues of the Goddess Sekhmet," *BMMA*, XIV (1919), October, part II.

MACADAM, M. F. L. *The Temples of Kawa* (*The Griffith Institute, Oxford Excavations in Nubia*). 2 parts (4 vols.). London, 1949, 1955.

MEKHITARIAN, A. "Statues d'Aménophis III?" *Chronique d'Égypte*, XXXI (1956), pp. 296-298.

MERCER, S. A. B. *The Tell el-Amarna Tablets.* 2 vols. Toronto, 1939.

MÖLLER, G. "Das Dekret des Amenophis, des Sohnes des Hapu," *Sb. Berlin*, 1910, pp. 932-948.

MORET, A. "La Dédicace du temple d'Aménophis III à Louxor," pp. 119-121 in *Studies Presented to F. Ll. Griffith* (*The Egypt Exploration Society*). London, 1932.

NEWBERRY, P. E. "Extracts from My Notebooks," nos. 3, 14, 15, 21, 31, 56, 63, *PSBA*, XXI-XXV (1899-1903), XXVII (1905), *passim.*

——— "The Sons of Tuthmosis IV," *JEA*, XIV (1928), pp. 82-85.

PENDLEBURY, J. D. S. *Tell el-Amarna.* London, 1935. See pp. 1-21.

PHILLIPS, D. W. "Cosmetic Spoons in the Form of Swimming Girls," *BMMA*, XXXVI (1941), pp. 173-175.

QUIBELL, J. E. *Tomb of Yuaa and Thuiu* (*CCG*, nos. 51001-51191). Cairo, 1908.

RANKE, H. "Ištar als Heilgöttin in Ägypten," pp. 412-418 in *Studies Presented to F. Ll. Griffith* (*The Egypt Exploration Society*). London, 1932.

REISNER, G. A. "Inscribed Monuments from Gebel Barkal," *ZAS*, LXVI (1931), p. 81.

ROBICHON, C., AND VARILLE, A. *Le Temple du scribe royal Amenhotep, fils de Hapou*, I (*FIFAO*, XI). Cairo, 1936.

SÄVE-SÖDERBERGH, T. *Four Eighteenth Dynasty Tombs* (*Private Tombs at Thebes*, I). Oxford, 1957.

SCHÄFER, H. "Die angebliche Basilikenhalle des Tempels von Luksor," *ZAS*, LXI (1926), pp. 52-57.

——— "Das Simonsche Holzköpfchen der Königin Teje," *ZAS*, LXVIII (1932), pp. 81-86.

SCHROEDER, O. *Die Tontafeln von el-Amarna* (*Vorderasiatische Schriftdenkmäler der Königlichen Museen zu Berlin*, XI, XII). Leipzig, 1914, 1915.

SCOTT, N. E. "Recent Additions to the Egyptian Collection," *BMMA*, n. s. XIV (1955-1956), pp. 79-92.

SETHE, K. "Amenhotep, der Sohn des Hapu," *Aegyptiaca* (*Festschrift für Georg Ebers*), pp. 107-116. Leipzig, 1897.

SPIEGELBERG, W. "Die Inschriften des grossen Skarabäus in Karnak," *ZAS*, LXVI (1931), pp. 44-45.

TYTUS, R. DE P. *A Preliminary Report on the Re-excavation of the Palace of Amenhetep III.* New York, 1903.

VARILLE, A. "L'Inscription dorsale du colosse méridional de Memnon," *ASAE*, XXXIII (1933), pp. 85-94; XXXIV (1934), pp. 9-16.

——— "Nouvelles Listes géographiques d'Aménophis III à Karnak," *Ibid.*, XXXVI (1936), pp. 202-214.

——— "Le Tombeau thébain du vice-roi de Nubie Merimes," *Ibid.*, XL (1941), pp. 567-570.

——— "Une Statue de Ptahmôse, grand prêtre d'Amon sous Aménophis III," *Ibid.*, pp. 645-648.

——— "Toutankhamon, est-il fils d'Aménophis III et de Satamon?" *Ibid.*, pp. 651-657.

——— "L'Hymne au soleil des architectes d'Aménophis III Souti et Hor," *BIFAO*, XLI (1942), pp. 25-30.

——— "Les Trois Sarcophages du Fils Royal Merimes," *ASAE*, XLV (1947), pp. 1-15.

WHITE, H. G. E. "The Egyptian Expedition 1914-15. II. Excavations at Thebes," *BMMA*, X (1915), pp. 253-256.

WIEDEMANN, K. A. "Die Uschebti-Formel Amenophis' III," *Sphinx*, XVI (1912), pp. 33-54.

WINLOCK, H. E. "The Work of the Egyptian Expedition," *BMMA*, VII (1912), pp. 184-189.

WINLOCK, H. E., *continued*

——— "A Scarab of Amen-ḥotpe III," *Ibid.*, XXVII (1932), p. 236.

DE WIT, C. "Un Scarabée commémorant la chasse aux lions d'Aménothès III (E. 2368)," *Bulletin des Musées royaux d'art et d'histoire* [Brussels], 4th series, XXVIII (1956), pp. 28-30.

WOLF, W. "Vorläufer der Reformation Echnatons," *ZAS*, LIX (1924), pp. 109-119. See also pp. 157-158.

28. The ʿAmārneh Period[1]

ALDRED, C. "The End of the El-ʿAmārna Period," *JEA*, XLIII (1957), pp. 30-41.

——— "Year Twelve at El-ʿAmārna," *Ibid.*, pp. 114-117.

ANTHES, R. *Die Maat des Echnaton von Amarna* (*Supplement to the Journal of the American Oriental Society*, 14). Baltimore, 1952.

——— *The Head of Queen Nofret-ete.* Translated by Kathleen Bauer. Berlin, 1954.

BADAWY, A. "Maru-Aten: Pleasure Resort or Temple?" *JEA*, XLII (1956), pp. 58-64.

VON BISSING, F. W. *Der Fussboden aus dem Palaste des Königs Amenophis IV zu El Hawata im Museum zu Kairo.* Munich, 1941.

BLACKMAN, A. M. "Preliminary Report on the Excavations at Sesebi, Northern Province, Anglo-Egyptian Sudan, 1936-37," *JEA*, XXIII (1937), pp. 145-151.

BORCHARDT, L. *Ausgrabungen in Tell el-Amarna*, 1911-1914 (*Mitteilungen der Deutschen Orient-Gesellschaft*, Nos. 46, 50, 52, 55). Berlin, 1911-1914.

——— *Porträts der Königin Nofret-ete aus den Grabungen 1912-13 in Tell-el Amarna* (*44. Wissenschaftliche Veröffentlichung der Deutschen Orient-Gesellschaft*). Leipzig, 1923.

——— "Amenophis IV. Mitkönig in den letzten Jahren Amenophis' III.?" pp. 23-29 in Borchardt, *Allerhand Kleinigkeiten.* Leipzig, 1933.

BOURIANT, U. *Deux Jours de fouilles à Tell el Amarna* (*MMAF*, I, 1). Paris, 1884.

———, LEGRAIN, G., AND JÉQUIER, G. *Monuments pour servir à l'étude du culte d'Atonou en Égypte.* I. *Les tombes de Khouitatonou* (*MIFAO*, VIII). Cairo, 1903.

BRUNNER, H. "Eine neue Amarna-Prinzessin," *ZAS*, LXXIV (1938), pp. 104-108.

BULL, L. S. "Two Letters to Akhnaton, King of Egypt," *BMMA*, XXI (1926), pp. 169-176.

COONEY, J. D., AND SIMPSON, W. K. "An Architectural Fragment from Amarna," *The Bulletin of the Brooklyn Museum*, XII, 4 (Summer, 1951), pp. 1-12.

COTTEVIEILLE-GIRAUDET, R. *Rapport sur les fouilles de Médamoud, 1932. Les reliefs d'Aménophis IV Akhenaton* (*FIFAO*, XIII). Cairo, 1936.

DAVIES, N. DE G. *The Rock Tombs of el Amarna* (*The Egypt Exploration Fund: Archaeological Survey of Egypt*, 13th-18th Memoirs). 6 vols. London, 1903-1908.

——— "Akhenaten at Thebes," *JEA*, IX (1923), pp. 132-152.

——— "The Graphic Work of the Expedition," *BMMA*, XVIII (1923), December, part II, pp. 40-53.

DERRY, D. E. "Note on the Skeleton Hitherto Believed to

[1] See also the works of Davies, Engelbach, Gardiner, Glanville, Helck, Knudtzon, Mercer, Pendlebury, and Schroeder listed in the preceding section.

be that of King Akhenaten," *ASAE*, XXXI (1931), pp. 115-119.

DORESSE, M. "Les Temples atoniens de la région thébaine," *Orientalia*, XXIV (1955), pp. 113-135.

ENGELBACH, R. "The So-called Coffin of Akhenaten," *ASAE*, XXXI (1931), pp. 98-114.

FRANKFORT, H. (ed.) *The Mural Painting of El-ʿAmarneh* (*The Egypt Exploration Society. F. G. Newton Memorial Volume*). London, 1929.

GARDINER, SIR ALAN, "The So-called Tomb of Queen Tiye," *JEA*, XLIII (1957), pp. 10-25.

GHALIOUNGUI, P. "A Medical Study of Akhenaten," *ASAE*, XLVII (1947), pp. 29-46.

GORDON, C. H. "The New Amarna Tablets," *Orientalia*, XVI (1947), pp. 1-21.

GRIFFITH, F. LL. "A Contract of the Fifth Year of Amenhotep IV," *PSBA*, XXX (1908), pp. 272-275; XXXI (1909), pp. 42-43.

GUNN, B. "Notes on the Aten and His Names," *JEA*, IX (1923), pp. 168-176.

HALL, H. R. "Egypt and the External World in the Time of Akhenaten," *JEA*, VII (1921), pp. 39-53.

HAMZA, M. "The Alabaster Canopic Box of Akhenaten and the Royal Alabaster Canopic Boxes of the XVIIIth Dynasty," *ASAE*, XL (1941), pp. 537-543.

KAMAL, M. "Fouilles du Service des antiquités à Tell el-Amarna en 1934," *ASAE*, XXXV (1935), pp. 193-196. See also *Ibid.*, XXXIX (1939), pp. 381-382.

LANGE, K. *König Echnaton und die Amarna-Zeit. Die Geschichte eines Gottkünders* (*Gesellschaft für Wissenschaftliches Lichtbild m.b.H.*). Munich, [1951].

LANSING, A. "Two Egyptian Royal Portraits," *BMMA*, n. s. V (1946-1947), pp. 188-192.

LEEUWENBURG, L. G. "De grensstele's van Amarna," *Jaarbericht van het vooraziatisch-egyptisch Gezelschap "Ex Oriente Lux,"* IX (1944), pp. 39-49.

——— *Echnaten* (*Cultuurhistorische Monografieën*, 5). The Hague, 1946.

——— *Indexes on Bibliotheca Aegyptiaca VIII* (*M. Sandman, Texts from the Time of Akhenaten*). Leiden, 1943.

LEGRAIN, G. "Notes d'inspection: I. Les stèles d'Aménôthès IV à Zernik et à Gebel Silsileh," *ASAE*, III (1902), pp. 259-266.

MERCER, S. A. B. *The Tell el Amarna Tablets*. 2 vols. Toronto, 1939.

PEET, T. E., FRANKFORT, H., PENDLEBURY, J. D. S., AND OTHERS *The City of Akhenaten* I-III (*The Egypt Exploration Society*, 38th, 40th, and 44th Memoirs). 4 vols. London, 1923-1951.

PENDLEBURY, J. D. S. *Tell el-Amarna*. London, 1935.

PETRIE, W. M. F. *Tell el Amarna*. London, 1894.

PILLET, M. "À propos d'Akhenaten," *Cahier complémentaire à la Revue d'égyptologie*, 1950, pp. 63-82.

ROEDER, G. "Amarna-Blöcke aus Hermopolis," *Mitt. Kairo*, XIV (1956), pp. 160-174.

SANDMAN, M. *Texts from the Time of Akhenaten* (*Bibliotheca Aegyptiaca*, VIII). Brussels, 1938.

SCHÄFER, H. "Kunstwerke aus der Zeit Amenophis' IV," *ZÄS*, LII (1914), pp. 73-87.

——— *Die Religion und Kunst von El-Amarna. Mit Übersetzung des Sonnengesangs*. Berlin, 1923.

——— *Amarna in Religion und Kunst* (*Deutsche Orient-Gesellschaft, Sendschrift*, 7). [Leipzig], 1931.

——— *Kunstwerke aus El-Amarna* (*Meisterwerke in Berlin*). 2 vols. Berlin, n. d.

SCHULMAN, A. R. "Egyptian Representations of Horsemen and Riding in the New Kingdom," *JNES*, XVI (1957), pp. 263-271.

SETHE, K. *Beiträge zur Geschichte Amenophis' IV* (*Nachrichten der Königliche Gesellschaft der Wissenschaften zu Göttingen*, Philologisch-historische Klasse, 1921). Berlin, 1921.

VANDIER, J. "Les Stèles frontières d'El-Amarna, à propos d'une nouvelle acquisition du Musée du Louvre," *Monuments et mémoires publiés par l'Académie des inscriptions et belles-lettres* (*Fondation Eugène Piot*), XL (1944), pp. 5-22.

WILLIAMS, C. R. "Wall Decorations of the Main Temple of the Sun at el-ʿAmarneh," *Metropolitan Museum Studies*, II (1930), pp. 135-151.

——— "Two Egyptian Torsos from the Main Temple of the Sun at el-ʿAmarneh," *Metropolitan Museum Studies*, III (1931), pp. 81-99.

WINLOCK, H. E. "A Gift of Egyptian Antiquities," *BMMA*, XVII (1922), pp. 170-173.

DE WIT, C. *La Statuaire de Tell el Amarna*. Antwerp, 1950.

29. The End of the Eighteenth Dynasty[1]

BENNETT, J. "The Restoration Inscription of Tutʿankhamūn," *JEA*, XXV (1939), pp. 8-15.

BOTHMER, B. V. "The Dwarf as Bearer," *BMFA*, XLVII (1949), pp. 9-11.

CAPART, J. "The Memphite Tomb of King Ḥaremḥab," *JEA*, VII (1921), pp. 31-35.

CARTER, H. *The Tomb of Tut·ankh·Amen, Discovered by the Late Earl of Carnarvon and Howard Carter*. 3 vols. (Vol. I with A. C. Mace). London, 1923-1933.

CHEVRIER, H. "Découvertes à Karnak en 1953-1954," *Bulletin de la Société française d'égyptologie*, 18 (July, 1955), pp. 41-51.

——— "Chronologie des constructions de la Salle Hypostyle," *ASAE*, LIV (1956), pp. 35-38.

CLARK, C. R. "Costume Jewelry in Egypt in the XVIII Dynasty," *BMMA*, n. s. VIII (1949-1950), pp. 154-156.

COONEY, J. D. "A Relief from the Tomb of Ḥaremḥab," *JEA*, XXX (1944), pp. 2-4.

DAVIES, NINA DE G., AND GARDINER, A. H. *The Tomb of Ḥuy, Viceroy of Nubia in the Reign of Tutʿankhamūn* (*No. 40*) (*The Egypt Exploration Society. The Theban Tombs Series*, 4th Memoir). London, 1926.

DAVIS, T. M., MASPERO, G., AND OTHERS *The Tomb of Queen Tîyi* (*Theodore M. Davis' Excavations: Bibân el Molûk*). London, 1910.

——— *The Tombs of Harmhabi and Touatânkhamanou* (*Ibid.*). London, 1912.

EATON, E. S. "A Fragment from a Statue of King Eye (Recent Discoveries in the Egyptian Department, I)," *BMFA*, XL (1942), pp. 42-45.

EDEL, E. "Neue keilschriftliche Umschreibungen ägyptischer Namen aus den Boğazköytexten," *JNES*, VII (1948), pp. 11-24. See pp. 14, 15.

EDWARDS, I. E. S. "A Fragment of Relief from the Memphite Tomb of Ḥaremḥab," *JEA*, XXVI (1940), pp. 1-2.

[1] See also the works of Borchardt, Clark, Edwards, Engelbach, Glanville, Hayes, Helck, Macadam, Pendlebury, Schäfer, and Varille listed in § 27 above, and those of Aldred and Gardiner in § 28.

ENGELBACH, R. "A Hitherto Unknown Statue of King Tutʿankhamûn," *ASAE*, XXXVIII (1938), pp. 23-28; XXXIX (1939), p. 199.

ERMAN, A. "Aus dem Grabe eines Hohenpriesters von Memphis," *ZAS*, XXXIII (1895), pp. 18-24.

FOX, P. *Tutankahmun's Treasure*. London, 1951.

GARDINER, SIR ALAN "The Memphite Tomb of the General Ḥaremḥab," *JEA*, XXXIX (1953), pp. 3-12.

——— "The Coronation of King Ḥaremḥab," *Ibid.*, pp. 13-31.

GÜTERBOCK, H. G. "The Deeds of Suppiluliuma as Told by His Son, Mursili II," *Journal of Cuneiform Studies*, X (1956), pp. 41-68, 75-98, 107-130.

HALL, H. R. "Objects of Tutʿankhamūn in the British Museum," *JEA*, XIV (1928), pp. 74-77.

HAYES, W. C. "Minor Art of the Egyptian New Kingdom. A Perfume Jar and a Pair of Cosmetic Boxes," *BMMA*, XXXV (1940), pp. 81-82.

HELCK, W. "Das Dekret des Königs Haremhab," *ZAS*, LXXX (1955), pp. 109-136.

HÖLSCHER, U., AND ANTHES, R. *The Temples of the Eighteenth Dynasty. The Excavations of Medinet Habu*, II (*The University of Chicago Oriental Institute Publications*, XLI). Chicago, 1939.

LANSING, A. "Accessions to the Egyptian Collection," *BMMA*, XXIII (1928), pp. 158-160.

——— "A Faience Broad Collar of the Eighteenth Dynasty," *Ibid.*, XXXV (1940), pp. 65-68.

——— "An XVIII Dynasty Saluki Hound," *Ibid.*, XXXVI (1941), pp. 10-12.

——— "An Egyptian Painting on Linen," *Ibid.*, n. s. III (1944-1945), pp. 201-203.

——— "A Head of Tutʿankhamūn," *JEA*, XXXVII (1951), pp. 3-4.

LUCAS, A. "The Canopic Vases from the 'Tomb of Queen Tîyi,' " *ASAE*, XXXI (1931), pp. 120-122.

NEWBERRY, P. E. "Akhenaten's Eldest Son-in-law ʿAnkhkheprurēʿ," *JEA*, XIV (1928), pp. 3-9.

——— "King Ay, the Successor of Tutʿankhamūn," *Ibid.*, XVIII (1932), pp. 50-52.

PFLÜGER, K. *Haremhab und die Amarnazeit. Teildruck: Haremhabs Laufbahn bis zur Thronbesteigung* (*Abhandlung zur Erlangung der Doktorwürde der Philosophischen Fakultät I der Universität Zürich*). Zwickau, 1936.

——— "The Edict of King Haremhab," *JNES*, V (1946), pp. 260-276.

PIANKOFF, A. *Les Chapelles de Tout-Ankh-Amon* (*MIFAO*, LXXII). 2 vols. Cairo, 1951, 1952.

——— *The Shrines of Tut-Ankh-Amon* (*Bollingen Series*, XL, 2). New York, 1955.

ROEDER, G. "Thronfolger und König Smenh-ka-Rê," *ZAS*, LXXXIII (1958), pp. 43-74.

ROWE, A. "Inscriptions on the Model Coffin Containing the Lock of Hair of Queen Tiji," *ASAE*, XL (1941), pp. 623-627.

SCHÄFER, H. "Die Simonsche Holzfigur eines Königs der Amarnazeit," *ZAS*, LXX (1934), pp. 1-25.

SCOTT, N. E. "Recent Additions to the Egyptian Collection," *BMMA*, n. s. XV (1956-1957), pp. 79-92.

SEELE, K. C. "King Ay and the Close of the Amarna Age," *JNES*, XIV (1955), pp. 168-180.

SIMPSON, W. K. "The Head of a Statuette of Tutʿankhamūn in The Metropolitan Museum," *JEA*, XLI (1955), pp. 112-114.

STEINDORFF, G. "Die Grabkammer des Tutanchamun," *ASAE*, XXXVIII (1938), pp. 641-667.

VANDIER, J. "Deux Fragments de la tombe memphite d'Horemheb conservés au Musée du Louvre," pp. 811-818 in *Mélanges syriens offerts à Monsieur René Dussaud*. Paris, 1939.

VAN DE WALLE, B., AND PFLÜGER, K. "Le Décret d'Horemheb," *Chronique d'Egypte*, XXII (1947), pp. 230-238.

WINLOCK, H. E. "A New Egyptian Room," *BMMA*, XI (1916), pp. 84-86.

——— "Harmhab, Commander-in-Chief of the Armies of Tutenkhamon," *Ibid.*, XVIII (1923), October, part II.

——— "A Statue of Horemhab before His Accession," *JEA*, X (1924), pp. 1-5.

——— *Materials Used at the Embalming of King Tut-ʿankh-Amūn* (*The Metropolitan Museum of Art, Papers*, No. 10). New York, 1941.

WOLF, W. *Das schöne Fest von Opet; die Festzugdarstellung im grossen Säulengange des Tempels von Luksor* (*Veröffentlichungen der Ernst von Sieglin Expedition in Ägypten*, V). Leipzig, 1931.

30. The Earlier Ramessides

ALBRIGHT, W. F. "The Smaller Beth-Shan Stela of Sethos I (1309-1290 B.C.)," *Bulletin of the American Schools of Oriental Research*, 125 (February, 1952), pp. 24-32.

ALT, A. "Die Deltaresidenz der Ramessiden," *Festschrift für Friedrich Zucker zum 70. Geburtstage*, pp. 1-13. Berlin, 1954.

ANTHES, R. "Der Wesier Paser als Hoherpriester des Amon in Hermonthis," *ZAS*, LXVII (1931), pp. 2-9.

VON BECKERATH, J. "Das Thronbesteigungsdatum Ramses II," *ZAS*, LXXXI (1956), pp. 1-3.

BONOMI, J., AND SHARPE, S. *The Alabaster Sarcophagus of Oimenepthah I, King of Egypt, now in Sir John Soane's Museum, Lincolns Inn Fields*. London, 1864.

BULL, L. "Fragment of a Statue of Ramesses II," *BMMA*, n. s. I (1942-1943), pp. 219-221.

CALVERLEY, A. M., BROOME, M. F., AND GARDINER, A. H. *The Temple of King Sethos I at Abydos*. 4 vols. London, 1933-1959 (?).

ÇAPART, J. *Le Temple de Séti Ier (Abydos)*. Brussels, 1912.

ČERNÝ, J. "L'Identité des 'Serviteurs dans la Place de Vérité' et des ouvriers de la nécropole royale de Thèbes," *Revue de l'Egypte ancienne*, II (1929), pp. 200-209.

——— "Graffiti at the Wādi el-ʿAllaki," *JEA*, XXXIII (1947), pp. 52-57.

——— "Prices and Wages in Egypt in the Ramesside Period," *Journal of World History* [Paris], I (1954), pp. 903-921.

CHEVRIER, H. "Chronologie des constructions de la Salle Hypostyle," *ASAE*, LIV (1956), pp. 35-38.

CHRISTOPHE, L.-A. "La Carrière du prince Merenptah et les trois régences ramessides," *ASAE*, LI (1951), pp. 335-372.

CLÈRE, J. J. "Notes sur la chapelle funéraire de Ramsès I à Abydos et sur son inscription dédicatoire," *Revue d'égyptologie*, XI (1957), pp. 1-38.

COUROYER, B. "La Résidence ramesside du Delta et le Ramsès biblique," *Revue biblique*, LIII (1946), pp. 75-98.

DARESSY, G. "L'art tanite," *ASAE*, XVII (1917), pp. 164-176.

DARESSY, G., *continued*
——— "La Trouvaille de Sen-nezem: Objets séparés de l'ensemble," *Ibid.*, XXVIII (1928), pp. 7-11.
DAVIES, N. DE G. *Two Ramesside Tombs at Thebes* (*Publications of The Metropolitan Museum of Art Egyptian Expedition. Robb de Peyster Tytus Memorial Series*, V). New York, 1927.
EDEL, E. "Die Rolle der Königinnen in der ägyptisch-hethitischen Korrespondenz von Bogazköy," *Zeitschrift für Indogermanistik und allgemeine Sprachwissenschaft*, LX (1949), pp. 72-85.
——— "KBo I 15 + 19, ein Brief Ramses' II mit einer Schilderung der Ḳadešschlacht," *Zeitschrift für Assyriologie und vorderasiatische Archäologie*, n. s. XV (XIX.) (1949), pp. 195-212.
——— "Ein Brief aus der Heiratskorrespondenz Ramses' II," *Jahrbuch für kleinasiatische Forschung* (*Internationale orientalische Zeitschrift*), II, 3 (1952), pp. 262-273
——— "Weitere Briefe aus der Heiratskorrespondenz Ramses' II: KUB III 37 + KBo I 17 und KUB III 57," *Geschichte und Alten Testament* [Tübingen], 1953, pp. 29-63.
EDGERTON, W. F. "The Nauri Decree of Seti I. A Translation and Analysis of the Legal Portion," *JNES*, VI (1947), pp. 219-230.
ERMAN, A. "Beiträge zur Kenntniss des ägyptischen Gerichtsverfahrens," *ZÄS*, XVII (1879), pp. 71-83.
FAIRMAN, H. W., AND SHINNIE, P. L. "Preliminary Report[s] on the Excavations at ʿAmārah West, Anglo-Egyptian Sudan," 1938-1950, *JEA*, XXV (1939), pp. 139-144; XXXIV (1948), pp. 3-11; XXXVII (1951), pp. 5-11.
FAKHRY, A. "Three Unnumbered Tombs at Thebes. 3. Tomb of User-Montu," *ASAE*, XXXVI (1936), pp. 129-130.
FAULKNER, R. O. "The Wars of Sethos I," *JEA*, XXXIII (1947), pp. 34-39.
FRANKFORT, H., DE BUCK, A., AND GUNN, B. *The Cenotaph of Seti I at Abydos* (*The Egyptian Exploration Society*, 39th Memoir). 2 vols. London, 1933.
GARDINER, A. H. *The Inscription of Mes. A Contribution to the Study of Egyptian Judicial Procedure* (*Unters.*, IV, 3). Leipzig, 1905.
——— "The Map of the Gold Mines in a Ramesside Papyrus at Turin," *The Cairo Scientific Journal*, VIII (1914), pp. 41-46.
——— "The Delta Residence of the Ramessides," *JEA*, V (1918), pp. 127-138, 179-200, 242-271.
——— "Tanis and Pi-Raʿmesse: A Retractation," *Ibid.*, XIX (1933), pp. 123-128.
——— "Ramesside Texts Relating to the Taxation and Transport of Corn," *Ibid.*, XXVII (1941), pp. 19-73.
——— *Ramesside Administrative Documents* (*The Griffith Institute, Ashmolean Museum, Oxford*). London, 1948.
——— "Some Reflections on the Nauri Decree," *JEA*, XXXVIII (1952), pp. 24-33.
GAUTHIER, H. *La Grande Inscription dédicatoire d'Abydos* (*Institut français d'archéologie orientale, Bibliothèque d'étude*, IV). Cairo, 1912.
——— "Le Temple de l'Ouâdi Mîyah (el-Knaïs)," *BIFAO*, XVII (1920), pp. 1-38.
——— "Une Statue de Ramsès Ier défunt originaire d'Abydos," *ASAE*, XXXI (1931), pp. 193-197.
GHAZOULI, E. "Les Récentes Découvertes à Abydos," pp. 59-61 in *Les Grandes Découvertes archéologiques de 1954*. Cairo, 1955.
GOETZE, A. "A New Letter from Ramesses to Ḫattušiliš," *Journal of Cuneiform Studies*, I (1947), pp. 241-251.
GOYON, G. "Le Papyrus de Turin dit 'des Mines d'Or' et le Wadi Hammamat," *ASAE*, XLIX (1949), pp. 337-392.
GRDSELOFF, B. *Une Stèle scythopolitaine du roi Sèthos Ier* (*Études égyptiennes*, 2nd fascicle). Cairo, 1949.
GRIFFITH, F. LL. "The Abydos Decree of Seti I at Nauri," *JEA*, XIII (1927), pp. 193-208.
GRIFFITHS, J. G. "Shelley's 'Ozymandias' and Diodorus Siculus," *The Modern Language Review*, XLIII (1948), pp. 80-84.
GUNN, B., AND GARDINER, A. H. "New Renderings of Egyptian Texts. 1. The Temple of the Wâdy Abbâd," *JEA*, IV (1917), pp. 241-251.
HABACHI, L. "Khatâʿna-Qantîr: Importance," *ASAE*, LII (1954), pp. 443-562.
HAMZA, M. "Excavations of the Department of Antiquities at Qantîr (Faqûs District) (Season, May 21st-July 7th, 1928)," *ASAE*, XXX (1930), pp. 31-68.
HAYES, W. C. *Glazed Tiles from a Palace of Ramesses II at Kantīr* (*The Metropolitan Museum of Art, Papers*, No. 3). New York, 1937.
KAMAL, A. "Rapport sur les fouilles dans la montagne de Sheîkh Saîd," *ASAE*, X (1910), pp. 145-154. See pp. 153-154.
——— "Fouilles à Deir Dronka et à Assiout (1913-1914)," *Ibid.*, XVI (1916), pp. 65-144. See pp. 86-94.
KUENTZ, C. "La 'Stèle de Mariage' de Ramsès II," *ASAE*, XXV (1925), pp. 181-238.
——— *La Bataille de Qadech* (*MIFAO*, LV). Cairo, 1928-1934.
LANGDON, S., AND GARDINER, A. H. "The Treaty of Alliance between Hattušili, King of the Hittites, and the Pharaoh Ramesses II of Egypt," *JEA*, VI (1920), pp. 179-205.
LECLANT, J., AND YOYOTTE, J. "Les Obélisques de Tanis (deuxième article). Observations concernant la série des obélisques remployés," *Kêmi*, XI (1950), pp. 73-84.
LEFÉBURE, E. *Les Hypogées royaux de Thèbes*, I, II (*Annales du Musée Guimet*, IX, XVI). Paris, 1886, 1889.
LEFEBVRE, G. "Fouilles à Abydos. I. Déblaiement de la première cour du temple de Séti," *ASAE*, XIII (1914), pp. 193-214.
——— "Les Débuts du règne de Séti Ier," *Comptes rendus de l'Académie des inscriptions et belles-lettres*, 1950, pp. 246-253.
——— "Inscription dédicatoire de la chapelle funéraire de Ramsès I à Abydos," *ASAE*, LI (1951), pp. 167-200.
LEGRAIN, G. "Au Pylône d'Harmhabi à Karnak (Xe pylône). III. Les statues de [*Pꜣ-Rʿ-ms-sw*] Paramessou, fils de [*S̱ty*] Séti," *ASAE*, XIV (1914), pp. 29-38.
MAYSTRE, C. "Le Tombeau de Ramsès II," *BIFAO*, XXXVIII (1939), pp. 183-190.
MONTET, P. "La Stèle de l'an 400 retrouvée," *Kêmi*, IV (1931 [1933]), pp. 191-215.
——— *Tanis, douze années de fouilles dans une capitale oubliée du delta égyptien* (*Bibliothèque historique*). Paris, 1942.
——— *La Vie quotidienne en Égypte au temps des Ramessides* (*XIIIe-XIIe siècles avant J. C.*). Paris, 1946.
——— *Les Enigmes de Tanis* (*Bibliothèque historique*). Paris, 1952.
MORET, A. "La Campagne de Séti Ier au nord du Carmel, d'après les fouilles de M. Fisher," *Revue de l'Egypte ancienne*, I (1927), pp. 18-30.

NIMS, C. F. "A Stele of Penre, Builder of the Ramesseum," *Mitt. Kairo*, XIV (1956), pp. 146-149.

NOTH, M. "Die Wege der Pharaonenheere in Palästina und Syrien. Untersuchungen zu den hieroglyphischen Listen palästinischer und syrischer Städte." II. "Die Ortslisten Sethos I;" V. "Ramses II in Syrien," *Zeitschrift des Deutschen Palästina-Vereins*," LX (1937), pp. 210-229; LXIV (1941), pp. 39-74.

PARKER, R. A. "The Lunar Dates of Thutmose III and Ramesses II," *JNES*, XVI (1957), pp. 39-43.

PETRIE, W. M. F. *Tanis* (*The Egypt Exploration Fund*, 2nd and 5th Memoirs). 2 parts. London, 1885, 1888.

PIANKOFF, A. "Le Nom du roi Sethos en égyptien," *BIFAO*, XLVII (1948), pp. 175-177.

QUIBELL, J. E., AND SPIEGELBERG, W. *The Ramesseum* (*Egyptian Research Account*, 1896). London, 1898.

REISNER, G. A., AND REISNER, M. B. "Inscribed Monuments from Gebel Barkal," *ZAS*, LXVI (1931), pp. 76-100 (see p. 77); LXIX (1933), pp. 73-78.

ROWE, A. "The Two Royal Stelae of Beth-shan." *The Museum Journal* (*University of Pennsylvania*), XX (1929), pp. 89-98.

ROWTON, M. B. "Manetho's Date for Ramesses II" (with an appendix by H. Kees), *JEA*, XXXIV (1948), pp. 57-74.

SANDER-HANSEN, C. E. *Historische Inschriften der 19. Dynastie* (*Bibliotheca Aegyptiaca*, IV). Brussels, 1933.

SCHIAPARELLI, E. *Esplorazione della "Valle delle Regine"* (*Relazione sui lavori della Missione archaeologica italiana in Egitto, Anni* 1903-1920). Turin, n. d.

SCOTT, N. E. "Recent Additions to the Egyptian Collection," *BMMA*, n. s. XV (1956-1957), pp. 79-92.

SEELE, K. C. *The Coregency of Ramses II with Seti I and the Date of the Great Hypostyle Hall at Karnak* (*The University of Chicago Oriental Institute Studies in Ancient Oriental Civilization*, No. 19). Chicago, 1940.

SETHE, K. "Der Name Sesostris. 8. Der Kurzname Ramses' II," *ZAS*, XLI (1904), pp. 53-57.

——— "Die Berufung eines Hohenpriesters des Amon unter Ramses II," *Ibid.*, XLIV (1907), pp. 30-35.

——— "Die Jahresrechnung unter Ramses II und der Namenwechsel dieses Königs," *Ibid.*, LXII (1927), pp. 110-114.

SHORTER, A. W. "The Statue of Khā'emuas in the British Museum," pp. 128-132 in *Studies Presented to F. Ll. Griffith* (*The Egypt Exploration Society*). London, 1932.

SPIEGELBERG, W. *Hieratic Ostraka and Papyri found by J. E. Quibell in the Ramesseum, 1895-6* (*Egyptian Research Account*, Extra Volume, 1898). London, 1898.

——— "Bemerkungen zu den hieratischen Amphoreninschriften des Ramesseums," *ZAS*, LVIII (1923), pp. 25-36.

STRUVE, V. V., AND FRANTSEN, U. P. "New Data on the Chronology of the Ancient East," *Relazioni de Comitato Internazionale di Scienze Storiche*, VII (1955), pp. 122-124.

STURM, J. *Der Hettiterkriege Ramses' II* (*Wiener Zeitschrift für die Kunde des Morgenlandes, Beihefte*, 4). Vienna, 1939.

TODA, E., AND DARESSY, G. "La Découverte et l'inventaire du tombeau de Sen-nezem," *ASAE*, XX (1920), pp. 145-160.

TRESSON, P. *La Stèle de Koubân publiée avec notes, glossaire et reproduction du monument en trois planches phototypiques* (*Institut français d'archéologie orientale, Bibliothèque d'étude*, IX). Cairo, 1922.

VIROLLEAUD, C. "L'Orient au temps des Ramsès," *L'Ethnographie*, n. s. 50 (1955 [1956]), pp. 3-15.

WILSON, J. A. "The Texts of the Battle of Kadesh," *AJSLL*, XLIII (1927), pp. 266-287.

W[INLOCK], H. E. "The Statue of Iny and Rennut," *BMMA*, XIV (1919), pp. 32-35.

——— *Bas-reliefs from the Temple of Ramesses I at Abydos* (*The Metropolitan Museum of Art, Papers*, I, part 1). New York, 1921.

——— "Recent Purchases of Egyptian Sculpture," *BMMA*, XXIX (1934), pp. 184-187.

——— *The Temple of Ramesses I at Abydos* (*The Metropolitan Museum of Art, Papers*, No. 5). New York, 1937.

YOYOTTE, J. "Les Grand Dieux et la religion officielle sous Séti Ier et Ramsès II," *Bulletin de la Société française d'égyptologie*, 3 (February, 1950), pp. 17-22.

——— "Les Stèles de Ramsès II à Tanis," *Kêmi*, X (1949), pp. 58-74; XI (1950), pp. 47-62; XII (1952), pp. 77-90; XIII (1954), pp. 77-86.

31. The Late Nineteenth Dynasty

BARGUET, P. "Les Stèles du Nil au Gebel Silsileh," *BIFAO*, L (1952), pp. 49-63.

VON BECKERATH, J. "Die Reihenfolge der letzten Könige der 19. Dynastie, *ZDMG*, CVI (1956), pp. 241-251.

BURTON, H. "The Late Theodore M. Davis's Excavations at Thebes in 1912-13. 1. The Excavation of the Rear Corridors and Sepulchral Chamber of the Tomb of King Siphtah," *BMMA*, XI (1916), pp. 13-18.

CAMINOS, R. A. *Late-Egyptian Miscellanies* (*Brown Egyptological Studies*, I). London, 1954.

——— "Two Stelae in the Kurnah Temple of Sethos I," pp. 17-29 in *Ägyptologische Studien Hermann Grapow zum 70. Geburtstag gewidmet*. Berlin, 1955.

CARTER, H. "Report of Work Done in Upper Egypt (1902-1903)," *ASAE*, IV (1903), pp. 171-180.

ČERNÝ, J. "Quelques Ostraca hiératiques inédites de Thèbes au Musée du Caire," *ASAE*, XXVIII (1927), pp. 183-210.

——— *Ostraca hiératiques* (*CCG*, nos. 25501-25832). 2 vols. Cairo, 1930-1935.

——— *Catalogue des ostraca hiératiques non littéraires de Deir el Médineh* (*Documents de FIFAO*, III-VII). 5 vols. Cairo, 1935-1951.

——— *Late Ramesside Letters* (*Bibliotheca Aegyptiaca*, IX). Brussels, 1939.

——— AND GARDINER, A. H. *Hieratic Ostraka*, I (The Griffith Institute). Oxford, 1957.

CHABÂN, M. "Fouilles à Achmounéîn," *ASAE*, VIII (1907), pp. 211-223.

CHEVRIER, H., AND DRIOTON, É. *Le Temple reposoir de Séti II à Karnak*. Cairo, 1940.

CHRISTOPHE, L.-A. "Quatres Enquêtes ramessides," *Bulletin de l'Institut d'Égypte*, XXXVII (1956), pp. 5-37.

——— "La Fin de la XIXe Dynastie égyptienne," *Bibliotheca Orientalis*, XIV (1957), pp. 10-13.

COUROYER, B. "Dieux et fils de Ramsès," *Revue biblique* [Paris], LXI (1954), pp. 108-117.

DARESSY, G. "Quelques Ostraca de Biban el Molouk," *ASAE*, XXVII (1927), pp. 161-182.

DAVIS, T. M., MASPERO, G., AND OTHERS. *The Tomb of*

Siphtah; the Monkey Tomb and the Gold Tomb (*Theodore M. Davis' Excavations: Bibân el Molûk*). London, 1908.

DUNHAM, D. "An Osirid Figure of King Merenptah," *BMFA*, XXXVII (1939), pp. 6-9.

EDGAR, C. C. "The Treasure of Tell Basta," pp. 93-108 in G. Maspero, *Le Musée égyptien: Recueil de monuments et de notices sur les fouilles d'Égypte*, II. Cairo, 1907.

——— "A Building of Merenptah at Mit Rahineh," *ASAE*, XV (1915), pp. 97-104.

——— "Engraved Designs of a Silver Vase from Tell Basta," *Ibid.*, XXV (1925), pp. 256-258.

EMERY, W. B. "The Order of Succession at the Close of the Nineteenth Dynasty," *Mélanges Maspero*, I (*MMAF*, LXVI), pp. 353-356. Cairo, 1935-1938.

ENGELBACH, R. "A Monument of Prince Meneptaḥ from Athribis (Benha)," *ASAE*, XXX (1930), pp. 197-202.

FISHER, C. S. "The Eckley B. Coxe Jr. Egyptian Expedition," *The Museum Journal* (*University of Pennsylvania*), VIII (1917), pp. 211-237.

GARDINER, A. H. "The Stele of Bilgai," *ZAS*, L (1912), pp. 49-57.

——— *Late-Egyptian Miscellanies* (*Bibliotheca Aegyptiaca*, VII). Brussels, 1937.

——— "Ramesside Texts Relating to the Taxation and Transport of Corn," *JEA*, XXVII (1941), pp. 19-73.

——— *Ramesside Administrative Documents* (*The Griffith Institute*). London, 1948.

——— "The Harem at Miwēr," *JNES*, XII (1953), pp. 145-149.

——— "The Tomb of Queen Twosre," *JEA*, XL (1954), pp. 40-44.

GAUTHIER, H. "À Travers la Basse-Égypte: XVIII. Deux statues du roi Ménephtah à Kafr Matboul," *ASAE*, XXIII (1923), pp. 165-169.

HABACHI, L. "Amenwahsu Attached to the Cult of Anubis, Lord of the Dawning Land," *Mitt. Kairo*, XIV (1956), pp. 52-62.

HAYES, W. C. *Glazed Tiles from a Palace of Ramesses II at Ḳantīr* (*The Metropolitan Museum of Art, Papers*, No. 3). New York, 1937.

HELCK, W. "Zur Geschichte der 19. und 20. Dynastie," *ZDMG*, CV (n. s. XXX) (1955), pp. 27-52.

——— "Zwei thebanische Urkunden aus der Zeit Sethos II.," *ZAS*, LXXXI (1956), pp. 82-87.

HÖLSCHER, W. *Libyer und Ägypter: Beiträge zur Ethnologie und Geschichte libyscher Völkerschaften nach den altägyptischen Quellen* (*Ägyptologische Forschungen*, IV). Glückstadt, Hamburg, New York, 1937.

KEIMER, L. "Un Scarabée commémoratif de Mineptah," *ASAE*, XXXIX (1939), pp. 105-120.

VON KOMORZYNSKI, E. "Der Torso einer Statue Merenptaḥs im Luxortempel," *ASAE*, XXXIX (1939), pp. 401-402.

KUENTZ, C. "Le Double de la stèle d'Israël à Karnak," *BIFAO*, XXI (1923), pp. 113-117.

LEFÉBURE, E. *Les Hypogées royaux de Thèbes*, II. *Notice des hypogées* (*Annales du Musée Guimet*, XVI, 1). Paris, 1889.

LEFEBVRE, G. "Stèle de l'an V de Méneptah," *ASAE*, XXVII (1927), pp. 19-30.

——— "À propos de la Reine Taousert," *Le Muséon*, LIX (*Mélanges L. Th. Lefort*) (1946), pp. 215-221.

——— *Inscriptions concernant les grands prêtres d'Amon Romê-Roÿ et Amenhotep*. Paris, 1929.

MILOJČIĆ, V. "Das Sethosschwert kein gemeineuropäisches Griffzungenschwert," *Germania* [Berlin], XXX (1952), pp. 95-97.

MOSS, R. 'Iron-mines near Aswān," *JEA*, XXXVI (1950), pp. 112-113.

PETRIE, W. M. F. *Six Temples at Thebes*. London, 1896.

RICKE, H. "Der Geflügelhof des Amon in Karnak," *ZAS*, LXXIII (1937), pp. 124-131.

ROEDER, G. "Zwei hieroglyphische Inschriften aus Hermopolis (Ober-Ägypten)," *ASAE*, LII (1954), pp. 315-442.

SANDER-HANSEN, C. E. *Historische Inschriften der 19. Dynastie* (*Bibliotheca Aegyptiaca*, IV). Brussels, 1933.

SCHAEFFER, C. F.-A. "Une Epée de bronze d'Ugarit (Ras Shamra) portant le cartouche de Mineptah," *Revue d'égyptologie*, XI (1957), pp. 139-143.

SCHARFF, A. "Altes und Neues von den Goldschmiedearbeiten der ägyptischen Abteilung," *Berliner Museen, Berichte aus den preussischen Kunstsammlungen*, LI (1930), pp. 114-121.

SIMPSON, W. K. "The Tell Basta Treasure," *BMMA*, n. s. VIII (1949-1950), pp. 61-65.

SMOLENSKI, T. "Les Peuples septentrionaux de la mer sous Ramsès II et Minéptah," *ASAE*, XV (1915), pp. 49-93.

SPIEGELBERG, W. "Der Siegeshymnus des Merneptah auf der Flinders Petrie-Stela," *ZAS*, XXXIV (1896), pp. 1-25.

WAINWRIGHT, G. A. "Some Sea-Peoples and Others in the Hittite Archives," *JEA*, XXV (1939), pp. 148-153.

WINLOCK, H. E. "The Pharaoh of the Exodus," *BMMA*, XVII (1922), pp. 226-234.

——— "Ushabti Figures of Siphtah," *Ibid.*, XI (1916), p. 18.

WOLF, W. "Papyrus Bologna 1086. Ein Beitrag zur Kulturgeschichte des Neuen Reiches," *ZAS*, LXV (1930), pp. 89-97.

——— "Neue Beiträge zum 'Tagebuch eines Grenzbeamten,' " *Ibid.*, LXIX (1933), pp. 39-45.

32. The Twentieth Dynasty to the Death of Ramesses IV

ANTHES, R. "Die Vorführung der gefangenen Feinde vor den König," *ZAS*, LXV (1930), pp. 26-35.

BORCHARDT, L. "Einige astronomisch festgelegte Punkte zweiter Ordnung im Neuen Reiche. 4. Zwei Krönungstage aus der 20sten Dynastie," *ZAS*, LXX (1934), pp. 102-103.

——— "Wo wurde der grosse Papyrus Harris gefunden, und wer hat ihn zusammenstellen lassen?" *Ibid.*, LXXIII (1937), pp. 114-117.

BRUGSCH, E. "On et Onion," *Rec. trav.*, VIII (1886), pp. 1-9.

BRUYÈRE, B. "Neb-nerou et Hery-Mâat," *Chronique d'Égypte*, XXVII (1952), pp. 31-42.

DE BUCK, A. "Documenten betreffende een samenzwering in der Harem van Ramses III," *Jaarbericht van het vooraziatisch-egyptisch Gezelschap "Ex Oriente Lux,"* IV (1936), pp. 165-170.

——— "The Judicial Papyrus of Turin," *JEA*, XXIII (1937), pp. 152-164.

BURTON, H. "The Late Theodore M. Davis's Excavations at Thebes in 1912-13. II. Excavations at Medinet Habu," *BMMA*, XI (1916), pp. 102-108.

Carter, H., and Gardiner, A. H. "The Tomb of Rameses IV and the Turin Plan of a Royal Tomb," *JEA*, IV (1917), pp. 130-158.

Černý, J. "Fluctuations in Grain Prices during the Twentieth Egyptian Dynasty," *Archiv Orientální*, VI (1933), pp. 173-178.

——— "Datum des Todes Ramses' III. und der Thronbesteigung Ramses' IV.," *ZÄS*, LXXII (1936), pp. 109-118.

——— *Late Ramesside Letters* (*Bibliotheca Aegyptiaca*, IX). Brussels, 1939.

Chevrier, H. *Le Temple reposoir de Ramsès III à Karnak* (*Service des antiquités de l'Egypte*). Cairo, 1933.

Christophe, L. "La Stèle de l'an III de Ramsès IV au Ouâdi Hammâmât (No. 12)," *BIFAO*, XLVIII (1949), pp. 1-38.

——— "Ramsès IV et le Musée du Caire," *Cahiers d'histoire égyptienne* [Cairo], 3rd series, fasc. 1 (1950), pp. 47-67.

——— "Les Enseignements de l'Ostracon 148 de Déir el-Médineh," *BIFAO*, LII (1953), pp. 113-128.

——— "Les Fondations de Ramsès III entre Memphis et Thèbes," *Cahiers d'histoire égyptienne* [Cairo], 5th series, fasc. 4 (1953), pp. 227-249.

——— "Note à propos du rapport de M. Chevrier, Ramsès IV et la 'Salle de Fêtes' de Thoutmosis III à Karnak," *ASAE*, LII (1954), pp. 253-266.

——— "Deux Notes sur le rapport de M. Chevrier (Karnak, 1953-1954)," *Ibid.*, LIII (1955), pp. 43-48.

——— "Quatre Enquêtes ramessides," *Bulletin de l'Institut d'Égypte*, XXXVII (1956), pp. 5-37.

Daressy, G. "Plaquettes émaillées de Médinet-Habou," *ASAE*, XI (1911), pp. 49-63.

Edgerton, W. F. "The Strikes in Ramses III's Twenty-ninth Year," *JNES*, X (1951), pp. 137-145.

——— and Wilson, J. A. *Historical Records of Ramses III. The Texts in "Medinet Habu" volumes I and II* (*The University of Chicago Oriental Institute Studies in Ancient Oriental Civilization*, No. 12). Chicago, 1936.

Erichsen, W. *Papyrus Harris I, Hieroglyphische Transkription* (*Bibliotheca Aegyptiaca*, V). Brussels, 1933.

Gardiner, A. H. "Ramesside Texts Relating to the Taxation and Transport of Corn," *JEA*, XXVII (1941), pp. 19-73.

——— "A Pharaonic Encomium," *Ibid.*, XLI (1955), p. 30; XLII (1956), pp. 8-20.

Gauthier, H. "Un Vice-roi d'Éthiopie enseveli à Bubastis," *ASAE*, XXVIII (1928), pp. 129-137.

Griffith, F. Ll. "The Decree of Elephantine," *JEA*, XIII (1927), pp. 207-208.

Helck, W. "Zur Geschichte der 19. und 20. Dynastie," *ZDMG*, CV (n. s. XXX) (1955), pp. 27-52.

Hölscher, U. "Erscheinungsfenster und Erscheinungsbalkon im königlichen Palast," *ZÄS*, LXVII (1931), pp. 43-51.

——— *The Excavation of Medinet Habu.* I; *General Plans and Views;* III, IV: *The Mortuary Temple of Ramses III*, parts I and II (*The University of Chicago Oriental Institute Publications*, XXI, LIV, LV). Chicago, 1934-1951.

——— "Gessodekorationen, Intarsien und Kachelbekleidungen in Medinet Habu," *ZÄS*, LXXVI (1940), pp. 41-45.

Hölscher, W. *Libyer und Ägypter: Beiträge zur Ethnologie und Geschichte libyscher Völkerschaften nach den altägyptischen Quellen* (*Ägyptologische Forschungen*, IV). Glückstadt, Hamburg, New York, 1937.

Janssen, J. M. A. *Ramses III. Proeve van een historisch beeld zijner regering* (*Nederlandsch Instituut voor het Nabije Oosten*). Leiden, 1948.

Korostovtsev, M. "Stèle de Ramsès IV," *BIFAO*, XLV (1947), pp. 155-173.

Lansing, A. "The Museum's Excavations at Thebes," *BMMA*, XXX (1935), November, sect. II, pp. 4-16.

Lefébure, E. *Les Hypogées royaux de Thèbes.* II: *Notice des hypogées;* III: *Tombeau de Ramsès IV* (*Annales du Musée Guimet*, XVI, 1, 2). Paris, 1886-1889.

Lewis, H. "Tel-el-Yahoudeh," *Transactions of the Society of Biblical Archaeology*, VII (1882), pp. 177-192.

Maspero, G. "Notes de voyage. X," *ASAE*, X (1910), pp. 131-144.

Naville, E., and Griffith, F. Ll. *The Mound of the Jew and the City of Onias; The Antiquities of Tell el Yahûdîyeh* (*The Egypt Exploration Fund*, 7th Memoir. Extra Volume for 1888-9). London, 1890.

Nelson, H. H. "Three Decrees of Ramses III from Karnak," *Journal of the American Oriental Society*, LVI (1936), pp. 232-241.

——— "The Naval Battle Pictured at Medinet Habu," *JNES*, II (1943), pp. 40-55.

——— and others *Medinet Habu*, I-V (*The University of Chicago Oriental Institute Publications*, VIII, IX, XXIII, LI, LXXXIII). 5 vols. Chicago, 1930-1957.

——— and others *Reliefs and Inscriptions at Karnak*, I, II (*Ibid.*, XXV, XXXV). 2 vols. Chicago, 1936.

Pillet, M. "Le Temple de Khonsou dans l'enceinte de Mout, à Karnak," *ASAE*, XXXVIII (1938), pp. 469-478.

R[owe], L. E. "Egyptian Portraiture of the XX Dynasty," *BMFA*, VI (1908), pp. 47-50.

Sander-Hansen, C. E. "Bemerkungen zu dem juridischen Turiner-Papyrus," *Studia Orientalia Ioanni Pedersen*, 1953, pp. 316-317.

Sauneron, S., and Yoyotte, J. "Le Texte hiératique Rifaud," *BIFAO*, L (1952), pp. 107-117.

Schaedel, H. D. *Die Listen des grossen Papyrus Harris, ihre wirtschaftliche und politische Ausdeutung* (*Leipziger ägyptologische Studien*, VI). Glückstadt, 1936.

——— "Der Regierungsantritt Ramses' IV.," *ZÄS*, LXXIV (1938), pp. 96-104.

Schiaparelli, E. *Esplorazione della "Valle delle Regine"* (*Relazione sui lavori della Missione archaeologica italiana in Egitto, Anni* 1903-1920). Turin, n. d.

Seele, K. C. "Some Remarks on the Family of Ramesses III," pp. 296-314 in *Ägyptologische Studien Hermann Grapow zum 70. Geburtstag gewidmet* (*Deutsche Akademie der Wissenschaften zu Berlin, Institut für Orientforschung, Veröffentlichung* 29). Berlin, 1955.

Spiegelberg, W. *Arbeiter und Arbeiterbewegung im Pharaonenreich unter den Ramessiden* (*ca. 1400-1100 v. Chr.*). Strassburg, 1895.

Wilson, J. A. "Ceremonial Games of the New Kingdom," *JEA*, XVII (1931), pp. 211-220.

33. The End of the New Kingdom

Albright, W. F. "The Eastern Mediterranean about 1060 B.C.," *Studies Presented to David Moore Robinson* [St. Louis], I (1951), pp. 223-231.

Aldred, C. "A Statue of King Neferkarēʿ Ramesses IX," *JEA*, XLI (1955), pp. 3-8.

Borchardt, L. "Der Krönungstag Ramses' V," *ZAS*, LXXIII (1937), pp. 60-66.

Botti, G. "Who Succeeded Ramesses IX-Neferkerēʿ?" *JEA*, XIV (1928), pp. 48-51.

British Museum. *Select Papyri in the Hieratic Character from the Collections of the British Museum*, II. Prefatory remarks by Samuel Birch. London, 1860.

——— *Facsimile of an Egyptian Hieratic Papyrus of the Reign of Rameses III now in the British Museum*. Edited by S. Birch. 2 vols. London, 1876.

Capart, J., Gardiner, A. H., and van de Walle, B. "New Light on the Ramesside Tomb-Robberies," *JEA*, XXII (1936), pp. 169-193.

——— and Gardiner, A. H. *Le Papyrus Léopold II aux Musées royaux d'art et d'histoire de Bruxelles et le Papyrus Amherst à la Pierpont Morgan Library de New York*. New York and Brussels, 1939.

Černý, J. "A Note on the 'Repeating of Births,' " *JEA*, XV (1929), pp. 194-198.

——— "Zu den Ausführungen von Sethe über die *whm msw·t* Datierungen in den thebanischen Grabberaubungsakten der 20. Dynastie," *ZAS*, LXV (1930), pp. 129-130.

——— "Une Famille de scribes de la nécropole royale de Thèbes," *Chronique d'Égypte*, XI (1936), pp. 247-250.

Elgood, P. G. *The Later Dynasties of Egypt*. Oxford, 1951.

Faulkner, R. O. *The Wilbour Papyrus*, edited by Alan H. Gardiner, IV. *Index* (The Brooklyn Museum). Oxford, 1952.

Forbes, R. J. "The Coming of Iron," *Jaarbericht van het vooraziatische-egyptisch Gezelschap "Ex Oriente Lux,"* IX (1944), pp. 207-214.

Gardiner, A. H. *The Wilbour Papyrus* (*The Brooklyn Museum*). 3 vols. Oxford, 1941, 1948.

——— "A Protest against Unjustified Tax Demands," *Revue d'égyptologie*, VI (1951), pp. 115-133.

Guilmant, F. *Le Tombeau de Ramsès IX* (*MIFAO*, XV). Cairo, 1907.

Hayes, W. C. "A Canopic Jar of King Nesu-Ba-neb-Dēdet of Tanis," *BMMA*, n. s. V (1946-1947), pp. 261-263.

Helck, W. "Die Inschrift über die Belohnung des Hohenpriesters ʿ*Imn-ḥtp*," *Mitteilungen des Instituts für Orientforschung*, IV (1956), pp. 161-178.

Kees, H. *Herihor und die Aufrichtung des thebanischen Gottesstaats* (*Nachrichten von der Gesellschaft der Wissenschaften zu Göttingen*, Philologisch-historische Klasse, Fachgruppe I. *Altertumswissenschaft*, n. s. II, 1). Göttingen, 1936.

Labib, P. "Feudalismus in der Ramessidenzeit," *ASAE*, XLVIII (1948), pp. 467-484.

Lefebvre, G. "Sur Trois Dates dans les mésaventures d'Ounamon," *Chronique d'Egypte*, XI (1936), pp. 97-99.

Meyer, E. "Gottesstaat, Militärherrschaft und Ständewesen in Agypten. Zur Geschichte der 21. und 22. Dynastie," *Sb. Berlin*, 1928, pp. 495-532.

Newberry, P. E. *The Amherst Papyri*. London, 1899.

Nims, C. F. "An Oracle Dated in 'The Repeating of Births,' " *JNES*, VII (1948), pp. 157-162.

——— "Another Geographical List from Medīnet Habu," *JEA*, XXXVIII (1952), pp. 34-45.

——— Review of *Ägyptologische Studien* (Berlin, 1955) in *Bibliotheca Orientalis*, XIV (1957), pp. 136-139.

Parker, R. A. "The Length of the Reign of Ramses X," *Revue d'égyptologie*, XI (1957), pp. 163-164.

Peet, T. E. *The Mayer Papyri A and B, Nos. M 11162 and 11186 of the Free Public Museums, Liverpool* (The Egypt Exploration Society). London, 1920.

——— "A Historical Document of Ramesside Age," *Ibid.*, X (1924), pp. 116-127.

——— "The Supposed Revolution of the High-Priest Amenḥotpe under Ramesses IX," *JEA*, XII (1926), pp. 254-259.

——— "The Chronological Problems of the Twentieth Dynasty," *Ibid.*, XIV (1928), pp. 52-73.

——— *The Great Tomb-robberies of the Twentieth Egyptian Dynasty*. 2 vols. Oxford, 1930.

Piankoff, A. *La création du disque solaire* (*Institut français d'archéologie orientale du Caire, Bibliothèque d'étude*, XIX). Cairo, 1953.

——— *The Tomb of Ramesses VI* (*Bollingen Series XL*, 1. *Egyptian Religious Texts and Representations*, edited by N. Rambova). New York, 1954.

——— and Maystre, C. "Deux Plafonds dans les tombes royales," *BIFAO*, XXXVIII (1939), pp. 65-70.

Sauneron, S. "Trois Personnages du scandal d'Éléphantine," *Revue d'égyptologie*, VII (1950), pp. 53-62.

Vandier, J. Review of P. G. Elgood, *The Later Dynasties of Egypt* (Oxford, 1951), in *Bibliotheca Orientalis*, IX (1952), pp. 108-109.

Vandier d'Abbadie, J. "Un Monument inédit de Ramsès VII au Musée du Louvre," *JNES*, IX (1950), pp. 134-136.

van Wijngaarden, W. D. "Ein Torso von Ramses VI," *Studi in memoria di Ippolito Rosellini* [Pisa], II (1955), pp. 293-299.

Wilson, J. A. *The Collapse of an Ancient Civilization* (*Lecture delivered before the Alumni School of The University of Chicago, June 6, 1940*). Chicago, 1940.

Yoyotte, J. "À Propos des Scarabées attribués à Ramsès VIII," *Kêmi*, X (1949), pp. 86-89.

34. Music and Dancing

Brunner-Traut, E. *Der Tanz im alten Ägypten, nach bildlichen und inschriftlichen Zeugnissen* (*Ägyptologische Forschungen*, VI). Glückstadt, Hamburg, New York, 1938.

Cottevieille-Giraudet, R. "À propos du Nom de la harpe en vieil égyptien," *Comptes rendus du Groupe linguistique d'études chamito-sémitiques*, III (1938), pp. 32-33.

Drioton, É. "La Danse dans l'ancienne Egypte," *La Femme Nouvelle* [Cairo], October, 1948, pp. 24-32.

Garnot, J. Ste.-F. "L'Offrande musicale dans l'ancienne Égypte," pp. 89-92 in *Mélanges d'histoire et d'esthétique musicales offerts à Paul-Marie Masson*, I. Paris, 1955.

Hickmann, H. *La Trompette dans l'Egypte ancienne* (*Supplément aux ASAE, Cahier No. 1*). Cairo, 1946.

——— "Miscellanea musicologica," *ASAE*, XLVIII-LII (1948-1952), *passim*.

——— "Ägyptische Musik," *Allgemeine Enzyklopädie der Musik*, cols. 92-96. Kassel and Basel, 1949.

——— *Instruments de musique* (*CCG*, nos. 69201-69852). Cairo, 1949.

——— *Le Métier de musicien au temps des pharaons* (*Cahiers d'histoire égyptienne*). Cairo, 1954.

——— "Les Harpes de l'Égypte pharaonique: Essai d'une nouvelle classification," *Bulletin de l'Institut d'Egypte*, XXXV (1954), pp. 309-368.

HICKMANN, H., *continued*

——— "Le Problème de la notation musicale dans l'Égypte ancienne," *Ibid.*, XXXVI (1955), pp. 489-531.

——— "Die altägyptische Rassel," *ZÄS*, LXXIX (1954), pp. 116-125.

——— *Musicologie pharaonique. Études sur l'évolution de l'art musical dans l'Egypte ancienne* (*Collection des études musicologiques. Sammlung musikwissenschaftlicher Abhandlungen*, XXXIV). Kehl, 1956.

——— "Les Problèmes et l'état actuel des recherches musicologiques en Egypte," *Acta Musicologica* [Basel], XXVIII (1956), pp. 59-68.

VON KOMORZYNSKI, E. "Die Trompete als Signalinstrument im altägyptischen Heer," *Archiv für ägyptische Archäologie*, I (1938), pp. 155-157.

——— "Blinde als Musiker im alten Ägypten," *Weg ohne Licht: Organ des Österreichischen Blindenverbandes, Zeitschrift über das Blindwesen* [Vienna], VI (1951), no. 5, pp. 3-5.

KRAEMER, C. J., JR. "A Greek Element in Egyptian Dancing," *American Journal of Archaeology*, 2nd series, XXXV (1931), pp. 125-138.

LANSING, A. "Excavations in the Assasîf at Thebes," *BMMA*, XII (1917), May, Supplement, pp. 7-26.

LEXOVA, I. *Ancient Egyptian Dances.* Translated by K. Haltmar (*Oriental Institute, Czechoslovakia*). Prague, 1935.

METROPOLITAN MUSEUM OF ART, *Handbook No. 13: Catalogue of the Crosby Brown Collection of Musical Instruments.* New York, 1903-1907.

R[ANSOM], C. L. "Egyptian Furniture and Musical Instruments," *BMMA*, VIII (1913), pp. 72-79.

SACHS, C. *Altägyptische Musikinstrumente* (*Der alte Orient*, XXI, 3, 4). Leipzig, 1920.

——— *The History of Musical Instruments.* New York, 1940. See pp. 86-104.

SCOTT, N. E. "The Lute of the Singer Ḥar-mosĕ," *BMMA*, n. s. II (1943-1944), pp. 159-163.

STRACMANS, M. "Du Nouveau sur la musique et la danse des anciens Égyptiens," *Le Flambeau* [Brussels], 1954, 6, pp. 706-714.

WEGNER, M. *Die Musikinstrumente des alten Orients* (*Orbis Antiquus*, 2. *Schriften der Altertumswissenschaftlichen Gesellschaft an der Universität Münster*). Münster in Westfalen, 1950. See pp. 8-22.

WILD, H. "La Danse dans l'Égypte ancienne. Les documents figurés," pp. 227-230 in *Positions des thèses des élèves de l'Ecole du Louvre* (1911-1944). Paris, 1956.

35. Arts and Crafts of the New Kingdom[1]

ALDRED, C. *New Kingdom Art in Ancient Egypt during the Eighteenth Dynasty, 1590 to 1315* B.C. London, 1951.

ANTHES, R. *Äegyptischer Plastik in Meisterwerken* (*Die Sammlung Parthenon*). Stuttgart, 1954.

BADAWY, A. *Le Dessin architectural chez les anciens Égyptiens. Étude comparative des représentations égyptiennes de construction* (*Service des antiquités de l'Égypte*). Cairo, 1948.

——— "La Maison mitoyenne de plan uniforme dans l'Egypte pharaonique," *Bulletin of the Faculty of Arts* (Cairo University), XV (1954), part II, pp. 1-58.

BORCHARDT, L. "Metallbelag an Steinbauten," pp. 1-11 in Borchardt, *Allerhand Kleinigkeiten.* Leipzig, 1933.

[1] Supplementary to *The Scepter of Egypt*, Part I, pp. 355-374 (see especially §§ 18, 19) and to the works listed in the preceding sections of the present Bibliography.

BRUNNER-TRAUT, E. *Die altägyptischen Scherbenbilder* (*Bildostraka*) *der deutschen Museen und Sammlungen.* Wiesbaden, 1956.

BULL, L. "Two Egyptian Stelae of the XVIII Dynasty," *Metropolitan Museum Studies*, II (1929), 1, pp. 76-84.

Burlington Fine Arts Club *Catalogue of an Exhibition of Ancient Egyptian Art.* London, 1922.

ČERNÝ, J. *Egyptian Stelae of the Bankes Collection* (The Griffith Institute). Oxford, 1958.

DARESSY, G. *Ostraca* (*CCG*, nos. 25001-25385). Cairo, 1901.

DAVIES, N. M. *Picture Writing in Ancient Egypt* (*The Griffith Institute*). London, 1958.

DAVIES, N. DE G. "Egyptian Drawings on Limestone Flakes," *JEA*, IV (1917), pp. 234-240.

——— "The Town House in Ancient Egypt," *Metropolitan Museum Studies*, I (1929), pp. 233-255.

DESROCHES, C. "Un Modèle de maison citadine du Nouvel Empire (Musée du Louvre: No. E.5357)," *Revue d'égyptologie*, III (1938), pp. 17-25.

DESROCHES-NOBLECOURT, C. *Le style égyptien* (*Collection Arts, Styles et Techniques*). Paris, 1946.

DRIOTON, E. *Egyptian Art.* Photographs by Étienne Sved. New York, 1950.

EDGERTON, W. F. "Two Notes on the Flying Gallop," *Journal of the American Oriental Society*, LVI (1936), pp. 178-188.

Egypt: Paintings from Tombs and Temples. Introduction by J. Vandier. (*Published by the New York Graphic Society by arrangement with UNESCO*). Paris, 1954.

ENGELBACH, R. *The Aswân Obelisk, with Some Remarks on the Ancient Engineering* (*Service des antiquités de l'Egypte*). Cairo, 1922.

FARNSWORTH, M., AND RITCHIE, P. D. "Spectrographic Studies on Ancient Glass: Egyptian Glass, Mainly of the Eighteenth Dynasty, with Special Reference to its Cobalt Content," *Technical Studies in the Field of Fine Arts* [Cambridge, Mass.], VI (1938), pp. 155-173.

FRANKFORT, H. "Notes on the Cretan Griffin," *Annual of the British School at Athens*, XXXVII (1940), pp. 106-122.

GARNOT, J. STE.-F. "Le Lion dans l'art égyptien," *BIFAO*, XXXVII (1937), pp. 75-91.

GILBERT, P. "La Conception architecturale de la Salle Hypostyle de Karnak," *Chronique d'Egypte*, XVII (1942), pp. 168-176.

GOTHEIN, M. L. *A History of Garden Art.* Translated by Mrs. Archer-Hind. 2 vols. New York, 1928. See Chapter I, "Ancient Egypt."

HALL, H. R. "Some Wooden Figures of the Eighteenth and Nineteenth Dynasties in the British Museum," *JEA*, XV (1929), pp. 236-238; XVI (1930), pp. 39-40.

HELCK, H. W. "Die liegende und geflügelte weibliche Sphinx des Neuen Reiches," *Mitteilungen des Instituts für Orientforschung*, III (1955), pp. 1-10.

HEUZEY, L. AND J. *Histoire du costume dans l'antiquité classique. L'Orient* (*Egypte—Mesopotamie—Syrie—Phénicie*). Paris, 1935.

HORNEMANN, B. *Types of Egyptian Statuary*, I-III. 3 parts, Copenhagen, 1951-1957.

JÉQUIER, G. *Décoration égyptienne: Plafonds et frises végétales du nouvel empire thébain* (*1400 à 1000 avant J.-C.*). Paris, 1911.

——— *Les Temples ramessides et saïtes de la XIXe à la XXXe dynastie* (*L'Architecture et la décoration dans l'ancienne Egypte*, II). Paris, 1922.

KANTOR, H. J. "Narration in Egyptian Art," *American Journal of Archaeology*, LXI (1957), pp. 44-54.

KEIMER, L. "Remarques sur les 'cuillers à fard' du type dit à la nageuse," *ASAE*, LII (1952), pp. 59-72.
LACAU, P. "L'Or dans l'architecture égyptienne," *ASAE*, LIII (1955), pp. 221-250.
LANGE, K., AND HIRMER, M. *Egypt: Architecture, Sculpture and Painting in Three Thousand Years*. London, 1956.
LANSING, A. "The Theodore M. Davis Bequest. The Objects of Egyptian Art," *BMMA*, XXVI (1931), March, sect. II, pp. 4-12.
LEGRAIN, G. *Les Temples de Karnak* (*Fondation égyptologique Reine Élisabeth*). Brussels, 1929.
LEIBOVITCH, J. "Quelques Éléments de la décoration égyptienne sous le Nouvel Empire: I. Le Griffon; II. La Sphinge," *Bulletin de l'Institut d'Égypte*, XXV-XXVIII (1943-1947), *passim*.
LHOTE, A. *Les Chefs-d'oeuvre de la peinture égyptienne* (*Arts du Monde*). Photographs by Hassia. Preface by J. Vandier. Paris, 1954.
LUCAS, A. "Glass Figures," *ASAE*, XXXIX (1939), pp. 227-235.
LYTHGOE, A. M. "The Carnarvon Egyptian Collection," *BMMA*, XXII (1927), pp. 31-40.
MACE, A. C. "The Murch Collection of Egyptian Antiquities," *BMMA*, VI (1911), January, Supplement.
The Metropolitan Museum of Art *A Special Exhibition of Glass from the Museum Collections*. New York, 1936. See "Ancient Egyptian Glass."
MONTET, P. *Les Reliques de l'art syrien dans l'Égypte du nouvel empire* (*Publications de la Faculté des lettres, Université de Strasbourg*, LXXVI). Paris, 1937.
NAGEL, G. *La Céramique du Nouvel Empire à Deir el Médineh*, I (*Documents de FIFAO*, X). Cairo, 1938.
NELSON, H. H. "The Egyptian Temple, with Particular Reference to the Theban Temples of the Empire Period," *Biblical Archaeologist*, VII (1944), pp. 44-53.
VAN OS, W. "Die ägyptische Zeichenkunst," *Jaarbericht van het vooraziatisch-egyptisch Gezelschap "Ex Oriente Lux,"* VIII (1942), pp. 767-784.
OTTO, E. "Zur Bedeutung der ägyptischen Tempelstatue seit dem neuen Reich," *Orientalia*, XVII (1948), pp. 448-466.
PHILLIPS, D. W. *Ancient Egyptian Animals. A Picture Book* (*Metropolitan Museum of Art*). New York, 1942.
PILLET, M. *Thèbes. Karnak et Louxor* (*Les Villes d'art célèbres*). Paris, 1928.
PRITCHARD, J. B. *The Ancient Near East in Pictures Relating to the Old Testament*. Princeton, 1954.
RANKE, H. *Masterpieces of Egyptian Art*. London, [1951].
RIEFSTAHL, E. *Glass and Glazes from Ancient Egypt* (*The Brooklyn Museum*). Brooklyn, 1948.
ROEDER, G. "Freie Plastik aus Ägypten in dem Rijksmuseum van Oudheden," *Oudheidkundige Medeelingen uit het Rijksmuseum van Oudheden te Leiden*, n. s. XX (1939), pp. 1-23.
ROGERS, E. A. "An Egyptian Wine Bowl of the XIX Dynasty," *BMMA*, n. s. VI (1947-1948), pp. 154-160.
ROSTEM, O. R. "Remarkable Drawings with Examples in True Perspective," *ASAE*, XLVIII (1948), pp. 167-177.
SCHÄFER, H. "Ägyptische Zeichnungen auf Scherben," *Jahrbuch der königlich preussischen Kunstsammlungen*, XXXVII (1916), pp. 23-51.
SCHARFF, A. "Gott und König in Aegyptischen Gruppenplastiken," *Studi scritti in onore di Ippolito Rosellini* [Pisa], I (1949), pp. 303-321.
SCHWEITZER, U. *Löwe und Sphinx im alten Ägypten* (*Ägyptologische Forschungen*, XV). Glückstadt, 1948.
SCOTT, N. E. "Egyptian Cubit Rods," *BMMA*, n. s. I (1943-1943), pp. 70-75.
——— "Egyptian Accessions," *Ibid.*, VI (1947-1948), pp. 62-65.
SENK, H. "Von der Beziehung zwischen 'Geradvorstelligkeit' und 'perspectivischen Gehalt,' " *ZAS*, LXXIV (1938), pp. 125-132.
——— "Der Kopf als Einheit des ägyptischen Proportionskanons," *Archiv für Orientforschung*, XIII (1940), pp. 135-144.
——— "Fragen und Ergebnis zur Formgeschichte des ägyptischen Würfelhockers," *ZAS*, LXXIX (1954), pp. 149-156.
SMITH, W. S. *The Art and Architecture of Ancient Egypt* (*Pelican History of Art*). Harmondsworth, 1958. See pp. 121-229.
VANDIER, J. *Egyptian Sculpture* (*Bibliothèque Aldine des arts*, XXII). Paris, 1951.
VANDIER D'ABBADIE, J. *Catalogue des ostraca figurés de Deir el Médineh* (*nos. 2001-2733*) (*Documents de FIFAO*, II). Cairo, 1937-1946.
——— "Une Fresque civile de Deir el Médineh," *Revue d'égyptologie*, III (1938), pp. 27-35.
——— "Cuillères à fards de l'Égypte ancienne," *Recherches* [Paris], October, 1952, 2, pp. 20-29.
VERNIER, É. *Bijoux et orfèvreries* (*CCG*, nos. 52001-53855). 2 vols. Cairo, 1927.
WALLIS, H. *Egyptian Ceramic Art: The MacGregor Collection*. London, 1898.
——— *Egyptian Ceramic Art*. London, 1900.
WERBROUCK, M. "Ostraca à figures," *Bulletin des Musées royaux d'art et d'histoire* [Brussels], 4th series, XXV (1953), pp. 93-111.
WINLOCK, H. E. "Statue of the Steward Roy Singing the Psalm to Rēʿ," *JEA*, VI (1920), pp. 1-3.
——— "An Egyptian Flower Bowl," *Metropolitan Museum Studies*, V (1936), 2, pp. 147-156.
——— *Egyptian Statues and Statuettes. A Picture Book* (*The Metropolitan Museum of Art*). New York, 1937.
WOLF, W. *Die Kunst Aegyptens: Gestalt und Geschichte*. Stuttgart, 1957. See pp. 396-598.

36. Theban Tombs and their Decoration

BAUD, M. *Les Dessins ébauchés de la nécropole thébaine* (*au temps du Nouvel Empire*) (*MIFAO*, LXIII). Cairo, 1935.
BÉNÉDITE, G. "Tombeau de la reine Thiti," *MMAF*, V (1893), pp. 381-412.
BORCHARDT, L., KÖNIGSBERGER, O., AND RICKE, H. "Friesziegel in Grabbauten," *ZAS*, LXX (1934), pp. 25-35.
BRITISH MUSEUM. *Wall Decorations of Egyptian Tombs, Illustrated from Examples in the British Museum*. London, 1914.
BRUYÈRE, B. *Tombes thébaines de Deir el Médineh à décoration monochrome* (*MIFAO*, LXXXVI). Cairo, 1952.
——— AND KUENTZ, C. *Tombes thébaines. La Nécropole de Deir el-Médineh. La tombe de Nakht-Min et la tombe d'Ari-Nefer* (*MIFAO*, LIV). Cairo, 1926.

[1] Works on royal tombs are for the most part listed in the sections of the Bibliography pertaining to the periods involved.

Davies, Nina M. de G. *Ancient Egyptian Paintings*. Edited by A. H. Gardiner (*Special Publication of the Oriental Institute of The University of Chicago*). 3 vols. Chicago, 1936.

——— "Some Representations of Tombs from the Theban Necropolis," *JEA*, XXIV (1938), pp. 25-40.

——— and Gardiner, A. H. *The Tomb of Amenemhēt* (*No. 82*) (*The Egypt Exploration Fund* [*Society*]. *The Theban Tombs Series*, 1st Memoir). London, 1915.

——— and Gardiner, A. H. *The Tomb of Ḥuy, Viceroy of Nubia in the Reign of Tutʿankh-amūn* (*No. 40*) (*Ibid.*, 4th Memoir). London, 1926.

——— and Davies, Norman de G. *The Tombs of Menkheperrasonb, Amenmosĕ, and Another* (*Nos. 86, 112, 42, 226*) (*Ibid.*, 5th Memoir). London, 1933.

——— and Davies, Norman de G. "The Tomb of Amenmosĕ (No. 89) at Thebes," *JEA*, XXVI (1940), pp. 131-136.

Davies, Norman de G. "The Rock-cut Tombs of Sheikh Abd el Qurneh at Thebes," *BMMA*, VI (1911) pp. 53-59.

——— "The Work of the (Robb de Peyster) Tytus Memorial Fund," *Ibid.*, X-XVI (1915-1921), *passim.*

——— "The Graphic Work of the Expedition," *Ibid.*, XVII-XXIV (1922-1929), *passim.*

——— "The Work of the Graphic Branch of the Expedition," *Ibid.*, XXV-XXX (1930-1935), *passim.*

——— "Research in the Theban Necropolis: 1938-1939," *Ibid.*, XXXIV (1939), pp. 280-284.

——— *Five Theban Tombs* (*The Egypt Exploration Fund: Archaeological Survey of Egypt*, 21st Memoir). London, 1913

——— *The Tomb of Nakht at Thebes* (*Publications of The Metropolitan Museum of Art Egyptian Expedition. Robb de Peyster Tytus Memorial Series*, I). New York, 1917.

——— *The Tomb of Puyemrê at Thebes* (*Ibid.*, II, III). 2 vols. New York, 1922, 1923.

——— *The Tomb of Two Sculptors at Thebes* (*Ibid.*, IV). New York, 1925.

——— *Two Ramesside Tombs at Thebes* (*Ibid.*, V). New York, 1927.

——— *The Tomb of Ḳen-Amūn at Thebes* (*The Metropolitan Museum of Art Egyptian Expedition Publications*, V). 2 vols. New York, 1930.

——— "Teḥuti: Owner of Tomb 110 at Thebes," pp. 279-290 in *Studies Presented to F. Ll. Griffith* (*Egypt Exploration Society*). London, 1932.

——— *The Tomb of Nefer-hotep at Thebes* (*The Metropolitan Museum of Art Egyptian Expedition Publications*, IX). 2 vols. New York, 1933.

——— *Paintings from the Tomb of Rekh-mi-Rēʿ at Thebes* (*Ibid.*, X). New York, 1935.

——— *The Tomb of the Vizier Ramose* (*Mond Excavations at Thebes*, I). London, 1941.

——— *The Tomb of Rekh-mi-Rēʿ at Thebes* (*The Metropolitan Museum of Art Egyptian Expedition Publications*, XI). 2 vols. New York, 1943.

——— *Seven Private Tombs at Ḳurnah* (*Mond Excavations at Thebes*, II). London, 1948.

——— and Davies, Nina de G. *The Tombs of Two Officials of Tuthmosis the Fourth* (*Nos. 75 and 90*) (*Egypt Exploration Society: The Theban Tombs Series*, 3rd Memoir). London, 1923.

Engelbach, R. *A Supplement to the Topographical Catalogue of the Private Tombs of Thebes* (*Nos. 253-334*) *with Some Notes on the Necropolis from 1913 to 1924*. Cairo, 1924.

Fakhry, A. "Tomb of Nebamun, Captain of Troops (No. 145 at Thebes)," *ASAE*, XLIII (1943), pp. 369-379.

——— "A Report on the Inspectorate of Upper Egypt. 3. The Theban Necropolis," *Ibid.*, XLVI (1947), pp. 25-54.

——— "Tomb of Paser (No. 367 at Thebes)," *Ibid.*, pp. 389-414.

Foucart, G. "Sur Quelques Représentations des tombes thébaines découvertes cette année par l'Institut français d'archéologie orientale," *Bulletin de l'Institut égyptien*, 5th series, XI (1917), pp. 261-324.

——— *Tombes thébaines. Nécropole de Dirâʿ abû'n-Naga. Le Tombeau d'Amonmos*, I (*MIFAO*, LVII). Cairo, 1932.

Farina, G. *La pittura egiziana*. Milan, 1929.

Gardiner, A. H. "The Tomb of Amenemhet, High-Priest of Amon," *ZÄS*, XLVII (1910), pp. 87-99.

——— and Weigall, A. E. P. *A Topographical Catalogue of the Private Tombs of Thebes*. London, 1913.

Grapow, H. "Studien zu den thebanischen Königsgräbern," *ZÄS*, LXXII (1936), pp. 12-39.

Hermann, A. *Die Stelen der thebanischen Felsgräber der 18. Dynastie* (Ägyptologische Forschungen, XI). Glückstadt, 1940.

Klebs, L. *Die Reliefs und Malereien des neuen Reiches* (*XVIII.-XX. Dynastie, ca. 1580-1100 v. Chr.*). *Teil I: Szenen aus dem Leben des Volkes* (*Abhandlungen der Heidelberger Akademie der Wissenschaften*, Philologisch-historische Klasse, 9. Abhandlung). Heidelberg, 1934.

Lansing, A. *An Exhibition of Copies of Egyptian Wall Paintings from Tombs and Palaces of the XVIII and XIX Dynasties, 1600-1200 B.C.* (*The Metropolitan Museum of Art*). New York, 1930.

Lepsius, C. R. *Denkmäler aus Aegypten und Aethiopien, Text*, III. Edited by E. Naville, L. Borchardt, and K. Sethe. 5 vols. Leipzig, 1900.

Loret, V. "Le Tombeau de l'Am-xent Amenhotep," *MMAF*, I (1889), pp. 23-32.

——— "La Tombe de Khâ-m-hâ," *Ibid.*, pp. 113-132.

Lythgoe, A. M. "List of Private Tombs at Thebes Recorded by the Museum's Egyptian Expedition during the Years 1907-1927," *BMMA*, XXIII (1928), February, sect. II, pp. 73-75.

Mackay, E. "Proportion Squares on Tomb Walls in the Theban Necropolis," *JEA*, IV (1917), pp. 74-85.

——— "The Cutting and Preparation of Tomb-chapels in the Theban Necropolis," *Ibid.*, VII (1921), pp. 154-168.

Maspero, G. "Les Hypogées royaux de Thèbes," *Revue de l'histoire des religions*, XVII (1888), pp. 251-310; XVIII (1889), pp. 1-67.

Maystre, C. *Tombes de Deir el-Médineh. La tombe de Nebenmât* (*No. 219*) (*MIFAO*, LXXI). Cairo, 1936.

Mekhitarian, A. *Egyptian Paintings*. Translated by Stuart Gilbert (*Éditions d'art Albert Skira*). Geneva, Paris, New York, 1954.

——— "Personnalité de peintres thébains," *Chronique d'Egypte*, XXXI (1956), pp. 238-248.

Mond, R. "Report of Work in the Necropolis of Thebes during the Winter of 1903-1904," *ASAE*, VI (1905), pp. 65-96.

——— and Emery, W. B. "Excavations at Sheikh Abdel Gurneh 1925-26," *Annals of Archaeology and Anthropology* (*University of Liverpool*), XIV (1927), pp. 13-34.

——— and Emery, W. B. "The Burial Shaft of the Tomb of Amenemhāt," *Ibid.*, XVI (1929), pp. 49-74.

Moret, A. "Maspero et les fouilles dans la Vallée des Rois," *Revue égyptologique*, n. s. II (1924), pp. 38-59.

PIANKOFF, A. "Les Différents 'Livres' dans les tombes royales du Nouvel Empire," *ASAE*, XL (1940), pp. 283-289.

PORTER, B., AND MOSS, R. L. B. *Topographical Bibliography of Ancient Egyptian Hieroglyphic Texts, Reliefs, and Paintings*, I. Part 1: *Private Tombs;* part 2: *Royal Tombs and Smaller Cemeteries*. 2nd edition. Oxford, in preparation.

SCHEIL, J. V. *Tombeaux thébains de Mâi, des Graveurs, Rat'-eserka-Abasenb, Pâri, Djanni, Apoui, Montou-m-hat, Aba* (*MMAF*, V). Paris, 1894.

SCHIAPARELLI, E. *La tomba intatta dell'architetto Cha* (*Relazione sui lavori della Missione archaeologia italiana in Egitto, Anni 1903-1920*, II). Turin, [1927].

SCHOTT, S. *Wall Scenes from the Mortuary Chapel of the Mayor Paser at Medinet Habu*. Translated by E. P. Hauser. (*The University of Chicago Oriental Institute Studies in Ancient Oriental Civilization*, No. 30). Chicago, 1957.

SPIEGEL, J. "Die Entwicklung der Opferszenen in den thebanischen Gräbern," *Mitt. Kairo*, XIV (1956), pp. 190-207.

STEINDORFF, G., AND WOLF, W. *Die Thebanische Gräberwelt* (*Leipziger ägyptologische Studien*, IV). Glückstadt, 1936.

The Theban Necropolis. A set of 26 maps of Western Thebes, scale 1:1,000. Also 2 Tourist Maps of *El Qurna* and *Luxor and Karnak* at a scale of 1:10,000, published by *The Survey of Egypt* in collaboration with the *Service des Antiquités*. Cairo, 1926.

VANDIER, J. *Tombes de Deir el-Médineh. La Tombe de Nefer-Abou* (*MIFAO*, LXIX). Cairo, 1935.

VANDIER D'ABBADIE, J. *Deux Tombes ramessides à Gournet-Mourraï* (*MIFAO*, LXXXVII). Cairo, 1954.

——— AND JOURDAIN, G. *Deux Tombes de Deir el-Médineh*. I. *La chapelle de Khâ;* II. *La Tombe du scribe royal Amenemopet* (*Ibid.*, LXXIII). Cairo, 1939.

VIREY, P. "La Tombe des vignes à Thèbes, ou tombe de Sennofri, directeur des greniers, des troupeaux et des jardins d'Ammon," *Rec. trav.*, XX (1898), pp. 211-223; XXI (1899), pp. 127-133, 137-149; XXII (1900), pp. 83-97.

——— *Sept Tombeaux thébains* (*MIFAO*, V, 2). Paris, 1891.

WEGNER, M. "Stilentwickelung der thebanischen Beamtengräber," *Mitt. Kairo*, IV (1933), pp. 38-164.

WERBROUCK, M. *Les Pleureuses dans l'Egypte ancienne* (*Fondation égyptologique Reine Elisabeth*). Brussels, 1938.

——— AND VAN DE WALLE, B. *La Tombe de Nakht: Notice sommaire* (*Edition de la Fondation "Reine Elisabeth"*). Brussels, 1929.

WINLOCK, H. E. "The Tomb of Queen Inhapi" etc., *JEA*, XVII (1931), pp. 107-110.

37. Literature of the New Kingdom[1]

Aegyptische Hieratische Papyrussen van het Nederlandsche Museum van Oudheden te Leiden. Leiden, 1853-1862.

ALLEN, T. G. "Additions to the Egyptian Book of the Dead," *JNES*, XI (1952), pp. 177-186.

BACCHI, E. *L'Inno al Nilo* (*Pubblicazioni egittologiche del Regio Museo di Torino*). Turin, [1950?].

BAKIR, ABD EL-M. "The Cairo Calendar of Lucky and Unlucky Days (Journal d'entrée, no. 86, 637)," *ASAE*, XLVIII (1948), pp. 425-431.

1 Supplementary to *The Scepter of Egypt*, Part I, pp. 368-371 (§ 14-16).

BARNS, J. "Three Hieratic Papyri in the Duke of Northumberland's Collection," *JEA*, XXXIV (1948), pp. 35-46.

——— "The Nevill Papyrus: A Late Ramesside Letter to an Oracle," *Ibid.*, XXXV (1949), pp. 69-71.

BÉRARD, J. "Vérité et fiction dans le poème de Pentaour: Étude sur la formation des légendes," *Revue des études anciennes*, XLIX (1947), pp. 217-227.

VON BISSING, F. W. *Altägyptische Lebensweisheit, eingeleitet und übertragen* (*Die Bibliothek der alten Welt: Der alte Orient*). Zürich, 1955.

BLACKMAN, A. M., AND PEET, T. E. "Papyrus Lansing: A Translation with Notes," *JEA*, XI (1925), pp. 284-298.

BOTTI, G. "A Fragment of the Story of a Military Expedition of Tuthmosis III to Syria," *JEA*, XLI (1955), pp. 64-71.

——— AND PEET, T. E. *Il giornale della necropoli di Tebe* (*I papiri ieratici del Museo di Torino*). Turin, 1928.

BRITISH MUSEUM. *Select Papyri in the Hieratic Character from the Collections of the British Museum*. Prefatory remarks by S. Birch. 2 parts. London, 1844-1860.

——— *Facsimiles of Egyptian Hieratic Papyri in the British Museum*. Edited by E. A. W. Budge (*Department of Egyptian and Assyrian Antiquities*). 2 series. London, 1910, 1923.

BRUNNER, H., GRAPOW, H., KEES, H., AND OTHERS *Ägyptologie*, sect. 2: *Literatur* (*Handbuch der Orientalistik*, edited by B. Spuler, I). Leiden, 1952.

BRUNNER-TRAUT, E. "Ägyptische Tiermärchen," *ZAS*, LXXX (1955), pp. 12-32.

BUDGE, E. A. W. *The Book of the Dead. The Chapters of Coming Forth by Day*. 3 vols. London, 1898.

CAMINOS, R.A. *Late-Egyptian Miscellanies* (*Brown Egyptological Studies*, I). London, 1954.

ČERNÝ, J. "The Opening Words of the Tales of the Doomed Prince and of the Two Brothers," *ASAE*, XLI (1942), pp. 336-338.

——— "Nouvelle Série de questions adressées aux oracles," *BIFAO*, XLI (1942), pp. 13-24.

——— *Paper and Books in Ancient Egypt* (*Lecture delivered at University College, London, May 29, 1947*). London, 1952.

CHABAS, F. *Les Maximes du scribe Ani*. Chalon-sur-Saône, 1876-1878.

ERMAN, A. *Hymnen an das Diadem der Pharaonen aus einem Papyrus der Sammlung Golenischeff* (*Abh. Berlin*, 1911, I).

——— *Die ägyptischen Schülerhandschriften* (*Ibid.*, 1925) II).

GARDINER, A. H. "Hymns to Amon from a Leiden Papyrus," *ZAS*, XLII (1905), pp. 12-42.

——— *Egyptian Hieratic Texts, transcribed, translated and annotated*, I, 1: *The Papyrus Anastasi I and the Papyrus Koller, together with the parallel texts*. Leipzig, 1911.

——— *Late-Egyptian Stories* (*Bibliotheca Aegyptiaca*, I). Brussels, 1932.

——— "The Astarte Papyrus," pp. 74-85 in *Studies Presented to F. Ll. Griffith* (*The Egypt Exploration Society*). London, 1932.

——— *The Library of A. Chester Beatty. The Chester Beatty Papyri, No. 1: Description of a Hieratic Papyrus with a Mythological Story, Love-songs, and other Miscellaneous Texts*. London, 1931.

——— *Hieratic Papyri in the British Museum*, 3rd series: *Chester Beatty Gift*. 2 vols. London, 1935.

——— "A Lawsuit Arising from the Purchase of Two Slaves," *JEA*, XXI (1935), pp. 140-146.

——— *Late-Egyptian Miscellanies* (*Bibliotheca Aegyptiaca*, VII). Brussels, 1937.

Gardiner, A. H., *continued*

——— "A New Moralizing Text," *Wiener Zeitschrift für die Kunde des Morgenlandes*, LIV (1957), pp. 43-45.

Gaster, T. H. "The Egyptian 'Story of Astarte' and the Ugaritic Poem of Baal," *Bibliotheca Orientalis*, IX (1952), pp. 82-85, 232.

Gilbert, P. "Les Chants du harpiste," *Chronique d'Égypte*, XV (1940), pp. 38-44.

——— *La Poésie égyptienne*. 2nd edition revised and augmented. Brussels, 1949.

Glanville, S. R. K. "The Letters of Aaḥmōse of Peniati," *JEA*, XIV (1928), pp. 294-312.

Grapow, H. "Beiträge zur Untersuchung des Stils ägyptischer Lieder," *ZAS*, LXXIX (1954), pp. 17-27.

Grébaut, E. *Hymne à Ammon-Ra des papyrus égyptiens du Musée de Boulaq* (*Bibliothèque de l'École des hautes études*, XXI). Paris, 1874.

Hermann, A. *Die ägyptische Königsnovelle* (*Leipziger ägyptologische Studien*, X). Glückstadt, 1938.

——— "Beiträge zur Erklärung der ägyptischen Liebesdichtung," pp. 118-139 in *Ägyptologische Studien Hermann Grapow zum 70. Geburstag gewidmet*. Berlin, 1955.

Hintze, F. *Untersuchungen zu Stil und Sprache neuägyptischer Erzählungen* (*Deutsche Akademie der Wissenschaften zu Berlin, Institut für Orientforschung, Veröffentlichungen* 2, 6). Berlin, 1950, 1952.

——— "Ein Bruchstück eines unbekannten Weisheitslehre," *ZAS*, LXXIX (1954), pp. 33-36.

Kees, H. "Göttinger Totenbuchstudien," *ZAS*, LXV (1930), pp. 65-83; *Miscellanea Academica Berolinensia*, II, 2 (1950), pp. 77-96.

Lefebvre, G. "Une Conte égyptien: Vérité et Mensonge," *Revue d'égyptologie*, IV (1940), pp. 15-25.

——— *Romans et contes égyptiens de l'époque pharaonique. Traduction avec introduction, notices et commentaire*. Paris, 1949.

Lichtheim, M. "The Songs of the Harpers," *JNES*, IV (1945), pp. 178-212.

Loukianoff, G. *Poème heroique sur la bataille de Qadech* (*1288, av. J. C.*). *Traduction du texte hiéroglyphique complet avec étude sur l'auguste auteur du poème*. Cairo, 1930.

Malinine, M. "Notes juridiques (à propos de l'ouvrage de E. Seidl)," *BIFAO*, XLVI (1947), pp. 93-123.

Mariette, A. *Les Papyrus égyptiens du Musée de Boulaq publiés en facsimile sous les auspices de S.A. Ismaïl-Pacha, khédive d'Egypte*. 3 vols. Paris, 1871-1876.

Massart, A. *The Leiden Magical Papyrus I 343 + I 345* (*Oudheidkundige Medeelingen uit het Rijksmuseum van Oudheden te Leiden, Supplement op nieuwe reeks* 34). Leiden, 1954.

Maspero, G. *Hymne au Nil: transcrit et publié* (*Institut français d'archéologie orientale, Bibliothèque d'étude*, V). Cairo, 1912.

Maystre, C. *Les Déclarations d'innocence* (*Livre des Morts, Chapitre 125*) (*Recherches d'archéologie, de philologie et d'histoire*, VIII). Cairo, 1937.

——— "Le Livre de la Vache du Ciel dans les tombeaux de la Vallée des Rois," *BIFAO*, XL (1941), pp. 53-115.

——— and Piankoff, A. *Le Livre des Portes*, (*MIFAO*, LXXIV). Cairo, 1939-1946.

Müller, W. M. *Die Liebespoesie der alten Aegypter*. 2nd printing. Leipzig, 1932.

Nims, C. F. "Egyptian Catalogues of Things," *JNES*, IX (1950), pp. 253-262.

Peet, T. E. "The Legend of the Capture of Joppa and the Story of the Foredoomed Prince," *JEA*, XI (1925), pp. 225-229.

Peet, T. E., *continued*

——— "Two Eighteenth Dynasty Letters: Papyrus Louvre 3230," *Ibid.*, XII (1926), pp. 70-74.

Piankoff, A. "Le Livre du Jour et de la Nuit" (*Institut français d'archéologie orientale, Bibliothèque d'étude*, XIII). Cairo, 1942.

——— "Le Livre des Qererts," *BIFAO*, XLI-XLV (1942-1947), *passim*.

——— "The Theology of the New Kingdom in Ancient Egypt," *Antiquity and Survival* [The Hague], I (1955-1956), pp. 488-500.

Pirenne, J., and van de Walle, B. "Documents juridiques égyptiens," *Archives d'histoire du droit oriental*, I (1937), pp. 3-86.

Pleyte, W., and Rossi, F. *Papyrus de Turin*. Leiden, 1869-1876.

Posener, G. *Catalogue des ostraca hiératiques littéraires de Deir el Médineh* (*Documents de FIFAO*, I, XVIII). 2 vols. Cairo, 1934-1952.

——— "Recherches littéraires" I-VI, *Revue d'égyptologie*, VI-XI (1949-1957), *passim*.

——— "La Légende égyptienne de la mer insatiable," *Annuaire de l'Institut de philologie et d'histoire orientales et slaves*, XIII (1953 [1955]), pp. 461-478.

Scharff, A. *Aegyptische Sonnenlieder, übersetzt und eingeleitet* (*Kunst und Altertum: Alte Kulturen im Lichte neuer Forschung*, IV). Berlin, 1922.

Schiaparelli, E. *Il Libro dei funerali degli antichi Egiziani*. 3 vols. Turin, 1881-1890.

Schott, S. *Altägyptische Liebeslieder mit Märchen und Liebesgeschichten* (*Die Bibliothek der Alten Welt: Der Alte Orient*). Zürich, [1950]. French translation by P. Krieger. Paris, 1955.

Schröder, F. R. "Sakrale Grundlagen der altägyptischen Lyrik," *Deutsche Vierteljahrsschrift für Literaturwissenschaft und Gesitesgeschichte* [Stuttgart], XXV (1951), pp. 273-293.

Sethe, K. *Die Totenliteratur der alten Ägypter* (*Sb. Berlin*, 1931, XVIII). Berlin, 1931.

Shorter, A. W. *Catalogue of Egyptian Religious Papyri in the British Museum: Copies of the Book Pr(t)-m-hrw from the XVIIIth to the XXIInd Dynasty*. I. *Description of Papyri with Text*. London, 1938.

Spiegelberg, W. "Ein Brief des Schreibers Amasis aus der Zeit der Thutmosiden," *ZAS*, LV (1918), pp. 84-86.

Suys, E. *La Sagesse d'Ani, traduction et commentaire* (*Analecta Orientalia*, XI). Rome, 1935.

Turajeff, B. "Zwei Hymnen an Thoth," *ZAS*, XXXIII 1895), pp. 120-125.

Vikentiev, V. *La Légende de Deux Frères et la recherche de l'immortalité*. Cairo, 1941.

Volten, A. *Studien zum Weisheitsbuch des Anii* (*Det Kgl. Danske Videnskabernes Selskab*, Historisk-filologiske Meddelelser, XXIII, 3). Copenhagen, 1937-1938.

van de Walle, B. "Le Thème de la satire des métiers dans la littérature égyptienne," *Chronique d'Égvpte*, XXII (1947), pp. 50-72.

Wiedemann, K. A. *Hieratische Texte aus den Museen zu Berlin und Paris in Facsimile mit Uebersetzung und sachlichen Commentar*. Leipzig, 1879.

Würfel, R. "Die ägyptische Fabel in Bildkunst und Literatur," *Wissenschaftliche Zeitschrift der Universität Leipzig*, III (1952-1953), pp. 63-77, 153-160.

Zandee, J. "De Hymnen aan Amon van Papyrus Leiden I 350," *Oudheidkundige medeelingen uit het Rijksmuseum van Oudheden te Leiden*, n. s. XXVIII (1947), pp. 1-158.

INDEXES OF PROPER NAMES

Indexes of Proper Names

A. Egyptian and Foreign Kings

[1] Formerly referred to as Montu-ḥotpe II.
[2] Formerly referred to as Montu-ḥotpe III.

B. Egyptian and Foreign Personal Names

C. Divinities

Osiris, *continued*
representations, 48, 75, 89, 180, 329, 384, 391, 400, 417, 419, 420, 423, 428
Osiris Khenty-Amentiu (Khenty-Amentet), 272, 388, 391
"the Osiris . . .," 137, 146, 242, 261, 270, 330, 356, 386, 403, 418, 427
Osiris Wen-nefer, 330, 349, 350

Pakhet, 102
Ptaḥ, 11, 31, 43, 158, 185, 240, 250, 269, 274, 304, 308, 332, 354, 355, 379, 396, 400, 424
representations, 124, 142, 183, 185, 274, 340, 344, 368, 370, 391, 400, 404
in royal epithets, 303, 308, 333
Ptaḥ Sokar, 52, 113, 244, 293, 304, 384, 398
Ptaḥ Sokar Osiris, 53
Ptaḥ Ta-tenen, 340

Rēʿ, 4, 37, 52, 125, 161, 162, 172, 178, 182, 183, 213, 248, 250, 286, 292, 344, 395, 400, 412, 420, 431, 433
Rē, *continued*
in royal epithets, 127, 134, 233, 240, 244, 256, 286, 292, 308, 333, 337, 353, 392, 393, and *passim*
representations, 182, 278, 322, 344, 399
Rēʿ Atūm, 117, 262, 384
Rēʿ Ḥor-akhty, 43, 84, 118, 119, 129, 172, 242, 274, 279, 292, 386, 387, 423, 429, 432
Rēʿ Ḥor-akhty Atūm, 272
Resheph, 141, 251

Sakhmet, 124, 127, 180, 183, 185, 237-239, 274, 278, 304, 355, 398, 400, 402
Satis, 159
Serḳet, 183, 227, 357, 400, 417
Sēth̲, 4, 11, 183, 250, 273, 275, 310, 326, 332, 364, 400, 403, 431, 432
Sēth̲ ʿA-peḥty, 369
Shu, 72, 134, 183, 252, 286, 292, 322, 329, 359, 370, 396, 398, 412
Sobk, 36, 153, 154, 183, 308, 352, 391
Sobk-Rēʿ, 20, 124
Sokar, 58, 158, 170, 171, 178, 354, 384, 391
Sokar Osiris, 318
Sothis, Sothic, 46, 327
Sun god, the, *see* General Index

Ta-tenen, 340
Ta-weret, 13, 38, 100, 133, 134, 385; *see also* Thoueris
Tefēnet, 72, 134, 329, 359
Tḥōt, 172, 191, 250, 275, 304, 308, 322, 344, 350, 354, 400, 422, 428, 432
representations, 37, 150, 180, 183, 265, 344, 347, 380, 397, 399, 400, 402, 416, 417
ibis of, 400
Thoueris, 100, 183, 192, 196, 251, 268, 278, 385, 396, 400
amulets, 13, 180, 252, 254, 293, 322, 398, 402; *see also* Ta-weret
Tjenenyet, 170
Tree goddess, 417

Udōt, 7, 368
Up-wawet, 349, 350

Wen-nefer, 37, 183, 270, 271, 384, 400
Weret-ḥekau, 150, 258, 292
West, Sovereign or Mistress of, 419

Yuny(et), 170

D. Geographic and Ethnic Names

Abu Simbel, 307, 339, 432
Abydene, 112, 120, 272, 329, 330
Abydos, 8, 34, 70, 126, 221, 229, 332, 349, 387
temples, 9, 43, 44, 119, 326, 329-332, 334, 339, 344, 370, 371
tombs, 16, 19, 21, 22, 39, 40, 43, 44, 64, 113, 179, 185, 189, 193, 198, 203, 210, 214, 216, 219, 229, 277, 301, 307, 308, 322, 329, 404, 406, 407, 424
Achaeans, 353
Aegean, 37, 74, 111, 184, 245, 337
Africa, African, 40, 52, 74, 101, 116, 144, 150, 165, 211, 268, 295, 303
ʿAget, 239
Ahnāsyeh, 187, 342; *see also* Herakleopolis
Akhet-Aten, 281, 283, 285, 288-290, 293, 308; *see also* el ʿAmārneh
Akhmim, 260, 307, 403; *see also* Ipu
Akkadian, 295
Alexandria, 118, 327
Amada, 147
ʿAmāreh, 327
el ʿAmārneh (Tell), 237, 255, 256, 259, 260, 262, 271, 280-301, 307, 314-316, 319-324, 338, 374, 405
temples, 284, 285, 287, 288
tombs, 262, 284, 286, 289, 294, 319
school (of art), style, 236, 259, 282, 283, 285, 288, 290, 298, 300, 304, 306, 308, 310, 311, 313, 314, 317, 318, 325, 329
period, 192, 268, 280, 291, 309, 310, 316, 319
Letters, 295
America, 148, 238, 261, 294
Amorite, 327
ʿAmu, 3
ʿAniba, 115
Aphroditopolis, 401
Arabia, 74
Arabic, 22, 245
Argo, 75
Armageddon, 114; *see also* Ḥar Megiddon, Megiddo
ʿAruna, 114
Arzawa, 258, 295, 365
ʿAsāsīf (valley), 15, 19, 35, 61, 62, 65, 67, 73, 84, 97, 101, 176, 177, 202, 205, 272, 340, 371, 375, 409
Asia, 3, 4, 12, 25, 36, 74, 75, 114, 115, 136, 165, 197, 198, 231, 295, 327, 374
Asia Minor, 74, 337
Asiatic, 3, 4, 6-9, 11, 20, 24, 29, 35, 42, 52, 68, 74, 75, 102, 114-116, 124, 144, 147, 183, 192, 219, 233, 236, 237, 258, 261, 278, 279, 295, 303, 319, 334, 339, 343, 365, 367, 370, 373, 407, 420
Askalon, 353
Assyria, Assyrian, 115, 295, 344, 370, 434
Aswān, 39, 76, 92, 101, 159, 233, 373

GENERAL INDEX

General Index

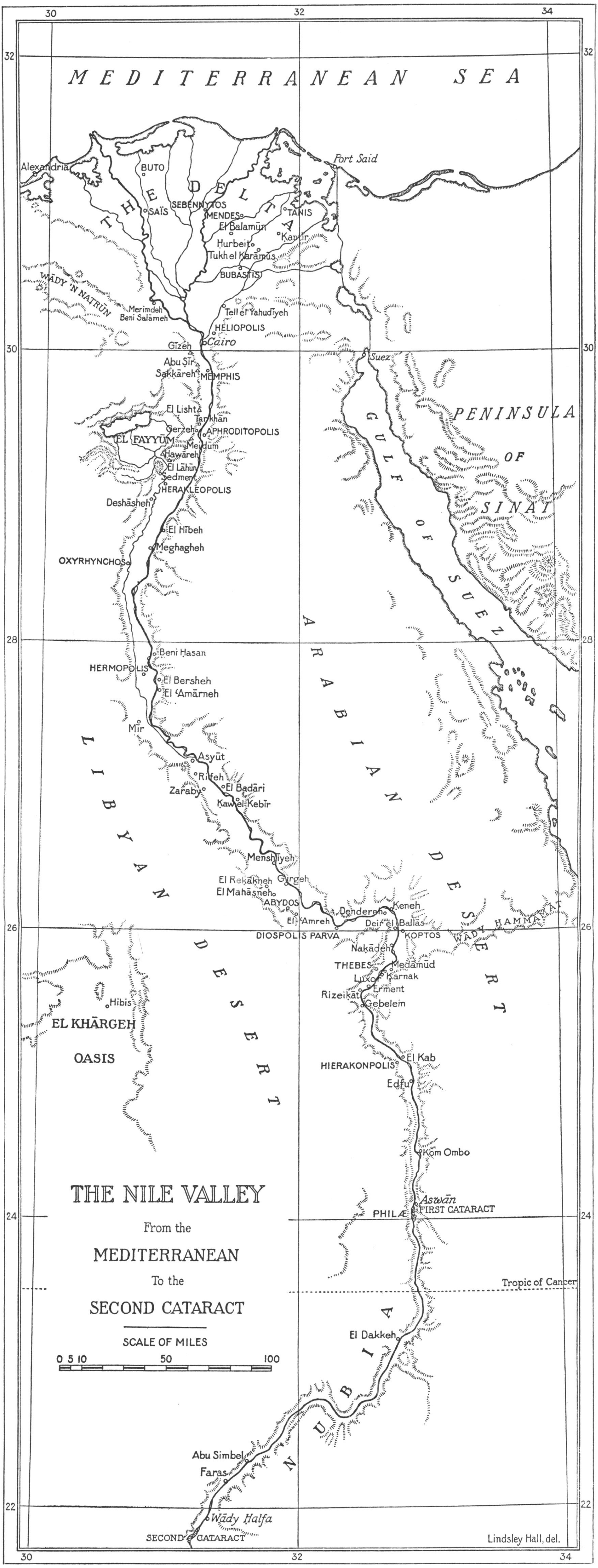

THE NILE VALLEY
From the
MEDITERRANEAN
To the
SECOND CATARACT
SCALE OF MILES
0 5 10 50 100
MEDITERRANEAN SEA
THE DELTA
Alexandria
BUTO
SAÏS
SEBENNYTOS
MENDES
TANIS
El Balamūn
Kantir
Hurbeit
Tukh el Karamus
BUBASTIS
Port Said
WĀDY 'N NATRŪN
Merimdeh
Beni Salāmeh
Tell el Yahudīyeh
HELIOPOLIS
Gīzeh
Cairo
Suez
Abu Ṣīr
Saḳḳāreh
MEMPHIS
El Lisht
Tarkhān
Gerzeh
APHRODITOPOLIS
EL FAYYŪM
Meydūm
Hawāreh
El Lāhūn
Sedment
HERAKLEOPOLIS
Deshāsheh
El Hībeh
Meghagheh
OXYRHYNCHOS
PENINSULA OF SINAI
GULF OF SUEZ
ARABIAN DESERT
Beni Ḥasan
HERMOPOLIS
El Bersheh
El ʿAmārneh
Mīr
LIBYAN DESERT
Asyūt
Rifeh
El Badāri
Zaraby
Kaw el Kebīr
Menshīyeh
El Reḳāḳneh
Girgeh
El Mahāsneh
ABYDOS
El ʿAmreh
Dendereh
Keneh
Deir el Ballās
DIOSPOLIS PARVA
KOPTOS
WĀDY HAMMAMĀT
Naḳādeh
THEBES
Medamūd
Luxor
Karnak
Rizeiḳāt
Erment
Gebelein
Hibis
EL KHĀRGEH OASIS
El Kab
HIERAKONPOLIS
Edfu
Kom Ombo
Aswān
PHILÆ
FIRST CATARACT
Tropic of Cancer
NUBIA
El Dakkeh
Abu Simbel
Faras
Wādy Halfa
SECOND CATARACT
Lindsley Hall, del.

Set in 10 point Linotype Baskerville,
with Bauer Weiss for display
Format by Peter Oldenburg
Printed by Plantin Press, New York
Reprinted in offset
by the Meriden Gravure Company, Meriden, Conn.